I0879545

Enchanting

A Global Academic Publishing Book

ENCHANTING

Beyond Disenchantment

Stephen David Ross

SUNY PRESS

Published by
STATE UNIVERSITY OF NEW YORK PRESS, ALBANY

© 2012 State University of New York

Global Academic Publishing
International Studies in Philosophy Series, Monograph VI

All rights reserved

Printed in the United States of America

No part of this book may be used or reproduced in any manner whatsoever without written permission. No part of this book may be stored in any retrieval system or transmitted in any form or by any means including electronic, electrostatic, magnetic tape, mechanical, photocopying, recording, or otherwise without the prior permission in writing of the publisher.

For information, contact
State University of New York Press, Albany, NY
www.sunypress.edu

Library of Congress Cataloging-in-Publication Data

Ross, Stephen David.
Enchanting : beyond disenchantment.
p. cm.
"A global Academic Press book."
Includes bibliographical references (p.) and index.
ISBN 978-1-4384-4510-6 (paperback : alk. paper)
ISBN 978-1-4384-4509-0 (hardcover : alk. paper) 1. Philosophy and civilization. 2. Philosophy, Modern. 3. Civilization—Forecasting. I. Title.
B59.R68 2012
190—dc23

2012018792

10 9 8 7 6 5 4 3 2 1

Contents

Preface

Disenchantment

> The fate of our times is characterized by rationalization and intellectualization and, above all, by the "disenchantment of the world."[1] (Max Weber, *SV*, 155)

Fates spinning weaving in our times through all times. Many fates many threads many times. Many reasons many intellects many passions many truths. Many expressings askings tellings. Many spirits gods beauties arts. Shall we insist on one? Can we imagine many? Why above all and for whom? Many disenchantments many enchantments endless askings tellings expressings surprises arrivals interruptions. Images proliferating...

What characterizes our fate our time? Death of the world death of the gods environmental catastrophe industrial depredation global disenchantment. Hope for ecology dream of ecosophy. If there be such . . .

One can, in principle, master all things by calculation. This above all is what intellectualization means. (Weber, 139)

What disenchantment means...

Accounting for all things...

Mastering by calculation. . .

Living by measure...

What is not mastered by rationalization? What interrupts its rule? What remains for enchantment?

Asking of all things...[2]

And telling...

Celebrate abundance and wonder. Sing the wonder and abundance of the earth. Cherish enchantment without sacrificing disenchantment...

Would you celebrate, will you sing dance chant with me? Ask tell with me? Enchantingly?...

For many years, in many ways, I have been exploring what others describe as the disenchantment of the world and its reenchantments.[3] I would now acknowledge this explicitly. Yet to name the goal *reenchantment* takes disenchantment for granted as the condition of modern life. On one side it responds to the modernization of the world by seeking to restore an enchantment disavowed in modernity. On another side it occupies an innocent space in which the earth was never disenchanted, in which modern reason imposed views on many who never accepted them, in which religion, theology, and the gods retain enchantment in their heart. All enchantment belongs to the gods and their chosen. On this view, the mind belongs to reason, disenchanted, the heart belongs to the divine, enchanted. On the former view, disenchantment is the defining condition of contemporary life in the midst of countless faiths. On this view modern religion is disenchanted, the gods are dead.

Neither of these images evokes the enchantments I ask for. One takes the earth as if it were magical without asking of the meaning of disenchantment. The other takes disenchantment for granted without asking after the pervasiveness of enchantment. It is as if they took the spheres of god and reason as given, no matter how different their work, and sought divine reenchantment on the one hand or disenchanted reason on the other. Complicating this dichotomy is another, that the modern public sphere is given over almost everywhere to reason, disenchanted, while coexisting everywhere with enchanted private spheres.

What is modern modernity modernization? Who would not desire to be modern, perhaps without modernization industrialization rationalization? Without disenchantment filled with desire. Yearning for appearances simulacra virtualities as if perhaps they were enchanting...

Magic superstition wizardry illusion all contaminated. Perhaps. Unreal irreal appearances virtualities simulacra. As if reality were not them all as if enchantment might be cut away. With what knife? By which surgeon with what techniques? The incisions of disenchantment...

Once upon a time the world was enchanted but is now disenchanted...

The world was always disenchanted...

Once upon a time the world was enchanted and now is still enchanted...

The world was always enchanted...

The world was enchanted the world was disenchanted the world was neither enchanted nor disenchanted the world was both enchanted and disenchanted...

The world is neither enchanted... nor disenchanted... The world is both enchanted... And disenchanted...

Let us suppose there is no choice here, nothing to settle, but endless askings and tellings concerning enchantment and disenchantment; endless images of disenchantment and enchantment; endless interruptions, and more; moreover, that enchantment offers endless askings while disenchantment presents endless others. I understand disenchantment to pose critical questions for modernization, rationalization, globalization, and technologization, and enchantment to pose endless askings for life and practice—and disenchantment. In particular, enchantment does not presuppose disenchantment's view of reason, even where it takes place in a world given over to that view. It is as if the natural world presented itself as if always in its mysteriousness, understanding economic, technical, and scientific rationality neither to eliminate nor to discount the mysteries. Nor on the other side do god and religion establish mysteries, but invoke them beyond themselves. An enchanted universe is mysterious because it is abundant in wonder, full of askings and tellings, multifarious, expressive, because it sings, bellows, chants, speaks in many tongues,[4] because its languages are unknown, because its images proliferate beyond themselves, because its ingredients exceed any accounts, mundane or divine, interrupting their rule.[5] Humanity and its disenchantments are among these enchantments. An enchanted universe is never innocent, betrays itself as disenchantment, offers itself in laughter to betrayal.

Enchantment embraces the multifariousness of the world—the fairies dance christ is nailed to the cross. (Alfred North Whitehead, *PR,* 338)...

Enchantment embraces irreverence. Learn to laugh!...

Learn to laugh! Learn to betray! Learn to betray irreverence irreverently! Learn to enchant enchantingly!...

Learn a language halfway between gesture and thought. (Antonin Artaud, *TC1,* 242–3)...[6]

Learn to sing! Learn to hear!...[7]

I would tell and sing in wonder and abundance of this betrayal as the caesura between disenchantment and enchantment.[8] I would imagine that it belongs to all ingredients of the earth including humanity and nature themselves, if there be such, if nature can be taken whole and if humanity can be taken apart. I doubt it, and doubt that such a wholeness is compatible with enchantment. That is another story, still to come.[9] It pertains to local and global movements mobilized today under the heading of ecological practices. If nature and earth are inert, disenchanted, then ecological questions rest finally upon how they bear upon the conditions of human life. If earth and nature are enchanted, transformative and creative, then ecological askings bear upon creatures and things beyond humanity in unaccountable ways without finality. Ecology is enchanting, unaccountable beyond accounting, asking beyond questions, telling beyond knowing, relational beyond relations. The enchanted earth exceeds all accounts, proliferates its images beyond attachment and possession.

Ways of living, of relating, of relationality. Ecological ecosophical multiple autopoietic ruptures of meaning. Enchanted and enchanting...
Interrupting...

> The Earth is undergoing a period of intense techno-scientific transformations. If no remedy is found, the ecological disequilibrium this has generated will threaten the continuation of life on the planet's surface. Human modes of life, both individual and collective, are progressively deteriorating. The relationship between subjectivity and its exteriority—be it social, animal, vegetable or Cosmic—is compromised.
>
> Only an ethico-political articulation—which I call *ecosophy*—between the three ecological registers (the environment, social relations and human subjectivity) would be likely to clarify these questions.
>
> Henceforth the ways of living on this planet are in question. (Félix Guattari, *TE*, 27–8)

The refoundation of politics will have to pass through the aesthetic and analytical dimensions implied in the three ecologies. We cannot conceive of solutions to the poisoning of the atmosphere and to global warming due to the greenhouse effect, or to the problem of population control, without a mutation of mentality, without promoting a new art of living in society. We cannot conceive of international discipline without solving the problem of hunger and hyperinflation in the Third World. We cannot conceive of a collective recomposition of the socius without a new way of conceiving political and economic democracies that respect cultural differences. We cannot hope for an amelioration in the living conditions of the human species without a considerable effort to improve the feminine condition. The entire division of labour, its modes of valorisation and finalities need to be rethought. And to learn the intimate workings of

> this production, these ruptures of meaning that are auto-foundational of existence—poetry today might have more to teach us than economic science, the human sciences and psychoanalysis combined. (*C*, 20–1)

Enchanting ways of living are ecological aesthetic artistic poetic...
Enchanting stories interrupt our lives today...

The future is to come, is coming, coming and going, interrupting and proliferating. Interruption is proliferation...

The questions we may ask today are how to think of enchantment under the conditions of contemporary reason, how to live an enchanting life, a life of wonder, asking, transformation, multiplicity, interruption, relationality, alterity. The mark of enchantment—but not its soul—is that it exceeds all accounts. Every ingredient, moment, thing, and creature of the earth exceeds every account, including every account of enchantment. This does not entail that accounts are useless, that knowledge is impossible. To the contrary, enchantment is the condition of the inspirations that make knowledge possible, that make truth accessible. Plato calls it *wonder*. I call it *asking*. In the midst of the disenchantments gathered under the heading of Platonism—I do not imagine it as Plato[10]—messages as if from the gods appear throughout the dialogues, filling the earth with wonder, augmenting its abundance, exposing its uncontainability.[11] Wonder is the condition of abundance whereby a disenchanted philosophy is possible. As Derrida says of responsibility and Heidegger says of truth. The impossibility of knowledge is the condition of its possibility, untruth the condition of truth. The wonder of things inspires us to seek to know them and to master them, to disenchant them. This sad and irresistible condition[12] is interrupted by enchantment, understood not to reenchant what was disenchanted, but by the uncontainable tellings through which the enchantments of the earth are augmented and exposed. Enchantment is the exposition in images and language of the earth in wonder and abundance without which nothing can be known, including everything disenchanted.

Exposition... as exposure expression ecology asking telling as aisthēsis mimēsis poiēsis catachrēsis technē as image aesthetics beauty art as unearthing revelation disclosure calling as giving interrupting in betrayal...

Interrupting... for asking... and telling...

Ask and you shall receive...
Seek as if you may find...

Give beyond gifts...
Tell what you do not know...
Perhaps...

In English as well as other languages, *asking* performs diverse gestures. One evokes questioning, examining, inquiring, investigating, and presupposes, expects, insists on answers. A second evokes entreaty, solicitation, invocation, supplication, yearning, seeking, hospitality, welcome, and if it hopes for response, presupposes neither answers nor resolutions. The first drives toward control and violence, promotes forcible inquisition, and in the extreme elicits torture. The second answers of itself to the earth's deepest desires, and in the extreme offers itself as prayer. Similarly, *telling* suggests claiming, proving, demonstrating, establishing, explaining; yet also intimates revealing, sharing, presenting, exposing, expressing, opening, giving.

From the standpoint of command and response, these figures appear opposing. One exerts control, sometimes forcibly, and demands answers to the point of violence. The other expresses generosity and vulnerability, bequeaths control to others who are implored to assist and care. Yet in this juncture, if we ask of asking itself to assist us in living and being—all the way from before birth to death, and beyond; all the way from ethics to science, and back—the two join hands at the point of their departure. I mean that to insist on answers where there are none, or too many, is violence beyond questions. To plead and implore when we are asked to know is another violence, this time to reason. In other words, asking and telling on this doubled landscape, together with calling and giving and other expressive figures, reflect limitless possibilities for human beings and others, limitless askings for giving and telling, endless undoings for every doing, limitless promises of curiosity.

In these ways *asking* and *telling* present a doubly doubled gesture, proliferating before us, multiple figures of intimacy and separation, revelation and betrayal. Each is double, and each doubles the other, and multiples again. Asking seeks answers, seeks where there are no answers, sometimes answers without seeking. On another register, asking opens itself and the world, welcomes asking and telling beyond seeking and having. Telling claims answers, even where there are no answers, tells the answer of what has no answer, responds to asking with telling. On another register, telling expresses itself beyond claims and answers, beyond asking, responds to limitless asking with limitless expressing, endlessly asking of what may be inexpressible, if anything. Asking and telling together proliferate beyond any telling and any asking—moreover, each propagates beyond itself and the other.

The proximity of asking and telling is a separation that does not disconnect, a double that multiplies without division. In other words, the figure of their intimacy expresses—and unexpresses—what each might hope to say, to ask and tell, apart from the other—if that were possible. The point is that it is not possible, impossible beyond possibilitiy. Asking is always telling: every asking is a telling, and every telling is an asking. That is, no claim, assertion, indication of truth can present itself without questions, without asking beyond itself, beyond questions, beyond answers, without expressing beyond expression. Conversely, every asking is a telling, expresses something unexpected, surprising, wondering.

Together, asking and telling express wonder and abundance, not in the abstract sense of an unknown, but in the concrete sense of what is known and claimed. To tell is to claim; to tell is to ask; to tell is to express; to tell is to beseech. And conversely, of asking. Asking and telling cannot be separated, cannot be identical, cannot be evaded, cannot be destroyed. Together they make up the world—that world of which we ask and tell, is it human? what of animals? what do stones tell? what do the stars ask of us? how are we to live? and the others, how are they?

In these ways we see that asking and telling exceed any account as *exposition*:[13] as expression, asking, calling, telling.[14]

What you do not know, you may ask...

What you need, you should tell...

What you desire, go and ask...

What you hope, you may seek...

And so forth...

Asking in the generosity of calling, expressing, responding, betraying...

If we could only imagine asking, or understand asking—and of course we am asking these of asking. Not a logic of questions, not a theory of asking, not even a language or poetry of asking and questioning—though there is goodness in all of them. Ask of and what and why of asking, and perhaps in that asking to find or hear or envisage or express something unknown, unknowable, beyond possession, given beyond having, telling beyond knowing. And in that way touch by asking upon what we may hope to know, how we may hope to live, what we may hope to give and receive—again, our deepest desires. By asking and telling. Not from asking—receiving what we ask, receiving because we ask; not from telling—claiming what we need—but imagining human being as promised by asking in the generosity of expressing and responding, in wonder and abundance. Betrayed as human and beyond.

We live in a time in which Enlightenment reason appears to many to be under grave attack, from those who have never admired it to those who employ it to undermine itself. Some say that human beings are fundamentally not rational, those who disagree with us are deeply irrational, political and economic forces show that human beings act and believe from desire and feeling, not reason. Some say we should be saved by reason—those who are rational shall rule. Some say we cannot be saved by reason—reason itself is irrational, imposes itself on the world in the name of some human authority. Some say that reason claims an authority it cannot possess.

> How is it that humankind throws up, generation after generation, a cadre of thinkers slightly further from God than Ramanujan, but capable nevertheless, after the designated twelve years of schooling and six of tertiary education, of making a contribution to the decoding of the great book of nature via the physical and mathematical disciplines? If the being of man is really at one with the being of God, should it not be cause for suspicion that human beings take eighteen years, a neat and manageable portion of a human lifetime, to qualify to become decoders of God's master script, rather than five minutes, say, or five hundred years? Might it not be that the phenomenon we are examining here is, rather than the flowering of a faculty that allows access to the secrets of the universe, the specialism of a rather narrow self-regenerating intellectual tradition whose forte is reasoning, in the same way that the forte of chess players is playing chess, which for its own motives it tries to install at the centre of the universe? (J. M. Coetzee, *EC*, 69)

None of these suggestions can be told without asking. Certainly there will be no answers without asking—where there are answers—and no doing without undoing. Perhaps it is worth imagining that asking and telling, with or without answers, is the reason—and unreason—I mean the life we may be seeking. To ask, and to ask of asking; to call, and to call of calling; to tell, and to tell of telling; to know that every asking, calling, telling divides, and divides again; betrays and betrays again. These might be science, or philosophy, more likely they may be poetry, or art, or love. In any case, the asking goes beyond itself.

The project I am undertaking here is asking and telling.[15] And I am asking it of others. Asking after asking, asking of and about asking, asking by telling. And yet, not too quickly—or ever—expecting to answer, to say what asking is, to define asking, to explain telling. The point of asking, as against questioning or problem solving, is that we may ask and not answer, not because we do not have the answer, not because there is no answer, not because not answering is lacking, but because asking and telling is the thing itself, that which goes beyond itself. This going beyond, this generosity, is what I hope to seek, asking and telling as thought and life and being going beyond themselves, undoing themselves, multiplying and dividing. Asking and telling multiply, proliferate other askings and tellings. Questioning and answering call for resolution and settling in place. Asking in daily life, in intimacy and community, encompasses science, philosophy, performance, poetry, and religion, yet perhaps not in their own terms, in the ways they have come to answer to the asking, but as expressing, responding, giving, telling, enchanting. The asking I would ask goes back to the beginning of recorded thought, to the asking and not the answers, not in a historical sense of what is past, but in the historical sense of what is now and to come.

There is, then, a project of asking, asking of and after asking, present as limitless desire and endless generosity, betrayed as telling, exposition and expression. Yet it does not begin with asking itself. And it may not end with asking itself. Instead I mean to explore the landscape of asking, its topography and flora and fauna if you will. The telling beyond, undoing beyond doing.

Nevertheless, the gist of asking, its life and promise, and of telling, is that, rooted in the soil of the human world, human experiences, languages, and cultures, it overflows beyond any boundaries. Overflowing is the mark of asking and telling; teeming is their manifestation.

Some day there may be an answer to asking, what it is to ask, what it might be to tell. Yet why should there be, why expect to have the answer to asking where asking is beyond answers?

Some day there may be an answer to humanity, what it is to be human; an answer to being, what it is to be, human or otherwise, living or nonliving. Yet why should there be, why expect to have the answer where asking of them is beyond answers?

Asking is expressing, imagining, giving, performing, telling, enchanting, undoing, unsettling, desiring, proliferating, calling, surprising, etc. etc....

Asking is exposition... as exposure expression ecology asking calling performing... as aisthēsis mimēsis poiēsis catachrēsis technê... as image aesthetics beauty art... as unearthing revelation disclosure telling... as giving interrupting betraying...

Asking is expressing and responding beyond questions and answers, beyond knowing and unknowing, beyond doing and undoing, beyond being and nonbeing, where beyond is always more and other in the wonder and abundance of enchantments...

Here, then, are some of the prospects, one after the other. And of course, in the nature of asking, nothing can be taken for granted. Here is where asking with telling promises to take us, linked terms surpassing every limit and themselves:

asking as giving, giving as enchanting;...
asking as performing, performing as undoing;...
asking as desiring, desiring as proliferating;...
asking as expressing, expressing as imagining, imagining as telling;...
asking as promising, promising as surprising;...
asking as undoing, undoing as queering, queering as betraying;...
as calling, invoking, responding, saying, knowing;...
as coming, becoming, going, staying;...
as giving, having; possessing, dispossessing;...
in wonder, abundance, profusion, proliferation;...
in flourishing, compassion, cherishment, sacrifice, plenishment;...
in enchanting, wandering, traveling, resisting;...
in mystery, surprise, unsettling, unknowing, conjuring; not to mention:...
human asking (what does it mean that human beings ask and tell?);...
beyond human asking (how do other creatures ask and tell?);...
asking asking;...
telling telling;...

and finally, if only to mark a certain asking familiar to us as a university:

asking and telling as disciplining...

A world of asking for giving and telling, celebrating and betraying enchantment and unsettling.[16]

Returning from this second interruption...

These expositions themselves exceed every account. So from the first we glimpse the paradoxical forms in which enchantment appears enchanted. The enchantment of the earth gives to us the possibility of its disenchantment. Enchantment exceeds every account, including the account I hope to give. In this enchanting discourse, we encounter three recurrent themes. The excessiveness of enchantment is its prevailing condition; it appears as given, in giving, interrupting having; and it appears in expression, through exposition, in asking and telling. The enchantments, the inspirations that exceed all accounts, are the ways in which the things of the earth are given to us, as gifts, in asking, by telling, in performing and giving, impossible to hold or grasp, images proliferating in wonder and abundance. Giving and generosity are among the recurrent thematic expositions of enchantment and its excesses, as are expressing, performing, asking, and telling. Generosity and giving are among the ways in which we may speak of how things exceed every account—as giving exceeds possession, as expressing exceeds knowing, as asking exceeds responding, as becoming interrupts being, as ecology exceeds relationality. As if...

Generously the earth in wonder and abundance offers its enchantments to us to the gods offers us to the gods offers the gods to us and more than the gods as the sacred spiritual pagan divine secular ecological ingredients of our time endless images in proliferation...

It follows that the task of exposition in which the earth and its ingredients are expressed is itself ecological beyond accounting. The task is endless, every offering is called into question in the ways in which it becomes disenchanted, every image multiplies and proliferates. Disenchantment here is not uniquely a function of the modern world but of its reflections upon enchantment. To know, to understand, is not as such to disenchant, but to bring enchanted things into our possession, where they may be disenchanted. I mean that they do not cease to be enchanted though they may appear so. Among the terms—I will not say *concepts*—that are required to express enchantment are those that express its relations with disenchantment. The term *betrayal*, an enchanting word, expresses that relation as violation and revelation.[17] Enchanted things are betrayed by disenchantment; disenchanted things betray the enchantments at their heart, reveal them, interrupt them, transgress them. This complex relation entails that enchantment and disenchantment are not oppositional in a binary relation—nor for that matter synthetic, reciprocal, or dialectical—but inhabit the transgressive relation described by betrayal. It entails as well that no binary relations—perhaps of reason—can express enchantment and its relations to disenchantment. Nor can any nonbinary relations, relations absolutely without rupture. Enchantment is the rupture in the world that on the one side opens it up to asking and giving, on the other betrays it. Enchantment interrupts every account including every account of its impossibility. Here enchantment is not a way of being, and disenchantment is not its betrayal into being. Each betrays the other, frames it and reframes it.

Betrayal betrays the order of things. In interruption. The disenchantment of the earth betrays every ingredient in the perhaps and as if of telling and asking that marks their generosity affirms the ruptures disruptions caesuras of their identities betrays them defiles them reveals them frames them. Betrayal betrays itself...

For these reasons I have engaged in the endless task of articulating something enigmatic and elusive through different ways and avenues and terms of art. No account of enchantment can settle its nature and being, no account of the earth and its ingredients. Many accounts have been given, many more are to come, including the most technical and scientific reports, in which betrayal and enchantment are present obliquely, and many other expositions, many ecologies,[18] in which enchantment and betrayal are foregrounded. All must succeed, and all must fail. Moreover, success and failure are not oppositional and binary, but are enchanting beyond any disenchantments, asking beyond any answers.[19]

For these reasons again, my writings of the past decades, my life work so to speak, form an ongoing encounter with enchantment, by means of diverse interruptions. In the reworking of that project here I will retrace those gifts to present them in an enchanted light. I begin with disenchantment as weber made it explicit in "Science as a Vocation," the work in which he discusses it extensively. I begin with such a disenchantment so as to extend its reach back and forward in time. I mean to ask whether science can be a vocation without enchantment.[20] I take for granted that it is impossible for philosophy, the arts, and life itself to be what they are without enchantment, without endless asking, though it is possible—indeed irresistible—to disenchant them.[21] Similarly, reflective human life—I mean ethics, politics, arts, religions, and sciences—affirms the enchantments of the earth even as they have become disenchanted. The death of the gods is one of the defining events of the modern world. That is why I speak repeatedly of the secular enchantment of the earth, of how secularization betrays enchantment in ways beyond the reach of religion or theology.

Secularization enchants the world in abundance... Wonder proliferates in exposition... Reason interrupts the rule of the gods... Asking disrupts the rule of truth...

Returning from this first interruption...

"Science as a Vocation" is addressed to graduate students in the modern academy. It avows to advise them on the conditions they must meet to become successful scientists and the conditions they will face and under which they will live. Weber describes such conditions as *external* and *internal,* and among the latter includes the disenchantment of the world, by which he

> means that principally there are no mysterious incalculable forces that come into play, but rather that one can, in principle, master all things by calculation. This means that the world is disenchanted. One need no longer have recourse to magical means in order to master or implore the spirits, as did the savage, for whom such mysterious powers existed. Technical means and calculations perform the service. This above all is what intellectualization means. (139)

One might summarize this far too briefly as that enchantment is belief in spirits[22] invested with mysterious powers, and that disenchantment is mastery over all things by technical means and calculation. Disenchantment removes the magic from things, making them knowable and calculable. Enchantment in this way is beyond calculation.

No incalculable forces in principle as if principles were not disenchanted from the first. As if enchantments knew principles did not betray them...

Following a line of thought from Friedrich Nietzsche through Martin Heidegger and Theodor Adorno into Michel Foucault, one might emphasize that mastery takes precedence here. Enchantment and disenchantment are conceived by weber as forms of domination, competing for control. Imploring, pleading, and praying are other masterful ways of obtaining goods from recalcitrant gods or events. One might imagine that science and religion compete for authority and mastery in the contemporary world. Such a view leaves state authority aside, an authority I regard as neither scientific and technical nor religious even in states dominated by clergy. The contemporary state is disenchanted, but by no means because it accounts for everything. To the contrary, it is because government originates its own forms of mastery and its own techniques of control.[23]

One might suppose that modern reason and its disenchantment both follow from insistence on mastery, and that another view of reason, perhaps an enchanted one, might be possible if we turned from mastery to generosity, from knowing to asking and telling, and from possession to dispossession. One might suppose that reason as such is disenchanted in its insistence on control. We no longer strive for control through magical means because reason is the greater master.[24] The critique of technical rationality must acknowledge the masterful force of reason. I suggest that reason itself is enchanted, even when it is calculation and mastery, and that these too are enchanted. In an enchanted world we do not know where exclusion and mastery will take us. Every journey exceeds expectations. Including the journeys of disenchantment.

We journey together and apart filled with violence injustice destruction cruelty mastery domination as if perhaps journeying must be. Filled with joy love celebration wonder abundance ecstasy rapture responsibility generosity, affirming journey's enchantments. Being's journey yours and mine is abundant wonderful cruel exposition's wonder and abundance...

It may be productive in the context of a disenchanted world to address the mastery associated with religion and the divine as well as with academic disciplines and sciences. It may be productive to view the debate between disenchantment and enchantment as one of authority.[25] Who controls and who possesses authority? I would think of enchantment as unsettling all forms of mastery and authority, divine authority and priestly mastery as well as academic authority and scientific mastery. I would imagine the wonder and abundance of the earth as exceeding all mastery and authority, even as these are irresistible, as they always return. Here the language of generosity reappears: enchantment is given from the earth to give, in giving, ecological beyond possession; mastery is received from the earth to have. Here the earth is given in abundance and wonder while the spirits and gods are held up by institutional religions and their elites as something to hold onto.

Gods spirits disciplines sciences rend us rip open the fabric of the world to its wonders and abundances, grip us grasp us coerce us persuade us make all of us theirs. Enchantments become masteries become our masters become disenchantments. We succumb we war we struggle are broken in their grip are comforted in their grasp are awakened we sleep the long sleep...

It is time to evoke a different relation to the spirits whose presence marks the enchantment of the earth, at least as human beings encounter it.

Another interruption...

> Someone, you or me, comes forward and says: *I would like to learn to live finally (enfin).*
>
> *To learn to live*: a strange watchword. Who would learn? From whom? To teach to live, but to whom? Will we ever know? Will we ever know how to live and first of all what "to learn to live" means? And why "finally"?
>
> But to learn to live, to learn it *from oneself and by oneself,* all alone, to teach *oneself* to live, is that not impossible for a living being?
>
> And yet nothing is more necessary than this wisdom. It is ethics itself, to learn to live—alone, from oneself, by oneself.
>
> If it—learning to live—remains to be done, it can happen only between life and death. Neither in life nor in death *alone.* It can only *maintain itself* with some ghost, can only *talk with or about* some ghost (s'entretenir *de quelque fantôme*). So it would be necessary to learn spirits. Even and especially if this, which is neither substance, nor essence, nor existence, *is never present as such.* To live otherwise, and better. No, not better, but more justly. But *with them.* No *being-with* the other, no *socius* without this *with* that makes *being-with* in general more enigmatic than ever for us. And this being-with specters would also be, not only but also, a *politics* of memory, of inheritance, and of generations. (Derrida, *SM,* xvii–xviii)

> Could one *address oneself in general* if already some ghost did not come back? If he loves justice at least, the "scholar" of the future, the "intellectual" of tomorrow should learn it and from the ghost. He should learn to live by learning not how to make conversation with the ghost but how to talk with him, with her, not to let them speak or how to give them back speech, even it if is in oneself, in the other, in the other in oneself: they are always *there,* specters, even if they do not exist, even if they are no longer, even if they are not yet.
>
> *Thou art a scholar, speak to it, Horatio.* (176)

These ghosts or spirits, if they enchant us, are to be neither mastered nor implored, but spoken with and to. And never finally. There are always ghosts, and more, the earth is enchanted, spirits come back, interrupt our comfort.

To learn to live ecologically enchantedly relationally with spirits with ghosts with...

In the modalities of as if and perhaps as if many ghosts perhaps as if they return as if we might speak with them as if they might speak perhaps to us perhaps for us. Never finally. As if and perhaps as asking...

Derrida calls our attention to these ghosts as uniquely present in the academy. The enchantments of the earth present tasks to the modern intellectual, if there be such, tasks of unmastery and dispossession perhaps, as if that were possible.

Dead spirits returning with the gods. Dead gods the gods are dead the gods return perhaps the spirits too. Gods and spirits and the return are infinite eternal questionable beyond accounting as if to be accounted for in another return another accounting. Ecstatically the gods return us to ourselves to themselves beyond accounting beyond possession to speak with address comfort ask with the ghosts who restlessly reappear. There is no rest the world proliferates at rest...

Before venturing a closer reading of weber's understanding of disenchantment, I would recall the audience of his speech[26] to explore the possibility that disenchantment does not pertain to humanity in general, that it is not human beings as such or ordinary europeans and americans, but academics and especially scientists who are disenchanted. The question is whether disenchantment pertains to contemporary life as such, to ordinary people who believe in different kinds of things, many regarded by academics as superstitions, or whether it pertains to academics as such, to those who have chosen science as a vocation, for whom calculation represents the form of their knowledge but not all the ways in which they relate to the earth. Not finally.

I will content myself here with asking this question. I am not in a position to answer it nor must I do so to approach enchantment as I hope to. The question is less whether contemporary life has been taken over by technical means and calculation in all walks and ways, and more whether the academy, including philosophy, has made itself disenchanted in order that it may be scientific, resisting interruption of reason's rule.[27] In other words, the question is again of the divide between the university and the world, the ivory tower and life, in the form of the commitments of secular rationality to guarding its authority tightly in the form of disenchantment. *We who know the earth best know it as disenchanted.* Such a claim is directed against those who believe in magic and superstition, in strange and incredible things, by those whose knowledge confers authority upon them. That such knowledge confers little authority in the world at large—in state, church, military, or corporation—is a minor issue. The scientist would possess authority in the academy. The schools must be ruled by disenchantment.

In this way I will keep the academy in mind in my celebration of enchantment. I believe the earth to be a magical, enchanted place for many people in their daily lives, whether in their churches or in the rituals and incantations that mark their social relations. I draw inspiration from Michel de Certeau's understanding of marginality.

> Marginality is today no longer limited to minority groups, but is rather massive and pervasive; this cultural activity of the non-producers of culture, an activity that is unsigned, unreadable, and unsymbolized, remains the only one possible for all those who nevertheless buy and pay for the showy products through which a productivist economy articulates itself. Marginality is becoming universal. A marginal group has now become a silent majority.
>
> This does not mean the group is homogeneous. The procedures allowing the re-use of products are linked together in a kind of obligatory language, and their functioning is related to social situations and power relationships. (Certeau, *PEL*, xvii)

Marginal behaviors are resistant to mainstream institutions of authority. That means they are superstitious, magical, enchanted. In certeau's words, they are "everyday practices that produce without capitalizing, that is, without taking control over time" (xx). They interrupt the rule of time.

> our society is characterized by a cancerous growth of vision, measuring everything by its ability to show or be shown and transmuting communication into a visual journey. It is a sort of *epic* of the eye and of the impulse to read.
>
> In reality, the activity of reading has on the contrary all the characteristics of a silent production: the drift across the page, the metamorphosis of the text effected by the wandering eyes of the reader, the improvisation and expectation of meanings inferred from a few words, leaps over written spaces in an ephemeral space. Words become the outlet or product of silent histories. The readable transforms itself into the memorable. A different world (the reader's) slips into the author's place.
>
> This mutation makes the text habitable, like a rented apartment. It transforms another person's property into a space borrowed for a moment by a transient. Renters make comparable changes in an apartment they furnish with their acts and memories; as do speakers, in the language into which they insert both the messages of their native tongue and, through their accent, through their own "turns of phrase," etc., their own history; as

> do pedestrians, in the streets they fill with the forests of their desires and goals. In the same way the users of social codes turn them into metaphor and ellipses of their own quests. (xxi–xxii)

Marginality expresses powerlessness illusion unreality as if powerful actual real always perhaps. People live as if perhaps among powers beyond possession beyond the rulers of culture. We are displaced, enchanted agents beyond the rulers of culture...

Interrupting the organized spaces of everyday life, framed by technical means and calculation, readings and practices are transformed into metaphors and ellipses of alternative quests, magical and enchanted in their ways. These ways—crucial for enchantment—are social, collective, collaborative, shared. But they are shared outside the authorized institutions of disenchantment, including churches. They are shared as enchanted transformations.

Returning from this interruption...

Weber is explicit that the institutions that carry the weight and history of enchantment have become disenchanted, and the gods they worship have become disenchanted as well.

> Today the routines of everyday life challenge religion. Many old gods ascend from their graves; they are disenchanted and hence take the form of impersonal forces. They strive to gain power over our lives and again they resume their eternal struggle with one another. What is hard for modern man, and especially for the younger generation, is to measure up to workaday existence. The ubiquitous chase for "experience" stems from this weakness; for it is weakness not to be able to countenance the stern seriousness of our fateful times. (149)
>
> The fate of our times is characterized by rationalization and intellectualization and, above all, by the "disenchantment of the world." Precisely the ultimate and most sublime values have retreated from public life either into the transcendental realm of mystic life or into the brotherliness of direct and personal human relations. It is not accidental that our greatest art is intimate and not monumental, nor is it accidental that today only within the smallest and intimate circles, in personal human situations, in pianissimo, that something is pulsating that corresponds to the prophetic pneuma, which in former times swept through the great communities like a firebrand, welding them together. If we attempt to force and to "invent" a monumental style in art, such miserable monstrosities are produced as the many monuments of the last twenty years. If one tries intellectually to construe new religions without a new and genuine prophecy, then, in an inner sense, something similar will result, but with still

> worse effects. And academic prophecy, finally, will create only fanatical sects but never a genuine community. (155)

No room exists for enchantment in the academy, there religion produces fanaticism but not prophecy. Religion in the state does so as well. Enchantment comes when and where it chooses, and becomes fanaticism when secular disenchanted authorities claim its authority. Given the rest of the 20th century, weber's academic prophecy foretold many truths.

The gods are dead. That is known to all religions and faiths known and felt in every faith no matter how deep. Always perhaps. Always as if a death not of religion but of enchantments and expressions...

I have mentioned the link between disenchantment and the critique of reason. Those who have most prominently discussed disenchantment have interpreted calculation, technical rationality, mastery, and control as marks of a reason out of control.

That other form of madness by which men in an act of sovereign reason confine their neighbors and communicate and recognize each other through the merciless language of non-madness. (Foucault, *MC*, ix–x)...

I share the critique that would question the authority of modern reason, but I do not question its grandeur—let me call it *enchanted.*[28] Modern science and technology have contributed to terrible events—as have many religions. Science and technology claim to disenchant the world in the name of knowing everything, insist that everything is knowable by science and doable by technology. This inflated claim exceeds any possibility of credence. Why, then, would it not be enchanted, marking the mania weber describes?[29] The inflation of scientific knowledge can be accomplished only by magical means, and indeed, there is magic in the presentations of science and in the advertisements for new technologies. What they are is enchanted enough, what is claimed for them in the mimetic images that surround them is enchanting beyond enchantment. Enchantment is uncontrollable, together with mimesis and exposition. Uncontrollability includes fanaticism, domination, violation. There are no guarantees against evil spirits and violent demons.

No assurances against evil spirits violent demons cruel ghosts oppressive gods mad scientists. The death of the gods is not the end of evil or its beginning...

The critique of disenchanted reason and its defenders inhabits a line of thought from descartes to habermas. The defenders of reenchantment inhabit a line of thought largely restricted to religion and the arts. The possibility of reason's enchantment in the context of its disenchantment—an enchanted science, secularity, rationality—remains largely ignored.[30] Yet it is of immense importance for science and reason and for the struggle for mastery between church and academy. Each guards its authority against the other—two possessive forms of disenchantment. Against this guarding is an enchantment that glitters in art, the uncontainability of exposition and mimesis, the opening of the earth in language and exposition that inhabits every expression, every ingredient, with a wonder and abundance beyond attachment, enclosure, and possession. This is the enchantment of the earth—as world, as nature, ecological enchantments in and through humanity and culture. It knows no bounds even as it finds itself bounded on every side. Its enchantment requires the disenchantment of every world. This is another picture of the academy, filled with disenchanted disciplines whose limits are evident everywhere, in and out of the academy. This disenchantment neither struggles with enchantment nor is diminished by it. Instead, disenchantment fulfills enchantment in the context of a human academy. Disenchantment betrays enchantment.

Disenchantment betrays enchantment fulfills enchantment enchants itself. Enchantment betrays disenchantment betrays itself interrupts itself disenchants itself...

It is time to return again to weber, for I have passed over where he speaks of something that falls from the sky under the rule of enchantment: inspiration, creativity—indeed, intoxication, passion, enthusiasm, frenzy. The "inward calling for science" calls for all of these from its practitioners even as it presents itself and them as disenchanted.

Inspiration creativity intoxication passion frenzy enthusiasm calling asking telling inhabit science express the wonder of science interrupt its disenchantments betray its enchantments. Science disenchants the world to betray enchantments hidden in an enchanted world...

> Nowadays in circles of youth there is a widespread notion that science has become a problem in calculation, fabricated in laboratories or statistical filing systems just as "in a factory," a calculation involving only the cool intellect and not one's "heart and soul." First of all one must say that such comments lack all clarity about what goes on in a factory or in a laboratory.
>
> On the other hand, and this also is often misconstrued, inspiration plays no less a role in science than it does in the realm of art. It is a childish notion to think that a mathematician attains any scientifically valuable results by sitting at his

> desk with a ruler, calculating machines or other mechanical means. The mathematical imagination of a Weierstrass is naturally quite differently oriented in meaning and result than is the imagination of an artist, and differs basically in quality. But the psychological processes do not differ. Both are frenzy (in the sense of Plato's "mania") and "inspiration." (135–6)

Imagination and inspiration are madnesses in Plato's sense of *mania*, inseparable from wonder. Weber does not imagine a science without them and is scathing toward those who believe that science and reason are nothing but calculation. The earth is disenchanted by the madness of science. We are at a point at which it may be possible to discern the dividing line between one disenchantment and another—an enchanted one if there be such. Modern science and reason have given us to believe that everything can be known, everything can become an object of calculation. Yet they are not of themselves calculable, and depend on movements beyond technique and calculation. Inspiration, imagination, creativity, intoxication, passion, enthusiasm, frenzy—madnesses in wonder—are enchanted and uncontrollable requisites of a reason that offers the earth to us as a calculable possession.

Such a view suggests an enchanted reason and enchanted science, yet not in the sense that what science tells us of the earth in its voice is that it is enchanted. I believe that voice is enchanted, that abundance and wonder pervade the earth radiantly and ecologically viewed through the lens of scientific reason. There is always more to know and more to be known, new and surprising ways in which the earth is given to us to ask. Here, however, science passes itself off as disenchanted in its procedures and calculations all the while steeped in wonder and abundance in the frenzies of inspiration and passion, the madnesses of asking. The wonder and abundance of the earth are the conditions of the disenchantment of reason. The calling of reason elicits disenchantment in the midst of endless enchantments.

Asking as exposition giving generosity beyond containment echoing sounding resonating speaking singing...

It seems that scientific rationality inhabits several pairs of oppositions. Here are just a few of many that touch upon enchantment and disenchantment: between secular reason and religious commitment, between modernity and what comes before and after, between technical, instrumental calculations and unbounded asking, between knowledge and value. Disenchantment names the first term of each of these, and depending on other commitments, enters into a preexisting dialogue. Weber himself inhabits all of these, but his commitments as a sociologist bring him to the last: the disparity between the work of science and the values by which we hope to live.

> What stand should one take? Has "progress" as such a recognizable meaning that goes beyond the technical, so that to serve it is a meaningful vocation? The question must be raised. But this is no longer merely the question of man's calling for science, hence, the problem of what science as a vocation means to its devoted disciples. To raise this question is to ask for the vocation of science within the total life of humanity. What is the value of science? (140)

> the ultimately possible attitudes toward life are irreconcilable, and hence their struggle can never be brought to a final conclusion. Thus it is necessary to make a decisive choice. Whether, under such conditions, science is a worth while "vocation" for somebody, and whether science itself has an objectively valuable "vocation" are again value judgments about which nothing can be said in the lecture-room. To affirm the value of science is a presupposition for teaching there.
>
> Science today is a "vocation" organized in special disciplines in the service of self-clarification and knowledge of interrelated facts. It is not the gift of grace of seers and prophets dispensing sacred values and revelations, nor does it partake of the contemplation of sages and philosophers about the meaning of the universe. This, to be sure, is the inescapable condition of our historical situation. We cannot evade it so long as we remain true to ourselves. And if Tolstoi's question recurs to you: as science does not, who is to answer the question: "What shall we do, and, how shall we arrange our lives?" or, in the words used here tonight: "Which of the warring gods should we serve? Or should we serve perhaps an entirely different god, and who is he?" then one can say that only a prophet or a savior can give the answers. If there is no such man, or if his message is no longer believed in, then you will certainly not compel him to appear on this earth by having thousands of professors, as privileged hirelings of the state, attempt as petty prophets in their lecture-rooms to take over his role. (152–3)

Not grace not gift not seeing not prophecy not sacredness not valuing not how we shall arrange our lives. Science arranges the lives of scientists arranges the lives of children knowledge classifies both knower and known...

In other words, the integrity of science depends on its disenchantment, on its commitments to knowledge and not to asking, to truth and not to life. The greatness of science, disenchanted, makes it unfit to serve as prophecy. Weber does not recoil from the other side of this equation, that science is worthless from the side of those who seek how to live. He then poses a possibility that we should not shirk from, that while *disenchanted* means devoid of values, *enchantment* does not give us life. To the contrary, enchantment, wonder, and abundance may be too full and too empty to tell us how to live. Especially finally. There are too many spheres of value, too many different ways of being, too many questions, too many others in their otherness for any system of values to coordinate. The academy cannot do so, but neither can the church. Wonder and enchantment are too abundant for reason on the one hand and for life on the other. In return, they are wonderful and abundant beyond any of the limits they establish for themselves.

Too much multiplicity diversity disparition caesuras askings tellings wonder abundance. How can there be too much too many? How can there be enough? What is our ecology?...

Let us imagine, if we can, that intellectualization and rationalization manifest themselves as disenchanted in an enchanted world, but manifest that world as disenchanted. Let us imagine that rationalization and intellectualization have so defined themselves as to reject all enchantments as magical, illusory, and superstitious. Let us imagine further that the space of enchantment is presented to us carried by religion and theology in the name of divinity and god. This is a view of the disenchantment of religion in the specific sense that what is beyond accounting is accounted for in a particular place and by a particular cluster of disciplines and practices. In other words, disenchantment marks a fixity of appearance, enchantment is mobile and transgressive. Here, where weber reminds us that "Scientific progress is a fraction, the most important fraction, of the process of intellectualization which we have been undergoing for thousands of years" (138), we must distinguish the claims of reason from its accomplishments and effects, and in particular the claim that everything can be known by calculation from that knowledge itself. Rationalization has become a meta-narrative here,[31] marking scientific progress. Yet as such it is highly controversial, especially whether it owns the right to give that mark. In relation to the institutions that influence daily life—governments, corporations, bureaucracies, economies, etc.—reason frequently plays a minor role, waning and expanding to suit institutional needs. Foucault calls it *governmentality*, and its presence calls into question intellectualization and rationalization as forces in contemporary life.[32] They become forms of governmentality, population control, among the ways in which citizens are managed. Disenchantment becomes a figure under which populations are regulated, corresponding on the other side to the figure of the divine under which other populations are regulated. Enchantment resists governmentality[33] by resisting all the binary oppositions under which disenchantment is mobilized. At the extreme we may hazard the hypothesis that binarity is disenchantment and that magic, sacredness, rapture, and love are enchanted, interrupting binary oppositions. Contemporary religion is disenchanted in the ways in which it is organized by the oppositions of sacredness and secularity and of religion and reason. As if these complex, questionable terms wore a single general meaning.

Religion is disenchanted disenchantment is enchanted we are all you and they are all disenchanted...

Here, then, weber's understanding of contemporary religion in Europe, especially after the protestant reformation, presents the disenchantment of this world as a long term process "which has continued to exist in Occidental culture for millennia, and, in general, [as] 'progress,' to which science belongs as a link and motive force" (139). Progress and continuity here are disenchantment, tightly linked with enlightenment reason on the one hand and secular modernization on the other. This is another major stake of the question of disenchantment, whether the world we live in is advancing. Many deeply religious people do not think so, do not believe in scientific, rational, or technical progress. The world is god's and is just fine the way it is. Its eschatological narrative has nothing to do with rational progress. I am asking whether there is another enchanted story of the earth that interrupts its rational progression without an eschatological meta-narrative of enchantment. Each of these is a disenchanted meta-narrative in the sense that it accounts for what there is. Each remains in the disenchanted opposition between disenchantment and enchantment. I am asking whether there is another enchanted tale that multiplies these oppositions to infinity and interrupts their rule. Weber does not think so.

To infinity multiply to infinity divide to infinity add and subtract to infinity as if infinity were a place to go to. Why does enchantment disenchant? Why does infinity become finite? All betrayals all betrayed...

> Under these internal presuppositions, what is the meaning of science as a vocation, now after all these former illusions, the "way to true being," the "way to true art," the "way to true na-

> ture," the "way to true God," the "way to true happiness," have been dispelled? Tolstoi has given the simplest answer, with the words: "Science is meaningless because it gives no answer to our question, the only question important for us: 'What shall we do and how shall we live?'" That science does not give an answer to this is indisputable. The only question that remains is the sense in which science gives "no" answer, and whether or not science might yet be of some use to the one who puts the question correctly. (143)

This "no" can be organized under the opposition between reason and value with the qualification that the illusions have been disenchanted and dispelled by reason. To dispel them as illusions and superstitions is to disenchant them. Reason here gives itself the right to disenchant the earth's enchantments as illusions, where one might imagine that they might remain vigorous and wonderful. This is not nietzsche's polarity between apollo and dionysus, where the illusions of apollo represent one sweeping realm of enchantment—transformed into disenchantment by reason. Apollo and dionysus offer two different realms of enchantment, two different realms of illusion, opposed neither to each other nor to reason's realm of truth. Only reason—*Socratism* to nietzsche—insists on this opposition. Modernity does not except where reason is given governmental authority. Marginalization reenchants.

This insight marks both the critique of reason and its account of modernity. Put another way, modernization—with industrialization, economization, technologization—all can take place without insisting on reason's authority. All can take place without disenchantment. Reason's disenchantment insists on opposition with illusion, magic, superstition, and religion in ways that undermine their authority. Religion in turn insists on its authority within another opposition with the claims of secular modern authority. In this way contemporary religion is disenchanted. It claims to know with authority what cannot be known. Disenchantment gives authority to rational knowledge. Enchantment interrupts authority.

Here weber's understanding of disenchantment as failing to answer the ultimate questions of life and meaning may be kept separate from the impulse to transcendence and to final meanings—to a better philosophy and a more truthful metaphysics. A striking example—another interruption—is found in peter dews, where the "widespread deflationary tendency of contemporary thinking" (Peter Dews, *LD*, ix) is linked to "attempts to restore meaning to a disenchanted universe," offering "inauthentic meanings to compensate for a meaningless world" (1 [quoted from Charles Taylor, *SS*, 458]). Astonishingly, this understanding of nietzsche's critique of 19th century Germany becomes a critique of derrida and deconstruction, following dews's insistence that disenchantment is loss of meaning. "The dominant paradigm of hostility to meaning in recent European philosophy has undoubtedly been deconstruction, which initially appeared on the scene as a radicalization of Heidegger's overcoming of metaphysics. The thought of the early Derrida is marked by a determination to go beyond Heidegger to abandon the philosophical quest for meaning" (2). Dews's faith in philosophy as a giver of meaning puts him at a distance from weber and derrida, though he seems to hold a view of meaning close to tolstoi and weber:

> One might have thought that the disenchantment of the world as the collapse of belief in a cosmic order whose immanent meaning guides human endeavour, would constitute a cultural trauma of such magnitude that philosophy could do little other than struggle to come to terms with it—and indeed, the shock waves of this collapse have reverberated throughout nineteenth- and twentieth-century thinking. (1–2)

One might have thought that most of contemporary philosophy and science have nothing to say about the collapse of belief in a cosmic order or transcendent meanings. Philosophy—possibly dews's philosophy as well—is as disenchanted as science, possibly especially so in philosophy of religion. Dews never imagines, as I will insist, that what he understands as derrida's rejection of meaning might be understood as resistance to disenchantment, understanding enchantment as the interruption of all transcendent, cosmic meaning. Where dews calls upon adorno to insist that "meaning implies *givenness*—it is something we encounter and experience, not something we can arbitrarily posit" (2)—if anyone holds such a view, without ghosts so to speak—I would insist that such meaning implies *havingness*, something to own and to possess. Enchantment is the impossibility of having meanings, possessing and owning them; loss of meaning is not disenchantment but the interruption of values we wish to grasp and the multiplication of values beyond grasping. Derrida's emphasis on the trace calls attention to the impossibility of grasping meaning or being, under their names or of transcendence or god.

Possessing having grasping meanings beings realities. Are these disenchantments dispossessings givings ungraspings illusions simulacra appearances virtualities? Are they enchantments? The enchantments of the world cannot be grasped or fixed or named...

Dews praises "Taylor's insistence on the indispensability and irreducibility of the human encounter with transcendent, empowering moral sources such as freedom, nature or—ultimately—God" (11) side by side with habermas's and derrida's quite different language:

> The trivial must be allowed to shatter against the sheerly alien, abyssal, uncanny which resists assimilation to what is already understood, although no privilege can now install itself behind it. (Dews, 11; quoted from Jürgen Habermas, *VV*, 630–1)

> Derrida seeks to hold open the space of an "experience of the impossible." Derrida interprets this experience in various ways—as a messianic promise, which presupposes "hospitality without reserve" towards the singularity of the event as a basic pre-ontological structure of receptivity and donation which has *intrinsic* ethical significance. (Dews, 11)

Here he reads derrida's language of the impossible as a late gesture toward ethical meaning and away from disenchantment. He fails to note that derrida speaks of what is impossible throughout his writing as the condition of possibility, as if enchantment were the condition of disenchantment. I understand the ethical significance of the promise and singularity of the event as a hospitality beyond knowledge or calculation to the arrival of the unexpected: "welcoming salutation accorded in advance to the absolute surprise of the *arrivant* from whom or from which one will not ask anything in return" (Derrida, *SM*, 65). Absolute surprise at being given what cannot be taken, even asked to have. Is this meaning, transcendent or otherwise, is it a transcendent, empowering source—ultimately god—or is it the impossibility of meaning—not perhaps its loss—that makes meaning possible—its openness to what cannot be known, possessed, or accounted for? The messianic promise is always to come, never to arrive, interrupting every arrival. If it is a meaning it is one never to be grasped. If there is transcendent meaning must it not resist grasping?

Loss of meaning is meaning found. Finding meaning takes place in loss. Meaning is always on the edge of being lost. (Kathy Acker, *AOL*, 21)...

Loss of meaning is meaning not absence of meaning. Impossibility of meaning makes meaning mean. Meaning is present, lost, neither present nor lost, both present and lost. Interrupting. Asking...

In this light I would imagine that meanings are all disenchanted for us today insofar as we would possess them, secure them, and that enchantment dislocates every meaning from possession—including all transcendent meanings and the gods—insofar as they take possession of us and our world. Science is not just a vocation if it has possessed us and disenchanted our world. I am by no means sure it has done so for any but a few academics, scientists and philosophers. If it has done so it has taken on the work of the gods and has given some of us meaning, reason's meaning. I do not see how to deny that the contemporary world is filled with meanings—too many, perhaps. I believe that science's, technology's, and philosophy's meanings are all disenchanted figures of and in an enchanted earth.

Disenchanted figures lost meanings lost times dispossessions enchant the earth expose the world to enchanting expositions...

I have pressed weber's account of disenchantment in order to illuminate some of the ambiguities that circumscribe it—in particular, the oppositions in which it is located that engender one ambiguity after another: between secular reason and religious commitment, between modernity and what comes before and after, between technical, instrumental calculations and tellings, between knowledge and value. How, for example, are secular reason and modernity linked in relation to modern religion? Is secular reason the source of knowledge and religion the source of value? Many ambiguities haunt such conceptions, thereby haunting modern life and academic discipline. All inhabit a larger ambiguity, that given by the term *disenchantment* itself. It appears as a forsaken term, forsaking eternity, infinity, meaning, value. Yet secular modernity would insist that disenchantment is the condition of scientific knowledge and rational secular society. In this way it marks progress far beyond that of science, marks unceasing improvement in human life. Disenchantment is the name of art that marks the values of science as science and of secularization as civil society.

Magic disenchantment illusion are the conditions of secular reason and scientific knowledge. All lost...

Here the critiques of modern reason and of technical thinking represent one response to a world seen as advancing toward higher perfection through disenchantment. In other words, the valuelessness and objectivity of disenchanted reason are the root of its accomplishments. Reenchantment appears here as regression to a view of the earth that insists on knowledges that do not exist and cannot be had. The paired oppositions between secular reason and religion on the one hand and knowledge and value on the other present us with choices that define the modern world, past, present, and future. Here in the extreme one may imagine that in the name of disenchantment secular reason claims monopoly over all knowledge of the natural world, including human life, and in the name of reenchantment religion claims monopoly over ultimate values, including the natural world. Here is one example from the contemporary debate on intelligent design and evolution (if such a debate exists), given in quasi official form:

> "To speak of chance for a universe which presents such a complex organization in its elements and such marvelous finality in its life would be equivalent to giving up the search for an explanation of the world as it appears to us. In fact, this would be equivalent to admitting effects without a cause. It would be to abdicate human intelligence, which would thus refuse to think and to seek a solution for its problems." (quoted from Pope John Paul, 1985)
>
> Throughout history the church has defended the truths of faith given by Jesus Christ. But in the modern era, the Catholic Church is in the odd position of standing in firm defense of reason as well. In the 19th century, the First Vatican Council taught a world newly enthralled by the "death of God" that by the use of reason alone mankind could come to know the reality of the Uncaused Cause, the First Mover, the God of the philosophers.
>
> Now at the beginning of the 21st century, faced with scientific claims like neo-Darwinism and the multiverse hypothesis in cosmology invented to avoid the overwhelming evidence for purpose and design found in modern science, the Catholic Church will again defend human reason by proclaiming that the immanent design evident in nature is real. Scientific theories that try to explain away the appearance of design as the result of "chance and necessity" are not scientific at all, but, as John Paul put it, an abdication of human intelligence. (Christoph Schönborn, *FDN*)

Reason and religion claim authority over spheres of life and nature that understood ecologically and enchantingly admit to no such authority.

Weber is explicit that the claims of disenchanted science to give the truth of an enchanted world of values and ends are arrogant and fruitless. The roman catholic cardinal archbishop of Vienna offers fruitless and arrogant claims in reverse, insisting that human reason from the standpoint of the catholic church can establish immanent design. Weber takes for granted that the valuelessness of disenchantment promotes the values of scientific knowledge—and they are magnificent: evidence, proof, reliability, documentation, theory, vision. Science and religion achieve their goals by separation. Against this schönborn claims church authority over science in the realm of scientific knowledge, making any secular academic reaffirm separation.

> We live as did the ancients when their world was not yet disenchanted of its gods and demons, only we live in a different sense. As Hellenic man at times sacrificed to Aphrodite and at other times to Apollo, and, above all, as everybody sacrificed to the gods of his city, so do we still nowadays, only the bearing of man has been disenchanted and denuded of its mystical but inwardly genuine plasticity. Fate, and certainly not "science," holds sway over these gods and their struggles. One can only understand what the godhead is for the one order or for the other, or better, what godhead is in the one or in the other order. With this understanding, however, the matter has reached its limit so far as it can be discussed in a lecture-room and by a professor. Yet the great and vital problem that is contained therein is, of course, very far from being concluded. But forces other than university chairs have their say in this matter. (Weber, 148)

An ambiguity here concerns disenchantment, a term that appears to offer only negative values. Yet modernity, rationality, and technological practice all appear to support social progress, and if disenchantment and secularity are requisites, they too are progress. Moreover, the negation of magic, superstition, sorcery all appear as positive advances over illusion, madness, and delusion. That is the standard, secular academic position, and it can be opposed only by such claims as schönborn's, not because contemporary religion has nothing to say of value but because it seems unable to separate value from knowledge. If, as weber insists, the ends of life are inaccessible to science, where are we to turn for knowledge of how to live—finally? And if we do so by turning (back) to religion, is this reenchantment an abdication of contemporary science? *Neo-Darwinism* is the name of a dogma against which schönborn claims a higher and more truthful reason. The death of god is another, as if the enigmas of god and death might dissipate into another truth.

Living creatures walk the earth fly swim. Human beings walk the earth swim fly ride. Why do human beings need to be superior to the animals when they are animals? How indeed are they superior? What enchanted miracle brought about intelligence in the midst of inert matter—proving that matter is enchanted?...

Indeed, some believe, as I do, that science augments the wonder and is enchanting:

The most important thing about studying evolution is that the endeavor contains a profound optimism. We have an invitation to imagine, to play, to experiment and explore. To my mind, this only enhances the wonder. (Olivia Judson, *OE*)...

The magic of the microscope is not that it makes little creatures larger, but that it makes a large one smaller. We are too big for our world. The microscope takes us down from our proud and lonely immensity and makes us, for a time, fellow citizens with the great majority of living things. It lets us share with them the strange and beautiful world where a meter amounts to a mile and yesterday was years ago. (Judson, *PD*; quoted from A. E. Treat, *MMB*. Ithaca, NY: Cornell University Press, 1975)...

Facts do not float in sterile solitude are embedded in reality tainted with everyday life stained with history inextricable like darwin's web. We are here so briefly awake for a moment unique for an instant then we return to the generosity of this universe and its great making power. That is love. And not even the merest particle reveals itself without it. (Anne-Marie MacDonald, *BM*, 147–8)...

Enchantment is love. Love is enchanting...

The still ambiguous question of whether disenchantment is the condition of any reason that can claim epistemic authority, of modernity and modernization itself, founders on the question of authority over knowledge and truth. Put in this form, it is not merely that the academy and science claim to exercise authority over their truths as churches, temples, and mosques claim another and greater authority. It is that the struggles and conflicts within the sciences and academies are brought under the umbrellas of objectivity and valuelessness even as these are scrutinized by those sciences and in the academies as more complex than they may seem. Disenchantment is a more complex phenomenon in the contemporary epistemological landscape than it appears to be, and if it is a laudable condition for any science, just how it is and what it must be to be so remain open questions. Reason too remains an open question—what it is, how its own values can be sustained under an image of freedom from value, how it bears on all those forms of life and thought it has excluded in the name of unreason. Here is an example returning us to madness:

> We have yet to write the history of that other form of madness, by which men, in an act of sovereign reason, confine their

> neighbors, and communicate and recognize each other through the merciless language of non-madness; to define the moment of this conspiracy before it was permanently established in the realm of truth, before it was revived by the lyricism of process. We must try to return, in history, to that zero point in the course of madness at which madness is an undifferentiated experience, a not yet divided experience of division itself. We must describe, from the start of its trajectory, that "other form" which relegates Reason and Madness to one side or the other of its action as things henceforth external, deaf to all exchange, and as though dead to one another.
>
> What is constitutive is the action that divides madness, and not the science elaborated once this division is made and calm restored. What is originative is the caesura that establishes the distance between reason and non-reason; reason's subjugation of non-reason, wresting from it its truth as madness, crime, or disease, derives explicitly from this point. We shall have to speak of this act of scission, of this distance set, of this void instituted between reason and what is not reason, without ever relying upon the fulfillment of what it claims to be. (Foucault, *C*, ix–x)[34]

This caesura between reason and nonreason, perhaps between enchantment and disenchantment, is the site I would occupy—if it is anything to claim, a place to be, if it is not mobile and uninhabitable, interrupting every location.

Reason remains an open question remains an oppressive madness insists on its authority beyond all other authorities...

The view that what is at stake in disenchantment is the authority of reason and its political implications is the theme of habermas's *Theory of Communicative Action*, where he discusses weber and disenchantment at length.[35] The lines of thought that organize his discussion are the critique of enlightenment reason as instrumental and technical in lukács, horkheimer, and adorno, and habermas's own theory of communicative rationality. Thomas McCarthy is clear about this in his introduction:

> The first classical social theorist Habermas discusses in this book, Max Weber, directly challenged all these tenets of the Enlightenment faith in reason and progress in ways that remain relevant for us today. In his view, the rationality that defines modernity is at bottom a *Zwechrationalität*, a purposive or means/ends rationality, the inherent aim of which is the mastery of the world in the service of human interests. As a consequence, the growth and spread of reason does not, as Enlightenment thinkers supposed it would, furnish a new, nonillusory center

> of meaning to modern culture. It does, to be sure, gradually dissolve traditional superstitions, prejudices and errors; but this "disenchantment of the world," as Weber calls it, does not replace traditional religious worldviews with anything that could fulfill the functions of, for instance, giving meaning and unity to life. Rather, the disenchanted world is stripped of all ethical meaning; it is devalued and objectified as the material and setting for purposive-rational pursuit of interests. The gain in control is paid for with a loss of meaning. And the control that we gain is itself value-neutral—an instrumental potential that can be harnessed from any one of an unlimited number of value perspectives. This subjectivization of "ultimate" ends means that the unity of the world has fallen to pieces. In place of the one God or the unitary ground of being, we have an irreducible plurality of competing, often irreconcilable values.
>
> The realization of reason that the eighteenth-century philosophers envisioned as a Kingdom of God on earth has turned out to be an "iron cage" in which we are henceforth condemned to live. Disenchantment and rationalization are irreversible, as are the loss of meaning and the loss of freedom that accompany them. (Thomas McCarthy pref., xvii–xviii)

Kingdom of god on earth reigning ruling. Sovereign reason sovereign authority. Loss of meaning loss of freedom. Can freedom coexist with reason's sovereignty authority domination oppression? Can enchantment coexist with disenchantment, with unity in life and meaning?...

Can a god coexist with enchantment?...

What mccarthy says about disenchantment and value is worth considering, as if traditional religion's enchantments provided unity to life and meaning. Against this I am pursuing a line of thought in which unity and meaning are hegemonic in traditional and contemporary societies, and where enchantment offers resistance, interrupting every authority. The problem with reason is not its wonderful accomplishments and glorious revelations—though it would not describe itself that way—but the excessive authority ascribed to it over its competitors, whatever they may be. The enchantments of reason interrupt this authority while at the same time opening reason up beyond the limits of its claims to authority. Enchantment occupies the caesura.

In this context, habermas's concern is restricted almost entirely to more and less adequate views of rationalization. Moreover, he reads weber to posit disenchantment first of all in relation to religion:

> Weber analyzes the *process of disenchantment in the history of religion,* which is said to have fulfilled the necessary internal conditions for the appearance of Occidental rationalism; in doing so he employs a complex, but largely unclarified concept of rationality. (Habermas, *TCA* I, 143)

habermas does not explore the range of enchantments in and out of religion against which disenchantment is mobilized. Instead, he restricts himself to issues of social rationalization:

> On the one hand, Marx, Weber, Horkheimer, and Adorno identify societal rationalization with expansion of the instrumental and strategic rationality of action contexts; on the other hand, they all have a vague notion of *an encompassing societal rationality*—whether in the concept of association of free producers, in the historical model of an ethically rational conduct of life, or in the idea of fraternal relation with a resurrected nature—and it is against this that they measure the relative position of empirically described processes of rationalization. But the concepts that Marx, Weber, Horkheimer, and Adorno take as basic are not complex enough to capture all those aspects of actions to which societal rationalization can attach. The rationalization of action orientations and lifeworld structures is not the same as the expansion of the "rationality," that is, complexity of action systems. (144–5)

This describes habermas's orientation toward disenchantment—not in relation to an enchantment that would be both regressive and irrational, but the rectification of inadequate views of rationalization. The possibility of an enchanted reason disappears into the complexity of action systems. One might wonder whether the complexity of life systems might surpass any sphere of action—let us say *mimetically* and *enchantingly.* Habermas does not neglect this, though he classifies it under the names of horkheimer and adorno, especially the latter. Here first is horkheimer, then habermas's reading of adorno.

> What has been referred to as subjective reason is that attitude of consciousness that adjusts itself without reservation to the alienation between subject and object, the social process of reification, out of fear that it may otherwise fall into irresponsibility, arbitrariness, and become a mere game of ideas. The present-day systems of objective reason, on the other hand, represent attempts to avoid the surrender of existence to contingency and blind hazard. But the proponents of objective reason are in danger of lagging behind industrial and scien-

> tific developments, of asserting meaning that proves to be an illusion, and of creating reactionary ideologies. (Max Horkheimer, *ER*, 173–4; Habermas, *TCA*, 381)

> As the placeholder for primordial reason that was diverted from the intention of truth, Horkheimer and Adorno nominate a capacity, *mimesis*, about which they can speak only as they would about a piece of uncomprehended nature. They characterize the mimetic capacity, in which an instrumentalized nature makes its speechless action, as an "impulse."
>
> The paradox in which the critique of instrumental reason is entangled, and which stubbornly resists even the most supple dialectic, consists then in this: Horkheimer and Adorno would have to put forward a *theory* of mimesis, which, according to their own ideas, is impossible. (*TCA*, 382)

> It is the task of critique to recognize domination as unreconciled nature even within thought itself. But even if thought mastered the idea of reconciliation, even if it were not in the position of having to let this idea come to it from without, how could it transform mimetic impulses into insights, discursively, in its own element, and not merely intuitively, in speechless "mindfulness?" How could it do so if thought is always identifying thought, tied to operations that have no specifiable meaning outside the bounds of instrumental reason—all the more so today when, with the triumphal procession of instrumental reason, reification of consciousness seems to have become universal? (384)

How can thought master what it does not master master mastery master the very thought of mastery as knowledge as if the enchantments of mastery and thought were known only through disenchantment?...

As if disenchantment emerged from fear feared enchantment as reason fears unreason as if order were not as fearful as disorder reason as unreason disenchantment as enchantment...

Here the different terminologies—mimesis, mindfulness, impulse—express the subjective side of enchantment. Habermas does well to remind us that on the subjective side enchantment does not have a voice, that the voice belongs to the subject and its affects. The polarity of subject and object, inherited from kant through the third *critique*, leaves enchantment aside for a subjective aesthetics. It is perhaps in heidegger's reinstatement of being in response to modern subjectivation that we can find a gesture toward enchantment that is neither subjective nor objective, but enchanted being always moving beyond itself.

Habermas's argument concerning the positive critique of reason that would uphold mimesis as its alternative is a familiar one, and except for the prejudice that underlies it—what Foucault calls the madness of reason—allows itself to be reversed. If we can defend mimesis against the critique of reason only on reason's terms, if mimesis is silent regarding itself, then reason must be silent that we do so, no matter how eloquently or loudly it squawks. This is where *The Philosophical Discourse of Modernity* is important: it represents habermas's insistence, under the heading of the *problem of reflection* in hegel, that reason validates itself—*and only reason can do so.* His argument against mimesis is that it is not reason, does not have rational and discursive resources at its disposal—the very condition for which Adorno praises it—and is thereby silent where reason speaks. The reversal is that reason is silent where mimesis speaks. Moreover, this is not symmetric. The silence of reason is always given as unreason. Art—aesthetics, mimesis, exposition—does not exclude reason, not even instrumental reason, from its calling.

Exposition knows no opposite. Exposure expression asking calling telling as aisthēsis mimēsis poiēsis catachrēsis technē image aesthetics beauty art performance presentation interrupting calling giving asking telling have no opposites. Enchantment cannot be opposed by disenchantment...

Habermas has a point in saying that mimesis offers a subjective, archaic alternative to reason—if that is what it is and does. Adorno's explicit comments on mimesis suggest affinities with habermas's reading because he focuses on its implicit critique of instrumental reason:

> Art is a refuge for mimetic behaviour. In art the subject, depending on how much autonomy it has, takes up varying positions *vis-à-vis* its objective other from which it is always different but never entirely separate. Its ability to hold its own *qua* mimesis in the midst of rationality, even while using the means of rationality, is a response to the evils and irrationality of the rational bureaucratic world. The end of all rationality viewed as the sum total of all practical means would have to be something other than a means, hence a non-rational quality. Capitalist society hides and disavows precisely this irrationality, whereas art does not. It represents truth in the twofold sense of preserving the image of an end smothered completely by rationality and of exposing the irrationality and absurdity of the status quo. (Adorno, *AT*, 79)

It is clear that adorno does not ascribe irrationality to mimesis but to practical rationality (its "madness"). It is clear that Habermas cannot begin to entertain this critique, so he turns to the other side of mimesis, the silence that is its irrationality.

> The notion of direct intervention by the intellect in human affairs which recurs time and again throughout history is forsaken in art. But this does not mean that art can, through remembrance, simply and immediately turn to nature instead. It cannot, and it must not. Art's separation from nature can be undone, but only in virtue of this separation. This reinforces the rational moment of art while at the same time exculpating it, because it stands in opposition to real domination, even though art again and again falls into the position of an ideological ally of domination. (79–80)

This separation from nature echoes some of marx's most eloquent words. I will offer them here in the spirit of enchantment, knowing that adorno means separation as disenchantment.

> The first premise of all human history is, of course, the existence of living human individuals. Thus the first fact to be established is the physical organisation of these individuals and their consequent relation to the rest of nature. Men can be distinguished from animals by consciousness, by religion or anything else you like. They themselves begin to distinguish themselves from animals as soon as they begin to *produce* their means of subsistence. (Karl Marx, *GI*, 31).
>
> The way in which men produce their means of subsistence depends first of all on the nature of their means of subsistence they actually find in existence and have to reproduce.
>
> This mode of reproduction must not be considered simply as being the reproduction of the physical existence of the individuals. Rather it is a definite form of activity of these individuals, a definite form of expressing their life, a definite *mode of life* on their part. As individuals express their life, so they are. What they are, therefore coincides with their production, with *what* they produce and with *how* they produce. Hence what individuals are depends on the material conditions of their production. (31–2)

These words are read to express the separation of humanity from nature: as human beings live and express their lives, so they are, and so too is the earth they produce. What human beings are in nature and the world, thereby what the world and nature are, depends on the material conditions of their production. Use value is no more pristine nature than exchange value. In other words, there is no uncontaminated humanity or nature. Nature is disenchanted.

Life produces, life expresses. As human beings express and produce so they are so is the earth they produce. Expression production exposition are the conditions of being of humans and others. Production expression exposition are the enchantments of abundance and wonder...

If being unpristine is being disenchanted, then marx and engels must be read as disenchanting nature and humanity, no matter how different they are from weber. Moreover, they are by no means to be read as pessimistic about disenchantment—if that is how we choose to read weber. Yet in the light of weber's understanding of disenchantment as rationalization and intellectualization, thereby of enchantment as that which exceeds them, then while marx and engels reject religion as magic and superstition, the ways in which human beings produce and express themselves exceed any accounting. Expressiveness enchants the very world of humanity and nature that depends on material means of subsistence and production. Animals, people, things are what they are—mobile, effective, transitional—in virtue of changing means of production. It is not far from these understandings to gilles deleuze and guattari's understanding of the production of production, and to guattari's enchanted understanding of ecology:

> Everywhere *it* is machines—real ones, not figurative ones: machines driving other machines, machines being driven by other machines, with all the necessary couplings and connections. There is no such thing as either man or nature now, only a process that produces the one within the other and couples the machines together. Producing-machines, desiring-machines everywhere, schizophrenic machines, all of species life: the self and the non-self, outside and inside, no longer have any meaning whatsoever. (Deleuze and Guattari, *A-O*, 1–2)

> Hence everything is production: *productions of productions,* of actions and of passions; *productions of recording processes,* or distributions and of coordinates that serves as points of reference. This is the first meaning of process as we us the term: incorporating recording and consumption within production itself, thus making them the production of one and the same process. (4)

> It has become imperative to recast the axes of values, the fundamental finalities of human relations and productive activity. An ecology of the virtual is thus just as pressing as ecologies of the visible world. And in this regard, poetry, music, the plastic arts, the cinema—particularly in their performance or performative modalities—have an important role to play. (Guattari, *C*, 91)

> At the heart of all ecological praxes there is an a-signifying rupture. In the scenario of processual assemblages, the expressive a-signifying rupture summons forth a creative repetition that forges incorporeal objects, abstract machines and Universes of value that make their presence felt as though they had been always "already there," although they are entirely dependent on the existential event that brings them into play.
>
> We find this eco-logic equally at work in everyday life, in social life at every level. (Guattari, *TE*, 45–6)

Enchanted machines, if you will. Enchanting machines. Everywhere are machines expressing, desiring, asking, writing, and producing. Everything is producing, everything is expressing, everything is desiring, everything is enchanting and enchanted. The enchantment of the earth is given in the production and exposition of enchanting machines.

Enchanted machines machines are enchanting. Everywhere is machines everywhere is immanence immanence is enchantment immanent machines are enchanting. Everywhere machines express desire produce machines, everything is machines, machines interrupting machines. Everywhere machines express interrupt ask tell desire produce enchanted machines. Producing machines producing enchantments producing productions desiring desires mechanizing machines enchanting enchantments asking machines asking askings...

Separation for adorno is disenchantment, so that we may imagine that undone it becomes reenchantment. Here, however, weber's language and adorno's suspicion bring enchantment back to magic.

> There is a sense in which even the cliché about the "magic of art" rings true. The continued existence of mimesis defines art as a form of cognition. Since magic, which is being secularized by art, refuses to go along, art is threatened with destruction. The so-called crisis of art is in fact as old as the concept of art itself. Art cannot live up to its concept. (Adorno, *AT*, 80)

Art can't live up to its concept nor can magic and enchantment. Why should anything live up to its concept? Why should everything possess a concept—including art and disenchantment? Everything betrays its concept...

Moreover, this disparity between enchantment and concept may be a key to enchantment. That is, its name, every word that would grasp it—god, divinity, spirituality, magic—betrays it, interrupts it. And so with disenchantment, it proves to be impossible to grasp, as if it remained enchanted, as if it could be present only through what it excludes, mimesis and art. Much of what

Adorno says here can be read as mirroring the understanding of enchantment I will offer, not so much in the name of art's accomplishments as in the uncontainability of writing and mimesis and the impossibility of naming what in art and literature is their contribution to an enchanted earth. This earth and this enchantment do not resist the separation of art from nature but interrupt, embellish, and multiply it. Silence and speechlessness are not reticence but multiplicity and diversification.

> Mimesis is the ideal of art, not some practical method or subjective attitude aimed at expressive values. The epitome of expression is the linguistic character of art which is totally different from language as a medium of art. In fact, the true language of art is speechless. (164)

One may hear walter benjamin echoing in these words, a historical necessity. One may hear another echo in foucault, multiplying history to infinity.

> Nature creates similarities. One need only think of mimicry. The highest capacity for producing similarities, however, is man's. His gift of seeing resemblances is nothing other than a rudiment of the powerful compulsion in former times to become and behave like something else. (Walter Benjamin, *OMF*, 333)

> From time immemorial the mimetic faculty has been conceded some influence on language. Yet this was done without consideration of a further meaning, still less a history, of the mimetic faculty. In brief, it is nonsensuous similarity that establishes the ties not only between the spoken and the signified but also between the written and the signified, and equally between the spoken and the written. (334–5)

> In this way language may be seen as the highest level of mimetic behavior and the most complete archive of nonsensuous similarity: a medium into which the earlier powers of mimetic production and comprehension have passed without residue, to the point where they have liquidated those of magic. (336)

Liquidating magic is disenchantment, and mimesis returns to limit and foreclose it. Yet as exposition, if not art, perhaps not even language but always sensuous—nonsensuously sensuous—mimesis is uncontainable beyond limit. Foucault describes the prose of the world in this way:

> *Convenientia, aemulatio, analogy,* and *sympathy* tell us how the world must fold in upon itself, duplicate itself, reflect itself, or

> form a chain with itself so that things can resemble one another. (Foucault, *OT*, 25–6)[36]
>
> The semantic web of resemblance in the sixteenth century is extremely rich:
>
> *amicitia aequalitas (contractus consensus matrimonium societas pax et similia) consonantia concertus continuum paritas proportio similitudo conjunctio copula.* (17)...
>
> There is something in emulation of the reflection and the mirror: it is the means whereby things scattered through the universe can answer one another. The human face, from afar, emulates the sky, and just as man's intellect is an imperfect reflection of God's wisdom, so his two eyes, with their limited brightness, are a reflection of the vast illumination spread across the sky by sun and moon; the mouth is Venus, since it gives passage to kisses and words of love; the nose provides an image in miniature of Jove's sceptre and Mercury's staff. The relation of emulation enables things to imitate one another from one end of the universe to the other without connection or proximity: by duplicating itself in a mirror the world abolishes the distance proper to it; in this way it overcomes the place alloted to each thing. But which of these reflections coursing through space are the original images? Which is the reality and which the projection? It is often not possible to say, for emulation is a sort of natural twinship existing in things; it arises from a fold in being, the two sides of which stand immediately opposite to one another. (19–20)

Mimesis as enchantment as if enchanting as if it were uncontained uncontainable incalculable mimesis as the interruption of the world perhaps...

This uncontainable and incalculable mimesis is guarded by modern representation as if it were empty:

> First and foremost, the plethoric yet absolutely poverty-stricken character of this knowledge. Plethoric because it is limitless. Resemblance never remains stable within itself; it can be fixed only if it refers back to another similitude, which then, in turn, refers to others; each resemblance, therefore, has value only from the accumulation of all the others, and the whole world must be explored if even the slightest of analogies is to be justified and finally take on the appearance of certainty. And for this reason, from its very foundations, this knowledge will be a thing of sand. (30)

And indeed the emptiness of the infinite and the fullness of emptiness are worth pursuing. Here, however, emptiness still has explicit meaning. To be devoid of meaning is meaningful in the voices of exposition.

> There are no resemblances without signatures. The world of similarity can only be a world of signs. (26)

> Every resemblance receives a signature; but this signature is no more than an intermediate form of the same resemblance. As a result, the totality of these marks, sliding over the great circle of similitudes, forms a second circle which would be an exact duplication of the first, point by point, were it not for that tiny degree of displacement which causes the sign of sympathy to reside in an analogy, that of analogy in emulation, that of emulation in convenience, which in turn requires the mark of sympathy for its recognition. (29)

Imitating, mirroring, similitudes beyond similitudes produce endless multiplicities and differences. Perhaps only in the imagination—if that is a name of difference. Perhaps not without betrayal.

The one does violence to itself and guards itself against the other (Derrida, *PF*, ix). *The one betrays itself in betraying the others* (Ross, *GSSEB*, xxx)...

As exposition exposure expression calling aisthēsis mimēsis poiēsis catachrēsis technē image aesthetics beauty art asking telling giving interrupting...

The enchantment of the earth is its exposition perhaps not without betrayal. The speechlessness of mimesis betrays the emptiness of the earth and the fullness of exposition. Disenchantment does violence to itself and guards itself against enchantment. Enchantment opens itself to the other beyond containment but betrays it in every name every gesture every place and thing. Enchantment disenchants itself...

I do not believe that habermas is open to enchantment, closing himself off into the violence and guarding of disenchantment. I believe that he poses for us, in a disenchanted way, the possibility that reason is enchanted and that it is called to asking no matter how violently it struggles against it.

The madness of reason is that it struggles to destroy what it cannot be without...

I do not write primarily in the context of the critique of reason, instrumental or otherwise, but of the possibility of enchantment that remains, taking habermas's goal for granted that modernity has not lost the possibility of value—here understood as enchantment. With respect to reason, I am interested in an enchanted, secular reason. With respect to the world, however, I am interested in an enchanted nature, ecologically.

Before moving on from reason and its critique to that other pole of enlightenment history, the death of the gods, I would pause over the insistence in weber and habermas especially, but also in marx, horkheimer, and adorno, that history has been marked by disenchantment in an irreversible way. Reason has arrived and has changed everything—or perhaps the change in everything has brought disenchantment. In *The Conflict of the Faculties* especially, and in "What is Enlightenment?" kant insists on the irreversibility of reason in history as he insists on the end of art. The end of art, the death of god, the close of modernity, and disenchantment together frame the possibility of an event whose coming surpasses understanding.

> Without the mind of a seer, I now maintain that I can predict from the aspects and precursor-signs of our times, the achievement of this end, and with it, at the same time, the progressive improvement of mankind, a progress which henceforth cannot be totally reversible. A phenomenon of this kind in human history *can never be forgotten*. (Immanuel Kant, *CF*; quoted in Lyotard, *SH*, 408)

> In science, then, the greatest discoverer only differs in degree from his laborious imitator and pupil, but he differs specifically from him whom nature has gifted for beautiful art. And in this there is no depreciation of those great men to whom the human race owes so much gratitude, as compared with nature's favorites in respect of the talent for beautiful art. For in the fact that the former talent is directed to the ever advancing perfection of knowledge in this it has a great superiority over those who deserve the honor of being called geniuses. For art stands still at a certain point; a boundary is set to it beyond which it cannot go, which presumably has been reached long ago and cannot be extended further. (Kant, *CJ*, §47, 152)

Here disenchantment and its reason impose a permanent mark in history. Even foucault recognizes this permanence.

> I wonder whether we may not envisage modernity rather as an attitude than as a period of history. And by "attitude," I mean a mode of relating to contemporary reality; a voluntary choice made by certain people; in the end, a way of thinking and feeling; a way, too, of acting and behaving that at one and the same time marks a relation of belonging and presents itself as a task.
>
> The thread that may connect us with the Enlightenment is not faithfulness to doctrinal elements, but rather the permanent

> reactivation of an attitude—that is, of a philosophical ethos that could be described as a permanent critique of our historical era. (48–51)

A permanent critique appears to be disenchanted on both sides of its dyad: permanent and critical. Something may surpass critique in history, something in history may undergo transformation, an enchanted history and earth cannot be held fixed even within the freedom foucault defines as modernity. Yet he answers to this enchantingly in a disenchanted voice:

> The critical ontology of ourselves has to be considered not, certainly, as a theory, a doctrine, nor even as a permanent body of knowledge that is accumulating; it has to be conceived as an attitude, an ethos, a philosophical life in which the critique of what we are is at one and the same time the historical analysis of the limits that are imposed on us and an experiment with the possibility of going beyond them. (56)

Not a permanent doctrine or a body of knowledge, but an ongoing attitude, ethos, life so that we may experiment more radically and deeply with the possibility of becoming otherwise. Experimentation and becoming otherwise take enchantment for granted. Foucault expresses something of this in another voice:

> I hate to say it, but it's true that I am not a really good academic. For me, intellectual work is related to what you could call "aestheticism," meaning transforming yourself. I am not interested in the academic status of what I am doing because my problem is my own transformation. This transformation of one's self by one's own knowledge is, I think, something rather close to the aesthetic experience. Why should a painter work if he is not transformed by his own painting? (Foucault, *MF*, 130–1)

I would hazard that this is an enchanted transformation. I would hazard that it offers a place where enchantment meets disenchantment and religion meets secularity: the point of self transformation within the opening of the transformation of the world, of every thing.

Intellectual work perhaps all work perhaps life itself finally or otherwise are related to enchantment as if perhaps transforming oneself. An excessive exalted enchanted self. (Monique Wittig, *MG*, 87)...

I interrupt and approach conclusion by setting a disenchanted stage for enchantment with the death of god and radical theology's struggle with secularization. The death of god here is not secularity, radical theology is not the end of theology and the victory of academic reason over religion. It is the (en)closure of an epoch within its passing—within its life as well as its death. Like the (en)closure of the Western, European, Greek-Judaic-Christian Epoch of Metaphysics,[37] it can be thought and lived only from within, interrupting itself. It is not located, as it appears to be, in the space between the sacred and secular, religion and science, enchantment and disenchantment, nor between one religion and another—christianity and islam, for example, or monotheism and paganism. On the side of theology it remains entirely given over to religion. On the side of disenchantment, it rejects the link between enchantment and religion, and especially between the infinite and god. One of the crucial limitations of the discourse on disenchantment is this association of enchantment with religion and magic and of disenchantment with reason and science. I have spoken of a secular enchantment and an enchanted reason as well as of a disenchanted theology.

Here I would pursue the disenchantments of theology and the enchantments of its radicalization. Do radical theology and the death of god reenchant the world or do they interrupt its disenchantment? Another asking, more crucial here, is how secularity can open itself to enchantment given that it is founded on reason's disenchantment. Here in anticipation is a gesture from Emmanuel Levinas on the enchantment of reason:

> Non-indifference, humanity, the-one-for-the-other is the very signifyingness of signification, the intelligibility of the intelligible, and thus reason. The non-indifference of responsibility to the point of substitution for the neighbor is the source of all compassion. It is responsibility for the very outrage that the other, who qua other excludes me, inflicts on me, for the persecution with which, before any intention, he persecutes me. Proximity thus signifies a reason before the thematization of signification by a thinking subject, before the assembling of terms in a present, a pre-original reason that does not proceed from any initiative of the subject, an anarchic reason. It is a reason before the beginning, before any present, for my responsibility for the other commands me before any decision, any deliberation. Proximity is communication, agreement, understanding, or peace. (Emmanuel Levinas, *OB*, 166)
>
> Reason is the-one-for-the-other! (167)

The diachrony and immemoriality of the one for the other opens it beyond disenchantment to an anarchic, enchanted, pre-original reason. If there be such. If there be peace.

The one for the other is reason, immemorial diachronic infinite responsibility in proximity vulnerability beyond calculation or account-

ing anarchic before disenchantment. Proximity is communication agreement understanding peace all enchanted...

For the moment I will set levinas aside and turn to the event claimed as the death of god—and it is as event, becoming, transformation, caesura, interruption that this radical possibility offers itself enchantedly. All the *posts* of our time echo the possibility—known most visibly in the west as the advent of jesus—of a coming beyond expectation. Here is a sampling on the side of jesus:

> *Jesus Christ, the crucified reconcilor.* First of all this means that the whole world became god-less, without God, by rejecting Jesus Christ, and that by no effort of its own can the world remove this curse. The worldliness of the world received its signature once and for all through the cross of Christ. The cross of reconciliation means freedom to live before God in the midst of the godless world, that is, in genuine worldliness. (Dietrich Bonhoeffer, *MC*, 21)

> Already in the possibility of the knowledge of good and evil Christian ethics discerns a falling away from the origin. Man at his origin knows only one thing: God. It is only in the unity of his knowledge of God that he knows of other men, of things, and of himself. He knows all things only in God, and God in all things. The knowledge of good and evil shows that he is no longer at one with this origin.
>
> He knows himself now as something apart from God, outside God, and this means that he now knows only himself and no longer knows God at all; for he can know God only if he knows only God. The knowledge of good and evil is therefore separation from God. Only against God can man know good and evil. (*E*, 21–2)

Both the coming of jesus, with his crucifixion, and the possibility of ethics in this world give it to us as godless. In both cases, and despite bonhoeffer's personal suffering, the godless world is given to us in freedom and goodness, not in evil or disenchantment.

> A theology that chooses to meet our time, a theology that accepts the destiny of history, must first assess the theological significance of the death of God. We must realize that the death of God is a historical event, that God has died in our cosmos, in our history, in our *Existenz*. (Thomas Altizer, *RD*, 11–2)

> the time has now come to say that theology can know neither grace nor salvation; for a time it must dwell in darkness, existing on this side of the resurrection. Consequently the theolo-

> gian must exist outside of the Church: he can neither proclaim the Word, celebrate the sacraments, nor rejoice in the presence of the Holy Spirit. Before contemporary theology can become itself, it must first exist in silence.
>
> If theology is truly to die, it must will the death of God, must will the death of Christendom, must freely choose the destiny before it, and therefore must cease to be itself. Everything that theology has thus far become must now be negated; and negated not simply because it is dead, but rather because theology cannot be re-born unless it passes through, and freely wills, its own death and dissolution. (William Hamilton, *DGTT,* 15)

The death of god is an event, the time has come for theology to insist that god is dead, for christian theology—possibly not the world, not civilization, not all people in their spiritual practices—to undergo the event of the death of god. And in this undergoing to be reborn, through death and dissolution. In interruption. If death is the way through which christians are reborn, then it is time for christian theology to undergo its death in order to live again, to reenchant itself and the earth.

We have killed him—you and I. All of us are his murderers. But how did we do this? How could we drink up the sea? Who gave us the sponge to wipe away the entire horizon? What were we doing when we unchained this earth from its sun? Whither is it moving now? Whither are we moving? (Nietzsche, *GS,* #125)...

The question is how the death of god might reenchant the world and god. Perhaps as if that death might unleash a new paganism unlike the old.

> What does it mean to say that God is dead? Is this any more than a rather romantic way of pointing to the traditional difficulty of speaking about the holy God in human terms? Is it any more than a warning against all idols, all divinities fashioned out of human need, human ideologies? Does it perhaps not just mean that "existence is not an appropriate word to ascribe to God, that therefore he cannot be said to exist, and he is in that sense dead?" It surely means all this, and more.
>
> The hypothetical meanings suggested still all lie within the safe boundaries of the neo-orthodox or biblical-theology tradition, and the death of God group wants clearly to break away from that. It used to live rather comfortably there, and does so no longer. (Hamilton, *DGTT,* 26–7)

This notion of safe boundaries may be the cutting edge of both radical theology and disenchantment. The disenchanted world has become familiar, safe, on the side of theology and rationality.

Yet what is radical in theology is what is radical in god: god is not safety but calling and arrival, unfathomable mystery. As these pass from life god dies.

Is not the greatness of this deed too great for us? Must we ourselves not become gods simply to appear worthy of it? There has never been a greater deed; and whoever is born after us—for the sake of this deed he will belong to a higher history than all history hitherto! (Nietzsche, *GS*, #125)...

Enchantment looks to calling, arrival, mystery, and interruption everywhere, and hesitates at locating them uniquely in theology or god, in church or spirituality. To evoke the enchantments of the supernatural and divine against the disenchantments of the world is in effect to disenchant them all. If that be possible.

> Let theology rejoice that faith is once again a "scandal," and not simply a moral scandal, an offense to man's pride and righteousness, but, far more deeply, an ontological scandal; for eschatological faith is directed against the deepest reality of what we know as history and the cosmos. Through Nietzsche's vision of Eternal Recurrence we can sense the ecstatic liberation that can be occasioned by the collapse of the transcendence of Being, by the death of God. (Hamilton, *DGTT*, 30)

This is hamilton summarizing altizer, and for both I would refuse naming the scandal and the certainty of ecstatic liberation. The death of the gods opens up the arrival of the unknown and unknowable, liberation or confinement. The new age is by no means the enchanted answer to the death of the old. Nietzsche's madman echoes through these assurances of what the greatest deed ever will bring—assurances of what we can never be assured of.[38] That is clear where hamilton chooses to rest.

> I find myself unable and unwilling to separate myself from Christianity because, in part, it is Christians (and Jews) who are raising the questions today that I hold to be most important. And I wish to stand in the midst of that community. We are what we are because of our choice of comrades.
>
> *Just what is that community? Is it the church?*
>
> It can be for some; it is not, on the whole, for me. I am a Christian because I am deeply committed to many of the things that some Christians are committed to and know I cannot be without them. But I cannot now see in the church, even if renewed or underground, any trustworthy form for that new community. (Hamilton, *TGOD*, 17–8)

I might ask, which church? which christianity? where is it located? The spread of christianity throughout the world changes it drastically even where all believe in the living god. Could that be the death of god, its disenchantment?

Christianity was from the beginning, essentially and fundamentally, life's nausea and disgust with life. Hatred of "the world," condemnations of the passions, fear of beauty and sensuality, a beyond invented the better to slander this life, at bottom a craving for the nothing, for the end, for respite. (Nietzsche, *ASC*, 22–3)...

Fear as disenchantment...

I have suggested that the death of god offers itself as candidate for the event of all events, the arrival of what cannot be foreseen, the unknown, the strangest, the other in anomaly and alterity. The death of god repeats the coming of the messiah as if there might be another coming—not a second coming of the messiah, no matter how strange, but of a coming and yet another coming of what will be other, alter, anomalous, strange. This repetition repeats the coming of christ at the same time that it insists on the death of god. In this way all the *post*s that emerge in our time—postmodernity especially—signify this coming beyond any coming, as if to say that there might be no such coming but that strangeness, alterity, asking, telling, interruption, are always present and becoming. Postmodernity, poststructuralism, postcoloniality, postmarxism, postsecularity, postcritique, postgender—postfeminism-postmasculinism-post(hetero)sexualism (queering), postchristianity all express not so much the anticipation of what is to come but the extremity of becoming itself. Here are two enchanted examples, two examples of enchantment, however christian, interrupting this interruption:

> Love arrives, it comes, or else it is not love. But it is thus that it endlessly goes elsewhere than to "me" who would receive it: its coming is only a departure for the other, its departure only the coming of the other.
>
> What is offered is this arrival and this departure, this incessant coming-and-going. What is offered is the offered being itself: exposed to arrival and to departure, the singular being is traversed by the alterity of the other, which does not stop or fix itself anywhere, because it is nothing other than the coming-and-going. The other comes and cuts across me, because it immediately leaves for the other: it does not return to itself, because it leaves only in order to come again. The crossing breaks the heart. (Jean-Luc Nancy, *SL*, 98)

> Eternal return cannot mean the return of the Identical because it presupposes a world (that of the will to power) in which all previous identities have been abolished and dissolved. Returning is being, but only the being of becoming. The eternal return does not bring back "the same," but returning constitutes the only Same of that which becomes. Returning is the becoming-identical of becoming itself. Repetition in the eternal return, therefore, consists in conceiving the same on the basis of the different. Only the extreme, the excessive, returns; that which passes into something else and becomes identical. That is why the eternal return is said only of the theatrical world of the metamorphoses and masks of the Will to power. (Deleuze, *DR*, 40–1)

A third example, marking the queerness of enchantment as well as enchantments' queerness:

> My own suspicion is that the universe is not only queerer than we suppose, but queerer than we can suppose. (Haldane, *PW*, 298)
>
> What characterises queer apocal(o)ptic/isim? It is queer's relentless questioning of all categorical imperatives, including the ontology Queer itself. The unremitting desire to undo, disrupt and make trouble for norms. The recognition that queer is transitory and momentary and thus might be superseded or become defunct as an interpretative tool at some future date, as well as the dedication to examining the notion of utility itself. It is queer's commitment to the here and now, the present, not putting faith in the always postponed future but in making an immediate intervention. It is the anti-assimilationist bent in queer theory, the activist strain with its refusal to be defined by or in terms set down by the dominant culture in any given situation. It points to the fact that queer is brought into being through acts of resistance, the recognition of the potential futility of resistance because of the norm's propensity for cooption and reinvention, but the drive towards resistance all the same. It is the trace of queer's investments in deconstruction and psychoanalysis, the refusal to normative coherence as fantasy and the making visible of the instability that constitutes any one thing. (Giffney, *QA*, 57)

This is to say, in queering, queering queers itself, temporally, spatially, processually, intimately; and, moreover, queers time and space. Queering queering queering is the endless betrayal of asking and telling: queering as asking of anything told, as telling of anything asked. Not to mention human and inhuman.

And a fourth example, marking our time's enchantments in a secular voice, derrida's voice echoing hélène cixous's, enchanting in wonder:

> In this place, from which her work springs, and to which it points, the alleged disenchantment of the world (*Entzauberung der Welt*), which has been dinned into our ears since Max Weber and which opposes magic to technique, may no doubt have a lot of sense and pertinence up to this point but it loses any pointed relevance. Like the opposition between faith and knowledge. And the point where this opposition appears, can be thought, determined—and annulled—is the point where she enchants technique that has remained technique, where she thinks and writes. No distinction then can hold any longer between magic and technique, faith and knowledge, and so on. (Derrida, *HCL*, 119–20)

Not to mention between the dead and living gods. But I have mentioned them, written them, hope to write them in a magical, enchanting chant—if any chants are disenchanting, if every chant is not enchanting, perhaps.[39] Between enchantment and disenchantment, where enchantment chants.

> I was interested in what happens when "believe" is preceded by this subjunctive (*would that* I *might*, that I *might*, *would that* we *might*, *would that* you *might* believe), which seems to play between the possible and the impossible. If one hears the full might of meaning this word has, to believe should then lie and only reside in this impossible faith in the impossible. Then one could believe only in miracles. And to believe would be the miracle, the magical power of the miracle. The miracle would be the ordinary of belief. A belief agrees with, allies itself to, and promises itself to only the incalculable. If it were so, what would "would that I might believe" or "I wish I might believe" mean then? What does this subjunctive become? How would the mighty powers of this unbelievable belief in the impossible watch over what is called so glibly the fiction of a so-called literary event, over all that complies with the modality of a certain "as if?" And as each art entertains a different experience of fiction and therefore of belief, one may wonder what happens to believing and to the "would that I might believe" when arts graft, haunt, and mingle with one another. What happens when music becomes the very body of another art, of literature for instance? What happens to belief then? When one hears a piece of music, if one can hear it, for instance a song [*chant*], an "enchanting chant [*enchant*t]?" What happens then, as far as belief and the impossible are concerned, when the song of the

> enchanting chant can no longer be dissociated from the whole body of words and from what still presents itself as the literality of literature? When literature becomes an enchanting chant? (4–5)

When literature interrupts itself. As if literature (and writing) were not always chanting, interrupting, where the opposition between one literature and another, one enchantment and another (another disenchantment) were another enchantment (or disenchantment).

Under the heading of belief, if you will, the might of belief as enchantment. I mean the chants of *might* performed in the modalities of *as if* and *perhaps*.

> "singing the song of enchantment," these are the words of *OR*, and the mighty power of the *might* of which we are speaking, as of Hélène Cixous's poetics in fact, is the enchantment, the arrival as if by an enchantment, where the poetic song, the charm, the *carmen*, and magical power are allied to *kommen Lassen*, make come in letting come, if one insists on formulating in the language of the mother or of the uncle this formula of the miracle of a chant of enchantment, which is also a song of songs. (79)
>
> > We are bodies in minds fast as the radio. Now I call up the name.
> > Watch out!
>
> This exclamation, "Watch out!" is extraordinary, truly magical, and it would merit centuries of analysis. Three lines earlier, there was the word "magic," you heard it, and the phrase "I call the number and, by a magic. . . ." Now [*or*] here she has just said: "Now I call up the name." She begins a new paragraph and exclaims or cries out: "Watch out!"
>
> This warning, "Watch out!" is the conjurer's exclamation or injunction: address or skill, agility, dexterity, digital writing. On a stage, while the trapeze artist carries on with his acrobatic exercises, this magician talks to his public as he is about to pull his trick and conjure the thing out of himself, in a moment, right now, it is imminent, as if by an enchantment. Watch out, the impossible thing will take place under your eyes in a moment:
>
> > Now I call up the name.
> > Watch out!
> >
> > Provided you watch carefully—but in any case you will not see a thing, since it goes so fast and the mighty power escapes you. (100–1)

Where the enchantment's mighty power is right now, here, where *right now here* has become enchanting. Right now, here, where the gods are living or dead. I mean the animals. Today.

> are there more telephones or animals in the life and works of Hélène Cixous? Answer: animals are telephones and sometimes the other way around, and they multiply, in the prolifauny of all their animal, human, and divine metamorphoses. (102)

In the cacophony of all metamorphoses. In the voice of derrida reading cixous reading (uncle) freud (if this is reading and not singing):

> > ...Here is the reason why one can love an animal: (beyond all the differences of organic development) we are next of kin by the same enchantment. I am really talking about the enchanting chant, this unlimited sentenceless willful language comparable to God's unknown language. So my uncle Freud thought.
> >
> > "That's why often, while caressing Jofi, I caught myself humming a melody that I know well although I am no musician..."
>
> The musician of this *enchanting chant*—the musician that the subject of utterance says he is not, although he is humming, as Freud would hum—is a male musician. Not a female musician. We would have—a truly infinite work—to deal with the truth of the sex of this masculine, like that of the author who is the daughter of the dead-fathers, as with the trouble, the instability, the infinitely intertwined, criss-cross multiplicity of the sexual identities that share the signature of this work, replacing one another anywhere with unspeakable craft, tricks, and subtleties—making all the more difficult or improbable a reading that would not make the same expenditure—and with reading comes the political strategy that would instrumentalize this enchanting chant like a feminist theorem or a philosophical thesis. (106)

This political-religious-secular strategy can exist only in the instrumentality of an enchanting chant. So we may ask, what is the end of the enchantment? Perhaps a (feminist) theorem or a (philosophical) thesis. Perhaps an (enchanting) disenchantment, or a (dis)enchanting chant(ment). Perhaps the (death of the) gods.

Returning from this interruption inside an interruption:

The dead gods chant the gods disenchant the gods enchant and disenchant. Who could believe in disenchantment in the might of belief?...

The death of the gods comes in the strangeness of things their endless enchantments another strangeness beyond the gods. The gods have lost their strangeness we know too well who is god what the gods want of us we know and we do not know and do not know what we do not know. That is death as the disenchantment of the gods. That is enchantment as interruption the coming and going of love and spirits and ghosts the arriving of gods beyond the desire to know...

Kant marks the end of art in a gesture that insists on the perpetuity of science and reason.[40] Hegel marks the end of art in a gesture that insists on the gathering of spirit beyond the death of the gods.

> The religion of art belongs to the spirit animating the ethical sphere,. . . .
>
> But this self, through its being empty, has let the content go. It is consciousness of the loss of everything of significance in this certainty of itself, and of the loss even of this knowledge or certainty of self—the loss of substance as well as of self; it is the bitter pain which finds expression in the cruel words, "God is dead."
>
> The statues set up are now corpses in stone whence the animating soul has flown, while the hymns of praise are words from which all belief has gone. The tables of the gods are bereft of spiritual food and drink, and from his games and festivals man no more receives the joyful sense of his unity with the divine Being. They are themselves now just what they are for us—beautiful fruit broken off the tree; a kindly fate has passed on these works to us, as a maiden might offer such fruit off a tree. Their actual life as they exist is no longer there, not the tree that bore them, not the earth. Our action, therefore, when we enjoy them is external; it consists in wiping off some drop of rain or speck of dust from these fruits, not in order to enter into their very life, but only to represent them ideally or pictorially within ourselves. But just as the maiden who hands us the plucked fruits is more than the nature which presented them in the first instance since in a higher way she gathers all this together into the light of her self-conscious eye, and her gesture in offering the gifts; so too the spirit of the fate, which presents us with those works of art, is more than the ethical life realized in that nation. For it is the *inwardizing* in *us*, in the form of conscious memory, of the spirit which in them was manifested in a still *external* way;—it is the spirit of the tragic fate which collects all those individual gods and attributes of the substance into the one Pantheon, into the spirit which is itself consciousness of itself as spirit. (G. W. F. Hegel, *PM*, 751–4)

The death of the gods takes place in the emergence of the modern spirit who turns from the certainty of nature and the divine to itself. It loses itself in its loss of god. But this loss gives way to the emergence of another gathering: the presenting and offering of the fruits of the past in the light of a self-conscious eye. Here the death of the gods is the lighting of the modern, individual self, the collection and presentation of past works in the present. What gathers is everything that can be gathered, that can be preserved. The death of the gods is the preservation of what can be gathered of them in the time to come.

This is hegel, it is supersession and sublimation. Self-conscious spirit emerges from death to a new life. In this way, then, it is more than hegel, for in the death of the ancient gods life comes to all, especially christians. The death of the gods here marks the coming of an event, the arrival of a world-transforming occurrence, an interruption after which the earth will never be the same and that can never be forgotten. In this case it is the arrival of the messiah. Christianity as well as western rationality occur as if irreversibly and unexpectedly. Disenchantment is this event, albeit in the name of god. The death of god is a radical event, still in the name of god. That is how everyone who follows—nietzsche especially but also the radical theologians—understands it. The death of god is the unexpected arrival of what cannot be anticipated or known. Heidegger and his followers speak of it as the event, the happening, the arrival. Radical theologians speak of it as death but what they mean is life. The question is what we hope to mean by holding onto the name of god for what has no name, and what it means to name the unexpected arrival, the other, with any name.

The death of god is the arrival of disenchantment in such a way as to enchant every moment and place with the aura of a coming that is always on the way and that can never be held in place. This is why the announcement of the death of god is received by Zarathustra with disappointment. It is announced as if it is to be anticipated, but cannot be. The death of god suffers the same fate as the gods, gathered and regathered at the point of its ungathering.

> "And what is the saint doing in the forest?" asked Zarathustra.
>
> "Could it be possible? This old saint in the forest hath not yet heard anything of this, that *God is dead!*" (Nietzsche, Z, Prologue, #2)

Even so, he laughs irreverently.

> The madman jumped into their midst and pierced them with his eyes. "Whither is God?" he cried. "I will tell you! *We have killed him*—you and I. All of us are his murderers. But how

> did we do this? How could we drink up the sea? Who gave us the sponge to wipe away the entire horizon? What were we doing when we unchained this earth from its sun? Whither is it moving now? Whither are we moving? Do we hear nothing as yet of the noise of the gravediggers who are burying God? Do we smell nothing as yet of the divine decomposition? Gods, too, decompose. God is dead. God remains dead. And we have killed him.
>
> "How shall we comfort ourselves, the murderers of all murderers? What was holiest and the mightiest of all that the world has yet owned has bled to death under our knives: who will wipe this blood off us? What water is there for us to clean ourselves? What festivals of atonement, what sacred games shall we have to invent? Is not the greatness of this deed too great for us? Must we ourselves not become gods simply to appear worthy of it? There has never been a greater deed; and whoever is born after us—for the sake of this deed he will belong to a higher history than all history hitherto!"
>
> Here the madman fell silent and looked again at his listeners and they, too, were silent and stared at him in astonishment.... "I come too early," he said then; "my time is not yet. This tremendous event is still on its way, still wandering; it has not yet reached the ears of men. Lightning and thunder require time; the light of the stars requires time; deeds, though done, still require time to be seen and heard. This deed is still more distant from them than the most distant star—*and yet they have done it themselves*."
>
> "What after all are these churches now if they are not the tombs and sepulchers of God?" (Nietzsche, *GS*, #125)

> The greatest recent event—that "God is dead," that the belief in the Christian God has become unbelievable—is already beginning to cast its first shadows over Europe. But in the main one may say: The event itself is far too great, too distant, too remote from the multitude's comprehension even for the tidings of it to be thought of as having *arrived* as yet. Much less may one suppose that many people know as yet *what* this event really means—and how much must collapse now that this faith has been undermined because it was built upon this faith, propped up by it, grown into it: for example, the whole of our European morality. (#343)[41]

Of course, god is dead, jesus is dead, and his followers killed him, all who love and follow him kill him over and over, and know that he is dead, that he comes back as dead. Nietzsche does not turn away from the dead god to jesus but reminds us that all of us in the eyes of gods are ugly, ugly in our depths and nooks, ugly as the murderer of the god. The death of god is not the end of christianity but its meaning—if there is meaning after the death of god, if there was ever meaning in the death of a god, if there is meaning in christianity today, and tomorrow. The event, the coming after the death of god, remains to come, always coming. Our whole being, our whole morality, who we will become comes after the death of god.

Coming-and-going. The other comes and cuts across me and leaves immediately for the other. It does not return to itself because it leaves only in order to come again...

The superman comes in nietzsche, the girl comes in hegel, the end of art arrives in kant, the earth is disenchanted in modern reason, a coming that marks the end of the past, the death of the gods, the reign of secularity, the coming of that which will never pass away. Impossible, one might imagine. Or instead, all too possible, understanding that this coming of that which will never go is disenchantment. The gods come and go, and when they come the earth trembles. Disenchantment comes and never goes, and from that moment the earth never trembles.

Fates spinning weaving in our times through all times. Many fates many threads many times. Many reasons many intellects many passions many truths. Many spirits many gods many beauties many arts. Shall we insist on one? Can we imagine many? Why above all and for whom? Many disenchantments many enchantments endless askings surprises arrivals interruptions. Images proliferating...

Disenchantment is the death of the gods, the end of enchantment, if that be possible. This very death, announced by Nietzsche and then by radical theologians, announces the coming of the new, the coming of the unknown, the arrival of that which cannot be anticipated. In the name of god, whose death means nothing other than this coming of what in the name of the god cannot be recalled. Enchantment then is interrupting, coming and going, always coming and always going, everywhere coming and everywhere going, the possibility and the actuality and the reality and the illusion of the arrival of that which cannot be anticipated: the other, the others, the herald, the transfiguration.

In this light, postmodernity is not an event that marks the end of modernity but the death of the gods that circumscribe it—here the disenchantment of the earth. It is not so much that disenchantment claims the abolition of enchantment—as if that were possible—as that it claims the end of the end, the disappearance of becoming, the loss of the other who might appear, of the enchantments that might enchant us. Postmodernism, poststructuralism, postcoloniality, post-this and post-that all announce in an enchanted voice the coming of what cannot be expected.

Hamilton calls it *revolutionary*, after Raymond Williams and Northrup Frye.

> It seems to me that we are living through a long revolution, transforming men and institutions. Yet it is a difficult revolution to define, and its uneven action is taking place over so long a period that it is almost impossible not to get lost in its exceptionally complicated process. (Raymond Williams, *The Long Revolution*, New York: Columbia University Press, 1961, x, xiii)
>
> The earlier closed mythology of the Western world was a religion, and the emergence of an open mythology has brought about a cultural crisis which is at bottom a religious crisis. Religion tends increasingly to make its primary impact, not as a system of taught and learned belief, but as an imaginative consistency and imaginative informing power. In other words, it makes its essential appeal as myth or possible truth, and whatever belief it attracts follows from that. (Northrop Frye, *MC*, 118–20; Hamilton, *TGOD*, 220–2)

What is open about an open mythology is that there are always limits but they do not limit absolutely. God is one of those limits, and is taken absolutely. But so is the human imagination, when it claims to possess enchantment. Enchantment cannot be possessed, that is what the death of god, the end of modernity, the questioning of disenchantment mean. If anything.

The gods are fugitive guests of literature. They cross it with the trail of their names and are soon gone. Every time the writer sets down a word, he must fight to win them back. The mercurial quality that heralds their appearance is token also of their evanescence. Everything ends up as history of literature. (Roberto Calasso, *LG*, 3)...[42]

The world—the time has come to say it, though the news will not be welcome to everyone—has no intention of abandoning enchantment altogether, if only because, even if it could, it would get bored. (23)...

The earth—it is time to say it—is disenchanted and has always been disenchanted. The earth is enchanted has always been and always will be enchanted. Through and through. The living gods the dying gods the dead gods secular rationality all are enchanted all enchant...

God is binary, my god not yours, god not nature, transcendence beyond immanence. God is nonbinary, beyond divisions, dichotomies, distinctions. Everything is god, everything is divine, many gods beyond any gods all the same all different all enchanted all enchanting. Everything is divine everything is religious everything is secular everything is disenchanted everything is enchanted...

Our enchantment is to question disenchantment in the name of religion and god from the standpoint of scientific and technological rationality. Secularization is as enchanted as religion. Both are disenchanted. And enchanted.

> With the history of religions and its central notion, religion, what is in question is, in fact, nothing more or less than certain pretensions of modern Western science to conceive of humankind and the world according to codes that it has elaborated and to points of reference that it has fixed. Or, if we prefer to turn this observation into a blunter question, is Western anthropology, religious anthropology in particular, in its quest for the Other and for our very humanity, capable of discovering anything but itself—that is, anything other than its own categories and its own ways of conceiving the world? (Daniel Dubuisson, *WCR*, 6)

> Just like the notion itself, the most general questions concerning religion, its nature and definition, its origins or expressions, were born in the West. From there, they were transferred, much later and at the cost of daring generalizations, to all other cultures, however remotely prehistoric or exotic.
>
> The exclusively Western history of questions relative to religion is, of course, inseparable from the intellectual history of the West, since it is from its own history that the West drew a complex of systematic reflections (from philosophy to theology, from anthropology to sociology or psychology) that were to lead to the universalization of a concept born of Christian apologetics dating from the first centuries of our era. Before retracing these historical steps, it is crucial to pause for a moment to address three questions that should normally open any debate devoted to this subject:
>
> — Is Christianity the special form taken in the West by something that has always existed and that similarly exists elsewhere, if not everywhere, namely, religion or the religious phenomenon?
> — As the legitimate daughter of Christianity, is religion not rather an element wholly unique to Western civilization, one of its most original creations?
> — Should we not, moreover, go somewhat farther and ask whether religion is not effectively the West's most characteristic concept, around which it has established and developed its identity, while at the same time defining its way of conceiving humankind and the world? (9)

Are these not enchanting askings? Might what has always existed everywhere be an original creation an enchanting chantment? What could interrupt christianity's rule?...

From this point of view, simply by raising these questions without insisting on their answer, religion, its history, and its philosophy are all disenchanted—westernly. Western religion's philosophy and its science. Religion is disenchanted and disenchants its offspring, science and philosophy.

> If we indulged ourselves by listing those chief works, literary or artistic, as well as the most general moral, political, scientific, or philosophical conceptions that escape the grasp of religion or its influence (if only to distance themselves from or oppose this influence), we would probably end up with very meager results. Around this privileged notion, the Christian West, spiderlike, has continued to spin its web of concepts, to wind the successive variations of its learned discourse, to superimpose its palimpsests of speculations, in brief, to affirm its own identity.
>
> Religion, that is to say, the entire universe that the word summarizes (theological subtleties, conceptions of the human being and human destiny, the role of providence, moral choice, retribution in the beyond, the immortality of the soul, the discipline of the body), has never ceased to nourish our major controversies and ever appears as the essential locus, that on which all others with very rare exception depend. (11–12)

> If there is one point on which history and anthropology can understand each other and agree, it must be this: every human group, in order to exist and to perpetuate itself as such, is obliged to develop and preserve a set of ideas, opinions, and diverse theses, themselves passed on and deepened by images, symbols, and myths concerning humankind, the world, and society. And this complex set, formed of a tangled multitude, is so indispensable, so intrinsically tied to the existence of the group itself that it finally appears (even if it is, from a metaphysical point of view, perfectly contingent) as its exclusive reference. *A fortiori*, this illusion is fundamental for its proponents, who have no other way to think themselves and the world than to draw from its own repertory of ideas and notions.[43] (69)

Enchantment and disenchantment agree that every human group must take possession of the world in a disenchanted way so that what is contingent, local, specific to that group—disenchanted—is at the same time and in the same ways infinite, necessary, inescapable, enchanted...

Everything remains religious—including secularity, philosophy, and science. Everything remains christian—including buddhism, confucianism, islam. Everything remains western—including the rest of the earth. Science repeats its relation to religion in dismissing it as not science. Philosophy claims independence in a voice of repetition. What if science were not disenchantment but an other enchantment? What if secularity were not unreligion but took heed of the pervasiveness of religion in asserting its own authority? Would this be more or less enchantment, less or more disenchantment?

Everything is religious. Everything is enchanted. Everything is secular. Everything is disenchanted...

Harvey Cox denies belonging to the death of god and radical theology movement(s) while acknowledging that he is a "radical" theologian who rejects the death of god (as well as its radicalism) (*SS*, 169). The meaning of radical theology he affirms is "to be in touch with those people who are ordinarily seen as 'losers.'" (169–70). This is an important meaning of radicality, and might be interpreted as the radicalization of the radical theology movement in the name of the dispossessed. Such a double gesture in the name of marginalization must remind us of certeau as well as of dubuisson. It is as if to say that radicalization cannot take place except in the context of religion and theology, at least on the world stage and in the history of the world as we know it. That is another story. The story here concerns enchantment, without which nothing radical is possible, but which pursues a different inheritance.

Cox does not address enchantment directly, nor weber's arguments concerning disenchantment, but he does discuss secularization at length.

> Contemporary man has become the cosmopolitan. The world has become his city and his city has reached out to include the world. The name of the process by which this has come about is *secularization*. It is the loosing of the world from religious and quasi-religious understandings of itself, the dispelling of all closed world-views, the breaking of all supernatural myths and sacred symbols. It is what Dietrich Bonhoeffer in 1944 called "man's coming of age." (Cox, *SC*, 1–2)

What he has to say of enchantment is perhaps more promising, albeit in another genre and to satisfy a different need.

> All human beings have an innate need to tell and hear stories and to have a story to live by. Religion, whatever else it has done, has provided one of the main ways of meeting this abiding need.

> There are two kinds of stories that are especially important as vehicles for religious experiences. The first is *autobiography*, or "testimony," the first-person account of the teller's struggle with the gods and the demons.
>
> The second religiously significant mode of storytelling is what I call "people's religion." It is the collective story of a whole people.
>
> There is a third type of religion which is neither testimony nor folk expression but which serves an important purpose. It is the religion that is coded, systematized, controlled and distributed by specialists. Religion in this form, though it still bears certain marks of a story, has actually become a system of what I call "signals." Most of the great religions of the world are a mixture of story and signal. (*SS*, 9–10)

It is possible to understand such a view in terms of enchantment and disenchantment, and moreover to do so twice—the double gesture of enchantment. The stories—autobiographical or collective—are *stories*, expressive, imaginative, enchanted; and *as stories, tellings, language, or mimēsis*, are tales of enchantment. Correspondingly, signals, specialization, totalization, and collective self-identifications may be interpreted as disenchantments. In this context, religion is not the condition of enchantment but a site of enchantment and disenchantment. And it has always been so. Our time, that of the secular city, is disenchantment run amok, with religion one of its casualties, but by no means the issue at hand. We can speak of the death of god here not as the decay of religion or loss of belief in divinity, but as the decline of the spirit that pertains to what the tales evoke and express *as stories*, that is, as what surpasses economic rationality.

This is a somewhat different understanding of disenchantment than the critique of modern reason. It overlaps with it in relation to the poor and dispossessed. More interesting, perhaps, for us here is cox's account of the human spirit, separated from religion and theology in an account of enchantment as *perhaps* and *as if*:

> The human spirit will undoubtedly continue to spawn myths and weave symbolic meanings, without much regard either to intellectual attacks or to zealous defenses, as long as the species exists. Though in the short run the spirit is catastrophically subject to trickery, coercion and exploitation, in the long run it can neither be exterminated nor domesticated.
>
> The future of theology, however, does not seem as secure as the future of the spirit. Theology, after all, is the expression of a particular form of thought—reflective, analytical, objective—

> that has arisen only in recent centuries and will probably not last forever. Sciences, mental forms and modes of thinking come and go, but the creativity of the spirit continues.
>
> The theology of the future should be a kind of play.
>
> 1) As "making fun of," theology is a satirizing activity which debunks destructive myths.
>
> 2) Theology is play not just as making fun of but also as "making believe," as fantasizing, pretending or imagining.
>
> "Make-believe" involves setting aside for a brief period the role, self-image, identity and world view within which one operates most of the time and trying out another way of being.
>
> 3) Theology can become play in a third sense, namely as non-instrumental, non-productive, "useless" activity. As an enterprise which, like play, serves no goal beyond itself, theology rightly defines the modern prejudice which decrees that only useful things have a right to exist. (318–25)

Disenchantments come and go, expressions of the enchanted spirit. As if to make believe in every moment open to fantasy alienness alterity without cessation. Uselessly. Playfully. Enchantingly. Beyond limit...

Limits limit but never absolutely. That is finiteness, infinitely. That is disenchantment, enchantedly. The (un)absoluteness of the absolute is the enchantment of its disenchantment...

If anything. With this kind of thinking I would turn to Morris Berman,[44] whose *Reenchantment of the World* poses its disenchantments as deeply as any. Another interruption:

> The view of nature which predominated in the West down to the eve of the Scientific Revolution was that of an enchanted world. Rocks, trees, rivers, and clouds were all seen as wondrous, alive, and human beings felt at home in this environment. The cosmos, in short, was a place of *belonging*. A member of this cosmos was not an alienated observer of it but a direct participant in its drama. His personal destiny was bound up with its destiny, and this relationship gave meaning to his life. This "participating consciousness" involves merger, or identification, with one's surroundings, and bespeaks a psychic wholeness that has long since passed from the scene.
>
> The story of the modern epoch is one of progressive disenchantment. From the sixteenth century on, mind has been progressively expunged from the phenomenal world. The reference points for all scientific explanation are matter and motion. Scientific consciousness is alienated consciousness: there is no ecstatic merger with nature, but rather total separation from it. Subject and object are always seen in opposition to each other. This world is not of my own making; the cosmos cares nothing

> for me, and I do not really feel a sense of belonging to it. What I feel, in fact, is a sickness in the soul. (Berman, *RW*, 16–7)

The story of the modern epoch is more complex, as I shall imagine. Enchantment is more than mind in nature. Many magical peoples felt alienated, out of place and home in nature, an earth not of their making. Scientific consciousness is in many ways unalienated, and as weber emphasizes, frequently ecstatic in inspiration. Belonging and merging are dionysian but also totalizing. Exstasis, being away from oneself, is by no means belonging to something transcendent, and the rule of the latter evokes endless questions of authority and control. Most of all, especially in the psychoanalytic model on which berman depends, finding oneself at home in the world involves separation, and enchantment is more than belonging, but journeying toward an earth that forever exceeds one's grasp. The world and cosmos that care for us remind us of gods as if they never died, gods who give us answers as if they were not disenchanted. The death of the gods does not appear here as the promise of enchantment, posing endless questions and questioning every answer.

We know ourselves to be made from this earth. We know this earth is made from our bodies. For we see ourselves. And we are nature. We are nature seeing nature. We are nature knowing nature. Nature weeping. Nature speaking of nature to nature. All that I know, I know in this earth, the body of the bird, this pen, this paper, these hands, this tongue speaking, all that I know speaks to me through this earth and I long to tell you, you who are earth too, and listen as we speak to each other of what we know: the light is in us. (Susan Griffin, *WN*, 226–7)...

Even so, I read berman as offering a picture of disenchantment close to mine, structurally speaking, if a different picture of enchantment. Without caesura. As weber and he insist, the world according to modern reason is no longer enchanted. Yet such a sense of what was once experienced is no longer possible for us, and I believe for good reason. I won't go into hostile gods, blood sacrifice, aggressive wars, the plunder of nature by indigenous peoples. Nor will I insist as many have that the gods are dead for us and we cannot return. Instead I would insist that reenchantment not return to an enchantment that is but another picture of the entire world, animistic and enchanted instead of alienated and mechanical. The earth has never ceased to be enchanted and has never been fully disenchanted. At all times and places disenchantments offered themselves in resistance to an enchantment that elusively slipped away, filled with surprises and unexpected arrivals. Berman replaces a modern scientific metaphysics with another. I would abolish neither and would expect both to continue, yet I would guard against their hegemony by reminding us that the earth is enchanted and that enchantment interrupts every metaphysics. Metaphysics is a view of the world that we grasp, a clutching, fixing, possession of things under a world view—god's view again. The disenchanted world is the world as this kind of picture. The enchanted earth is not a picture but the earth in pictures, pictures that escape and multiply and proliferate. The enchanted earth is in the caesura, as far beyond berman's alternative as it (and he) are beyond disenchantment.

> Here, then, is the crux of the modern dilemma. We cannot go back to alchemy or animism. *Some* type of holistic, or participating, consciousness and a corresponding sociopolitical formation have to emerge if we are to survive as a species. (Berman, *RW,* 23)

I am far more sympathetic to alchemy and animism—enchanted by multiplicity and heterogeneity—than I am to holism, which seems to me to be entirely unqualified. Here, for example, is a critique of the image of holism.

> one of the most important features of the whole Earth image is the vantage point from which it is obtained: from the outside. We have left the Earth in order to get a better view, in order to see it all at once. (Jacob Garb, *PE,* 265)
>
> We were once surrounded by our world, experiencing it with all our senses, participating in it with devout attention to its details—but we have left the cathedral. (266)
>
> Feminists (and postmodernists in general) have become wary of complete pictures, of single unifying viewpoints from which everything can be seen all at once. (269)
>
> Yet the whole Earth image was brought to light and is still being used by those who rebel *against* what is destructive in the Western relationship to the Earth: by peace activists, environmentalists, and proponents of a new Earth-based spirituality. The image, they claim, shows us the incredible beauty of the Earth. (275)

And a critique of the world as picture, engaged with its disenchantment:

> The fundamental event of the modern age is the conquest of the world as picture. The word "picture" [*Bild*] now means the structured image [*Gebild*] that is the creature of man's pro-

> ducing which represents and sets before. Because this position secures, organizes, and articulates itself as a world view, the modern relationship to that which is, is one that becomes, in its decisive unfolding, a confrontation of world views; and indeed not of random world views, but only of those that have already taken up the fundamental position of man that is most extreme, and have done so with the utmost resoluteness. (Heidegger, *AWP*, 134–5)
>
> the fact that world becomes picture at all is what distinguishes the essence of the modern age. (130)
>
> A fifth phenomenon of the modern age is the loss of the gods. This expression does not mean the mere doing away with the gods, gross atheism. The loss of the gods is so far from excluding religiosity that rather only through that loss is the relation to the gods changed into mere "religious experience." When this occurs, then the gods have fled. (116–7)

I have taken issue with this picture of the image of the earth, the world as picture.[45] I would align myself with this picture of the disenchantment of the earth as image of its totality, in its entirety, joined by heidegger with representation and the loss of the gods. A representation that sets before, secures and organizes, holds fast and grasps. If these are disenchantment, then picturing the world in its entirety is that disenchantment again. Enchantment resists totality and, as garb suggests, interrupts the multiplication and proliferation of the enchanted world. Participation here is in its place and time, as if without entirety or totality.

The image sees. The image feels. The image acts ... (Lerone Bennett, Jr., *CB*, 195)...

The image gives. The image is given. The image asks. The image proliferates. The image interrupts. The image betrays. The image for gives. The image is for giving. The image is for exposition. The image is for beauty. The image is from the good. The good is enchanting...[46]

The image is mother and is father is both mother and father and neither mother nor father for it is the child. The image is the parent and the children both parent and children and neither parent nor children. (Ross, *WAP*, xxx)...

Berman's most striking reading is his account of alchemy.

> Alchemy was first and foremost a craft, a "mystery" in medieval terminology, and all crafts, from the most ancient of times, were regarded as sacred activities.
>
> From these ancient sources came the central notion of alchemy: that all metals are in the process of becoming gold, that they are gold *in potentia*, and that men can devise a set of pro-

> cedures to accelerate their evolution. The practice of alchemy is thus not really playing God but is a type of midwifery. The set of procedures came to be called the "spagyric art," the separating of the gross from the subtle in order to assist evolution and obtain the gold that lay buried deep within the lead.
>
> Transmutation consisted in the following set of operations: purification, solution, putrefaction, distillation, sublimation, calcination, and coagulation. However, the order and content of them is unclear, and not all alchemists employed all the techniques. Circumstances, especially the nature of the ores, always seemed to alter the methods. (Berman, 88–9)

This operational account is more fragmentary than the theory of totality and participative consciousness. A connoisseur of secrets works with the minutest things in the most transformative ways. Alchemy was on one side the infinite secret of the promise of matter, on the other side the secrets of transmutation and alteration. The secret order of things was on the one hand that which modern science proposed to reject, on the other hand another order—many orders and disorders and transmutations—than the one that authoritative knowledge claimed to possess. In other words, alchemy followed the infinite orders of an infinite universe described by foucault as the prose of the world[47] together with a search for the secret order that would join all together in an all-encompassing magical embrace.

> The alchemist is thus like a miner, probing deeper and deeper veins of ore. One vein leads to another, there is no right answer. Life, and human personality, are inherently crazy, multifaceted; neurosis is the inability to tolerate this fact. The traditional model of the healthy soul demands that we impose an order or identity on all of these facets, but the alchemical tradition sees the result as an aborted metal that sulfur fixed too quickly. *Solve et coagula*, says the alchemist; abandon this prematurely congealed persona that forces you into predictable behavior and a programmed life of institutionalized insanity. If you would have real control over your life, says the tradition, abandon your artificial control, your "identity," the brittle ego that you desperately feel you must have for your survival. Real survival, the gold, consists in living according to the dictates of your own nature, and that cannot be achieved until the risk of psychic death is confronted directly. (90–1)

One might imagine alchemy as affording two different visions of enchantment, one the promise of material abundance in which the stability of things pledged transformation and transmutation, alterity and variation—alchemical ecology if you will—the other an expert knowledge on the truths of material reality. In the latter form modern science insisted on its authority, in the former on representational certainty against the plethora of mysteries. The enchantments of material things are revealed and betrayed alchemically in the *perhaps* and *as if* of our uncertainties and their becomings, in their proliferations, comings and goings.

One vein leads to another one thing evokes another things emulate each other signify each other interrupt each other promise infinite unimagined transformations...

Berman fears what he calls radical relativism in the name of enchantment. He resists the vision of endless transmutation and insists on an alternative reality. The plethora is too abundant. Participating consciousness, putting mind back in nature, some holistic, undivided understanding and relation to the world is better, resolves the splits of alienated, binary consciousness. I would resist binary consciousness but I do not imagine a better consciousness nor a better view or relation to nature. Not better in general, certainly not best. Better is binary. An enchanted earth is filled with destructive as well as beneficent forces, with jealous as well as propitious gods, with demons as well as fairies. Enchantment is not better than disenchantment but multiplies it and betrays it. What berman rejects as radical relativism is filled with enchantments—plural, multiple, diverse, proliferating, surprising, asking, telling, transgressing, betraying enchantments—that take us on journeys—not enclosures—of better and worse. Except where relativism is another form of grasping.

Animism and mind in nature are among the enchantments of the world, but become disenchanted when grasped. Reenchantment for berman marks both an impossible return—as he frequently insists—and a metaphysics. Can there be an enchanted metaphysics, an enchanted science? Can we replace the divided subject-object metaphysics and alienated sciences of our day with holistic, participatory sciences and metaphysics? Garb speaks of *participation* but against holism. Instead, to participate in the earth is to be there with all one's senses, devoted not to its totality but participating in the ecological abundance of its enchanted details. And of all the ways of thought of our time, science appears to care for things intricately, in detail, even as it seeks abstraction and engages in representation. Perhaps, then, it is representation in place of sense that disenchants, abstraction in place of participation. Perhaps *participation* is an abstract word for a metaphysics of multiple reenchantments. Perhaps we need to pay more attention to the wonder and abundance of things in the earth.

All that I know speaks to me through this earth and I long to tell you you who are earth too and listen as we speak to each other of what we know the light is in us. (Griffin, *WN*, 226–7)...

The chapters of berman's book are:

The Modern Landscape
The Birth of Modern Scientific Consciousness
Consciousness and Society in Early Modern Europe
The Disenchantment of the World
Prologomena to Any Future Metaphysics
Eros Regained
Tomorrow's Metaphysics
The Politics of Consciousness

His heroes are Wilhelm Reich and Gregory Bateson, His focus is on fusion more than proliferation, on holism more than diversification—though he does not neglect these:

> Participation is self and not-self identified at the moment of experience. The pre-Homeric Greek, the medieval Englishman (to a lesser extent, of course), and the present-day African tribesman know a thing precisely in the act of identification, and this identification is as much sensual as it is intellectual. It is a totality of experience: the "sensuous intellect," if the reader can imagine such a thing. (76)

> We also now know that a field of colors, called an "aura," surrounds every living thing, and that children perceive it up to a certain age. It is likely that auras are still commonly perceived in nonindustrial cultures, and probable that yellow halos painted around the heads of various saints in medieval art were something actually seen, not (according to a modern formulation) a metaphor for holiness "tacked on" for religious effect. (186–7)

We now know, it is true that, the modern world is mistaken, there is a better, more truthful view—as if to preserve the distinction between the true and the false, the binary distinction essential to the view of the world he opposes.

This view, the one he advocates, is holistic and experiential. My view is fragmentary, dispersed, proliferating, and experiential. Not truer, not better, but true and untrue, enchanted and disenchanted in the ways it is, in the asking, in the caesura. Among these proliferations for me are the disenchanted scientific and rational views berman considers to be alienated and alienating, as well as the holistic and experiential views he advocates. The latter are not more enchanted on my view but among the enchantments of the earth. Enchantments give us wonder and abundance, and these come in diverse forms and hues and proliferate in others.

> I cannot formulate a new, fully articulated paradigm, but I believe that the holistic exploration of such inexhaustible subjects as color, heat, or electricity, will give us a whole new world of questions. The key scientific question must cease to be "What is light?," "What is electricity?," and become instead, "What is the *human experience* of light?" "What is the *human experience* of electricity?" "What is the human experience of nature?" must become the rallying-cry of a new subject/object-ivity.
>
> The late twentieth century may be a difficult time to be alive, but is not without its exciting aspects. At the very point that the mechanical philosophy has played all its cards, and at which the Cartesian paradigm, in its attempt to know everything, has ironically exhausted the very mode of knowing which it represents, the door to a whole new world and way of life is slowly swinging ajar. (187)

The door to enchantment. Perhaps.

I come to philosophy and its enchantments through the understanding that objectivity cannot be separated from subjectivity, that nature is given to us as experience. I am speaking of john dewey and whitehead as well as reich and r. d. laing. The latter three are praised by berman, but I take from dewey especially along with some of the others a suspicion of philosophy, of abstraction, reflection, and metaphysics—most of all of totality. Holism and totality are as disenchanted as are bifurcation and alienation. In the enchanted earth every theory proliferates beyond any metaphysical grasp. Enchantment is interruption and betrayal.

Things are objects to be treated used acted upon and with enjoyed and endured even more than things to be known. They are things had before they are things cognized. (Dewey, *EN*, 21)...

Things are before and beyond (as if ~~not~~ beyond) their disenchantments...[48]

A vital question is whether science and metaphysics must be disenchanted. Weber appears to believe that in its nature science disenchants, perhaps philosophy as well. Berman appears to share that judgment even while proposing a whole new world of science and its questions. I believe that if the earth is enchanted, then its fruits are enchanted, no matter how mistaken and alienated. A disenchanted science is still enchanted, enchants the world it touches, belongs to the world strangely. Strangeness is as close to enchantment as anything may be.

Here I find myself far from berman:

> The most striking aspect of the medieval world is its sense of closure, its completeness. Man is at the center of a universe that is bounded at its outermost sphere by God, the Unmoved Mover. God is the only entity that, in Aristotle's terminology, is pure actuality. Everything moves and exists in accordance with divine purpose. All of nature, rocks as well as trees, is organic and repeats itself in eternal cycles of generation and corruption. As a result, this world is ultimately changeless, but being riddled with purpose, is an exceptionally meaningful one. (50–1)

I do not believe the earth was ever changeless, certainly not an enchanted one. I do not accept closure and completeness as achievements much less values. I do not imagine a changeless world in the midst of endless cycles. I do not imagine the medieval world as more meaningful than a modern or contemporary world—perhaps different meanings and values, different hierarchies and dominations. Participation and meaning take place in the midst of sensory encounters, and these are what and where they are. Enchantment resists changelessness, totality, and closure in the medieval world and in the modern one—closed and familiar in the totality of reason.

It is as if berman would wish for us to be once again at the center of a familiar universe in the name of reenchantment. I would resist any center and insist on transformation, transgression, surprise, and wonder as the conditions of enchantment. Here two views of money offer themselves to our view, one disenchanted the other quite different:

> Because we ourselves live in a society so completely dominated by a money economy, because the cash value of things has become their only value, it is difficult for us to imagine an age not ruled by money and almost impossible to understand the formative influence that the introduction of a money economy exerted on the consciousness of early modern Europe. Georg Simmel argued that the money economy "created the ideal of exact numerical calculation," and that the "mathematically exact interpretation of the cosmos" was the "theoretical counterpart of a money economy." (54–5)

> Just as in the order of representations the signs that replace and analyse them must also be representations themselves, so money cannot signify wealth without itself being wealth. But it becomes wealth because it is a sign; whereas a representation must first be represented in order subsequently to become a sign. (Foucault, *OT*, 177)

> The whole system of exchanges, the whole costly creation of values, is referred back to the unbalanced, radical, and primitive exchange established between the advances made by the landowner and the generosity of nature. It would be untrue to say that nature spontaneously produces values; but it is the inexhaustible source of the goods that exchange transforms into values, though not without expenditure and consumption. (195)

> The creation of value is therefore not a means of satisfying a greater number of needs; it is the sacrifice of a certain quantity of goods in order to exchange others. Values thus form the negative of goods.
>
> But how is it that value can be formed in this way? What is the origin of this excess that makes it possible for goods to be transformed into wealth without being effaced and finally disappearing altogether as a result of successive exchanges and continual circulation? (192)

Among the answers I am proposing to these final questions of circulation, exchange, and excess are that money and capitalism are enchanted even as they disenchant everything they touch. This phenomenon—not a contradiction—is for me the heart of betrayal. More of this later.

Beyond our immediate ends, man's activity pursues the useless and infinite fulfillment of the universe. The living organism receives more energy than is necessary for maintaining life; if the excess cannot be absorbed it must be spent, willingly or not, gloriously or catastrophically. (Georges Bataille, *AS*, 21)...

A series of profitable operations has absolutely no other effect than squander. (22)...

On the surface of the globe, for living matter in general, energy is always in excess. (23)...

Changing from the perspectives of restrictive economy to those of general economy accomplishes a copernican transformation, the possibility of pursuing growth is subordinated to giving. (25)...

General economy makes apparent that excesses of energy are produced, and that these excesses cannot be utilized. The excessive energy can only be lost without the slightest aim, consequently without any meaning. (Bataille, *MM*, 233, n. 1)...

General economy is economy beyond use and meaning: enchanted economy, in wonder and abundance. Restricted economies are economies of meaning and use: disenchanted economies...

General economy betrays restricted economies beyond meaning and use as the earth's enchantments. Restricted economies betray general economy as the human world's disenchantments...

General and restricted ecologies interrupt the wonder and abundance of general and restricted economy...

Berman does not hold this kind of view. Even so, his images are frequently intensely attractive:

> The "secret" that lies at the heart of the occult world view, with its sense of everything being alive and interrelated, is that the world is sensual at its core; that this is the essence of reality. Tactile experience can be taken as the root metaphor for *mimesis* in general. When the Indian does a rain dance, for example, he is inviting the clouds to join him, to respond to the invocation. He is, in effect, asking to make love to them, and like any normal lover they may or may not be in the mood. *This is the way nature works.* (Berman, 177)

> What do I know in my heart, then? I know that in some relational sense, everything is alive; that noncognitive knowing, whether from dreams, art, the body, or outright insanity, is indeed knowing; that societies, like human beings, are organic, and the attempt to engineer either is destructive; and finally, that we are living on a dying planet, and that without some radical shift in our politics and consciousness, our children's generation is probably going to witness the planet's last days. (269)

> Ego-consciousness, let alone the tradition of modern individualism, is a phenomenon with a comparatively short history; it is hardly essential for human survival or for a rich human culture, and may ultimately be inimical to both. We may be on the verge of a period of dynamic devolution, in which what is emerging is not merely a new society but a new species, a new type of human being. In the last analysis the present species may prove to be a race of dinosaurs, and ego-consciousness something of an evolutionary dead end. (298)

This final picture, of a new species and a new type of human being, seems to me the greatest disenchantment of reenchantment. I would explore the possibility that together with all the things of the earth we are enchanted in the midst of ego-consciousness. This does not make it good, not even the best alternative. But it may not be more enchanted or more disenchanted.

What is emerging is a new species of human enchantment. Human enchantments are not all the enchantments there are all the enchant-

ments known. Divine enchantments are not all the enchantments there are all the enchantments known. Disenchantments are included...

The wonder and abundance of things is their enchantment, and these are uncontainable. Together with the disenchantment of the world I would envisage containment, domination, hegemony, and oppression as closely linked in thought and practice. The disenchantment of the modern world is the hegemony of a certain view of reason, frequently in conflict with current rational practices. Here it is evident that enchantment entails other practices, other views, other images—of reason and unreason, of science and unscience. Unreason, superstition, illusion all proliferate in the enchantments of things, interrupting the rule of reason.

Disenchantment cannot eliminate imagination—science requires it. Yet it can blunt its wonder and proscribe its abundance. This is true in science but it is also true in organized religion and in the state. The call to enchantment is a call to calling itself, the calling of things to asking beyond any institutional limits and proscriptions—most of all, perhaps, to normalization, understanding this to reach beyond Foucault's early account of it into the institutional practices of governmentality.[49] Wherever being a person, human, or self is organized by institutional forces that claim control over truth, enchantments are brought into fixtures that claim to contain the uncontainable, to disenchant the enchanted. The greatest danger of disenchantment always is where church or state or other overarching institution claims to possess the key to enchantment.

The thesis of this book is that enchantment is uncontainable, that disenchantments take place hegemonically and insidiously in the midst of what they cannot contain, that the achievements of scientific and technical rationality are as enchanted as magic and ecstasy, and finally, that there is no theory or truth of enchantment. In wonder and abundance there is always more beyond any accounting. The key to enchantment in our age is to reach it through a secular lens, not because that is better but because that is our age's lens. There is another reason, that secularization's enchantments open up a wonder and abundance of transformations and transgressions, of tellings, beyond those fixed in theology and religion. The only enchanted religion is paganism, understood not to claim the spirituality of all things but to deny any claim to locate spirits and gods in an enchanted world. Paganism affirms the enchantments of things by denying its institutionalization. No community of pagans![50]

> I think that pagans are artists, that is, they can move from one game to another, and in each of these games (in the optimal situation) they try to figure out new moves. And even better, they try to invent new games. What we call an "artist" in the usual sense of the term proposes new rules of the painting game. Same thing for the so-called independent cinema, or for music. (Jean-François Lyotard and Jean-Loup Thébaud, *JG*, 61)

> If one is pagan, it is certainly not because one thinks that one game is better than another; it is because one has several kinds of games at one's disposal. It is in this way that something like the imagination, or the will, I do not know, could develop. (61)

> when I speak of paganism, I am not using a concept. It is a name, neither better nor worse than others, for the denomination of a situation in which one judges without criteria. And one judges not only in matters of truth, but also in matters of beauty (of aesthetic efficacy) and in matters of justice, that is, of politics and ethics, and all without criteria. That's what I mean by paganism. (Lyotard and Thébaud, *JG*, 16)

Paganism as affirmation in enchantment beyond accounting proliferation beyond multiplicity beyond measure counting beyond large and small. Exposition in betrayal...

The modality of this affirmation beyond is that of *perhaps*, the *as if* of enchantment, its performativity, interruption, asking, and betrayal. It is a perhaps and as if that is not fictiveness and unreality, nor what will never arrive, but what is always arriving, becoming, before and beyond the other. It is the exposition that can neither be foreclosed nor terminated, the enchantment of the image, the performance in its proliferation. It is the modality of enchantment always to be more than and beyond itself, in exposition and betrayal. It is exposition and betrayal affirmed and performed in the mode of *as if* and *perhaps*.

> No response, no responsibility, will ever abolish the *perhaps*. The perhaps must open and precede, once and for all, the questioning it suspends in advance—not to neutralize or inhibit, but to make possible all the determined and determining orders that depend on questioning (research, knowledge, science and philosophy, logic, law, politics and ethics, and in general language itself). (Derrida, *PF*, 38)

> What is going to come, *perhaps*, is not only this or that; it is at last the thought of the *perhaps*, the *perhaps* itself. The *arrivant* will arrive *perhaps*, for one must never be sure when it comes to *arrivance*; but the *arrivant* could also be the *perhaps* itself the unheard-of, totally new experience of the *perhaps*. Unheard-of,

> totally new, that very experience which no metaphysician might yet have dared to think. (29)

It is impossible to say what enchantment is, both because it proliferates, multiplies in wonder and abundance beyond naming and because of the *perhaps* and *as if* that haunt asking and telling. What is to come, what is coming and going, what is performing and performed, remains surprising even after arrival.

Coming and going giving beyond gifts proliferating beyond identity dispossessing beyond possessing having fixing performing presenting express the perhaps and as if and beyond of enchantment as if ~~not~~ beyond any place or time or name, as if ~~not~~ beyond any name or word or presentation or performance or identification. As if betrayed ~~beyond~~. Perhaps asking beyond. Perhaps...

Every name, every knowing, every gift betrays the enchantments it would grasp—reveals and violates them. Secular disenchantment betrays the enchantments it would deny. The earth is enchanted everywhere in the midst of the disenchantments that would interrupt it. That is the difficult conflict in which all ecological, ecosophical, and ecospiritual practices and discourses are located. They betray what they would nourish. Learning to live with betrayal as a living practice is living enchantedly. Enchantment interrupts every disenchantment.

Introduction

Death of Nature

> philosophy begins in wonder. (Plato, *Theaetetus*, 155d)
>
> There are more things in heaven and earth, Horatio,
> Than are dreamt of in your philosophy. (William Shakespeare, *Hamlet*, Act 1, Scene 5)

More. Things. More things. Interrupting heaven and earth. Heaven. Earth. Dreaming. Knowing. Philosophy. More than philosophy. More than science. More than reason. In wonder beyond themselves...

Horatio. Poor horatio. Wondering horatio. Wonderful horatio. To live and ask in wonder...

Closely allied with the death of the gods and its disenchantments is the death of nature.[1] If such a death be possible. In both cases the disenchanted claim is not that god or nature once lived and now has died—that would be enchanting—but that a certain view of nature has become predominant, replacing a prior view ascribed to premodern peoples. The modern view of nature is of a dead material world made up of inert particles and mechanical forces subsumed under universal concepts or laws. The living gods have vanished from such a view, along with the spirits that haunted every rock and bush and stream. Natural things are lifeless, dead, inert, abstract—disenchanted. Once (it was thought that) nature was enchanted, human beings inhabited an enchanted world that enchanted their own. Now (it is thought that) nature is composed of lifeless and lawful atoms and particles, whose being and reality are universal not singular. Many believe that human beings are natural in this way as well, composed of lifeless particles subject to universal laws. Living things are no more than mechanical assemblages of nonliving atoms. Others believe that human beings are complex and sensitive assemblages, individual spirits. To still others, human beings possess living souls that inhabit the empty spaces in nonliving bodies. And to others, human—but not animal—life is a divine gift that pervades every crevice of human bodies, every moment of human experience. In these ways, the world remains enchanted and nature remains alive, pulsing with vitality.

In these ways the earth interrupts every picture of itself...

The secular image remains of unliving, disenchanted things, not the dead who were once alive, not natural things whose blood has been sucked out by hostile forces. Things of the earth are natural ingredients that were never alive never inspirited disenchanted mechanical assemblages of atoms and particles. What if mechanical assemblages were enchanted? What of enchanting machines?...

An overarching purpose of this book is to expose ways in which material things, lawful assemblages of atoms and particles, may be encountered and understood as inspirited, living, enchanted, instead of dead, inert, moribund—all questioning as well as questionable terms. The purpose of this introduction is to extend the disenchantment of the world from human experience into nature, and to do so in a historical voice. Such a voice touches upon deep and pervasive ambiguities and uncertainties that surround the oppositions that encompass scientific rationality and its disenchantments, interrupting their rule. The historical form of the question is when and how the world became disenchanted, when and how nature died, how it was possible for us—in the words of nietzsche's madman—to perform such a monumental act. Weber suggests that modern science and technology have brought about disenchantment, marking the disenchantment of christianity in the rise of a capitalist economy. Heidegger speaks of the age of the world picture as that moment in modernity where the world becomes picture and art becomes subjective—moments of modern culture joining the rise of science and the middle classes. Yet he also looks back to the greeks for the origin of modern technology, following nietzsche's suggestion that in Plato, especially through the figure of Socrates, we can see the beginnings of the insistence that the world is rational, thereby disenchanted.

It is remarkable—and evident in nietzsche—that the philosopher who wrote what many regard as the most enchanted philosophical texts concerning the enchantments of the earth is read by others, indeed canonically, as the source of its disenchantments. The wealth of passages in plato that celebrate inspiration and ecstasy is routinely subordinated to the passages that celebrate binary division and argumentative persuasion. Both kinds of writings occur in plato, and one of the enchanted features of his work is that dialogues that work by ironic indirection and misdirection, whose narrators frequently cannot be trusted and who frequently say so, is read as supporting a linear, disenchanted discourse.

This combination in plato of enchantment and disenchantment reflects not only the ambiguous relation of betrayal I have proposed as characteristic of enchantment,[2] but also the enigmatic relations-otherwise between enchantment and disenchantment. These are not oppositional or binary; the world cannot be divided up into enchanted and disenchanted things or spheres, enchanted and disenchanted knowledges, beliefs, or discourses. To the contrary, if everything is enchanted, then so is disenchantment. Each interrupts the other. This is the truth of enchantment as I understand it, betraying the caesura: disenchantment is enchanted, and enchantment expresses itself in disenchantment. In the language of betrayal, each betrays the other, and enchantment betrays itself; each reveals and interrupts and corrupts the other and itself.[3] This means that if we are to mark a difference between enchantment and disenchantment, it will be that disenchantment knows nothing of enchantment, seeks to hide or mask or obliterate it, all the while betraying it as itself. It is perhaps a question of what we are ethically responsible for obliquely that we cannot know yet still betray, and a question of what we are epistemologically responsible for obliquely in what we reveal that exceeds what we know. Historically speaking, it is not only the question of when disenchantment began but of history's transformations and effects. In the case of plato, it is the divergence between Plato the man and author and "Plato" the historical figure of disciplinary history, between *plato* and *Plato*. This must in any case remain ambiguous and uncertain, but especially in the wealth of dialogues we have available to us and in the receptions and transformations that subsequent philosophers have offered to *Plato* in their name. This means that the relation between *plato* and *Plato* (as well as between *Platonism* and *Socratism*, not to mention *platonism* and *socratism*) is a blurred, mobile, and shifting relation—betraying enchantment if you will. If *plato* is an enchanted name, so must *Plato* be, and so must every other name, canonical or forgotten.[4]

On the side of enchantment, then, here is *plato* enchanted, beginning with *wonder.*

Wonder is the feeling of a philosopher philosophy begins in wonder iris [the messenger of heaven] is the child of thaumas [wonder]. (Plato, *Theaetetus,* 155d)...[5]

Plato is not alone in dwelling in wonder. Even descartes, whose separation of soul appears to many to have disenchanted matter, endures in wonder. If philosophy can be reenchanted, it will surely be through betraying wonder.

When our first encounter with some object surprises us and we find it novel or very different from what we formerly knew or from what we supposed it ought to be this causes us to wonder and to be astonished at it. Wonder is the first of all the passions. (René Descartes, *PSO,* 350)...

Here, for example, in betrayal?

Wonder is the passion of that which is already born and not yet reenveloped in love? The passion of the first encounter and of perpetual rebirth? The place of incidence and junction of body and spirit which has been covered over again and again hardened through repetitions that hamper growth and flourishing? The forgotten ground of our condition between mortal and immortal men and gods creatures and creators in us and among us???. (Luce Irigaray, *ESD,* 81–2)...

Askings—question marks—???—enchantments...

Perhaps questioning and problematizing are largely disenchanted, while asking is enchanted. Asking without answering, without demanding answering. Some answers are enchanted. As are many questions and problems.

Yet plato has socrates say in *phaedo* that philosophy begins with death. And as enchanted as *phaedo* makes death, as enchanted as *phaedo* is, filled with death's enchantments, this appearance of death at the origin of philosophy has appeared to many to disenchant it.

The truth rather is that the soul which is pure at departing and draws after her no bodily taint [this secreting of the self by means of which the soul retreats from the visible body to assemble itself within itself—separation and invisibility the criteria for secrecy], having never voluntarily during life had connexion with the body which she is ever avoiding herself gathered in herself all this means that she has been a true disciple of philosophy and therefore has in fact been always practising how to die without complaint for is not such a life the practice of death? (Plato, *Phaedo,* 80e; Jowett trans.; interpolation from Derrida, *GD,* 15)...

Continuing and interrupting:

> This canonical passage is one of the most often cited, or at least evoked, in the history of philosophy. For it is indeed a matter of care, a "keeping-vigil-for," a solicitude for death that constitutes the relation to self of that which, in existence, relates to oneself. For one never reinforces enough the fact that it is not the psyche that is there in the first place and that comes thereafter to be concerned about its death, to keep watch over it, to be the very vigil of its death. No, the soul only distinguishes itself, separates itself, and assembles within itself in the experience of this *melete tou thanatou*. It is nothing other than this concern for dying as a relation to self and an assembling of self. It only returns to itself, in both senses of assembling itself and waking itself, becoming conscious [*s'éveiller*], in the sense of consciousness of self in general, through this concern for death. (Jacques Derrida, *GD*, 16)

Concern for death, perhaps enchanted; concern for Death, disenchanted...

Such a reading does not succeed in disenchanting plato or philosophy. To the contrary. Nietzsche offers a more disenchanted reading, if *disenchantment* is a word to describe his revulsion toward Christianity and Socrates, if not socrates and christianity.

> Christianity was from the beginning, essentially and fundamentally, life's nausea and disgust with life, merely concealed behind, masked by, dressed up as, faith in "another" or "better" life. Hatred of "the world," condemnations of the passions, fear of beauty and sensuality, a beyond invented the better to slander this life, at bottom a craving for the nothing, for the end, for respite—a sign of abysmal sickness, weariness, discouragement, exhaustion, and the impoverishment of life. (Friedrich Nietzsche, *ASC*, 22–3)

> To fathom the depths and to separate true knowledge from appearance and error, seemed to Socratic man the noblest, even the only true human vocation. And since Socrates, this mechanism of concepts, judgments, and inferences has been esteemed as the highest occupation and the most admirable gift of nature, above all other capacities. (*BT*, #15, 97)

> Is the irony of Socrates an expression of revolt? Of plebeian *ressentiment*? Does he *avenge* himself on the noble people whom he fascinates? (Nietzsche, *TI*, p. 476)

This is Socrates, Socratism, and Platonism, perhaps not plato or socrates. Others guard the name of Plato with Platonism and neoPlatonism. Plato is another story—many enchanted stories. And so is socrates, if we listen to plato. The irreverence is enchanting. Again in laughter. I read Nietzsche's savage rendering of Socrates as expressing nietzsche's own enchantments. Here is another:

> Well, to begin with, he stood the hardships of the campaign far better than I did, or anyone else, for that matter. And if we were cut off from our supplies, there was no one who put such a good face on it as he. But when there was plenty to eat he was the one man who really seemed to enjoy it. There's not a man living that's ever seen Socrates drunk. And I dare say he'll have a chance to show what he's made of before this party's over.
>
> Then again, the way he got through that winter was most impressive, and the winters over there are pretty shocking. There was one time when the frost was harder than ever, and all the rest of us stayed inside, or if we did go out we wrapped ourselves up to the eyes and tied bits of felt and sheepskins over our shoes, but Socrates went out in the same old coat he'd always worn, and made less fuss about walking on the ice in his bare feet than we did in our shoes.
>
> Well, there's a lot more to be said about Socrates, all very peculiar and all very much to his credit. You'll never find anyone like Socrates, or any ideas like his ideas, in our own times or in the past—unless, of course, you take a leaf out of my book and compare him, not with human beings, but with sileni and satyrs—and the same with his ideas. (Plato, *Symposium*, 219e–221d)

In Alcibiades' words, socrates is ugly, unprepossessing, ordinary looking, yet he—socrates—is extraordinary, enchanted, godlike. No doubt alcibiades' love for socrates is speaking, and we are asked in *symposium* and *phaedrus* to remember the divine enchantments of love in the enchanted voice of plato, which never speaks in a disenchanted voice, never says plainly what it means to say, interrupts itself repeatedly, yet repeatedly insists that that is what philosophy must do—always in the midst of ambiguity. Plato's enchanted voice never says what it means to say yet says wonderfully enchanted, serious things.

No serious man will ever think of writing about serious realities for the general public. When anyone sees anywhere the written work of anyone, whether that of a lawgiver in his laws or whatever it may be in some other form, the subject treated cannot have been his most serious concern—that is, if he is himself a serious man. His most serious interests have their abode somewhere in the noblest region of the field of his activity. If, however, he really was seriously concerned with these matters and put them in writing, "then surely" not the gods, but mortals "have utterly blasted his wits." (*Letter 7*, 344cd)...

This famous passage suggests to many that Plato wrote dialogues to mask his words, which might have been expressed differently, more seriously and directly. Seriousness is disenchantment. Yet if we take *mimēsis* seriously, then every exposition is expressed with blasted wits, in a noble and enchanted region. Pursuing this ambiguity:

> The mimetic art is far removed from truth, and this, it seems, is the reason why it can produce everything, because it touches or lays hold of only a small part of the object. A painter will paint us a cobbler, a carpenter, and other craftsmen, though he himself has no expertness in any of these arts, and would deceive children and foolish men, and make them believe it to be a real carpenter. (*Republic*, 598bc)
>
> All the poetic tribe, beginning with Homer, are imitators of images of excellence and of the other things that they "create," and do not lay hold on truth, but, as we were just now saying, the painter will fashion, himself knowing nothing of the cobbler's art, what appears to be a cobbler to him and likewise to those who know nothing but judge only by forms and colors? (600e–601a)
>
> we must reach a decision whether we are to suffer our poets to narrate as imitators or in part as imitators and in part not, and what sort of things in each case, or not allow them to imitate at all. (394d)
>
> unless I mistake, the same men cannot practice well at once even the two forms of imitation that appear most nearly akin, as the writing of tragedy and comedy. (Plato, *Republic*, 395a)
>
> Socrates was arguing that the same man might be capable of writing both comedy and tragedy—that the tragic poet might be a comedian as well. (Plato, *Symposium*, 223cd)
>
> The art of contradiction making, descended from an insincere kind of conceited mimicry, of the semblance-making breed, derived from image making, distinguished as a portion, not divine but human, of production, that presents a shadow play of words—such are the blood and lineage which can, with perfect truth, be assigned to the authentic Sophist. (Plato, *Sophist*, 268cd)

To this hesitation—if that is what it is—the betrayal—I mean enchantment—of writing is the condition of its truth. Derrida calls our attention to its performativity.

> My friends there is no friend. (Derrida, *PF*, 1)

> It has often been noted that there is no cut-and-dried reportive utterance. Some "primary" performative value is always presupposed in it: an "I am speaking to you," "I am telling you that," "I assure you or promise you that." It was indeed necessary that the assertion be *addressed* and that the address contain some performative force. (214)

> this is why we have stressed the performative force which had to prevail in both versions of a sentence which in any case, in addressing another, could not count on any assurance, any purely theoretical criterion of intelligibility or accord; it *could not* count on such assurance, but above all *it had to* and *desired not to want* to count on such an assurance, which would destroy in advance the possibility of addressing the other as such. (219–20)

Derrida speaks of a performative contradiction. I would speak of a performative interruption, interrupting the contradiction in wonder and abundance. That we perform when we speak, that we say one thing and at the same time mean and express and say another, can be understood in the language of paradox and contradiction. In the language of madness, however, in the madness of love and its enchantments, the madness of which Derrida speaks reminds us of enchantments from a disenchanted point of view. From such a disenchanted point of view we speak of contradiction and reason's madness. From an enchanted point of view madness is divine, interrupting the continuity of reason.

The greatest blessings come by way of madness, indeed of madness that is heaven-sent. (Plato, *Phaedrus*, 244ab)...

We distinguished four types of madness ascribing them to four gods: the inspiration of the prophet to apollo, that of the mystic to dionysus, that of the poet to the muses, and a fourth type which we declared to be the highest, the madness of the lover, to aphrodite and eros. Moreover we painted, after a fashion, a picture of the lover's experience, in which perhaps we attained some degree of truth, though we may well have sometimes gone astray. (265bc)...

It follows that when we read plato's enchantments together with disenchanted accounts of a disenchanted reason, it is from a disenchanted point of view that they may be distinguished. With this in mind, here is enchanted plato on the one hand and disenchanted Plato on the other, with the understanding that enchantment interrupts each and the third hand, itself:

Toward the end he will suddenly perceive a nature of wondrous beauty [phusin kalon], which in the first place is everlasting, not growing and decaying, or waxing and waning; secondly, not fair in one point of view and foul in another, or at one time or in one relation or at one place fair; but beauty absolute, separate, simple, and everlasting, which without diminution and without increase, or any change, is imparted to the ever-growing and perishing beauties of all other things. (Plato, *Symposium*, 210e–211a)...

Socrates, even before I met you they told me that you are a perplexed man yourself and reduce others to perplexity. At this moment I feel you are exercising magic and witchcraft upon me and positively laying me under your spell until I am just a mass of helplessness. I think that not only in outward appearance but in other respects as well you are exactly like the flat sting ray that one meets in the sea. Whenever anyone comes into contact with it, it numbs him, and that is the sort of thing that you seem to be doing to me now. (*Meno*, 80)...

The gift which you possess is not an art [technē], but an inspiration; there is a divinity moving you. (*Ion*, 533d)...

For the poets tell us, don't they, that the melodies they bring us are gathered from rills that run with honey, out of glens and gardens of the muses, and they bring them as the bees do honey, flying like the bees? And what they say is true, for a poet is a light and winged thing, and holy, and never able to compose until he has become inspired, and is beside himself, and reason [nous] is no longer in him. So long as he has this in his possession, no man is able to make poetry or to chant in prophecy. (534b)...

These are passages of transcendent mystery, and it is tempting to assimilate them to prior theories of transcendence and mystery. Christianity has done so, and so has secular philosophy, which assigns mystery and transcendence to religion and to Christianity in particular. This means that philosophy and reason need not pay attention to these enchantments in plato, only to his rational arguments. I would insist on the enchantments in the caesura, interrupting both rationality and religion.

Phaedrus is a dialogue that can be read to present this kind of reading and this kind of choice. If there is a choice. More of that later. Here in interruption I would juxtapose, as plato does, several different approaches to the world, philosophy, and *phaedrus* itself, reduced for the moment to two. Some correspond to those just above, in a supremely enchanted voice:

The greatest blessings come by way of madness indeed of madness that is heaven-sent. (*Phaedrus*, 244b)...

The men of old who gave things their names held madness to be a valuable gift, when due to divine dispensation. (244c)...

The souls that are called immortal, so soon as they are at the summit, come forth and stand upon the back of the world, and straightway the revolving heaven carries them round, and they look upon the regions without. (247c)...

Such is the life of the gods. (248a)...

For only the soul that has beheld truth may enter into this our human form, and such understanding is a recollection [anamnēsis] of those things which our souls beheld aforetime as they journeyed with their god, looking down upon the things which now we suppose to be, and gazing up to that which truly is...

Therefore is it meet and right that the soul of the philosopher alone should recover her wings, for she, so far as may be, is ever near in memory to those things a god's nearness whereunto makes him truly god. If a man makes right use of such means of remembrance, and ever approaches to the full vision of the perfect mysteries, he and he alone becomes truly perfect. (249cd)...

There is a third form of possession or madness, of which the muses are the source. This seizes a tender, virgin soul and stimulates it to rapt passionate expression, especially in lyric poetry. If any man come to the gates of poetry without the madness of the muses, persuaded that skill alone will make him a good poet, then shall he and his works of sanity with him be brought to nought by the poetry of madness, and behold, their place is nowhere to be found. (245ab)...

Enchanted in its erotic splendors:

When one who is fresh from the mystery beholds a godlike face or bodily form that truly expresses beauty, first there come upon him a shuddering and a measure of that awe which the vision inspired, and then reverence as at the sight of a god. Next, with the passing of the shudder, a strange sweating and fever seizes him. For by reason of the stream of beauty entering in through his eyes there comes a warmth, whereby his soul's plumage is fostered, and with that warmth the roots of the wings are melted, which for long had been so hardened and closed up that nothing could grow; then as the nourishment is poured in, the stump of the wing swells and hastens to grow from the root over the whole substance of the soul, for aforetime the whole soul was furnished with wings. Meanwhile she throbs with ferment in every part, and even as a teething child feels an aching and pain in its gums when a tooth has just come through, so does the soul of him who is beginning to grow his wings feel a ferment and painful irritation. Wherefore as she gazes upon the boy's beauty, she admits a flood of particles streaming therefrom—that is why we speak of a 'flood of passion'—whereby she is warmed and fostered; then has she respite from her anguish, and is filled with joy. But when she has been parted from him and become parched, the openings of those outlets at which the wings are sprouting dry up likewise and are closed, so that the wing's germ is barred off. And behind its bars, together with the flood aforesaid, it throbs like a fevered pulse, and pricks at its proper outlet, and thereat the whole soul round about is stung and goaded into anguish; with madness upon her she can neither sleep by night nor keep still by day, but runs hither and thither, yearning for him in whom beauty dwells. At last she does behold him, and lets the flood pour in upon her, releasing the imprisoned waters; then has she refreshment and respite from her stings and sufferings, and at that moment tastes a pleasure that is sweet beyond compare. (251a–252a)...

The story is that once upon a time the cicadas were men—men of an age before there were any muses—and that when the latter came into the world, and music made its appearance, some of the people of those days were so thrilled with pleasure that they went on singing, and quite forgot to eat and drink until they actually died without noticing it. From them in due course sprang the race of cicadas, to which the muses have granted the boon of needing no sustenance right from their birth, but of singing from the very first, without food or drink, until the day of their death, after which they go and report to the muses how they severally are paid honor among mankind, and by whom. (259bd)...

Some correspond to the most disenchanted understandings—forgetting the divine madnesses:

> [T]he subject we proposed for inquiry just now was the nature of good and bad speaking and writing, so we are to inquire into that. (259d)
>
> Any discourse ought to be constructed like a living creature, with its own body, as it were; it must not lack either head or feet; it must have a middle and extremities so composed as to suit each other and the whole work. (264c)
>
> Suppose someone said, "I know how to apply such treatment to a patient's body as will induce warmth or coolness, as I choose." What do you imagine they would have to say to that?
>
> They would ask him, of course, whether he also knew which patients ought to be given the various treatments, and when, and for how long.
>
> Then what if he said, "Oh, no, but I expect my pupils to manage what you refer to by themselves"?
>
> I expect they would say, "the man is mad; he thinks he has made himself a doctor by picking up something out of a book, or coming across some common drug or other, without any real knowledge of medicine." (268c)

Some insist on interruptions, and on interrupting interruptions.

As for the words "just" and "good"—don't we diverge and dispute not only with one another but with our own selves?. (263)...

Could this be enchantment? Interrupted everywhere by disenchantments? Could this be asking? Asked everywhere by knowings?...

> Now suppose someone went up to Sophocles or Euripides and said he knew how to compose lengthy dramatic speeches about a trifling matter, and quite short ones about a matter of moment, that he could write pathetic passages when he chose, or again passages of intimidation and menace, and so forth, and that he considered that by teaching these accomplishments he could turn a pupil into a tragic poet. (268d)

> My good sir, it is true that one who proposes to become a master of harmony must know the things you speak of, but it is perfectly possible for one who has got as far as yourself to have not the slightest real knowledge of harmony. You are acquainted with what has to be learned before studying harmony, but of harmony itself you know nothing. (268e)

> there is a nature that we have to determine, the nature of body in the one, and of soul in the other, if we mean to be scientific when we apply medicine and diet to induce health and strength, or words and rules of conduct to implant such convictions and virtues as we desire. (270b)

> [W]hen he is competent to say what type of man is susceptible to what kind of discourse; and when, on top of all this, he has further grasped the right occasions for speaking and for keeping quiet, then and not till then has he well and truly achieved the art. (271d–272b)

> You know, Phaedrus, that's the strange thing about writing, which makes it truly analogous to painting. The painter's products stand before as if they were alive, but if you question them, they maintain a most majestic silence. It is the same with written words: they seem to talk to you as though they were intelligent, but if you ask them anything about what they say, from a desire to be instructed, they go on telling you just the same thing forever. And once a thing is put in writing the composition, whatever it may be, drifts all over the place, getting into the hands not only of those who understand it, but equally of those who have no business with it; it doesn't know how to address the right people, and not address the wrong. And when it is ill-treated and unfairly abused it always needs its parent to come to its help, being unable to defend or help itself. (275de)

> For serious purposes wouldn't he behave like a scientific farmer, sow his seeds in suitable soil, and be well content if they came to maturity within eight months? (276b)
>
> And are we to maintain that he who has knowledge of what is just, honorable, and good has less sense than the farmer in dealing with his seeds? (276c)
>
> Then it won't be with serious intent that he "writes them in water." (276c)
>
> First, you must know the truth about the subject that you speak or write about; that is to say, you must be able to isolate it in definition, and having so defined it you must next understand how to divide it into kinds, until you reach the limit of division. (277b)

As if writing desired to be disenchanted but wandered madly and asked enchantingly.

Serious disenchantments appear surrounded by unserious enchantments. How can we tell what is serious and what is not? How can we choose? What pharmakon shall we follow? What pharmakeus interrupts our rule?...

> I regard such theories as the invention of clever, industrious people who are not exactly to be envied, for the simple reason that they must then go on and tell us the real truth about the appearance of centaurs and the Chimera, not to mention a whole host of such creatures, Gorgons and Pegasuses and countless other remarkable monsters of legend. If our skeptic, with his somewhat crude science, means to reduce every one of them to the standard of probability, he'll need a deal of time for it. I myself have certainly no time for the business (229de)
>
> [and speaking of two procedures whose significance (*dynamin*) may be seized in a] scientific fashion—
>
> The first is that in which we bring a dispersed plurality under a single form, seeing it all together— (265d)
>
> [And then] the reverse of the other, whereby we are enabled to divide into forms, following the objective articulation; we are not to attempt to hack off parts like a clumsy butcher, but to take example from our two recent speeches. The single general form which the postulated was irrationality; next, on the analogy of a single natural body with its pairs of like-named members, right arm or leg, as we say, and left, they conceived of madness as a single objective form existing in human beings. (266a)

As if we might imagine madness seriously as a single, objective form, as if madness were not mad, as if we might know its recipe together with writing...

> when it came to writing Theuth said, "Here, O king, is a branch of learning that will make the people of Egypt wiser and improve their memories; my discovery provides a recipe for memory and wisdom." But the king answered and said, "If men learn this, it will implant forgetfulness in their souls. What you have discovered is a recipe [*pharmakon*] not for memory, but for reminder." (275)

Let us stay for the moment with the image of two and more hands.[6] Let us imagine being asked how many? Sometimes plato insists on one, sometimes on dividing on the left hand and the right hand—hunting on the right and left.[7] As God only knows.

> Believe me, Phaedrus, I am myself a lover of these divisions and collections, that I may gain the power to speak and to think, and whenever I deem another man able to discern an objective unity and plurality, I follow "in his footsteps where he leadeth as a god." Furthermore—whether I am right or wrong in doing so, God alone knows—it is those that have this ability whom for the present I call dialecticians. (265d–266c)

I have to this point neglected *mimēsis*—I mean not only the uncontainability of imitation and art, but the indefinite number that surrounds all categories and divisions. In *Philebus*, for example, after these divisions and collections, we are to let them all pass away, in stories of old.

There is from old [palaia] a quarrel [diaphora] between philosophy and poetry. (Plato, *Republic*, 607b)...

Let us suppose the world to be the very image of that whole of which all other animals both individually and in their tribes are portions. (*Timaeus*, 30c)...

When the father and creator saw the creature which he had made moving and living, the created image of the eternal gods, he rejoiced, and in his joy determined to make the copy still more like the original, and as this was an eternal living being, he sought to make the universe eternal, so far as might be, wherefore he resolved to have a moving image of eternity. (37c)...

There is a gift of the gods that they let fall from their abode. The men of old [palaioi], who were better than ourselves and dwelt nearer the gods, passed on this gift in the form of a saying. All things, so it ran, that are ever said to be consist of a one and a many, and have in their nature a conjunction of limit and unlimitedness. (*Philebus*, 16c)...

Continuing:

> This then being the ordering of things we ought, they said, whatever it be that we are dealing with, to assume a single form and search for it, for we shall find it there contained; then, if we have laid hold of that, we must go on from one form to look for two, if the case admits of there being two, otherwise for three or some other number of forms. And we must do the same again with each of the "ones" thus reached, until we come to see not merely that the one that we started with is a one and an unlimited many, but also just how many it is. But we are not to apply the character of unlimitedness to our plurality until we have discerned the total number of forms the thing in question has intermediate between its one and its unlimited number. It is only then, when we have done that, that we may let each one of all these intermediate forms pass away into the unlimited and cease bothering about them. (16d–17a)

We interrupt the reign of every universal form with an intermediate and interrupt the flow of intermediates in the return of the unlimit...

Back to hunting and grasping after the sophist. There are:

> two kinds *(eidē)* of arts *(technōn)*, productive *(poiētikos)* and acquisitive *(ktētikos)*;
> two kinds of acquisitive arts, voluntary and coercive;
> two kinds of coercive arts, fighting and hunting *(thēraō)*;
> two kinds of hunting arts, pursuing living and nonliving things;
> two kinds of arts for hunting living things, land and water;
> two kinds of water animals, swimming and winged, giving the arts of fishing and fowling;
> two kinds of fishing, by net and by blow;
> two kinds of blow, by spear and by line. (Plato, *Sophist*, 219–21)

Moreover, in the stranger's words, "One half of all art was acquisitive"; "half of the acquisitive art was conquest or taking by force, half of this was hunting, and half of hunting was hunting animals; half of this was hunting water animals." The world is measured by halves.[8]

How enchanting is hunting to grasp and hold, possibly to kill? How enchanting is dividing by half, insisting on binary divisions? My ongoing argument is that much of what we understand to be taking place between enchantment and disenchantment, *poiēsis* and *technē*, dispossession and possession, is understood and described entirely on one side of these pairs: hunting, having, grasping, dividing. Art and magic divide and combine, but without insistence on the world's authority to do so. To the contrary, enchantments combine and divide to pluralize, ask, interrupt, put into play, multiply—much closer to the sophist than to the philosopher, if these can be divided enchantedly.

It is time for me to insist that *plato does not choose, that he presents these passages interwoven together, that one may interpret him as enchantedly giving into everyday dichotomies or as disenchantedly feeding poetry to his readers to make them happy...*

These are plato's two hands, and I have suggested that there is a third hand or more, not least because of the desire we may have to combine these in one or more ways. For example, under the name of plato, what did plato mean when he wrote dialogues in which enchantment and disenchantment appear together? What might we mean, how would we think of the relation between enchantment and disenchantment? Once we ask these questions, then we can see another multiplication, for they can be answered in an enchanted or disenchanted or an other voice.

The enchanted voice refuses to choose, knows nothing of opposition, interrupts and multiplies and divides to enchant, inspirit, inspire, to ask in wonder and abundance. The disenchanted voice insists on choice, on categories and classifications, does not know how to give plausibility and authority to enchantment. The third voice, the ecological voice of exposition and mimēsis, interrupts each again and again, enigmatically and disconcertedly. The third voice suggests that disenchantment can be looked at in abundance and wonder, as if enchanted, and that enchantment can give rise to disenchantment without losing its enchantments. The third voice asks of asking...

These are difficult thoughts to think and ways to be. They are expressed by plato himself in the indefinite dyad, another tale of old:

When we have discerned the total number of forms the thing in question has intermediate between its one and its unlimited number we may let each one of all these intermediate forms pass away into the unlimited and cease bothering about them...[9]

Disenchantment passes away into enchantment into wonder and abundance betrays restricted economy as general economy restricted ecology as general ecology. We must live and think disenchantedly in restricted ecologies, and we must cease bothering to do so. What a enchanting thought!...

In an enchanted world there is no authoritative choice, we cannot choose by principle or rule. I do not mean that we cannot decide, cannot determine, but that determination can never be given to us by rule or principle or knowledge or truth; moreover, the cut of decision does not cut off, but keeps asking. Enchantment adds and supplements and interrupts and augments in the midst of deciding. In other words, we decide in an enchanted world without ruling out what we have decided against. What is undecided returns, and we must decide where reason cannot, we must determine what remains undetermined. We can always make a choice, can always decide, but we do so beyond accounting and beyond discarding. Deciding and choosing are always made, accomplished, in the midst of risks that nothing can remove. One may say as if by art, where we grant that there is nothing in art that decides and chooses—yet artists choose repeatedly and insist that other artists and spectators choose.

When Derrida insists that there is no choice between the old name *politics* and a new one—*the political*—it is not to say that that it is impossible to choose. One may give one's life to such a choice, and many have done so.

> 1. *Either* to admit that the political is in fact this phallogocentrism in act. This structure can be combated only by carrying oneself beyond the political, beyond the name "politics" and by forging other concepts, concepts with an altogether different mobilizing force. Who would swear that this is not in progress?
>
> 2. *Or else* keep the "old name," and analyse the logic and the topic of the concept differently, and engage other forms of struggle, other "partisan" operations, and so forth.
>
> If there were a single thesis to this essay, it would posit that there could be no choice. (Derrida, *PF*, 158–9)

It is that such a choice is ungrounded, undetermined by anything other than the choice, and that it succumbs to a temptation to overlook, repress, the call of the other, the other choice, to cease asking. It is that choices are binary, disenchanted, interrupted by enchantments beyond binaries. Asking as if perhaps ~~not~~ beyond. There can be no choice between the old and the new, between remembering and forgetting, between enchantment and disenchantment, but there is a temptation to choose. And a responsibility to resist it.

Temptation indeed. It is that of the book you are reading—there can be no doubt about it—but it is also the temptation this same book owes itself to resist. We cannot and we must not exclude the fact that when someone is speaking, in private or in public, when someone teaches, publishes, preaches, orders, promises, prophesies, informs or communicates, some force in him or her is also striving not to be understood, approved, accepted in consensus—not immediately, not fully, and therefore not in the immediacy and plenitude of tomorrow, etc. (Derrida, *PF*, 217–9)...

There is a temptation to imagine that we can choose the one without also choosing the other. Disenchantment insists on choosing and imagines that something—calculation, technique, knowledge—can make the choice, can determine it so that what is unchosen can be cast aside. Enchantment knows that what is cast aside is enchanted by the call of the other. To decide as if by art is to decide without criteria, without rules, without authority, still to decide—at least for the moment. And in deciding for the moment we undecide for another moment, another time and place, we decide as if in and by and for the other in another moment. Here this other is unknown to us and remains unknown through all times and places: the arrival of the strange, the stranger, the unfamiliar, the anomalous.

Here the question of guarding the unity of the one returns in a disenchanted voice.

The one does violence to itself, and guards itself against the other. (Derrida, *PF*, ix)...

The one betrays itself in betraying the others. (Stephen David Ross, *GSSEB*, xxx)...

The one interrupts itself and interrupts every interruption...

Every one, and every many, is for asking for telling and for giving...

The disenchanted one guards itself before the other. The enchanted one—here plato the philosopher, the historical figure, the author of history—brings together in a single place what cannot be gathered. But no, that phrase *cannot be gathered* is disenchanted and describes a disenchanted place. The unity of plato—in particular here of *phaedrus*—is a unity of ungathering, where disenchanted figures cohabit with cicadas and madness, and where ungathering is asking.

Derrida describes the impossibility of gathering as madness, reminding us of enchantment's other aberrations.

> How is one to speak reasonably of a gift that could not be what it was except on the condition of not being what it was? On the condition of not being or appearing to be the gift of anything, of anything that is or that is present, come from someone and given to someone? On the condition of "being" a gift without given and without giving, without presentable thing and act? A gift that would neither give *itself,* nor give itself *as such,* and that could not take place except on the condition of not taking

> place—and of remaining impossible? To desire, to desire to think the impossible, to desire, to desire to give the impossible—this is obviously madness.
>
> This madness, let us recall, would also be that of a forgetting, of a given and desired forgetting, not as a negative experience therefore, like an amnesia and a loss of memory, but as the affirmative condition of the gift. How does one desire forgetting or the non-keeping of the gift if, implicitly, the gift is evaluated as good? (Derrida, *CF*, 35–6)

How can this madness negotiate with what it is not, how can it be protected and translated in the good sense of "things," in proofs, guarantees, concepts, symbols—in a politics, this politics and not another—this is the whole of history, of what is called history. But every time it will be singular, singularly iterable, as will the negotiation and contamination of singularity and concept, exception and rule. (*PF*, 219–20)...

Are there two madnesses here or one or more? Is it madness? Are there two madnesses in *phaedrus* or one or more? Are there one or two or four or more ones, the one that guards and the one that enchants, passing away into infinity? The one that asks, passing away into endless tellings and askings?

Perhaps the one is mad. Madness seems as if sometimes one sometimes two sometimes many sometimes passing away into infinity...

In *phaedrus* we find the madness of the *pharmakon*, against which good sense—if there be such—mobilizes its resources, and divine madnesses against which there can be no mobilization. Again and again we are asked to choose by disenchanted voices that go mad against what they would resist. These voices are mad, but which kind of madness? We cannot choose and must refuse a choice, no matter how strong the temptation. Or perhaps we must choose and cannot refuse a choice, no matter how disenchanting. Perhaps we must ask and cannot refuse asking, no matter the tellings. Enchantment cannot choose, does not choose, resists the temptation to choose, and in resisting asks.

In the name of plato, then, in dialogue performativity mimēsis exposition we must choose and cannot choose, we must ask and ask again. What we choose cannot be chosen we cannot choose enchantment over disenchantment because only disenchanted reason knows how to choose knows how to answer...

In socrates' words, describing a disenchanted city—perhaps one we would not choose to inhabit:

> If a man, then, it seems, who was capable by his cunning of assuming every kind of shape and imitating all things should arrive in our city, bringing with himself the poems which he

> wished to exhibit, we should fall down and worship him as a holy and wondrous and delightful creature, but should say to him that there is no man of that kind among us in our city, nor is it lawful for such a man to arise among us, and we should send him away to another city, after pouring myrrh down over his head and crowning him with fillets of wood, but we ourselves, for our souls' good, should continue to employ the more austere and less delightful poet and taleteller, who would imitate the diction of the good man and would tell his tale in the patterns which we prescribed in the beginning, when we set out to educate our soldiers. (Plato, *Republic*, 398ab)

> Do you want me, may I ask, to give way like a porter jostled and knocked about by the crowd, to fling open the doors and allow every sort of knowledge to stream in, the inferior mingling with the pure?
>
> I don't really see, Socrates, what harm one would suffer by taking all those other sorts of knowledge, providing one had the first sort.
>
> Then I am to allow the whole company to stream in and be gathered together in a splendid Homeric mingling of the waters? (Plato, *Philebus*, 62de)

The one, then, guards itself and commits violence in the name of reason's disenchantments. Plato and *phaedrus*, on the side of their enchantments, cannot be gathered into such a one, the one of disenchantment, but multiply enchantments in abundance and wonder, multiply to gather, gather to ask. To read plato enchantedly is to include his disenchantments, no matter how mad they may seem. Disenchantment augments enchantment's wonders. Plato's philosophy knows no bounds, multiplies its boundaries even as it claims to set them.

Here are some other extreme examples; I ask you to regard them as madly true, enchanted and disenchanted, interrupting time and being:

If the one is, it is in time. Time, moreover, is advancing. Hence since the one moves forward temporally, it is always becoming older than itself. And we remember that what is becoming older becomes older than something that is becoming younger. So, since the one is becoming older than itself, that self must be becoming younger. Therefore, in this sense, it is becoming both younger and older than itself. (Plato, *Parmenides*, 152ab)...

Such a thing cannot, then be either older than, or of the same age with, anything. Therefore the one cannot be younger or older than, or of the same age with, either itself or another. (141a)...

Therefore the one has nothing to do with time and does not occupy any stretch of time. (141e)...

In time, the one comes to be as if older and younger than the others. How both? How older and younger than itself? How older than time? The men and their tales of old are older and younger than themselves. And with their help we are younger and older than ourselves...

On the side of disenchantment, plato's *parmenides* is mad.[10] The least deranged reading is that the enigmas pave the way to an older and more sophisticated understanding of the Ideas. On the side of enchantment—including the indefinite dyad and the vision of the good—the one, the idea, the good, and the vision are beyond all binaries, untainted by opposition and variation. This one and anything said of it is impossible to say or know—in time, out of time, becoming and not becoming older and younger than itself—yet we say all this and more, in the mode of asking.

The good is nothing yet everything is given from it as enchanted...

The good is nothing but enchanting...

The good is nothing... Asking is everything...

This is nonsense, this is madness, this is enchantment from the side of disenchantment, which insists on calculation and accountability. How can we choose in such disorder, how can we live in such a vision, how can we ask without answers? The response is that we can and do and must, but it is not all there is and enchantment madly insists on disenchantment. We cannot choose between older and younger, time and eternity, and yet we do and yet we must, and in these ways we ask. The choice is mad, delirious, bizarre, both as choice and as enchantment, from the side of disenchantment. There is no choice in the madness of enchantment. This madness is not delirium but the wonder and abundance of the vision beyond division.

The one, then, plato's one, is disenchanted by his many dialogues, his letters in which he denies that he has ever written truthfully, his different characters and what they say at different times and different places: disenchanted and enchanted. The dialogues and plato and his characters—including socrates—are, like all such dialogues and performances, older and younger than themselves, visions beyond accounting.

One and many and more than one and less than many and gathered as one, all violent, guarded, oblique, betrayals beyond gathering. Wonder and abundance interrupt disenchantment's divisions in the multiplicities and anomalies of enchantment...

All this is to say that what plato says, what plato believes, what the dialogues show, is both enchanted and disenchanted and interrupts and betrays them both. Philosophy chose at some point to disenchant itself by reading plato disenchantedly. When did this take place? After nietzsche? Before the renaissance? Is this a modern reading? The greeks themselves did not know, read plato in different ways depending on their different concerns. One way to read plato—and not only plato—is as interposing apollinian disenchantment into a world of dionysian enchantments. This is how nietzsche reads him, insisting on greek versions of enchantment and disenchantment—I mean, of course, greek and german, 19th century german. Another way to read him is as the progenitor of disenchantments to come. As diotima says of love,

A very powerful spirit, socrates, and spirits, you know, are halfway between god and man...

They are the envoys and interpreters that ply between heaven and earth, flying upward without worship and our prayers, and descending with the heavenly answer and commandments. (Plato, *Symposium*, 202e)...

I would say this of enchantments and of enchanted philosophers such as plato. I would say that we who come after—whoever we are—interrupt ourselves in this caesura between past and future, Plato and plato, disenchantment and enchantment. We who come after come for asking.

Perhaps it is time to look ahead at what was and is to come, the disenchantments that were present in plato and aristotle, in greek life, drama, and philosophy, to imagine that enchantment and disenchantment coexist in any modernization of humanity and the world. To imagine also that both vary enchantedly where and when they occur, that modernity, modern reason, science, economics, and politics present themselves, sometimes by force, as disenchantedly authoritative, but that enchantments of language, life, experience, history, and art interrupt the authority of any disenchantment with askings.

For the moment the authority of disenchantment is in the foreground, with enchantment interrupting its reign. From the standpoint of wonder and enchantment, this is a profound misrepresentation, yet maybe it is the only way the subject can be presented in our time. We must pass through disenchantment on the way to its enchantments, and of course the others, because with everything apparently disenchanted it is essential to keep the subject open. The temptation is to choose what is enchanted and what is not and to imagine that we have chosen the one or the other. We must choose and it is impossible to choose, from the standpoint of the one or the other. Still we ask.

With asking in mind, I would trace a rapid line of disenchantments, following nietzsche's image of socratism. If I have been persuasive, I have argued—shown, demonstrated, revealed: disenchanted practices—that plato's writing is enchanted through and through, it is enchanted even when disenchanted, and gathering its multiplicity into one multiplies its enchantments and their disenchantments. Plato's dialogues do not merely appear enchanted but enchantment walks hand in hand with disenchantment, the wonders of philosophy interrupt and inspire its arguments and calculations, the abundances of the world transcend the classifications and categories of science. Philosophy and science reveal the wonder and abundance and enchantment and ecologies of the world even where they would deny them, or appear to deny them, or reject them as superstitions and illusions.

Continuing this line of thought, then, here is a rapid tracing after plato of the enchantments of disenchantment. By this, of course, I mean more than that these walk hand in hand, that we can find aristotle, descartes, and kant divided on asking and telling. I mean to bring to the fore the astonishing commitment on the part of western readings to disenchantment and the incredible resistance to it on the part of the philosophers who are read to support it. I will return to some of these philosophers—spinoza, kant, hegel, etc.—in later readings. I continue here my preliminary historical overview.

In the case of aristotle, then, we have what can only be described as an abominable attachment to disenchantment in the midst of some of the most eloquent revelations of it and its enchantments. Here are just a few:

> Where then there is such a difference as that between soul and body, or between men and animals, the lower sort are by nature slaves, and it is better for them as for all inferiors that they should be under the rule of a master. (*Politics*, 1254b)

> In like manner we may infer that, after the birth of animals, plants exist for their sake, and that the other animals exist for the sake of man, the tame for use and food, the wild, if not all, at least the greater part of them, for food, and for the provision of clothing and various instruments. Now if nature makes nothing incomplete, and nothing in vain, the inference must be that she has made all animals for the sake of man. (1256b)

> A question may indeed be raised, whether there is any excellence at all in a slave beyond those of an instrument and of a servant—whether he can have the excellences of temperance,

> courage, justice, and the like; or whether slaves possess only bodily services. A similar question may be raised about women and children, whether they too have excellences; ought a woman to be temperate and brave and just, and is a child to be called temperate, and intemperate, or not? For the slave has no deliberative faculty at all; the woman has, but it is without authority, and the child has, but it is immature. Clearly, then, excellence of character belongs to all of them; but the temperance of a man and of a woman, or the courage and justice of a man and of a woman, are not, as Socrates maintained, the same; the courage of a man is shown in commanding, of a woman in obeying, as the poet says of women,
>
> Silence is a woman's glory,
>
> but this is not equally the glory of man. (1259b–1260b)

> Hence we see that is the nature and office of a slave; he who is by nature not his own but another's man, is by nature a slave; and he may be said to be another's man who, being a human being, is also a possession. (1254a)

Here disenchantment is violence beyond the guarding of the one, against language, humans, animals, nature. It is not a violence for human fulfillment against the plenitude of nature but violence per se, in itself. In other words, attached to disenchantment are a hierarchy and a privilege in which some are claimed to be and are instituted as superior, higher than others, *by nature.* The disenchantment of nature is its ordering from high to low. Whenever science finds itself in opposition to religion, philosophy to life, it is essential to remember these stakes and to interrupt them by asking.

Yet the aristotle whose image of the disenchanted world by nature is of hierarchy and domination is also source of the image of the world beyond domination and hierarchy. The nature in which form and order walk hand in hand with rule is itself beyond rule.

Nature (phusis) is a source or cause of being moved and of being at rest in that to which it belongs primarily, and not in virtue of a concomitant attribute. (Aristotle, *Physics,* 192b)...

Heidegger reminds us of the necessity of form and of the abundance of nature in moving from and toward itself. This gesture is close to diotima's voice toward what surpasses all divisions: a nature everlasting, which without any change, is imparted to the ever-growing and perishing beauties of all other things. Nature, moving from itself, is enchanting beyond all disenchantment and the source of all other enchantments, of all ecologies. Form and plenitude coexist, allowing us to read aristotle and later spinoza as enchanted and disenchanted together, not in the confusion of their commitments but in the mingling of the waters of enchantment.

Something similar can be found in aristotle's *poetics*, which again is read to order, classify, and disenchant the wildness and confusion of art, to resist the ways in which art overpowers and disorders us.

> A tragedy, then, is the imitation of an action that is serious and also, as having magnitude, complete in itself; in language with pleasurable accessories, each kind brought in separately in the parts of the work; in a dramatic, not in a narrative form; with incidents arousing pity and fear, wherewith to accomplish its catharsis of such emotions. (Aristotle, *Poetics*, 1449b)

Yet aristotle is explicit that it is in the nature of art to enchant, overwhelm, and disorder.

The poet's function is to describe what is possible as being probable or necessary [as it were, another nature, a nature whose possibility, whose imitation, remains within it]. (Aristotle, *Poetics*, 1451)...

The most mundane and disenchanted accounts of imitation and metaphor give way to echoes of abundance.

> Imitation is natural to man from childhood, one of his advantages over the lower animals being this, that he is the most imitative creature in the world, and learns at first by imitation. And it is also natural for all to delight in works of imitation. The truth of this second point is shown by experience.

Though the objects themselves may be painful to see, we delight to view the most realistic representations of them in art, the forms for example of the lowest animals and of dead bodies (Aristotle, *Poetics*, 1448b)...

"Metaphor consists in giving the thing a name that belongs to something else" (Aristotle, *Poetics*, 1457b), while "the greatest thing by far is to be a master of metaphor. It is the one thing that cannot be learnt from others; and it is also a sign of genius" (Aristotle, *Poetics*, 1459a).

In a seemingly disenchanted voice—I will argue that it is wonderfully enchanted—derrida describes the pairing of nature's enchantments and disenchantments:[11]

Naturizing, originary, and productive phusis, nature can be on the one hand the great, generous, and genial donor to which everything returns, with the result that all of nature's others are still nature itself in difference; and, on the other hand, nature can be the order of so-called necessities, and the natural is again referred to the gift this time as the given. (Derrida, *GT,* p. 127)...

I am suggesting, enchantedly, that there is no such choice. I am asking, again enchantingly, what it means that there is no choice. The abundance and wonder of nature and its expositions are the enchantments that offer themselves up to disenchantment. One might go further and argue that reason's disenchantments are not necessary, no more than any other form, that if form is necessary to nature, disenchanted forms—ordered, accountable—are not necessary to humanity but to certain states of order and control. Many goods come of modern order, many sacrifices are called for. Disenchantment must be viewed as practical and useful and as dominating and coercive.

The view of nature that Aristotle finds in art, another nature, another story, is not just a poetics but also an ethics. It may be time to consider an enchanted ethics as well as a disenchanted one, an ethics of enchantments as well as of disenchantments. A disenchanted ethics is one that looks to decide and rests its decisions on accounting and calculation, on certain practices of reason, on authority and promulgation. An enchanted ethics requires action, but cannot account for its practices by reason or by commandment. This is not due to its elusiveness and illusoriness but to its abundance and ecology, to nuances, subtleties, the struggle to be ethical in a complex and multifarious world, the endless askings that ethics calls from us. This is by no means withdrawal from ethics but its saturation and enchantments. An enchanted ethics is more ethical than a disenchanted one, ethical interrupting ethics. It knows that the good surpasses any accounting in morality or law.

I have elsewhere suggested that we read aristotle's *poetics* as an ethics.[12]

I would consider the possibility that the painful, lowest, and dead, the delight and meaning given by art, come as gifts from the good, otherwise, beyond the mundane, not by making the divine mundane, which is what theology frequently does, and what art does not do except when mistaken for theology. That mistake is what i take socrates to criticize in books ii and iii of plato's republic. (Ross, *GBGA,* 105)...

This is another way to speak of enchantment and disenchantment, a giving from the good that gives us mundane gifts. As for art and poetry,

Nature's plenitude imposes on us an endless responsibility, fulfilled more poignantly for us in art than elsewhere in our experience, to un-

derstand and care for what we destroy, the sacrifices we must make, in order to live and choose. (114)...

Nature is a plenitude of things and events that does not divide into categories and kinds except in response to gifts from the good that resist the violence in every division. The good calls us to know, to ask, to care for, to respond to the low, the painful, the terrible, to what we regard as evil, to recognize the nature of things and kinds beyond the regulation of any authority...

I call this sense of the good in all things cherishment. It can do work in time only as sacrifice. The conjunction of cherishment and sacrifice is plenishment. On my reading, aristotle suggests in relation to art (but not to ethics) a sensitivity through poiēsis to the dark, difficult, terrible, forbidding side of things, of nature. And it is nature, indeed, that is in question. We could not live except by forgetting. But the good demands that we remember. And it is a demand so difficult that it requires all the resources of poiēsis for its expression. (114)...

This nature is a nature otherwise, in memory of divine and erotic madness, but in no other place. The otherwise in nature belongs to nature, belongs to the gods in nature, interrupting. It does not belong to the gods in their places. This is the truth of poiēsis beyond all other truths: that in reminding us of the good, responding to its call, circulating the giving of the good, art shows us the good here, where we are, as interruption. Aristotle speaks of painful and terrible things in nature that interrupt the order of technical production, the order of the state, teach us of meanings beyond any other meanings—here before us, where we are, in our places. The gift of the good, as read in aristotle's poetics, given by art under poiēsis, is given to us where we are, not in another place. This is what we may say is what art shows us more than anything else: that the gods and their madnesses are not away from being, in another place, even descending from that place to ours, but belong to nature, given as interruption for asking. (115–6)...

Plenishment in the earth is the enchantment of all things everywhere, including disenchanted and mundane things. Those who call upon us to relate to the world disenchantedly know and reveal its enchantments in vivid and joyous ways...

Here I would depart from the conviction that our world has ceased to be enchanted and has become disenchanted. It has indeed become so, but it remains enchanted. It has indeed become so, but not recently, it was disenchanted from the first. Disenchantment remains among the endless multiplicities and interruptions of enchantment. That is why art remains for us a place, a work, that will never lose its enchantments even when it becomes as disenchanted as possible.

In the remainder of this chapter I will pursue the enchantments of disenchantment by touching further upon a few writers, primarily philosophers, who have been accused of defining the disenchantment of our age. I mean to agree, and yet to disagree, to suggest that they remain visibly enchanted before our eyes.

If the modern world has become disenchanted, and disenchantment is the product of its modernity, then Descartes appears to be a progenitor of disenchantment as he is regarded as a progenitor of modernity. Here modernity is both the modernization of society and the enlightenment thought that gave rise to modern science. The reappearance of the modern in these related but different occurrences is of course the reappearance of different disenchantments. If so, then the most plausible possibility is that different enchantments are present in each.

In this context, enchanting treatments of disenchantment can be found in Carolyn Merchant's *The Death of Nature* and Susan Griffin's *Woman and Nature*. Nature has been disenchanted, deprived of vitality and life, so that it and some of its parts might be subjugated. Merchant and Griffin present the subordination of women as central to this process, as if to minimize the subjection of women in more religious and less modern secular societies; as if the subjugation of women were not more pervasive than modernization, present in it in modern ways. Merchant argues that modernization took place specifically as if in order to gain control over women and over nature as female. Her treatment is especially productive in that she does not approach the process of modernization as inherent only in thought, as fundamentally philosophical. The death of nature, the disenchantment of the world, is not just an attitude, set of beliefs, or way of thinking. It is the many ways in which the European world changed itself to become modern. After and by means of these changes, exploration and colonization spread European modernity throughout the earth, supplanting indigenous modernization trends in China and elsewhere. European thought, from Descartes to Kant, as well as Christianity from the beginning, was carried everywhere on earth.

We are the rocks, we are soil, we are trees, rivers, we are wind, we carry the birds, the birds, we are cows, mules, we are horses, we are solid elements, cause and effect, determinism and objectivity, it is said, are lost. Matter. We are flesh, we breathe, we are her body: we speak. (Griffin, *WN*, 48)...

We know ourselves to be made from this earth. We know this earth is made from our bodies. For we see ourselves. And we are nature. We are nature seeing nature. We are nature with a concept of nature. Nature weeping. Nature speaking of nature to nature. (228)...

All that I know, I know in this earth, the body of the bird, this pen, this paper, these hands, this tongue speaking, all that I know speaks to me through this earth and I long to tell you, you who are earth too, and listen as we speak to each other of what we know: the light is in us. (229)...

This is a rich and complex story, and I'll return to it in Merchant's and Griffin's voices. Here I would trace something of the pairing of disenchantment and enchantment in some of the authors who define modern philosophy for us, for the moment leaving modern science aside. Like Plato, Descartes offers ways of thinking that contributed powerfully to the advance of modern disenchantment. For example, Rule Seven for the direction of the mind defines calculation explicitly:

> In order to make our knowledge complete, every single thing relating to our undertaking must be surveyed in a continuous and wholly uninterrupted sweep of thought, and be included in a sufficient and well-ordered enumeration.
>
> This deduction sometimes requires such a long chain of inferences that when we arrive at such a truth it is not easy to recall the entire route which led us to it. So I must run through them several times in a continuous movement of the imagination, simultaneously intuiting one relation and passing on to the next, until I have learnt to pass from the first to the last so swiftly that memory is left with practically no role to play, and I seem to intuit the whole thing at once. In this way our memory is relieved, the sluggishness of our intelligence redressed, and its capacity in some way enlarged. (Descartes, *RDM*, 25)

I have suggested that weakness of memory and elusiveness of assurance haunt such passages, and that intuition—with its own elusiveness and uncertainties—plays the role of savior. But it is more direct and plausible to emphasize the sweep of thought and the sufficient and well-ordered enumeration. Descartes's insistence on certainty can easily support skepticism and resistance to calculation, but his emphasis on enumeration won out in the advance of disenchantment.

Similarly, Rule Twelve calls upon us to use all our human powers—possibly enchanted as well as disenchanted—but understands these solely within an image of an orderly intellect:

> Finally we must make use of all the aids which intellect, imagination, sense-perception, and memory afford in order, firstly, to intuit simple propositions distinctly; secondly, to combine

> correctly the matters under investigation with what we already know, so that they too may be known; and thirdly, to find out what things should be compared with each other so that we make the most thorough use of all our human powers. (39)

The philosophers and scientists who defined the model of disenchantment were no strangers to enchantment, but through effective history—their influence on their successors—promoted disenchantment far more widely.

The reasons for this are complex, but one reason is that while the modern world was advancing toward disenchantment—if that is advancement—it did so in the context of secularization and the consolidation of the nation state. Disenchantment, democratization, and secularization went hand in hand, and were identified with each other. This is problematic enough, and tenable if at all only from a disenchanted point of view. More problematic still is that enchantment, authority, and religion were similarly linked, so that all enchantment was ascribed to religion—and even worse, to Christianity first and monotheism thereafter.

Those with stakes in modernization, technology, and rationalization who pursued ways of thinking beyond institutional authorities found themselves in the difficult position of supporting one set of institutional authorities—state and secular academy—over others—temple and church; of denying that the authority of reason is an institutionalization of power; and of promoting disenchantment in the name of truth. This is an unenviable position, and I am trying to resist it by returning truth to enchantment and by separating it from institutional authorities.

Here Descartes (or descartes) may be read backward in resistance to Church authority and forward into academic authority. Certainty and enumerative reason play their role in disenchantment. More telling, perhaps, is his view of matter as disenchanted, contributing to the development of modern science's view of a mechanical view of material things, lifeless atoms and mechanical creatures. Descartes's view is famous:

> *I suppose the body to be nothing but a statue or machine made of earth, which God forms with the explicit intention of making it as much as possible like us.* (*TM*, 99)...
>
> I might consider the body of a man as a kind of machine equipped with and made up of bones, nerves, muscles, veins, blood and skin in such a way that, even if there were no mind in it, it would still perform all the same movements as it now does

> in those cases where movement is not under the control of the will or, consequently, of the mind. (*M*, 6, 58)

> I want the reader to have a general notion of the entire machine which it is my task to describe. So I will say here that the heat in the heart is like the great spring or principle responsible for all the movements occurring in the machine. The veins are pipes which conduct the blood from all the parts of the body towards the heart, where it serves to fuel the heat there. The stomach and the intestines are another much larger pipe perforated with many little holes through which the juices from the food ingested run into the veins; these then carry the juices straight to the heart. The arteries are yet another set of pipes through which the blood, which is heated and rarefied in the heart, passes from there into all the other parts of the body, bringing them heat and material to nourish them. Finally, the parts of the blood that are most agitated and lively are carried to the brain by the arteries coming directly from the heart in the straightest line of all; these parts of the blood make up a kind of air or very fine wind which is called the "animal spirits." These dilate the brain and make it ready to receive impressions both from external objects and from the soul; and in receiving these impressions the brain acts as the organ or seat of the "common" sense, the imagination and the memory. Next, this same air or these same spirits flow from the brain through the nerves into all the muscles, thus making the nerves ready to function as organs for the external senses; they also inflate the muscles in various ways and thus impart movement to all the parts of the body. (Descartes, *DHB*, 315)

Here human beings are thinking things and bodies are mechanisms. On the side of bodies, human and animal, material things have no spirit at all. This is not entirely a novel thought, and circulated throughout Christianity, but where God's divinity and love fell upon the earth it touched bodies as well as souls. Descartes offered as a truer and better view that only minds and souls were divine, inspirited.

Such a view of matter gave rise to more infamous and influential conclusions:

> I made special efforts to show that if any such machines had the organs and outward shape of a monkey or of some other animal that lacks reason, we should have no means of knowing that they did not possess entirely the same nature as these animals; whereas if any such machines bore a resemblance to our bodies and imitated our actions as closely as possible for all practical purposes, we should still have two very certain means

> of recognizing that they were not real men. The first is that they could never use words, or put together other signs, as we do in order to declare our thoughts to others. Secondly, even though such machines might do some things as well as we do them, or perhaps even better, they would inevitably fail in others, which would reveal that they were acting not through understanding but only from the disposition of their organs. (Descartes, *DM*, 139)
>
> Now in just these two ways we can also know the difference between man and beast. For it is quite remarkable that there are no men so dull-witted or stupid—and this includes even madmen—that they are incapable of arranging various words together and forming an utterance from them in order to make their thoughts understood; whereas there is no other animal, however perfect and well-endowed it may be, that can do the like. This shows not merely that the beasts have less reason than men, but that they have no reason at all. (140)
>
> It is also a very remarkable fact that although many animals show more skill than we do in some of their actions, yet the same animals show none at all in many others; so what they do better does not prove that they have any intelligence, for if it did then they would have more intelligence than any of us and would excel us in everything. It proves rather that they have no intelligence at all, and that it is nature which acts in them according to the disposition of their organs. (140)

Human beings' bodies are animal bodies, as mechanical as theirs. Bodies are lifeless, only reason is divine. Even so, descartes knows that if these lifeless bodies were made by god, they have something divine and enchanted in them.

For we may regard this body as a machine which, having been made by the hands of god, is incomparably better ordered than any machine that can be devised by man, and contains in itself movements more wonderful than those in any such machine. (139)...

These days such a view would be regarded by many as intelligent design: the world is made up of things that only a god could devise, no matter how mechanical they may be. Both of these views are disenchanted, refusing to things themselves qualities and capacities beyond the reach of any maker, knower, or associate. Although the sense of an enchanted world containing enchanted things of all kinds was expressed more explicitly by leibniz and spinoza, descartes must acknowledge that an infinite world—god's or nature's—is something we can only wonder at.

This pairing off of order and certainty on the side of disenchantment and of infinity and wonder on the side of enchantment continues throughout Descartes's writings. It is as if we must close off one side of our wondering mind in order to read him as disenchanted. For example, the figure of architect and city planner leans on one side toward building well, on the other side toward reaching too far, transporting us where we are to other places.

> Throughout my writings I have made it clear that my method imitates that of the architect. When an architect wants to build a house which is stable on ground where there is a sandy topsoil over underlying rock, or clay, or some other firm base, he begins by digging out a set of trenches from which he removes the sand, and anything resting on or mixed in with the sand, so that he can lay his foundations on firm soil. In the same way, I began by taking everything that was doubtful and throwing it out, like sand; and then, when I noticed that it is impossible to doubt that a doubting or thinking substance exists, I took this as the bedrock on which I could lay the foundations of my philosophy. (Descartes, *OR*, Obj. 7, 366)

This tempered account bears exalted expectations.

> Above all I delighted in mathematics, because of the certainty and self-evidence of its reasonings. But I did not yet notice its real use; and since I thought it was of service only in the mechanical arts, I was surprised that nothing more exalted had been built upon such firm and solid foundations. *On the other hand, I compared the moral writings of the ancient pagans to very proud and magnificent palaces built only on sand and mud.* (Descartes, *DM*, 114)...
>
> Ancient cities which have gradually grown from mere villages into large towns are usually ill-proportioned, compared with those orderly towns which planners lay out as they fancy on level ground. Looking at the buildings of the former individually, you will often find as much art in them, if not more, than in those of the latter; but in view of their arrangement—a tall one here, a small one there—and the way they make the streets crooked and irregular, you would say it is chance, rather than the will of men using reason, that placed them so. And when you consider that there have always been certain officials whose job is to see that private buildings embellish public places, you will understand how difficult it is to make something perfect by working only on what others have produced. Again, I thought, peoples who have grown gradually from a half-savage to a civilized state, and have made their laws only in so far as they were

> forced to by the inconvenience of crimes and quarrels, could not be so well governed as those who from the beginning of their society have observed the basic laws laid down by some wise law-giver. Similarly, *it is quite certain that the constitution of the true religion, whose articles have been made by god alone, must be incomparably better ordered than all the others.* (116)...

The desire for solid foundations so that a serviceable and commodious habitation might be built passes into images of palaces and towers, public buildings instituting the authority of great civilizations, gathering all their subjects under their rule. The figure framing this desire for greatness comes from enforced solitude, another figure of madness.

> I stayed all day shut up alone in a stove-heated room, where I was completely free to converse with myself about my own thoughts. Among the first that occurred to me was the thought that there is not usually so much perfection in works composed of several parts and produced by various different craftsmen as in the works of one man. Thus we see that buildings undertaken and completed by a single architect are usually more attractive and better planned than those which several have tried to patch up by adapting old walls built for different purposes. (*DM*, 116)

Similarly, nature's mechanical order gives way as it must to repeated figures of what exceeds human expectations.

I am taking nature to be something more limited than the totality of things bestowed on me by god. For this includes many things that belong to the mind alone—for example my perception that what is done cannot be undone, and all other things that are known by the natural light; but I am not speaking of these matters. It also includes much that relates to the body alone, like the tendency to move in a downward direction, and so on; but I am not speaking of these matters either. (*M*, 6, 56)...

When I distinctly see where things come from and where and when they come to me, and when I can connect my perceptions of them with the whole of the rest of my life without a break, then I am quite certain that when I encounter these things I am not asleep but awake. But since the pressure of things to be done does not always allow us to stop and make such a meticulous check, it must be admitted that in this human life we are often liable to make mistakes about particular things, and we must acknowledge the weakness of our nature. (61)...

Indeed, Descartes is no stranger to wonder, the figure of enchantment that, historically and beyond, in plato's name pervades philosophy. If descartes's view of wonder is less enchanted than plato's, it goes far beyond the mechanical disenchantments he is read to invoke.

When our first encounter with some object surprises us and we find it novel, or very different from what we formerly knew or from what we supposed it ought to be, this causes us to wonder and to be astonished at it. Since all this may happen before we know whether or not the object is beneficial to us, I regard wonder as the first of all the passions. (PS, 350)...

I identify enchantment with wonder, if not only wonder—because the terms of enchantment endlessly betray themselves. Terms of transcendence, surpassing, and overwhelming exceed our capacity to grasp them. In this way, wonder as the passion that moves us with astonishment can be identified less with the impulse and more with the amazement. Even so, although himself enchanted by wonder, Descartes chooses disenchantment.

> More often we wonder too much rather than too little, as when we are astonished in looking at things which merit little or no consideration. This may entirely prevent or pervert the use of reason. Therefore, although it is good to be born with some inclination to wonder, since it makes us disposed to acquire scientific knowledge, yet after acquiring such knowledge we must attempt to free ourselves from this inclination as much as possible. There is no remedy for excessive wonder except to acquire the knowledge of many things and to practise examining all those which may seem most unusual and strange. (355)

> This passion seems to diminish with use, for the more we encounter unusual things which we wonder at, the more we find ourselves accustomed to stop wondering at them and to regard any we subsequently come upon as common. (355)

Although beset by extraordinary doubts, Descartes brings his asking to rest by doubting too little.

Of the enchanting readings of descartes's wonder, irigaray's is perhaps most wondering.

Wonder is the motivating force behind mobility in all its dimensions. (Irigaray, *W*, 73)...

This first passion is indispensable not only to life but to the creation of an ethics. Through sexual difference. This other, male or female, should surprise us again and again, appear to us as new, very different from what we knew or what we thought he or she should be. Who are thou? I am and I become thanks to this question. Wonder goes beyond that which is or is not suitable for us. (74)...

Wonder is the passion of that which is already born and not yet reenveloped in love. It is the passion of the first encounter. And of perpetual rebirth? The place of incidence and junction of body and spirit, which has been covered over again and again? This would be possible only when we are faithful to the perpetual newness of the self, the other, the world. A third dimension. An intermediary. Neither the one nor the other. Which is not to say neutral or neuter. The forgotten ground of our condition between mortal and immortal, men and gods, creatures and creators. In us and among us. (81–2)...

And she wonders from other places:

As soon as a woman leaves the house, someone starts to wonder, someone asks her: how can you be a woman and be out here at the same time?. (Irigaray, *Q*, 144)...

How can a woman be equal in public? Wonder is perhaps the answer.

This passion has no opposite or contradiction and exists always as though for the first time. Thus man and woman, woman and man are therefore always meeting as though for the first time because they cannot be substituted one for the other. (W, 12–3)...

Who or what the other is, I never know. But the other who is forever unknowable is the one who differs from me sexually. This feeling of surprise, astonishment, and wonder in the face of the unknowable ought to be returned to its locus: that of sexual difference. (13)...

Who or what the other is I never know but I know the other is another sex. Perhaps this other and the other's sex is enchanting. I wonder if the enchanting other has a sex.

Let us wonder in other places...

In *The Age of the World Picture* Heidegger speaks of "[t]he fundamental event of the modern age [a]s the conquest of the world as picture" (134).[13] He comments:

> One of the essential phenomena of the modern age is its science. A phenomenon of no less importance is machine technology. Machine technology remains up to now the most visible outgrowth of the essence of modern technology, which is identical with the essence of modern metaphysics.
>
> A third equally essential phenomenon of the modern period lies in the event of art's moving into the purview of aesthetics.
>
> A fourth modern phenomenon manifests itself in the fact that human activity is conceived and consummated as culture.
>
> A fifth phenomenon of the modern age is the loss of the gods. The loss of the gods is so far from excluding religiosity that rather only through that loss is the relation to the gods

> changed into mere "religious experience." When this occurs, then the gods have fled. (116–7)

> world picture, when understood essentially does not mean a picture of the world but the world conceived and grasped as picture. What is, in its entirely, is now taken in such a way that it first is in being and only is in being to the extent that it is set up by man, who represents and sets forth. (129–30)

> For the sake of this struggle of world views and in keeping with its meaning, man brings into play his unlimited power for the calculating, planning, and molding of all things. Science as research is an absolutely necessary form of this establishing of self in the world; it is one of the pathways upon which the modern age rages toward fulfillment of its essence. (134–5)

> Everywhere everything is ordered to stand by, to be immediately on hand, indeed to stand there just so that it may be on call for a further ordering. We call it the standing-reserve [*Bestand*]. It designates nothing less than the way in which everything presences that is wrought upon by the revealing that challenges. Whatever stands by in the sense of standing-reserve no longer stands over against us as object. (*QTOE*, 17)

It is possible—perhaps obligatory—to read this view of the modern age, world picture, science, representation, calculation, and technology as expressing the disenchantment of the modern world and of its salvation as reenchantment.

The closer we come to the danger, the more brightly do the ways into the saving power begin to shine and the more questioning we become. For questioning is the piety of thought. (35)...

The loss of the gods, their flight, is disenchantment. It is as if the gods still manifested enchantment for us, as if the Greek world knew enchantment as the modern world no longer does, as if the fourfold has passed away in picture and standing reserve.

Sky and earth, mortals and divinities. The four are united primally in being toward one another, a fourfold. The things let the fourfold of the four stay with them. This gathering, assembling, letting-stay is the thinging of things. The unitary fourfold of sky and earth, mortals and divinities, which is stayed in the thinging of things, we call—the world. (*L*, 199)...

It is possible to read heidegger as directing his critique of the modern age against the disenchantment of the world and as directing asking toward its reenchantment. In the fourfold with sky and earth, things remain in their thinging beyond any reserve and accounting. Science here is part of the process of disenchantment—otherwise called *metaphysics*—in which the withdrawal of being passes over into being on call.

The key word here, perhaps, is *questioning*. And it may be read as a philosophical word. Philosophers question, ordinary people live. Or it may be read as enchantment, philosophical and something else, read as *asking*. To ask, asking beyond asking, asking questions that call beyond any answers, may be the heart of enchantment,[14] that which calls us to language and to art.

The question framing *The Origin of the Work of Art* is of the origin: "Origin here means that from and by which something is what it is and as it is. What something is, as it is, we call its essence or nature. The origin of something is the source of its nature" (Heidegger, *OWA*, 17). The answer Heidegger gives to this seemingly metaphysical question of art is the happening of truth.

> The origin of the work of art—that is, the origin of both the creators and the preservers, which is to say of a people's historical existence, is art. This is so because art is by nature an origin: a distinctive way in which truth comes into being, that is, becomes historical. (Heidegger, *OWA*, 78)

Not the artist, not art itself, art comes to be from neither humanity nor nature, neither subjectively nor objectively, but in the rift between them, between world and earth. The rift we may know as enchantment. Happening happens as interruption, in the caesura, between enchantment and disenchantment, between asking and telling. Asking and telling are the exposition of an event that happens beyond fixing and having.

The world is the self-disclosing openness of the broad paths of the simple and essential decisions in the destiny of an historical people. The earth is the spontaneous forthcoming of that which is continually self-secluding and to that extent sheltering and concealing. World and earth are essentially different from one another and yet are never separated. The world grounds itself on the earth, and earth juts through world. (48–9)...

The opposition of world and earth is a striving. In the struggle, each opponent carries the other beyond itself. (49)...

This pairing, this striving, this struggle between appearing and secluding, is expression, as interruption.

World appears and withholds itself in its expression, in its appearance. It is more and other than it appears, but it appears. Expression, appearing, exposition are the manifestations of things. I understand this struggle not as conflict but as movement, irruption, emergence, forgetting...

> To be a work means to set up a world. (Heidegger, *OWA*, 44)
>
> The *world worlds.* (44)
>
> *The work lets the earth be an earth.* (46)

What emerges is appearance, art brings appearance forth in the withholding of the earth, in forgetting.

The strife that is brought into the rift and thus set back into the earth and thus fixed in place is figure, shape, gestalt. (64)...

Thought cuts furrows into the soil of being. (*NL*, 70)...

The earth, being, nature, world exceeds any accounting, any appearance, any name, but appear in a struggle over appearing itself.

For some time I have understood *The Origin of the Work of Art* as a reworking of Kant's *Critique of Judgment*.[15] The origin of the work of art is not the genius of the artist nor the subjectivity of the perceiver, but the withdrawing of the work beyond the reach of any concept, the enchanting of asking and telling. Here is a summary of Kant's view of aesthetic judgment through the moments or images of taste:

> (1) Taste is disinterested satisfaction; beauty is the object of such a satisfaction. (2) Beauty pleases universally without requiring a concept. (3) Beauty is the form of the purposiveness (or finality) of an object without representation of a purpose. (4) Beauty is the object of a necessary satisfaction independent of a concept. In other words, beauty falls under no concept, scientific or ethical; pleases disinterestedly, without a purpose; pleases universally; consequently, it is the universal object of a subjective universality, taste.

Each of these negations can be understood to express withdrawal: from practice, concept, and purpose. Each can be understood to express forthcoming as opening, enchanting as exceeding. Heidegger emphasizes not the production of an aesthetic object for consumption but happening as withdrawing into its open, the showing of the object beyond accounting. If this is enchantment, then enchanting takes place by withdrawing beyond accounting. Asking and telling multiply in art as events of becoming and expressing.

It is impossible to think of the third critique without the others, so it may be productive to pose the possibility that the first two critiques, of pure and practical reason, largely express disenchantment, while the third evokes enchantment. If this reading is to be pursued, it would be based on a reading of the limits of reason that both establishes its authority and disrupts it at the limit. Here every critique plays the same explicit role, to define the limits of the universal and to establish its authority—under concepts in the first two critiques, without a determinate concept in the third. The concept rules over phenomena in the first two critiques but not in the third, which repeatedly carries the force of the universal beyond the limits that define it under a concept.

Kant's role in the advance of the disenchantment of enlightenment reason has always been ambiguous. On the reading of disenchantment that establishes science's authority, kant is both a prominent resource in favor and a source of its unsettling. The authority of science is gained at the expense of the natural world, which appears—if only through a fog—as enchanted.

We have not merely explored the territory of pure understanding, and carefully surveyed every part of it, but have also measured its extent, and assigned to everything in it its rightful place. This domain is an island, enclosed by nature itself within unalterable limits. It is the land of truth—enchanting name!—surrounded by a wide and stormy ocean, the native home of illusion, where many a fog bank and many a swiftly melting iceberg give the deceptive appearance of farther shores, deluding the adventurous seafarer ever anew with empty hopes, and engaging him in enterprises which he can never abandon and yet is unable to carry to completion. (Kant, *CPR*, [NKS 257; M 180])...

We have found, indeed, that although we had contemplated building a tower which should reach to the heavens, the supply of materials suffices only for a dwelling-house, just sufficiently commodious for our business on the level of experience, and just sufficiently high to allow of our overlooking it. The bold undertaking that we had designed is thus bound to fail through lack of material—not to mention the babel of tongues, which inevitably gives rise to disputes among the workers in regard to the plan to be followed, and which must end by scattering them over all the world, leaving each to erect a separate building for himself, according to his own design. (Kant, *CPR*, [NKS 573; M 406])...

Let us call this modernity's architectural|political|epistemological project,[16] to found authority vertically, reaching to the sky. As founding, the project is disenchanted; as reaching, enchanting beyond disenchantment.

Both of these figures can be read as establishing the authority of the universal as if it were not threatened by its own limits. Both can be read as establishing that authority only by figures that reach beyond it. The critical project is a project of disenchantment, but it succeeds only through gestures toward enchantment. In this way, kant may treat the transcendences of things themselves as illusions, but they cannot be empirical or aesthetic illusions; they are the primordial withdrawal of things to themselves. Heidegger's response is to bring this withdrawal back into appearing in the production of art.

It follows on such readings that the authority of disenchanted reason—science and philosophy—is given by its refusal to open itself to what it claims exceeds it. It struggles to refuse this reading, and to claim that what exceeds it is superstitious and irrational, as if the label *reason*—again, *science and philosophy*—exceeded itself in becoming authority of itself. The figure of dispersion, of the babel of tongues and scatterings, carries so much truth that the authority of science is always presented in excessive ways. The critical method in kant establishes scientific reason, as it should, in a rift between what is known and what it says cannot be known—asking as shape and figure, exposition. The exposition of science marks the enchantments of its own disenchantment.

Such a view of philosophy more than science appears in Vattimo's *The End of Modernity*. *Modernity*, in the present context, marks the sweep of disenchantment far beyond the academic plane. *The end* marks something enigmatic, so extensive that *reenchantment* does not suffice yet cannot be rejected.

> "post-" signifies precisely that attitude which Nietzsche and Heidegger have tried to establish in regard to the heritage of European thought. Both philosophers call this heritage into question in a radical manner, but at the same time refuse to propose a means for a critical "overcoming" of it. For both philosophers, the reason for this refusal is that any call for an "overcoming" would involve remaining captive to the logic of development inscribed in the tradition of European thought. (Gianni Vattimo, *EM*, 2)

Vattimo situates nietzsche and heidegger at the moment of post-modernity as if they marked the greatest possibility of reenchantment. Yet the *post-* expresses at best an "overcoming," calling modernity's disenchantment into question but at the same time refusing to name the overcoming as such. In other words, what follows modernity, modernization, and modern science—all disenchantments—is not known, not present, never perhaps fully present, an enigmatic—enchanting—overcoming, if an overcoming at all. Every name of this event, *reenchantment* especially, remains within the logic of disenchantment, as if we can know what we cannot know.

It must seem strained to identify postmodernity with enchantment, especially the different movements that resist modernity. Yet the logic of disenchantment, identified with the logic of modernity, requires that the *dis-* be resisted and transcended, no matter how enigmatically or enchantedly.

The "post-" in the term "post-modern" indicates in fact a taking leave of modernity. In its search to free itself from the logic of development inherent in modernity—namely the idea of a critical "overcoming" directed toward a new foundation—post-modernity seeks exactly what nietzsche and heidegger seek in their own peculiar "critical" relationship with western thought. (Vattimo, 3)...

This conjecture—and as a conjecture is how I will read it—evokes multiple questions of the event that Vattimo is naming, in particular whether the post-modern is the postmodern, whether it is critical or something more promising, whether and how it is an overcoming, but most of all, perhaps, whether it is an event named properly by nietzsche and heidegger.

I hazard the conjecture that these are all related, though perhaps not as vattimo would have it.

We may read nietzsche and heidegger to resist the disenchantment of the modern world in evoking a taking leave and a healing (verwindung) that may not depart in any particular way or return to any particular place or heal any particular disease; an overcoming or taking leave that marks not so much a departure, novelty, or distance, but an enchantment that remains in disenchantment, the pre- and post- and other disparitions that remain in modernity...

This is congenial with the sense that enchantment is not the opposite of disenchantment, that only disenchantment insists on opposites, that the other to disenchantment is an enigmatic event of asking. Call it *post-* if you will, as that which does not resolve its strangeness.

In philosophical language—and Vattimo insists on philosophy—this is described as an event:

> Nietzsche and Heidegger radically conceive of Being as an event; for both of them it is vitally important, in order to be able to speak of Being, to understand at "what point" we are, and at "what point" Being itself is. Ontology is nothing other than the interpretation of our condition or situation, since Being is nothing apart from its "event," which occurs when it historicizes itself and when we historicize ourselves. (3)

I do not want to question this historicization of the event—more truthfully, perhaps, the eventization of history—but to reenact the disruptions of enchantment beyond the name of the event, beyond history and historicization. There is no point where being is disenchanted because time and history are not the conditions of enchantment. The *post* of postmodernity is not a moment, event, or historical arrival, but a very different kind of eventuality.

Always on the way, always present, always to come, always coming, always already here. Words for this are enchantment, promising, asking, telling, perhaps, maybe, as if. Enchantment exceeds the conditions of the event, exceeds the modernity of the modern...

In other words:

No justice is possible or thinkable without the principle of some responsibility beyond all living present, within that which disjoins the living present, before the ghosts of those who are not yet born or who are already dead. Victims of the oppressions of capitalist imperialism or any of the forms of totalitarianism. Without this non-contemporaneity with itself of the living present, without that which secretly unhinges it, without this responsibility and this respect for justice concerning those who are not there, of those who are no longer or who are not yet present and living, what sense would there be to ask the question "where are we going, what shall we do?" (Derrida, *SM*, xviii).

Enchantment exceeds itself, exceeds every enchantment and disenchantment...

This is a strong thing to say. So let me back up just a bit to make this point properly—I mean, in terms of proper names—although it cannot be proper as it stands. Let me hazard after vattimo that nietzsche and heidegger resist modernity and its disenchantments, that the dionysian is enchantment as enchantment is the origin of art. In this way, vattimo's contribution is to evoke postmodernity's aftermath of modernity in both its succession and its enchantments. "[I]t may probably be said that the postmodern—in Heideggerian terms, post-metaphysical—experience of truth is an aesthetic and rhetorical experience" (Vattimo, *EM*, 12). It may perhaps improbably be said that truth remains enchanted in the midst of the most disenchanted methods and procedures. It may perhaps be improbably said that the possibility of enchanted truth lies in the enchantments that dislocate it. The *post* dislocates the accountability that disenchantment would institute.

Vattimo's reading allows us to see not only a possible place for nietzsche and heidegger in relation to the grip of disenchantment in modernity, but also the obliqueness of the resistance to this grip—by which I mean it remains oblique as such, in itself, in its nonidentity with itself. Postmodernity is not after modernity nor before nor the same nor different, but *other*, unaccountable. The relation of the *post* is as obscure and mobile as of enchantment to the world.

It is the nature of enchantment not to have a place, but always to be seeking its place...

It is enchanting to be other, ~~not~~ beyond itself, in the modalities of ~~as if~~ and ~~perhaps~~, where even these are other to themselves, other as ifs, perhaps other perhaps...

What is going to come, perhaps, is not only this or that; it is the thought of the perhaps, the perhaps itself. The arrivant will arrive perhaps. The arrivant could also be the perhaps itself the unheard-of, totally new experience of the perhaps. Unheard-of, totally new. (Derrida, *PF*, 29)...

That we are heirs does not mean that we have or that we receive this or that, some inheritance that enriches us one day with this or that, but that the being of what we are is first of all inheritance, whether we like it or know it or not. To bear witness to what we are insofar as we inherit, and that—here is the circle, here is the chance, or the finitude—we inherit the very thing that allows us to bear witness to it. (68).

To be enchanted is to inherit—nothing in particular; not to receive or have but to give, ask, bear witness, express—perhaps, as if—the unheard-of as if and perhaps...

This means that we must—it is necessary, it is good—to keep nietzsche and heidegger in mind and to forget them and to look at others. Enchantment has no place even as it insists on replacing disenchantment. Replacing here does not mean obscuring or eliminating, but—in heidegger's language—resituating the disenchantment of the world upon the enchantments of the earth. The enchantments of nature and the earth exceed any accounting, any return. They exceed any image of healing the dis-ease of disenchantment.

With this image of healing I will return to Merchant and the death of nature. I will come back to Griffin in a later chapter to evoke her enchanted voice. Merchant's voice is disenchanted even as it is disenchantment of which she speaks. Even so, her understanding of ecology offers prospects for enchantment.

> Today, a global ecological crisis threatens the health of the entire planet. Ozone depletion, carbon dioxide buildup, chloroflurocarbon emissions, and acid rain upset the respiration and clog the pores and lungs of the ancient Earth Mother Gaia. Toxic wastes, pesticides, and herbicides seep into ground water,

> marshes, bays, and oceans, polluting Gaia's circulatory system. Tropical rainforests and northern old-growth forests disappear at alarming rates as lumberers shear Gaia of her tresses. Entire species of plants and animals become extinct each day. A new partnership between humans and the earth is urgently needed.
>
> During the past decade, women over the entire globe have emerged as ecological activists. Simultaneously, feminist scholars were producing an explosion of books on ancient goddesses that became the basis for a renewed earth-rooted spirituality.
>
> Yet these celebrations of the connection between women and nature contain an inherent contradiction. If women overtly identify with nature and both are devalued in modern Western culture, don't such efforts work against women's prospects for their own liberation? Such actions seem to cement existing forms of oppression against both women and nature, rather than liberating either.
>
> What these developments point to is the possibility of a new world view that could guide twenty-first-century citizens in an ecologically sustainable way of life. A nonmechanistic science and an ecological ethic, however, must support a new economic order grounded in the recycling of renewable resources, the conservation of nonrenewable resources, and the restoration of sustainable ecosystems that fulfill basic human physical and spiritual needs. Perhaps Gaia will then be healed. (Merchant, *DN*, xv–xviii)

The figure of healing, suggesting a mutilated, diseased, or broken earth, evokes a conservative, conserving, conservationist perspective instead of surprise and enchantment. It will be important to consider healing and repair as figures of enchantment, and I will do so momentarily. First, however, I would keep merchant in the foreground evoking a transformation of the current scene. Ecology offers the reenchantment of the earth through its restoration together with the liberation of women.

> Environmentalists, warning us of the irreversible consequences of continuing environmental exploitation, are developing an ecological ethic emphasizing the interconnectedness between people and nature. Juxtaposing the goals of the two movements can suggest new values and social structures, based not on the domination of women and nature as resources but on the full expression of both male and female talent and on the maintenance of environmental integrity. (xix)

The figure of Gaia is one of enchantment, if perhaps a restricted one. It suffers from the image of holism that runs throughout merchant's book.[17] Gaia, the earth, is whole. Modern science is mechanistic; its objects are fragmented, divided into parts. The death of nature is its division against its totality.

> The mechanistic view of nature assumes that nature can be divided into parts and that the parts can be rearranged to create other species of being. "Facts" or information bits can be extracted from the environmental context and rearranged according to a set of rules based on logical and mathematical operations. The results can then be tested and verified by resubmitting them to nature, the ultimate judge of their validity.
>
> The most important example of holism today is provided by the science of ecology. The idea of cyclical processes, of the interconnectedness of all things, and the assumption that nature is active and alive are fundamental to the history of human thought. No element of an interlocking cycle can be removed without the collapse of the cycle. The parts themselves thus take their meaning from the whole. Each particular part is defined by and dependent on the total context. The cycle itself is a dynamic interactive relationship of all its parts, and process is a dialectical relation between part and whole. Ecology necessarily must consider the complexities and the totality. It cannot isolate the parts into simplified systems that can be studied in a laboratory, because such isolation distorts the whole. (290–3)

She equates holism with relationality, and does not explore how relations might exceed the totality: the infinity of relation in levinas's voice, the noncontemporaneity with itself of any living present in derrida's voice, how a multiplicity of enchantments might exceed the whole of any grasp in mine. She speaks of healing and returning gaia to her wholeness, as if humanity once cared for the earth as an enchanted place and did not mutilate it; and she speaks of a new understanding and practice where "the future distribution of energy and resources a communities should be based on the integration of human and natural ecosystems. Such a restructuring of priorities may be crucial if people and nature are to survive" (295). I envisage wholeness as another figure of disenchantment.

The one does violence to itself and guards itself against the other...

I would conclude this chapter with the figure of healing. Healing and repairing are figures of making whole, as if what was once present before modernity, industrialization, and globalization was complete and good. A bit too nostalgic for me, but far worse, it assumes what disenchantment takes for granted, that the whole is whole, there, restorable to its familiar wholeness, another form of accountability. The whole earth, the whole world, the whole truth all are figures of completion. Enchantment revels in partiality, incompleteness, and multiplicity, the wonders of the finite, its infinite abundance.

In a fascinating and long overdue book, Elizabeth Spelman asks us to look closely at *repair*, beginning with its craft and domestic figures, extended to a sweeping way of being in the world. So sweeping, indeed, that it is productive to view enchantment and disenchantment through its lens, productive and ecological. We have seen this already, the compelling sense in which the violences of disenchantment may be responded to by healing, yet in which this healing occupies an ambiguous space between returning to a state of completion and ease and ministering to the living body so that it may take on new tasks and responsibilities, so that it may dance. Similarly, repair occupies an ambiguous ecological space between fixing and augmenting.

The human being is a repairing animal. Repair is ubiquitous, something we engage in every day and in almost every dimension of our lives. Homo sapiens is also homo reparans. (Spelman, *R*, 1)...

Repair is reenchantment, disenchanting-enchanting-reenchanting...

> Perhaps the most obvious kinds of repair are those having to do with the inanimate objects with which we surround ourselves—the clothes calling out for mending, the automobiles for fixing, the buildings for renovating, the works of art for restoring. But our bodies and souls also are by their very nature subject to fracture and fissure, for which we seek homely household recipes for healing and consolation, or perhaps the expert ministrations of surgeons, therapists, and other menders and fixers of all manner of human woes. Relationships between individuals and among nations are notoriously subject to fraying and being rent asunder. From apologies and other informal attempts at patching things up to law courts, conflict mediation, and truth and reconciliation commissions, we try to reweave what we revealingly call the social fabric.
>
> No wonder, then, that *H. reparans* is always and everywhere on call: we, the world we live in, and the objects and relationships we create are by their very nature things that can break, decay, unravel, fall to pieces. (Spelman, 1–2)

If repair is associated with returning to a whole state from unravel and decay, then in response to disenchantment it would appear to suggest either another disenchantment—fixing according to specifications—or returning to a prior state of enchantment. If repair is more closely related to the unraveling and decay, if making whole means making things work in the midst of unworking, if we imagine the disenchantment of the world as the world so thoroughly known that it never needs mending, then repair is a double figure of enchantment, both the breaking and fragmenting that this disenchanted world cannot escape and the mending, fixing, and renovating that are required, both of which exceed accounting.

This second view appears vividly in the three examples with which spelman begins: a handyman who makes anything work somehow—she calls it *bricolage;* a motorcyclist who wants a vintage motorcycle restored to its most pristine state; a museum restorer who must bring a damaged work back to its original state without obscuring the restorations. In all these cases the image of restoration is strong, yet repairing does not mean recovering the original. In every case that is impossible, even in the second, where the original has to be so authentic as to be entirely beyond any usefulness as a vehicle. Spelman understands bricolage as "mak[ing] do with what is at hand by envisioning new uses for remnants and leftovers" (11), acknowledging—celebrating—the ways in which the finite world is fragmented and broken and in which we make it new—not whole.

> The story of *H. reparans* throws into sharp relief how we humans have responded to the fact of being creatures who are inherently limited by the resources at our disposal, who are subject to the ever present possibility of failure and decay, who sometimes seek continuity with the past, and who face the necessity of deciding whether or not to patch up relationships with our neighbors—in short, it reminds us of some facts about the human condition that perhaps we tend to find disturbing. (139–40)

Repairing exposes an enchanted world of multiplicity, fragmentation, and decay. Repair is required in the midst of a broken world in which fractured things can be made to do all manners of surprising things, some of which we know in advance, many of which we do not. The language of reparation is restitutive—repair, restoration, rehabilitation, renovation, correction, reconciliation, redemption, healing, fixing, mending...

All things make reparation to one another for their injustice according to the ordinance of time. (Anaximander)...[18]

Reparation is surprising... Justice is astonishing...

> Repair is conservative: It makes it possible for what has existed in the past to continue into and beyond the present. Re-

> pair gets the car running again, the friendship back on its legs, the community able to resume civil functioning. But in order to bring about this link to the past, in order to undo the damage, repair has to do something about those breakdowns, ruptures, and collapses. In this sense, repair is interventionist. Curators of historical buildings have been taught by authorities in the field to think of options before them in terms of degrees of intervention: "We can classify levels of intervention according to a scale of increasing radicality, thus: (1) preservation; (2) restoration; (3) conservation and consolidation; (4) reconstitution; (5) adaptive reuse; (6) reconstruction; (7) replication." (Spelman, *R*, 124)

Every one of these terms falls into an enchanted world broken, ecologically open to transformations and interventions.

> To repair, then, is to enact a complicated attitude toward the past and the preexistent: Repair is conservative, but also interventionist; humble, but also presumptuous; it honors some moments in the past while erasing others. In its service to the past and the preexistent we find reasons to distinguish repairing something from creating it or replacing it, and in the conservative commitment of repair to continuity we note its difference from destruction.
>
> This profile of repair suggests that human beings, like the rest of the natural world of which we are part, exhibit at least three kinds of impulses, embody at least three kinds of forces, which we can observe in our ability to create, to destroy, and to repair. (125–6)

I would bring this understanding of what appears familiar into play between enchantment and disenchantment. Here, disenchantment means a way of thinking and being that never needs repair, never needs bricolage, understands in advance the forces that work and can measure them and guard against them. It doesn't assume that human beings or nature are perfect, only the knowledge that is available to guard against imperfections.

An enchanted world is a world of bricolage. Forces are immeasurable. Everything falls to pieces, into decay, loss with the multiplication of causes and effects, motions and transformations, unexpectednesses and broken promises. It is in the nature of language, exposition, and enchantment to promise broken promises. That is the joy as well as sorrow of enchantment, its ecology. Repair promises return, but in returning departs, in restoring the promise, relocates, takes place in a world in which it is impossible to hold on to the promise and in which it is impossible to repair every break, multiplying options for further enchant-

ment. The conservative impulse that drives repair is the impossibility of holding on that expresses its enchantments...

I would conclude with Blanchot's enchanted words on the image in its decay:

The image, at first sight, does not resemble the cadaver, but it is possible that the rotting, decaying, cadaverous strangeness might also be from the image. (Maurice Blanchot, *TVI*, 256 [*el*, 344; my translation])...

On the worldly plane ambiguity is the possibility of give and take: meaning always escapes into another meaning. We never come to an understanding once and for all...

On the second level it is no longer a question of perpetual double meanings—of misunderstandings aiding or impeding agreement. Here what speaks in the name of the image "sometimes" [tantôt: presently, soon, in a little while, yet to come, maybe someday, ever; deferring, postponing—all as if, perhaps] still speaks of the world, and "sometimes" [perhaps someday] introduces us into the undetermined milieu of fascination. However, what we distinguish by saying sometimes, sometimes [« tantôt, tantôt »], ambiguity introduces by always, here on the third level meaning does not escape into another meaning, but into the other of all meaning. Because of ambiguity nothing has meaning, but everything seems infinitely meaningful. Meaning is no longer anything but semblance; semblance makes meaning become infinitely rich. It makes this infinitude of meaning have no need of development—makes meaning immediate, which is also to say incapable of being developed, only immediately void [vide: empty] (263)...

Perpetual double meanings meanings in endless decay endless procrastination the undetermined milieu of fascination meaning is endless semblance incapable of being developed immediately empty is this not enchantment—nothing at all yet everything seems infinite? Is this not asking asking? Who can tell?...

Chapter 1

Nature's Enchantments

> There has only ever been one ontological proposition: Being is univocal. A single voice raises the clamor of being. (Gilles Deleuze, *DR*, 35)

The clamor of being sings enchantingly...

> The essential in univocity is not that Being is said in a single and same sense, but that it is said, in a single and same sense, *of* all the individuating differences or intrinsic modalities. Being is said in a single and same sense of everything of which it is said, but that of which it is said differs: it is said of difference itself. (36)

Being is asked enchantingly...

> A single and same voice for the whole thousand-voiced multiple, a single and same ocean for all the drops, a single clamor of being for all beings: on condition that each being, each drop and each voice has reached the state of excess. (303–4)

The state of excess is nature's voice each drop each voice resounds enchantingly...

In the caesura... Asking interruptingly...

The earth is enchanted the world disenchanted...

The earth is disenchanted the gods enchanted...

The earth is enchanted the earth disenchanted...

The world is disenchanted the world is enchanted...

Being is enchanted disenchanted neither enchanted nor disenchanted both enchanted and disenchanted...

Becoming is enchanted disenchanted neither enchanted nor disenchanted both enchanted and disenchanted...

The earth is infinite the earth is finite the earth is neither infinite nor finite the earth is both infinite and finite...

The earth is general economy restricted economy neither general nor restricted economy both general and restricted economy...

The earth is all and none of these in betrayal in the enchantments of disenchantment in the caesura...

All as if perhaps asking telling betraying...

Enchantments shimmer everywhere, covered over with disenchantment. Disenchantment darkens every place, irradiated by enchantments. Enchantment echoes everywhere, obscured by disenchantments. In the introduction I explored this coupling in the context of authors who represent for many the origins and depths of disenchantment, to unfold the enchantments at their heart. Here I would offer this pairing again in the context of authors who have been read by many as alternatives to mainstream Western philosophy, alternatives I interpret as enchantments, to explore the inevitability of the disenchantments that return.

Exploring is asking...

I have named these alternatives *earth and world, being and becoming, finite and infinite.* One might begin by asking whether these pairs are alternatives or complementary, if they represent coordinate concepts of understanding. All such ways of understanding them are disenchanted. One might ask instead if earth and world are neither alternatives nor complements nor coordinates, but struggle together disenchantedly in the enchantments of the unveiling of being. In the caesura. I understand the *and* as interruption, endless questions for asking.

The infinite, perhaps, is where we may look for enchantment. Yet that image bends traditionally toward having, fixing, firming up the infinite, thereby disenchanting it. The finite, full of experience and language, multiplies the infinite, propagates enchantments to infinity, from the nature of its finiteness. Finiteness is finite, it can never be fixed, never be grasped, grasping and fixing it are finite, the finiteness of finiteness is unlimited. Its disenchantments are all enchanted because they are limited.

Unlimit outstrips every attempt to fix it, grasp it, in greek or later in latin, german, french, english, etc. One might imagine that *apeiron* in *greek—heraclitus, parmenides, anaxagoras, anaximander...* —returns enchantments in the teeth of one disenchantment after another. I have taken the words of *philebus,* storied words of old, as the exemplar of this movement, the wonder of the indefiniteness of a dyad that does not insist on knowing whether it is enchanted or disenchanted.

All things have in their nature a conjunction of limit and unlimitedness (apeiron) after we have discerned the intermediate forms we may let them pass away into the unlimited and cease bothering about them. (Plato, *Philebus*, 16c–17a)...[1]

Let them pass away in asking...

Before seeking a language, writing, presentation, production that might enchant those moments at which enchantment begins to unravel into disenchantment, I would pause briefly at another historical transition in which some of the most famous writers we know, together with some of their followers, resisted manifest disenchantment with explicit enchantments, only to become victims to a *Zeitgeist* of disenchantment. Such a phenomenon has always remained strange, and spinoza is perhaps the most visible member of the philosophical pantheon, if there be such. Perhaps grinding lenses made him acutely aware of enchantment, perhaps not. But the most ordinary ways in which such an extraordinary mind might present itself to a disenchanted academic history have been difficult for that academy to accept in the plethora of its enchantments. Spinoza remains an anomaly, as enchantments must always be. Anomaly, aporia, heresy, antinomy all retain enchantments of old that do not pass away into oblivion. More of that presently.

Not passing away from enchantment to disenchantment or the reverse means more than that both work together, that each remains present, on the scene. It means that each undercuts the force of the other in the way that an opposition or a dichotomy cannot. An example might be leibniz, who is taken—with good reason—as an exemplar of enlightenment rationality, yet much of whose work may be read as an enchanted answer to disenchanted Cartesian reason.

> 1. The *monad* of which we shall here speak is merely a simple substance, which enters into composites; *simple*, that is to say, without parts.
>
> *56. Each simple substance has relations which express all the others, consequently, it is a perpetual living mirror of the universe...*
>
> *57. There are as it were so many different universes, which are nevertheless only the perspectives of a single one, according to the different points of view of each monad...*
>
> 64. Thus each organic body of a living being is a kind of divine machine or natural automaton, which infinitely surpasses all artificial automata.
>
> 65. Each portion of matter is not only divisible *ad infinitum*, but also each part is actually endlessly subdivided into parts.

> *66. Whence we see that there is a world of creatures, of living beings, of animals, of entelechies, of souls, in the smallest particle of matter...*
>
> *67. Each portion of matter may be conceived of as a garden full of plants, and as a pond full of fishes...* (G. W. F. Leibniz, *M*)

From the standpoint of the universe as a whole, indeed from a far more grandiose, divine perspective, all the simple parts cohere. At least so it seems. The world is made up of simple things without parts coordinated into one universe ordered from a comprehensive standpoint under the principles of sufficient reason and preestablished harmony. Even so, the simple monads without parts have no windows yet mirror all the others and the universe itself, each a perspective on the whole with all its parts. The universe as a whole is but one of many different points of view of each monad. And no matter the condition of unity, there is in the simple monad a plurality of affections. Even so, together with this plurality in ourselves, in the simple substance, each is an entelechy, a certain perfection, a certain source of itself.

Together with this plurality—of simple substances, their affections and perceptions, perspectives, points of view, and internal movements—there is a supreme substance, God, which is unique, universal and necessary, absolutely perfect, source of all existences and essences, beyond all limits and askings. Moreover, all creatures have their perfections from God and their imperfections from themselves. Leading to a striking figure:

> 47. Thus God alone is the primitive unity or the original simple substance; of which all created or derived monads are the products, and are generated, so to speak, by continual fulgurations of the Divinity, from moment to moment, limited by the receptivity of the creature, to whom limitation is essential.

On the side of the universe is a multitude of universes, all emerging by continual fulgurations from God. On the side of individual monads is a multitude of perspectives, points of view, mirrors of a universe that is but one among the many. As in spinoza, if less directly, leibniz's god presides over infinitely infinite infinites, an image of the enchantment of the world. The infinitely infinite, not merely infinite, very large, but immeasurably beyond measure, is beyond accounting in such a way as to give that beyond to us in a certain definite way. In other words, it is not just that we do not and cannot know, but we can know something of what and why we cannot: the multitude of creatures exceeds any knowing. I would say possibly including god's. More important is leibniz's figure of enchantment. There is a world of creatures, of living beings, of animals, of entelechies, of souls, in the smallest particle of matter.

Each portion of matter is a garden full of plants a pond full of fishes the world teems with abundance every thing is composed of countless other living things, infinite mirrors, representations, of a universe without windows...

Leibniz belongs to a pantheon of disenchantment. In that pantheon the principle of perfection is a principle of accounting: as great a variety as possible with the greatest possible order—if order can be accounted for. In the nonpantheon of enchantment the principle is one of excess: no matter how well ordered, variety exceeds it in abundance; uncontainable ecological abundance includes a condition of order.

The principle of perfection is then either a higher level principle of order, ordering the relation between variety and order, or it is excessive on both sides, in its questionability. Order too can be excessive. Here enchantment and disenchantment themselves conform to a principle—more precisely, two principles, one on the side of enchantment, the other on the side of disenchantment. From the standpoint of enchantment, perfection exceeds all order and indeed all perfection. From the standpoint of disenchantment, god's vision of the world is extreme enchantment, choosing by perfection the one universe among the infinitely many. This enchantment is not a repetition of the complementarity of variety and order but disorders every relation. Disorder here is not nonorder, not the contradictory of order, but ecological abundance interrupting itself for asking.

I am reading leibniz as I will read spinoza, on the side of their enchantments. I have suggested that human beings encounter the unaccountable everywhere, and they seek to account for it as best they can. In other words, not just great philosophers, great thinkers and writers, but all human beings struggling to live and express their lives encounter what is unaccountable and render it accountable. In a secular world, this experience is no longer governed by church or temple. In a secular world, the figure of what is beyond all beyonds, perfect beyond perfections, infinite beyond infinites, may no longer take the name of any gods. Secular institutions—academies and bureaucracies—have taken responsibility for accountability.

This infinite beyond infinites takes us to spinoza, who seems to me to offer up enlightenment reason and mechanical order as infinite beyond containment. In this way, infinite beyond accounting, immanent beyond transcendence, spinoza's world is endlessly enchanted. In the same way, no matter how strange that world appears to us, no matter how heretical, most philosophers take it to be disenchanted. No philosopher has more forcefully appeared as mad, enchanted, anomalous, strange, in a tradition that regards him disenchantedly.

Much of this can is evident in spinoza's *ethics* from the beginning, in all the definitions of Part 1.

> D1: By cause of itself I understand that whose essence involves existence, or that whose nature cannot be conceived except as existing. (Baruch Spinoza, *E*, 1, D1)
>
> D3: By substance I understand what is in itself and is conceived through itself, i.e., that whose concept does not require the concept of another thing, from which it must be formed.
>
> D4: By attribute I understand what the intellect perceives of a substance, as constituting its essence.
>
> D5: By mode I understand the affections of a substance, or that which is in another through which it is also conceived.
>
> D6: By God I understand a being absolutely infinite, i.e., a substance consisting of an infinity of attributes, of which each one expresses an eternal and infinite essence.
>
> Exp.: I say absolutely infinite, not infinite in its own kind; for if something is only infinite in its own kind, we can deny infinite attributes of it; but if something is absolutely infinite, whatever expresses essence and involves no negation pertains to its essence.

I leave aside arduous questions of what it means to be cause of itself, to conceive something through itself, as if everything were not limited, even infinite, and as limited required something else to be and to be conceived. I leave aside asking what it is to be conceived as well as what it is to be, as if these were not infinite, complex, beyond calculation. Instead, I would associate spinoza's nature with the univocity of being.

Being is said in a single and same sense of everything of which it is said, a single clamor of being, univocal being as nomadic distribution and crowned anarchy. (Deleuze, *DR*, 37)...

The univocity of being is the principal condition which permits difference to escape the domination of identity, which frees it from the law of the same as a simple opposition within conceptual elements. Being is that which is always said of difference; it is the recurrence of difference. (Foucault, *TP*, 192)...

Nature, substance, god is an abundance of difference, multiplicity, diversity, variety, abundance as infinity, unicity as disparition. Being as cause of itself, conceived through itself, whose essence involves existence, is infinite beyond infinities, beyond disenchantment...

In this way spinoza is the least binary of philosophers, where binarity is disenchantment and enchantment is the unity of ungathering.

P7: The order and connection of ideas is the same [*idem est*] as the order and connection of things. (Spinoza, *E*, 2, P7)

Ideas and things are the same, ideas and things are different, ideas and things are neither same nor different, ideas and things are both same and different...

Throughout, spinoza speaks of identities that cannot be identities, disparities that are identical, ways of being one or two that outstrip any accounting. The result is an intensely concrete way of being unlimited, infinite, multiplied infinitely.

God is absolutely infinite consisting of infinite attributes each infinite expressing infinite essence...

God, substance, nature is absolutely and infinitely infinite, expressed in infinite attributes each of which is infinite—again, not large, immense, but unlimited: unlimitedly unlimited in unlimitedly unlimited ways. It is as if the world, substance, nature, god were infinitely one in such a way that its expression—by world, substance, nature, or god—required infinitely infinite ways, infinite numbers of infinite attributes, unlimited expressions, endless askings; as if god and nature required expression—the condition of enchantment—and expressed their infinite unity in infinitely many infinite ways.

Substance is this infinity, existing in a unity of infinite multiple abundances. Moreover, this existence is expression, exposition.

The world expresses itself in its attributes, god and nature are expressed, exposed, in infinite attributes...

The ways in which substance is conceived through itself are infinitely many and infinitely one. The unity of nature, god, substance, being is infinitely infinite beyond infinity itself.

This is only a part of nature's infinity. For every finite thing is multiply infinite, not only in relation to god and substance, to infinite numbers of attributes each of which is infinite, but in relation to finiteness itself.

> P28: Every singular thing, or any thing which is finite and has a determinate existence, can neither exist nor be determined to

> produce an effect unless it is determined to exist and produce an effect by another cause, which is also finite and has a determinate existence; and again, this cause also can neither exist nor be determined to produce an effect unless it is determined to exist and produce an effect by another, which is also finite and has a determinate existence, and so on, to infinity.
>
> P29: In nature there is nothing contingent, but all things have been determined from the necessity of the divine nature to exist and produce an effect in a certain way.
>
> Schol.: I wish to explain here what we must understand by *Natura naturans* and *Natura naturata*. By *Natura naturans* we must understand what is in itself and is conceived through itself, or such attributes of substance as express an eternal and infinite essence, i.e., God, insofar as he is considered as a free cause.
>
> But by *Natura naturata* I understand whatever follows from the necessity of God's nature, or from any of God's attributes, i.e., all the modes of God's attributes insofar as they are considered as things which are in God, and can neither be nor be conceived without God.

Finite, individual things are what they are in relation to other finite things, *ad infinitum*, and also in relation to nature's infinite power. All this is by necessity, and I have argued that what one finds in spinoza is that infinite necessity produces contingency, that necessity is contingency and freedom.[2] *Natura naturans* and *natura naturata* are each infinitely infinite. Each and both together are enchantments of an infinitely disenchanted mechanical world.

Enchantment here means beyond accounting, what we cannot and will never know—even where we know. Spinoza's language is corporeal, material. God is material, corporeal. Infinitely corporeal.

> P2: Thought is an attribute of God, or God is a thinking thing.
>
> P3: Extension is an attribute of God, or God is an extended thing. (Spinoza, *E*, 2, P2, 3)
>
> For indeed, no one has yet determined what the Body can do. The Body itself, simply from the laws of its own nature, can do many things which its Mind wonders at. (Spinoza, *E*, 3, P2, Sch)[3]

Enchantment also means infinite, where infinite means beyond limits and where every limit is transgressive beyond itself.

Transgression carries the limit right to the limit of its being: transgression forces the limit to face the fact of its imminent disappearance, to find itself in what it excludes, to recognize itself for the first time, to experience its positive truth in its downward fall? And yet, toward what is transgression unleashed in its movement of pure violence, if not that which imprisons it, toward the limit and those elements it contains? (Foucault, *PT*, 34–5)...

Transgression is the exposition of enchantment, the finite asking of the limit...

If so, then as strange as it may be to think of transgression as the mark of spinoza's *ethics*, of his mark on disciplinary philosophy, the relation of this mark to disenchanted secular philosophy remains transgressive, dislocated. This means that the most familiar images of familiar places are enchanted, transgressive. Spinoza offers one of these.

> Now let us imagine, if you please, a tiny worm living in the blood. The worm would be living in the blood as we are living in our part of the universe, and it would regard each individual particle as a whole, not a part, and it would have no idea as to how all the parts are controlled by the overall nature of the blood and compelled to mutual adaptation as the overall nature of the blood requires, so as to agree with one another in a definite relation.
>
> Now all the bodies of Nature can and should be conceived in the same way as we have here conceived the blood. Now since the nature of the universe, unlike the nature of the blood, is not limited, but is absolutely infinite, its parts are modified by the nature of this infinite in infinite ways and are compelled to undergo infinite variations. (Spinoza, *ESL*, Letter 32, 245–6)

Let me rest with the infinite variations. The infinite universe, infinite in its nature, looks orderly from the standpoint of a tiny worm, from our standpoint, looks and is orderly by necessity. Yet our standpoint is limited and we cannot begin to imagine the overall nature of anything. Moreover, that overall nature is unlimited, an infinite whose nature is to vary in infinite ways and to undergo infinite variations.

Infinite variations from the standpoint of the whole are manifested as diverse enchantments from the standpoint of the part. Fairies dance, magic reigns, in the meadows and the fields. Every flower, every insect, every tiny work enchants and is enchanted...

Spinoza speaks directly to this enchantment in what some hear as a disenchanted voice.

> P38: Whatever so disposes the human Body that it can be affected in a great many ways, or renders it capable of affecting external Bodies in a great many ways, is useful to man; the more

> it renders the Body capable of being affected in a great many ways, or of affecting other bodies, the more useful it is; on the other hand, what renders the Body less capable of these things is harmful. (Spinoza, *E*, 4)

> P39: He who has a Body capable of a great many things has a Mind whose greatest part is eternal. (Spinoza, *E*, 5)

The adaptation and disposition of human bodies among material things is a relation to eternity. This is incomprehensible from a disenchanted point of view, perhaps because eternity is incomprehensible. It is, perhaps, enchanting that finite things might be in their play infinite and eternal. Eternity here surely does not mean living forever, lasting forever, never passing away. Those are all terms of disenchantment. Eternity must mean something so far beyond temporality and succession as to open up onto transgression and enchantment.

Finally, then, at least for our reading of spinoza, we may recall other movements to infinity, beyond any disenchantments reason can offer. I must interject, though I will not pursue it here, that reason in spinoza, as in levinas—perhaps because they were jewish—must be understood in its enchantments. That is an important story, the enchantments of reason, that I will postpone till later. I have been suggesting it throughout, that it is not reason, not calculation and accountability, not mechanism or technology that disenchant the world. They are all enchanted. It is human beings who do so, and they do so as if they could—though of course they cannot. So we may pose the question of reason for us here as if one of enchantment. What would an enchanted reason be? Would it be different from what reason is taken traditionally to be, from a disenchanted reason? How would an enchanted reason change the world?[4]

Spinoza gives an answer, as do leibniz and plato, against the expectations from a disenchanted world, a certain kind of academy. Indeed, the very idea of an academy that might control and regulate the enchantments of philosophy so as to disenchant them began with plato, an extreme example of the disenchantment of the most enchanted visions, of the academicization of the wildest profusions, the codification of the most extreme askings and tellings.

Be that as it may, it is spinoza who is before us now, in his wild enchantments. And I would conclude my discussion of them with two of his most questionable and extreme disorders: the enchantments of power, *potentia* and *potestas*, and the extremities of striving, *conatus*. Both are situated in the caesura between enchantment and disenchantment, finite and infinite, a space that is itself disenchanted and enchanted. Historically, these are read as theories of power and of desire. Textually they speak directly to the impossibility of containing spinoza's view of god and nature under intelligible categories.

Potentia and *potestas* correspond to *natura naturans* and *natura naturata*, nature naturing, nature natured, to the power of god and nature and to their productions, to the opening between the infinite succession of things and the finite powers of a productive and generous nature. We are required to imagine two important things, that every finite thing is given from the powers of nature in the infinity of its finiteness, and that this two is one, this separation is not a separation, nature itself is infinite both on the side of the infinity of its power and on the side of the infinity of its products.

Power and desire permeate spinoza's world, our world, god and nature's world. God or substance or nature is power.

> P34: God's power (*potentia*) is his essence itself. (Spinoza, *E*, 1, P34)
>
> P6: Each thing, as far as it can by its own power (*potestas*), strives to persevere in its being. (*E*, 3, 6)
>
> P7: The striving (*conatus*) by which each thing strives to persevere in its being is nothing but the actual essence of the thing.
>
> P8: The striving by which each thing strives to persevere in its being involves no finite time, but an indefinite time.
>
> we neither strive for, nor will, neither want, nor desire anything because we judge it to be good; on the contrary, we judge something to be good because we strive for it, will it, want it, and desire it. (P9n)
>
> Desire is man's very essence, insofar as it is conceived to be determined, from any given affection of it, to do something. (Def Aff 1)

In every case, throughout spinoza, but here in relation to power and desire, the infinite—creative, productive, giving *natura naturans*—yields an infinite number of infinite kinds of finite individual things—produced, created, provided *natura naturata*. All follows from god or nature, from this infinite power, individual things each produce, are productive in infinite different ways (*potestas*). In the same way and inseparably the infinite creativity of *natura naturans* gives rise to infinite singular desires. *Conatus* is the finite manifestation of infinite creativity.

All this means that *no matter how limited, finite, determinate, settled any finite thing may be, it is irradiated, permeated, by infinite others, infinite variations and transformations...*

While it is plausible in virtue of spinoza's language and geometric structure to imagine that he neglects process and becoming, *the nature of the infinite manifests itself in infinite becomings, infinite enchantments beyond imagining...*

In contrast with being, infinite and finite, becoming exceeds it infinitely...

In contrast with becoming, finite and infinite, being exceeds it...

In contrast with the finite, the infinite exceeds...

In contrast with the infinite, the finite exceeds...

In contrast with the infinite, excess exceeds being, becoming, finite, infinite, knowledge, feeling, power, desire...

Excess is surprising, astonishing, unknown, the otherness of the other, surpasses all expectations...

Excess is enchantment disenchantment exceeds enchantment enchantment exceeds any imagination any religion any science any philosophy any asking. There is more on earth in the sky beneath the sea in our words and dreams and images in our imaginations than can be asked or told...

If unlimit expresses the enchantment of being in the context of its historical disenchantments, then process and becoming, with other forms of multiplicity, do so as well. Here let us consider first whitehead and dewey then some of their enchanted successors.

On the one hand, then, whitehead unmistakably describes his goal as disenchanted.

> This course of lectures is designed as an essay in Speculative Philosophy.
>
> Speculative Philosophy is the endeavour to frame a coherent, logical, necessary system of general ideas in terms of which every element of our experience can be interpreted. (Alfred North Whitehead, *PR*, 3)

This is by no means a language of enchantment, though we may speculate whether *every element* might include enchantments—it certainly includes fairies and gods—and whether interpretation might be more enchanted than disenchanted. This would be a way to show that every point of view, no matter how disenchanted on the surface, is enchanted at its heart.

We do not need to dig that deep in whitehead to bring enchantments to the surface. For in the same way in which levinas suggests, in reading heidegger, that secularization does not mean ignoring religion, whitehead—together with james and dewey—understands the multiplicity of experience to include enchantments as well as disenchantments.

The final facts are actual entities (aka actual occasions): drops of experience, complex and interdependent. (18)...

The ultimate is creativity god is its primordial nontemporal accident one side makes process ultimate the other side fact. (7)...

Experience is enchanted the universal is enchanted creativity novelty ultimacy primordiality process are enchanting and enchanted...

This is a material universe. Actual occasions emerge in the midst of things. This midst is a world of corporeal feelings, and feelings of feelings, material feelings of material things, creative transformations of creative things. Whitehead's term for feeling is *prehension,* and it is central to his work.

> The first phase [of concrescence, the becoming of an actual occasion] is the phase of pure reception of the actual world. In this phase there is the mere reception of the actual world as a multiplicity of private centres of feeling. (212)

An actual occasion originates in the feeling of past occasions' feelings. Actual occasions feel (or prehend), and what they feel are other actual occasions' feelings (or prehensions). Feelings are feelings of feelings. Feelings of feelings of feelings on the one hand reproduce the given world as if it were disenchanted, and on the other transform and enrich it as if it were enchanted.

"A prehension reproduces in itself the general characteristics of an actual entity: it is referent to an external world, and in this sense will be said to have a 'vector character'; it involves emotion, and purpose, and valuation, and causation" (19).

Creativity is the universal of universals, the ultimate principle by which the many, the universe disjunctively, become the one actual occasion, the universe conjunctively. (21)...

Creativity is the principle of novelty. An actual occasion is a novel entity. Creativity introduces novelty into the context of the many. (21)...

Fact is ultimate process is ultimate neither fact nor process is ultimate both fact and process are ultimate...

Disenchantment is ultimate enchantment is ultimate neither disenchantment nor enchantment is ultimate both disenchantment and enchantment are ultimate...

All are for asking and for giving...

An actual entity arises within an external world and prehends or feels the past entities that compose it. Such prehension is the heart of corporeality, expresses relations of touch, body to body. It is vectoral, from a past entity to the present, filled with bodies, emotions, purposes, and valuations. With spinoza in mind, whitehead understands prehension as desire. Bodies feel, select, value, strive for ends, all in response to, prehending, touching, exposed to other bodies. Here is one meaning of being as perspective that resists disenchantment: to be is to prehend, to relate to, touch, be imprinted by infinite numbers of other beings and their bodies from the standpoint of the prehending body, filled with its vectoral feelings, feeling other bodies' feelings, prehending prehensions. Being is perspective as standpoint and reproduction but also as production, expression and feeling, creativity and transformation. All are corporeal, expression as material exposure. Bodies are expressive, always more than we can know.

To express to feel; to portray inscribe imprint; to receive, welcome open toward material bodies; opening is inscriptive expressive full of meaning. Bodies touch each other in proximity every body is nearby touching other bodies that touch touching them touching where touch is exposition expression full of purpose emotion valuation. Touch is corporeal enchantment...

Prehensions prehending prehensions, feelings feeling feelings, perspectives perspecting perspectives, touch touching touch, asking asking asking. All undo the limits of their conditions, unbind them from their disenchantments. The limits of the limits of limits are the enchantments of enchantment...

Creativity is the principle of novelty and of the many becoming one. These are realized in nine categoreal obligations that can be read as conditions of both disenchantment and enchantment. The first three pertain to the initial phase of concrescence and are largely categories of fact defining reproductive conditions for becoming.

> (i) *The Category of Subjective Unity.* The many feelings which belong to an incomplete phase in the process of an actual entity are compatible.
>
> (ii) *The Category of Objective Identity.* There can be no duplication of any element in the objective datum of the "satisfaction" of an actual entity.
>
> (iii) *The Category of Objective Diversity.* There can be no "coalescence" of diverse elements in the objective datum of an actual entity. (26)

From these emerge the categories of conceptual valuation and conceptual reversion, expressions of diversity:

> (iv) *The Category of Conceptual Valuation.* From each physical feeling there is the derivation of a purely conceptual feeling whose datum is the eternal object determinant of the definiteness of the actual entity physically felt.[5]
>
> (v) *The Category of Conceptual Reversion.* There is secondary origination of conceptual feelings with data which are partially identical with, and partially diverse from, the eternal objects forming the data in the first phase of the mental pole. The diversity is a relevant diversity determined by the subjective aim. (26)

These represent the movement of becoming in each occasion from what it inherits to what it creates, first on the level of form, then beyond. Conceptual valuation is reproduction, image of the past as datum; conceptual reversion is the production of new entities and their feelings.

In the final analysis, there is the primordial nature of god, "the unconditioned conceptual valuation of the entire multiplicity of eternal objects" (31)—the valuation, feeling, prehension of the entire multiplicity of images; and there is the consequent nature of god, "the fulfillment of his experience by his reception of the multiple freedom of actuality into the harmony of his own actualization" (349), god's image of the entire actual world in its becoming and its multiplicity.

In its totalities on both sides of its experiences, primordial and consequent, god expresses disenchantment. At least that is how I understand totality. I have suggested a god—if there be such—dependent in its primordiality on the changing world and a god whose experience of that world can never reach fulfillment, both exceeding any anticipations.[6]

The last three categoreal obligations are explicit expressions of enchantment:

> (vii) *The Category of Subjective Harmony.* The valuations of conceptual feelings are mutually determined by the adaptation of those feelings to be contrasted elements congruent with the subjective aim.
>
> (viii) *The Category of Subjective Intensity.* The subjective aim, whereby there is origination of conceptual feeling, is at intensity of feeling.
>
> (ix) *The Category of Freedom and Determination....* That in each concrescence whatever is determinable is determined, but

> that there is always a remainder for the decision of the subject-superject of that concrescence. (27–8)

All the feelings in becoming, all the feelings of feelings of feelings, are contrastive, a play of identities and differences, *contrasts of contrasts of contrasts...* Contrasts give rise to intensity, feelings heightened by differences.[7] There is always a remainder beyond whatever is determined for a becoming.

Feelings feelings feelings...

Contrasts contrasting contrasts...

Intensities intensifying intensities...

Enchantments enchanting enchantments...

Becoming of differences intensification of feelings leaving a remainder beyond any accounting intensity of feeling as aesthetic. Art aims at intensity of feeling, becoming is intensified in feeling, feelings of feelings of feelings are manifested for us in art but not in great art alone. Art is for telling giving and asking...

The enchanted world is an aesthetic phenomenon—known to nietzsche and whitehead among others...[8]

Intensity is disparition as the enchantment of the earth the intensification of a harmony otherwise inaudible perhaps beyond disparition and harmony perhaps beyond gathering and ungathering...

> Beauty is the mutual adaptation of the several factors in an occasion of experience. There are gradations in Beauty and in types of Beauty. (Whitehead, *AI*, 324)

> All realization is finite, and there is no perfection which is the infinitude of all perfections. Perfections of diverse types are among themselves discordant. Thus the value of Discord is a tribute to the merits of Imperfection. (330–1)

> Beauty is a wider, and more fundamental, notion than Truth. Truth is the conformation of Appearance to Reality. In other words, a truth-relation is not necessarily beautiful. It may be evil. Thus Beauty is left as the one aim which by its very nature is self-justifying. (341–2)

Beauty is the enchantment of the world the earth's enchantments are its beauties beauty is enchanted beyond truth truth and beauty are given from the good in the intensifications of feeling feeling feeling touch touching touch enchantments enchanting enchantments...

Dewey and whitehead shared a time in history in which the disenchantments of the world meant more than the accountings of academic reason, in which the industrialization of Europe threatened to dull if not kill the possibilities of ecstasy in human life. Against this they mobilized experience itself as a source of rapture, enchanted experiences in an enchanted nature in which things far surpassed any of the knowledges that reached out to grasp them. Frequently in a disenchanted voice.

> *Experience* is what James called a double-barrelled word. Like its congeners, life and history, it includes *what* men do and suffer, *what* they strive for, love, believe and endure, and also *how* men act and are acted upon, in short, processes of *experiencing*. It is double-barrelled in that it recognizes in its primary integrity no division between act and material, subject and object, but contains them both in an unanalyzed totality. (John Dewey, *EN*, 8)

> Experience is *of* as well as *in* nature. It is not experience which is experienced, but nature—stones, plants, animals, diseases, health, temperature, electricity, and so on. Things interacting in certain ways *are* experience; they are what is experienced. (4a)

> What is really "in" experience extends much further than that which at any time is *known*. (20)

> For things are objects to be treated, used, acted upon and with, enjoyed and endured, even more than things to be known. They are things *had* before they are things cognized. (21)

Things are before they are known, enchanted before they are disenchanted, enchanted before time, nothing is before time everything is before time...

The world in which we live in which we strive succeed and are defeated is pre-eminently a qualitative world. (Dewey, *ENF*, 176)...

An enchanted world...

Means are disenchantments, qualities and ends enchantments. What if this were our watchword?

Human experience has for one of its most striking features preoccupation with direct enjoyment, feasting and festivities; ornamentation, dance, song, dramatic pantomime, telling yarns and enacting stories. (Dewey, *EN*, 78)...

Feasting festivities ornamentation dance song drama pantomime telling enacting are among the earth's enchantments...

It is said that knowing, meaning, inquiry disenchant an enchanted world and make it available for use. So it is said. The world is composed of contexts, perspectives, and perspectives of perspectives. These are disenchanted, but also enchanted. The world is multiplied in its perspectives, knowings, inquiries, feelings, situations, multiply enchanted.

> In responding to things not in their immediate qualities but for the sake of ulterior results, immediate qualities are dimmed, while those features which are signs, indices of something

> else, are distinguished. The very conception of cognitive meaning, intellectual significance, is that things in their immediacy are subordinated to what they portend and give evidence of. (Dewey, *EN*, 128)

The very conception of intellectual significance is that things are disenchanted...

> Philosophy, like all forms of reflective analysis, takes us away, for the time being, from the things had in primary experience as they directly act and are acted upon, used and enjoyed. (19)

Takes us away from our enchantments...

> What is already known, what is accepted as truth, is of immense importance; inquiry could not proceed a step without it. But it is held subject to use, and is at the mercy of the discoveries which it makes possible. It has to be adjusted to the latter and not the latter to it. When things are defined as instruments, their value and validity reside in what proceeds from them; consequences not antecedents supply meaning and verity. Truths already possessed may have practical or moral certainty, but logically they never lose a hypothetic quality. They are true *if.* (154–5)

They are true as if... Perhaps... For asking...

> When the claim of meanings to truth enters in, then truth is indeed preeminent. But this fact is often confused with the idea that truth has a claim to enter everywhere; that it has monopolistic jurisdiction. Poetic meanings, moral meanings, a large part of the goods of life are matters of richness and freedom of meanings, rather than of truth; a large part of our life is carried on in a realm of meanings to which truth and falsity as such are irrelevant. (*EN*, 410–1)

Poetic meanings moral meanings living meanings are enchanted truth is enchanted and enchanting...

> The chief characteristic trait of the pragmatic notion of reality is is is precisely that no theory of Reality in general, *überhaupt,* is possible or needed. *Reality* is a word used to designate indifferently everything that happens. (*NRP*, 59)

> Examination discloses three deepening levels or three expanding spheres of context. The narrowest and most superficial is that of the immediate scene, the competitive race. The next deeper and wider one is that of the culture of the people in question. The widest and deepest is found in recourse to the need of general understanding of the workings of human nature. (Dewey, *CT*, 108–9)

Everything is real reality exceeds any account of reality any account of experience exceeds experience any telling exceeds. Life being becoming world earth finite infinite exceed themselves...

Everything is local perspectival contextual multiple nothing is in general or knowable in general...

The earth's enchantments exceed themselves the earth exceeds itself excess exceeding itself is the earth's enchantment...

If meanings are selective, for an end, if every truth is situated and situational, then so is pragmatism, so is dewey's thought, so is mine, and so is every thought of disenchantment and enchantment. It is limited and its limits are limited. It is enchanted and its enchantments are disenchanted, its disenchantments enchanted. It cannot be the whole story—of itself or of its others. Enchantment does not offer itself as means or knowledge but as excess. It is limited, local, and everything about it is limited, local, inexhaustible. It betrays disenchantment and itself.

A striking and neglected form of thought to enter into and transfigure this enchanted tradition from emerson through james, santayana, and dewey to whitehead—if it is one tradition or many, if these can be gathered together except in a disenchanted way—is that of natural complexes.[9] I call it *striking* to express a hesitation at its enchantments, knowing that no matter how disenchanted it may appear to those who dance with it, it and they are enchanted. I express this hesitation because I was drawn to it in its enchantments at a time I knew little of enchantment. A disenchanted theory of enchantment, from which emerge the mysteries of disenchantment.

Whatever is, in whatever way, is a natural complex. Relations, structures, processes, societies, human individuals, human products, physical bodies, words and bodies of discourse, ideas, qualities, contradictions, meanings, possibilities, myths, laws, duties, feelings, illusions, reasonings, dreams—all are natural complexes. Whatever is discriminated in any respect is a natural complex. (Justus Buchler, *MNC,* 1)...

Whatever is is real, whatever is is natural, ask not whether but how and what, unreality is real, unnaturalness is natural, disenchantment is enchantment...

Nature is the presence and availability of complexes, the provision and determination of traits, providingness but not providence or providentness. (3)...

Whatever is discriminated in any way is a natural complex and no complex is more real, more natural, more genuine, or more ultimate than any other. This is ontological parity. (31)...

From a standpoint of utmost metaphysical generality—if there be such—there is ontological parity...

Natural complexes do not contrast with non-natural or supernatural complexes. (6)...

Whatever is is natural, whatever is is complex, whatever is is inexhaustible, inexhaustibly natural inexhaustibly complex...

Such a theory—and it is a theory—permits us to refuse to limit our perspectives in principle to some things—complexes—and not to others, and at the same time to identify, discriminate, classify, etc.—in other words, to know them by the finest details and the widest generalities, to relate to them in the most varied ways. What could be more enchanting?

> The concept of natural complex not only permits satisfactory generic identification: it permits various distinctions and categorizations. It encourages striving after the functions of generalizing precisely and portraying uniquely. Precise generalization is twin to precise differentiation. (3)

The key words, in the present context, are *satisfactory and precisely*, terms of disenchantment. Buchler's is a disenchanted language, a disenchanted theory, a nontraditional metaphysics that offers itself as adequate in traditional, disciplinary terms yet addresses philosophy and the world as if they were radically enchanted.

Whatever is is a natural complex: ordinary things, clear and precise satisfactory objects of knowledge, things we cannot discriminate clearly, know well, define strictly. Nature is providingness, provides whatever and wherever and whenever we encounter it and its ingredients, leaving it for us to struggle with, to master, to disenchant—and perhaps to find enchanting, astonishing, exceeding every accounting including the theory of natural complexes. Every natural complex—every order, every thing—is as real as anything else, a recipe for enchantment, a formula for surpassing any categories, any restrictions, for inexhaustibility, including those of mastering and of ordering. The central term that explicates natural complex is that of *order*—always many orders, always at least one more order, always orders, ordinality: inexhaustibly inexhaustible complexes and orders. A disenchanted language expressing enchantment.

Every complex is an order and belongs to an order of complexes. orders are inclusive and belong to more inclusive orders. (Buchler, *MNC*, 93)...

Should we speak of nature as a complex of complexes? if this can be justified, it cannot be justified all at once. Any complex is a complex of complexes. (2)...

Belonging to an order, being located in an order, being in various orders, being an order, are indissociable from natural complex, ways of representing its ordinality. (93–4)...

Ordinality is the condition of being knowable, categorizable, subject to identification, discrimination, analysis, inexhaustibly; and of being multiple, complex, resistant to accounting. Ordinality is a trait—of nature, natural complexes, orders, and philosophy—that limits and unlimits, disenchants and enchants.

If the concept of god is viable it must signify a natural complex. (6)...

If there is enchantment it must be a natural complex, an order, ordinality...

Enchantment is ordinality, ordinality is enchanting...

On the side of disenchantment, then:

> The term "trait" probably is the most satisfactory of the terms that can serve to identify a constituent of a natural complex. (12)

> Traits require for their being a natural complex in which they are "located" (as subaltern complexes). (13)

Traits are orders, complexes and subaltern complexes are orders of orders and orders located in orders. Ordinality is a metaphysics of relation.

> An order is a sphere of (or for) relatedness. It is what "provides" extent, conditions, and kinds of relatedness. (95)

> Whatever the boundaries or limits of complexes may happen to be, whatever may be the conditions under which these limits obtain, wherever these limits may lie, any complex has just the status, just the relations, just the constitution that it has. This is its integrity, that in which its being "a" complex and "that" complex consists. Integrity entails both uniqueness and commonness. (21–2)

> A complex has an *integrity* for each of its ordinal locations. The continuity and totality of its locations, the interrelation of its integrities, is the *contour* of the complex. The *identity* of a complex is the continuous relation that obtains between the contour of a complex and any of its integrities. (22)

If there be such a continuity and such a totality. But that is a question of enchantment. Is there something that surpasses even this exceptionally multiple, supple, and inclusive metaphysics?

Here are its categories, its terminology: *natural complex, trait, constituent, order, ordinality, integrity, contour, identity, scope, prevalence, alescence, possibility, actuality,* all disenchanted as categories, all pertaining to a world of enchantment, if that be possible. It is important to emphasize the categories and the terminology. An ordinal metaphysics, a metaphysics of natural complexes, inhabits that tradition in western philosophy exemplified by spinoza and whitehead in which the invention of a new system of categories and a new terminology represents the creative endeavor of philosophy—one mode of its enchantments, its askings and tellings.

> A complex has not only an integrity but also a "scope." (22)
>
> The scope of a complex, its pervasiveness and comprehensiveness, may be regarded as its "inclusiveness." Every complex is inclusive, regardless of the way in which it is inclusive. (39)
>
> Every natural complex prevails, is ineluctable; it has a sphere of primacy and domination; it is restrictive and exclusive of other complexes. (53)
>
> Now when a complex located in a given order is not prevalent in that order or ceases to be prevalent in that order, we shall say that it is *alescent*, or an *alescence*. (55)
>
> A possibility is that prevalent extension or continuation of the contour of a natural complex, whereby certain traits that are related (or, not related) to certain other traits will be related (or, not related) to the other traits. By contrast, an actuality is that prevalence of a natural complex whereby certain traits are related (or, not related) to certain other traits. (165)

As I have said, this is an enchanted theory expressed in the disenchanted language of categoreal metaphysics. In its terminology, the structure of its categories, its emphasis on precision and rigor—more precisely and rigorously, in the rejection of imprecision and unrigor—this is a traditional, disenchanted form and writing of philosophy. If it opens onto enchantment—and I shall insist that it does so explicitly—it does so in a dismissive voice, a voice that does not openly betray its own betrayals.

Embedded in it are several principles of enchantment, at least as I have understood them to express ordinality: ontological parity, inexhaustibility, and locality.[10] One might say that each and all together present the fairies dancing. That at least is what I would say. Even more important, perhaps, they all together and each present the voice of traditional philosophy, metaphysics and ontology—including a metaphysics of natural complexes—as belonging to another dance. Not the best or most general or most adequate, not the most precise and most rigorous—except perhaps in certain ways—but one of the enchanted dances of philosophy, of thought, in a world of enchanted dances beyond number. Perhaps.

This is a relational theory, a theory in which whatever is is in relation, is as relation, in which relation is both precise and rigorous, and uncertain, expansive, and excessive; in which *perhaps* and *as if* pertain to every relation, to relation as such. Every pair of categories is a complement of definite and indefinite, limit and unlimit, unitary and multiple, determinate and indeterminate, where every one of these terms and every one of Buchler's categories is itself determinate in certain ways and indeterminate in others, especially indeterminate in any future that would implement them in any way, any other time and any other place.[11] This pairing of determinateness and indeterminateness, in their own determinateness and indeterminateness, limit and unlimit, is the pairing of enchantment and disenchantment. I once spoke of it as *mystery* (see my *PM*).[12] It offers the world up to endless query interrogatively, endless questioning—I mean asking and telling.

> Products or judgments are the ramifications of the individual. As judgments ramify the being of the individual, so individual judgments may be ramified or developed. When pursued systematically or methodically, the process of ramifying judgment is the process of query. (Buchler, *NJ*, 57–8)

> We shall think of query as a process expectative of or inclusive of invention. And we shall think of invention as the methodical process of actually producing in consummation of query. (59)

Buchler is openly expressive in wonder, if in a disenchanted, critical pose:

> My chief purpose in this book is to attain better philosophic understanding of an elusive domain of art. Poetic utterance, and artistic utterance in general, have simply never been dealt with satisfactorily on the foundational level. (Buchler, *ML*, 3)

> One of the objectives of these first four chapters is to engage a group of ideas rendered sacrosanct by long tradition, functioning without vitality, often without meaning, and with the force only of slogans: ideas hardened into a sterile language. (4)

> A poem, or work of poetry in whatever form, is an exhibitive judgment wrought in language. We may speak of exhibitive judgments within the poem. And we may speak of a sequence of poems, or an entire body of poetry, as an exhibitive judgment of greater sweep, multifariously constituted. As a linguistic contrivance, a poem must be distinguished from non-poetic forms of literature. But initially we must think of it in the way we may think of all literature, as exemplifying a non-assertive mode of discriminating natural complexes, a mode which is itself diversified and continuingly defined by the range of literary products. (102)

This is the language of satisfactoriness, as if it were the task of philosophy to grasp the nature of something as enchanted as poetry once and for all, the language of disenchantment. Even so it is in wonder.

> That a complex should prevail is the source of poetic wonder. That, generally speaking, what prevails should prevail, that it should be what prevails, is a further source of poetic wonder; but on this general level it can be formulated philosophically as the basal sense of mystery. (131)

> The poem as poem arouses query through its contagion of seeking, in any mode, any medium, any degree. (115–6)

> All the poetry of Rimbaud, all poetry, is interrogative in its process of probing and in the radiation of wonder. All poets communicate the interrogative strain, even those whose manner is categorical, and those in whom we find a verbal order that seems to incarnate assertiveness. (114)

All poets and perhaps all philosophers, even those whose manner is disenchanted.

For the traits that concern him the poet defines an order, an ordinal location. He maps a road by which such an order can be reached. He communicates a sense of ontological parity, a sense of the reality of all the complexes he deals with. Poetic imagination is the power of shaping complexes in ways that compel an assent peculiar to exhibitive query. The orders that the poet builds are perspectives to be occupied. (ML, 126–7)...

To arouse the spirit of query. To compel assent. These two forces which poetry sets in motion to bear fruit are two forms of the same power. Far from being self-sufficient and terminal, artistic assent is the renewal of query. It is the beginning of articulation. The spirit of query lies in the urge to make a work relevant in new ways—relevant to one's situation in life, to one's disciplinary concerns, and to one's sense of the world at large. We have accepted the poetic climate: we have become permeated by a sense of the parity of all complexes. We accept the contrivance of the poet and extend the sphere of its influence. (127)...

In the climate of ontological parity, poetic endeavor can build orders of complexes with a freedom belonging to no other form of query involving language. Herein lies one reason for the uniqueness of poetic judgment and for the monumental amount of bad poetry in the world. (127)...

In the context of poetry, then, foregrounding the mistakes of his predecessors on both the nature of poetry and bad poetry, buchler expresses the sense of wonder that lies in ontological parity, *that there are complexes, that they prevail as and as what they are*—the *as if* and *perhaps* of complexity and complexes that betray enchantment. Poetry exhibits, explores, interrogates, seeks, asks, tells in endless query the determinate sense of an inexhaustible complex in its orders and their orders. Ordinality in its specificities—locality and inexhaustibility—is the site of wonder.

In the context of poetry, then, Buchler identifies a sense of wonder, exploration, asking and telling that I would identify with enchantment. These are to be understood in terms of ontological parity and ordinality, with their locality and inexhaustibility. In this sense, the determinate sense of a complex or order as prevalent answers to its locality in the context of the inexhaustibility of ontological parity and ordinality, evoking the inexhaustibility of asking and telling.

Ordinality, locality, inexhaustibility are the generosity of wonder, abundance, mystery, enchantment, of asking and telling, thereby of the restrictiveness and cruelty of disenchantment...

Told on the side of mystery as enchantment, then:

To be is to be an order, thereby a constituent of other orders. Can a order then not be? In the theory of orders all orders are orders. Not to be is not to be a constituent of one order and to be a constituent of another order. (Ross, *TOM*, 93)...

An order is a function of its constituents and of its location. Relative to its constituents, it is an order; relative to its location it is a constituent. (95)...

Being is ordinal, functional, local, inexhaustible...

To be is to be an order, to be an order is to be located, every order is multiply located, inexhaustibly, there is no all encompassing order of the world, nature, being. Ordinality is locality and inexhaustibility...

In what sense are events beings? In what sense are fictions beings? (101*) In what sense are enchanted things enchanted, disenchanted* *things enchanted, enchanted things disenchanted? There are many senses of being. Inexhaustible senses, none is more real, more primary, more truthful. Is this not to tell the enchantment of the world, its locality, inexhaustibility, ontological parity? Always more. Always other, other askings...*

All orders are real, none is more or less real. There is no order of non-being but there is ordinal location. Every order is a constituent of some orders and not others. The universe is no order: thus there is no order of being and no order of non-being. (109)...

There is no world to be known through metaphysics, but there is knowledge and there is metaphysics. There are no "most general" traits pervasive of all orders, but there are general traits that may be articulated as metaphysics. There are many orders some of which encompass others. Ordinality entails that there are no categories that apply to everything. (141–2)...

An order encompasses its constituents but not all their constituents. Relevance is not in general transitive (58)...

What makes this theory enchanted? How does it express enchantment? Ordinality is relational, excessive, conditioned, local, and inexhaustible. Locality and inexhaustibility designate location and excess, as if location determined both enchantment and disenchantment, and as if inexhaustibility enchanted each again. There is no world in general, there is no world order, to be is to belong to a sphere of relevance, many spheres of relevance, and there is no total world for relevance. In this way, enchanted things have their places and exceed them, belong where they belong, can be encountered, experienced, sometimes here, sometimes there, can be present, can be missing, can be familiar, are frequently unfamiliar. Always *perhaps* and *as if*. Always other askings and tellings. Inexhaustible orders and locations leave inexhaustible room for inexhaustible enchantments, always in their places, where we might meet them and know them and wonder at them, inexhaustibly exceeding their places, inexhaustible locales of betrayal and excess.

It must be added that some enchanted things are terrible, terrifying, destructive, not charming at all, and some are dull—boring fairies, for example. The dullness of the categories of locality and inexhaustibility does not dull enchantment but augments it. Dullness comes in diverse tastes and flavors.

Whatever is in any way is an order of constituents. Every order is a constituent of other orders. Whatever is relevant to an order is one of its constituents. Not every order is relevant to any given order. There is no totality of orders. (Ross, *PM*, 67)...

Ordinal pluralism entails that no being has an essence but many, many integrities expressing that being's relations to many orders of which it is a constituent. An unqualified essence commits us to a world order in which all beings have one role. Every order plays different roles relative to different orders, to its different locations. (69–70)...

Every order is at least doubly relational: in its constituents and relative to orders in which it is located. (71–2)...

The principles of ontological parity and of inexhaustibility—that there is no world order—are equivalent. To say that something is unqualified in any respect whatever is to assume a world order relative to which it bears this unqualified character. (83–4)...

To say that something is unqualified in any respect whatever is disenchanting.

Being is always plural and qualified and there is no absolute, wholly determinate or unqualified sense of being, no sense inclusive of all the other senses of being. (90)...

The fairies dance among the inexhaustible senses of being...

Every order is inexhaustible, indeterminate in many ways and determinate in many ways. No exhaustive determination can express the nature of an order. (98)...

Ordinality is the source of mystery: inexhaustibility, functionality, relationality. (100)...

Mystery is the source of asking and telling.

Everything is limited, qualified, including limits and qualifications. Everything is mysterious. In the ways in which these mysteries are strange and unfamiliar, surprising, astonish us with their deviations, they and all things are enchanted. Among these enchantments are disenchantments...

There are no ultimate mysteries, there is no ultimate ground of enchantment. There is an indefinite plurality of mysteries, and there can be no order and no mode of judgment without its mysteries and enchantments, full of askings and tellings. Each mystery is penetrable, amenable to indefinite revelation. God, the world, being, life are mysteries. None can be given a final explanation. All can be given inexhaustible interpretations and understandings. Reason is inexhaustibly mysterious and the inexhaustible source of all understanding (118–9)...

Query is inventive interrogative activity—asking and telling. Science, ethics, art, and philosophy are modes of query, interrogative judgment for its own sake. Endless questions, questionings, askings. Questions never cease and nothing is outside interrogation...

The inexhaustibility of orders and of query entails that mysteries are ubiquitous, that the conditions of life that promote determinateness engender new possibilities of understanding and action, new uncertainties and indeterminations, inexhaustibly surprising mysteries. (141)...

I would now read this view of ordinality and mystery as a disenchanted writing of enchantment, knowing that all disenchantments are enchanted and that enchantment falls into the world disenchanted. I would read it as lacking a strong enough sense of its own betrayals. Still, the terms and categories of an ordinal metaphysics, the ways in which mysteries exceed our truths, delimit the possibilities whereby enchantments outstrip any familiar place of refuge. A disenchanted theory of the enchantments of the world hides from its own disenchantments and thereby fails to express their enchantments. What is perhaps in question is style, meter, categories of the ways in which writing and thought surpass any categories.

Here are some examples of such surpassings, first in voice and song:

How may we represent representation? What task unfolds from that endeavor? Do we presuppose an end, a measure, to which any representation may be subjected, or does such a representation exceed any scale? Can we speak in a neutral voice that does not represent its own representativity, or does representation's voice drown out any neutrality? Shall we employ a familiar voice that resonates harmoniously in our ear, or a voice that echoes the discordances between any representation and its representativity? And familiar to whom? Who are the "we" so represented? Will "you" listen to an unfamiliar voice that seeks to sound the excesses of its representativity? Will "you" find yourself subjected once more to an alien representativity? (Ross, *RR*, 1)...

What if we were to represent representation's representativity in a sonorescent voice, listening to the ring of representation, echoing the sonance of nature? Would representativity become more aware of itself in its reverberations? Would we make ourselves more familiar with its cacophony? (1)...

Nature's nature rings as poiēsis, echoing in human life as judgment and query. We do not know if nature must reverberate only in that form, even in human life, or whether there may echo other forms of sonorescence. The representation of nature and judgment, of power, desire, time, and materiality, all ring of limits and their limits, in that way metaphysical. Here the nature of nature sings at a time and place through judgments that exceed themselves. This excess echoes the excesses of metaphysics, nature, and artifice over themselves: none at all. A nothing that makes all the difference in the world. Our sonorescence sounds each of these words inexhaustibly. Nature rings as a no thing that makes all the difference in the world. The cacophony of the world. The ring of nature's representations (214)...

It is time to ask the following question in the context of enchantment:

What is the task of thought, of philosophy, of academic and other knowledges in relation to what cannot be mastered? To master anyway? To disenchant, to bring under the supervision of reason? Perhaps...

Philosophy has always insisted upon thinking its other. Its other: that which limits it, and from which it derives its essence, its definition, its production. Does the limit, obliquely, by surprise, always reserve one more blow for philosophical knowledge? Perhaps. (Derrida, *T*, x–xi)...

To enchant, to unmaster, no matter how impossible. And indeed, impossibility is the condition of enchantment. Perhaps...

Awaiting without horizon of the wait, awaiting what one does not expect yet or any longer, hospitality without reserve, welcoming salutation accorded in advance to the absolute surprise of the arrivant from whom or from which one will not ask anything in return; messianic opening to what is coming, that is, to the event that cannot be awaited or recognized in advance to the event as the foreigner itself, to her or to him for whom one must leave an empty place, always. Such a hospitality without reserve is the impossible itself, and this condition of possibility of the event is also its condition of impossibility. Without this experience of the impossible, one might as well give up on both justice and the event (Derrida, *SM*, 65)...

What is going to come perhaps is not only this or that it is at last the thought of the perhaps the perhaps itself. The arrivant will arrive perhaps for one must never be sure when it comes to arrivance but the arrivant could also be the perhaps itself the unheard-of totally new experience of the perhaps. Unheard-of, totally new, that very experience that no [one] might yet have dared to think (Derrida, *PF*, 29)...

Enchantment is unmasterable—perhaps...

Every gesture, task, expression, exposition masters and re-masters—perhaps...

Asking and telling is mastery—perhaps...

Asking and telling is mystery—perhaps...

Exposition unmasters and enchants—perhaps...

Art and literature master and unmaster, enchant and disenchant—if that were possible, perhaps...

Asking and telling is unmastery—perhaps...

Philosophy masters—and unmasters; strives to unmaster—and masters; transgresses its limits as if betrayed beyond mastery and unmastery—perhaps...

Music, song, meter all surpass mastery—with another; enchant—toward another disenchantment; impose a disenchanted rigor, harmony, order—as if beyond any order, in cacophony—perhaps...

Religion claims to master enchantment—perhaps...

God is offered as master of enchantment—perhaps...

Mastery disenchants every enchantment—perhaps...

Always as if another perhaps...

CHAPTER 2

Truth's Enchantments

> I have heard from men and women who understand the truths of religion. All nature is akin, and the soul has learned everything, so that when a man has recalled a single piece of knowledge—learned it, in ordinary language—there is no reason why he should not find out all the rest, if he keeps a stout heart and does not grow weary of the search, for seeking and learning are in fact nothing but recollection (*anamnēsis*). (Plato, *Meno*, 81ae)

In greek, truth and knowledge are unforgetting (*anamnēsis*). Knowledge and truth emerge from darkness, forgetting, untruth. With religion. If we take this seriously—I mean of course enchantedly—then against the view that truth is given, untruth its failing, that knowledge is the standard, error the departure, our view must be that knowledge, truth, and memory are given in the light of a primordial darkness and loss. It is as if it took the death of the gods for asking and telling to emerge in truth—the death of the gods or of something more enchanted. We forget, we err, we do not know—and from this forgetting emerge remembrance, truth, and understanding. This emergence of asking and telling is a wonder, in that sense enchanted, one that we will never know or understand or recall because we are always given it too late.

There is nothing here of skepticism, that we cannot know. Indeed we can, indeed we do. Skepticism is the disenchanted form of the recognition that knowledge, memory, and truth are enchantments. Enchantments here bear the weight of two marvels—or curses: the *un-* of untruth and unforgetting, and the *in-* of the injustice (*adikia*) present in all things.

All things make restitution to one another for their injustice according to the ordinance of time. (Anaximander)[1]...

The curse is injustice, the miracle is justice. Injustice is first, dark on the face of things. All things are unjust in their coming to be, their being, their passing away. This injustice is the curse that every being, every becoming betrays. The miracle is justice, for there might be none. Justice comes to be in the restitution each thing makes to others past and present for its becoming. Injustice is beyond all accounting, enchanted. Justice is the accounting, no matter how infinite. Asking and telling emerge from injustice in the forgetting of truth.

This means that ethics as practice, the performance of ethics, is disenchanted, as if it were possible to account for goodness, as if there were a measure of ethics that accounted for us, to us, as if the good gave measure. What I call *the good* is the inexhaustible, unaccountable, immeasurable, immemorial, enchanted call from injustice to justice, the infinite, unaccountable, immeasurable, immemorial, enchanted ways in which injustice is in justice, as if, as justice and injustice, they were inseparable on the side of their enchantment, and distinct on the side of their disenchantment.

Perhaps this is the story of betrayal:

Justice and injustice betray each other and themselves beyond any distinction or separation. And still we separate, distinguish, and judge, still we betray, still we are betrayed...

More of the good and its betrayals later. Here we are before the court of truth.

All things come in truth from the enchanted darknesses of untruth...

The un- of untruth and unforgetting is the condition of truth and understanding...

The curse—no curse at all—is the un- of truth and the in- of justice, the revelation of their betrayal. The wonder of disenchantment is that there is truth, memory, and justice...

The form in which the enchantment of truth appears has many names, perhaps an endless number. I have noted *wonder* and *abundance.* Others, well-known, are *imagination, intuition, insight.* Let us imagine that *anamnēsis* mobilizes for us not the routine disenchantment of recollection—familiar reproduction and recall—but the infinite and immemorial marvel that takes place in every emergence of truth from untruth, every asking and telling. What emerges is an asking and a telling that has never appeared in this place and time before, whether in human life, divine providence, in this child's or adult's mind. Some truth or connection or communication shatters the darkness with light, the silence with voice, brings the *un-* forth into another place. Some enchanted image crosses the caesura.

> Of all things, communication is the most wonderful. That things should be able to pass from the plane of external pushing and pulling to that of revealing themselves to man, and thereby to themselves; and that the fruit of communication should be participation, sharing, is a wonder by the side of which transubstantiation pales. When communication occurs, all natural events are subject to reconsideration and revision; they are re-adapted to meet the requirements of conversation, whether it be public discourse or that preliminary discourse termed thinking. Events turn into objects, things with a meaning. (John Dewey, *EN*, 166)

Exposition changes everything. Telling is most wonderful. As if perhaps...

> Man is first of all "thrown" from Being itself into the truth of Being, so that ek-sisting in this fashion he might guard the truth of Being, in order that beings might appear in the light of Being as the beings they are. Man does not decide whether and how beings appear, whether and how God and the gods or history and nature come forward into the lighting of Being, come to presence and depart. the advent of beings lies in the destiny of Being. (Martin Heidegger, *LH*, 210)

Man does not decide, god does not decide, being does not decide, nothing decides. The advent of beings is enchanted. Deciding is disenchanted...

Understanding is an unforgetting of those things that our souls beheld aforetime as they journeyed with their god. (Plato, *Phaedrus*, 249c)...

Living is forgetting...

Knowing is anamnēsis...

Truth is recollection...

Recollection is unforgetting...

In the modality of perhaps and as if...

In the proliferation of the image...

In the unforgettings of enchantments. (Ross, *UM*, xxx)...

Multiplicities of knowledges...

Multiplicities of truths...

Multiplicities of understandings...

Multiplicities of askings, questions, queries, experiments, perceptions...

Multiplicities of reasons...

Multiplicities of expositions, expressions, exposures, tellings...

Knowledges of knowledges...
Truths of truths...
Unforgettings of unforgettings...
Images of images...
Understandings of understandings...
Questions of questions...
Queries of queries...
Askings of askings...
Reasons of reasons...
Tellings of tellings...
Enchantments of enchantments...

Overlapping, interweaving, reciprocating, revolving, turning back, turning over...

Expositions of exposition, expressions of expression, exposure exposing exposition, touch touching touch, telling telling telling...

Multiplying, shattering, reinforcing, augmenting, undermining, unearthing, unfounding...

Enchantments disenchanting, disenchantments enchanting, etc. etc....

In greek, memory is *mnēmē*; recollection is *anamnēsis*; remembrance is *mnēmosunē*; forgetfulness is *amnēmosunē*; *anamnēsis* is bringing back to memory from forgetting. And so we may ask, what is it to bring back, what is brought back from forgetting? The answer, perhaps, is *nothing, nothing in particular—that is, as if it were everything, as if in the caesura, the caesura of enchantment...*

Unforgetting is the exposition of things as images beyond themselves, coming back in the caesura, in the modality of *as if*.

Unforgetting is doubly triply multiply ambiguous present and not present here and there now you see it now you don't. Unforgetting is beyond choice is all the freedom of the world present as if it were disaster. (Ross, *U*, xxx)...

What if human beings were in the process of, constrained into, becoming inhuman? And what if what is "proper" to humankind were to be inhabited by the inhuman?. (Lyotard, *I*, 2)...

Which would make two sorts of inhuman. The inhumanity of the system which is currently being consolidated under the name of development (among others) must not be confused with the infinitely secret one of which the soul is hostage. (2)...

Development imposes the saving of time. But writing and reading are slow. One loses one's time seeking time lost. Anamnesis is the other pole—not even that, there is no common axis—the other of acceleration and abbreviation. (3)...

Anamnēsis is the enchanted pole of disenchanted knowledges, the enchantments excesses proliferations of exposition: exposure as expression, asking, telling; as aisthēsis, mimēsis, poiēsis, catachrēsis, technē; as image, aesthetics, beauty, art; as unearthing, revelation, disclosure; calling as giving; interrupting in betrayal; as if perhaps...

That knowing, appearing, language, images, communication, expression, exposition are wonders, uncontainable and immeasurable; that remembering is unforgetting, *anamnēsis*; that untruth, unforgetting, injustice are enchanted, owes nothing to skepticism. Unlike levinas, who understands the recurrence of skepticism as sign and betrayal of immemoriality, I understand it as the disenchantment of enchanted askings, of captivating tellings, of expressions always on the way to elsewhere and the endless proliferation of images.

We have been seeking the otherwise than being from the beginning, and as soon as it is conveyed before us it is betrayed in the said that dominates the saying which states it.[2] (Levinas, *OB*, 7)...

Not to be otherwise but otherwise than being. (3)...

Skepticism, at the dawn of philosophy, set forth and betrayed the diachrony of this very conveying and betraying. To conceive the otherwise than being requires, perhaps, as much audacity as skepticism shows, when it does not hesitate to affirm the impossibility of statement while venturing to realize this impossibility by the very statement of this impossibility. (7)...

Skeptical discourse, which states the rupture, failure, impotence or impossibility of disclosure, would be self-contradictory if the saying and the said were only correlative, if the signifyingness of proximity and the signification know and said could enter into a common order. (168)...

The enchantment of knowledge and truth is not their absence but the impossibility of their gathering. Knowledge is a reality, a fact, science provides us with valuable insights, everyday life is filled with knowings, many impossible to articulate. These are all useful, reliable, effective in the ways in which they are tenuous, mobile, transformative, transgressive. Enchanted truths are transgressive. They cannot be fixed in place.

This means that they cross unfamiliar boundaries, that they cannot be held in place, that the reliability that we may seek through knowledge—constancy, durability, stability—are all dangers that work against the knowledges they would support.

Knowledge as perception, concept, comprehension, refers back to an act of grasping. The immanence of the known to the act of knowing is already the embodiment of seizure, belongs to that unit of knowledge in which Auffassen (understanding) is also, and always has been, a Fassen (gripping). The mode of thought known as knowledge involves man's concrete existence in the world he inhabits, in which he moves and works and possesses. (Levinas, *EFP,* 76)...

Heidegger, with the whole of western history, takes the relation with the other as enacted in the destiny of sedentary peoples, the possessors and builders of the earth. Possession is preeminently the form in which the other becomes the same, by becoming mine. Ontology becomes ontology of nature, impersonal fecundity, faceless generous mother, matrix of particular beings, inexhaustible matter for things. (Levinas, *TI,* 46)...

Ontology becomes faceless, uniform, all things gathered together. Surprise and wonder withdraw. Knowledge and truth answer to a call given and giving beyond any grasping. So we may say that truth is enchanted and disenchanted, enchanting and disenchanting, and that the knowledge we seek to have, the knowledge we would grasp under the headings of science, method, analysis, synthesis, confirmation, even critique all are disenchanted, accounted for under the headings that grasp them, and disenchant what they would grasp.

Yet grasping and having are impossible, knowing and being exceed any grasp, the most disenchanted of understandings enchant the world in wonder. Enchantment always returns, remains present beyond any presence, in the inspiration and wonder of any asking including science, and the transgressions of every telling in its mobilities and proliferations. Knowledge, truth, being are all nomadic, impossible to settle down. *Images proliferate and proliferate again, as if betrayed beyond themselves...*

Dewey speaks of the nomadism of knowledge in the language of inquiry.

> What is already known, what is accepted as truth, is of immense importance; inquiry could not proceed a step without it. But it is held subject to use, and is at the mercy of the discoveries which it makes possible. It has to be adjusted to the latter and not the latter to it. When things are defined as instruments, their value and validity reside in what proceeds from them; consequences not antecedents supply meaning and verity. Truths already possessed may have practical or moral certainty, but logically they never lose a hypothetic quality. They are true *if.* (*EN,* pp. 154–5)

Truth if is the disenchanted form of enchanted truth *as if, perhaps*—and even more, perhaps, of the *as if* of *as if,* and *perhaps* of *perhaps,* where the displacements themselves are displaced, and the enchantments enchanted.

The arrivant could also be the perhaps itself the unheard-of totally new experience of the perhaps. Unheard-of, totally new, that very experience which no [one] might yet have dared to think. (Derrida, *PF*, 29)...

Inquiry here is hypothetical, transitory, mobile, not just on the surface but in its nature, deeply and pervasively. On the one hand, there is knowledge. On the other hand, it is dispossessive, always on the move. It is not the flaw of inquiry that it fails to put knowledge in our grip, it is its wonder.

This is another way to celebrate the wonder of the impossibility of justice and the inescapability of untruth. They do not fail to accomplish what they might accomplish, what we might hope they would accomplish—justice and truth. Injustice is the pervasive condition of being—and still there is justice, divine or human, divine and human, human without the divine. Untruth is the pervasive condition of inquiry—and still there is knowledge, truth, divine or human. We know and know yet more. Levinas speaks of this in the language of responsibility:

The infinity of responsibility denotes not its actual immensity, but a responsibility increasing in the measure that it is assumed; duties become greater in the measure that they are accomplished. (Levinas, *TI*, 244)...

We know less the more we know, and still we know what we know...

The enchantment of truth is its anamnēsis...

I understand the notion of query to answer to this pervasive nomadism in the circulation of truth, while perhaps not as visibly presenting its unforgetting and untruth, its inescapable enchantments. Query is inventive and methodic, terms of disenchantment. Yet query's inventions and methods enchant whatever they touch. Query asks and tells.

Here, then, disenchantment and enchantment in alternation:

> Science is articulation; it is also query. A true scientific theory is true in relation to a given order, true by virtue of the methods involved, and true in terms of available evidence. Its truth is relational and qualified, a function of ordinal location.
>
> The primary function of query is to provide validation through methodic and inventive judgment. And the way in which validation is achieved is through further articulation and query. A work of art may articulate some aspect of experience; a critic may articulate the work of art; another artist may imitate its style; another may go on to new works of art and styles in response to the first work. All are articulations of the work. All

> are query. Articulation is the enhancement of judgments by further judgments, and foreshadows further articulations. Query fulfills the promise of articulation through ongoing and inventive interrogative judgment. (Ross, *TOM*, 146–7)

Query is methodic and inventive judgment. If this is disenchanted, it reenchants itself. Every query, every truth, is local, thereby inexhaustible, inexhaustibly expressive. Invention invents and reinvents itself, making understanding uncanny. Method appears organized, orderly, structured, yet new methods are invented, invention, organization, order, and structure are orderly in the most unaccountable ways. There is no one form of query, no superior method, no orderly invention. All are multiple, all are haunted by *perhaps* and *as if*.

This is worth unfolding. Disenchantment appears as if to claim that everything is accountable and measurable, as if measure and accounting were determinate and determinable once and for all, as if scientific and technological rationality had been decided finally, both in their inescapable grip and in what and how they are, as if *perhaps* and *as if* did not haunt them through and through. Yet they are successful, valid, accomplish their tasks through the modalities of *as if* and *perhaps*, in asking and telling, following derrida's suggestion that both of them, *perhaps* and *as if*, remain open, as if perhaps they remain open, as if the *perhaps* and *as if* themselves were haunted by *perhaps* and *as if*. As if, then, another *perhaps*, as if perhaps the proliferation of images, virtualities, simulacra; the simulation of simulation; exposition beyond exposition. *Asking and telling as if and perhaps...*

In the language of query, truth and validation are accomplishments of highly determinate procedures—methods and inventions if you will. The multiplicity of queries, the inventiveness of methods and inventions, the methodicality of invention—indeed, the determinateness and disenchantment of every form of query, including science—transform it, transfigure it, put it forward in the mode of *perhaps* and *as if*, perhaps on the three levels of ambiguity of which Blanchot speaks,[3] as if perhaps it were asking and telling.

Still, then, in the disenchanted language of query:

> Query is ongoing methodic judgment concerned with validation and emphasizing invention. Its ontological conditions are the conditions of ordinality: the complementarity and functionality of determinateness and indeterminateness. Every order is determinate in some respects and is in these respects available for judgment and query, for knowledge and truth, provided that

> epistemic conditions are propitious. Every order is also indeterminate in certain respects, both within any ordinal location and in virtue of other ordinal locations. If it were not indeterminate in some respects, an order would be unknowable, for it would lack the possibility of becoming known. Now what is indeterminate in one location may be determinate in another; but conversely, what is determinate in a particular location is indeterminate in another. Every order is determinate in some respects and indeterminate in others for any and all of its locations. (Ross, *TOM*, 87–8)

In other words, the determinateness of query provides us with knowledge and reason, and the indeterminateness of query, its inventions and proliferations, produce inexhaustible askings and tellings beyond any accountings. In the language enchanted by query, *the inexhaustibility of orders entails an inexhaustibility to query—especially, an inexhaustibility to metaphysical query.* (129)...

This is said of metaphysics in the teeth of its critique. Metaphysics—with science, philosophy, technical rationality—brings everything to presence, under concepts, categories, structures, essences, makes everything accountable. It does so as query, therefore it cannot do what it is said to do, a *cannot* that is its greatest glory, its greatest achievement, to be more than what is said of it, to express more than what it says of itself, always more. This always more is enchantment, the enchantments of a disenchanted reason, of a philosophy and science and knowledge that know truth only in disenchanted form, but that must be enchanted to know anything.

In other words, the nature of knowing here, and of reason, especially including philosophy and metaphysics, is to outstrip any grasping. On the way, then, to enchantment:

> An ordinal metaphysics provides a more active role for the understanding—query not simply discovering order but inventing it; not simply reflecting order but providing it. Here metaphysics is the synthetic achievement of reason, seeking to encompass through its ongoing capabilities inexhaustibly diverse orders. Metaphysics cannot achieve a total embrace, but it can bring into a unified, synthetic order what was separate and disordered. Order here is created; intelligibility is achieved, not found. The rational life is a project of coordination, never to be completed, always pregnant with novel opportunities. (151)

> By query I mean not only that there is an indefinite number of questions, but that everything may be called into question. Query involves unremitting interrogation in the two senses that

> questions never cease and that nothing is outside interrogation. (Ross, *PM*, 64)

This conjunction of what can never be settled conclusively, either inside or outside query, is dispossession and enchantment on its epistemological side. It is by no means the magic of enchantment in relation to the image or its proliferation.

Here then are two images of enchantment in knowing, perhaps of enchanted knowing—a very different matter. Query is enchanting, on the way to enchanted knowing, no matter how obscured the enchantment may be by science's insistences. We may think of them again as possessions and dispossessions. Science cannot possess its knowledge, cannot possess knowing or wisdom but questions incessantly. Incessant asking is dispossession, right in the midst of science's exposition of scientific truth.

We began our discussion of disenchantment in the context of weber's account of science for those who would choose it as a vocation. In the midst of asserting that the contemporary academic, scientific, and religious world is disenchanted, and will remain so, weber insists on the side of science that many understand as enchanted:

Inspiration plays no less a role in science than it does in the realm of art. Both are frenzy in the sense of plato's "mania" and "inspiration." (Weber, *SV*, 136)...[4]

Inspiration imagination intuition insight discovery creativity invention asking are madnesses frenzies passions agitations transportations beyond accounting...

How can science be sane when scientists are mad? How can science be disenchanted at the point at which scientific reason's truth concretely appears in enchanted telling?

How can we trust a mad enchanted science, how can we depend on irrational enchanted truths, how can such a telling be knowledge?

How can disenchanted knowledge be anything but enchanted in exposition: exposure as expression, asking, calling, telling; as aisthēsis, mimēsis, poiēsis, catachrēsis, technē; as image, aesthetics, beauty, art; as unearthing, revelation, disclosure; calling as giving; interrupting in betrayal?...

All the forms of knowledge, academic and nonacademic, are disenchanted, and in this inescapable condition are gathered all the enchantments of the world...

Multiplicity perspectivity alterity all appear in asking as generosity, giving beyond grasping, betrayed in choosing...

How can we know what we do not know? How can we learn it and know that we have learned it? The paradox of learning asks these questions from the standpoint of disenchantment directed toward a world of enchantment.

> The paradox insists that the line between ignorance and knowledge is hard and fast, that there is no way to cross it, that knowledge is a state or possession. Instead, the line is fundamentally and systematically blurred, we are always partly ignorant, partly knowledgeable, engaged in an unending process in which novel questions are continually asked and new answers proposed. (Ross, *LD*, 41)

I would speak here briefly in a voice I have not allowed myself before, to say that unending askings and novel tellings, the blurring of the line between ignorance and knowledge, untruth and truth, dispossession and possession, and indeed, enchantment and disenchantment, is a radical, uncanny state. It is nothing ordinary, no matter how common, nothing familiar, no matter how frequent. In the surprises of appearance and becoming lie the most extreme enchantments. The truth I have spent most of my life promulgating is that the most enchanted discoveries require disenchanted preliminaries. The world of science is disenchanted in the ways in which it organizes its knowledge. The world of science is then miraculously enchanted in the askings it engenders and the tellings that it gives. In the non-contemporaneity with itself of the living present.[5] In the caesura.

Leaving this voice behind, I mean to insist that any voice that would speak enchantingly of enchantment must speak in an enchanted voice, that disenchantment struggles to do so in vain. Yet what it shows in its inadequacies—and in the context of disenchantment they are failings—reveals the enchantments of its own struggles. Weber is clear. The possibility of a disenchanted science rests on madnesses it can speak of only at a distance, never in its disenchanted voice. Madness haunts scientific and academic knowledge twice, first in its possibility, its emergence, and second in the disruption of its own languages and codes when it has to answer to itself.

> Learning and understanding are grounded in insight, in immediacy, relationality, and fallibility. Insight is a power of judgment. It comes with no guarantees and there is no way of providing such guarantees. It is not only fallible, but often wrong, in whole or in part, and is modifiable only by other in-

> sights. All understanding depends on insight, all learning is the development of insight. (Ross, *LD*, 96)

Knowledge learning understanding are powers of enchantment in the heart of disenchantment, disenchanted powers in the soul of enchantment...

> Knowledge is produced by insight and invention. Even learning by memorization and repetition can become knowledge only through insight and understanding. The difference between novice and expert does not lie in the presence of insight and invention, but in the questions they ask and the activities they undertake. (98)

> The purpose of education is to develop the mind, to expand its powers and enrich its capabilities. At every level, this is attained through query leading to insight, realized in invention and discovery. Learning is the fulfillment of the mind: development of the capacity through discovery to make further discoveries; expansion of the powers of query through further query. (115)

I would now say that the purpose of asking is to enchant and disenchant the mind and more than the mind: to live between enchantment and disenchantment, life and death, knowledge and ignorance, one knowledge and another. Between. In the modalities of *perhaps* and *as if*. Well beyond what I have said before.

> Education offers human beings the possibility of expanding and magnifying themselves. They learn to influence and comprehend diverse and separate things. They see profound relationships between diverse elements in precise and analytic clarity. They make subtle and attractive designs, of novel shape and form. They become capable of considered and valid actions, in diverse areas of existence. Education offers them a chance to become more than they were: the determination of a given perspective for an individual, and the diversification of powers and capacities of sharing other perspectives. (Ross, *ME*, 40)

> Science, ethics, and art form an interrelated set of perspectives. And as each of these perspectives is capable of universal applicability, so the rational life is the expansion of them all in their indefinite interaction. The only coherence possible may be that provided by the application of as wide a range of perspectives as possible to every subject matter. Thus scientific knowledge about psychology and choice is relevant to religion and morality, while a given scientific theory may be judged aesthetically or ethically. What good is science? How true is *Hamlet*? Is not

> the realization of the breadth of possibility the only truly humane life? (*SP*, 153)

There are always more perspectives, other perspectives, expressing enchantment and disenchantment. Learning as discovery takes place between disenchantment and enchantment. Knowledge, understanding, truth occupy the caesura between enchantment and disenchantment. In the aporias of telling and asking.

Either learning is a supreme and unconditioned value, or it is asking beyond value, telling beyond grasping, enchanted, endless giving from the good, in the call to exposition...

All systems of philosophy are personal, temperamental, accidental, and premature. They are human heresies. (Santayana, *PH*, 94)...

All knowledge is personal temperamental accidental premature perspectival emotional heretical. The aporias of asking are the exposition of its tellings...

Reason is heretical. (Ross, *MAPH*, 2)...

Every tradition includes and synthesizes within itself manifold divisions and differentiations. Every tradition is filled with negations and discontinuities, and seeks to establish rules to control their risks and dangers. To deny a tradition its heresies is to entomb it (6).

Where heresy remains at the heart of philosophy aporias remain at the heart of being and truth, reality is aporetic. (7)...

> By *aporia*, I mean the moments in the movement of thought in which it finds itself faced with unconquerable obstacles resulting from conflicts in its understanding of its own intelligibility. Such conflicts cry out for a resolution that cannot be achieved within the conditions from which they emerge. The result is either the termination of thought or heresy: a break in the limits of intelligibility. The question is whether such heretical disruptions are at the limits of reason or, aporetically, its fullest expression. (Ross, *MAPH*, 3–4).

Are aporia and heresy enchanted or disenchanted? Do they occupy the space between? Is there a caesura between? Does enchantment meet disenchantment at the point of aporia, is the outcome heresy? We do not know and may never know. But we may ask, and tell.

> While the forms aporia may take are inexhaustible, three recurrent forms are worth noting. One is that of contradiction. The second is that of multiplicity dividing identity, same and other.

> *Here, finiteness is inexhaustibility and inexhaustibility is aporia the limit of every limit the indeterminateness of every determination the determinateness in every indetermination...*
>
> The third recurrent form, then, is that of limitation, the limits of every limit, the reciprocity of determinateness in every indeterminateness. (4)

We may never know because the questions are aporetic, because the answers are heretical, because the askings and tellings take place where enchantment meets disenchantment, and can be offered from either side, incongruently, aporetically, and heretically, while the site is unstable and unresolvable.

An example is the question of the end of philosophy, a question of the limits of traditional philosophy and of the possibility of a break—aporia in the first place, heresy in the second.

> A central assumption in such an understanding is that the philosophic tradition is sufficiently coherent that it may be characterized as a whole, to be supplanted by another form of thought that forbids totality. Because being is aporetic and metaphysics is heretical, no totality is intelligible. Metaphysics is heretical, deeply and inexhaustibly pervaded by aporia, in its most systematic works as thoroughly as in those that iconoclastically call for its end. (282)

Recurrently tradition disenchants the earth with disenchanted knowings. Recurrently enchantment flickers at the heart of every knowing as the disruption that allows it to be disenchanted and be knowledge...

> The greatest heresy of science is science itself: the form of reason that proclaims consensus as its only norm while filled with conflict and controversy, even violence. (7)

> How to understand a tradition that has recurrently engaged in heresy against itself, whose intelligibility, even intelligibility itself, is always profoundly in question? (8)

How to understand an enchantment that disenchants itself? Is it something to understand? Is its understanding enchanted or disenchanted?...

Knowing is aporetic because being is aporetic; knowing is heretical because truth is heretical. To show the aporias of any being and the heresies of any truth; to expose the aporias of aporia, the heresies of heresy. (303)...

To be is to be local: located and locating. Multiple locality is the origin of aporia and heresy, no origin at all, if an origin aporetic and heretical. (306)

Locality is limitation multiple location is inexhaustibility the limitation of every limit. Locality and inexhaustibility are local, inexhaustibility and locality are inexhaustible, limitation is limited, inexhaustibility is inexhaustible, finite, local, aporetic and heretical. (Ross, *MAPH*, 307)...

Being is divided by multiple enchantments, judgment and reason are divided by multiple disenchantments, there are always many knowings, many askings and tellings, many modes and kinds of enchantment and disenchantment, judgment inexhaustibly demands disenchantment while its desires are enchanted...

Unlimit is limited limitation is unlimited stability is openness finiteness is transcendence, locality is inexhaustibility, sameness is otherness aporias heresies...

> Knowing can be knowing, query can be query, reason can be reason, only insofar as it is heretical. Heresy is the form judgment wears to express the inexhaustibility of local being (*MAPH*, 323).

> 1. Where truth is freedom from aporia, or where there is a truth of aporia itself, then one truth may be imagined to constitute truth itself, whether we have yet conceived it or not. Where truth is aporetic, thought is constituted by multiplicity, always on the way, always coming, never arrived. Metaphysical truth is heresy.
>
> 2. No truth can be entirely adequate, no understanding can be a proper self-understanding, meaning is always indeterminate, engendering future heresies.
>
> 3. Every truth is a divided truth, Every knowing is heretical. Every understanding is aporetic.
>
> 4. The aporia of aporetic thought is intrinsic, divided inexhaustibly. There is no final truth of aporia, however aporetic, no final truth of enchantment or its enchantments. There is no thought of the limits of disenchantment, at the limits of intelligibility, that is free from the aporias that enchant it. (341–2)

Aporia heresy irrationality unreason unintelligibility hover at the limits of reason and representation. A recurrent figure of enchantment is madness the madness beyond reason the madness of reason the desire that surpasses every reason and every other madness. An exceptionally sane madness still mad. An exceptionally mad reason, still sane. Enchanted and disenchanted. In the caesura...

What kind of writing thinking exposition asking telling answers to the locality of writing thinking exposition and its inexhaustibility? What may be expected of the aporias that pervade every tradition that would know and express and tell of locality and inexhaustibility? Of disenchantment and enchantment? Every writing thinking exposition telling is one of many expressions proliferates as other images other expressions. Every expression is disenchanted proliferates as endless enchantments. Every expression is enchanted proliferates as endless disenchantments. Enchantment is exposition endlessly exposing itself and others. (*MAPH*, 343–4)...

In *Phaedrus*, the madness of love is contrasted with the nonmadness of the nonlover in the name of truth. The nonlover perhaps offers certain advantages, but love is mad, given from the gods.[6] Might truth, then—philosophy's, science's, reason's truth—be divine and mad, mad and divine? Might science's truth be magical, might witchcraft be at the heart of science, might the ambiguity of the *pharmakon* haunt the truths of science, might enchantment reenchant every disenchantment of science? Could it do so and still be science? Could it do so in the name of truth?

Pharmakeia as medicine, drug, madness, remedy, poison, potion, agent, dye, pigment, color; pharmakos as sacrifice, scapegoat; pharmakeus as wizard. Desire circulates as poison and cure, madness and remedy, menace and magic, enchantment and disenchantment, in the colors of the rainbow. (Ross, *IR*, 223)...

What represents the wings of desire the life of the soul but pharmakeia mania erōs poiēsis circulating together? What follows the climax of love with its mad yearning for beauty and its recollection of true being? What but truth but asking telling? What but the enchantments of disenchantment?...

Phaedrus reveals and offers the wings of living truth in the animate soul as against dead science, dead technē, dead art, dead writing, dead memory, dead repetition, perhaps even dead gods. All dead! What gives them life, lifts their wings? What madness animates the wings of their desire? What economy? What telling?. (Ross, *IR*, 250)...

What is disenchantment but death? What is enchantment but life, love of living, the madness of loving, the poiēsis of technē, the calling of asking and telling?...

Science's knowledge is an enchanted truth that appears before us disenchanted, unjust, as if dead. It would not be truth without the fire that burns the soul that touches it, the love that inspires it, the madness required for any truth to make its appearance, the endless asking of truth. The facts of science—and the fact of science—the fact in science of its knowledge, the technicalities of its expertise, all are the dead, disenchanted face of the irruption from the call of the world to know that knows no limits. Science imposes limits, attempts to murder the spirit that moves it. It murders many things, but that spirit cannot be slain.

The possibility of knowledge, the reality of truth—no matter what kind—echo from the enchanted voices that surround them. (Ross, *IR*, 251??)

After we soar to the heavens on mad wings of desire, we fall back into disenchantment and law, into law's authority and unending injustice, but not altogether, not as if we had never known, never been disturbed by, the madness of truth, but remember madness and injustice. We remember pharmakeia as science's spell. We remember endless injustice in justice...

What, on such a reading, can we say of science's authority? That its public law represents the death of living truth—an inevitable death? That its rules and laws represent the death of god—an inevitable death? That its accountability represents the death of memory as reminder? What kind of science might circulate unending injustice as its truth?. (Ross, *IR*, 252)...

What kind of science might circulate unending disenchantment as its enchanted truth? What kind of science might ask and tell?...

What kind of science? Enchanted science. All science is enchanted—magical, bewitched, mad, demonic, salvatory. All science is disenchanted—accountable, authoritative, accomplished, technical. Disenchanted science then, just science. That science does not know its enchantments, that it passes off its enchantments as disenchantments, that it passes itself off as authoritative when it is simply science, do not obliterate enchantment, though they may disenchant it and repossess it. Obliteration is emptiness, the emptiness of emptiness and the oblivion of oblivion. Science belongs to the wizards and witches as much as it belongs to science graduate students. Each unforgets the other, unforgets science, in the name of knowing and disclosing.

None of these insights into the enchantments of science inhibit or support an enchanted critique. Without an extra step, without what heidegger means by questioning and derrida means by the question before the question, without what foucault means by a permanent critique of our historical era and endless unforgetting, without endless images in proliferation, askings and tellings, critique goes back to disenchantment. Which is not perhaps to say that it leaves enchantment behind, as if it could.

Here then is a critique of science, feminist critique, which addresses science on the one side as a vocation, right in the heart of disenchantment, and on the other as a life, a world, containing men and women in proximity.

> What, one may ask (and, as feminists know, many have), has feminism to say about—what *could* feminism have to say about—physics (or chemistry, mathematics, or logic)? Physics, after all, seems pure of any content that would (or could) be affected by sex-gender and politics.
>
> There are two short answers to the question. The most obvious is *we simply don't know yet*. (Lynn Nelson, *WK*, 250)

We don't know yet. Could we ever know, satisfactorily and truthfully, and what would such knowledge tell? What happens to the pharmakon, to pharmakeus and pharmakos, when we gain such knowledge? and why would we wish to do so?. (Ross, *IR*, 268)...

> Would it be *good news* if it turned out that only physics, mathematics, logic, chemistry, or whatever, show no evidence of our experiences of politics and sex/gender? Are we willing to say "if physics is all right, so is science?" Does it save science? (Nelson, *WK*, 250)

What if feminist women were witches, as socrates was pharmakeus and as so many women were burned as witches? As socrates began an epoch of magic in the name of reason, askings and tellings of sexual difference and gender and other historical and cultural differences may open another epoch of knowledge and science. And life. (Ross, *IR*, 268–9)...

The threat of feminist criticism of science presents the possibility that science's practices subjugate women. The next step extends that critique from the west to its nonwestern others, suggesting that science's hegemony subjugates nonwestern forms of knowledge at the same time that it subjugates nonwestern peoples and ways of life. This critique does not belie science's effectiveness or expertise, does not ask us to repudiate science, but calls upon us to acknowledge the injustices of its techniques, the dangers of the most "enlightened" forms of knowledge, menaces that haunt various economies of knowledge, instrumental and technical, anarchical or social. (Ross, *IR*, 268)...

Such a critique opens up unfamiliar askings and tellings of science, on the way to who knows where?...

In the name of its rationality science disenchants the world. In the name of its rationality science subjugates women, other people and their ways of life. Does it do so in the name of disenchantment? Might disenchantment oppress and subjugate people and ways in the name of reason? Might the successes and effectiveness of scientific knowledge and its rationality be in this way unethical? Unscientific? Might reason itself be mad,[7] in passion and inspiration, and in cruelty and violence? In reverse, can science answer from itself to the caesura between enchantment and disenchantment, can science and reason be scientific and rational in the caesura?

Science's reason is science's madness the madness of silence and subjugation. Let us seek another madness in science, science's madness in the caesura...

Would this other science be a more rational science, a less rational science, a different reason and a different science, a more knowing, better science? Could it be a witches' science, enchanted, dangerous, intimidating, joyful?[8] Could the injustice of science—its disenchantments and more, beyond disenchantment and reenchantment—haunt it to its depths, pervade every nook and cranny of science, as if, for example, frogs had no perspectives from the standpoint of science while science were a frog perspective; as if, another example, women had no scientific perspectives. All askings to which we know no tellings?

Let's ask again, perhaps with greater irony, would it be good news that science might be objective, that politics might be by rule? What goodness of rules except by disenchantment? What science might take up the witches' critique—a better or another science? One magically transformed by endless enchantments, transfigured as a pharmakon, where we cannot tell, decisively by rule, the difference between good and bad science, cannot tell even in ourselves, for ourselves, the truth?...

What if knowledge, especially science, circulated with desire and magic? Would that make science more or less dangerous? Would it make truth more or less fearsome? What if, as the witches say, science judged by taste, a recipe, a pharmakon, a witches' brew?. (Ross, *IR*, 271)...

What of these endless askings and their tellings?...

Within truth we know an ideality that allows for and demands endless askings expressing and circulating its ideality, the ideality of truth, always present as saying, telling, gathering, assembling, and as error and untruth. (Ross, *GTGG*, 197)...

This ideality is cherishment, the infinite call from everywhere and every thing toward endless enchantments. The endless enchantments of truth and the endless truths of enchantment...

In the name of endless askings let us interrupt the ideality of truth with another critique of science and scientific rationality. I mean of course sciences and scientific rationalities, for there is always more than one. If there be one, if reason be one, there must be more, *plus d'un*.

> For this will be our hypothesis or rather our bias: *there is more than one of them, there must be more than one of them.* (Derrida, *SM*, 13).

> There is then *some spirit*. Spirits. And *one must* reckon with them. One cannot not have to, one must not not be able to reckon with them, which are more than one: the *more than one/no more one* ["le *plus d'un*"]. (xx)

Enchantment is this *plus d'un*. Always more than one, than any one, than itself. Always an other.

In interruption, then, here is another critique of science in the name of its enchantments. Beginning with another view of enchantment:

> Enchantment is a fascinating spell that takes over consciousness, a state of feeling that immerses the soul in dreamy reverie or fearful anxiety. You walk into a sun-drenched field in a forest and feel the wonder of that magic circle. You stumble upon a glorious waterfall, gaze at the immensely distant stars, float naked in a hot springs. You fall in love and are captivated by your lover's charms. You are possessed by a vision of a successful career, a brilliant invention, a dazzling work of art, a passionate determination. Enchantment brings life-enhancing ecstasy, and the soul demands it, thrusting us into reverence, adventure, dance, drink, or rebellion. The heart cannot survive without enchantment's nourishment. Quests to feast at that banquet drive us to passionate impulses, including fascinations with technologies.
>
> Like a wizard's spell in a folktale, enchantment can also be destructive, seizing us with murderous jealousy, furious rage, deep disappointment, defensive fear, foolish denial, or exaggerated suspicion. It can cloud judgment and wreak havoc. (Lee Bailey, *ET*, 1)

> As mortal beings, we cannot be free of enchantments. There can be no non-enchantment, since all thought, even from the deepest sources, comes through earthly imaginative forms and the brain's desires, as basic as bodily survival and as refined as an elegant symphony. The goal is to free ourselves from the destructive and crude passions so we can flourish in the garden of the deepest, truest, most refined enchantments. (4)

And another, perhaps without dreams of the deepest, truest enchantments, yet in other gardens and landscapes:

> As a consumer, you can do many things today that you could not do several decades ago, including

> Shopping in an immense, brightly lit, colorful mall with several hundred shops many of them part of well-known chains and with literally millions of goods and services from which to choose.
>
> Spending a day or more in an even bigger and more dazzling mega-mall that encompasses not only shops but also an amusement park.
>
> Gambling the day (and night!) away in a casino that not only is an enormous hotel but also includes a shopping mall and an amusement park on the grounds of the complex.
>
> Whiling away a week on a deluxe, 100,000-ton cruise ship that offers the expanse of the sea and the beauty of tropical islands and also hotel-like facilities, a casino, a mall, a health spa, amusements, and many other places to spend money.
>
> Eating in a "theme" restaurant, part of an upscale chain, where the setting, the accoutrements, the staff, and the food bring to mind a tropical rain forest or the world of rock music.
>
> Vacationing at a theme park where the restaurants and everything else—attractions, costumes, employees' utterances—portray such themes as life in the future, life in other parts of the world, or animals of the world.
>
> Wandering about for a week, or more, in a "landscape of consumption" such as Pigeon Forge, Tennessee, or the Las Vegas Strip that encompasses a number of cathedrals of consumption.

A revolutionary change has occurred in the places in which we consume goods and services, and it has had a profound effect not only on the nature of consumption but also on social life. (George Ritzer, *EDW*, ix)

The new means of consumption can be seen as "cathedrals of consumption"—that is, they have an enchanted, sometimes even sacred, religious character. To attract ever-larger numbers of consumers, such cathedrals of consumption offer increasingly magical, fantastic, and enchanted settings in which to consume. (7)

it is also important to examine landscapes of consumption, or geographic areas that encompass two, or more, cathedrals of consumption. Just as we have witnessed revolutionary new developments in the cathedrals of consumption, we have seen dramatic changes in the immediate geographic areas that encompass them. (149)

Bailey insists that our need—our fate requires it—is to choose the better enchantments from the worse. If there be such. Ritzer wonders at the multiplication of enchantments. The world is full of enchantments in the most disenchanted places, disenchantment is a myth.

Bailey understands the earth as full of enchantments because we are enchanted, because our mortality brings us enchantments, because everything we encounter is surrounded by passions, desires, impulses, dreams, including things to make and buy and consume. The earth is enchanted because things enchant us.

> Once upon a time the world was filled with enchantments, many of them beautiful and harmonious, such as a wondrous sense of participating in nature guided by invisible spirits. But some were destructive, such as the ancient fears that drove tribes to bloody sacrifices. Religions were the homes of many of these negative enchantments, so discrediting religion was a goal of scientific and technological progress in order to clear the way for new foundations for thought. We can be glad that many of these ancient enchantments have been discredited and the horizons of knowledge have expanded. Today, many fervently believe that we have removed all enchantments, but we have not. They are simply different, now located in technologies, and they still have a powerful effect on us, including the demand for sacrifice. (Bailey, *ET,* 6)

The earth is filled with enchantments, we are driven by enchantments to enchantments, yet our time insists on its disenchantments.

> After millions of years of enchantment with the spirit nyads in rivers, dragons in mountains, ancestors in the stars, and gods throwing thunderbolts, it seems that humanity has, in a few remarkable centuries, shoved aside this world of transcendent wonder. Industrial societies, it seems, have rapidly replaced it with an awesome, immense surge in technological power held in human hands, from new medicines and computers to nuclear weapons and space travel.
>
> Since the European Renaissance, the traditional history goes, one religious and mythic belief after another fell before the logic of humanistic, rational, and technological discoveries that reshaped the world from superstitious dogmatism into a cultural world of enlightened freedom and technological wonders. (6–7)
>
> Strictly rational, analytical thought built on the metaphysics of a disenchanted world that has succeeded in building tech-

> nologies and sees them as determinative is not the best mode of consciousness for understanding its own deeper cultural context. Technical consciousness cannot see outside of its own self-imposed boundaries, so it is incapable of solving its deepest problems. Reason is necessary but inadequate, for logic and technological fixes are insufficient. An entirely new consciousness is needed. Imagination is not to be brushed aside as subjective, romantic sentiment. Rather, enchantments necessarily pervade and feed the heart of technological culture. There is no technical thought without enchantment because technological culture is teeming with dreams, visions, hopes, goals, expectations, and imaginative premises. Awakening to this realm will require a radical shift in consciousness. (16–7)

I do not believe that we are the sources of enchantment. I do not believe we can choose the better enchantments from the worse: enchantments remain dangerous, risky, uncontrollable. I believe that choosing as if we can choose, as if we can know how to choose, belongs to disenchantment. Enchantment is beyond choice. We cannot choose and yet we must. We cannot choose reason over unreason, science over other knowledges, the deepest, truest, most refined enchantments from the shallow, false, and coarse. We cannot choose and yet we must and yet we do. The choices we make must be imbued with the impossibility of the choice, the transportations and transgressions of enchantment, the ways in which enchantment exceeds every choice including itself, including every account of the source of enchantment, and every account of rational disenchantment.

We are told repeatedly that we must choose, reason over magic, enchantment over disenchantment, better enchantments over worse. A radical shift in consciousness is another choice. Against this way of thinking, I imagine enchantment as refusing every binary, including these. Bailey rejects binary thinking, yet he reintroduces it between enchantment and disenchantment. Let us reject this binary as belonging to disenchantment, reject every binary as disenchanted without reinstating nonbinariness as better, not even as enchantment.

Such an enchantment comes back to deneutralize science's objectivity.

> Technology does not inhabit a neutral world of pure space, time, causation, and reason. Rather, technology's lifeworld is fully imbued with imagination, purpose, ethics, motivation, and meaning. Technologies are embodiments of imaginative,

> collective desires as much as utilitarian, rational designs—not just fact, but fascination. (18)

Sciences do not inhabit a neutral world of pure space, time, causation, and reason. Their lifeworlds are imbued with imagination, purpose, ethics, motivation, and meaning. Sciences are embodiments of imaginative, collective desires as much as utilitarian, rational designs—not just facts, but fascinations...

Not just fact, not just objectivity, not just rationality, but fascination, enchantment, imagination: all beyond the bounds of knowledge, truth, accountability. The enchanted earth is beyond bounds. Enchanted reason is beyond limits. Disenchanted reason insists on limits.

> Some say that each culture, including ours, is indoctrinated with a kind of hypnosis, an unconscious enchantment that prevents its members from accepting the reality of "unthinkable" phenomena outside its worldview. I will argue what to such people is "unthinkable": that the subject/object dichotomy itself is an enchanted, dangerously inadequate description of the foundation of the technological worldview, for it has all along been displaced by being constantly bridged and conjoined by a more primordial ontological union, like a wound that heals from below. (18)

I insist that every disenchantment, and every disenchanted view—of enchantment or of disenchantment—is enchanted; that below, or above, or displaced, or bridged, or conjoined, or interrupted, torn apart, and fragmented is a more primordial enchantment that knows nothing of union or above and below, or for that matter of healing and wounding. Enchantment is more than any, more than itself, refuses every boundary by whatever means it can devise: askings, tellings, stories, myths, magic, or science, technology, and reason themselves.

> Behind the bastion of reason lurks a zoo full of passions, desires, and enchantments, barely disguised by conventional consciousness. These unthinkable dynamics are numerous and beyond adequate description. They have endless names, such as obsessions, fascinations, crazes, fetishes, fixations, phobias, and so forth.
>
> Our machines are products of numerous unthinkable enchantments that use reason to fill passionate needs. The disenchanted, neutral world itself is not a factual reality or even a rational principle but a highly imaginative value, a mythic image promoted by industrial culture. (18–9)

In reason's disenchantments lurks a zoo of passions desires enchantments undisguised by consciousness. These unthinkable transgressions are beyond accounting and description. With endless names. Stories myths expressions obsessions fascinations crazes fetishes fixations phobias and more. Fairies wizards hobgoblins...

Fascinations charms captivations mystiques trances wizardries sorceries magics. All science...

> The conscious part of science is what most scientists would insist is all there is to science. [But] the unconscious parts of the mind of science emerge as fantasies and obsessions shared by scientists in these fields. Science is the product of the unconscious sources of imagination and introspection as much as it is the product of a set of rules. Science engages the whole mind of each scientist, both the conscious and the unconscious parts; fears, fantasies, dreams, and memories are as important to a scientist as any measurement or model. (Robert Pollack, *MM*, 58, 75; quoted in Bailey, *ET*, 25)

The conscious part, the rational part, the arguments, documentation, experiments, sources—all the academic and disciplinary paraphernalia—are but visible disenchanted fragments of a concatenation of scraps and pieces and a cacophony of noises and sounds.

> "Magic" in a scientific world is interpreted as a peripheral, harmless entertainment enacted by stage performers doing explainable tricks. But even materialistic science and technology are cloaked with the mantle of magic. Electricity, speedy vehicles, dramatic communications technologies, and supersonic flight embody many of the dreams of magic. Science and technology have not despiritualized the world nearly as much as we think, for they have enacted dreams such as flight.
>
> When we look at the large gaps in our knowledge, unexplained aberrations, and rapid changes in quantum physics, we need not readily accept the claim of the universal explanatory power of science. Most people still imagine the world in a mechanical, materialistic way that has been outmoded by new relativity and quantum theories in physics. Large gaps remain in the lag between those theories and daily life. The dance of energy that holds the world together is an overwhelming mystery. We know only a useful fragment. (39)

Mystery is another name for enchantment—in this context let us say an epistemological name, setting aside the sacred mysteries. Or let us say that mystery is the epistemic part of enchantment—truth's enchanted fragments. Enchantment stretches, multiplies, fragments, disperses in all directions, askings and tellings in and beyond knowing, science, and truth. All sorts of names are invented to describe the discredited fragments that science and its colleagues hold at bay. Mysticism is one of these names.

> "Magical," "mythic," "hypnotic," "mystical"—these are hardly expected descriptions of science and technology, but these words express a new layer of understanding reason as part of human culture, with all its passions, beneath the sophisticated rational analysis. The imaginative and hypnotic dimension of thought is so fundamental that there is no question of eliminating it as such. It has always been there. The question is what quality of depth and mystery will prevail and command our faith? (40)

The disenchanted world is infinite, but does not express infinite infinities. In this way it can deny that we know everything, but not that our knowledge might be inexhaustible or that the world is enchanted. Enchantment is infinitely infinite, each part of the whole is infinite while the whole itself is nothing. We desire in truth to have truth, as if it could be had. Yet desire and truth are inexhaustible, enchanted in infinitely enchanted ways. Including science.

Science as we know it is an inexhaustible response to the inexhaustible desire for truth. Science is one of the ways in which we are immeasurably exposed to the earth's abundance, the teeming abundance of life in every drop, the worlds in every world, the play of forces throughout nature, and more. If we have lost something of the awe we might feel before the olympian gods, we have gained something of awe before the fecundity of things. It is science's task to reveal something of the earth's abundance as truth. (Ross, *GTGG*, 198)...

Yet that task has imposed constraints on the scope of science. The ideality of the task to gather and show the world's truths has imposed restrictions on the possibilities of science. Only this method, some say, shows us truth, the ideality of method, of science. One route, then, to the ideality of truth leads to disenchantment and the reign of scientific truth, instituting its overweening authority, excluding everything that is not science, every possibility of truth that does not conform to the rule of science.

The other route toward scientific truth recalls the inexhaustible debt that truth imposes on science to seek ever more hidden, forgotten, obscured truths, to pursue the very small and the very large, but especially those truths covered over by science's authority and scientific practices.

The earth's abundance promotes the abundance of science and more abundance, more truths than any science, any institution of sciences, can gather in any place. In this extreme sense, science interrupts the gathering of truth in any one place, including that of science's authority. An anarchistic, enchanted science returns to resist the rules that grant it authority, not against the truth of science but against the excesses of its authority, the reign of its disenchantments. (Ross, *GTGG*, 198)...

What rationality might resist the rules that grant it authority? What would be an anarchistic science, an enchanted knowledge? At least the following: a reason without rules that designate its authority: rules that might make it more efficacious at a certain time and place, perhaps, but not rules that define its might. A science imbued with the modality of *I wish I might*, of *as if* and *perhaps*, but not one that would be mighty. A science that takes for granted the enchantments of the world, the subtle, invisible, transitory, strange and unfamiliar events and creations of the natural world that exceed every scientific truth and expectation. A science whose knowledge and reliability—the truths of science—are profoundly relational, transpiring among scientists, in other social relations, and between humanity and what it would know, the natural and human worlds. Here other people belong to science as active members; the scientific community is open, not closed; creatures and things to be known look back, touch back, are active in the ways they play a role in scientific knowledge. Every truth of science is hypothetical and mobile, every asking and telling wanders through endless relations and communities, endless activities and agencies, endless inscribings and reinscribings, every image proliferates endlessly. This is the enchantment of the world of science, its enchantments and the enchantments of the activities of the living things that a disenchanted science knows as dead.

The gathering of being in abundance as truth emerges in inexhaustible debt to seek to know to respond beyond every limit. Truth emerges within our exposure to others within the touch of others upon our skins and of others touching each other, inexhaustible exposure and desire. Truth calls from within the gift of exposure within a desire and movement toward things of the earth that goes beyond every established limit. Truth gathers in being as the limits that constitute truth's enchantments, moved by desire toward a responsiveness beyond every limit. (Ross, *GTGG*, 201)...

Truth is the gathering of being in the exposure of things to each other, inexhaustible exposure and debt beyond any given touch, any limits. Relation to the other, the asking and telling of the good, is touch touching the other in its skin reaching toward its depths a touch beyond the revelation of any touch a touch beyond the limits known as exposure. This limitless touch is the exposure known as truth, gathering and interruption. (202)

Some guidelines to enchanted truth as given from the good, anarchistic guidelines to the gift of truth, expressive of and resistant to their disenchantment.[9]

> 1. We find ourselves as individuals who belong to many different kinds, mixed kinds, kinds belonging to other kinds, by birth, by history, by blood, by choice, and by the activities and representations of others. This is our condition, our abundance, the abundance of the earth. We find ourselves surrounded by, touching, working for the sake of many different individuals and kinds, which we constitute by our activities and representations, and by which we and they constitute who we are, as human and as individual. To be is to be individual among kinds, individual in virtue of complex and mobile kindred relations. Our relation to knowledge and truth is a relation to kinds, heterogeneous kinds to which we may belong, other kinds in our proximity to which we know we will never belong. Truth gathers in the limitless abundance of heterogeneous kinds, nature's general economy; truth gathers its authority in restricted economy. Individuals and kinds circulate together in nature's general economy, all included, gathered under the curse of exclusion.
>
> 2. Truth gathers in nature's abundance. In its plenitude nature calls to us in endless desire to pursue its truth. It follows that everything matters in truth, everything is inexhaustibly, heterogeneously relevant, every individual thing and every kind. Everything matters in truth beyond any gathering. Everything in the earth touches others in inexhaustible ways, Everything responds beyond any gathering. To revere, to know, the truth of things is to know that they pursue their own truths and bear a debt, an obligation, to respond to that pursuit in endless exposure, for their own sake and the sake of others, for the sake of something otherwise, with three qualifications.
>
> 3. (a) They may not know their own truth, though nothing, no one else can know it better. The good resists the better and worse of truth. (b) Such a truth, one's own proper truth, is multiple, heterogeneous, impure, bound to others face to face, constituted by memberships, practices, representations, and mobilities, heterogeneous beyond any gathering in any place. (c) The kinds of the earth, human and other kinds, spiders, frogs, and bats, with their truths, circulate everywhere in nature in fourfold relations: constituted by their members, constituting their

members' identities, in virtue of their mobilities and circulations, related heterogeneously; touching each other in every place, exposed to each other as individuals and kinds in multiple, heterogeneous ways, exposed to, touching others for their sake, called by something beyond measure.

It follows that:

4. The good gives rise in time to the impossibility of knowing the truth of all strange and heterogeneous things together, and to the impossibility of any measure of fulfillment, the impossibility of achieving truth, holding it in place, within the circulation of countless truths in restricted places. Our responsibility in truth, toward truth, is to gather things together with limitless care in truth joined with limitless resistance to the authority of any gathering. The institution of truth and knowledge betrays knowledge and truth, mourning for endless disasters.

5. Among creatures who can know their truth, they must know it for themselves, exposed to, touching others in abundance, resisting every truthful authority. None can know the truth of another with authority, especially another individual and kind; no one can authorize the truth for another, especially not the heterogeneous truths of others, foreigners and strangers. Imposing the authority of truth on others brings about endless disaster.

6. Nothing can justify the sacrifice of any individual and kind or its truths to others' truth, of any kind, women, children, animals, Jews, not even the AIDS or smallpox virus. Nothing can justify the destruction of an individual and kind or its truths in the march of history. Yet history is the recurrence of such catastrophes. Truth gathers in memories of endless disasters.

7. In the places where we compose ourself and others in proximity, exposed in face and touch, we may know our truths to whatever extent they are knowable and we may hope to ask and tell the truths of others, touched by others. Especially, we bear a debt to ask and tell of the weight of our injustices in the struggle for truth.

8. Truth gathers within a double debt, each unlimited in its exposure: to institute truth beyond the reach of any authority, and to challenge the institution of every authority in the name of truth. Our utmost desire in truth, given from the good, must be to gather truth without authority, a profoundly anarchistic truth whose sovereignty is nothing, whose truth is the curse, whose work is disaster, whose origin is enchantment. This asking and telling beyond authority always institutes sovereign authority, in the name of truth, desiring its own destruction in the promulgation of truth.

> 9. Heterogeneity works face to face, in proximity and touch, arising in the wounding and joy of love, in unbounded desire, passing away into the general economy of goods, circulating everywhere. Heterogeneity complicates the identity of every kind in proximity, the indefiniteness and impurity of every truth. Authority, sovereignty, and truth all do their work upon bodies, work through representation upon material and embodied things. Truth gathers in the touch of flesh as desire, reaching beyond itself, exposed in flesh and bodies beyond any limits. The body of truth and desire circulates in the exposure of embodied touch. The will to truth is the body of truth.
>
> 10. Abundant truth is strange in the double sense that familiar truth is always touched by strangeness and that the asking and telling of truth gathers friends and strangers together in place. Gathering the good bears the endless debt to gather and to know the impossibility of gathering friends and strangers together in truth. (207–10)

Do you remember?[10]—

An enchanted ethics regards every thing, complex, order, trait, ingredient, as ethical, inexhaustible beyond accounting...

As cherishment...

And now—

An enchanted science regards every thing, complex, order, trait, ingredient, as inexhaustibly truthful beyond accounting...

As cherishment...

Let us then think of evolutionary biology in a different way, as opening the inexhaustible wonders and enchantments of the world to us from within themselves, without external authority. In an ethical voice.

Everything matters beyond accounting. Every truth calls beyond measure...

The world is abundant in every thing and place, living and dead. Evolutionary and ecological theories offer ways of thinking about abundance responsive to the diversity of living creatures. In responding to their surroundings, they adapt and change in myriad ways, frequently surprisingly and unpredictably. In the world of evolutionary biology, the mechanism is frequently understood as random, the adaptive advantage as highly specific. Both of these understandings regulate the abundance—perhaps unduly. Might there be mechanisms other than random genetic modifications? Might selective advantage be conferred in subtle and complex ways?

Selective adaptation offers diverse ways in which random mutations can produce effective, stable forms. It does so at the expense of clear accounts of the generating transformations. This lack of accountability in evolutionary explanations is in no way a liability. To the contrary, it offers a more powerful way of understanding the abundance of life forms than any more determinate mechanism can provide. Even so, recent developments in evolutionary science suggest that a variety of mechanisms supplement those of genetic mutation without curtailing the abundance. Moreover, adaptive advantages are themselves abundant, and lend themselves to askings that are immensely productive at some levels and unaccountable at others. I am as sure as I can be of anything that language, thinking (including but not restricted to reason: argument, analysis, distinctions, oppositions, all the panoply of binary logic; story telling, image construction, gestures and performances), expression, performance, telling, are highly adaptive, but I am also dubious that any of these can be separated sharply from the others and adaptive on their own. Much depends on how *adaptive* and *advantage* are understood, once given the complexity of human social and cultural conditions.

With respect to the adaptive mechanisms, then:

> Our basic claim is that biological thinking about heredity and evolution is undergoing a revolutionary change. What is emerging is a new synthesis, which challenges the gene-centered version of neo-Darwinism that has dominated biological thought for the last fifty years.
> We will be arguing that
>
> > there is more to heredity than genes;
> > some hereditary variations are nonrandom in origin;
> > some acquired information is inherited;
> > evolutionary change can result from instruction as well as selection.
>
> Molecular biology has shown that many of the old assumptions about the genetic system, which is the basis of present-day neo-Darwinian theory, are incorrect. It has also shown that cells can transmit information to daughter cells through non-DNA (epigenetic) inheritance. This means that all organisms have at least two systems of heredity. In addition, many animals transmit information to others by behavioral means, which gives them a third heredity system. And we humans have a fourth, because symbol-based inheritance, particularly language, plays a substantial role in our evolution. It is therefore quite wrong to think about heredity and evolution solely in terms of the genetic system. Epigenetic, behavioral, and symbolic inheritance also

> provide variation on which natural selection can act. (Jablonka and Lamb, *EFD*, 1)

Such a view is controversial, but it is important to understand such controversiality as lending support to uncertainty and unaccountability without undercutting evolutionary science or any other scientific understanding. What we understand by science and scientific explanation becomes more complex, less accountable, through time. Science evolves, less perhaps at the DNA level—though that should not be excluded—and more at other levels. That is one of the striking ways in which evolutionary and ecological thinking pertain to enchantment. The ways in which such thinking can explain science (not to mention philosophy, art, religion, narrative, storytelling) render it more abundant and less accountable.

The more we know the more we ask the more asking the more telling the more telling the more understanding the more understanding the less accountable are things science knowledge truth enchant the world through disenchantment...

We live for truth we live in truth truth offers the enchantments of the world the enchantments of all things living and dead. This truth enchanted truth belongs to hobgoblins and fairies witches and demons lesser and greater gods. It belongs to them because it belongs to all things, in their nooks and crannies, in their caesuras, the breaks and ruptures that compose their bodies, that interrupt their minds and spirits. The world is full of wonder, its wonder and ours, we wonder at the wonders of the earth, the enchantments of the things that surprise us and the things that have ceased to surprise us because we have disenchanted them. Disenchantment science academic knowledge familiar practices all are miracles strange and wonderful in the ways in which we have made them familiar and ordinary...

The most ordinary things are miraculous when looked at closely, obliquely, in the light of poetry and art, in the eyes of painters and dreamers including scientists. The greatest miracle and wonder by far is that they are ordinary, enchanted in their ordinariness. Everydayness is a wonder, that anything could become ordinary, everyday, that we could frame it so as to dim its splendors, obscure its radiances, block its surprises. And still it surprises, astonishes, astounds us when we drop our guard. And so we ask.

Among the enchantments of enchantment are the disenchantments of the world. Among the enchantments are the limits of reason, the miracles of meaning, the wonders of knowing, the tellings of askings. That things should mean, that we can ask and tell, that reason can light up the darkness, all are enchanted, all are enchanting...

Bringing us to another telling, of un-forgetting and re-membering, another saying of asking and telling:

The light that brings the image back to memory transfigures distorts obscures reveals it. The image can never be what it is without transfiguration without dis-appearance. Remembering is re-membering transformation transsubstantiation re-presents the gifts of the earth in other modalities times places keeps them on the move. The volatility of memory is its reality transformation truth, its transsubstantiation its preservation. (Ross, *U*, 10)...

Re-membering is for-getting forgetting is remembering its truth is untruth the untruth of truth is forgotten the forgetting of memory the betrayal of exposition. Nothing appears nothing is recalled revealed except in exposition as if in language except as image. The unearthing of expression takes place as the unforgetting of the image. The image proliferates the exposition betrays the recollection transfigures. Transcendence transfiguration transformation are the remembrances of memory, its forgettings in the modalities of perhaps and as if. (10)...

Something is always forgotten, we can never remember or know everything, time and history are forgettings; we desire to know, to remember, with such a will that we forget the fascination of unforgetting even as we are fascinated by it; forgetting is constitutive of being always everywhere past present future here and elsewhere. In this forgetting everything is unforgotten, returning differently. Forgetting proliferates everywhere as remembering and unforgetting. (10–1)...

Unforgetting is itself forgotten, and in the caesura of this second forgetting everything comes back as if it were remembered. Everything comes back to truth beyond any remembering and forgetting, in the caesura of as if and perhaps. (26)...

To unforget is to return from forgetting to re-member nothing as if it were anything to interrupt oblivion with expression to re-call the sound of silence and unearth the depths of loss. Memory is another matter. Perhaps. Memory appears as if it were something fixed by the past elusive but fully present. If anything can be fully present. Unforgetting passes through the caesura of absence on the way to an other presence. (43)...

What kind of knowledge might be provided by a forgotten memory? Not the assurance of presence not retention as if ready to hand. Perhaps the inassurance of presence or the assurance of absence as well as presence perhaps a retention that is always on the edge of loss. Perhaps the subject of memory is not of time as held and fixed but always as if being lost always as if disappearing forgetting as this losing. Not as if losing what might be retained as the disappearance of what has appeared or might reappear but loss and disappearance as the asking and telling of being and truth. (52–3)...

What kind of knowledge would this be? What kind of truth or recollection? Not a knowledge that we can be certain can be known again but one on the verge of disappearance transformation creation transfiguration interruption. Not a recollection of an earlier presence but the invention of a disparity in the disparition of the collection. (53)...

To bear witness... to what? What is it to bear witness? To remember to write to speak to tell perhaps to unforget? In witness to what is constitutively forgotten as if witnessing were disconstitutively unforgetting as if perhaps by unremembering?. (61)...

As if unremembering were... what? Perhaps we cannot say but ask. Perhaps we can tell it in relation to injustice and disaster. What we are to remember perhaps to unforget is the trauma that constitutes our selves kin and kind. As if we could forget. (61)...

The disaster is the forgotten beyond remembering and forgetting. Witnessing is asking and telling beyond forgetting and remembering. Let us go under in affirmation and wonder to the disaster that allows us to be. Let us go under in disaster to the wonder and affirmation whose being we are...

Chapter 3

The Good Enchanting

The good is not a thing, or event, or being; does not belong to human beings; and is not God—though many have spoken of the good in terms of the sacred or divine. It is neither in this world nor out, inhabits no immanent or transcendent place, but is giving in abundance, beyond having, the unlimit of every limit and the displacement of every place, exposing each creature and thing to others. The good is not a category, does not oppose the bad or war with evil, but interrupts the authority of judgment. The good is not good opposed to bad, right opposed to wrong, justice opposed to injustice. It expresses what is priceless, irreplaceable, beautiful in local, contingent, heterogeneous things and kinds, worth cherishing throughout nature, all born in immeasurable exposure to others. It haunts the limits of individuals in their identities and relations and of the kinds and gatherings of the earth, belongs to nature everywhere, composing the circulation of goods beyond having. The good is enchanted and enchanting. (Ross, *GBGA*, 2)

The earth calls in every time and place from every place in every time from every ingredient small and large near and far. Calling is endless enchantment inexhaustible asking telling ecological transmigration...

Calling is exposition... exposure expression ecology asking telling aisthēsis mimēsis poiēsis catachrēsis technē image aesthetics beauty art unearthing revelation disclosure calling giving interrupting betraying...

Calling is enchanting, expressing beyond accounting, multiplying beyond division. As if perhaps ~~not~~ beyond.[1] *Calling is ethical, responding beyond asking, responsive beyond telling, caring beyond care, com-*

passionate beyond compassion. The beyond in every place is the endless call to its enchantments. As if perhaps ~~not~~ beyond...

Expressivity and responsivity are the enchantments of the earth asking telling beyond any question answer caring loving beyond care and love. Cherishment beyond cherishment compassion beyond compassion love beyond love ethics beyond ethics enchanting beyond enchantments. As if perhaps ~~not~~ beyond...

Cherishment calls from the good, the good is nothing, nothing but ethical, nothing but calling; asking, telling, expressing, responding, enchanting; as if ~~nothing~~; imperative beyond command, urgent beyond the moment, passive beyond passivity, passionate beyond feeling, enchanting as if perhaps ~~not~~ beyond. Everything is expressive, everything matters, everything is inexhaustible, infinite in its ways, as if ~~not~~ perhaps beyond accounting. Nothing can be more ethical, more demanding, more impossible, more enchanting...

Cherishment is the endless inexhaustible impossible call of the earth's enchantments in every place, from every ingredient, to what we will never know or be, asking telling us to be and know. The finite realization of the inexhaustible call of cherishment is sacrifice, to take the place of another, to usurp a space a life instead of another, to be to ask to tell to choose. Choosing is never good, always cruel, and still we choose, and still we must, and in choosing we affirm in joy and love the call of cherishment, the enchantments of the earth. Sacrifice answers to the call of cherishment under the name of plenishment in infinite betrayal...

Plenishment is the endless responsivity in the earth that answers to the inexhaustible expressivity of the call to cherishment, echoing in every enchanting place from every ingredient every thing toward an unknown proliferation of images, beginnings and endings, askings and tellings, endlessly betraying, endlessly betrayed. Cherishment is asking, expressivity and calling; plenishment is telling, expressivity and responsivity. Nothing is more ethical this is ethicality itself. Nothing is more truthful this is truth itself. Nothing is more enchanted this is enchantment enchanting itself. As if ~~not~~ perhaps beyond...

Cherishment calls from the good as general economy. beyond accounting. Sacrifice responds as restricted economy, accounting for everything.[2] Enchantment calls from the good as cherishment. Disenchantment responds as sacrifice. Disenchantment betrays enchantment—reveals it in violation, desecration.

Plenishment responds in the caesura between cherishment and sacrifice, in the betrayal between enchantment and disenchantment, in endless expressivity, responsivity, exposition: exposure, expression, calling, giving, asking, telling.

Plenishment is the enchantment of disenchantment, in betrayal...

Others call it impossible, excessive, the impossible, the excessive. The good, responsibility, ethics, the calling of the good beyond any call, any hearing, any exposition, exceeds every realization.

> Responsibility carries within it, and must do so, an essential excessiveness. It regulates itself neither on the principle of reason nor on any sort of accountancy. (Derrida, *EW*, 272)
>
> I repeat: responsibility is excessive or it is not a responsibility. A limited, measured, calculable, rationally distributed responsibility is already the becoming-right of morality; it is at times also, in the best hypothesis, the dream of every good conscience, in the worst hypothesis, of the petty or grand inquisitors. (286)
>
> The origin of the call that comes from nowhere, an origin in any case that is not yet a divine or human "subject," institutes a responsibility that is to be found at the root of all ulterior responsibilities (moral, juridical, political), and of every categorical imperative. Something of this call of the other must remain nonreappropriable, nonsubjectivable, and in a certain way nonidentifiable, a sheer supposition, so as to remain *other*, a *singular* call to response or to responsibility. (276)

Something of this call of and from the other must remain nonreappropriable, nonidentifiable, must remain *other*, a singular asking for response or responsibility. At the heart of the world lie two enchantments, expressivity and responsivity, calling beyond calling, from and of and toward the other in betrayal. In the caesuras of asking and telling.

> It would be easy to show that a hospitality without reserve is the impossible itself, and that this *condition of possibility* of the event is also its *condition of impossibility*. But it would be just as easy to show that without this experience of the impossible, one might as well give up on both justice and the event. (Derrida, *SM*, 65)[3]

It is impossible, accomplishing the good is impossible, the good is nothing, nothing to accomplish, empty of everything including itself, empty beyond emptiness, full beyond fullness. In this way cherishment is beyond being, beyond having, beyond ethics, beyond binaries, as if betrayed beyond itself. Perhaps.

As if betrayed beyond accounting. As if impossible beyond performing. As if enchanting beyond enchantment. As if ~~not~~ beyond...

Perhaps...

As calling. The good calls, calling calls, the earth rings, ringing rings out, peals, solicits, asks, tells. The expressivity of the earth, of each ingredient among the others, of and from the others, is asking from the good as ethical beyond ethics. Cherishment calls from the other—and the others—to respond beyond response. The calling is from the good against neutrality. The calling of cherishment from the good echoes the enchanting of things against the neutrality of the earth. In the caesura.

The calling of the good echoes multiple reverberations. Heidegger's call (Ruf) of conscience, the disclosedness of Dasein as constituted by state-of-mind, understanding, falling, and discourse. Another example is saying in Levinas, understood as interruption, exposure, and proximity. The caesura that breaks the hold of the living present. A third is the debt in memory of the injustices that Anaximander says compose the ordinance of time. A fourth is the call from nowhere that must remain nonreappropriable, nonsubjectivable, and nonidentifiable to mark the nowhere and nothing in particular of the other. Calling is from nowhere, toward nothing, as if betrayed beyond everything and anything. As ethics, from the good, the expressivity of the ingredients of the earth in their enchantments. (Ross, *GPHG*, 255–6)...

A profusion of other reverberations: the call of music, echoes of wind and rain, movements of celestial spheres, timbres of bodies touching; sounds of life; tones of voices and instruments; songs, carols, melodies, cries, shouts and yells; screams bellows roars, screeches shrieks of animals and birds; debts and obligations, demands to act, to strive, brought by necessity to performances, to deeds, summoned for the sake of something beyond show; events promised, heralded, greeted, announced; being taken to task, obligated indebted evoked cited served by decree under law, in the name of judgment; naming and designation, questioning and interrogation, being asked to respond; community, calls to mingle and gather, echoing the assembling of being and language as dissembling; calling to augur, foretell, most of all, perhaps, to prophesy and to divine—despite the death of God; calling to work, to task, to art, to labor, to master, demanding knowledge, skill, craft, technē, and more, always more, poiēsis or beauty; callers, those who call out, those who call to enter—guests, visitors, or strangers; another memory of gathering and community; repeated interruptions: welcoming, giving, generosity; expression, bodies squeezing, saying, meaning, touching, evoking responsiveness to touch, a responsivity known to human beings as responsibility in the name of the good, where the good gives and calls but is nothing, no thing, no being; giving and calling as interruption and betrayal. As asking and telling. As mimēsis. In enchantment. (256)...

The calling of the good is exposition, exposure and expression, corporeal movements and enchantments, betraying neutrality.

The calling of the good is the enchanting of the earth and its ingredients. The ingredients of the earth call out, here I am, here we are, we are enchanting, we are given, we give, we ask, tell me your responses, give me your cherishment...

Let us give ourselves an ethic of inclusion, a responsibility toward the good everywhere, a cherishment of heterogeneous creatures and things throughout human life and nature. An ethic of difference, of heterogenous, enchanted creatures and things, enchanting heterogenous ingredients.

An ethic of inclusion bequeaths an archaic memory of the impossibility of caring for all things together in a harmony in which none are harmed. Heterogeneous ingredients come together by selection and exclusion. To live in memory of cherishment is to experience endless joys and sorrows, fulfillments and injustices, betrayed in the name of the good. To undertake the good is to face unceasing sacrifice and loss: the deaths of some that others may live, the suffering of some that others may know joy. Sacrifice knows the enchantments of cherishment, works within the good, but never becomes sacred, never brings us to safety, never eludes asking. Sacrifice never escapes from the betrayals of injustice. Responsibility for sacrifice refuses every comfort in the name of the good. (Ross, *PE*, 1)...

Plenishment crosses cherishment and sacrifice, inhabiting their borders: inexhaustible care for heterogeneous ingredients and kinds joined with endless impossibilities of fulfillment, producing boundless possibilities of love and joy, haunted by memories of disaster. (2)...

Cherishment sacrifice plenishment speak together in an archaic voice of an inescapable call from the good that ethics can neither resist nor fulfill, expressing something enchanted and immemorial. This immemoriality is older than any law, the call of things and kinds to us from where we find ourselves together. From its enchantments, it repeatedly asks us to wonder who we are. From its memories of injustices, it repeatedly asks us to exceed ourselves in the earth, to reach out beyond ourselves to others. (2)...

Cherishment includes the heterogeneous ingredients of the earth, expresses the call of the good. Sacrifice is exclusion, the work of the good in time, divides the world into good and bad, right and wrong, excludes some that others may thrive, expresses the impossibility of accomplishing the good without betrayal. Plenishment is cherishment joined with this impossibility. An ethic of inclusion undertakes the difficult thought of cherishment and sacrifice together in plenishment, of inclusion joined with exclusion, of injustice in justice, of enchanting disenchantment. (2)...

No ethics is possible without care for the things of the earth, for every ingredient, large or small. God—many gods are needed, and more—takes care of these things, small and large, sparrow and mountain, cares for them in betrayal. Cherishment reaches out to every thing. Ethical responsibility, love and care, reach toward every ingredient, small and large, every plant in every garden, every garden in every plant. Our ethicality is to be responsive to every ingredient everywhere, our capacity to touch and to be touched, exposure to the things of the earth, an exposition, a touch that does not halt at any skin, in any place, toward any time. It does not halt but reaches, touches, extends itself toward the broken, fragmented, shattered, and lame. All enchanted.

No just life is possible in the glare of this ethics, in the demand of this imperative to respond to everything, to care for everything, to ask of everything, to make everything whole. It is impossible. Our being is permeated by injustice and betrayal. And yet the truth of this ethics, of this imperative, is that the fate and possibility of justice rests on this impossibility, on its asking, on the injustice in justice, on the betrayal of enchantment in disenchantment.

This is another way to say that justice is impossible, that we are surrounded by injustice. It is another way to mark the endlessness of injustice and of the betrayals it calls forth. Justice is betrayal, betraying and betrayed, beyond any achievement or accomplishment. This beyond is impossibility. But it is more than any possibility, more than any actuality. It is the unlimits beyond unlimit, enchantments beyond enchantment, askings beyond asking, tellings beyond telling, perhaps beyond perhaps, as if ~~not~~ beyond the exposition of injustice in justice. Justice is revealed in every injustice, reveals and betrays itself.

Enchantment is betrayal. Enchantment cannot be trusted except to betray. More enchantingly, betrayal is enchantment, and this is difficult to know, to say, to believe, to feel. It is the laughter of Zarathustra, the affirmation of *Zusage,* that while we cannot trust betrayal it betrays itself in truth, betrays its enchantments in endless ways. Betrayal is endless asking, calls for endless telling.

Plenishment is this endless asking and telling. Every thing in every place, every ingredient in every time and every place, is what it is—and more, betrays itself as itself—and more, escapes itself—as if ~~not~~ beyond. Every more and beyond is enchantment, not just magic, wizardry, prophecy, divinity. Religion has no monopoly on enchantment, and in our age is disenchanted. Disenchantment denies a beyond beyond the beyond—as if, perhaps. Disenchantment names a ~~not beyond~~ as if without betrayal—perhaps, as if enchantment had a name. Secularization would deny enchantment in the image of its disenchantments. Religion claims to own enchantment in the image of god, as if enchantment were not all images, every image, beyond any naming and any owning.

The disenchantment of the world is the claim to possess the world under a category or institution or practice—let us say again, betrayed under a given name. To own and possess the name. That is the greatest magic, to insist on a name. It is the insistence on disenchanting the name of enchantment. So let us insist in return that every name escapes itself, that every thing and every ingredient and the earth itself escapes every name including itself—including the names *escape* and *it* and *self* not to mention the name of the *name*.

The emptiness of emptiness, then, is enchanting, while emptiness itself is one of its names. Enchantment outstrips itself under any name, including *enchantment* and *emptiness*. Enchantment outstrips every asking and telling, including *enchantment, asking,* and *telling*.

In Mahāyāna Buddhism, emptiness (*sūnyatā*) is one of these names, itself empty (and non-empty).

> The emptiness of what is called "emptiness" is referred to as "the emptiness of emptiness" *(sūnyatāsûnyatā)*, and it is explained in this way for the purpose of controverting any understanding of emptiness as a[n ontological reference to] "being." (Candrakirti, *EMW*, 180)
>
> *Everything is such, not such, both such and not such, and neither such nor not such; this is the Buddha's admonition...* (Nāgārjuna, *PMW*, 269)
>
> If all this is empty, then there exists no uprising and ceasing. These imply the non-existence of the four noble truths. (326)
>
> If all this is non-empty, there exists no uprising and ceasing. These imply the non-existence of the four noble truths. (342)

Cherishment is another of these names, no better and no worse than the rest. But like emptiness it names its own outstripping, its disownership and dispossession. *As if perhaps ~~not~~ its own*. It resides in the being of each thing and ingredient beyond—*as if per-*

haps ~~not~~ beyond—every being and every ingredient, not to mention every time and place. More to the point, every time and place and ingredient and being cannot be mentioned, have no name, even as we give them a name. Every name is empty, including emptiness. The love and care we give to each thing and ingredient in its time and place—cherished themselves—are always as if perhaps ~~not~~ beyond, as if ~~not~~ out of time and place, interrupting and disrupting the hold of every identification. And it is identification—one of the names of the disenchantments of enchantment—that insists that we should be able to give anything a name, identifying as asking and telling. The name belongs to exposition, as if anything had a name, perhaps as if every name were not enchanting and empty as if ~~not~~ not beyond enchantment and emptiness.

God told Adam to name everything, the first disenchantment of the unnamed enchantments of the earth. At least in the judeochristian tradition. From that moment—if there were such, if disenchantment ever took place—being and naming belonged to exposition, not as possessions but as dispossessions. Named as possessions, as if ~~not~~ perhaps dispossessions. Affirmed as dispossessions. Celebrated as the enchantments of disenchantment.

Each thing among the others every ingredient men and women among the others circulates excessively inexhaustibly. This inexhaustible excessive circulation is cherishment. Cherishment is the cacophony of inexhaustibility the music of endless spheres among other spheres, endless tellings among endless askings. It can be heard as the rests, the remains, of the earth, we have listened to its song. This song I understand as ethical, each thing every kind is inexhaustible precious in its general circulation beyond all circulations. (Ross, *PE*, 127).

Disenchantment is sacrifice, as if it were good, as if, perhaps, it were possible to take sacrifice into one's possession, as if it were truth, as if it were not endless dispossessions. Plenishment is cherishment and sacrifice together as if, perhaps, they could not be possessed, could not be had, yet still we might live joyfully, affirmatively, in the midst of untruth and pain. Not to celebrate pain, as if it were something to possess, but to affirm the asking, the joy of dispossession, the impossibility of cherishment, the inescapability of sacrifice, the enchantments of disenchantment as if they were life itself, joy itself, as if they were enchanting love.

Cherishment is love for the enchanting things of the earth. In loving generosity...

All the others that obsess me face to face in heterogeneity express the depths of responsivity. Each of us all of us in our skins find it difficult to reach to know to care for all the others, to find our way to cherishing all the other ingredients in nature, except through face to face body to body relations with some. In cherishing the other as other I experience the insistence and impossibility of cherishing the others. Conversely, I cannot cherish any without cherishing some. Responsibility to the others imposes on me an unlimited responsibility to care for touch some in my proximity. The reach of the neighbor is everywhere in proximity. Cherishment depends on a sense of place, somewhere and everywhere, resting in place. The return to place, from elsewhere, returns us from the unlimit of plenishment to the intermediate number, in proximity, face to face. (*PE*, 132)...

The infinite dyad, the intermediate number, the caesura that restlessly rests between but does not mediate, the place where I meet the other, is right here in this place, in my skin, the place of displacement where the other's heterogeneity, the alterity of otherness, appears before me to call me out of myself, out of my place, disrupting my place. All this is cherishment, love and care for the other's otherness. All this is sacrifice, the call for me to respond to the impossibility of sharing the other's otherness. All this is plenishment, the exposition of dispossessing the good, of sacrificing sacrifice, from a love beyond all loves. All this is enchantment beyond all disenchantments, asking beyond all telling.

The plenishment that gives itself forth as an ethic of inclusion pertains to our places everywhere, at rest, in place displaced responsible everywhere, fulfilled in cherishment demanding sacrifice, selection and choice, because not all things are possible together, not all can be enchanted together. Our greatest responsibility is to refuse to undertake a destructive choice, in relation to others or ourselves, without pursuing beyond all other pursuits the possibility of plenishment. Refusing the choice and the temptation to choose. Refusing disenchantment. (188)...

An ethic of inclusion an ethic of difference an ethic of sexual and racial and other difference institutes a profound difference in how we think of ethics sexuality gender race etc., how we think of humanity nature enchanting. Perhaps. Displacing the course of oppositional thinking of exclusion that has defined Western and other thought. Not to eliminate dyadic thought but to displace it to its unlimit, to understand that the places of dyads are elsewhere as well as somewhere. Not as if to eliminate the dyads of race and gender and humanity and nature but to resist the hold of oppositional and exclusionary thinking and feeling. Rights and duties have their place, as do care and trust, local places and inexhaustible displacements. Both an ethic of care and an ethic of rights seem, in the places traditionally assigned them, not to know that their place is elsewhere. (188–9)...

An ethic of care, an ethic of rights, all ethics as we know them that judge on right and left, good and bad, are in their places, sites of possession and having, surrounded and permeated by sites of dispossession, interruption, disruption, asking, and telling. Ethics of inclusion, cherishment, sacrifice, and plenishment have no places, are here and there, nowhere and everywhere, places of interruption and transgression. All things call us, cry out to us, all things living and dead, past, present, and future, call and cry and ask not only in our responsibility, our responsivity, but in their meanings for us, their dances before us, the fairies' enchantments that call them to us out of themselves, that call us to them out of ourselves. The call is enchanted, calling is enchanting, the good is enchantment. It falls into the world as disenchantment. Whatever is in the world is disenchanted and in this way is enchanting beyond all enchantments.

Sacrifice is disenchantment. Plenishment is the sacrifice of sacrifice, the disenchantment of disenchantment, disenchantment betraying disenchantment, asking asking, enchanting enchanting. Like the emptiness of emptiness and the enchantment of enchantment, all these foldings and refoldings exceed the limits of the folds that provoke them. Enchantment exceeds its limits, interrupts the limits of disenchantment, disenchants disenchantment so as to betray its endless enchantments. As if to betray the language, the words, the images that would reveal enchantment. Impossible, still betrayed.

An ethic of difference emerges from the inexhaustibility of things and kinds, each and every enchanting creature, imposing upon us an inexhaustible responsibility face to face with each and every ingredient, in love and respect, a responsibility and care toward it as other to ourselves, heterogeneous. This inexhaustible responsibility is cherishment cherishing the inexhaustible alterity of each and every ingredient. In our face-to-face experiences we encounter wounding we impose ruin. This is sacrifice, but it bears cherishment within itself, response to the immemorial and unlimited injustice in things and ourselves. Cherishment with sacrifice together is plenishment ethical difference in work intimately obsessed by inexhaustible betrayal, employing sacrifice against sacrifice resisting neutrality. (Ross, *PE*, 238)...

An ethic of difference bears unlimited obsessive responsibility toward heterogeneity, face to face with another person or creature, other in species genus kind. Heterogeneity between genera and kinds falls repeatedly into proximity, bears the weight of immemorial injustice in proximity. (238–9)...

Ethical difference is the enchantment of the other, heterogeneously. Enchantments call to us enchantedly, ask of us in mystery, tell us to disenchant, to work, ask to us to care, to cherish, to live ethically surrounded by endless disenchantments. The calling, the asking call, is enchantment, exposition: exposure as expression, asking telling. The call, the calling, is exposition: ethical beyond ethics, cherishment beyond cherishing, sacrifice beyond sacrificing, plenishment beyond possessing. As if ~~not~~ beyond.

Calling is endless, enchantment is infinite.

Calling is giving beyond gifts, beyond having, possessing, owning, being.

Giving is asking from the good, which is nothing, nothing but enchantment, nothing perhaps but as if asking, asking perhaps as if nothing...

The enchantments of the earth call to us beyond us we are called by them beyond them beyond ourselves. This calling is enchanted is enchanting the earth calls enchantingly beyond possession having owning belonging. Enchanted things—all things—are given beyond possessing belong to no one and nothing, not even themselves. This is enchantment, it is their enchantment, to be given and giving beyond having enchanting beyond enchantment...

Enchantment, calling, and giving in this way express and expose themselves to each other and to us, are the ways in which ingredients—not just creatures, things, and kinds: also events, qualities, dreams; things that come and go—are always coming, ingredients that are nothing except coming and going, calling and giving and asking and telling, enchanted and enchanting. Calling and giving are the enchantments of things, ingredients call and give their enchantments to themselves and others, calling and giving are always beyond themselves, beyond any having.

> a gift is a thing we do not get by our own efforts. We cannot buy it; we cannot acquire it through an act of will. It is bestowed upon us. (Lewis Hyde, *G*, ix)

> The only essential is this: *the gift must always move*. There are other forms of property that stand still, that mark a boundary or resist momentum, but the gift keeps going. (Hyde, *G*, 4)

The gift keeps giving, giving keeps moving, every stasis, identification, name, every boundary resists the disruption of giving. Calling and giving speak of becoming against its neutrality, against every neutrality, cherishment evokes compassion beyond love and care.

Giving calls from the good against the neutrality of having, exposes the nonneutrality of having and the enchantment of disenchantment. Exposition is this giving, the expressivity everywhere that disrupts the contentment of owning. Against the contentment of owning—by no means as secure as its contentment requires—giving enchants beyond contentment, delights beyond ecstasy, threatens beyond danger. Always perhaps. Always asking. The giving of the earth offers its beauties as if beyond compare, its goodnesses as if beyond measure, its truths as if beyond accounting, its enchantments as if beyond disenchantment. And still it disenchants in the name of its enchantments. Still it is impossible beyond its impossibility.

> the gift is the impossible. Not impossible but *the* impossible. The very figure of the impossible. It announces itself, gives itself to be thought as the impossible. (Derrida, *GT,* 7)

> this is the impossible that seems to give itself to be thought here: These conditions of possibility of the gift (that some "one" gives some "thing" to some "one other") designate simultaneously the conditions of the impossibility of the gift. And already we could translate this into other terms: these conditions of possibility define or produce the annulment, the annihilation, the destruction of the gift. (Derrida, *GT,* 11).

We have seen something like this before in relation to hospitality.[4] Like but not the same. As hospitality is in relation to giving, similar but not the same.

The impossible is beyond possibility. Giving is beyond possessing, even in the mode of lack—as if not having, not possessing. Giving is positively impossible beyond not having, as if in the affirmation that impels it, the enchantment that fascinates it. Giving is ~~not~~ not having...

Let us imagine that calling and giving are everywhere, and everywhere impossible beyond impossibility—*the* impossible as Derrida says. Let us imagine that calling and giving are exposition: exposure, expression, asking, calling; image, aesthetics, beauty, art; calling as giving, as telling. Let us imagine that all of these, and more, are enchanting. Let us imagine that giving, generosity, hospitality are enchanting, enchanted, that enchantment is hospitality, generosity, giving, exposure and expression, things touching each other expressively, expressivity and responsivity in an ethical register. The impossibility of enchantment, giving, calling, is ethical, as asking and telling.

Let us return to the impossibility of giving as the impossible itself. This is to deny that any gift can accomplish the good or express enchantment disenchantingly. Everything is enchanted means that each is irreplaceable in its ways and those ways are inexhaustible. Enchantment calls in each place from a good beyond measure to an exposure beyond containment, evoking an asking beyond telling. The exposition beyond limit, the beyond of enchantment, must be said, expressed, exposed in a responsivity that echoes the expressivity from all things, the expressivity and responsivity that are enchantment's enchantings.

Here nothing can be had, held onto, grasped, possessed. Having, possession, property, attachment are bonds that fix the places of disenchantment against the mobilities, displacements, and becomings of enchantment. Giving and generosity are names of this dispossession in the enchanting of the good, as are cherishment and love. Cherishment and love express the impossibility of the good as task and accomplishment. Generosity and giving express the dispossessiveness of becoming in the light of the injustice everywhere in justice. Exposition and enchantment express the ways in which expressivity expresses itself beyond any expression, in which responsivity responds beyond any response, the ways in which asking and telling fold back onto themselves and unfold beyond themselves. In this way enchantment is endless exposition and betrayal, in a giving beyond having.

The letter *g* here adopts an enchanting supplementarity, in the light of giving, generosity, and gift—in the genitive, let us say.[5] Here *g* comes before the *h* of having, *g* in all its complexity. One might say in a certain mythic space, where the earth is given in an act of surprising generosity. Again as if, perhaps. A telling filled with endless asking.

> *In the beginning* was property, so it is said. In the genitive.[6] Yours, mine, ours, theirs. Claiming divine authority. Or if not the very beginning, with darkness on the face of the deep, then soon after, on the second day, with the tree yielding fruit *after its kind*; or perhaps not long after that, on the fifth day, with every living creature, every plant and beast, *after its kind*, a kind that insists on the genitive; surely soon after that, when humanity arrived on the scene, in the greatest production known to the earth, when God created man *in his own image*. The institution of owning and having comes to pass as the appearance of an image: property and *mimēsis* together, at the beginning. Genitivity as *mimēsis*. Props of property.

> Immediately after their appearance in the genitive image of God, human beings were given dominion over all things of the earth, theirs to subdue, to possess, to own, to betray. All genitive marks of property, I would say. *Mimēsis* again. Culminating in the epochal event of history: the covenant in which Abraham together with his progeny are to be given the land wherein they are strangers, all the land of Canaan, *for an everlasting possession.* Genitivity forever.
>
> All things in the earth become the rightful possessions of human beings. (Ross, *GPHG,* 1–2)

Become. And in this miraculous arrival, this enchanting *parousia,* other arrivals and becomings are abolished. The earth arrives in the genitive, with what can be had and possessed. On the side of possession is the demand to own and have, to possess the goods of the earth, to prosper in our possessions. On the side of dispossession is openness to other arrivals, other becomings, to surprises and transportations. To the generosity of the earth. Giving comes before having, and after.

Openness to *parousia* is enchanting, to the coming of what cannot be known, cannot be anticipated, except the anticipation of the unexpected and unknown. To what is given to us as this anticipation of a coming and a going, a giving that exceeds every having. We attempt to have, to hold on, to grasp; we attempt to make the world familiar, attempt to know it and to claim it; we attempt to make it a different place than we find it. All of these are temptations to have in a world that cannot be had, which gives itself to us beyond any grip.

> Heidegger, with the whole of Western history, takes the relation with the Other as enacted in the destiny of sedentary peoples, the possessors and builders of the earth. Possession is preeminently the form in which the other becomes the same, by becoming mine. Ontology becomes ontology of nature, impersonal fecundity, faceless generous mother, matrix of particular beings, inexhaustible matter for things. (Levinas, *TI,* 46)
>
> It is in generosity that the world possessed by me—the world open to enjoyment—is apperceived from a point of view independent of the egoist position. (75)

> Essence stretching on indefinitely, without any possible halt or interruption, the equality of essence and justifying, in all equity, any instant's halt, without respite, without any possible suspension, is the horrifying *there is* beyond all finality proper to the thematizing ego. It is the incessant buzzing (*bourdonnement*) that fills each silence, where the subject detaches itself

from essence and posits itself as a subject in face of its objectivity. (Levinas, *OB*, 163–4)

The whole of history enacts the relation with the Other in the destiny of sedentary peoples the possessors and builders of the earth...

The whole of another history performs the relation with the Other in the subjectivity of subjects in face of other ingredients of the earth...

An enchanting story of enchantment takes its departure from this passage on sedentariness, in its intricacies and complexities, with disenchantment given in possession and enchantment given in dispossession, where the *dis-* marks an endless rupture and break. *Diachrony* is Levinas's name. The other shatters my time and place. The enchanting call of the other in exposition.

Let us listen to this call and respond to its exposition. Slowly and enchantedly.

First *Heidegger*, who presents his time, still perhaps our time, as the *Gestell*, the frame of modern technology, modern rationality—let us say, though he does not use the word—as *disenchanted*. The *Gestell* as disenchantment. Against this Heidegger speaks of the saving power, the power in which the destiny of technological peoples may be transformed. Again.

The closer we come to the danger, the more brightly do the ways into the saving power begin to shine and the more questioning we become. For questioning is the piety of thought. (35)...

Could the saving power be enchanted, could it be enchanting? How does asking evoke enchantment? What might make it pious? How does asking pertain to enchantments more than disenchantments? Does the exuberance of telling overwhelm the piety of thought? What kind of powers does enchantment wield?

Too many questions, too few answers. Just right for enchantment. Without mentioning it Heidegger opens his discourse onto enchantment, more than into poetry, more perhaps than away from technology and metaphysics. Let us imagine that Heidegger speaks of enchantment without a name, and of disenchantment under the name of the *Gestell*. Let us imagine it without nostalgia.

For the saving power did not save Heidegger, he came too close to danger, the shining of the saving power dimmed for him under National Socialism and Hitler, he could not tell the difference between violence of thought and piety, he ceased to question, forgot the vigilance of questioning. As do we all, sometimes. Sometimes we must. Perhaps not on so visible a world stage.

According to Levinas, Heidegger comes too close to the danger on another side, not the loss of vigilance, forgetting asking, but in the faceless, neutral buzzing of being. The infinite call of the otherwise becomes impersonal: inexhaustibility without heterogeneity, being without alterity, time without diachrony, exposition without betrayal. Only subjectivity can save us.

Essence stretching indefinitely without interruption, equality without alteration, the horrifying *there is* beyond all finality, the incessant buzzing (*bourdonnement*) that fills each silence, disenchantment without betrayal, truth beyond asking.

Perhaps. But why should subjectivity be what saves us against the inexhaustible heterogeneity of beings? What interrupts the incessant humming of subjectivity, the endless betrayals of humanity?

Enchantment gives beyond having, in betrayal, evoking endless asking, telling.

Giving enchants beyond any having, buzzing, subjectivity, identity. Enchantment calls beyond neutrality.

What is beyond neutrality? Nothing, perhaps enchantment and exposition are nothing. Everything. The fullness of emptiness. Perhaps and as if.

Then *western history*, indeed, *the whole* of western history, and more, the possibility of the whole of human history, of any history, of history itself as disenchantment, destiny and possession. Sedentary peoples, sedentary history, sedentary being possessed by neutrality. Disenchantment offers itself as neutrality.

It is as if the whole of history, perhaps, were sedentary, neutral, sought to possess history itself, sought to have history as its own identity, disenchanted history to possess it. It is as if the whole of humanity sought by means of history—for us today as a discipline, for others before as a legacy—to settle down in its place. As if, for example, a god offered Adam a place to settle, as if the chosen people were promised a place to have as they wandered in the desert and through history, as they marked their history by the promise as if they were a sedentary people even when they had no place of their own. Not as if the promise remained open beyond any settling in the questioning of what they might be and become beyond any possession. In a judeochristian voice:

> The Exodus is about to be completed. The promise is about to be fulfilled. Landless sojourning is about to end. Nothing is more radical than this, that the sojourner becomes a possessor. Land entry requires of Israel that it cease to be what it had been in

> the wilderness and become what it had never been before. Land makes that demand. (Walter Brueggemann, *L*, 45).
>
> Israel lives under gift, not gift anticipated, but gift given. That is its new consciousness, and nothing is more radical, especially to landed, empowered people, than to discover they are creatures of gift. (51).
>
> Israel's central temptation is to forget and so cease to be an historical people. Settled into an eternally guaranteed situation, one scarcely knows that one is indeed addressed by the voice in history who gives gifts and makes claims. And if one is not addressed, then one does not need to answer. (54)
>
> The central temptation of the land is coveting. The central question at the boundary is this: Can Israel live in the land without being seduced by the gods, without the temptation of coveting having its way? Can Israel live in the land with all the precarious trust of landlessness? (59)

This is an enchanted reading in one tradition—partly Levinas's, partly other. It offers the possibility of an understanding of the promise of gift, of giving, beyond any possession. Israel coveted land and settled down, once in Biblical times and now again. Israel coveted, as perhaps do all in Western, Greek-Judeo-Christian history, as perhaps do all in every society and every history. As if sociality and history were possessive, coveting and disenchanting. The temptation is to covet, the question of giving and promising—perhaps of enchanting—is whether coveting must have its way. Can human beings, and not just human beings, live in the earth with all the precarious trust of landlessness, dispossession, enchantment, of asking and telling?

Enchantment is the precarious trust in asking beyond any gifts, beyond anything given, including land and knowledge, including enchantment itself. In this context, Greek-Judeo-Christianity's coveting interposes itself into a long history in which foragers, hunter-gatherers, and nomads did not settle down, or did so temporarily, for a season perhaps. Humanity's long history—in this context again, *pre*-history, non-sedentary history, unsettled and unsettling lives and generations—was neither settled in a given place, enacted by building and possessing, nor written down. All these settlings fail to settle. All these settlements decay. All writings wander. Human life, through time, leaves a record of non-sedentariness and non-settlement. Sedentariness belongs to Western, Greek-Judeo-Christian history, perhaps including all settled societies, not the whole of humanity, perhaps not western, greekjudeochristian societies. Perhaps the very possibility of a society is sedentary, possessive, disenchanted, seeking to build itself in a place, even a nomadic place that moves.

Giving is beyond having; nomadism is beyond settling; generosity is beyond coveting; enchantment is beyond disenchanting; westerngreekjudeochristianity is beyond Western Greek-Judeo-Christianity.

What is lost in the temptation, buried by coveting and yearning for possession, buried under one's feet in settling down, sedentarily, is *the relation with the other,* both as relation and as other, each beyond itself. Relationality is mobile, transitory, collective; it takes one out of oneself away from the boundaries that delineate its identity. This is true for a people—Israel—and for an individual, and it is true between an individual and a people.

The relation with the other as other is inexhaustible, impossible to fulfill, to grasp, always on the move, giving and given, never gotten and never grasped. The other's otherness, the otherwise than being, is beyond any identity or identification. The buzzing of being, the stretching of essence, neutralizes the other's alterity, distinctiveness, infinite expressiveness.

The key term for the other, Levinas's term, is *face*. Sedentary being, neutral essence stretching indefinitely, the neutral buzzing of being, is without face, impersonal. More of that later. Here the relationality of giving is more pressing. The relation with the other is relation as well as alterity. Sedentariness cuts into the earth to rest, against the mobilities and transitorinesses of relation. Relation is not only collective but impossible to fix and grasp, in its multiplicities, transitions, nuances, exteriorities, ecologies, and especially in its fixings and graspings. At the boundaries of relation, inside and out, are promises of transformation, transportation, in and out of one's skin. Skin at the boundary promises to divide and reaches out to touch. Skin divides and binds, touches inside and out, generously brings the world inside, reaches outside to the world. Touch touches itself, touches things, touch touches touch as corporeal generosity, as ecological hospitality. Generously as bodies, matter.

Every body is a face...

Every face asks and tells and promises infinitely...

Every body is enchanting beyond any face, any grasp, any gathering...

Touch touches us with excess, enchanted. (Ross, *GTGE*, xviii)...

Wherever bodies are they touch other bodies. The endless folding, unfolding, refolding of bodies is plenishment in the earth, for the sake of the good, in memory of enchantment's abundance and wonder. (303)...

The being of each being, the endless matter of each faceless thing, is *enacted* in the *destiny* of peoples. It does not arrive from nowhere, empty of direction or place, and it does not pass away to nothing, empty again in place or direction. Being is not faceless, objective, neutral but acts and enacts, performs and reforms, brings being into being, brings about disenchantment. Enchantment and disenchantment are enactments, performances, emergences, constitutions. If this be so, and we take the being of disenchantment as constituted historically in exposition, then there is no being of disenchantment that is itself disenchanted, objective, neutral, but belongs to a culture and a world that is never all of culture and never the totality of things even as history strives to make it so. That the world is disenchanted is enacted as a claim, instituted at a time and place, brings itself into being by expressing itself as a claim in truth.

In this way, the disenchantment of weber's claim to disenchantment, together with all the ensuing affirmations of disenchantment on the one side—academic, scientific, economic, political, global, rational—and of enchantment on the other as its resistance—religious, pagan, magical, spiritual, alchemical, aesthetic, postmodern, the enchantments of post-disenchantment—are enacted as disenchantments in a history—and perhaps a destiny—of a given people who would thereby institute their rule over all peoples and all things. In this way as well, the disenchantment of disenchantment, understood as performed in a time and place and culture, exposes the enchantments that define the borders of disenchantment. Disenchantment performs and cuts and defines itself in and against and alongside its other, its otherwise, what is beyond itself. The enactment of disenchantment is exposition, exposure as expression, calling as giving, unearthing, revelation. All impossible to disenchant, impossibly enchanting, the impossible itself.

Enacted in the *destiny* of peoples. *Destiny (Geschick)* is Heidegger's word. After Hitler and National Socialism a very dangerous word. Let us define this danger not as Heidegger's injustice, his failure to live up to his word. Instead, let us regard it as the danger of a disenchanted word—*destiny*—becoming enchanted, taking on magical, archaic, immemorial, violent characters, tellings surpassing askings. It works against the revelation that it and disenchantment are enacted, at a time and place—by Hitler and during National Socialism in mid-twentieth-century Germany for example. Destiny is enacted in this Germany and for a century before as falling upon the German people in the name of striving to be a people, in full knowledge that they were not such a people and would never be so except in a violent act of self-mutilation.

Let us say, then, that the forced enchantment of a destiny that has no meaning except as instituted and as disenchanted—the delineation of a multiplicity of peoples and languages into a single destiny by force—is the inexhaustible betrayal of that destiny and that enchantment. Let us acknowledge as well that Germany, with all its struggles, has never been more German than after Lagers, gas chambers, and tortured memories. The inexhaustible enchantment that is Germany today and Germany or something else tomorrow rests on the disenchantment of a plan to account for all the Jews and homosexuals and gypsies in Europe. If there be such an account. If it is not the devil's work to imagine such an accounting *and to enact it*.

An enchanted people has no destiny, has nothing to name or enact as its destiny, not even a history or a language. Many languages, many histories, many names, regions, cultures, minorities bear the weight of enacting the futures of such a people, possibly its nationalities, destinies, and democracies—to come, always coming. An enchanted people's destinies, perhaps the destinies of the greekjudeochristian west (marked again by lower case letters) are its enchanting promises of becoming what it will become, what it chooses and what it does not choose to become, multiple destinies—if there be such—that are nothing until they become, and in coming enchant every disenchantment.

Geschick is Heidegger's word, in Levinas's hands a word of scorn. The destiny of a people overshadows, betrays the face, denies the enchanting promise of the other who is not just any other. The destiny of the world, its being and its becoming, betrays the cherishment of the other, every being and every thing and every ingredient who is not just any other. The destiny of the earth is its disenchantment, and in that disenchantment—sometimes glorious, sometimes disastrous—reveals the enchantments that undergird and transfigure every destiny.

I have spoken of the disenchantment of history as such, history as a discipline or knowledge, as an account of what is unaccountable in the diachrony of time and the multiplicity of ingredients, conditions, elements, and forces. Diachrony is inexhaustible, asking and telling, interruption and departure. Multiplicity is inexhaustible, excess and augmentation. Heterogeneous, enchanted things cannot be gathered. Enchanting is ungathering.

Let us say that destiny is the collective promise of a people coveting themselves as a people, coveting all things as theirs, belonging to their destiny. Even if they do not imagine ruling over all things, their destiny relates to all and every thing in the gathering of themselves into their destiny. They enact themselves in coveting.

Let us imagine that in responding to such a destiny we mobilize the possibility inherent in every promise of living in a generosity without destination, without coveting. Let us imagine that israẹl's destiny—no destiny at all—was to receive the promise of land without ever having land—land without land, destiny without destination. Let us imagine that nomadic peoples receive the gift of life and death without coveting either or any thing in particular, but live as well as they can coming and going, in the openness of a destiny without destination, no destiny at all.

This is giving without having, generosity without sedentariness, asking beyond answers and telling beyond knowing, a promise of being given without certainty of receiving anything in the trust and affirmation of living and giving. And dying. The affirmation of dying without grasping too tightly to life. The affirmation of enchantment beyond anything that may be claimed under the weight of disenchantment.

We come, then, to the *sedentary peoples, the possessors and builders of the earth,* in whose memory we hope to participate in the giving, dispossessing, and unbuilding. Sedentary peoples first are peoples, destinary peoples, collective beyond the cherished uniqueness of each and every relational singular party. Singular individuals, unique in who and what they are, relate, are what they are in relation, before and from the other, and I would say others. Always more others, always more relationality. Sedentary peoples settle down among their neighbors, among their folk; among their many possessions are communities, neighbors, social environs.

The question for a sedentary people is whether their relationality imposes community, whether they can be relational without having or possessing collectivity, whether an enchanted and dispossessive relationality disrupts both individuality and collectivity. Not to mention destinality.

It is possible to think of relation and relationality as a matrix, disenchanted, regulated by structure and rule. Kinship appears to be such a relation, and for many who live in such a system, relationality offers little promise of enchantment, little space for transfiguration—though enchantment and transfiguration are always present, always pregnant. The key to relationality for Levinas and for enchantment here is *relation with the other, otherwise, relationality as alterity and transgression*. In this way, relationality is enchantment, both in the otherness of the other that transgresses every boundary, and in the relations whose bonding disrupts the boundaries of the individual person or thing.

Relationality arrays itself against the hegemony of the ego. Enchantment arrays itself against the hegemony of disenchantment. Hegemony belongs to relationality and to enchantment, but obliquely, through the structures that arise around them—social institutions and supernatural forces. Otherwise relationality enchants itself in the otherness of the relations.

> Community means, consequently, that there is no singular being without another singular being, and that there is, therefore, what might be called an originary "sociality" that extends far beyond the simple theme of man as a social being. For it is not obvious that the community of singularities is limited to "man" and excludes, for example, the "animal" (even in the case of "man" it is not a fortiori certain that this community concerns only "man" and not also the "inhuman" or the "superhuman"). (Jean-Luc Nancy, *IC*, 28)

> singular beings *[Daseins]* are themselves constituted by sharing, they are distributed and placed, or rather *spaced*, by the sharing that makes them *others*: other for one another, and other, infinitely other for the Subject of their fusion, which is engulfed in the sharing, in the ecstasy of the sharing "communicating" by not "communing." Thus, the communication of sharing would be this very dis-location. (25)

No community but sharing, where what is shared is singularity, the presence and relation of other beings, others in their otherness, spaced and placed by their alterity, other for and in one another, ecstatic in their relations, enchantingly enchanted. To be one is to be other. To be one is for there to be others, others without community, destiny, and history but in relationality. Relationality without community is dislocation, dispossession.

Community, here, is sedentary, disenchanted, a place where singular and heterogeneous beings settle down in their places. Relationality is nomadic, mobile, enchanting, togetherness without commonality. Commonality is sedentary, disenchanted, together with communion and community, insisting on a place to have. Relationality is dispossessive, ecstatic, always outside oneself in singularity. And it is important to say again that singularity is relationality, that there is no singular without another, consequently enchanting in relation. I am here, I am who I am, exposed as I must be by the presence and reality of some other singular being.

The singularity of sharing presents itself as the relationality of love, in the enchantments of love. Love is impossible to have, cannot settle down, is never sedentary.

> Love arrives, it comes, or else it is not love. But it is thus that it endlessly goes elsewhere than to "me" who would receive it: its coming is only a departure for the other, its departure only the coming of the other.
>
> What is offered by transcendence, or as transcendence, is this arrival and this departure, this incessant coming-and-going. What is offered is the offered being itself: exposed to arrival and to departure, the singular being is traversed by the alterity of the other, which does not stop or fix itself anywhere, neither in "him," nor in "me," because it is nothing other than the coming-and-going. The other comes and cuts across me, because it immediately leaves for the other: it does not return to itself, because it leaves only in order to come again. The crossing breaks the heart: this is not necessarily bloody or tragic, it is beyond an opposition between the tragic and serenity or gaiety. The break is nothing more than a touch, but the touch is not less deep than a wound. (98)

And the wound, more than anything perhaps, is the wound of mineness, having, genitivity. *Possession is the form in which the other becomes the same, by becoming mine.* The transcendence of the other is the enchantment of dispossession. In the name of love.

> Love defines itself as the absolute opposite and as the destruction of self-love. Self-love is not simply the love of the self. One can love oneself with a real love, and it might even be that one must do so. But self-love is the love of possession. It is the love of the self as property. (94–5)

The love of the singular as property, in the genitive, is the form in which the other becomes the same, by becoming mine. The other becomes mine, I myself am my self, I insist on holding onto myself, the most sedentary act of betrayal possible—betraying everything including myself.

> The ideas of being "true to oneself," of being one's own person, of being a self-actualized individual each refer us to the assumption that what is essential about the self is its separation from others:

> that it is "ownness" or "mineness" which defines the experience of self. (John Wikse, *AP*, 1)

> At the extremes of individuation, the essential characteristic of identity is that it is one's own. In my separation from others, in private and "alone with myself," deprived of others, this self with which I am alone is conceived on the logic of private property: it is my own unique possession, exclusively mine. (1)

The sedentariness of a people becomes the mineness of a self against its shattering, its emptiness, its generosity.

> It is different for whoever comes after the subject, whoever succeeds to the West. He *comes*, does nothing but come, and for him, presence in its entirety is coming: which means, not "having come" (past participle), but a *coming* (the action of coming, arriving). Presence is what is born, and does not cease being born. Of it and to it there is birth, and only birth. This is the presence of whoever, for whomever *comes*: who succeeds the "subject" of the West, who succeeds the West—this coming of another that the West always demands, and always forecloses. (Nancy, *BP*, 2)

> Being is at stake there, it is in shatters, offered dazzling, multiplied shrill and singular, hard and cut across: its being is there. (Nancy, *SL*, 104–5)

Again in the name of love:

> Love arrives then in the promise. In one sense (in another sense, always other, always at the limit of sense), it always arrives, as soon as it is promised, in words or in gestures. Love arrives in all the forms and in all the figures of love; it is projected in all its shatters.
>
> There are no parts, moments, types, or stages of love. There is only an infinity of shatters: love is wholly complete in one sole embrace or in the history of a life, in jealous passion or in tireless devotion. It consists as much in taking as in giving, as much in requiring as in renouncing, as much in protecting as in exposing. It is in the jolt and in appeasement, in the fever and in serenity, in the exception and in the rule. It is sexual, and it is not: it cuts across the sexes with another difference that does not abolish them, but displaces their identities. Whatever my love is, it cuts across my identity, my sexual property, that objectification by which I am a masculine or feminine subject. (101)

The expressiveness of the world is given in shatters, giving as shatters, falling upon the exposed self who betrays those shatters twice, forming itself against their multiplicity and dispersion, betraying that formation in its shatters. The shattering of love is the shattering of the self, not because the only way in which the self is shattered is in love, but because the self shatters in love, shatters enchantingly in love, is exposed in shatters in beauty and love. Beauty returns us to the asking that constitutes enchantment's betrayal, whether self or love or exposure otherwise. Beauty is the affirmation of shattering. (Ross, *GSSEB*, 210)...

Being is in shatters, exposure is disparition, shattering, transgression as love. The promise of love—as being with, sharing with others—is shattering. Shattering is enchanting. (211)...

Love, self, identity—all in the plural—cut across and shatter every possession, dispossess every having, overflow every genitive.

Enchantment is overflowing overflowing every genitive every possession every having every ruling...

Enchanting overflows every building durability is disenchanted...

We may ask of shatters: why love? We may ask of love: why shatters? We may ask of asking: why love and shatters? I respond that love and shatters—and being and beauty and enchantment and self—are shattered, shattering, exposed and betrayed into shatters. The shattering of being and self is the shattering of love and beauty and shatters. The astonishing return from the humming and buzzing betrayal of being and self, from their regathering, is to the impossible-to-gather nonneutrality of being here, shattered here and there beyond shattering, enchanting there and here beyond enchantment. (219)...

Sedentary peoples are *the possessors and builders of the earth.* In this way everything that we prize—buildings, states, institutions, regulations, laws, works, writings, documents, archives—are sedentary, created and built to last. Especially the institutions organized around their preservation—preservation societies, governments, corporations, courts, libraries. All histories, all contributions to history. In this way history is sedentary, holding on to events and works that make it history, make it documentable.

I do not say *memorable*—we remember more than history. I do say forgettable. We forget, we must forget what makes history history in order to escape its disenchantment. If only for a moment. If only partly, obliquely, tangentially. Unforgetting—*anamnēsis*—is the shattering of memory and history, the enchantment of truth.

Building is the production of the human world, a durable, repeatable, reliable world. *Reliability,* Heidegger says, reminding us of its abundance, the abundance of reliability, the enchantment of disenchantment, what makes the earth inexhaustible, strange, and unfamiliar. Reliability, that which makes the earth familiar, is uncanny and unfamiliar. Returning us to asking and telling.

> The equipmental quality of the equipment consists indeed in its usefulness. But this usefulness itself rests in the abundance [*Fülle*] of an essential being of the equipment. We call it reliability. (*OWA*, 34)

> The repose of equipment resting within itself consists in its reliability. (35)

> Bestowing and grounding have in themselves the unmediated character of what we call a beginning.
>
> A beginning, on the contrary, always contains the undisclosed abundance [*Fülle*] of the unfamiliar and extraordinary, which means that it also contains strife with the familiar and ordinary. (76)

> [A]t bottom, the ordinary is not ordinary; it is extra-ordinary, uncanny, (54)

What is ordinary is enchanting. As is art. Under the headings of *art* and *aesthetics* the earth and all its works, its buildings and possessions, expose their unfamiliarities and strangenesses, give us the abundance of their enchantments. That is worth another chapter, an enchanting chapter of enchantment. Still to come.

The name aesthetic marks the interruption of the stretching on indefinitely the incessant buzzing filling each silence shattering the there is beyond finality...

Building is having, something to be seen, to stand up, to present itself as what it is, as something to possess. Being right here is having, a place to grasp. Building for the future, durable and reliable, is again something to have. Enchanting is giving, beyond anything standing up right here as what it is—always something else, otherwise; giving to and for an unknown future, an uncontrollable, unregulatable, unanticipatable, unaccountable future, an uncontrolled, unregulated, unanticipated, unaccounted place in a spacing in which we do not insist on settling down, in which we cannot settle down when and where we insist.

The earth is full of wonder and abundance including building and possessing, building and possessing are disenchanting the enchanted earth is full of disenchantment, the abundance and wonder of disenchantments...

Possession is the form in which the other becomes mine. Enchantment is the way in which the other remains other never mine to have giving beyond grasping...

Ontology of nature impersonal fecundity faceless generous mother matrix of particular beings inexhaustible matter for things...

I have presented enchantment as abundant beyond every boundary including the face. Emptiness and being and empty matter are all inexhaustibly enchanting, beyond the face but not faceless. This is cherishment, giving from the good, where the good marks every creature, living and nonliving, with and without a face, as inexhaustible, enchanted, immemorial. Cherishment knows no criteria, not even that of face. In Derrida's words:

> Discourses as original as those of Heidegger and Levinas disrupt a certain traditional humanism. In spite of the differences separating them, they nonetheless remain profound humanisms *to the extent that they do not sacrifice sacrifice.* The subject (in Levinas's sense) and the Dasein are "men" in a world where sacrifice is possible and where it is not forbidden to make an attempt on life in general, but only on human life, on the neighbor's life, on the other's life as *Dasein. Mitsein* is not conferred, if we can say so, on the living in general, but only on that being-toward-death that also makes the *Dasein* into something more and better than a living (thing). (Derrida, *EW,* 279)

Derrida speaks of animals, of life in general, of the divide between humanity and everything else living. He calls this virile insistence on human superiority *carnophallogocentrism,* echoing eating, sacrifice, and the control of language in the assembling of being. In this context, in our greek-judeo-christian western culture, it is good to sacrifice animals (and others) and to eat meat. In the context of enchantment, of sacrificing sacrifice, it is to ask whether sacrifice is disenchantment and whether enchantment sacrifices sacrifice in refusing to allow humanity to account for itself in this way.

In the context of Levinas—not Heidegger—the condition of generosity is personal, in the human face. Only humans can be other, only humans as neighbors can demand or insist or solicit generosity. Ethics is first philosophy not as being but as subjectivity—subjectivation if you will. The possibility that first philosophy is ethics in the way in which each and every being, every ingredient, the earth in every part and every whole, is to be cherished, infinitely what it is, is not a possibility that shows itself even in endless asking and telling.

> One cannot entirely refuse the face of an animal. It is via the face that one understands, for example, a dog. Yet the priority here is not found in the animal, but in the human face. We understand the animal, the face of an animal, in accordance with *Dasein*. The phenomenon of the face is not in its purest form in the dog. (Levinas, *PM*, 169).

> It is clear that, without considering animals as human beings, the ethical extends to all living beings. We do not want to make an animal suffer needlessly and so on. But the prototype of this is human ethics. Vegetarianism, for example arises from the transference to animals of the idea of suffering. The animal suffers. It is because we, as humans, know what suffering is that we can have this obligation. (172).

Cherishment betrays this unasking, asks of it intensely. It is not the personality of the other but its otherness, and animals and trees, not to mention clouds and stones and scraps in heaps, are all other. *Tout autre est tout autre* (Derrida, *GD*, 68); every other is enchanting.

We think we make the material world familiar in knowing it and using it. That is its disenchantment. Heidegger and Levinas accept this familiarity of the everyday, material world even as they give us enchanting tools for rendering it unfamiliar, tools of enchantment that resist the disenchantment of knowing and using.

Knowing and using are enchanted, otherwise we could not use them. Knowing and using are asking and telling...

In an enchanted earth every ingredient is enchanting beyond any knowing and using, beyond any neutrality or neutralization. Enchantment de-neutralizes every neuter.

Look a snake in the face and know the world it inhabits is not ours. Look into an insect's eyes and see a seeing that we cannot see. Animals are other. *Tout autre est tout autre...* Every other is abundantly other. This otherness gives enchantment to us, gives us to enchantment. Other living creatures. all things that become, that come and go. enchant the earth in exposition, call to us in wonder.

Cherishment and sacrifice expose the enchantments of plenishment. The earth asks us everywhere to listen, we ourselves are speakers and listeners, every speaking and listening is a double crossing—as language itself, always as if perhaps ~~not~~ beyond language, betraying itself. Exposition is the expressivity of the earth, abundance beyond abundance, as if perhaps ~~not~~ beyond, to which we our selves respond, again as if perhaps ~~not~~ beyond any self and any responses. Responsivity and expressivity are the abundance of abundance, crossing, interrupting, double crossing themselves and each other, enchanting themselves as this double crossing, betrayal betraying itself. It does not matter if we call this double crossing exposition, language, bodies, expressivity, responsivity, asking, cherishment, or enchantment. It does not matter what we call it; we will betray it, because the calling, naming of any of these is betraying and enchanting. (Ross, *GSSEB,* 306)...

Cherishment tells that enchantment matters infinitely, that abundance calls and asks and yearns for responses and other responses, that where things touch each other touch makes a difference, addresses others in the abundance of touching. Cherishment, touch, expressivity, enchantment—again, it does not matter what we call it or if we call it anything or nothing: each is a betrayal, a double crossing in the touch and name. The betrayal betrays, crosses and recrosses, and reveals enchantment in the double crossing. Enchantment is a name—one among countless others—of betrayal, double crossing, on the side of responsivity. If we respond, if we are called to respond, if we and others respond in the earth to others as like and other to ourselves, this responsivity constitutes who we are and who the others are in relation to ourselves. (307)...

The giving of being, the opening of the earth to others, happens everywhere and always. Every opening is new; every opening is beyond itself. And among these advents and beyonds is cherishment, the giving from the good that insists that we respond. Cherishment is singular, unique, and local in that what is expressed, the responses called for, are different in endless ways from every other place or ways: enchantment is always beyond itself. Cherishment is common, shared, inseparable from others in that it can be present as a call only from others, in the midst of others, including the strangeness and otherness of oneself to oneself. (307)...

Cherishment is enchantment...

The earth gives itself as asking, beyond answering, calling and responding. All these calls give enchantment to us as something to respond to, something to care for, give us the earth in cherishment, giving as enchanting...

The world is grasped as disenchanted, something to own and have, including knowledge, peace, and goodness. The earth is nothing to have, the good is nothing, nothing to grasp. Generosity, unattachment, and emptiness are figures of enchantment. As are cherishment, sacrifice, and plenishment. As are asking, telling, truth, peace, and goodness. All beyond accounting, beyond grasping, shattered figures of betrayal...

Enchantment shatters the attachments of the world into the emptiness of the earth. Enchantment gives rise to endless askings, tellings, betrayals. Enchantment betrays every identity, every having, every possession: giving beyond having, asking beyond answering, telling beyond any questions and any answers, the enchanting that calls perhaps as if ~~not~~ beyond...

Chapter 4

Art Enchanting

> the existence of the world is justified only as an aesthetic phenomenon. (Nietzsche, *ASC*, 22)

> art represents the highest task and the truly metaphysical activity of this life. (*BT*, 31–2)

> *Under the charm of the Dionysian, in song and dance, humans express themselves as members of a higher community; they have forgotten how to walk and speak and are on the way toward flying into the air, dancing. Their very gestures express enchantment. Just as the animals now talk, and the earth yields milk and honey, supernatural sounds emanate from them, too: they feel themselves a god, they walk about enchanted, in ecstasy, like the gods they saw walking in their dreams. They are no longer an artist, they have become a work of art: in these paroxysms of intoxication the artistic power of all nature reveals itself to the highest gratification of the primordial unity.* (#1, 37)...

> The image sees.
> The image feels.
> The image acts. (Bennett, *CB*, 195)

The world as aesthetic phenomenon calls into question every name that would mark the possibility of its expression: world, aesthetic, art, phenomenon, metaphysics; existence, justification, highest, life; not to mention only and truly. It urges those who are exposed to the call of phenomena to envisage multiplicity and inclusion in the midst of classification and exclusion, to imagine the enchantment of the world around us, to recall the ingredients of the earth's abundance, to evoke sound and image in the name of truth, to participate in the unfolding and refolding of being. It asks those who care for others and themselves to reimagine a point before reason and its disenchantments divided itself from unreason and the enchantments and beauties of the world. It reminds us that in archaic Greek and in many aboriginal languages, the world of natural things teems with life, vitality, expression: enchantment. The earth swarms with abundance. Gods, divinities, spirits. A world of unsurpassable beauty. Of exposition... Of calling and giving and asking and telling... The image calls and gives and feels and expresses. (Ross, *WAP,* 3)...

Let us call this ethics. Let us call it aesthetics. Let us call it art. Let us call it literature. Let us call it beyond ethics, aesthetics, literature, and art as if perhaps ~~not~~ beyond names, divisions, identifications, binaries. Let us call it enchantment...: ethics|aesthetics|sciences|enchantments... As if we lived as fully as possible and ethics, science, art, and enchantment were not divided from each other, but images multiplied in proliferation beyond gathering. The world is ethical through and through. The world is aesthetic through and through. The world is enchanting, expressing, fascinating through and through. The world is social, natural, relational through and through, asking and telling through and through. All things are enchanted without exclusion: abundant in wonder. Everything is beautiful in its ways, wonderful in abundance. Yet we cannot speak of this ethics or aesthetics or art or science, of this enchanting exposition, in a modern, disciplinary voice. In politics and reason we are at war, inside and out, right over wrong, true over false. Only some can rule. Some benefit more from institutional conformations than others. Life is to the swift and strong. Only great artists produce masterpieces. In ethics we must judge good from bad, right from wrong, just from unjust. (4)...

The world is enchanted as an aesthetic phenomenon...

The image proliferates...

The image enchants...

The beauty of the earth is its enchantment...

Suzi Gablik presents *The Reenchantment of Art* as "a sustained meditation on how we might restore to our culture its sense of aliveness, possibility and magic" (Gablik, *RA,* 1). Aliveness, possibility, and magic are names of enchantment—I do not say reenchantment. More significant, perhaps, is the assumption that the earth was once enchanted and is no longer, that modern science, industry, technology, rationality—modernity as such, including modern art—are disenchanted.

> Reenchantment, as I understand it, means stepping beyond the modern traditions of mechanism, positivism, empiricism, rationalism, materialism, secularism and scientism—the whole

> objectifying consciousness of the Enlightenment—in a way that allows for a return of soul. Reenchantment implies a release from the affliction of nihilism. It also refers to that change in the general social mood toward a new pragmatic idealism and a more integrated value system that brings head and heart together in an ethic of care, as part of the healing of the world. (11)

Another assumption is that art has an important role to play in reenchanting the world, but not because it is enchanting.

> If modern aesthetics was inherently isolationist, aimed at disengagement and purity, my sense is that what we will be seeing over the next few decades is art that is essentially social and purposeful, art that rejects the myths of neutrality and autonomy. The subtext of social responsibility is missing in our aesthetic models, and the challenge of the future will be to transcend the dis-connectedness and separation of the aesthetic from the social that existed within modernism. (4–5)

Against the possibility that art today is enchanting, that it offers enchantments in the midst of disenchantments, art must find its social purpose, must take on its responsibilities. It is time for another purposeful change. It is time for a different collective project that

> attempts to engage the whole being—not just the intellect but the emotional, psychological, ethical and spiritual parts of us as well. I see it as a collective project, giving voice to what many people already believe and feel; ideas are expressed and woven together that are very much "in the air," seeking their proper articulation in the community. (2)

> As a culture, we seem to be approaching a certain awareness that things must change, and not just superficially. Rather, the most basic assumptions underlying modern society are in flux; and, as these assumptions shift, the need for a new philosophical framework is being felt by many people. In arguing for the necessity of moving beyond the whole world view of an epoch, this book looks to the possibility that individuals can reject certain prevailing cultural attitudes and embrace new myths. The question is no longer how did we get here, and why? but, where can we possibly go, and how? (3)

The need for a new and proper framework, new ways of life, different cultural attitudes and mythologies, is widely felt. And yet, is it not modern to seek such a framework? Disenchanted? Another architectural|political|epistemological project?[1] As if innocent of betrayal? Is it not intimidating to be in the grip of such a sweeping framework, no matter how well meant? To insist that things must change and to know just how? Is it not disenchanted? Is knowing how to heal the world not disenchanted, as if we could know without betrayal? Is promulgating new myths not disenchanted, as if we had them in hand? Can we look for a new and better way to live without the tools at hand that modernity provides? How does this new framework betray? Can we imagine all these askings as if without grasping at tellings, repeatedly asking *as if* and *perhaps* and still more *perhaps* and *as if*?

Two of the many meanings of myth are the illusions that guide our ideologies, enchanted and disenchanted, and the narratives that constitute the margins and remainders of enchantment. We must choose—if we can, if such a choice is possible under the myths of enchantment, if we can choose without unending asking, as if ~~not~~ perhaps and as if.

Some say modernity is disenchanted, that the tools at hand disenchant. This would appear to include the new and the framework and the collectivity and the mythologies. If they are better, who decides and how? With what judgments and accountings, with what remainders? Perhaps better and worse are disenchanted terms, or perhaps for us today, in modern times, it is as if we can accept only forms of better and worse to account for and to choose. Including the new framework, new ways of life, proper articulations, different cultural attitudes and mythologies.

> Many of the difficulties and conflicts we experience as personal in this regard are related to the framework of beliefs and standards of behavior provided by our culture to serve as guidelines for individual lives. We tend to pattern ourselves and our world view after our culture, taking as self-evident certain beliefs, values and behaviors; thus, if our model of culture is faulty or disordered, then we ourselves are disordered in precisely the same way. Since cultural conditioning strongly influences individual behavior and thought, to begin to move toward a different framework of assumptions that would change the basis of our experience is extremely difficult. (3)

Perhaps not just because it is difficult to think and act differently—indeed it is—but because political, social, and cultural forces oppose us. And this will be true under any new framework as well. Disenchantment is not an innocent belief in rational procedures but includes dominating forms of thought and practice. Rationality insists that it owns the only forms of justification and dependability. As bizarre as may appear, to insist on a world dominated by magic and enchantment owned by a single religion, art, or culture is disenchanted, both in the claim that everything can be accounted for in that framework—the mark of many sects—and in the unbounded authority of the framework. The name *enchantment* can be disenchanted by practices that inscribe its own authority too forcibly, that insist on a paradigm instead of an asking. "The new questions that are being raised are no longer issues of style or content, but issues of social and environmental responsibility, and of multiculturalism, or 'parallel' cultures, rather than a dominant monoculturalism" (4). And perhaps other askings, and other tellings.

Enchantment does not insist on better over worse, does not know better myths, but invents and spreads old and new myths because they are inventive, interruptive, transgressive, astonishing in wonder, abundant in surprises. New is not better than old but proliferates askings. Asking does not stop with better and does not run from worse but enchants their enchantments endlessly. It does not need to reenchant them because they have never failed to be enchanting. The disenchantment of the world is enchanting. Art has never gone away, and hovers at the edges of disenchantment as the enchanted energies that give them life. And for that matter, that there is art and literature, that there is science, that disenchantment and modern technology might hold us in its grasp, testifies to their force and power and enchantment. If we listen. If we listen with an artist's eye and look with an artist's ear. Taking art piece by piece, enchantingly.

And perhaps piece by piece is what we need to keep in mind as art on one side and as enchantment on the other. Piece by piece, fragment by fragment, artist by artist, work by work, avoiding the modern demand for Art and Value, not to mention Fame and Money. As if perhaps they were ~~not~~ disenchanted.

> Individualism, freedom and self-expression are the great modernist buzz words. To highly individualistic artists, trained to think in this way, the idea that creative activity might be directed toward answering a collective cultural need rather than a personal desire for self-expression is likely to appear irrelevant, or even presumptuous. But I believe there is a new, evolving relationship between personal creativity and social responsibility, as old modernist patterns of alienation and confrontation give way to new ones of mutualism and the development of an active and practical dialogue with the environment. (6)

Against exalted individualism we need collectivity. Against individualism, freedom, and self-expression we need social responsibility. We need collectivity and sociality as if we no longer had them, as if the world was once enchanted and is no longer. We must seek the lost fairies and good witches, and above all the socially responsible artists as if they were not everywhere around us, as if artists did not know as well as she what gablik wants us to know, as if every work of art, good or bad, famous or unknown, failed to displace us from the prevailing winds of disenchantment if only for a moment, failed to betray us and itself, failed to ask us to ask, to remind us of perhaps.

> Some artists have taken offense at what I write because it doesn't appear to validate what they are doing; but a paradigm shift can't occur without consequences to the way we see and do things, and the uprooting of accustomed habits of thinking often has uncomfortable personal consequences. It is not part of our legacy to view ourselves as powerful agents of change; however, we are being confronted with the necessity of transforming our old modes of understanding if we are to survive the predicaments that are our collective fate right now. To create today is to create with responsibility. (8)

To create is to create with responsibility. To live is to live responsibly. Yet perhaps there are many different responsibilities, many different kinds and directions and practices. Perhaps responsibility is excessive, enchanted, so that those who would insist on its fulfillment are disenchanted, those who insist on a certain kind of collectivity must possess the right to claim such authority—always disenchanted.

Is communitarianism better than individualism? Or are they both disenchanted? Is the question itself disenchanted? And the answer? Would we ask such a question in an enchanted world? What would it mean? Whose better, and for what? Who would decide, and how?

> I see the task of this book as encouraging the emergence of a more participatory, socially interactive framework for art, and supporting the transition from the art-for-art's-sake assumptions of late modernism, which kept art as a specialized pursuit devoid of practical aims and goals. (7)

And yet, such art has always been the locus of political dissent and social critique. Not so much the individualized center of artists' quests for fame and wealth—so much part of our corporate culture—but the right of artists to detach themselves in whole or part from the dominant culture itself while benefiting from it.

> It would seem that a single philosophy no longer accurately represents our culture, which is more accurately revealed right now in the interplay of its opposing tendencies; this means dancing through some of the most conspicuous contradictions in the present scene and considering opposite points of view. (9)

It would seem that a single philosophy for our culture and a single aesthetics for art would claim to account for everything disenchantingly.

Let us imagine the following: that individuality is on one side disenchanted, insisting on the accountings and judgings that individuals do, as if they performed all the judgments in the world; and that individuality is on the other side relational, every individual is related, relating: acting, knowing, behaving, creating relationally. In the face of and through the touch of others, other people, other things. Things speak to artists, no matter how individual those artists wish to be, speak to them and relate to them from the depths of their being; things are enchanted for artists, no matter how individual those artists imagine themselves to be. No matter how individual, the world is relational for art and for artists. No matter how disenchanted, the earth is enchanted for art and for artists. And not for them alone.

> The necessity for art to transform its goals and become accountable in the planetary whole is incompatible with aesthetic attitudes still predicated on the late-modernist assumption that art has no "useful" role to play in the larger sphere of things. But the fact is that many artists now conceive their roles with a different sense of purpose than current aesthetic models sanction, even though there is as yet no comprehensive theory or framework to encompass what they are doing. (7)
>
> The collective task of "reenchanting" our whole culture is one of the crucial tasks of our time, and I should like to offer what I have written as one more contribution to a collective project, a vision that I perceive is shared by many others. If it is accurate to trace many of our present dilemmas to what has been called the "disenchantment of the world," then the solution must somehow involve a process that breaks the spell and circle of routines built up by modern culture and begins the transition into a different stream of experience. (11)

We are all faced with a collective task—all of us together including artists—to reenchant our whole culture. As if it were possible. As if it were desirable. As if there were a single culture, a single task, a single collectivity to gather, a single world to enchant. And what if that were disenchanted? What if totality were the enemy? What if enchantment disrupted the totality and hegemony of individuality and corporate control without replacing it with another hegemony and another totality? What if ungathering in disunity were enchanting?

Let us imagine the following: the disenchantment of the world has already taken place and, no matter how overwhelmed and desperate we may feel, it has been accomplished. We face the task of undermining it and accomplishing another, greater task, reenchanting our whole culture, other cultures, the whole world. We must then ask whether there is another, better accomplishment measured on another scale than that of disenchantment, than that of science; and whether we can be strong enough to win. It is as if we again must pit art and science against each other. It is as if we can choose.

Let us imagine the following: the disenchantment of the world has already taken place and, no matter how overwhelmed and desperate we may feel, it has only partly been accomplished, so that enchantment peers out from every nook and cranny. Among the nooks and crannies are those of the great art museums and famous artists. As disenchanted as the museum and art worlds are, as disenchanted as the economic and corporate and elite forces are that control and direct art and artists, art is enchanting everywhere, in the margins, artists who never hope to sell, never hope to live as artists, never follow a fad. People go to museums and galleries, not to buy, not even to learn to follow art, but to open spaces in their lives for asking and telling that are not economic and corporate and elite, but something otherwise. No matter how disturbed gablik may be at the corporate culture of art and its withdrawal from the urgent problems of our time—AIDS, 9/11, global warming, toxic wastes, environmental racism—art is one of the places to which people go to be aroused from their disenchanted complacencies.

Let us imagine that art and aesthetics and images are as disenchanted, contaminated, controlled, and corrupted as possible; still they are enchanted, still they are enchanting, still they offer enchantments. Not reenchantments, as if art was once more social, more relevant, more mythic; or as if society was once more meaningful, more transcendent, more magical. Every society, every culture, every art is magical, meaningful, transcendent, enchanted and enchanting in its ways. As if we cannot choose between enchanted and disenchanted art.

Isn't it amazing that the most disenchanted art, in the most disenchanted, toxic culture, is surprising, wonderful, abundant? Isn't it enchanting, isn't it enchanted? No matter its betrayals, modern and contemporary art is breathtaking, magical, transcendent...

It is time for our culture, perhaps, to open up some new ways of being a culture. The ways we have been following are too dangerous, too destructive, too overwhelming—and too fascinating, enchanting, desirous, erotic. They betray too much.

> We cannot heal the mess we have made of the world without undergoing some kind of spiritual healing. Before proceeding to tackle the "arguments," however, it might be useful to pause for a moment and consider what your concept of a "successful" artist is. What qualities does she have? What sort of "stance" in the world? Is the image that forms in your mind one that you can believe in? Is there anything about it that you would like to change? (Gablik, *RA*, 12)

Surely, artists are as spiritual and committed to healing the mess of the world as any other people, possibly more than many. Surely, artists seek fame and glory. At least, in both cases, some are and some do. Moreover, it is because art is enchanting that gablik can ask artists to turn toward healing. All of us need healing, all of us need to learn how to heal, and we need magical gifts to do so. Art and literature are among those gifts, if they are not the gift itself.

Under the headings of art and aesthetics the earth and its ingredients, its works, its buildings, its possessions, expose their unfamiliarities and strangenesses, proffer their enchantments...

A work of art is a gift, not a commodity. Where there is no gift there is no art...[2]

With the *es gibt* of being in mind, derrida speaks of the impossibility of the gift, in the extreme. "Not impossible but the impossible. The very figure of the impossible. It announces itself, gives itself to be thought as the impossible" (Derrida, *GT*, 7).[3] The giving of being is the impossibility that bing might be given as a present, given to presence.

The giving of being is the enchanting that allows art to be art, the enchanting of the impossible, the impossible of time and being and exposition...

The giving of being, the enchanting of the earth, is impossible, unnameable, giving and enchanting are the impossible, the unnameable, beyond possibility and impossibility, beyond naming and unnaming, beyond enchanting and disenchanting, as if perhaps ~~not~~ beyond any beyond...

The impossible is endless asking, asking for impossible telling...

Gifts circulate between two impossibles: the gift of being and human gifts, given by someone to another. "For this is the impossible that seems to give itself to be thought here: These conditions of possibility of the gift (that some 'one' gives some 'thing' to some 'one other') designate simultaneously the conditions of the impossibility of the gift" (Derrida, *GT*, 11). A gift "cannot take place between two subjects exchanging objects, things, or symbols. One would even be tempted to say that a subject as such never gives or receives a gift" (24). The gift cannot be exchanged, cannot be returned. "It must not circulate, it must not be exchanged, it must not in any case be exhausted, as a gift, by the process of exchange, by the movement of circulation of the circle in the form of return to the point of departure" (7).

I would speak of an enchanting-asking-giving-telling-proliferating-betraying that comes from no subject and returns to none, is not present and does not come to presence. I would speak of enchanted gifts that always move, enchanted, that circulate as intermediary figures, from one place to another, proliferate in disenchanted economies. I would speak of gifts in abundance overwhelming the identity of subjects, things, and kinds, all given from the good. I would explore the possibility that in human life we meet this abundance in images, beauty, art. If it were possible so to speak. And ask. (Ross, *GBGA*, 21–2)...

I would speak of enchantment in an enchanting voice as if the words broke off from the language in which they were said; as if words and images proliferate without return, without owning; as if our lives were lived in generosity, in telling and asking...

If it were possible that I might speak enchantingly and live generously...

> The relation of the gift to the "present," in all the senses of this term, also to the presence of the present, will form one of the essential knots in the interlace of this discourse. That a gift is called a present, that "to give" may also be said "to make a present," "to give a present," this will not be for us just a verbal clue, a linguistic chance or *alea*. (Derrida, *GT*, 10)

Present, gift; present, presence; presence, discourse; discourse, image, exposition; asking, telling, enchantment. To give a gift is to make a present, to make present, to expose the presentness of presence as proliferating enchantment, to present telling as asking. As time. In time. As images given in time. (Ross, *WAP*, 472)...

> It seems that "re-present-ation" is the process without there being any prior "present-ation" to back it up. Instead, "representation" (taking-the-place-of) is only one moment in a giftgiving

> process which is both linguistic and non-linguistic. We can indeed substitute one gift for another, but the whole process from the identification of the need to the fashioning of the particular gift—words or sentences—which will satisfy it, involves much more than taking-the-place-of or substitution. It involves other-orientation, the ability to recognize others' needs in relation to the world, and things in the world as relevant to those needs. A patriarchal point of view would see the world as made up only of things for which we should compete, not things as having value as relevant to the satisfaction of others' needs. (Genevieve Vaughan, *F-G*, 73)

It seems that re-present-ation takes place without present-ation, without giving, without asking, that exposition... (exposure as expression... image, aesthetics, beauty, literature, art... calling as giving...) proliferates beyond itself as if enchanting beyond gifts. Representation is not the appearance again of the thing or model in substitution and exchange but another gift, another present, generosity toward others, asking betraying enchantment. Presence before representation is presents, giving is exposition, enchanted in abundance. Being, presence, is for giving as the wonder and abundance of asking. (*WAP*, 472)...

I would imagine presence as asking and telling—enchantments in abundance. I would evoke the present as giving, enchanting beyond any gift in time. I would understand presence, gift, and present in terms of general economy, asking beyond exchange and restricted economy, as enchantment beyond disenchantment, representation as if perhaps ~~not~~ beyond itself. Representation is exposition, the ungathering of disenchantment and enchantment, asking and telling beyond themselves. Representation proliferates from itself to other representations, from images to other images, enchantments enchanting enchantments and disenchantments. Language, image, aesthetics, art give and are given beyond any gift, any presence, any moment, now, or present, enchanted perhaps as if ~~not~~ beyond disenchantment. (472)...

> The King takes all my time; I give the rest to Saint-Cyr, to whom I would like to give all. (Derrida, *GT*, 1)

> Here Madame de Maintenon is *writing*, and she says *in writing* that she gives the rest. What is the rest? *Is* it, the rest? She gives the rest which is nothing, since it is the rest of a time concerning which she has just informed her correspondent she has nothing of it left since the King takes it all from her. And yet, we must underscore this paradox, even though the King takes all her time, she seems to have some left, as if she could return the change. "The King takes all *my* time," she says, a time that belongs to her therefore. But how can a time belong? What is it

> *to have time*? Time already begins to appear as that which undoes this distinction between taking and giving, therefore also between receiving and giving, perhaps between receptivity and activity, or even between the being-affected and the affecting of any affection. (3)

In the midst of writing about time and giving, derrida writes of writing together with the impossibility of having time for disenchantment—never time enough, always more time. In the midst of calling our attention to the ways in which time disrupts the economy of taking and receiving that is having and possessing, derrida speaks of writing. It is *in writing*—I mean *in exposition...*—that the impossibility of having time is given; it is in exposition...—art, language, aesthetics, images—that the impossibility of having meaning is given as asking in the impossible caesura of enchantment. Perhaps as if there is never asking enough. As if enchantment were never enchanting enough. As if it were impossible—the impossible of exposition. Or betrayal. (*WAP*, 473)

> It must not circulate, it must not be exchanged, it must not in any case be exhausted, as a gift, by the process of exchange, by the movement of circulation of the circle in the form of return to the point of departure. If the figure of the circle is essential to economics, the gift must remain *aneconomic*. Not that it remains foreign to the circle, but it must *keep* a relation of foreignness to the circle, a relation without relation of familiar foreignness. It is perhaps in this sense that the gift is the impossible.
>
> Not impossible but *the* impossible. The very figure of the impossible. It announces itself, gives itself to be thought as the impossible. (Derrida, *GT*, 7)

The impossible here is not the impossibility of generosity, as if we would like to give gifts but cannot, as if we fail in what we desire. The gift is not impossible or even difficult, but is the impossible itself, the impossible as the unhaving of the gift, the unity of ungathering, as if ~~not~~ beyond the enchanting of enchantments—and disenchantments: the betrayal of betrayal. All perhaps. This impossible does not make it impossible to give a gift but is the condition, the being, of giving; this enchantment of giving is the condition, the being, of disenchantment. In other words, the gift and giving are the betrayal of the presence, immanence, and reality of enchantment, giving what is impossible to give, given in the propagation of enchantments. *As if. Perhaps. Asking and telling.* (Ross, *WAP*, 474)

> For there to be a gift, there must be no reciprocity, return, exchange, countergift, or debt. If the other *gives* me *back* or *owes* me or has to give me back what I give him or her, there will not have been a gift. (Derrida, *GT*, 12)
>
> For there to be a gift, *it is necessary [il faut]* that the donee not give back, amortize, reimburse, acquit himself, enter into a contract, and that he never have contracted a debt. (13)

Again, this does not suggest that one cannot be generous, one cannot give gifts generously, that the ingredients of the earth are not enchanted and enchanting. To the contrary, people give gifts, make presents, do favors, and there is always more than they can accomplish, than they can possess or have. They cannot be sure, it is impossible to be sure, that there is no reciprocity. We cannot be sure that what appears enchanting is not disenchanted, cannot be accounted for. In many cultures gifts must be reciprocated at a level comparable to the gift, so that giving is exchanging, and not to return a gift properly is to incur a dangerous debt. The gift is dangerous because it must be repaid. Everything must be accounted for, explained, organized and balanced, summed up. It would appear that there is, then, no gift, that generosity is taking and receiving rather than giving and asking. It would appear that what appears enchanting is organizing and exchanging. And in many cultures that is so. For there to be a gift it is necessary that there be no return, no debt. Generosity requires it. Yet in many cultures generosity imposes a debt, as if to be generous required generosity from others. Yet we know that that is rare: even gratitude much less generosity is not returned. (Ross, *WAP*, 474)

In a certain sense, this is what anaximander says of time: All things must make reparation to one another for their injustice. It is impossible and all things must. In a certain sense, it is what levinas says of the face. The asymmetry before the face requires nothing from the other. I am hostage, I am required, I am obliged, I am vulnerable, I must be generous regardless of what the other does, despite the other's stinginess and ungenerosity. I am responsible to the other though the other would harm me. I must be responsible though it be impossible, because it is impossible. Generosity is openness to the other in enchantment whereby the impossible promise is exposed, proliferating images in enchantment. In a certain sense, this is what hyde says of art. The gift, the work of art, must always move. Yet works are collected and displayed. The impossibility that art can never come to rest is the condition that allows it to be displayed in its space on the walls of the museum, and to exceed that and any space. The impossibility of enchantment is the condition of its disenchantment. (474–5)

The impossibility of responsibility is the condition of responsibility. That is what derrida says. Responsibility is excessive and impossible, and these conditions or images are the possibility and reality of responsibility and ethics. Enchantment is excessive and impossible and is thereby the condition of disenchantment. (475)

> Responsibility carries within it, and must do so, an essential excessiveness. It regulates itself neither on the principle of reason nor on any sort of accountancy. I believe there is no responsibility, no ethico-political decision, that must not pass through the proofs of the incalculable or the undecidable. (Derrida, *EW*, 272–3)

> I repeat: responsibility is excessive or it is not a responsibility. A limited, measured, calculable, rationally distributed responsibility is already the becoming-right of morality. (286)

> It would be easy to show that a hospitality without reserve is the impossible itself, and that this *condition of possibility* of the event is also its *condition of impossibility*, but it would be just as easy to show that without this experience of the impossible, one might as well give up on both justice and the event. (Derrida, *SM*, 65)

Enchantment is excessive or it is not enchanting. A limited, measured, calculable, rationally distributed enchantment is already becoming disenchanted. A limited, measured, calculable, rationally distributed asking is already becoming dogmatic. And yet it must be limited, knowable, disenchanted, and yet it cannot be and be enchanted. And this impossible—this madness, caesura, impossible relation between enchantment and disenchantment—is the condition of the possibility of disenchantment—and of enchantment.

This impossible is giving, this impossible is enchanting, this impossible is asking, this impossible is literature, art, aesthetics, exposition—in their possibility and actuality and reality and impossibility. This is the impossibility of art and aesthetics, which are nothing more—that is, everything—than this possibility and impossibility, in the caesura between asking and telling...

This immensely difficult thought is as far from disenchantment as it is possible to go, in the reverse direction so far as if again to come near: the proximity of the impossible. It is repeated with respect to enchanting and asking. It is in light of a giving beyond generosity that gifts are given. It is in light of enchantment, no matter how impossible, that the earth can be disenchanted. The enchantments of exposition—exposure as expression, asking, calling, telling; as *aisthēsis, mimēsis, poiēsis, catachrēsis, technē*; as image, aesthetics, beauty, art; as unearthing, revelation, disclosure; calling as giving; interrupting in betrayal (Ross, *WAP*, 475).

Two imperatives drive gablik's vision. One is her critique of modernism and of other critiques—postmodernism in particular. The other is her commitment to a single vision and an overarching paradigm.

> A lot of deconstructive postmodern art is about stripping away the ideological myths that held modernism together, particularly the hegemonic, masculine authority that has been vested in Western European culture and its institutions. (*RA*, 17)

> "Endgame" art embodies a retrospective reading of modernism that is fully aware of its limitations and failed political ambitions; we can no longer depend on the avant-garde to institute change. To replace modernism's utopian mission of social transformation with subversive complicity raises the question of what "a truly conscious postmodern practice"—what the substance of radicality—really is, after the closure of modernism. What future, if any, does it hold? How do we conceive of the post-avant-garde artist? (21)

This endgame art is critical of modernity and modern art but understands that corporate culture is overwhelming.

> to imagine at this point that art can somehow transcend the power structure, or that it can change anything, is quite simply self-delusion. There is no longer any possibility of escape from the system, and the nondeluded individual of today is the one who has given up naive hopes, and any pointless idealizing of the artist's role. The post-avant-garde doesn't try to conquer new territories or concern itself with radical new futures; it understands that the modernist impulse has exhausted itself, but makes no predictions about where our culture is going, or what will take modernism's place. (14)

This is disenchanted indeed, in more ways than that of accountability and rationality. It is disenchanted toward all futures and all possibilities. Even so, enchantment is betrayed inside such a view, though gablik cannot see it even when she quotes it.

"Here is a course of action," writes the French postmodern philosopher Jean-François Lyotard in *Driftworks*: "harden, worsen, accelerate decadence."

> Adopt the perspective of active nihilism, exceed the mere recognition—be it depressive or admiring—of the deconstruction of all values. Become more and more incredulous. Push decadence further still and accept, for instance, to destroy the belief in truth under all its forms. (Gablik, *RA*, 16; quoted from Lyotard)

Another example can be found in foucault, who when criticized for not telling us what to do responds that there are thousands of things to do.

> I worry about comprehending the effective mechanisms of domination; and I do it so that those who are inserted in certain relations of power, who are implicated in them, might escape them through their actions of resistance and rebellion, might transform them in order not to be subjugated any longer. And if I don't ever say what must be done, it isn't because I believe that there's nothing to be done; on the contrary, it is because I think that there are a thousand things to do, to invent, to forge, on the part of those who, recognizing the relations of power in which they're implicated, have decided to resist or escape them. From this point of view all of my investigations rest on a postulate of absolute optimism. I do not conduct my analyses in order to say: this is how things are, look how trapped you are. I say certain things only to the extent to which I see them as capable of permitting the transformation of reality. (Foucault, *RM*, 174)

Thousands of things to do, thousands of moments of transformation: endless, absolute optimism. Perhaps this is more enchanted than disenchanted: thousands of resistances and not one new disenchanted paradigm. Perhaps it is more aesthetic than political—or political because it is aesthetic. For foucault speaks of art when he speaks of transformation. As we have seen.

> For me, intellectual work is related to what you could call "aestheticism," meaning transforming yourself. I am not interested in the academic status of what I am doing because my problem is my own transformation. This transformation of one's self by one's own knowledge is, I think, something rather close to the aesthetic experience. Why should a painter work if he is not transformed by his own painting? (Foucault, *MF*, 130–1)[4]

What is the point of transformation if it is not of one's self by one's knowledge? Is this not art? Is this not aesthetics? Is this not enchantment?

What if lyotard's active nihilism were not giving up life, as gablik takes it to be, but abandoning belief in a total, better, innocent practice? Giving up the dream of living finally. Every dream of living finally is finally disenchanted: total, hegemonic, accounting for everything. Enchantment, like art, is full of what cannot be accounted for, and what we may resist in our active nihilism and our hardened and accelerated decadence is the insistence that everything is technological, economically rational, politically accounted for. The truth that is to be destroyed is replaced by many truths, none with claims upon us all, many askings and tellings. Decadence is anti-authoritarianism carried to such an extreme as to resist any possibility of disenchantment, an enchanting figure of enchantment. Resisting every finality.

> It all comes down, finally, to the kind of culture we take to be the most desirable, and to whether we are prepared to say what sort of world view would support the creation of a future different from our present situation. History provides many examples of monolithic social systems that changed: feudalism, slavery, colonialism. At this point, it is rapidly becoming obvious to many people that the achievements of modern technocratic society have been a mixed blessing, and that our profit-maximizing, competitive attitudes will have to be transformed, because the present values of growth, power and domination are not sustainable. (Gablik, *RA*, 23–4)

It seems to come down, finally, to whether a single kind of culture and a single world view is the alternative to modern technocratic disenchanted society. Perhaps an enchanted one—meaning not single but multiple points of view, many worlds if you will, all overflowing their barriers. Mixed blessings. Never finally. Perhaps perhaps. As if as if.

In the 21st century, after modern rationality has arrived, in what voice may one speak of "two postmodernisms," each opposite to the other?

> The question of whether postmodernism offers any real break with the "disenchantment" of the modern world view, cannot be adequately addressed, I feel, without an understanding that there are two postmodernisms—a deconstructive and a reconstructive version—each representing the pole opposite to the other, and each believing that its scenario and view of the future is the correct one. (21)

Are we in a battle of titans for the future, or a balancing of ledgers and accountings? Who can speak and in what modality of the correct view of the future?

I think that only a disenchanted voice can do so, and I fear that some of the most *interesting* artists—nietzsche's word—speak in a disenchanted voice of the future and of their art. Their art is another matter. A disenchanted voice seeks to be correct. An enchanted voice squawks and squeals. A voice gablik hears.

> The shaman can hear the voice of the stones and trees that are speaking—the voices of things unheard to us all. The shaman does not live in a mechanical, disenchanted world, but in an enchanted one, comprised of multiple, complex, living, interacting systems. Modern man, however, has left the realm of the unknown and the mysterious, and settled down in the realm of the functional and the routine. The world as an emanation of spirit, of visionary powers and mythical archetypes, is not congruent with the world of mechanization, which requires matter-of-factness as the prevailing attitude of mind. (45)

Perhaps she does not favor squeals and squawks when it comes to the future of the earth, or for that matter the future of art. Yet she speaks here of a world of multiple, complex, living, interacting systems, an abundance and multiplicity more than a unity and a framework. A driving force of deconstructive postmodernism—if there be such—is that speech and writing strive for more authority than they can rightly claim, that there is légerdemain—enchantment—in the voices of disenchantment, including all accountings for reenchantment.

> Much of my text is devoted to creating a framework for reconstructive postmodern practice, which, although less visible in the mainstream than deconstructive art, implicates art in the operative reframing of our entire world view and its Cartesian cognitive traditions. Reconstructivists are trying to make the transition from Eurocentric, patriarchal thinking and the "dominator" model of culture toward an aesthetics of interconnectedness, social responsibility and ecological attunement. "If there is any bond among the elements of this 'counter culture,' it is the notion of recovery of our bodies, our health, our sexuality, our natural environment, our archaic traditions, our unconscious mind, our rootedness in the land, our sense of community, and our connectedness to one another." (Gablik, 22; quoted from Berman, *RW*, 279)

I have spoken with berman, now with gablik. It might well be fulfilling to recover our bodies, our rootedness, and our connectedness. And it might be stifling. There is also the question of whether we have lost them, or whether they have gone underground, slid to the margins, turned sideways almost invisibly, but always present. More to the point, if they become prominent and visible, will they become disenchanted? Is not every modern and postmodern authority disenchanted—and for that matter terrible and destructive? How are we to speak of the betrayals of enchantment? In an enchanting or disenchanting voice? Reverently or irreverently?

It all comes down, finally, to the kind of culture we take to be the most desirable. It all comes down, perhaps, to the insistence that one kind of culture is superior to another and that we must do anything in our power to bring it about. One might call that attitude *modern*. One might call it *disenchanted*. One might call it unquestioning.

> We live in a toxic culture, not just environmentally but spiritually as well. If one's work is to succeed as part of a necessary process of cultural healing, there must be a willingness to abandon old programming—to let go of negative ideas and beliefs that are destructive to the planet and to life on earth. But what does this mean for art? (Gablik, 24)

We live in a toxic culture, becoming more toxic all the time. (Who is the *we* of this toxicity, does it include asia, africa, the middle east, and latin america as well as north america and europe?) One of the toxicities I fear, given from modernity itself, comes from those who know the solution and are prepared to impose it. On art and artists for example, including those who have been calling attention to the toxicities, long before and after and more widely than gablik and berman. She has a message for them too.

> In our present situation, the effectiveness of art needs to be judged by how well it overturns the perception of the world that we have been taught, which has set our whole society on a course of biospheric destruction. Ecology (and the relational, total-field model of "ecosophy") is a new cultural force we can no longer escape—it is the only effective challenge to the long-term priorities of the present economic order. I believe that what we will see in the next few years is a new paradigm based on the notion of participation, in which art will begin to redefine itself in terms of social relatedness and ecological healing, so that artists will gravitate toward different activities, attitudes and roles than those that operated under the aesthetics of modernism. (27)

It is one thing to ask everyone including artists to resist the toxicity of our culture. It is another to condemn art and artists and aesthetics as the toxicity of our culture, and another to insist that artists carry the weight of social transformation.

> This book represents my own attempt to look at what changes are necessary or desirable, how we might achieve them, and what the role of art and artists might be in accelerating this process. (4)

> I participated in a one-day invitational forum in New York, organized by the Rockefeller Foundation, for the purpose of discussing a possible new funding program for environmental and socially concerned art. Some of the questions put to us for consideration were: Are political and social concerns in the arts informing a new aesthetic? Are artists becoming more engaged in work that addresses social issues? Is there a new relevance to this art? Are artists actively invoking nature and issues of the environment in new ways? What is the relationship of their work to environmental activism? (4)

Even if I entirely agreed with the social programs advocated here—and in many ways I do—I would hesitate at the prescriptiveness for art and artists as well as for the rest of us. Not so much as—or under the heading—of environmental fascism or garbage police[5] as in relation to the enchantments of art. For while anyone may advocate that anyone else become more socially responsible, it is different when that claim is made in the name of art. That art must become more socially responsible is the form in which the state takes control of art, the way in which community standards impose their toxicity disenchantingly on the diversity of art. Enchantment emerges from the multiplicities and pluralities of arts and artists and ecologies and ecosophies. If there be such.

Perhaps it would be helpful if political and social concerns informed a new aesthetic. Whose concerns, what justifies their authority, how plural and how authoritarian is this new aesthetic? Are artists becoming more engaged in work that addresses social issues? Are you and I? In how many different ways? And what of religious groups and community organizations? Is it always better that this should be so? Does it depend on who is excluded, who is crushed, whose point of view and life don't matter? The one thing art always does, less of course after it has been authorized and institutionalized, is to present other points of view. As other. In the plural. And in this way to ask and tell. Otherness as other, in the plural, is the condition of enchantment, in the modalities of *as if* and *perhaps*, and every point of view that crushes otherness as other, that halts the proliferation of exposition, that replaces *as if* and *perhaps* by *must* and *real*, institutes disenchantment. *As if* and *perhaps* do not go away, enchantment cannot be crushed by disenchantment. But people can, including artists.

Gablik believes that literature and art and artists and aesthetics in our toxic culture are toxic, that modern art has failed along with the industrial modern culture that has spawned it.

> I wish to argue that the rational framework of modern aesthetics has left us with an ontology of objectification, permanence and egocentricity, which has seriously undermined art's inherent capacity to be communicative and compassionately responsive, or to be seen also as a process, rather than exclusively as fixed forms. I am, of course, aware that the new terms of interdependence and relatedness implied by reenchantment will not be suitable for every artist, however alluring they may seem to some: there will always be individuals for whom the autonomy of the aesthetic attitude, which needs no social or moral justification, is more correct. Nevertheless, I am proposing that our model of aesthetics needs therapeutic attention, because it has lost its sensitivity not only to the psychological conditions of individuals and society, but also to the ecological and process character of the world. (60–1)

I believe that art can only fail standards imposed upon it, that modern, western (and worldwide) art over the past century has been abundant, imaginative, wonderful in many ways. The toxicity of the culture indeed has limited its imagination. The toxicity of the culture also has spawned astonishing achievements and added to the abundance of the world. Art in its most individualized and toxic roles—and they are just an ingredient of the production of art in our toxic culture—is one of the most visible sites of its enchantments.

Here is a principle of enchantment—and every principle is disenchanted:

Enchantment creativity arrival require form, form disenchants. Form creates enchantingly, arrives disenchantingly...

From disenchanted toxic destructive violent forms emerge enchantments beyond accounting. Enchantments follow disenchantments. In this way and others disenchantment is enchanting...

Form is enchanting form is disenchanting form is neither enchanting nor disenchanting form is both enchanting and disenchanting...

Art is not the only enchanted practice in our industrialized, technologized, politicized culture, nor the most enchanted. Aesthetics is not the only modern, secular name of enchantment. Yet with all their restrictions and toxicities, art and aesthetics are experienced by many as unmistakably enchanted. Not for all or always the same arts, wealthy elites prefer institutionalized works, ordinary people work with ordinary crafts and everyday materials, religious people surround themselves with spiritual works with sacred themes. Yet for all, the ordinary and everyday, the disenchanting, is enriched and captivated by works of art made by artists, whether by images, fictions, writings, bodies, gestures, performances, whatever, you name it. In the arts, somewhere, something is enchanting for someone. Sacred, secular, or profane; scientific or humanistic; technological or handmade.

We do not know what art means, what art can do, it can do and mean anything, even when we try to prevent it. We do not know what art is, it can be and do anything: inspire, create, delight, offend, wound, hurt, open, crush, enlighten, illuminate, teach, ask, tell. It can give information about butterflies and whales, about guns and teas, teach about life and death. You name it, art can be and do and mean it. Even if you don't know the name. Art is where the superfluity of humanity, life, and nature resonates, proliferates, magnifies, contracts...

Would you want an artist to cut your appendix out, to treat you for AIDS? Is it that art makes for bad surgery and medicine, or that certain experiences are necessary for surgery and medicine, and art might be one of them? Would you want a surgeon without a sense of humor or magic to cut you open, or would you want a skillful surgeon full of enchantment? Why do you imagine they are in conflict?

Against *mimēsis*, exposition, art, aesthetics, again:[6]

> The art of contradiction making, descended from an insincere kind of conceited mimicry, of the semblance-making breed, derived from image making, distinguished as a portion, not divine but human, of production, that presents a shadow play of words—such are the blood and lineage which can, with perfect truth, be assigned to the authentic Sophist. (Plato, *Sophist*, 268cd)

The reason, disenchanted, is that:

> The mimetic art is far removed from truth, and this, it seems, is the reason why it can produce everything, because it touches or lays hold of only a small part of the object and that a phantom, as, for example, a painter, we say, will paint us a cobbler, a carpenter, and other craftsmen, though he himself has no expertness in any of these arts, but nevertheless if he were a

> good painter, by exhibiting at a distance his picture of a carpenter he would deceive children and foolish men, and make them believe it to be a real carpenter. (Plato, *Republic*, 598bc)

> Shall we, then, lay it down that all the poetic tribe, beginning with Homer, are imitators of images of excellence and of the other things that they "create," and do not lay hold on truth, but, as we were just now saying, the painter will fashion, himself knowing nothing of the cobbler's art, what appears to be a cobbler to him and likewise to those who know nothing but judge only by forms and colors? (600e–601a)

Looked at with eyes of disenchanted truth, the uncontainability of *mimēsis* is its scandal. Looked at with enchanted eyes, exposition..., expression, asking, telling, calling, *aisthēsis, mimēsis, poiēsis, catachrēsis, technē,* image, aesthetics, beauty, art are all enchanting, and more. Enchantment... is always more..., including all the goods of disenchantment. Art is always more..., exposing the limits of accountable truths.

I do not say that disenchanted truths are worthless, only disenchanted voices say such things, they say that enchanted truths are untruthful, unscientific, unworthy. Enchanted voices sing and squawk and chant and moan. They dissemble semblances, assemble and disassemble them into more and more semblances, truths and semblances, including every disenchanted truth we have found. They can produce anything and leave it to us to produce something more. In this way they ask and tell beyond every asking and telling.

What are you afraid of, why are you so fearful of being deceived, whom do you want to protect you from deception?...

Gablik's image of reenchantment follows berman's: restoring the lost paradigm in which perception is magical.

> One of the peculiar developments in our Western world is that we are losing our sense of the divine side of life, of the power of imagination, myth, dream and vision. The particular structure of modern consciousness, centered in a rationalizing, abstracting and controlling ego, determines the world we live in and how we perceive and understand it; without the magical sense of perception, we do not live in a magical world. We no longer have the ability to shift mind-sets and thus to perceive other realities—to move between the worlds, as ancient shamans did. The important thing is whether a shift in awareness occurs, creating a point of departure, an opening for numinous or magical experience that can never be obtained by cultivating intellectual skills; the world of magical perception has to be

> explored experientially, with wholehearted participation of the entire being. (Gablik, *RA*, 42–3)

She undertakes a "reenchantment project":

> At this point, the Reenchantment project reflects a more holistic outlook that is very much "in the air," but breaking the spell of dualism is no easy matter. Even though we are already changing the idiom of our culture away from the linear and the mechanistic and toward the ecological and the compassionate, dualistic ways of thinking continue to dominate all our discourses, myths and ideologies, so that it is not particularly easy to see the beginning of something that is being shaped by a truly different awareness. (164)

My image of enchantment is of unknown and undiscovered points of transgression and transfiguration, endlessly open to surprise, permeated by endless asking and telling. My image of art, no matter how commodified and institutionalized, is that it arises from and promotes shifts of awareness, creates points of departure, opens onto experiences beyond intellectual skills, arises from sensible feelings, perceptions, and explorations calling for the wholehearted participation of the entire being of artist and audience. I do not view art as subordinated to an overarching vision or project but as singularly, uniquely, and specifically enchanting—as art, if not art alone or especially. Religion, too, is enchanting—less so when it claims to possess the key to enchantment in the name of sacredness and spirituality, and almost not at all in the name of its institutions.

I consider disenchanted any fixed or total vision or institutionalization of the world and of life, no matter how magical it claims itself to be. The magic and transformations are either under the control of a central authority that guards them closely, or they are passages to the unknown—moments, arrivals, transfigurations, transgressions—beyond any vision or institution. Moreover, these are uncertain, hesitant, surprising, variable. Shifts in awareness and feeling come unexpectedly. Points of departure go elsewhere. Openings to transformative experiences unfold onto unknown and unfamiliar places, uncontrollable by intellect and reason. Experience offers a richness and wonder and abundance that calls forth our entire being, and helps us to discover that it is always more than we understood it to be, more than any gift can show it to be, no matter how magical or sacred. Enchantment exceeds any gift and art is one of its handmaidens. Not the only one, by any means, but certainly in our culture and many others among the most potent and pervasive.

Perhaps it is time, from the standpoint of art and aesthetics as well as ecology and philosophy, to think of the new paradigm of enchantment as directed against paradigms themselves, especially those that claim the right over others. Perhaps it is time to remind ourselves that art and aesthetics and ecology and philosophy all succumb to authoritarian paradigms yet are known in our culture, and others, to be sites at which authority is challenged. Perhaps overturning can take place without replacement, perhaps enchantment does not seek to replace disenchantment but to displace, multiply, and proliferate it. Perhaps we need more ecologies, perceptions, and arts than our toxic and stunted, disenchanted world can allow itself. More perhaps. Art and aesthetics are perhaps a perhaps of the proliferation of other paradigms and other aesthetics. Again perhaps.

Perhaps it is time to ask what a reenchanted art would be. In her final chapter gablik suggests the following:

> The essence of ecological thinking is not linear, but finds its identity in a continuous flow of mutually determined interactions: the self-in-relationship. Caring, here, is a quality of attention—a total commitment to looking and listening. The healing power rests not so much in the object exchanged, but in the path of mutuality and understanding that is created. (173)

This is ecology and enchantment, and art is given over to it. I am by no means sure of this giving over.

> In shedding conventional notions of self and self-interest like an old skin or a confining shell, we engage more effectively with the forces and pathologies that imperil planetary survival, as the ecologist and Buddhist scholar Joanna Macy describes it in *World as Lover, World as Self*. For Macy, as for many others, the crisis that threatens our planet, whether in its military, ecological or social aspects, derives from a dysfunctional and pathogenic notion of the self. Awakening to our larger, ecological self will give us new powers, according to Macy, undreamed of in our squirrel cage of the separate ego. But, she adds, because these new powers are interactive in nature, they manifest themselves only to the extent that we recognize and act upon our interexistence. (175)

Like gablik, macy begins with the wounds, but she has another relationship to offer. The world is our lover, we love it and it loves us. With all the complications of western love and of buddhist compassion, macy asks us to think of, participate in, and share this love beyond all loves.

> I would like to reflect on four particular ways that people on spiritual paths look at the world. These are not specific to any particular religion; you can find all of them in most spiritual traditions. These four are: world as battlefield, world as trap, world as lover, world as self. (Joanna Macy, *WLWS*, 5)

While she rejects the first two relations and identifies the last two, macy dwells in multiplicity, thereby in asking. One might crave and identify with the earth as love and self in a multiplicity beyond any self and any love; one might see love and self as multiplicity itself. In this way they would be aesthetic, and it would be artistic and aesthetic to embody and present this multiplicity.

> It is my experience that the world itself has a role to play in our liberation. Its very pressures, pains, and risks can wake us up—release us from the bonds of ego and guide us home to our vast, true nature. For some of us, our love for the world is so passionate that we cannot ask it to wait until we are enlightened.
>
> So let us discuss the world as lover. Instead of a stage set for our moral battles or a prison to escape, the world is beheld as a most intimate and gratifying partner. In Hinduism, we find some of the richest expressions of our erotic relationship to the world. (8)

The world as lover is as complex as any lover can be. She/he/it is our lover, we love her/him/it, it/he/she loves us. I emphasize this in the registers of both love and loving—we hope our lovers love us; love is complex, uncertain, unpredictable: impossible. We have no message, derrida insists, that we can offer in certainty in love, every message is impossible, every love is impossibly love. This thought of the impossible is not evident in gablik and macy, yet it is love—shattered and shattering beyond any telling.[7]

And all the more for us here, the world as lover loves us. macy quotes a long passage from calvino's *Cosmicomics,* at the moment of the big bang when we were *All at One Point* together, understanding the explosion as love:[8]

> We got along so well all together, so well that something extraordinary was bound to happen. It was enough for her to say, at a certain moment, "Oh, if I only had some room, how I'd like to make some noodles for you boys!" And in that moment we all thought of the space that her round arms would occupy moving backward and forward over the great mound of flour

> and eggs while her arms kneaded and kneaded, white and shiny with oil up to the elbows, and we thought of the space the flour would occupy and the wheat for the flour and the fields to raise the wheat and the mountains from which the water would flow to irrigate the fields of the space it would take for the Sun to arrive with its rays, to ripen the wheat; of the space for the Sun to condense from the clouds of stellar gases and burn; of the quantities of stars and galaxies and galactic masses in flight through space which would be needed to hold suspended every galaxy, every nebula, every sun, every planet, and at the same time we thought of it, this space was inevitably being formed, at the same time that Mrs. Ph(i)Nk$_0$ was uttering those words: the point that contained her and all of us was expanding in a halo of distance in light years and light centuries and billions of light millennia and we were being hurled to the four corners of the universe and she dissolved into I don't know what kind of energy-light-heat, she, Mrs. Ph(i)Nk$_0$, she who in the midst of our closed, petty world had been capable of a generous impulse, a true outburst of general love, initiating at the same time the concept of space and, properly speaking, space itself, and time, and universal gravitation, and the gravitating universe, making possible billions and billions of suns, and planets, and fields of wheat, and Mrs. Ph(i)Nk$_0$s, scattered through the continents of the planets, kneading with floury, oil-shiny, generous arms and she lost at that very moment, and we, mourning her loss. (Italo Calvino, *AAOP*, 46–7; quoted in Macy, *WLWS*, 10)

What love offers, in the figure of a pasta-making woman, is all the particularities of the beings and becomings of the world, particularities in which every becoming and every being is loved, and every thing and condition and possibility of that being and becoming is loved, so that love makes the world go round—in this case, produces the world in its inexhaustible particularities.

One might imagine this figure as a goddess. One might imagine it as a personification of impersonal forces. But they are love, they love us, and they are there for us to love them. In this way they are divine, they are personifications, they are symbolizations, they appear in art, literature, appear aesthetic; and their appearances are askings and tellings beyond every disenchantment. Calvino could not offer us this love except as literature. To our sorrow we must go to literature to find it, cannot find it in today's philosophy or physics; yet to our joy literature and art offer it to us.

And what they offer is enchantment. Love, world, self are all enchanted, all enchantment, all enchanting. The earth is enchanting in calvino's hands, in the hands of art and literature, in the mind and soul, in language and images, in proliferation. In this moment, however, enchantment is love, and love is self, and self is world, and world is enchanting—as love and self, in art.[9]

> Since, as Calvino reminds us, we were "all in one point" to begin with, we could as easily see the world as self. Just as lovers seek for union, we are apt, when we fall in love with our world, to fall into oneness with it as well. Hunger for this union springs from a deep knowing, to which mystics of all traditions give voice. The tree that will grow from the seed, that art thou; the running water, that art thou, and the sun in the sky, and all that is, that art thou.
>
> Mystics of the Western traditions have tended to speak of merging self with God rather than with the world, but the import is often the same. When Hildegard of Bingen experienced unity with the divine, she gave it these words: "I am the breeze that nurtures all things green. I am the rain coming from the dew that causes the grasses to laugh with the joy of life." (Macy, *WLWS*, 33)

Do we know what love and self and world and earth and spirit and enchantment are? Conclusively? Do the mystics? Or do they feel something of them all beyond any, beyond themselves? This beyond itself is enchantment, and the experience of it is enchanting. Art frequently enchants us, and it does so in the midst of the most toxic surroundings. It is not alone, but it is visibly present. And it enchants every place and time, no matter how mundane or toxic, no matter how secular.

The reenchantment project is different:

> How, then, can we shift our usual way of thinking so that we create more compassionate structures in our culture? How do we achieve the "world view of attachment" to the world, continuity with the world? At this point we lack any practical personal blueprint for action, unless we are willing to act as architects and engineer a new conceptual framework for our lives. The compassionate, ecological self will need to be cultivated with as much thoroughness as we have cultivated, in long years of abstract thinking, the mind geared to scientific and aesthetic objectivity: distant, cold, neutral, value-free. (Gablik, *RA*, 179–80)
>
> We are in transitional times, an undefined period between detachment from the old and attachment to the new. It is a good moment to attend to the delineation of goals, as more and more people now imagine that our present system can be replaced by

> something better: closeness, instead of distancing; the cultivation of ecocentric values; whole-systems thinking; a developed discipline of caring; an individualism that is not purely individual but is grounded in social relationships and also promotes community and the welfare of the whole; an expanded vision of art as a social practice and not just a disembodied eye. I have tried to show that none of these intentions is irrelevant to a value-based art, and that all of them are crucial to its reenchantment. The sacredness of both life and art does not have to mean something cosmic or otherworldly—it emerges quite naturally when we cultivate compassionate, responsive modes of relating to the world and to each other. (181)

We are in transitional times, not perhaps from one failed framework to a better, but in transition itself, one transitional object after another without certainty of fulfillment. It may be that this is where gablik and berman on the one hand and I on the other part. Disenchantment for me is not only toxic, is not toxic as such, but grasping. Enchantment offers us the world in wonder filled with transitions, transitional objects and selves, selves and objects that cannot be grasped because they are mobile, fragmentary, and displaced. Enchantments are in the caesura.

I think of disenchantment not as humanity gone awry—there are glories associated with it and wounds of enchantment. I think of it as I would think of the catholic church or of islam. They are enchanted and enchanting as are science and philosophy, modern knowledges and technologies. In their way, however, they are crushing, brutally repressing toward other ways of life and being. Disenchantment closes off the reach of the world, not in itself—except where it destroys—but in what humanity allows to touch its heart and its imagination, to limit what may be asked and told. As glorious as jesus may be it would seem that he has to die again in order that other glories may come to pass. As grand as modern reason may be it would seem that it has to pass away in order that other modernities and other rationalities may arrive. Perhaps.

Enchantment does not offer another modernity, another church, another god—but many, and many others. It offers them in the fragments, interstices, and caesuras of the other ways, the residues and incompletenesses of every way, every temple, every god, offers them for asking, multiplies them in telling. Art is enchanted in this way, enchanted when sold to the highest bidder on the altar of mammon, when shut up in great museums and corporate headquarters. Other artists do not join, those that do can inspire those who do not, art exists in the margins, enchanting a world that pretends that it can do without it, that it can kill enchantment, knowing that art and artists and aesthetics are always on the verge of disenchantment. In this way—it is not true of art alone—it reveals the absurdity of reenchantment, the absolute nihilism at its heart. This is because enchantment has never gone away, but constantly takes on new forms, new directions, opens up new wonders and abundances right in the midst of that which claims to kill abundance and wonder, to count abundance and to account for wonder.

The words that offer enchantment to us—words of generosity beyond gifts—are impossible, beyond possibility and impossibility. The impossible, which is to say, not impossible, not merely impossible, not on the register of possible and impossible, good and bad, high and low, pro and con, but other, otherwise, archaic, old and new. Enchantment's enchanting is much stranger—and yet not strange, not unfamiliar, but beyond familiarity, strangeness, and impossibility.

Disenchantment speaks of possibility and impossibility, reality and unreality, true and false, good and bad. Enchantment chants, moans, squawks, shrieks, sings, shrills, sighs enchantingly. The impossible is not in disenchantment's register, nor is the exposition of art. The impossible is enchantingly aesthetic...

Here, then, is enchantment, offered to us beyond disenchantment, other to religion. Beauty, art, aesthetics—all that is named for us as image—intersect science on one side and religion on the other without accepting their authorizations as disenchanted or enchanted. Art, literature, aesthetics are enchanting, and in their enchanting ways enchant everything they touch, in their disenchanting ways disenchant everything they touch. Religion, science, and art are more than what they claim to be. If religion and the gods are enchanted, then in our time religion is disenchanting. Yet disenchantment is no more opposite to enchantment than enchantment is to truth and goodness. These are all enchanting, these are all disenchanting. If science claims that everything is knowable, accountable, explainable, if reason claims authority over all the creatures and things of the earth, then in the touch of pigments, the wail of instruments, the beat of drums, disenchanted reason betrays itself as enchanting and enchanted.

Human enchantments are not more enchanting than other enchantments, enchantments produced by other living and nonliving things or the living and nonliving things themselves. Not *more* than they, but more than would be otherwise. *Otherwise* bears this double meaning, levinas's meaning,[10] not to be other but otherwise, the enchanting otherwise of abundance and wonder, in asking and telling. This is wandering, enchantment is the wandering of exposition, the proliferation of image, meaning, work, etc., the otherwise of the etc.

The image interrupts.
The image proliferates.
The image betrays.
The image for gives.
The image calls.
The image gives.
The image expresses.
The image exposes.

The image gives.
The image is given.
The image enchants.
The image betrays.
The image for gives.

The image is for giving.
The image is for exposition.
The image is for beauty.
The image is from the good. (Ross, *WAP*, 469)

The image is enchanting...

Enchantment interrupts.
Enchantment proliferates
Enchantment betrays.
Enchantment for gives.

The image is enchanting...

Enchantment calls.
Enchantment gives.
Enchantment expresses.
Enchantment exposes.

The image is enchanting...

Enchantment gives.
Enchantment is given.
Enchantment enchants.
Enchantment betrays.
Enchantment for gives.

The image is enchanting....

Enchantment is for giving.
Enchantment is for exposition.
Enchantment is for beauty.
Enchantment is from the good.

Everywhere is the image...
The image is enchanting...

The image is mother and is father, is neither mother nor father and both mother and father, for it is the child. The image is the parent and the children, is neither parent nor children and both parent and children... Here, perhaps, is what we might say of the image, of men and women, of enchantment and of art. The image is in the plural, always other images, images that copy, imitate, replicate; other men and women, other cultures, histories, languages; enchantments in wonder and abundance. Images, in their enchantments, fold back, return, in their multiplication. They do not stand off, object from subject. The image is parent, images the children, every image parent and child. Images are the abundance, fecundity, expressivity, affectivity, plurality, multiplicity, inexhaustibility, wonder, abundance, enchantment of the image, each image together with other images, folded upon and unfolding other images, endless enchantments. The image does not resemble but imitates, reproduces, repeats, refolds, proliferates. The image propagates by reproduction and transfiguration, telling and asking. Enchantment enchants by proliferation...

Children are not less real than their parents. The image in the singular is not more real than images in the plural. The origin, the parent, the cause is no more real—and no less—than the image, the images, the children who are its copies. Moreover, it is a copy and proliferates into other copies. The copies multiply the reality, express the reality as if perhaps ~~not~~ more than itself, enchant every disenchantment. The images are the enchantments that expose the disenchantments of reality—ask it tell it betray it. The difference between image and reality, enchantment and disenchantment, is no difference at all—and every difference, the differences that betray reality as expressive, as exposition, in the caesura. The image copies the reality and makes it more and less than itself, folds it up and unfolds it out, exposes and interrupts it as hyperreality. Reality is hyperreality in the proliferations of images, pictures, words, sounds, gestures, and so on to infinity. Reality is inexhaustibly abundant in the offspring—imitations and copies—it engenders, in the enchantments it proffers. The image—the aesthetic in the phenomenon—knows nothing of any distinction between it and reality, between the image and the thing itself. The solidity, savor, and fecundity of the earth are betrayed as the profusion of images promised to generations to come. Infinity betrays totality. Hyperreality betrays reality. Enchantment enchants disenchantment. (Ross, *WAP*, 6–8)...

The earth gives itself in wonder and abundance. The earth is given in the abundance and wonder of enchantment. The earth is giving and is given in asking and telling as if from the image. The earth, giving, abundance, and wonder are the image in proliferation, proliferation in enchantment. This is to express that we cannot know them and their meaning as such, that they wander in wonder and abundance, that they and every other meaning and sign are in the mode of perhaps, as if, to come, deferred, betrayed, on the way, still to arrive, always arriving. The as if of the image, the fictiveness, fascination, ambiguity, emptiness, and fullness of the image, are expressed and betrayed as if in images that are enchanted and enchanting. Perhaps. (469–70)...

How do we work for the proliferation? How do we fulfill the promise?

The image proliferates.

The image gives.

The image betrays.

The image is given.

Pandora is for giving.

As perhaps are you and I. (504)...

In the name of enchantment I would be pantheist, spiritualist, animist, pagan—or none of these, too secular for any, too aesthetic, too immanent. Immanence is not not-transcendence but enchantment, enchanting enchantment. God or nature as Spinoza says, immanently enchanting (201–)...

Can one be a pantheistic pagan without theism, without God, without gods? That is the secular question. Why should we imagine that God—even pagan gods—can undergird the promise of the universe? Why should we imagine the enchantment of things as if to endlessly repeat images of the divine?

Here is a secular version: the being of things is to promise themselves as if they were enchanting beyond themselves, beyond any accounting, any beginning. The being of things is the promise of proliferation from the image so far beyond as if the image—even if it were God—no longer held claim to the proliferation. The promise... and exposition... of things proliferates as if perhaps ~~not~~ beyond any image of god. That is pagan. If it is anything. It is necessary. If anything is necessary...

As if it were enchanting to be necessary...

That is the difference, then, with nietzsche and dionysus in mind. The world that emanates from God—the transcendent and glorious vision of plotinus and schelling among others—insists that it is God's, insists on the genitive claim of God. The world of pseudo-dionysus—who may have been an image of the god—proliferates the expressivity of all things that answer endlessly to each other.[11] We could say that they answer in the name of god, but it is perhaps as if they answer to each other with the name of god a call to enchantment beyond any asking and any telling. (*WAP*, 201–)

This is *enchanting perhaps as if it were pagan, pantheist, spiritualist, animist* etc. etc.... But it proliferates beyond any label, any name, proliferates from each as image to other images. The promise is fulfilled—and betrayed—in the proliferation. So we may say instead: the betrayal is the insistence on a genitive, the name or truth or identification of God. The proliferation betrays that betrayal. So the name of god may return—as pagan, pantheist, spiritualist, and animist... But these are now no longer what they were but enchanting images in proliferation. These now no longer promise what they were said to promise—God as if perhaps the one of all without remainder. These now promise a proliferation from god or nature or world or image into endless other enchantments with endless remainders.

Yet the promise and the image do not guarantee fulfillment. Proliferation is betrayal, guarantees neither completion nor transformation. I have not said that well: guarantees both completion and transformation, but in no specifiable ways; guarantees both repetition and transfiguration, but in no definite ways. I say this in full knowledge of predictability, do not mean to pretend that science cannot predict the movement of the planets and the completion of material processes. Even so, science, matter, processes, all are images: some of the proliferations are predictable, familiar, determinate, proper; others are anarchic, improper, transgressive; still others are social, individual, variable with context and perspective; all are images, proliferating in unexpected ways where the expected and familiar are as unfamiliar and unexpected and improper as the others.

Images repeat and transform and transfigure and betray. Betrayal reveals the imaging of the image as a proliferation that cannot be controlled even in its propriety—too proper, too controlled, too determinate. The image betrays its overdetermination—by which I mean its transgression and transfiguration—in the promises of asking and telling...

I would be a pantheist, light on the theism...

I would be a pagan, light on the gods...

I would be an aesthete, light on museums and on art...

I would be an artist, heavy on the medium...

I would be a betrayer, heavy on responsivity and responsibility...

I would be enchanted and enchanting as if betraying themselves beyond disenchantment...

I would be a secular pantheist, pagan, animist, spiritualist—if there be such. I would be secular, would be pantheist-pagan-animist-spiritualist, would be neither secular nor pantheist-pagan-animist-spiritualist, would be both secular and pantheist-pagan-animist-spiritualist...

I would be enchanting, would be disenchanting, would be neither enchanting nor disenchanting, would be both enchanting and disenchanting. I would betray these all as images of each other, images of proliferation. They betray themselves as images in proliferation. I would be an aesthete without aestheticization—if there be such. I would betray these all as images in proliferation. That is the point. The world as aesthetic, the imaging of the image, the proliferation of images, express the vitality, efficacy, transgressiveness, multiplicity, heterogeneity, and impropriety of the most familiar experiences and things. The necessary, conditioned, restrictive economies of the world are excessive, evocative, expressive as if perhaps ~~not~~ beyond themselves. (*WAP*, 201–3)...

CHAPTER 5

Enchanting Bodies

> For indeed, no one has yet determined what the Body can do, i.e., experience has not yet taught anyone what the Body can do from the laws of nature alone, insofar as nature is only considered to be corporeal, and what the body can do only if it is determined by the Mind. For no one has yet come to know the structure of the Body so accurately that he could explain all its functions—not to mention that many things are observed in the lower Animals that far surpass human ingenuity, and that sleep-walkers do a great many things in their sleep that they would not dare to awake. This shows well enough that the Body itself, simply from the laws of its own nature, can do many things which its Mind wonders at. (Spinoza, *E*, 3, P2, Schol.)[1]

We do not know what bodies can do. This largely political insistence, famous in spinoza, can be read as—*as if* and *perhaps*—an alchemical formula for enchantment.

As a political insistence, we do not know what bodies can do speaks against the attempt to regulate and control them. As an epistemological insistence, it speaks against every claim to know them finally. Under the name of enchantment, it speaks against the claim that material things are disenchanted.

We do not know what bodies can do, not just because of the limits of knowledge and reason but also because of the enchantments of bodies. We do not yet know, we will never know, bodies do things from their own nature that are filled with wonder and abundance.

The laws of corporeal nature are filled with wonder, bodies and bodily things are infinitely infinite, the earth is enchanting. As are a tiny worm and you and I...

Let us imagine a tiny worm living in the blood. The worm would be living in the blood as we are living in our part of the universe. Since the nature of the universe is absolutely infinite, its parts are modified by the nature of this infinite in infinite ways and are compelled to undergo infinite variations.[2] (Spinoza, *ESL*, Letter 32, 245–6)...

Absolutely infinite, infinite modifications, infinite variations...

Absolutely enchanting, enchanting modifications, enchanting variations...

On the side of disenchantment, we can understand infinite variations as inexhaustible variety and plurality. Absolute infinity, infinitely infinite, is either transcendence or plurality. Bodies obey their laws, laws are universal, infinite variety is universality.

On the side of enchantment, universality is absolute infinity, absolute infinity is enchanting. Not transcendence, beyond finiteness, but infinitely otherwise *as if ~~not~~ beyond* finite and infinite. Infinite infinites are neither infinite nor finite. Infinite infinites are not finite, not infinite, neither finite nor infinite, both finite and infinite. That is, enchanting, full of wonder and abundance.

Spinoza speaks at length of bodies from the point of view of their composition and identity. Beginning:

> A1′: All bodies either move or are at rest.
> A2′: Each body moves now more slowly, now more quickly.
> L1: Bodies are distinguished from one another by reason of motion and rest, speed and slowness, and not by reason of substance.

Continuing:

> L6: If certain bodies composing an Individual are compelled to alter the motion they have from one direction to another, but so that they can continue their motions and communicate them to each other in the same ratio as before, the Individual will likewise retain its nature, without any change of form.
>
> L7: Furthermore, the Individual so composed retains its nature, whether it, as a whole, moves or is at rest, or whether it moves in this or that direction, so long as each part retains its motion, and communicates it, as before, to the others.
>
> Schol.: By this, then, we see how a composite Individual can be affected in many ways, and still preserve its nature. So far we have conceived an Individual which is composed only of bodies which are distinguished from one another only by motion and rest, speed and slowness, i.e., which is composed of the simplest bodies. But if we should now conceive of another, composed of

> a number of Individuals of a different nature, we shall find that it can be affected in a great many other ways, and still preserve its nature.

Concluding:

> But if we should further conceive a third kind of Individual, composed of many individuals of this second kind, we shall find that it can be affected in many other ways, without any change of its form. And if we proceed in this way to infinity, we shall easily conceive that the whole of nature is one Individual, whose parts, i.e., all bodies, vary in infinite ways, without any change of the whole Individual. (Spinoza, *E*, 2, P13, L1–7)

We can easily conceive the whole of infinite nature as composed of parts that vary in infinite ways. But perhaps we may be less sure that the whole of nature is one individual that does not change with infinite changes in its parts. Perhaps change does not pertain to an enchanting whole, or to its individuality.

The enchanting whole of nature is one individual, is many individuals, is neither one individual nor many individuals, is both one individual and many individuals...

The whole of enchanting nature changes, does not change, neither changes nor does not change, both changes and does not change...

The whole of nature is infinitely infinite, wonderful and abundant...

More particularly:

bodies move and rest
quickly and slowly
agree and disagree
cause and follow
are determined in motion or rest by other bodies to infinity
compose and are composed
are fluid, soft, and hard
affect and are affected
impress and trace
move and affect
perceive, dispose in many ways
are simple and complex
remain the same under substitution of like bodies in like motions
a composite individual can be affected in many ways and still preserve its nature
the whole of nature is one (composite) individual whose parts vary in infinite ways

and in another voice:

bodies do
bodies produce
bodies express
bodies strive
bodies feel
bodies become
bodies compose
bodies decompose
bodies enchant
bodies are enchanting
bodies are otherwise than being
bodies do not become
bodies make
bodies happen
bodies relate, are relational
bodies are what they are in relation (metaphysically)
bodies relate as a verb (not metaphysically)
bodies become as a verb (not metaphysically)
bodies change, transform, transfigure (beyond metaphysics)
etc.

and still another:

bodies touch
bodies speak
touch is enchanting
in bodies, touch touches touch, etc.
for bodies, enchantment enchants enchantments
bodies evolve
bodies adapt
bodies learn
bodies are media, bodies are medial, bodies mediate (relate, intermediate, are intermediary, are mediums)
bodies are (in) the caesura
etc. etc.

Motion and rest, quick and slow, seem disenchanted. In a disenchanted voice they appear knowable, infinite but not infinitely infinite. Let us imagine them to be enchanted, infinitely infinite, varying in infinite ways, where varying and infinite here mean surpassing comprehension and prediction—beyond accounting otherwise. Nature is as if it were one composite individual—perhaps—whose parts vary in infinite ways beyond knowing, beyond accounting, beyond ordering, beyond universality, calling for asking and telling beyond grasping, and for giving beyond having.

Lucretius's swerving of atoms in the void may be understood as arbitrary deviation. That is disenchanted. The swerving of atoms in the void may be understood as the subtle departure of bodies moving and coming to rest, elusive, minuscule, too small to be detected—the very small as otherwise, the alteration as alterity, the transformation as transgression: enchanting and enchanted.

If it is thought without reflection that contradiction is absurd,[3] it will be thought that arbitrariness is absurd as well. And if the first is indefensible without reflection, perhaps so is the second. From the standpoint of disenchantment, arbitrariness is irrational and absurd. That is the way disenchantment divides up the world: reasonable and absurd. Contradiction and arbitrariness are irrational from the standpoint of a reason and a logic that demands to know its place at any time. From the standpoint of enchantment, contradiction and arbitrariness are enchanting, absurdity and weirdness open up new forms of asking and of telling. Indeed, the aporias that mark them can be distinguished in this way, those that block asking and those that ask more, ask anew, take nothing for granted.

Disenchantment takes everything for granted. Enchantment knows nothing to take for granted. Everything is ungranted, ungathered, present as a giving even when given as a gift...

If we think of bodies discretely, as separate, individual bodies composing and composed of other discrete bodies, and if we think of laws of nature as formulas describing variations in position and velocity, then such a view would appear not only deterministic—in the sense that all properties of such bodies, velocities, positions, motion and rest, would be determined and predictable—but it would suggest that what we do not know is not a function of bodies and their properties but of our inadequacies. Such a reading of spinoza is not implausible. It offers a certain understanding of both bodies and the infinite infinites that pertain to them.

If we think of bodies relationally, in terms of fields and systems; as gases, fluids, or waves; perhaps statistically, in terms of wave functions; perhaps ecologically—and above all, evolutionarily, so that motion and rest are not changes in position but variations and adaptations—then all the laws of nature, no matter how strict and invariant themselves,[4] give rise to infinite variations of infinite uncertainties that evoke abundance and richness more than inadequacies. It is not our inadequacies, or the incompleteness of natural laws, or the indeterminateness of bodies that makes it impossible to know all their properties rationally and scientifically, but their infinite infinity as bodies—here understanding composition as transfiguration, relationality as multiple identity, ecology as variation and adaptation, and finally, as if bodies touch each other less as discrete individuals and more as members of assemblages. Touching is assembling, and the model of assembling is emergence and adaptation.

Reason and science are also enchanting, infinitely infinite, relational and adaptive. As bodies...

Let us imagine that the world is composed of bodies and that the model of this composition is evolutionary. Bodies survive because of variation and adaptation—or put another way, bodies compose and decompose by learning, perceiving, repeating, adapting. Larger bodies are more the result of such adaptation, like societies and species, and smaller bodies are the driving engine, fully lawful, under laws of relation, system, interaction, assembling. Individual bodies are relational, systemic, interactive, social. Individual bodies learn, adapt, vary.

Let us imagine that the world is composed of bodies and that the mode of this composition is geometry. Bodies are physical, geometrical, and in this way they adapt and evolve. Perhaps laws of nature too adapt and evolve, not to mention geometry, mathematics, form itself and their laws. Put another way, in an evolutionary universe, where everything is evolving strictly according to the laws in effect at any time, but in which the forms of the things that behave according to law are selectively adaptive as well, the laws of nature even in their generic formulations pertain to things adaptively.

Some extraordinary discoveries, quite controversial, suggest that inorganic bodies evolve. Other extraordinary discoveries, controversial in other ways, suggest that microorganisms evolve extremely rapidly, that the stability of the perceived, organic world masks rapid transformations of mixed organic and inorganic systems—ecological and evolutionary. And finally, these extraordinary discoveries are by no means rare in nature: they are common and widely influential.

We do not know what bodies can do because they do wonderful things, and others...

So without giving up the dream that bodies behave as lawful bodies, that their properties and their behavior are amenable to scientific inquiry, we may know them and their properties as far as we seek, yet know them to be doubly enchanted: we will never know all their properties, because those properties are emergent, relational, variable, adaptive, systemic, contextual; because those bodies and their laws and properties are infinitely infinite.

Bodies move or rest; move quickly or slowly; agree with each other or disagree; remain the same or differ; are related to other bodies, are determined to act by them and determine them to act, to move and rest; compose and decompose and are composed and decomposed by other bodies; all this to infinity, and beyond.

Motion and rest pertain to certain kinds of bodies in familiar ways, changes of velocity and position. Motion and rest pertain to other kinds of bodies in other ways, adaptive variations in species. Motion and rest pertain to still other kinds of bodies in relational ways, where composition and decomposition transform motions into variations and conditions of rest into stability of form through time. Etc. etc. We do not know what bodies can do, we do not know what motion and rest are and can do, we do not know what composition and decomposition can produce, we do not know how fluid bodies behave from the behavior of the soft and hard bodies that compose them. Bodies are wonderful and abundant, exceed our knowing infinitely and otherwise.

And yet we know. And know that the properties of all these and other bodies are determined in motion and rest—cause and follow—from other bodies. We know that there are only bodies. We know that bodies are infinite, infinitely infinite. And among these infinites are minds, infinite in bodies. And so the infinite in bodies wonders at their infinity. How could it be otherwise?—it is otherwise itself. Enchantment otherwise...

Bodies affect and are affected by other bodies—in infinitely infinite ways. Bodies are impressed by and leave impressions on other bodies—in infinitely infinite ways. Here it is worth pausing for a moment on the brink of exposition. For this infinite tracing of impressions on bodies is split historically—in many related senses of history—between indenting and marking, where the first assumes the touching of bodies as if it were not language, and the second understands all affection as language, exposition, marking, imprinting, tracing—not to mention feeling.

Right here disenchantment and enchantment present themselves again at the heart of material things in the restrictions a disenchanted science would impose on the nonadaptive, nonlinguistic, noninformational, nonintelligent material part of the world. Perhaps there is no such separable or discernible part, perhaps indentation is always marking, perhaps marking is always language, or protolanguage, or subject to interpretation, variable with time and history and relation and composition and assemblage. Perhaps the difference between indentation and impression is the difference expressed by *as if* and *perhaps*. Perhaps, that is, as if always perhaps. Perhaps, in a world of life, knowledge, interpretation, language, exposition, everything is enchanting, in wonder and abundance. Everything is perhaps. And everything is bodies. Bodies are enchanted, infinitely infinite, always as if and perhaps.

This recognition marks the advent of modernity as its refusal. Except in spinoza, the least binary of all modern philosophers, modern representation depends on guarding the boundary between signifier and sign, representation and represented, being and meaning. Marking shatters this boundary, and with it modern representation.[5] Everything is expressive, we do not know what bodies or representations or language or words are and can do, we do not know the difference between doing and saying, at least we do not know how to say it, it cannot be said, it does not exist. Perhaps. This is the *as if* at the heart of *perhaps*.

Bodies perceive, bodies dispose, when bodies adapt and dispose in many ways, their infinity, their enchantment, multiplies.

> The human Mind is capable of perceiving a great many things, and is the more capable, the more its body can be disposed in a great many ways. (Spinoza, *E*, 2, P14)

> P39: He who has a Body capable of a great many things has a Mind whose greatest part is eternal. (Spinoza, *E*, 5)

Eternity here is an enchanted thought: who could know what it might mean? Perhaps it means timeless duration, unchanging in perpetuity. Perhaps it means relation to the unchanging laws of nature. Perhaps it links the changing, adapting, variable body to the unchanging nature whose parts vary in infinite ways. Perhaps a unity of ungathering. Perhaps the wonder and abundance of enchantment.

The whole of nature is one composite individual whose parts vary in infinite ways. Nature is composed of bodies whose relations, impressions, and affects vary in infinite ways.

What does it mean to vary in infinite ways? Many familiar ways, beyond counting? Ways that are so otherwise, unexpected, unimaginable as if to be beyond thinking—as if, perhaps, enchanted? Ways of life, humanity, thought, reason, imagination, myths, language, affects, feelings, emotions, etc. etc.? As if to be beyond asking and telling?

Here is another alternative, still with spinoza in mind, marking adaptation and disposition verbally:

bodies do
bodies produce
bodies express
bodies strive
bodies feel
bodies affect and are affected
bodies become
bodies enchant, bodies are enchanting
bodies come and go
bodies are otherwise than being, etc.
bodies make, happen, etc.
bodies relate, are relational, etc.
bodies change, transform, transfigure, etc.
bodies compose and decompose, etc.
bodies give, offer, are given, etc.

Here composition and decomposition, motion and rest, are adapted to spinoza's understanding of power (*potentia, potestas*), striving and desire (*conatus, laetitiam*), feeling (*adfectio*), and expression. Most of all, however, they are adapted to motion and rest themselves, that is, to bodies moving, producing, affecting, doing, making. Not to bodies' *be*-ing but to their be-*ing*, changing, transforming, transfiguring; to happening, producing, affecting, not to the states produced.

John dewey suggests that science states meanings while art expresses them (*AE*, 84).[6] Yet if bodies are expressive, perhaps science expresses them. And if art expresses bodily meanings in imaginative media, perhaps bodies are expressive even in science.

> An act of discharge or mere exhibition lacks a medium. The act that *expresses* welcome uses the smile, the outreached hand, the lighting up of the face as media. Acts that were primitively spontaneous are converted into means that make human intercourse more rich and gracious—just as a painter converts pigment into means of expressing an imaginative experience. Everything depends upon the way in which material is used when it operates as medium. (63)

Material and matter and bodies are expressive, and must be so for there to be art. And perhaps the expressiveness of bodies is the condition of science. Everything depends upon the way material is expressive and transformed expressively.

> Nature does not present us with lines in isolation. As experienced [through bodies touching other bodies (SDR)], they are the lines of objects; boundaries of *things*. They define the shapes by which we ordinarily recognize objects about us. Hence they carry over the meaning of the objects of which they have been constituent parts. They are expressive of the natural scenes they have defined for us. They express the ways in which things act upon one another and upon us; the ways in which, when objects act together, they reënforce and interfere. For *this* reason, lines are wavering, upright, oblique, crooked, majestic; for this reason they seem in direct perception to have even moral expressiveness. They are earthbound and aspiring; intimate and coldly aloof; enticing and repellent. They carry with them the properties of objects. (100-1)

The expressiveness of lines and colors, the expressiveness of the materials of art, are the expressiveness of things intensified and multiplied. In art, in artistic experience, in experience in general, the line between experience and the world is porous—intensified and multiple.

Because objects of art are expressive, they are a language, many languages (106). Art expresses the materiality of bodies in artistic mediums.

> For each art has its own medium and that medium is especially fitted for one kind of communication. Each medium says something that cannot be uttered as well or as completely in any other tongue. Each art speaks an idiom that conveys what cannot be said in another language and yet remains the same. (106)

Perhaps this is true whether languages are the same or different, whether meanings translated from one language to another are different. Whether mediums and works and bodies are the same and different at different times and places and in different relations are questions of disenchantment. The expressivity of bodies is their enchantment, exposed in art. Perhaps the expressivity of bodies is exposed in science as well as art, in religion as well as science.

Art expresses bodies enchantingly...
Science expresses the enchantments of bodies disenchantingly...
Religion organizes and controls the enchantments of bodies...

Enchantment cannot be organized or controlled, but is always betrayed...

Some betrayals:

From the standpoint of enchantment meanings are always the same, meanings are always different, meanings are either the same or different, meanings are both same and different...

From the standpoint of expression, bodies are the same in different mediums, bodies differ in different mediums, bodies are either the same or different in different mediums, bodies are both the same and different in different mediums...

Bodies are expressive, bodies are enchanting, bodies are medial, composed of matter in infinite mediums...

Bodies mediate, bodies express, bodies are mediums, bodies are expressive, bodies are relational, bodies are excessive...

Bodies are mediate as if ~~not~~ beyond themselves...

Bodies give themselves mediately as if ~~not~~ beyond any giving...

Bodies give themselves in betrayal...

Bodies give themselves in the caesura...

> All language, whatever its medium, involves *what* is said and *how* it is said, or substance and form. The great question concerning substance and form is: Does matter come first ready-made, and search for a discovery of form in which to embody it come afterwards? Or is the whole creative effort of the artist an endeavor to form material so that it will be in actuality the authentic substance of a work of art?
>
> The *material* out of which a work of art is composed belongs to the common world rather than to the self, and yet there is self-expression in art because the self assimilates that material in a distinctive way to reissue it into the public world in a form that builds a new object. (Dewey, *AE*, 106–7)

Is the whole disclosive effort of the artist an endeavor to form material into a work of truth? Might the whole disclosive effort of the scientist be an endeavor to form expressive material into a work of truth?

Let us imagine bodies as expressive, relational, medial, mediate, intermediary...

Let us imagine bodies speaking, enchanting, mediating because that is what bodies are and do...

Let us imagine bodies touching mediately, expressively, enchantingly...

Let us touch enchantingly...

Matter composes and decomposes, bodies move and rest, bodies touch other bodies. Bodies compose, decompose, neither compose nor de-

compose, both compose and decompose. Bodies move, rest, neither move nor rest, both move and rest. Bodies touch other bodies in composition and decomposition, in motion and rest, in enchantment and disenchantment, in exposition... Touch... and exposition... and bodies... and (de) composition... are (dis)enchanting...

Instead of bodies being what they are in relation—a metaphysical condition—bodies relate as a verb, come and go (or become) as a verb, and finally, bodies touch, verbally, actively, transfiguringly, transgressively, enchantingly. Bodies touch, touch other bodies, other bodies touch them, touch is expressive and constitutive, so that when bodies touch other bodies they touch themselves and touch those other bodies touching themselves, feel other bodies feelings, feel feelings, feel feelings feeling feelings, etc. etc., askings asking askings, tellings telling tellings, etc. etc. Such a touching, folding back and down, unfolding and refolding, is exposition. As exposing it is enchanting...

The expressiveness of bodies is their enchantment. The expressiveness of bodies is the medium of art. We are, we live, the earth is filled with expressive bodies, the expressiveness of bodies as media is their enchanting...

Maurice Merleau-Ponty imagines "opening onto a tactile world"; "a veritable touching of the touch, when my right hand touches my left hand while it is palpating the things, such that the touch is formed in the midst of the world and as it were in the things" (Maurice Merleau-Ponty, *VI*, 133–4); "a set of colors and surfaces inhabited by a touch caught up in the tissue of the things" (135).[7] He speaks of his left hand touching his right hand when his right hand touches his left, speaks of that which is touched or seen as touching or seeing in return, a way of expressing the expressiveness of touch and of bodies, perhaps a way of expressing enchantment. (Ross, *GTEG*, 6)

Touch touching touch, in the tissues of things, things touching everywhere in every place excluding nothing, ruling over nothing. Touch touches however it does, by contact, sensorily or organically, and more. Expressively. Inscriptively. Enchantingly. Wherever bodies are, they touch other bodies, at their surfaces and skins, across space and time, and more, below and between their surfaces and boundaries, interrupting the folds and pleats of their corporeality, unraveling and unskinning, still touch, still through the skin, through contact—but contact does not exclude, excludes no more than touch. Understood as proximity. As exposition. (7)...

Expression, exposition, inscription, images, virtuality, simulacra, all bodies, bodies' expressiveness, inscribed on bodies, bodily traces...

> *Herkunft* is the equivalent of stock or *descent*; it is the ancient affiliation to a group, sustained by the bonds of blood, tradition, or social class. (Foucault, *NGH*, 145)

> to follow the complex course of descent is to identify the accidents, the minute deviations—or conversely, the complete reversals—the errors, the false appraisals, the faulty calculations that gave birth to those things that continue to exist and have value for us; it is to discover that truth or being do not lie at the root of what we know and what we are, but the exteriority of accidents. (146)

> Finally, descent attaches itself to the body. It inscribes itself in the nervous system, in temperament, in the digestive apparatus; it appears in faulty respiration, in improper diets, in the debilitated and prostrate body of those whose ancestors committed errors, because the body maintains, in life as in death, through its strength or weakness, the sanction of every truth and error, as it sustains, in an inverse manner, the origin—descent. (147)

As exposition, descent inscribes itself on bodies. As history, descent bears the weight of time upon bodies, the weight of memory and of kind. It inscribes itself upon bodies, every body human and otherwise, every body bears the weight of kind, of memory, of inscription, and of time, in touching other bodies and as touched. The image of an innocent body—any body—weightless of descent, empty of inscription, is no body, none that can be touched by humanity, none that can be touched by any other body, no body at all, without memory, time, descent, or kind.

An innocent, disenchanted body is no body at all. Bodies are enchanted, expressive, inscribed in touch...

Descent is genealogy inscribed on bodies by asking and telling: identifications, accidents, deviations (too minute perhaps to be grasped); or conversely, reversals, errors, falsities, appraisals, calculations and measures (the minutiae of disenchantments), that produce value and being; these minutiae, these disenchantments, are not the root of what we are and what we know but the exteriority of accidents: unstable, excessive, in the caesuras of enchantments.

The language of reversal, error, and appraisal is disenchanted. The phenomena of which it speaks are enchanting and enchanted. The body, bodies, corporeal things all are deviant from the norms of disenchantment. They are departures, excesses, transfigurations in the normless productions of enchantments.

Inscription is exposition, enchanting and enchanted. Bodies are inscribed, exposed, expressive, productive. As any of these, nature and the earth as composite bodies—including fields, velocities, scalars and vectors—are enchanting, productive, expressive, exposed, inscribed, as exposition...

The miracle of the human body is the miracle of bodies...

The miracle of expression unfolds from the body...

> It is the body which points out, and which speaks. This disclosure of an immanent or incipient significance in the living body extends, as we shall see, to the whole sensible world, and our gaze, prompted by the experience of our own body, will discover in all other "objects" the miracle of expression. (Merleau-Ponty, *PP*, 197)

Merleau-ponty imagines the miracle of touch as bringing one close to what one touches, images of proximity entwined with intimacy. Proximity, expression, touch, and intimacy are images of inscription. I write, and send, and descend from and toward the other. I touch the other, the other touches me, entwined touches without mastery. They interrupt each other with the miracle of expression, that which cannot be known or gathered because we do not know, may never know, what bodies can do, the meaning, expression, inscription of touch. Touch is otherwise within the proximity of intimacy. Embracing, caressing know nothing of neutrality, duplication, or domination. Touch is interruption in reciprocity, impossible to gather into neutrality, yet enables gathering to take place. Gathering achieves the distance work demands within the intimacy of touch in proximity.

Merleau-ponty also speaks of the miracle of flesh in the chiasm—caesura—between touching bodies.

> Between the alleged colors and visibles, we would find anew the tissues that lines them, sustains them, nourishes them, and which for its part is not a thing, but a possibility, a latency, and a *flesh (chair)* of things. (Merleau-Ponty, *VI*, 132–3)

> Already in the "touch" we have found three distinct experiences which subtend one another, three dimensions which overlap but are distinct; a touching of the sleek and of the rough, a touching of the things—a passive sentiment of the body and of its space—and finally a veritable touching of the touch, when my right hand touches my left hand while it is palpating the things, where the "touching subject" passes over to the rank of the touched, descends into the things, such that the touch is

> formed in the midst of the world and as it were in the things. (133–4)

A thought of my body touching other bodies that exceeds the greatest gathering.

> This domain, one rapidly realizes, is unlimited. If we can show that the flesh is an ultimate notion, that it is not the union or compound of two substances, but thinkable by itself, if there is a relation of the visible with itself that traverses me and constitutes me as a seer, this circle which I do not form, which forms me, this coiling over of the visible upon the visible, can traverse, animate other bodies as well as my own. And if I was able to understand how this wave arises within me, how the visible which is yonder is simultaneously my landscape, I can understand a fortiori that elsewhere it also closes over upon itself and that there are other landscapes besides my own. (140)

The miracle of the body, my human body, is a miracle of expression. And its miracle—its enchantment—is not mine alone, not human alone, but the miracle of bodies, other bodies, other landscapes, of materiality and being.

Let us imagine touch, formed in the world and among things, as that which bodies do. Touch puts me in touch with bodies; my body touches other bodies, touches my own body touching other bodies touching mine, and in this way—not so much mutuality and reciprocity as the persistence, the abundance, the wonder of touch—touch touches in desire and debt. To be in the world is to be in touch, in the caesura of flesh, crossing every boundary knowledge insists on drawing. To be in the world is to be, in flesh and body, circulating enchantingly, called upon to keep things moving.

> We understand then why we see the things themselves, in their places, where they are, according to their being which is indeed more than their being-perceived—and why at the same time we are separated from them by all the thickness of the look and of the body; it is that this distance is not the contrary of this proximity, it is deeply consonant with it, it is synonymous with it. It is that the thickness of flesh between the seer and the thing is constitutive for the thing of its visibility as for the seer of his corporeity; it is not an obstacle between them, it is their means of communication. The thickness of the body, far from rivaling that of the world, is on the contrary the sole means I have to go unto the heart of the things, by making myself a world and by making them flesh. (Merleau-Ponty, *VI*, 135)

This glowing passage speaks enchantingly of the places where we must be in touch with other bodies, our bodies together with other bodies, in the heart of things, where bodies touch. Corporeity is communication, expression, exposition as asking and telling, intimacy in proximity. (Ross, *GTEG*, 127–8)

> If there is an animation *of* the body; if the vision and the body are tangled up in one another; if, correlatively, the thin pellicle of the *quale*, the surface of the visible, is doubled up over its whole extension with an invisible reserve; and if finally, in our flesh as in the flesh of things, the actual, empirical, ontic visible, by a sort of folding back, invagination, or padding, exhibits a visibility, a possibility that is not the shadow of the actual but is its principle, that is not the proper contribution of a "thought" but is its condition, a style, allusive and elliptical like every style, but like every style inimitable, inalienable, an interior horizon and an exterior horizon. (Merleau-Ponty, *VI*, 152)

It is tempting to read these enchanting words regarding bodies as pertaining only to human bodies, to fleshy bodies of human subjects. It is a temptation we must resist, though it may also, perhaps, be inescapable. For if the human body is enchanted, and what it touches looks back, touches back, then the folding back takes place in expression, exposure, and intimacy—enchantingly. From the standpoint of the knowing subject, the knowing subject's body enchants the world chiasmatically. From the standpoint of the artist, the artist's body touches the artist's materials and enchants them—or is enchanted by them. From the standpoint of enchantment, the materials and bodies, no matter how physical—*no matter how well they are known to physics*—are enchantingly physical, and physics too is enchanting.

Every atom, every particle is enchanted, different from every other particle, different in descent, time, exposition...

Let us imagine the enchantments of bodies, materiality, matter. What do physical bodies do enchantingly?

Bodies mediate, bodies relate, bodies touch other bodies, come and go and compose and decompose themselves between other bodies, etc. When we speak of bodies touching, mediating, relating, etc. bodies are, relate, compose, and touch other bodies expressively...

Bodies inhabit the middle, the chiasm, between; always in the middle way; relating, expressing, dividing, etc., in the caesura. The caesura is the richness of the mediate, the wonder and abundance of intimacy, the movement and coming of the other, the expression and exposition of relating. Etc....

Bodies touch, touch other bodies, touch other bodies touching, touch touching touch, bodies embodying bodies, etc. The etcetera is the excess of bodies as bodies, matter as matter, by no means human bodies only, by no means any only. We do not know what bodies can do because bodies interrupt every only. Inexhaustibly exceeding any only is enchanting...

Bodies speak, exposit, express, ask, tell etc. as they move and touch and come and go. Coming and going is enchanting. Touching expressingly...

> Before orality comes to be, touch is already in existence. No nourishment can compensate for the grace of work of touching. Touch makes it possible to wait, to gather strength, so that the other will return to caress and reshape, from within and from without, a flesh that is given back to itself in the gesture of love. The most subtly necessary guardian of my life is the other's flesh. (Irigaray, *FC*, 187)

> And if I have so often insisted on negatives: *not, nor, without,* it has been to remind you, to remind us, that we only touch each other naked. And that, to find ourselves once again in that state, we have a lot to take off. So many representations, so many appearances, separate us from each other. They have wrapped us for so long in their desires, we have adorned ourselves so often to please them, that we have come to forget the feel of our own skin. Removed from our skin we remain distant. You and I, apart.
>
> Two lips? *Retouching*: the unclosed containment of the body. The envelope of the skin is neither sutured nor open on to a "canal" which takes or rejects, but opening on to the touch of at least two, or four, mucous membranes: the upper and lower lips.
>
> If the skin is peeled off or folded back, there is no more retouching. The mucous membrane of one becomes that which surrounds the other. The skin inside out? The absence of any possible caress and the capture of the intimacy of the body, consumption of the flesh becoming a placentary envelope for the other. (Irigaray, *WOLST*, 217–8)

So much to take off, perhaps to take off disenchantment—no matter how enwrapped, enfolded, no matter how adorning—to re-evoke our enchantments, perhaps to take off disenchantingly. So much to take off to reach the skin, the lips of the skin that always touch, enchant, speak, expose themselves, ourselves to the bodies with skin and lips to enchantment. Bodies that touch and caress intimately.

Women's, men's, all bodies touch, caress, are enchanting as bodies...

Some bodies touch through instruments. Some bodies are instruments, some use instruments, touch mediately, deny their mediateness, relationality, seek instruments and techniques of relation as if they were not relational as bodies.

> In order to touch himself, man needs an instrument: his hand, a woman's body, language. And this self-caressing requires at least a minimum of activity. As for woman, she touches herself in and of herself without any need for mediation, and before there is any way to distinguish activity from passivity. Woman "touches herself" all the time, and moreover no one can forbid her to do so, for her genitals are formed of two lips in continuous contact. Thus, within herself, she is already two—but not divisible into one(s)—that caress each other. (Irigaray, *TSWNO,* 24)

Imagine that women's and men's and other bodies touch, caress, relate as bodies, enchantingly enchanted...

> Open your lips; don't open them simply. I don't open them simply. We—you/I—are neither open nor closed. We never separate simply: *a single word* cannot be pronounced, produced, uttered by our mouths. Between our lips, yours and mine, several voices, several ways of speaking resound endlessly, back and forth. (Irigaray, *WOLST,* 209)

Open your lips—don't open them simply—open them enchantingly—open your enchanting body. Bodies—enchanted, enchanting bodies—are neither open nor closed, cannot be expressed by a single word—disenchanted? disenchantingly? essentially? Many voices, yours and mine—I am many voices, you are many voices, bodies' voices are many—echo, resonate, materialize endlessly, back and forth and...

> The memory of touching? The most insistent and the most difficult to enter into memory. The one that entails returning to a commitment whose beginning and end cannot be recovered. (Irigaray, *ESD,* 215)

> To each wounding separation, I would answer by refusing the holocaust while silently affirming, for myself and for the other, that the most intimate perception of the flesh escapes every sacrificial substitution, every assimilation into discourse, every surrender to the God. Scent or premonition between my self and the other, this memory of the flesh as the place of approach means ethical fidelity to incarnation. To destroy it is to risk the suppression of alterity. (217)

Memories of touching, enchanting touching. Wounding separating affirming. Ethical fidelity to incarnation. Always forgetting always remembering. Bodies touching enchantingly...

Touch touching touch, enchantments enchanting enchantment. Bodies embodying bodies...

> The universe, that is, the whole mass of all things that are is corporeal, that is to say, body; and hath the dimensions of magnitude, namely, length, breadth, and depth: also every part of body, is likewise body, and hath the like dimensions; and consequently every part of the universe, is body; and that which is not body, is no part of the universe: and because the universe is all, that which is no part of it, is nothing; and consequently no where. Nor does it follow from hence, that spirits are nothing: for they have dimensions, and are therefore really bodies; though that name in common speech be given to such bodies only, as are visible, or palpable; that is, that have some degree of opacity. But for spirits, they call them incorporeal; which is a name of more honour, and may therefore with more piety be attributed to God himself; in whom we consider not what attribute expresseth best his nature, which is incomprehensible; but what best expresseth our desire to honour Him. (Thomas Hobbes, *Leviathan*, Pt. 4, Ch. 46, 689)

All that is is body, in nature or the universe or anywhere, and there is nothing that is not body. The body of the earth is filled with bodies, bodies touching other bodies, bodies touching themselves, everywhere. But perhaps no body touches every body everywhere; perhaps no aggregate of bodies is everywhere, as if all that is composed a totality. Anywhere is elsewhere, not totality but mobility, circulation, expression, unfolding and refolding. The full body of the earth is endless unfolding, refolding, circulating; generation and regeneration; but not totality. Endless touching and retouching. Endless exposure. Endlessly enchanting. (Ross, *GTEG*, 283)...

And perhaps not only bodies, where that epithet expresses something containable, knowable, masterable, disenchanting, as if mechanical bodies, touching other bodies everywhere, did so in ways less remarkable, less multifarious, less enchanting, than gods or spirits or minds. Bodies have limits, as do minds and spirits and gods, and those limits are limited, so that limits, boundaries, restrictions, with all their weight, are porous, transgressive, expressive, excessive. Bodies are contained in their envelopes, and those envelopes touch other envelopes, containing other bodies, finite and excessive, composing bodies, decomposing bodies, dividing into bodies, envelopes of envelopes of envelopes, bodies of bodies of bodies touching. This containment is uncontainable; the ne-

cessities of bodies, compelling, delimiting corporeal necessities, cannot hold, but multiply, divide, integrate, fracture and fragment inexhaustibly. Flows flow back upon themselves, augment and divide themselves, multiply and limit themselves. Bodies touch, touch enfolds, unfolds, refolds, in endless ways, all expressed as touch, in touch, to touch, in bodies in proximity, but where the nature of bodies endlessly refolds itself in multiple ways. Where nature and bodies compose multiply refolded folds. All expressive, enchanted and enchanting. (283–4)...

If everything is bodies, made up of bodies, touching and folding, we may not know what bodies can do, what bodies express. Yet we do know something of what bodies do within this incomprehensibility. And we know that we do not know, and something of what we do not know. (284)...

Bodies touch everywhere, touch themselves inside and out, touch themselves touching other bodies, inside and out, a welter and panoply of touchings, foldings, refoldings, all expressive, responsive, calling for other responses, other expressions, other touches, other enchantments. Bodies build and compose other bodies. Bodies divide, break down, destroy, ingest, devour, fragment other bodies. All in touch, by touch. Touch is unfolding, refolding, folding back, resisting the fixity and imperviousness of boundaries. Bodies touch and respond to other bodies, inside and out, expressive of bodiliness and corporeality, influencing, changing, responding to other bodies, demanding responses in return. Bodies change as they are touched, in predictable and unpredictable ways, sometimes in channeled, restricted ways, sometimes in flexible, uncertain ways, sometimes in multifarious, anarchistic ways, enchanted ways. Bodies embrace, enfold, touch, show themselves to other bodies, where every touch refolds, where every fold touches other folds. Folding and refolding are the expressiveness of touch, the enchantments in corporeal things. (285)...

Knowledge, expression, and truth are everywhere, in every corporeal place and thing, as philosophy has somehow always understood, in every culture. This everywhere and everything, however, is not totality but infinity, abundance beyond measure, surprise and wonder. Material bodies respond to each other in countless ways, and respond to their own responses. They represent themselves and others, express and represent other expressions and other representations. In these responses, knots and pleats form identities and truths amid countless unfoldings, refoldings, untyings and retyings of other identities and truths. The flows and entanglements of corporeal bodies and their expressions do not undo knowledge and truth but fold them back into and down upon every site and knot and fold and pleat into which they may be gath-

ered for a while, subsequently unfolding into other pleats and folds and knots. Materiality is expressivity. (287–8)...

It is time to return with bodies and their materiality to ecology and ecosophy.[8] For ecological science offers enchantment in all directions—living things in their habitats—but especially along two major axes: evolutionary transformations—enchanted becomings—and systems of interaction—enchanting relations. Entwinings and becomings are enchanted and enchanting wherever they are expressive, and material bodies, natural creatures and things, express themselves in all directions. Ecology and ecosophy express some of these ways.

Here then are three enchanting images reminding us of enchanted bodies, followed by another, recalling merleau-ponty:

> how do we change mentalities, how do we reinvent social practices that would give back to humanity—if it ever had it—a sense of responsibility, not only for its own survival, but equally for the future of all life on the planet, for animal and vegetable species, likewise for incorporeal species such as music, the arts, cinema, the relation with time, love and compassion for others, the feeling of fusion at the heart of the cosmos? (Guattari, *C*, 119)

> We are carriers of history, and that means carriers of marks from our own past and from the world around us. No wonder it seems strange to think of persons as having value in themselves—for the notion of "self" implicit here seems forever to elude proper description. (Andrew Brennan, *TTN*, 181)

> *We know ourselves to be made from this earth. We know this earth is made from our bodies. For we see ourselves. And we are nature. We are nature seeing nature. We are nature knowing nature. Nature weeping. Nature speaking of nature to nature. All that I know, I know in this earth, the body of the bird, this pen, this paper, these hands, this tongue speaking, all that I know speaks to me through this earth and I long to tell you, you who are earth too, and listen as we speak to each other of what we know: the light is in us.* (Griffin, *WN*, 226–7)...

How do we change mentalities to reenchant the earth and ourselves? It is unnecessary to do so, they are enchanting. We may open ourselves and our senses to them—in love.

Love is enchanting, love is enchanted, love makes the world go round disenchantedly, love disrupts everything it touches, enchantingly...

I have spoken repeatedly of love's enchantments. Here I would speak of bodies and their enchanting proliferations. First félix guattari, then andrew brennan, both employing a disenchanted rhetoric to ask and tell of enchantment. Thereafter, susan griffin and david abram, magical tellings of enchanted askings.

First, then, a material expression of subjectivity in disenchanted language, filled with enchantments if we listen:

> At this stage, the provisional definition of subjectivity I would like to propose as the most encompassing would be: "The ensemble of conditions which render possible the emergence of individual and/or collective instances as self-referential existential Territories, adjacent, or in a delimiting relation, to an alterity that is itself subjective." We know that in certain social and semiological contexts, subjectivity becomes individualised; persons, taken as responsible for themselves, situate themselves within relations of alterity governed by familial habits, local customs, juridical laws, etc. In other conditions, subjectivity is collective—which does not, however, mean that it becomes exclusively social. The term "collective" should be understood in the sense of a multiplicity that deploys itself as much beyond the individual, on the side of the socius, as before the person, on the side of preverbal intensities, indicating a logic of affects rather than a logic of delimited sets. The conditions of production sketched out in this redefinition thus together imply: human inter-subjective instances manifested by language; suggestive and identificatory examples from ethology; institutional interactions of different natures; machinic apparatuses (for example, those involving computer technology); incorporeal Universes of reference such as those relative to music and the plastic arts. This non-human pre-personal part of subjectivity is crucial since it is from this that its heterogenesis can develop. [I]t's a question of being aware of the existence of machines of subjectivation which don't simply work within the "the faculties of the soul," interpersonal relations or intra-familial complexes. Subjectivity does not only produce itself through the psychogenetic stages of psychoanalysis or the "mathemes" of the Unconscious, but also in the large-scale social machines of language and the mass media—which cannot be described as human. (Guattari, *C*, 8–9)

For in this strange and technical, seemingly disenchanted language lurks a jungle of images. Here are a few:

provisional, contingent...
proposing, defining...
subject, subjectivity, subjectivation...
encompassing...
ensemble...
conditions...

possibility, actuality...
emergence...
individual, collective...
self-reference, self-referential...
existence, existential...
territory, geography, adjacency, spatiality...
delimiting, bounding, boundaries, borders...
alterity, otherwise...
semiology, signs, exposition...
individuals, individualization, singularities...
persons, selves, agents...
family, kin, genealogy...
habits, customs...
laws, rules, norms...
juridicality, normativity...
collectivity, sociality, multiplicity...
intensities...
affects, emotions, feelings...
logic...
production...
humanity...
language...
suggestion...
identification...
examples...
ethology...
institutions...
interactions...
natures...
machines, machinic apparatuses...
computers...
technology...
incorporeality...
universes...
reference...
music...
plastic arts...
nonhuman...
prepersonal...
heterogenesis...
faculties...
soul...
psychogenesis...

stages...
psychoanalysis...
unconscious...
mass media...

So many unfamiliar images and terminologies.... So many novelties and incongruities... So many disconnected images proliferating...

We might imagine that these come together into a coherent, disenchanted narrative, that guattari's key term and title, *chaosmosis*, gathers together these other images. Yet we cannot escape the image of a chaosmosis from which this multiplicity of images proliferates other multiplicities.

Chaosmosis is for giving—asking, telling, enchanting...

The subtitle of *Chaosmosis* is *an ethico-aesthetic paradigm*. So the two images of proliferation return: one a paradigm that gathers and brings together these different images—in particular, *chaosmosis* as ethical, aesthetic, ecological, where the last includes three ecologies—"the environment, the socius and the psyche" (p. 20); and *ecosophy* as "an ethico-political articulation between the three ecological registers (the environment, social relations and human subjectivity)" (Guattari, *TE*, 28). Here a single image may be taken as the outcome and consummation of a multiplicity.

An alternative is that ethicc and aesthetics express the multiplicity of the image, that *ecosophy is the multiplication and the multiplier, not the gathered or the gathering, but for giving...*

Here the work of aesthetics as a paradigm is to shift the center of gravity, not to another center but to moving, transforming, asking, giving, "shifting the human and social sciences from scientific paradigms towards ethico-aesthetic paradigms" (Guattari, *C*, 10), from disenchanted to enchanted images (Ross, *WAP*, 491–3), to asking and telling.

Here are some examples:

> I intend to consider a multiplicity of expressive instances, whether they be of the order of Expression or Content. Rather than playing on the Expression/Content opposition this would involve putting a multiplicity of components of Expression, or substances of Expression in parallel, in polyphony. (Guattari, *C*, 23–4)
>
> Expressive, linguistic and non-linguistic substances install themselves at the junction of discursive chains and incorporeal registers with infinite, creationist virtualities. We are actually confronted by a non-discursive, pathic knowledge, which pres-

> ents itself as a subjectivity that one actively meets, an absorbent subjectivity given immediately in all its complexity. (24–5)

An enchanted subjectivity absorbed in its polyphonic corporeality...

Machines are expressive. Machines are expression. Machines are images in proliferation. Machines are gifts, machines are giving. Instead of deterritorialized machines let us think of images of subjectivation. Instead of categories and concepts, abstract machines, let us think of categories and concepts, abstractions and concretions, images in proliferation. Instead of enunciation let us imagine semiology, semiotics, biology, technology, aesthetics all as images of images. Instead of images of subjectivation let us think of images propagating throughout science, philosophy, art, and poetry. Instead of the production of subjectivity let us think of its propagation...

Think of ecosophy as endless images proliferating in multiple ecological registers, multiplying endlessly, endlessly enchanting, ethical and aesthetic, endlessly expressive...

Where but in art can enchanted bodies perform their enchanting dances?

> Performance art delivers the instant to the vertigo of the emergence of Universes that are simultaneously strange and familiar. It shoves our noses up against the genesis of being and forms, before they get a foothold in dominant redundancies—of styles, schools and traditions of modernity. In a more general way, every aesthetic decentring of points of view, every polyphonic reduction of the components of expression passes through a preliminary deconstruction of the structures and codes in use and a chaosmic plunge into the materials of sensation. Out of them a recomposition becomes possible: a recreation, an enrichment of the world (something like enriched uranium), a proliferation not just of the forms but of the modalities of being. (90)

Recreation, enrichment, proliferation as the enchantments of the modalities of being...

> In our era, aesthetic machines offer us the most advanced models—relatively speaking—for these blocks of sensation capable of extracting full meaning from all the empty signal systems that invest us from every side. It is in underground art that we find some of the most important cells of resistance against the steamroller of capitalistic subjectivity—the subjectivity of one-dimensionality, generalised equivalence, segregation, and deafness to true alterity. This is not about making artists the new heroes of the revolution, the new levers of History! Art is

> not just the activity of established artists but of a whole subjective creativity which traverses the generations and oppressed peoples, ghettoes, minorities.... I simply want to stress that the aesthetic paradigm—the creation and composition of mutant percepts and affects—has become the paradigm for every possible form of liberation, expropriating the old scientific paradigms. (90–1)

Underground art is the proliferation of enchanted images beyond any institution or ground... The creation and composition of mutant percepts and affects, of every form of liberation...

> In the scenario of processual assemblages, the expressive a-signifying rupture summons forth a creative repetition that forges incorporeal objects, abstract machines and Universes of value that make their presence felt as though they had been always "already there," although they are entirely dependent on the existential event that brings them into play.
>
> We must emphasize that the work of locating these existential refrains is not the sole province of literature and the arts. (Guattari, *TE*, 45–6)

We might ask, how can we be sure? How can even the best new relations be made secure? But more than these questions that return to grasp the image are the proliferations themselves: *images and more images, chaosmotic images and ecological images, virtual ecologies and virtual images. Aesthetics here is the ethical, and is the only possibility of the political...*

> Strange contraptions, you will tell me, these machines of virtuality, these blocks of mutant percepts and affects, half-object half-subject, already there in sensation and outside themselves in fields of the possible. They have neither inside nor outside. They are limitless interfaces which secrete interiority and exteriority and constitute themselves at the root of every system of discursivity, a play of bifurcations between becoming woman, becoming plant, becoming cosmos, becoming melodic. One gets to know them not through representation but through affective contamination. (Guattari, *C*, 92–3)

We might pause before the intense utopian affect of these images unless one understood the utopia and the affect to be the image again. It is not for us to say what these images are, to express the certainty and security they provide when understood and grasped, but to participate in what these images do, which is to cross and transport and induce and flash. In other words, the images coruscate and proliferate. The images are the sweeping, giving, and becoming in their propagation...

Now, then, brennan, another bodily image:

How do we mark ourselves as carriers of history? Of marks from our past? It is impossible not to do so. We do not know what bodies can do, our bodies and other bodies, in the wonder of their abundance...

A different picture—if a picture at all—can be found in brennan's ecosophical view of the world. In the context of a book written primarily from a philosophical point of view toward the environment, motivated by the sense of an acute environmental crisis, he urges that we adopt an ecological framework toward each of the following terms: the environment, of course, regarded ecologically, but also philosophy and the environmental crisis.

What would it mean to look at everything—including asking and looking—from an ecological point of view? One result would be epistemological: as there are systems of systems and perhaps no overarching ecological system, there are frameworks, and frameworks of frameworks, and no overarching framework, not even an ecological framework:

> If we distinguish different *frameworks* of ideas, theories and principles from each other, then we can say that [any given frameworks] are only a small selection from the number of frameworks available to us when we think about a situation. (Andrew Brennan, *TAN*, 2)

> 1. There are an indefinite number of frameworks that can be brought to bear on human life, conduct and society
> 2. When we restrict our modes of thinking to just one framework, we thereby choose to ignore the perspective supplied by other relevant frameworks
> 3. Except when dealing with frameworks of the same sort, no straight choices can be made among frameworks.
> 4. The weighing given to one framework for approaching a given subject matter can always be challenged on the grounds that some other relevant scheme or framework has been ignored or weighted too lightly (3)

Everything is ecological... Everything is ecosophical... Everything is relational, variable, multiple, organic, dynamic, transitional... Including ecology. Ecology is asking, telling, enchanting...

Brennan's framework is enchanting in presenting an ecological approach to ecological theories

> [E]cology can be regarded as a method of approaching problems, and as supplying a metaphysics that applies to far more than living systems. In this sense, ecology has application to academic disciplines and even to political and moral matters. (31)

It is becoming common to apply evolutionary theory to ethics and politics, possibly to everything human, everything living. That mode of adaptive explanation is only a part of what brennan is advocating. I would not minimize such an approach given my own ways of thinking enchantedly of them.[9] For I believe that evolutionary biology—which brennan treats critically under the heading of sociobiology—does not so much explain the reasons why we do what we do as it identifies the moments of emergence and disruption that arise in the history of natural processes, human practices, and social relations. The view that everything—not perhaps just living things—adapts, and that things adapt in astonishing and unpredictable ways, is a theory of enchantment. That is worth close consideration, but it is not my concern here.

Adaptation, transformation, emergence, inheritance are all surprising. We do not know what bodies can do, even when we know. Even when we know, what we know is that we do not know what bodies can do. Adaptation is conformation and variation, disenchantment and enchantment. Evolutionary biology asks us to ask and tell, tells too much as if beyond asking...

With qualifications, then, we may imagine scientific ecology as *the study of those interactions with their environment that determine characteristics, distribution and abundance of organisms and systems of organisms* (Brennan, 35). The key terms are interactions, organisms, systems of organisms, characteristics, distribution, and abundance. In other words, this is a relational theory, with systems of systems and orders of orders.[10] More important is that we are addressing not only human beings and their behaviors—moral and ethical—in such systems, but also the theories and truths and knowledges of such behaviors as themselves such behaviors. What human beings believe, including philosophers and scientists, artists and producers, is the result of adaptive, systemic, ecological, historical processes of interacting with their environments.

> What I wish to consider is the influence that science might have on ethics. By "ethics," I mean not just the principles that we claim to follow in actions, but the ideals, kinds of intentional behaviour and roles that we regard as characteristic of a person's moral style. We can thus ask whether the biological sciences in particular provide a framework within which certain distinctive ethical attitudes, styles of response and principles of conduct are motivated. (133–4)

I would read this far beyond the examples brennan gives to imagine frameworks derived from the sciences that help us understand and interpret not only what we do and the values and ideals we form but also the forms of thought and expression that we engage in when we pursue these activities. How we relate to the environment is irreducibly complex and inexhaustible. How we relate to anything else is also irreducibly inexhaustible and complex. The irreducibility is intensely specific and highly determinate. The more we know, the more irreducible and inexhaustible are the conditions of our lives and practices. This is an important aspect of enchantment, directly contrary to Weber's interpretation of disenchantment. The more we know the less accountable are things.

The more we know disenchantedly the more we question ask know enchantedly...

In brennan's disenchanted voice:

> In what way, then, can the biological, or life, sciences extend our awareness and make a revisionary impact on our moral beliefs and attitudes? Ecology is in a particularly powerful position since it is a fine example of an interdisciplinary subject. It thus provides us with an image of the world which is drawn jointly from the resources of biology, geology, chemistry and biochemistry. (136)

> *One of the central pieces of ecological insight is that each thing is what it is in part by being where it is.* (173)

> But living things likewise bear the marks of evolution. Each of us thus carries the marks of the past evolution of our species. These are all aspects of the truth that organisms and environment are complementary, each inseparable from the other. (173)

Complementary not only in ethical but in scientific, rational, argumentative, discursive, and expressive ways. Everything is where it is in inexhaustibly complex and multiple local relations, including expressive as well as propositional forms. All these forms of life and thought have evolved in ecological systems of life and thought.

> my complaint is that notions like *good, rationality, interest, desire, obligation, freedom* and the other key notions of ethical theory have been applied in ecologically careless ways. Theorists have taken little care to make sure that these notions are realistic for creatures that live in real social and biological surroundings, and are what they are by virtue of their location in such surroundings. (174)

Brennan reads this insight as providing a better theory:

> Persons are what they are by doing what they do, having the friends they have, forming the relationships they do, carrying out various projects, undertaking various commitments. My current experiences, then, would not be what they are were I not living at this time, in this society, of this species and carrying within me a distinctive history of previous experiences. To be me, then, involves the continuous reconstruction of this, my life, throuogh me-ish experiences.
>
> The other side of the same coin, however, is that my experiences and doings essentially involve the social and physical world that I inhabit. My friends, relationships and environing objects have played their part in constituting my "identity" (for want of a better word). (180)

We are on the verge of passing from ecological explanation to something more enchanted—forever eluding proper description—*as if and perhaps descriptions of human beings or of anything else might be proper, as if impropriety did not haunt us with its inexhaustibility and betrayals...*

> My "ecological humanism," to give the position a name, urges that human nature is tremendously rich and complex, for it is partly what we are born with and partly what we make for ourselves as we live (184)...

Asking of enchantment tells that human beings, the earth, and its ingredients are inexhaustibly rich and complex, endlessly proliferating. We inhabit multiple systems of relation, including those constituted by ecological sciences—in the double plural—directed toward systems of relation—in the inexhaustible plural—that have constituted human life and expression to this point and continue to proliferate. Ecological sciences enchant our world again and again in the face of those who think of this activity as disenchanted...

Inexhaustibly many, inexhaustibly diverse natural and social systems, constituted and reconstituted by interactions among epistemic, ethical, aesthetic, expressive systems upon each other, transforming each other for the future and throughout the past. Each natural, social, and expressive system and framework disenchants the others—and enchants them, reveals them to be surprising, multiple, mysterious. They in turn disenchant and enchant the others...

What is an enchanted ethics, then, but one that regards every thing, every ingredient, as ethical, thereby inexhaustible beyond accounting?...

What is an enchanted science, then, but one that regards its work as an enchanted ethics and an enchanted aesthetics?...

Leading us to griffin's enchanting voice:

We are made from this earth. The earth is made from our bodies. We are nature, we are bodies, all we know in the enchantment of the earth is in us we and the earth are enchanting...

He says that woman speaks with nature. That she hears voices from under the earth. That wind blows in her ears and trees whisper to her. That the dead sing through her mouth and the cries of infants are clear to her. But for him this dialogue is over. He says he is not part of this world, that he was set on this world as a stranger. He sets himself apart from woman and nature. (Griffin, *WN*, 3)

We are women. We rise from the wave. We are gazelle and doe, elephant and whale, lilies and roses and peach, we are air, we are flame, we are oyster and pearl, we are girls. We are woman and nature. And he says he cannot hear us speak...

But we hear. (3)...

We hear the enchantments of the earth. Whoever we are. He cannot hear. He is separated from us and the earth, and our enchantments...

Disenchanting...

It is decided that matter is transitory and illusory like the shadows on a wall cast by firelight; that we dwell in a cave, in the cave of our flesh, which is also matter, also illusory; it is decided that what is real is outside the cave, in a light brighter than we can imagine, that matter traps us in darkness. That the idea of matter existed before matter and is more perfect, ideal. (7)

It is decided that matter is passive and inert, and that all motion originates from outside matter.

It is decided that the nature of woman is passive, that she is a vessel waiting to be filled.

And the demon resides in the earth, it is decided, in Hell, under our feet. (5–9)

What is decided is disenchanted. The earth is enchanting beyond deciding and choosing. Still we must decide. And choose. And resist...

It is observed that women are closer to the earth. (9)

That women lead to man's corruption.

And we are reminded that we have brought death into the world.

And it is seen that the senses are deceptive.

And it is said that women are the fountain, the flood and the very root of deception, falsity and lies.

It is decided that matter cannot know matter.

That matter "is but a brute thing and only capable of local motion."

That matter has no intellect and no perception. (9–16)

We live observing, perceiving, and deciding, disenchanted. We live in our bodies, materially and physically, enchanted...

Griffin writes enchantingly of terrible decisions, cruel disenchantments. Disenchantment is cruelty.

There is nothing more useless than an organ.[11] With a body without organs, you will be delivered to your true liberty...

We must put an end to the subjugation of the theater to the text, and rediscover a unique language halfway between gesture and thought...

Without organs a body is enchanting. Speaking a language halfway between gesture and thought. Halfway between. In the caesura...

Returning from this caesura, to another.

1382	
1431	Joan of Arc
1468	The Pope defines witchcraft as *crimen exceptum,* removing all legal limit to torture
1482	
1523	One thousand witches burn in a single year in the diocese of Como
1543	
1571	
1572	
1583	Witch Burnings in two villages leave one female in habitant each.
1589	
1581–91	Nine hundred burned in Lorraine. (That nature must be bound into service, he persuades.)
1600	
1603	
1609	Galileo constructs a telescope (It is urged that nature must be hounded in her wanderings before one can lead her and drive her.)
1609	The whole population of Navarre is declared witches. (He says that the earth should be put on the rack and tortured for her secrets.)
1615	
1619	The first black slaves are introduced in America (She is asked if she signed the devil's book. She is asked if the devil had a body. She is asked whom she chose to be an incubus.)
1622	
1628	One hundred fifty-eight burned at Würzburg.

1637	
1638–1640	
1644	
1670	Rouen witch trials
1687	
1666	
1704	
1717	
1738	Dean of Faculty of Law at Rostock demands that witches be extirpated by fire and sword.
1745	Witch trial at Lyons, five sentenced to death.
1749	Sister Maria Renata executed and burned.
1778	Anna Maria Schnagel executed for witchcraft. (Griffin, *WN*, 17–9)

Where witches meet disenchanted powers are other cruelties...

It is argued now that animals do not think. That animals move automatically like machines. That passion in animals is more violent because it is not accompanied by thought. That our own bodies are distinguished from machines only by "a mind which thinks without reference to any passion." (19)

And it is further argued that if animals could think, they might have immortal souls.

But it becomes obvious that animals do not have immortal souls (and cannot think), since if one animal had an immortal soul, all might, and that "there are many of them too imperfect to make it possible to believe it of them, such as oysters, sponges, etc."

And it is said the souls of women are small.

It is decided that matter is dead.

Everything in the universe, it is perceived, moves according to the same laws: the earth, the moon, the wind, the rain, blood, atoms.

And it is decided that what makes God divine is his power.

And it is written in the law that "Women should be subject to their men."

And it is written that in the inferior world of brutes and vegetables man was created to act as the viceroy of the great God of heaven and earth, and that he should then name the brutes and the vegetables. For he who calls the creatures by their true names has power over them.

(Thus it is decided that earth shall be called land; trees, timber; animals to be called hunted, to be called domesticated; her body to be named hair, to be named skin, to be called breast, vulva, clitoris, to be named womb.)

All nature, it is said, has been designed to benefit man.

That nature has made it natural for a woman to seek only to be a good wife and mother, and "nature's darling" woman stays at home, it is pointed out.

And so all the species are named according to their sexual parts.

Yes, nature is merciless and insatiable, it is said, red in tooth and claw, it is written.

And it is stated that woman's nature is more natural than man's, that she is genuine with the "cunning suppleness of a beast of prey."

And we learn to be afraid.

It is stated that if women were not meant to be dominated by men, they would not have been created weaker.

Slavery is said to be a condition of every higher civilization

A woman should be an enthusiastic slave to the man to whom she has given her heart, it is declared. (19–33)

It is decided it is said it is written it is declared it is stated disenchanted women animals nature the earth are his he names them owns them possesses them enslaves and dominates them...

And yet they are enchanted and enchanting...

Enchanting and disenchanting...

We are the rocks, we are soil, we are trees, rivers, we are wind, we carry the birds, the birds, we are cows, mules, we are horses, we are Solid elements cause and effect, determinism and objectivity, it is said, are lost. *matter. We are flesh, we breathe, we are her body: we speak.* (48)

Her body—woman nature earth—is exposition, expressive animate enchanting. And disenchanting...

Her body is a vessel of death. Her beauty is a lure. Her charm a trap. She is irresistible. Her voice is deceit. Her word a plot. Her gesture a snare. She will eat the flesh she appears to love. Her hunger is never satisfied. She is a plague. A disease. The color of her blood is the color of calamity, of fire, of evil. The smell is offensive, the smell is a warning. She loves blood. She devours even herself. Her passion is endless, without reason, without boundary, existing only for itself. She would consume herself; in her body is the seed of nothingness. (84–5)

Enchanting...

Because we know ourselves to be made from this earth. See this grass. The patches of silver and brown. Worn by the wind. The grass

reflecting all that lives in the soil. The light. The grass needing the soil. With roots deep in the earth. And patches of silver. Like the patches of silver in our hair. Worn by time. This bird flying low over the grass. Over the tules. The cattails, sedges, rushes, reeds, over the marsh. Because we know ourselves to be made from this earth. Temporary as this grass. Because we know ourselves to be made from this earth, and shaped like the earth, by what has gone before... (225)

This bird with the scarlet shoulders. This bird with the yellow throat. And the beautiful song. The song like flutes. Like violoncellos in an orchestra. The orchestra in our mind. The symphony which we imagine. The music which was our idea. What we wanted to be. Because we know ourselves to be made of this earth, because we know sunlight moves through us, water moves through us, everything moves, everything changes, and the daughters are returned to their mothers...

Though we may cage her, though we may torture her with our will, with the boundaries we imagine, this bird will never be ours, he may die, this minute heart stop beating, the body go cold and hard, we may tear the wings apart and cut open the body and remove what we want to see, but still this blackbird will not be ours and we will have nothing. For we did not invent the blackbird, we say, we only invented her name. And we never invented ourselves, we admit...

We know this earth is made from our bodies. For we see ourselves. And we are nature. We are nature seeing nature. We are nature with a concept of nature. Nature weeping. Nature speaking of nature to nature. The red-winged blackbird flies in us, in our inner sight. We see the arc of her flight. We measure the ellipse. We predict its climax. We are amazed. We are moved. We fly. And yet the blackbird does not fly in us but is somewhere else free of our minds, and now even free of our sight, flying in the path of her own will...

Because I know I am made from this earth, as my mother's hands were made from this earth, as her dreams came from this earth and all that I know, I know in this earth, the body of the bird, this pen, this paper, these hands, this tongue speaking, all that I know speaks to me through this earth and I long to tell you, you who are earth too, and listen as we speak to each other of what we know: the light is in us... (225–9)

We are enchanted, enchantment is us, all the things of the earth are enchanting, enchant us, we and they are made from this enchanting earth...

Here now with merleau-ponty in mind is another story of enchantment—there are always many—not too many to tell, but too many to count. The senses are too many to count.

Late one evening I stepped out of my little hut in the rice paddies of eastern Bali and found myself falling through space. Over my head the black sky was rippling with stars, densely clustered in some regions, almost blocking out the darkness between them, and more loosely scattered in other areas, pulsing and beckoning to each other. There seemed no ground in front of my feet, only the abyss of star-studded space falling away forever.

I was no longer simply beneath the night sky, but also above it—the immediate impression was of weightlessness. I might have been able to reorient myself, to regain some sense of ground and gravity, were it not for a fact that confounded my senses entirely: between the constellations below and the constellations above drifted countless fireflies, their lights flickering like the stars, some drifting up to join the clusters of stars overhead, others, like graceful meteors, slipping down from above to join the constellations underfoot, and all these paths of light upward and downward were mirrored, as well, in the still surface of the paddies. I felt myself at times falling through space, at other moments floating and drifting. I simply could not dispel the profound vertigo and giddiness; the paths of the fireflies, and their reflections in the water's surface, held me in a sustained trance. Even after I crawled back to my hut and shut the door on this whirling world, I felt that now the little room in which I lay was itself floating free of the earth.

Fireflies! It was in Indonesia that I was first introduced to the world of insects, and there that I first learned of the great influence that insects—such diminutive entities—could have upon the human senses. (David Abram, *SS*, 3–4)...

In his magical voice abram allows us to hear—to sense and be sensed—touch and be touched—touching the earth and its enchanting bodies. Bodies, nature, the earth all are enchanting, sensing, touching.

As much as we may imagine disenchanting sense and touch, as much as we may suffer their estrangements and alienations, touch and sense are relational, emergent, transformative, enchanting.

Abram's agenda recalls gablik's—when it is an agenda: the world is in crisis, we are doing our utmost to destroy it, we need to restore wholeness to our relations, ecology to our being. Tribal being is whole.[12]

> The traditional or tribal shaman acts as an intermediary between the human community and the larger ecological field, ensuring that there is an appropriate flow of nourishment, not

> just from the landscape to the human inhabitants, but from the human community back to the local earth. To some extent every adult in the community is engaged in this process of listening and attuning to the other presences that surround and influence daily life. But the shaman or sorcerer is the exemplary voyager in the intermediate realm between the human and the more-than-human worlds, the primary strategist and negotiator in any dealings with the Others. (7)

This is a wonderfully enchanting image of the human community and the larger field of forces in which disenchanted humanity is embedded. Sometimes malevolent and terrifying, but always abundant beyond abundance. In this image ecology and enchantment meet, as if the enchanted world were ecological—whole, magical, interrelated.

In another image—local and sensual—each and every body, each and every body touching, sensing body is relational, and relationality is enchanting. Relationality is relational beyond any accounting.

The breathing, sensing body draws its sustenance and its very substance from the soils, plants, and elements that surround it; it continually contributes itself, in turn, to the air, to the composting earth, to the nourishment of insects and oak trees and squirrels, ceaselessly spreading out of itself as well as breathing the world into itself, so that it is very difficult to discern, at any moment, precisely where this living body begins and where it ends. As we actually experience and live it the body is a creative, shape-shifting entity. It has its finite character and style, its unique textures and temperaments that distinguish it from other bodies; yet these mortal limits in no way close me off from the things around me or render my relations to them wholly predictable and determinate. On the contrary, my finite bodily presence alone is what enables me to freely engage the things around me, to choose to affiliate with certain persons or places, to insinuate myself in other lives. Far from restricting my access to things and to the world, the body is my very means of entering into relation with all things...

Ultimately, to acknowledge the life of the body, and to affirm our solidarity with this physical form, is to acknowledge our existence as one of the earth's animals, and so to remember and rejuvenate the organic basis of our thoughts and our intelligence. (45–7)...

To live in a body—and where else can we live?—is to live relationally, to belong to the earth's living creatures—animals and plants—and for that matter to live with the nonliving. Relationality is lawful, determinate and predictable, and in the nature of those very same laws, the very same relationality is indeterminate and unpredictable, relational beyond relations. Far from restricting my relations to things, my body's enchantments are the means whereby I am related to other bodies, by sense and touch.

Reversing this relation, abram shows us how the sensuousness of the earth in touch and relation open it and us to enchantment. First as language and exposition, which cannot be separated from sense and relation, then as departure and caesura:

The chorus of frogs gurgling in unison at the edge of a pond, the snarl of a wildcat as it springs upon its prey, or the distant honking of Canadian geese veeing south for the winter, all reverberate with affective, gestural significance, the same significance that vibrates through our own conversations and soliloquies, moving us at times to tears, or to anger, or to intellectual insights we could never have anticipated. Language as a bodily phenomenon accrues to all expressive bodies, not just to the human. Our own speaking, then, does not set us outside of the animate landscape but—whether or not we are aware of it—inscribes us more fully in its chattering, whispering, soundful depths. (80)...

Each thing, each phenomenon, has the power to reach us and to influence us. Every phenomenon, in other words, is potentially expressive. Thus, at the most primordial level of sensuous, bodily experience, we find ourselves in an expressive, gesturing landscape, in a world that speaks. (81)...

We regularly talk of howling winds, and of chattering brooks. Our own languages are continually nourished by these other voices—by the roar of waterfalls and the thrumming of crickets. If language is not a purely mental phenomenon but a sensuous, bodily activity born of carnal reciprocity and participation, then our discourse has surely been influenced by many gestures, sounds, and rhythms besides those of our single species. Indeed, if human language arises from the perceptual interplay between the body and the world, then this language "belongs" to the animate landscape as much as it "belongs" to ourselves. (82)

Languages, tellings, images, expressions "belong" to the animate landscape. Our feelings, relations, thoughts, being "belong" to the earth. This figure of belonging echoes possession where I have expressed giving as dispossession. Exposition does not anchor us in our dwelling place but is mobile, transformative, as are sense and touch. Touch touches other bodies and in that way relates and goes outside itself, where outside oneself is in the caesura...

We do not know what bodies can do, including the most disenchanted and disenchanting bodies. They too are enchanting and enchanted...

We and everything else are bodies, bodies are material, material things follow natural laws. These laws do not abolish enchantment. In their geometry, in their formality, the most mathematical of natural laws are determinate, deterministic, and enchanting...

With sense and touch and enchantment in mind—by which of course I mean in body—let us conclude with a return to evolution. Here is what might be said about evolution in an enchanting voice—and if it is said, its exposition is enchanting. In other words, let us enter the fray of religion and evolution in an enchanted voice:

Evolution is true; living things mutate, adapt, evolve; other things may also adapt and evolve.

The laws of mutation are physical, chemical, biological. That includes statistical regularities and probabilistic uncertainties. The laws of the physical, chemical, biological world are quantum mechanical.

Evolution is true, yet is filled with uncertainties and disagreements about how and what and when for every individual and species. Evolutionary theory is filled with alternative theories and contradictory evidence pertaining to what we do not know.

Alternative theories to evolution as such—creationism, intelligent design—are false, contradicted by much of the evidence pertaining to them.

Such alternative theories claim to be not only more truthful than evolutionary theory but to explain what it cannot explain—that is, to be more rational, more complete. As such they are more disenchanting than it is. They claim—in some of their forms—that everything can be accounted for in relation to religion and the gods.

Evolution as a process is enchanting, adaptation frequently takes place at an invisible level, in unaccountable ways. Organisms adapt, evolve, transform themselves, become new species in recognizable yet unpredictable ways.

Evolution may become a theory of everything, in which everything takes place at a level of quantum transformation and mutation producing assemblages that evolve, change, become in unpredictable ways. Mixtures of predictability and unpredictability, but in which we can never know which is which.

We do not know what bodies can do, bodies do according to natural laws, natural laws are infinitely infinite.

Evolution is an exposition of infinitely infinite bodies...

As are sense and touch and relation...

Everything is sense and touch and relation, is not sense or touch or relation, is neither sense and touch and relation nor not sense and touch and relation, is both sense and touch and relation and not sense and touch and relation...

All are evolving...

Let us ask... and tell...

Chapter 6

Betraying Enchantment

> The beyond being, *being's other* or the *otherwise than being*, here situated in diachrony, here expressed in infinity, has been recognized as the Good by Plato. The beyond being, showing itself in the said, always shows itself there enigmatically, is already betrayed. Its resistance to assemblage, conjunction and conjuncture, to contemporaneousness, immanence, the present of manifestation, signifies the diachrony of responsibility for another more ancient than all freedom. (Levinas, *OB*, 19)

> We have been seeking the *otherwise than being* from the beginning, and as soon as it is conveyed before us it is betrayed in the said which dominates the saying which states it. (Levinas, *OB*, 7)...

Betrayal is the way in which enchantment appears—in truth, goodness, beauty, and more. It appears in truth—obliquely, indirectly, misdirectingly, untruth as truth. It appears in justice—wearing ornaments of evil, injustice in justice.[1] *It appears in beauty—ugly, disgusting, rotting—still aesthetic, unbeauty's beauty. It appears elsewhere and otherwise, in betrayal. Betrayal is the double caesura of revelation and violation. We aim—and miss. We understand—and misunderstand. We do right—as evil. All given and giving from the good . . .*

The nature of enchantment is to betray...

The enchantment of enchantment is to disenchant...

Disenchantment betrays enchantment, enchantment betrays disenchantment, each betrays the other, and the others...

Betrayal is the caesura in abundance, the wonder in exposition, enchantment's disenchantments. Enchantment betrays itself obliquely—a monolithic god, a multiplicity of spirits, the wonder and abundance of each and every ingredient, expressed in every asking and telling...

Betrayal is cruel, betrayal is cruelty, betraying betrayal is cruelty to cruelty...[2]

I have questioned many proposals for reenchantment because they did not betray betrayal, because they imagined enchantment as if it were free and innocent, as if it did not betray innocence and freedom and itself. Human beings and animals have been sacrificed on the altar of gods and spirits, enchantment is not free from violence, indeed may not be good—nor for that matter bad—but is the abundance, wonder, proliferation, and impossibility of the asking and telling that make art and aesthetics, ethics and politics, science and philosophy possible. Betrayal betrays the impossibility that allows these infinite tasks to come and go, infinite expressions, endless expositions, infinitely infinite betrayals. They are infinite, infinitely infinite, they come and go by betrayal.

Enchantment is the infinite coming and going, the endless proliferation of images of images, the wonder and abundance of the earth. It takes place by betrayal in disenchantment, but not in disenchantment alone. Enchantments betray—in blood and violence, in suffering. The wounding and suffering of political institutions and religions, the rulers and priests who claim to guard them, have been present throughout human history. Now science, technology, academic institutions, economic practices and institutions—the forms of modern technology—promote their own wounding and suffering, present their own betrayals. That does not make them any less enchanting, though it may make them more disenchanted. Disenchantment is not incompatible with enchantment, but is the face of its betrayal. And not the only such face. Starvation, famine, war, imprisonment, concentration camps are other betrayals, as are disciplinary practices, religious, artistic, and scientific institutions, etc.

Etc....

Everything is enchanted and enchanting...

Etc....

Art, philosophy, science, politics, ethics, life are enchanting, and disenchanting...

Asking and telling are enchanted and enchanting...

Philosophy is enchanted and enchanting...

Every philosophy is enchanting and enchanted, even the most disenchanted, even when disenchanted...

Every philosopher is enchanted and enchanting, even when read in the most disenchanting ways...

Etc....

Here are some examples:

heraclitus: the flux...
parmenides: the one...
anaximander: injustice...
plato: wonder, the good, mimēsis, poiēsis...
aristotle: mimēsis, poiēsis, phusis, nous...
plotinus: the one...
augustine: god, himself...
aquinas: reason, god...
ockham: the univocity of being...
descartes: wonder...
leibniz: living monads, creatures in creatures...
spinoza: what bodies can do, infinite infinites, expression, corporeality...
hobbes: bodies, desire, nature, sovereignty...
locke: association, ideas, madness...
hume: knowledge, sympathy, identity, causation...
kant: noumena, thing in itself, sublime, immortality...
hegel: absolute, sublation, spirit...
schelling: art, potencies, inspiration, the one...
nietzsche: dionysian, forces...
buddhism, taoism, confucianism...
christianity, judaism, islam...
indigenous, native, spiritual, shamanistic practices...
all religions are enchanted...
all religions are disenchanted...
no beliefs or practices are religious as such...
no truths or beliefs or practices are enchanted as such, or disenchanted...
heidegger, derrida, foucault, levinas, blanchot, etc....
dewey, james, emerson, whitehead, etc....
etc....

Should these be read and understood in enchanting ways?

Should these be read and understood in disenchanting ways?

Should we live in enchanting or disenchanting ways?

Can we choose?

Who is to choose?

How can we choose?

Each betrays the others.

The forms, genres, disciplines in which these appear (in authors, texts, forms of knowledge) are betrayals...

Disenchantment betrays enchantment...

The mark of enchantment lies beyond—beyond accounting, beyond understanding, beyond containment, beyond disenchantment. There is no such mark, every mark is beyond itself; there is no such beyond, every beyond is beyond itself, every mark and beyond is as if ~~not~~ beyond, perhaps ~~as if not~~ beyond perhaps. The mark of beyond lies in its enchantments and betrayals. Beyond betrays—astonishes, shatters, reveals. Enchantment and betrayal shatter every boundary, border, identity, rupture its identifications.

To identify is to grasp and fix, to reidentify is to fix again—differently. To put in motion, to betray, transfigure, transgress. Always perhaps...

The mark of disenchantment is reverence for what is countable, accountable, identifiable, settleable. The mark of enchantment is irreverence, betrayal as irreverence, where reverence is not seriousness—though there can be too much of that—but fixing, stabilizing, identifying.

The mark of disenchantment is stability, order, grasping. Disenchantment hopes to grasp, modern thought and life seek to grasp, the world is too quick, too transgressive, always moving on, moving beyond, irreverent toward old gods, toward reason, toward science.

Modern philosophy, science, and technology are disenchanted, modern reason is disenchanted. Philosophy, science, art, and technology enchant disenchanted reason, reason is enchanted.

Philosophy, science, technology, reason, art all are ~~as if not~~ beyond themselves...

Enchantment, exposition, asking, telling, images proliferate in wonder and abundance. Disenchantment proliferates in the ~~betrayal of~~ the wonder and abundance of the image, the exposition of exposition, all as if ~~not~~ beyond expression. The ~~not~~ and the beyond proliferate in the wonder and abundance of asking and telling. In this way, the most disenchanted of sciences, philosophies, philosophers proliferate enchantment...

Russell, wittgenstein, quine, davidson, rawls, habermas, apel, etc. etc....

Is rational philosophy enchanted?
Is metaphysics enchanted?
Is analytic philosophy enchanted?
Is academic philosophy enchanted?
Is modern philosophy enchanted?
What is enchanted about them?
What in them betrays betrayal?

Could analytic philosophy be more disenchanted than science?

Every theory is disenchanted: scientific, rational, philosophical, academic.

Every theory, writing, saying, is enchanted and enchanting...

Some of the most disenchanting of philosophical writings have wandered into enchanted places in enchanting ways...

Some of the most authoritative of philosophical writings have given rise to irreverence. Does that not betray enchantments?...

I am an academic philosopher who would be enchanting. I am an academic philosopher who believes that academic philosophy is disenchanting...

I am a philosopher who betrays enchantment of necessity (by heresy and aporia), betrays philosophy, etc....

Betrayal is enchanting...

Under the headings of reenchantment and postmodernism, influenced by his reading of alfred north whitehead, David Ray Griffin has gathered stories of a reenchanted, postmodern science—if such a science exists, if enchantment and postmodernism and science are compatible with each other, if disenchantment can be reenchanted. As if perhaps after modernization. As if without betrayal.[3]

Griffin claims that an enchanted science is possible today, and we can think of it as postmodern. Such a view assumes that postmodernity comes after modernity, is no longer modern, that reenchantment replaces disenchantment, is no longer disenchanted.

What if postmodernity—if there be such—betrayed modernity—before and after? What if enchantment betrayed disenchantment? What would such an enchantment be? What of such a modernity?

> modern aesthetics is an aesthetic of the sublime, though a nostalgic one. It allows the unpresentable to be put forward only as the missing contents; but the form, because of its recognizable consistency, continues to offer to the reader or viewer matter for solace and pleasure.
>
> The postmodern would be that which, in the modern, puts forward the unpresentable in presentation itself; that which denies itself the solace of good forms, the consensus of a taste which would make it possible to share collectively the nostalgia for the unattainable. (Lyotard, *WPM?*, 81)

The postmodern inhabits the modern, it does not replace it. What then is their relation? It denies the solace and nostalgia of the unattainable in the modern—let us call it god. If god is enchanting, the postmodern is disenchanting, and insists on the death of god. If, however, modernity is disenchanting, and it is haunted by nostalgia for a reenchanted god, then postmodernity gives up that reenchantment and that god together with disenchantment in general, and betrays itself as enchanting beyond reenchantment.

This seems surprising, at least on griffin's reading. This seems a betrayal of god and reenchantment. The postmodern is the betrayal at the heart of the modern, does not offer itself up as better than or a replacement to the modern but betrays its disenchantments.

Here are some other expressions in lyotard of this betrayal. In the caesura.

> To bear witness to the differend. (Lyotard, *DPD*, xiii)

> Let us wage a war on totality; let us be witnesses to the unpresentable; let us activate the differences and save the honor of the name. (*WP?*, 82)

> [I]n witnessing, one also exterminates. The witness is a traitor. (*I*, 204)

> The differend is the unstable state and instant of language wherein something which must be able to be put into phrases cannot yet be. (*DPD*, 13)

> *La réalité comporte le différend* [Reality is made up of the *differénd* (translated by Georges Van Den Abbeele as "Reality entails the differend")]. (Lyotard, *D*, 50; *DPD*, 90)

Here is my thesis, if enchantment can bear a thesis, if a thesis can be enchanting: the postmodern is that which in the modern betrays it enchantingly. The postmodern—if there be such—betrays the enchantments in the disenchantments of modernity. And what it betrays as well are the enchantments of reality, the world, the earth. The earth is made up of enchantments betrayed, betrays enchantments, exposes what is impossible to know or say or gather. Reality is the unity of ungathering—as enchantment, in exposition.

This is not a thesis, it could not be a thesis, if anything it is an asking of the modern betrayed in telling. In betrayal enchantment betrays every thesis. It thereby betrays science, philosophy, religion, god, etc. etc. And in such betrayal it reveals the enchantments of the earth.

We may ask, what is an enchanting science, what does it enchant, what does it betray?—joy and sorrow, peace and war, delight and suffering, all perhaps as if ~~not~~ beyond themselves?

~~As if not~~ beyond is betrayal. Perhaps...

Let us laugh at modernity in the irreverence of postmodernity. Let us betray...

It is true, that is false, this is correct, avoid that error! You are wrong, that is right, this is good, that is bad! It is beautiful, that is ugly, how glorious you are, that work is disgusting! All are disenchanted...

Enchantment speaks the voices of disenchantment—what other voices can be spoken?—and betrays them, betrays the authority vested in them...

All binaries identifications judgments insistences claims are disenchanted...

When the gods or spirits tell us what to do, how to act, what to believe, they betray enchantments. Do not eat of the tree of knowledge, cover your hair, avoid adultery—all enchanted. When they are repeated in a human voice, when institutions claim authority over their accounts, when they punish, foster, promote, vilify according to rule, they are disenchanting. Authority as such—if there be such—is enchanted and enchanting. Authority betrays its institution and itself as disenchanting.

Enchantment may be radiant, glorious, amusing. It may be violent, cruel, disgusting, terrible. In any of these ways it cannot be accounted for, must be betrayed. Accounting is disenchanting. Betrayal occupies the caesura between enchanting and disenchanting...

It is not, then, that we cannot go back to an enchanted time, or that it would be undesirable to do so. Such a time was as disenchanted, in its own ways, as modern disenchantments. Before the disenchantments of modern science, technology, and rationality, disenchantment took place in other social practices. Magic, witchcraft, alchemy, ceremonies, rituals were all enchanting, and became disenchanted by authority. Where the enchantments loosened the hold of the world upon human lives—in disease, famine, death—multiplied in wonder, authority regripped the hold of instituted authorities as if there were a total accounting beyond betrayal.

Perhaps and as if betray the enchantments of authority and rule by askings beyond any telling...

Griffin is editor of a series in "constructive postmodern thought," which he contrasts with a "deconstructive or eliminative postmodernism":

deconstructive or eliminative postmodernism overcomes the modern worldview through an anti-worldview: it deconstructs or eliminates the ingredients necessary for a worldview, such as God, self, purpose, meaning, a real world, and truth as correspondence. While motivated in some cases by the ethical concern to forestall totalitarian systems, this type of postmodern thought issues in relativism, even nihilism.

I am interested in a postmodernism that can, by contrast, be called constructive or revisionary. This constructive or revisionary postmodernism involves a new unity of scientific, ethical, aesthetic, and religious intuitions.

The constructive activity of this type of postmodern thought is not limited to a revised worldview; it is equally concerned with a postmodern world that will support and be supported by the new worldview. A postmodern world will involve postmodern persons, with a postmodern spirituality, on the one hand, and a postmodern society, ultimately a postmodern global order, on the other. Going beyond the modern world will involve transcending its individualism, anthropocentrism, patriarchy, mechanization, economism, consumerism, nationalism, and militarism. Constructive postmodern thought provides support for the ecology, peace, feminist and other emancipatory movements of our time, while stressing that the inclusive emancipation must be from modernity itself. The term *postmodern*, however, by contrast with *premodern*, emphasizes that the modern world has produced unparalleled advances that must not be lost in a general revulsion against its negative features.

From the point of view of deconstructive postmodernists, this constructive postmodernism is still hopelessly wedded to outdated concepts, because it wishes to salvage a positive meaning not only for the notions of the human self, historical meaning, and truth as correspondence, which were central to modernity, but also for premodern notions of a divine reality, cosmic meaning, and an enchanted nature. From the point of view of its advocates, however, this revisionary postmodernism is not only more adequate to our experience but also more genuinely postmodern. It does not simply carry the premises of modernity through to their logical conclusions, but criticizes and revises those premises. Through its return to organicism and its acceptance of nonsensory perception, it opens itself to the recovery of truths and values from various forms of premodern thought and practice that had been dogmatically rejected by modernity. This constructive, revisionary postmodernism involves a creative synthesis of modern and premodern truths and values. (David Ray Griffin, *RC*, x–xi)

I could argue that such an understanding of deconstruction is fundamentally mistaken; that such a dream of adequacy, unity, and synthesis is utopian—and worse, totalitarian; that no matter how glowing and visionary, such a sense of superiority and fulfillment is disenchanted and disenchanting; that constructive and revisionary postmodernism is metaphysics and theology in another guise; that the enchanting promises of an organic view easily become disenchanted by equating organism with organization. Whitehead does not do this:

> Thus in an animal body the presiding occasion, if there be one, is the final node, or intersection, of a complex structure of many enduring objects. Such a structure pervades the human body. There is also an enduring object formed by the inheritance from presiding occasion to presiding occasion. This endurance of the mind is only one more example of the general principle on which the body is constructed. Tic route of presiding occasions probably wanders from part to part of the brain, dissociated from the physical material atoms. But central personal dominance is only partial, and in pathological cases is apt to vanish. (Whitehead, *PR*, 109)

Perhaps in other cases as well.

As I have argued in relation to gablik's reconstructive postmodernism,[4] the idea of a new and higher spirituality that will replace modernity fails to realize the ways in which deconstruction and the "post" in poststructuralism—also postphenomenology, postexistentialism, postmarxism, postcolonialism, posthistory—are historical, linguistic, far from innocent. That is, constructive and reconstructive postmodernism are disenchanted, and remain so despite their hope for reenchantment. They dream of enchantment without betrayal.

At another level I could argue that together with all process theology, griffin's reading of whitehead is mistaken,[5] at least one-sided; that such a systematic and theological interpretation is profoundly disenchanted; that process philosophy has done great disservice to whitehead in the limited possibilities it has explored—compared, for example, with the readings emerging from foucault, deleuze and guattari, stengers, and latour. In other words, to propose another theory of the world and reality under whose umbrella science will be reenchanted is very different from exploring moments of thought in which science itself, no matter how mechanistic, imperialistic, and self-serving, is itself enchanted and enchanting, betrays itself enchantingly and disenchantingly.

At still another level I could argue that for philosophers and theologians—some scientists are included in griffin's collection, notably David Bohm, but also Charles Birch, Rupert Sheldrake, and Brian Swimme—to define and delineate a new and better science is another example of philosophy's claim to know everything. Postmodernity as that which questions modern science's claim to be and to account for everything questions the superiority of all authorities, scientific, technological, philosophical, theological, ethical, or political.

All these disagreements with the ways in which griffin and other process theologians understand the possibility of philosophy, religion, science, and the future—postmodernism, what will come after modernism—view them as disenchanted theories as well as theories of disenchantment—and, moreover, are themselves disenchanted and disenchanting. There is nothing that exceeds accounting, but here is another account of what is accountable. These theories and their critiques offer nothing overt that betrays accounting, betrays enchantment and disenchantment, nothing of betrayal in this dream of what the future may hold. There is nothing irreverent about such a dream, either for the future or in it, but another dream of reverence.

I insist that betrayal takes place no matter whether it is recognized and in every place that would deny it. It is a contingent necessity of exposition, the impossible condition of asking and telling. I insist that disenchantment is enchanted no matter how firmly it insists on accounting for everything. Everything cannot be counted. It is a necessary contingency of exposition.

Everything can be counted, nothing can be counted, neither everything nor nothing can be counted, both everything and nothing can be counted...

Everything betrays, nothing betrays, everything or nothing betrays, everything and nothing betrays...

Apart from questions of the possibility of a postmodern world with postmodern persons, a postmodern spirituality, a postmodern society, ultimately a postmodern global order that will transcend individualism, anthropocentrism, patriarchy, mechanization, economism, consumerism, nationalism, and militarism, that will provide support for the ecology, peace, feminist and other emancipatory movements of our time, are questions of its goodness and superiority. Is it possible? Would it be suffocating? But also, is this not another metaphysics, another accounting? In proposing it as better, are we not disenchanting? Is metaphysics disenchanting?

I believe so. I believe that one way to understand the critique of metaphysics that emerged in nietzsche and came to visibility in heidegger and poststructuralism is from a sense of enchantment as what cannot be contained or accounted for. Bringing to full presence is disenchantment. Levinas calls it sedentary and possessive. Enchantment is uncontainable. It does not reject ethics, goodness, beauty, truth but rejects their possessiveness and insists on their dispossession. In the name of generosity and giving beyond gifts. In the name of what is beyond having. In the name of perhaps and as if. In the name of asking and telling. In the name of betrayal. Most of all, here, in the name of self-betrayal. If any of these are names. Not only must we betray ourselves in witness, but we must know it, must at least express it, must find ways to betray betrayal.

I believe this is possible for science, a dionysian science.[6] I believe it is possible for metaphysics, an enchanted philosophy. Nothing is more wonderful and abundant than philosophy, in the revels of its enchantments, in the wildness of its dances with science, art, in life, in the fecundity of its askings. I believe science and philosophy, especially metaphysics, are aporetic and heretical, marks of their enchantments, enchanting revelations, enchanting betrayals, enchanting tellings. Betrayal is the enchantment of enchantment. Irreverence is the enchantment of spirituality.

That is not griffin's view:[7]

> The postmodern world I advocate involves a new science, a new spirituality, and a new society. The full flowering of each of these dimensions will presuppose, and be presupposed by, the others. A reenchanted, liberating science will be fully developed only by people with a postmodern spirituality, in which the dualisms that have made modern science such an ambiguous phenomenon have been transcended, and only in a society organized for the good of the planet as a whole. Likewise, relational, ecological, planetary, postpatriarchal spirituality will only become dominant in the context of a postmodern society and with the support of a postmodern science. Finally, no possibility exists for the emergence of a society in which individualism, nationalism, militarism, anthropocentrism, and androcentrism have been transcended apart from the widespread acceptance of a postmodern science and the emergence of a postmodern spirituality. (Griffin, *RS*, xiii)

No matter how valuable, full flowering is disenchanting. Without betrayal, without being able to laugh at oneself and the superiority of one's views and practices, one seeks full accounting. In fulfillment is the possessiveness that betrays enchantment. I could argue against griffin, but that would be disenchanting. I could agree with him about the ills of individualism, nationalism, militarism, anthropocentrism, and androcentrism, if not about postmodern spirituality, science, and society. I would rather laugh with and toward him, most of all betray him. My concern in this chapter is with how enchantment demands betrayal, how enchanting betrayal is, and how we might go about betraying the human world. Irreverently. Enchantingly.

> At the root of modernity and its discontents lies what Max Weber called "the disenchantment of the world." This disenchanted worldview has been both a result and a presupposition of modern science and has almost unanimously been assumed to be a result and a presupposition of science as such. What is distinctive about "modern" philosophy, theology, and art is that they revolve around numerous strategies for maintaining moral, religious, and aesthetic sensitivities while accepting the disenchanted world-view of modernity as adequate for science. These strategies have involved either rejecting modern science, ignoring it, supplementing it with talk of human values, or reducing its status to that of mere appearance. The postmodern approach to disenchantment involves a reenchantment of science itself. (1)

The postmodern approach to disenchantment—griffin's approach, griffin's postmodernism—is to reenchant science, as if science were not already enchanted, as if science were not itself enchanting, no matter how disenchanting. The disenchantment of the world is taken for granted as modern science—together or distinguished from modern reason, modern technology, modern economy, and indeed from premodern reason and postmodern technology.

Science insists—it is not alone—that it has the truth and it is rational, defensible, dependable. Without betrayal. Reason, justification, reliability are in abundance (*Fülle*) as heidegger understands them, where abundance is enchanted beyond any accounting, infinitely infinite perhaps, where beyond any accounting is perhaps betraying.

Griffin insists—he is not alone—that he has the truth and it is rational, defensible, dependable. Without betrayal.

Betrayal resists any reversal of disenchantment that would reenchant. Enchantment is not the reversal of disenchantment, an enchanted science is not any less disenchanted, nor can an enchanted science be any less insistent on experimentation, validation, or clarity. Or more. The reversal of disenchantment is disenchanted. Reenchantment is not enchantment but disenchantment again. Enchantment is the slippage—the dionysian, anarchistic, uncontainable, unaccountable caesura—beyond grasping of the wonder and abundance of the earth and its ingredients. Enchantment is dispossessive. Reversals are possessions. Disenchantment is possessive.

Here from griffin is perhaps a telling example, where telling is betraying: mechanism as such is disenchanted. Its disenchantment is the absence of subjectivity and spirituality—and, indeed, purpose and value.

> In disenchanting nature, the modern science of nature led to its own disenchantment. This happened because the mechanistic, disenchanted philosophy of nature, which was originally part of a dualistic and theistic vision of reality as a whole, eventually led to the disenchantment of the whole world.
>
> What does the "disenchantment of nature" mean? Most fundamentally, it means the denial to nature of all subjectivity, all experience, all feeling. Because of this denial, nature is disqualified—it is denied all qualities that are not thinkable apart from experience.
>
> These qualities are legion. Without experience, no aims or purposes can exist in natural entities, no creativity in the sense of self-determination or final causation. With no final causation toward some ideal possibility, no role exists for ideals, possibilities, norms, or values to play: causation is strictly a matter of efficient causation from the past. With no self-determination aimed at the realization of ideals, no value can be achieved. With no experience, even unconscious feeling, there can be no value received: the causal interactions between natural things or events involve no sharing of values. Hence, no intrinsic value can exist within nature, no value of natural things for themselves. Also, unlike the way our experience is internally affected, even constituted in part, by its relations with its environment, material particles can have no internal relations. Along with no internalization of other natural things, no internalization of divinity can occur. (2)

These are the qualities—legion if you will but not perhaps in abundance: final causation, teleology, self determination, ideal realization, norms, values, natural purposes in all natural things; experience, feeling, values given and received, shared; internal relations, and perhaps above all no internalization of god.

I find more enchantment in blind particles coming together in evolutionary transformations than in a cosmic purpose guiding all things together. I wonder at what blindness might be so creative and farseeing, and at the social relationality of particles that come together in such wonderful ways. I mean, however, to emphasize the surprising aspects of the emergence, of the insistence on purposes as if they disenchanted the surprises by explanation. Final purposes are accountings, to some more satisfying than lawfulness. More to the point, however, multiple causations, infinitely infinite, present law and order beyond any accounting, surprising and astonishing beyond any human expectations. Is that not enchanting?

Griffin's model is whitehead, and I share his fascination with whitehead's theory. Yet I am drawn to the ways in which such a theory does not explain, presents what cannot be explained, offers creativity, emergence, intensity, and feeling enchanting every ingredient in the universe. Another disenchanted way to put this is that accountability has limits, but those limits also have limits, so that there is an anarchistic and unlawful component of the most lawful relations, and it pervades every level of the material universe. This is not griffin's view, driven by god on one hand and purpose on the other. Griffin does not acknowledge his own betrayal, nor does he betray it.

> If the ultimate individuals of the world are momentary events, rather than enduring individuals, a positive relation can exist between efficient and final causation. Efficient causation applies to the exterior of an individual and final causation to the interior. But because an enduring individual, such as a proton, neuron, or human psyche, is a temporal society of momentary events, exterior and interior feed into each other.
>
> In primary individuals, such as photons and electrons (or quarks, if such there be), final causation is minimal. For the most part, the behavior of these individuals is understandable in terms of efficient causes alone. They mainly conform to what they have received and pass it on to the future in a predictable way. But not completely: behind the epistemic "indeterminacy" of quantum physics lies a germ of ontic self-determinacy.
>
> From this perspective we can understand why a mechanistic, reductionistic approach has been so spectacularly successful in certain areas and so unsuccessful in others. The modern Galilean paradigm was based on the study of nonindividuated objects, such as stellar masses and steel balls, which exercise no final causation either in determining their own behavior or that of their elementary parts. Absolute predictability and reduction is possible in principle. As one leaves nonindividuated objects for individuals, and as one deals with increasingly higher in-

> dividuals, final causation becomes increasingly important, and regularity and hence predictability become increasingly less possible. Hence, nothing but confusion and unrealistic expectations can result from continuing to regard physics as the paradigmatic science. (23–5)

Much can be gained from rethinking physics as the paradigmatic science and the basis of all other sciences. On the way, however, is the question of what we are to think from the standpoint of the other sciences, paradigmatic or something else. Griffin, at the point of a transition to another understanding, another science, other ways of understanding and enchanting the world, knows with certainty at least one thing we must all know, that the categories of both final and efficient causation must be employed for the study of all actual beings. Final and efficient causation—and for that matter, external and internal relations—are a given for all understanding, all science, in the infinite future to come.

Such a view is another accounting, richer in some ways, less in others. It belongs on the same plane as all disenchanted sciences—and for that matter, all disenchantments fall on the same plane. Enchantments are orthogonal—and even stranger: alien, surprising, questionable, irreverent. Betrayals.

Here the historical question of science arises as a unified field of knowledge with a unified object—if there be such, if there be such a thing as science, if there be a distinctive unity to science as against many sciences, many forms of knowledge, many ways to know.

> What then is science—what constitutes its unity? The anarchistic or relativistic view that "anything goes," that there is no such thing as a scientific method, is surely too strong. But it serves a useful function, as indeed it was intended, to shake us free from parochial limitations on what counts as science. A description of science for a postmodern world must be much looser than the modern descriptions (which were really *pre*scriptions). (26)

Again, I might ask, who believes that anything goes in science or morality except those who fear that god is dead? Whether the gods are alive or dead, whether there is or is not a unity to science, we can take for granted that there is science (or many sciences) and scientific truth (or many such truths). What we cannot take for granted is that such a truth is complete, separate from other truths, other sciences and other forms of knowledge, that such a truth is without betrayal. Spinoza's understanding that we do not know what bodies can do depends on our knowing many things about what bodies can do. That science is not unified under the heading of physics does not mean that separate sciences fail to provide many forms of scientific knowledge, factual and lawful. That science is not distinct from society, history, the arts and humanities, from the rest of human experiences, does not mean that it is useless or incompetent. To the contrary.

That anything goes or does not go is not without betrayal on either side. To think that anything goes is to propound a position and a life in which not anything goes. To insist on rules and boundaries is to insist on controlling what cannot be controlled, here in the name of science. Science cannot police its boundaries against nonscience, no matter how insistently it would do so. Science cannot allow the world's abundance to appear within it without betrayal, no matter how insistently it would hope to betray it. Betrayal is the form in which abundance and wonder mark the unity of science as its disunity, mark the disunity of science with its unity.

What if there were no unity to science, nothing distinctive that is science separate from literature, art, or philosophy? What if there were a multiplicity of sciences with no overarching unity, but with links and connections among the sciences adding to the multiplication? Perhaps there is no unique object to a science or to science in general, perhaps there is no unique method to a science or to science in general. Perhaps, most critical of all in relation to modern reason, there is no strict boundary between science and nonscience, between reason and unreason, but sophisticated, thoughtful ways of asking, developing theories, formulating facts, and gathering evidence to support them. How would this be any less science? Perhaps it would be more enchanting, more multiple, less ambitious in its accountings, more ambitious in its multiplications.

Not according to griffin:

> Any activity properly called *science* and any conclusions properly called *scientific* must, first, be based on an overriding concern to discover truth. Other concerns will of course play a role, but the concern for truth must be overriding, or the activity and its results would better called by another name, such as *ideology*, or *propaganda*, or *politics*. (26)

Perhaps by the name *philosophy*, perhaps *art* and *literature*. Or perhaps not. Perhaps truth in some form haunts all human activities, including ideology, propaganda, and politics. Perhaps knowledge in some form offers itself everywhere in human life, perhaps too enchantingly.

> Second, science involves demonstration. More particularly, it involves testing hypotheses through data or experiences that are in some sense repeatable and hence open to confirmation or refutation by peers. In sum, science involves the attempt to establish truth through demonstrations open to experiential replication. What is left out of this account of science are limitations (1) to any particular domain, (2) any particular type of repeatability and demonstration, or (3) any particular contingent beliefs. (26)

Yet the domain, the validation, and the beliefs mark off each separate science from the others and from the whole. If there are many sciences, if there are many different forms of knowledge and ways to truth—as there are many different forms of life and ways to live them, many human forms and ways—if this multiplicity is itself beyond accounting, unaccountable as a unity, in the small or large, then the successes, knowledges, achievements of these sciences mark them on the one hand as enchanting and on the other as betraying any unity of science. The only unity of enchanted science is as a unity of ungathering, given for asking. Unity comes to be by betrayal.

Betrayal is the issue here. Griffin seems not to betray it.

> (1) Science is not restricted to the domain of things assumed to be wholly physical, operating in terms of efficient causes alone, or even to the physical aspects of things, understood as the aspects knowable to sensory perception or instruments designed to magnify the senses. As the impossibility of behaviorism in human and even animal psychology has shown, science must refer to experience and purposes to comprehend (and even to predict) animal behavior. (26)

Understanding a multiplicity of sciences and knowledges in betrayal, we might understand physical sciences *to betray themselves as physical,* understand experiences and purposes, efficient and final causation, as betraying causation itself. A science without causation. Many sciences betraying causation, betraying law and lawfulness, science beyond explanation, cause, and law—still sciences. There is more on heaven and earth than can be told in any science—still science betraying science.

> (2) While science requires repeatable experiential demonstration, it does not require one particular type of demonstration, such as the laboratory experiment. (27)

Perhaps not. Perhaps repeatability is not a standard for science, at least for all sciences. Perhaps repetition is as if deleuze and derrida describe it, the repetition of difference. In order for science—or any other form of telling—to be stable it must repeat not only the experiments but the expositions, must be able to repeat everything about itself as knowledge and truth. And in this repetition everything changes, shifts ever so slightly, changes ever so much.

> (3) Besides not being limited to one domain or one type of demonstration, the scientific pursuit of truth is not tied to any set of contingent beliefs, meaning beliefs that are not inevitably presupposed by human practice, including thought, itself. Science is, therefore, not limited to any particular type of explanation. For example, science is not tied to the belief that the elementary units of nature are devoid of sentience, intrinsic value, and internal relations, that the universe as a whole is not an organism which influences its parts, or that the universe and its evolution have no inherent meaning.
>
> However, the fact that science as such is not permanently wedded to these contingent beliefs that reigned during the modern period does not mean that there are no beliefs that science as such must presuppose. If beliefs exist that are presupposed by human practice, including human thought, as such, then scientific practice and thought must presuppose them. (28)

Something must be taken for granted, nothing can be taken for granted, either something must be taken for granted or nothing can be taken for granted, something must be taken for granted and nothing can be taken for granted...

This is enchanted, this is disenchanted, this is either one or the other, this is both one and the other. One always is the other even as the same. Including science. And philosophy giving the rule to science...

I would not take for granted that the universe is a whole; I would imagine that each singular thing is an organism filled with surprising enchantments...

> To illustrate the types of beliefs intended and to show that they are not limited to innocuous, noncontroversial issues, I propose five principles as candidates. The first three principles relate to the crucial issue of causality. First, every event is causally influenced by other events. This principle rules out, for example, the idea that the universe arose out of absolute nothingness or out of pure possibility! Second, neither human experience nor anything analogous to it is wholly determined by external events; rather, every genuine individual is partially

> self-determining. Incidentally, these first two principles, taken together, provide the basis for a scientific understanding of the activity of scientists themselves in terms of a combination of external and internal causes.
>
> Third, every event that exerts causal influence upon another event precedes that event temporally. This principle rules out the notion of particles "going backwards in time," the notion of "backward causation," and any notion of "precognition" interpreted to mean that an event affected the knower before it happened or to mean that temporal relations are ultimately unreal!
>
> The final two principles proffered deal with science's concern for truth. These are the traditional principles of correspondence and noncontradiction, which are recovered in a postmodern context.
>
> After all necessary subtleties and qualifications have been added, the principle [of noncontradiction] remains valid and is necessarily presupposed even in attempts to refute it. Accordingly, science must aim for coherence between all its propositions and between its propositions and all those that are inevitably presupposed in human practice and thought in general. (Obtaining such coherence is indeed the primary method of checking for correspondence.)
>
> All of these principles are in harmony with postmodern organicism. (28–30)

I could argue that such a view remains disenchanted despite its claims to reenchantment. I could argue that griffin's view is far too limited from the standpoint of contemporary science. Science is more enchanted in its disenchanted forms than is the view of science he describes. Current physical theories suggest a plausible meaning and scenario to becoming from absolute nothing or pure possibility.[8]

Every event is relational, in relation to itself and others, but perhaps not causally. Relation is betrayal...

Nothing is wholly determined by any relations whatever, but it is determined by relations. Determination is betrayal...

No one knows what bodies can do, what time is, or what is possible for science. And still we know. The future determines the past historically and linguistically. Knowing is betraying. Time betrays...

Language and reality are beyond accounting. And still we account for them. Still we betray...

Everything is contradictory—and noncontradictory. That is the disenchantment of enchantment—and its enchantments...

It is time for a story—perhaps for many stories. If we are not enchanted by griffin's reenchantments, perhaps we may be enchanted by other stories he presents—enchanting and betrayed. For example, Brian swimme betrays physical cosmology's understanding of the world as stories, stories we may ask, stories we have told, stories we might tell, stories of physics. Under the heading of *story* he imagines the truth of the creation of the world as told and betrayed in science, betrayed as science. In this way, as story, we betray the truth of cosmic creation, whatever it may be.

> my suggestion is that we tell stories—the many stories that comprise the great cosmic story. I am suggesting that this activity of cosmic storytelling is the central political and economic act of our time. My basic claim is that by telling our cosmic creation story, we inaugurate a new era of human and planetary health, for we initiate a transformation out of a world that is—to use David Griffin's thorough formulation—mechanistic, scientistic, dualistic, patriarchal, Eurocentric, anthropocentric, militaristic, and reductionistic. (Brian Swimme, *CCS*, 47)

I am not confident that stories will lead us out of our mechanistic, scientistic, dualistic, patriarchal, eurocentric, anthropocentric, militaristic, reductionistic world, if that is what our world is: they are part of it, though they betray it. They may not save us but they must betray it. I insist that cosmic creation stories in particular together with myth and story in general ask and tell and betray themselves as stories. They betray themselves in the fictiveness and mobility of stories, what they mean and mean to say, in the stories that might have been told instead, and in the many that have been and are being told. They betray the richness of language and meaning, of the possibilities of the future, of the unstable state of the caesura.

In this caesura, we may seek a transformation from a world that may be too mechanistic, scientistic, dualistic, patriarchal, etc. etc.—a transformation of and from and in that world, perhaps not away from it, any more than such a transformation might be away from a world of story.

> A *cosmic creation story* satisfies the questions asked by humans fresh out of the womb. As soon as they get here and learn the language, children ask the cosmic questions. Where did everything come from? What is going on? Why are you doing such and such anyway? The young of our species desire to learn where they are and what they are about in this life. They express an inherent desire to hear their cosmic story.
>
> By *cosmic creation story* I also mean to indicate those accounts of the universe we told each other around the evening fires for

> most of the last 50,000 years. These cosmic stories were the way the first humans chose to initiate and install their young into the universe. The rituals, the traditions, the taboos, the ethics, the techniques, the customs, and the values all had as their core a cosmic story. The story provided the central cohesion for each society. Story in this sense is "world-interpretation"—a likely account of the development and nature and value of things in this world.
>
> Why story? Why should "story" be fundamental? Because without storytelling, we lose contact with our basic realities in this world. We lose contact because only through story can we fully recognize our existence in time. (48)

Storytelling is enchanting, storytelling is plural, if there is one there are many stories. Swimme tells one, we have seen another, calvino's story.[9] Yet somehow, like griffin, swimme travels quickly from the many to the one, insists that to be human is to have a story.

> To be human is to be in a story. To forget one's story is to go insane. All the tribal peoples show an awareness of the connection between health and storytelling. Our ancestors recognized that the universe, at its most basic level, is story. Each creature is story. Humans enter this world and awaken to a simple truth: We must find our story within this great epic of being! (48)

I insist that to be enchanting is to tell many stories—ask, tell, retell, listen to, repeat, invent, inhabit endless stories. Endless betrayals. Swimme understands that storytelling is not alternative to science, that scientists tell stories, betraying themselves in the scene that they control.

> What about our situation today? Do we tell stories? We most certainly do, even if we do not call them stories. In our century's textbooks—for use in grade schools and high schools—we learn that it all began with impoverished primitives, marched through the technical inventions of the scientific period, and culminated in the United States of America, in its political freedom and, most of all, in its superior modes of production. We were drawn into an emotional bonding with our society, so that it was only natural we would want to support, defend, and extend our society's values and accomplishments. Of course, this was not considered story; we were learning the facts. (48)
>
> How could modern Western culture escape a 50,000-year-old tradition of telling cosmic stories? We discovered science. So impressed were we with this blinding light, we simply threw out the cosmic stories for the knowledge that the sciences provided. Why tell the story of the Sun as a God when we knew the sun

> was a locus of thermonuclear reactions? We pursued "scientific law!" relegating "story" and "myth" to the nurseries and tribes. Science gave us the real, and the best science was mathematical science. We traded myth for mathematics and, without realizing it, we entered upon an intellectual quest that had for its goal a complete escape from the shifting sands of the temporal world. (49)
>
> What a shock it has been to have *story reappear*, and this time right in the very center of the mathematical sciences! (49)
>
> we now realize that ours is a universe that had a beginning in time and has been developing from 15 to 20 billion years. And every moment of this universe is new. That is, we now realize that we live not in a static Newtonian space; we live within an ongoing cosmic story.
>
> Story forced its way still further into physics when in recent decades scientists discovered that even the fundamental interactions of the universe evolved into their present forms. The laws that govern the physical universe today and that were thought to be immutable are themselves the results of developments over time. We had always assumed that the laws were fixed, absolute, eternal. Now we discover that even the laws tell their own story of the universe. That is, the Cosmic Story, rather than being simply governed by fixed underlying laws, draws these laws into its drama. (50)

Let's take the key to story and world as their temporality. The world evolved from a beginning, including physical laws. Story evolved without beginning or end, including the transformations, uncertainties, and betrayals of laws and facts and theories, of physics and physical reality. We tell stories because the world is story—that is, exposition, expression, enchantment, betrayal. Some call it love.

> Story inserts itself still further into the consciousness of contemporary physicists when the very status of physical law is put into a new perspective. Where once we listed a set of laws that, we were certain, held everywhere and at all times, we now ponder the violations of each of these laws. What happens when physicists begin to value not just the repeatable experiment but history's unrepeatable events, no longer regarding each event as simply another datum useful for arriving at mathematical law but as a revelation all by itself? A reenchantment with the universe happens. A new love affair between humans and the universe happens. (51)

A new love affair, a new story, full of surprises. I mean irreverence, wonder, abundance, enchantment, transgression, betrayal. Love cannot be controlled, desire exceeds every possibility of its containment, obsession attaches itself to anything and everything.

> Only when we are surprised in the presence of a person or a thing are we truly in love. And regardless how intimate we become, our surprise continues. Without question we come to know the beloved better and are able to speak central truths about her or him or it, but never do we arrive at a statement that is the final word. Further surprises always occur, for to be in love is to be in awe of the infinite depths of things. (51)

Such a love so transcends the account science gives of itself as to open up the very dream that science imagines itself to foreclose. By betrayal.

> A central desire of scientists in the future will be to explore and celebrate the enveloping Great Mystery—the story of the universe, the journey of the galaxies, the adventure of the planet Earth and all of its life forms. Scientific theories will no longer be seen as objective laws. Scientific understanding will be valued as that power capable of evoking in humans a deep intimacy with reality.
>
> I am convinced that the story of the universe that has come out of three centuries of modern scientific work will be recognized as a supreme human achievement, the scientific enterprise's central gift to humanity, a revelation having a status equal to that of the great religious revelations of the past. (51)

This story of the universe has been provided to us by science, by physics especially. Swimme imagines it in familiar terms, as if it were one of the great religious revelations of the past. That is where the great mystery takes him. By betrayal. In another betrayal, I would imagine that enchantment and mystery remain surprising far beyond anything so familiar as a religious revelation. A surprising, enchanted revelation in which the mystery betrays something new beyond imagining and old beyond remembering. Perhaps, more truthfully, in which the mystery remains mysterious in every betrayal.

Swimme tells a story of an old woman storyteller, who tells a story of the earth, ending with enchantment and mystery. This is her story:

> No matter what happens, remember that our universe is a universe of surprise. We put our confidence in the power that

> gathered the stars and knit the first living cells together. Remember that you are here through the creativity of others. You have awakened in a great epic of being, a drama that is 15 to 20 billion years in the making. The intelligence that ignited the first minds, the care that spaced the notes of the nightingale, the power that heaved all 100 billion galaxies across the sky now awakens as you, too, and permeates your life no less thoroughly.
>
> We do not know what mystery awaits us in the very next moment. But we can be sure we will be astonished and enchanted. This entire universe sprang into existence from a single numinous speck. Our origin is mystery; our destiny is intimate community with all that is; our common species' aim is to celebrate the Great Joy which has drawn us into itself.
>
> Rocks, soils, waves, stars—as they tell their story in 10,000 languages throughout the planet, they bind us to them in our emotions, our spirits, our minds, and our bodies. The Earth and the universe speak in all this. The cosmic creation story is the way in which the universe is inaugurating the next era of its ongoing journey. (55–6)

My story, like swimme's, is one in which rocks, soils, waves, stars, in infinite numbers of infinite languages, tell their stories and betray and expose themselves in story to each other and to us. On the side of this infinitely infinite exposition we have science. On the side of betrayal we have mystery. On the side of enchantment we have asking, telling, giving, in story, enchantment, and betrayal. Including science as science.

In the light of this expression of enchantment and betrayal as story, other views of science are disenchanted. This does not mean that they lack understanding or truth.

There are infinite stories, stories are infinite, infinite numbers and kinds of infinite stories. In this way, in these stories, the world is infinitely infinite, stories and worlds and enchantments and betrayals in abundance...

There are, there once was, once upon a time, long long ago, there will be, a long time still to come, story gestures, gestures of stories. The giving of being is another story...

Remember *Cosmicomics*, calvino's cosmic stories?[10]

> *all the universe's matter was concentrated in a single point, before it began to expand in space.* (Calvino, *AAOP*, 43)
>
> Naturally, we were all there—*Old Qfwfa said,*—where else could we have been? Nobody knew then that there could be

> space. Or time either; what use did we have for time, packed in there like sardines?
>
> I say "packed like sardines," using a literary image: in reality there wasn't even space to pack us into. Every point of each of us coincided with every point of each of the others in a single point, which was where we all were. In fact, we didn't even bother one another, except for personality differences, becaus when space doesn't exist, having somebody unpleasant like Mr. Pber^t Pber^d underfoot all the time is the most irritating thing.
>
> How many of us were there? Oh, I was never able to figure that out, not even approximately. To make a count, we would have to move apart, at least a little, and instead we all occupied that same point. Contrary to what you might think, it wasn't the sort of situation that encourages sociability; I know, for example, that in other periods neighbors called on one another; but there, because of the fact that we were all neighbors, nobody even said good morning or good evening to anybody else. (43)

These personifications and literarizations are not only delightfully enchanting, but they express and betray the infinitely infinite enchantments of the most disenchanted view of the world. In the big bang are (in some sense of what is here an impossibly enchanted word) all the particular, concrete things, individuals, relations, processes, etc. etc, all the etceteras actual and possible and . . . , in short all the wonder and abundance, all the surprises and revelations, all the betrayals and excesses, actual and possible and more. Love—here Mrs. Ph(i)Nk_o's love—exceeds all imaginable love in the most concrete way.

> And for her: she contained and was contained with equal happiness, and whe welcomed us and loved and inhabited all equally.
>
> We got along so well all together, so well that something extraordinary was bound to happen. It was enough for her to say, at a certain moment: "Oh, if I only had some room, how I'd like to make some noodles for you boys!" a true outburst of general love, initiating at the same moment the concept of space and, properly speaking, space itself, and time, and universal gravitation, and the gravitating universe, making possible billions and billions of suns and of planets, and fields of wheat, and Mrs. Ph(i)Nk_os, scattered through the continents of the planets, kneading with floury, oil-shiny, generous arms, and she lost at that very moment, and we, mourning her loss. (46–7)

In this incredible image of cosmic creation and love appear endless images of other enchantments, noodles of course, and boys, also space, time, gravitation, suns, and planets, also fields of wheat, flour, oil, floury, oil-shiny, generous arms, not to mention loss and mourning.

In other, less enchanted words, the enchantments of the world appear in and follow from the most concrete, determinate, contingent, particular, disenchanted things. By love, calvino says. In enchantment, I say. That is, in betrayal. Obliquely, irreverently.

Calvino is irreverent to science, and in that way betrays—reveals, asks and tells—how enchanted is the world of science. In case you may have forgotten. Betrayal is the obliqueness, displacement, multiplication, excess of the world and its ingredients.

Betrayal is the irreverence of exposition: exposure as expression, asking, calling, telling; as aisthēsis, mimēsis, poiēsis, catachrēsis, technē; as image, aesthetics, beauty, art; as unearthing, revelation, disclosure; calling as giving; interrupting in betrayal: blasphemous, sacrilegious, disrespectful, heretical; audacious, bold, daring, impertinent...

Swimme insists on story, advocates (disenchantedly) a cosmic creation story, tells (enchantingly) a cosmic creation story. Even so, he imagines "an imaginary event—a moment in the future when children are taught by a cosmic storyteller. We can imagine a small group gathered around a fire in a hillside meadow. The woman in the middle is the oldest, a grandmother to some of the children present" (54). Enchanted as such an image may be, as rare in an industrial society as such an event perhaps may be, it is familiar, and swimme is reverent. Calvino is something otherwise.

For the one who tells his stories is also a story teller, old Qfwfq: *old Qfwfq cried, old Qfwfq confirmed, Qfwfq said, old Qfwfq said, Qfwfq confirmed, Qfwfq narrated, old Qfwfq recalled, Qfwfq explained, Qfwfq corrected, Qfwfq asked...*

Qfwfq is old, the name unpronounceable, the gender indeterminate, the discourse ambiguous, somewhere between being there, experiencing, living through events that no one could live through—crying, narrating, recalling—yet that took place—old science tells us—and a scientific discourse—confirming, saying, explaining, correcting—coming finally to the asking that is enchantment, to the betraying that is enchanting. In this unfamiliar telling, calvino betrays the enchantments of science and the cosmos enchantingly—impudently, laughingly, irreverently. Betrayal is violence, its appearance heretical.

The enchantments of the world are its heresies, against heresy as well...

Always another meaning, always another, always other. As if perhaps ~~not~~ beyond the world and itself...

In fascination, fascinating, will, desire, yearning. As if perhaps ~~not~~ beyond themselves...

The other of all meaning. The other of all being. The other. As if perhaps ~~not~~ beyond the world and itself...

In wonder and abundance. The enchantment and irreverence and betrayal of wonder, in abundance. The abundance of enchantment and irreverence and betrayal...

In the abstract, schematic, universal forms of natural laws lie all the concrete, individual, disenchanted things that betray them. In wonder and abundance. Including science—science betrays the laws that make it possible. Including nonscience. The wonder and abundance of the world is an expression of form, and of the forms of forms, that is, an expression of disenchantment. Without disenchantment, without disenchanted science, some enchantments, some enchanted things, some askings and tellings, human and otherwise, would not be possible...

Without the hegemony of the church, catholic music would never have been heard. Without the hegemony of the nation state, ceremonial events would neither have existed nor be remembered. Without modern technology and economy, many enchanting things would not exist, many enchanting activities would not take place. All at immense cost, not only in the violence each of these imposes on human lives, but on other hegemonies that might have exposed their enchantments. Those we owe it to them and ourselves to reenchant...

An enchanted science pays off that debt, no matter how inadequately. And indeed, in the realm of enchantment, what could adequacy be?

Quickly, then, before the world changes before our eyes, let us betray the reenchantments griffin and his collaborators bring before us.

> With the coming of the modern era, human beings' view of their world and themselves underwent a fundamental change. The earlier, basically religious approach to life was replaced by a secular approach. This approach has assumed that nature could be thoroughly understood and eventually brought under control by means of the systematic development of scientific knowledge through observation, experiment, and rational thought.
>
> So great is the change in the whole context of thought thereby brought about that some have described it as the onset of the modern mind. This mind is in contrast with the mind of the medieval period, in which it was generally supposed that the order of nature was beyond human comprehension and in which hu-

> man happiness consisted in being aware of the revealed knowledge of God and carrying out the divine commandments. A total revolution occurred in the way people were aiming to live.
>
> The modern mind went from one triumph to another for several centuries through science, technology, industry, and it seemed to be solidly based for all time. But in the early twentieth century, it began to have its foundations questioned. (David Bohm, *PSPW*, 57–8)

The key words for us here, I suggest, are *secular* and *control*. As if these were internally related, as if secularity, modernity, and disenchantment were identical, as if sacrality, premodernity, and enchantment were once inseparable. As if we knew what we cannot know, as if we had decided once and for all what we cannot decide in the face of repetition and variation. Bohm is speaking less of science—where we may imagine that science is the deepest asking of things—than of *technoscience*, the marriage between science and technology, where it is supposed and posited and insisted that science serve human purposes, that it bring the risky world under human control, that science through technology is the means to govern and manipulate the world for human purposes. The way to grasp it.[11]

This is another understanding of disenchantment, the means to control the uncontrollable, to order the disorderly, to govern the unruly, to own what cannot be owned. The disenchantment of the world is its subjection to human control—as if that were possible, perhaps. It has little to do with religion and art, even where art requires technical proficiency and for religions that understand the world as given to humanity to master.

We may imagine other purposes, other technologies, all disenchanted. We may imagine other human relations to the world than control—reverence, for example, as bohm suggests. We may imagine something quite different from both, celebrating the abundance of the earth and its wonders, including ourselves. Irreverently. Indeed, in the sense that we do not give up control, do not imagine living without disenchantment, but ask, tell, betray, transfigure every insistence on control. That we seek to give in abundance rather than to have and own. Here bohm has less to offer. For first he offers a reverent and unprovocative view of mechanism:

> The first point about mechanism is that the world is reduced as far as possible to a set of basic elements. Typically, these elements take the form of particles. Whatever they may be called, the assumption is that a basic element exists which

> we either have or hope to have. To these elementary particles, various continuous fields, such as electromagnetic and gravitational fields, must be added.
>
> Second, these elements are basically external to each other; not only are they separate in space, but even more important, the fundamental nature of each is independent of that of the other. The elements do not grow organically as parts of a whole, but are rather more like parts of a machine whose forms are determined externally to the structure of the machine in which they are working. (60–1)

Such a view repeats descartes's view of machines as clocks, impossible to maintain in a quantum mechanical or relativistic universe, not to mention one filled with chaotic processes and fractal structures.

Second, then, a reverent view of organicism with implicate (internally related) order:

> Third, because the elements only interact mechanically by sort of pushing each other around, the forces of interaction do not affect their inner natures. In an organism or a society, by contrast, the very nature of each part is profoundly affected by changes in the other parts, so that the parts are internally related. In the mechanistic view, this sort of organismic behavior is admitted, but it is explained eventually by analyzing everything into still smaller particles out of which the organs of the body are made, such as DNA molecules, ordinary molecules, atoms, and so on. This view says that eventually everything is reducible to something mechanical. (61)
>
> In my proposal of unbroken wholeness, I turn the mechanistic picture upside down. Whereas the mechanistic picture regarded discrete objects as the primary reality, and the enfolding and unfolding of organisms, including minds, as secondary phenomena, I suggest that the unbroken movements of enfolding and unfolding, which I call the *holomovement,* is primary while the apparently discrete objects are secondary phenomena. An essential part of this proposal is that the whole universe is actively enfolded to some degree in each of the parts. Because the whole is enfolded in each part, so are all the other parts, in some way and to some degree. Hence, the mechanistic picture, according to which the parts are only externally related to each other, is denied. The fundamental truth is the truth of internal relatedness, because it is true of the more fundamental order, which I call the implicate order, because in this order the whole and hence all the other parts are enfolded in each part. (66)

The negation of the view that everything is composed of independent atoms is not that everything is related to everything else. That is the same view upside down. Relationality does not imply that everything is internally related to every other, that every thing and other are parts of a whole. That would be totality and not infinity. Infinity entails that everything is related to others, constituted by them, but never as a totality. There is always excess, on the side of the part and on the side of the whole.

Relation is excess, excess is abundance, immeasurable and uncontainable. It gives the world to us in wonder. As it gives us to the world in enchantment...

Like calvino, bohm expresses this enchantment in love.

Love is enchanted, love is enchanting, love is beyond disenchantment—personally, humanly, and cosmically...

> I have stressed that everything is internally related to everything through mutual enfoldment. And evidently the whole world, both society and nature, is internally related to our thinking processes through enfoldment in our consciousness. For the content of our thought is just the world as we perceive it and know it (which includes ourselves).
>
> This content is not just a superficial part of us. Rather, in its totality, it provides us with the ground of all meaning in our lives, out of which arise our intentions, wishes, motivations, and actions.
>
> Indeed, it can be said that, as we are not complete without the world which is enfolded in us, so the world is not complete without us who are enfolded in it. It follows that if we approach the world through enfolding its wholeness in our consciousness and thus act with love, the world, which enfolds our own being within itself, will respond in a corresponding way. This can obviously happen in the world of society. But even the world of nature will cease to respond with degeneration, due to pollution, destruction of forests, and so on, and will begin to act in a more orderly and favorable way. (67)

Wholeness, totality, enfolding, connection—all are love. Reminding us of macy.[12] But *perhaps love is not wholeness but intimacy, is not totality but locality, is not orderliness but derangement. Perhaps folding, enfolding, unfolding are the corporealities of being, including mechanistic, mechanical, atomistic being...* Totality may not be the answer—if there were an answer—to mechanism, but something much stranger, unfamiliar, irreverent. Perhaps.

Detotalize totality, sacrifice sacrifice, betray betrayal, unrevere irreverence, enchant enchantment and disenchantment...

Bohm does not imagine the enchantments of fragments, shards of meaning, pre- or postmodern. He does not imagine the betrayals that mark fragments (of meaning and reality) as against atoms and parts. Parts (of wholes) and atoms (complete in themselves) are pieces without betrayal. Fragments betray every whole they would pretend to be. Asking and telling take place in fragments.

> We have seen that fragmentary thinking is giving rise to a reality that is constantly breaking up into disorderly, disharmonious, and destructive partial activities. Therefore, seriously exploring a mode of thinking that starts from the most encompassing possible whole and goes down to the parts (sub-wholes) in a way appropriate to the actual nature of things seems reasonable. This approach tends to bring about a different reality, one that is orderly, harmonious, and creative. For this actually to happen, however, a thoroughgoing end to fragmentation is necessary. (67)

I believe in internal—intimate—relations, I believe that all things are bodies, touching each other, touching each other touching each other. I believe that touch is constitutive, other bodies are constitutive of my body, of any body, and there is nothing that is not body. This is an enchanted view, bodies touching are enchanting. But it is not enchanted or enchanting because of its holism or its internal relations. Internal relations are as disenchanted as external relations. Love is enchanting in its fragments and intimacies...

Relationality is enchanting in excess. Relationality is enchanted in exposition...

We may continue with some other accounts of internal relations:

> The mechanistic model of life recognizes only one set of causes as operative in a living organism. These are external relations—those components of the organism's environment that push it or pull it. Descartes wanted to reduce the laws of biology to the laws of matter in motion. "Give me matter and motion," he said in effect, "and I shall construct a universe." Mind was recognized to exist only in human beings. The rest of the created things on our planet, including the human body, were understood in strictly mechanistic terms.
>
> The postmodern challenge to biology is to recognize a second set of causes in addition to external relations. This second set is internal relations. We recognize internal relations in ourselves when our lives are profoundly influenced by a compelling purpose. Human lives are changed by such influences. I am

> what I am partly as a consequence of all the external relations that have impinged on me since conception. But I am also what I am by virtue of internal relations—the ways I have chosen to respond to those external conditions. An internal relation determines the nature of the entity, indeed even its very existence. (Charles Birch, *PCB*, 70)

If external relations are one set of causes, then there is another, always more than one—and for that matter, always perhaps more than two. Relations are in abundance, excessive. Including countless (and surprising) ways in which things are constituted (by language, touch, enfolding, etc.). Internal relations here are purposes, final causes. They are also systems of organization at different levels, systems that transform and multiply the very meanings of *internal* and *relations*.

> As one moves up levels of organization—electrons, atoms, molecules, cells, etc.—the properties of each larger whole are given not merely by the units of which it is composed but also by the new relations between these units. It is not simply that the whole is more than the sum of its parts. The parts are themselves redefined and recreated in the process of evolution from one level to another. This means that the properties of matter relevant at, say, the atomic level do not begin to predict the properties of matter at the cellular level, let alone at the level of complex organisms. This introduces a principle unrecognized by the mechanistic model, that as well as interpreting the higher levels in terms of the lower, we also interpret the lower levels in terms of the higher. (71)

From a disenchanted, possibly from any scientific point of view, to interpret lower levels in terms of higher levels is to understand them better in the whole and in the part, especially to be able to control them better. On the side of enchantment, to interpret is to understand that different levels of organization escape each other. In the most mechanical ways, in the most accountable ways, in the most local, relational, and fragmentary ways, things escape the conditions of any system of organization, no matter how generic, in another system of organization. That is why there are many sciences, and why every science links with every other science—scientifically and unscientifically—and with every other form of exposition. Linking here includes unlinking; constitutive relations exceed the bounds of constitution. That is why every system of control, technoscientific or political, engenders its own disruption, promotes the means for controlling it and undermining it.

> Humanity does not progress from combat to combat until it arrives at universal reciprocity, where the rule of law finally replaces warfare; humanity installs each of its violences in a system of rules and thus proceeds from domination to domination.
>
> The nature of these rules allows violence to be inflicted on violence and the resurgence of new forces that are sufficiently strong to dominate those in power. (Foucault, *NGH*, 150–51)

As a solution to our political problems, such an account is disenchanted. As a mark of the excess and exposition that mark domination and violence, mark every inscription on bodies, such a figure is enchanting beyond any accounting. Control is domination, and domination turns back upon itself, folds back, refolds upon itself, not to cancel but to multiply and proliferate. Proliferation is enchanting, but it is perhaps not good for all who fall under it.

> The universe of classical physics, formulated near the outset of the modern age, was a vast and eternal machine, composed of indestructible particles of matter, propelled by indestructible energy, and governed by changeless mathematical laws.
>
> By contrast, the universe of the new cosmology is an evolving organism. It recalls the mythological accounts of the Cosmic Egg, from which the universal organism grew, forming within itself all that is. It is said to have arisen in a primal explosion about 15 billion years ago, and has been growing and cooling ever since. On at least one planet, living forms appeared in the primal oceans. Then within the seas and, later, on the land as well, evolved the vast diversity of microorganisms, plants, and animals that we find on the earth today. Human beings arose from primate ancestors; and human culture and technology evolved at first slowly, then more rapidly with the development of agriculture, and more rapidly still with the rise of industries, and so on at an ever-accelerating pace.
>
> We ourselves have grown up in a world preoccupied with development and innovation. Our culture is permeated with a consciousness of change, and all our major social, historical, economic, and political theories are cast in an evolutionary framework. Science itself has evolved, and within science, the evolutionary perspective has dominated geology and biology for well over a century. But, seemingly insulated from this pervasive evolutionism, physics has, until very recently, remained the stronghold of a very different vision: the vision of an eternal universe governed by immutable laws, with a changeless amount of matter and energy. (Rupert Sheldrake, *LNH*, 79–80)

> At present, we can only begin to imagine the consequences that will flow from moving beyond the modern model into a radically evolutionary, postmodern understanding. (86)

Everything evolves, everything changes, everything betrays. That thought does not appear in griffin's reconstructive postmodernism, though it is inescapable, I would think, for any postmodernism. We have seen it before in the context of ecology.[13]

> Everywhere *it* is machines—real ones, not figurative ones: machines driving other machines, machines being driven by other machines, with all the necessary couplings and connections. There is no such thing as either man or nature now, only a process that produces the one within the other and couples the machines together. Producing-machines, desiring-machines everywhere, schizophrenic machines, all of species life: the self and the non-self, outside and inside, no longer have any meaning whatsoever. (Deleuze and Guattari, *A-O,* 1–2)

> Hence everything is production: *productions of productions,* of actions and of passions; *productions of recording processes,* of distributions and of coordinates that serve as points of reference. This is the first meaning of process as we us the term: incorporating recording and consumption within production itself, thus making them the production of one and the same process. (4)

An enchanting spinozistic thought.

Everything is production. Everything is machines. Everything is recording, writing, desiring, producing machines. Everything and everywhere betraying themselves as machines. Everything and everywhere enchanted and enchanting machines...

Everything and everywhere evolving organisms. Not perhaps a secular thought. Nor a mechanistic one. Nor one filled with betrayal. We can hardly begin to imagine the consequences for living and producing machines of endless betrayal.

More likely a religious thought, again without betrayal. Indeed, perhaps religion does not know its own betrayals, insists on God's truth.

> By far the most anguishing effect of modern science on the religious confidence of the industrial civilization built by its technologies and shaped by its values is the sense of alienation from responsible agency, from community with nature, and from personal inwardness. The images of the universe that are naturally drawn from the ideals of modern science—ideals contributory to three centuries of intellectual and technological achievements—provide no home for such qualities. (Frederick Ferré, *RWMPS,* 87)

But of course they do, if only by betrayal. And if *only* by betrayal, then in other ways as well, ways and images betrayed otherwise, as if ~~not only~~ betraying themselves and the others. Responsible agency may well appear only by betrayal, in a secular and in a religious context.

Ferré knows too much, more, perhaps, than one can know. Here he knows what the images of the universe given from modern science provide homes to. Yet as soon as we name the images in the plural, we are given countless homes, proliferating as if and wherever they proliferate. Even in science. As ferré knows.

> Science cannot function without ideals. Every measurement, however carefully taken, is laced with error and only approximates the ideal of perfect precision. Every significant theoretical concept reflects an idealization—point masses, frictionless surfaces, instantaneous velocities, and the like—not directly met in the unkempt world of experience. These ideals generate images of how things are. For example, the scientific ideal that things be perfectly regular, despite the apparent randomness of much in crude experience, suggests the image of the Perfect Machine. The world modeled after such a machine supports that ideal and encourages the devotion of years to the search for the hidden regularities and subsurface connections, which comprise the triumph of scientific genius. The world model of the Perfect Machine has further consequences: it gives a sense of the ideal unity of all things, organized in principle within one great system; and it gives a sense, also, of the kind of security that comes from feeling that all things are working together and are continuing as they must without accident, flaw, or mischance.
>
> These last consequences, of course, are religious attitudes. The images that evoke or embody them are what I call religious world models when they are used not only to focus attitudes toward the world but also to think about it and to grapple with it through policies of life rooted in a vision of what the world is like. (88)

As religious attitudes, such images bear a weight of finality: Perfect Machine, Ultimate Particle, Pure Object. All, then, in their finality, completeness, and totality may perhaps be religious—godlike in their imperiousness and divine in their extravagance. In all these ways, scientific or religious, they are disenchanted. Totality is disenchanted, infinity disrupts the totality with enchantment.

Against this perfection, ultimacy, and purity is the image, which proliferates beyond any ideality—I mean, proliferates the image of ideality into inexhaustible profusion, proliferates each image subsumed under the overarching image of science into abundance. Perfection, ultimacy, purity; machine, particle, object; who is to say what each of these is, what each of these means, what is to follow in the profusion and abundance of the images to follow?

None perhaps can say, but any may ask, and others may tell...

It is time to pick up one of these images of science to pursue the proliferation in its abundance.

> Ecological science, first, involves a whole way of thinking that is radically different from the epistemological model of modern analytical science. Ecologists need and use analysis, of course, but these analyses always become means to a wider end, the end of a conceptual synthesis that preserves awareness of living systems in dynamic interaction.
>
> Second, ecological science involves a vision of reality wholly at odds with the sterile, alien images generated from the modern sciences. The postmodern images of reality that come from ecology portray the world as an endlessly complex network of organic and inorganic systems locked in constant interaction. Nonhuman centers of value exist in the ecologist's world. At the same time, alienation from the matter being studied is overcome; the ecologist is personally and inevitably part of the total subject matter.
>
> Third, the postmodern science of ecology involves a set of values that differ sharply from the manipulative and Promethean values characteristic of outlooks inspired by modern science. By contrast, the values appropriate to ecological consciousness are modest, self-limiting, and integrative. Human exploitation is not accepted uncritically as a justification for bending nature to our will. The world is portrayed neither as a mere resource pit to be mined nor as a sheer wilderness to be shunned, but as a complex garden to be tended, respected, harvested, and loved.
>
> The image of the Garden, then, bids to replace the religious world model of the Machine in postmodern consciousness, if holistic ecology becomes the paradigmatic science of our future. (93–5)

The image of the garden is a beautiful one, contaminated repeatedly in the west. It is not an image of wilderness or allowed to be wild as an image. Gardens are tended. I for one would hate to live in a world garden, and the possibilities of an anarchistic world of machines seem fascinating. Perhaps they are not religious enough, perhaps ferré's image of religion is a garden image, as if the gods did not wreak destruction in their anger.

Here is another image of ecology, and we can see not only its religious connections but that it is not everyone's image of either ecology or religion. To the sense of sterile machines, where actual machines are anything but, we may add a somewhat sterile sense of ecology as a practice, ecological systems as gardens and religion as well tended. The garden of eden has always seemed more attractive to me in the profusion of unruliness than in obedience to rules.

> The ecological movement is religious, and Biblical thought (like most religious thought), from which Christianity arose, is ecological. But on the whole, the ecological movement is not Christian and contemporary Christianity is not ecological. The explanation lies in the participation of Christianity in the modern worldview. (John Cobb, *ESR*, 99)

I mean obedience to its disenchantments. For there is something deeply disenchanted about the form in which ecology and religion compose a worldview.

> The dominance of the materialistic-mechanistic worldview has never been complete. Most of its supporters have made some place for human beings outside the otherwise all-inclusive machine—for example, by at least tacitly presupposing the distinct existence of the human mind. This place was greatly enlarged and developed in German Idealism. The Romantic movement challenged the view of nature as machine, appealing to some of the intuitions that had been expressed in the magical tradition. (104)

Some of the intuitions of the magical tradition are the intuitions of enchantment, though enchantment and magic are not identical. Neither can be identical with anything including themselves. They overspill. As do minds and machines. It is as if spinoza's fantastic image of the world cannot be considered in the enchantingly infinite infinity of its materialism, its mechanism, and its geometry.

Against such a radical materialism proliferating endless images of mind, cobb offers us two images of ecology, one deep or holistic, the other postmodern or relational:

> The first ecological worldview is sometimes called deep ecology. It stresses the interdependent and unified character of the ecosystem as a whole. It is in this total system rather than in individual creatures that value lies. The individuals exist as participants in this whole and have value as they contribute to the complex network of relations which is the whole. To this

> whole, a strong sense of sacredness attaches itself; to its violation, a strong sense of evil. Deep ecology, like most worldviews, is a profoundly religious vision. Its rituals and practices are only beginning to be worked out, but that it has radical implications for all of life cannot be questioned.
>
> The second form of ecological worldview does not depart as radically from the Western tradition. It calls for a modification of science and religion but retains recognizable continuity with existing trends and in some ways returns to classical religious sources. Instead of focusing initially on the whole, it attends primarily to the individuals comprising it. I call this the postmodern ecological worldview.
>
> The ecological worldview holds that all the units of reality are internally related to others. All units or individuals are constituted by their relations. (106–8)

Religious here means reverent. Relationality is orderly, not disruptive. The image of the individuals constituted by their relations is of a well tended civil society with a well ordered government, not a mobile world of anomalous singular individuals resisting normalization.

Normalization is perhaps a term that describes disenchantment's appearance without betrayal. The image of a religious, ecological, constructive postmodern world that composes the reenchantment of the world is of an orderly system in an orderly state—normal conditions in which human beings are secure—and a normality in which individuals are well behaved. My sense of enchantment is of mischievous, irreverent fairies and pixies who laugh at the world behind its back, who do not understand the words *normal* and *normality* and the idea of *normalization.*

The disenchantment of the world is its normalization...

The normalization of the world is the accomplishment of modernity. If that were possible...

The normalcy of the world is the world as one. The disenchantment of the world is its totality, no matter the name of ecology...

> The modern worldview initially intended the unity of natural science. But this unity was always only a hope and, in fact, the natural sciences multiplied.
>
> The ecological worldview tells us that our initial mistake was the supposition that we could isolate some elements from the whole and learn the truth about them in this abstraction. Only a knowledge that is ecologically related to all knowledge is appropriate to a reality that is ecologically interconnected. (110–1)

Let us imagine that every worldview is disenchanted, including religion and science, no matter how enchanted it would hope to be. Let us imagine that ecology is disenchanted, no matter how beneficial as a science or as a way of life, to the extent that it answers to the conditions of life on earth. Answers are always disenchanting.

Enchantments engender asking, encourage telling, hover at the edges, compound confusions, trick us with their misdirections, incite us with their fragmentations, proliferate in betrayal...

Let us imagine, then, that enchantment is heresy, that irreverence and betrayal mark the earth in wonder without cessation. When heresy becomes orthodoxy it disenchants its enchantments. I would imagine what might make enchantments enchanting and heresies heretical in the midst of disenchantments and betrayals.

> We are seeing, I believe, indications of a "new heresy" that is challenging modern secular authority at a level as profound as the "scientific heresy" challenged ecclesiastical authority in the seventeenth century. If so, this means that *the postmodern world will be as different from the modern world as that is from the world of the Middle Ages*. (Willis Harman, *PH*, 116)

> Oversimplifying for clarity, here are three alternative kinds of metaphysical assumption that might underlie science and society:
>
> *M-1 Materialistic Monism (Matter Giving Rise to Mind)*: The basic stuff of the universe is matter-energy. Whatever we can learn about consciousness must ultimately be reconciled with the kind of knowledge we get from studying the physical brain.
>
> *M-2 Quasidualism*: The fundamental stuff of the universe has matter-energy aspects and also mind-spirit aspects. The former are studied by something such as conventional science; the latter by a complementary science especially adapted to the exploration of "inner space."
>
> *M-3 Transcendental Monism (Mind Giving Rise to Matter)*: The basic stuff of the universe is mind or consciousness; the world of matter-energy is as a dream in universal mind. (126)

Such a view is not new—consciousness pervades the world in hinduism—nor is it heretical. Most of all it is disenchanted, does not betray betrayal. One can easily imagine a science of mind in which evidence is presented to show that mind influences matter and material events. The key to enchantment would be how *mind, matter, causation, and events* are betrayed, not to mention *science* and *metaphysics*. "The third kind of metaphysical assumption finds *the ultimate stuff of the universe to be consciousness*. Mind or consciousness is primary, and matter-energy arises in some sense out of mind" (124). The only part of this view that might be enchanting is the phrase "arises in some sense." *Metaphysics* and *primacy* are disenchanted in the monism they would promote.

What would be a metaphysics that betrayed reality and itself? Would it be metaphysics? Would it be enchanting?...

The stakes of such a heresy—which does not betray itself—are parapsychology, another would-be heresy that in its applications knows little of enchantment. Even so, what passes through other cultures and histories comes with enchanting names.

> To appreciate how much and how rapidly the cultural premises are changing, one has only to listen carefully to what is being said (about karma and reincarnation, power of holding a vision, meaning of near-death experiences, altered states of consciousness, transcendental meditation, and no end of other topics that simply were not on the agenda one-quarter century ago). (127)

These are all enchanting, yet become disenchanted under epistemic authority—let us say by normalization. Enchantment cannot be normalized, in betrayal it retains its heresies. Altered states of consciousness transfigure humanity, the world, and the gods. Under identification, and without betrayal, they define a culture of disenchanted states to aspire to. Like parapsychology.

> The old cultural mythologies performed four functions. They helped people comprehend and explain the natural environment in an understandable way. They provided a pathway for carrying people through the succeeding epochs of their lives. They established social roles that facilitated congenial personal relationships and fulfilling work patterns. They enabled people to feel that they were participating in the vast wonder and perplexity of the cosmos. Mythologies varied during the classical and medieval eras but still encompassed all four of these functions.
>
> Primitive or totemic thought conceptualized people as an integral part of nature; knowledge was mediated through tribal shamans who heard "voices," saw "visions," and dreamed of "other realities!" Later, for Greek and other people in the classical era, knowledge was obtained through rationally constructed metaphysical systems. In medieval times, knowledge was "scholastic," i.e., it was to be found in the correct interpretation of sacred revealed scripture.

> The modern approach to knowledge—proper application of the scientific method—regarded the previous approaches as sheer superstition. However, each of these epistemologies can be seen as mythic in nature, as positing an "absolute truth," much like the Holy Grail or the Golden Fleece, a "truth" that could be obtained through a heroic journey that would penetrate the changing flux of experience and disclose a universal, underlying essence. (Stanley Krippner, *PPS*, 130–1)

If we can say that absolute truth is mythic, then we can say that myth is disenchanted, while enchantments disrupt and betray every absolute and every truth. Finally, then, to return to griffin in conclusion to this exploration of the betrayals in the (non)(re)enchantment of science, I would consider his own conclusion in which he reevokes Whitehead under the heading of panexperientialism.

> When we think of a molecule as a nonexperiencing thing, we are thinking of it as experienced *by us*. Actually, we usually experience a large aggregation of molecules, as in a rock, and then try to imagine what an individual molecule would be like. In any case, we do not experience what it is to be a molecule. We only know it, insofar as we know it at all, from without.
>
> But when we think of mind as an experiencing thing, we are thinking of it from within. We know what a mind is by identity, by being one.
>
> This raises an intriguing possibility: Perhaps the whole contrast between *mind* and *matter* is the result of a *category mistake*: trying to compare one thing as known from within, or by identity, with another type of thing known only from without, by nonidentity.
>
> The confusion would be between *physical* and *metaphysical* categories. As I am using these terms here, *physical* categories seek to describe a thing's appearances as known from without, through sensory perception and the apparatus to magnify it. *Physical categories* are ones such as size, shape, color, mass, and velocity. *Metaphysical categories* seek to describe what something is in and for itself. Categories that we humans use to describe ourselves as known from within include emotion, perception, purpose, satisfaction, and thought. Perhaps the problem of how "nonexperiencing molecules can relate to experiencing minds" arises only because a purely *physical* description of molecules has been treated as if it were a *metaphysical* description. To assume that some things without any experience exist would hence be a category mistake. (Griffin, *MMPM*, 151–2)

It is difficult for me to understand—in a disenchanted way—why such a description between inner and outer is not dualism in a different voice, or for that matter how to defend the distinction between physical and metaphysical categories in a panexperiential view in which physical properties are largely social, belonging to atoms in the aggregate, and in which metaphysical properties belong to individual atoms. Emotion, perception, purpose, satisfaction are feelings that pertain to atoms and to aggregates, if in different ways, as are size, shape, color, mass, and velocity as well.

I am drawn to some version of griffin's whiteheadian picture. More accurately, I think there are ways in which this is an attractive picture of singularity and relationality. I say an attractive picture to emphasize that as a picture or image, it proliferates enchantedly, and that each proliferating image betrays the others—reveals and violates them. This is true no matter how physical or metaphysical we claim an image to be. However, it betrays that betrayal to expose the proliferation, to call attention to the *perhaps* and *as if* of exposition—here, of speculation. It marks the enchantment of the specular image *as if perhaps ~~not~~ beyond itself and others* in betrayal, and further betrayal.

Perhaps this is once more the disenchantment at the heart of metaphysics, which in its history has been filled with heresy, yet which has marked its history by positions and choices. It is one thing to impose a heresy marked to take over the world, another to proliferate heresy without end, enchantingly, evoking endless asking and telling. The heresy that gives rise to endless others does so by betrayal—they betray it in repeating and restoring it, they transcend it in reinstituting it. They do so inevitably and in any case, it is necessary—that is, the contingency of proliferation is necessary. It is necessary to betray and proliferate and enchant as if ~~not~~ beyond any image, any singularity, any physics or metaphysics. Asking and telling are contingent, yet it is necessary to ask and tell.

Let us not speak of panexperientialism but of panenchantment—enchantments enchanting enchantingly—everywhere in full betrayal—betrayal betraying betrayal as if ~~not~~ beyond itself. It is language, it is exposition, it is being, reality, earth, and world... It is necessary to enchant. It is language, exposition, being, etc... It is necessary to disenchant. In language, exposition, being, etc... Enchantment and disenchantment are ~~life and being~~ themselves. The proliferation of asking and telling...

Perhaps...

This proliferation is perhaps how we may think of physics and metaphysics enchantingly.

> Three ideas make Whiteheadian-Hartshornean panexperientialism less counterintuitive than it otherwise would be. First, a clear distinction is made between *aggregates* and *genuine individuals*, with the insistence that only the latter have (or are) experiences.
>
> Second, great differences are allowed between levels of experience. To say that a molecule has experience means only that it has some vague feeling-response to its environment. Nothing remotely approaching the clear and distinct impressions of conscious sense-perception is implied.
>
> Third, this position rejects the assumption of the modern paradigm that perception is essentially sense-perception. Panexperientialism says that *sensory organs add precision and reliability* to perception but are *not the basis* of the most primitive form of perception. (Griffin, *MMPM*, 152–3)

A clear distinction is made, only genuine individuals have experiences, aggregates do not experience but are made up of individuals with experiences, great and insurmountable differences are allowed between levels of experience, between human and mouse consciousness and feeling, only human experiences are made up of clear and distinct perceptions. All disenchanted.

I understand whitehead's view as that human sense perception comes at a great loss of richness, complexity, and sensitivity, that the feelings of mice and trees and stones are richer and more nuanced—that is, more concrete—than human experiences, which are more abstract. One appears as if more enchanted, the other less.

This is another disenchanted position. Enchantment and disenchantment do not represent positions, neither physical nor metaphysical positions, theories, visions, etc. Betrayal betrays that possibility. Every position is disenchanted, poses itself against its betrayal. This means that every understanding, theory, position betrays itself despite itself, is enchanted and enchanting in spite of itself—and indeed, this *in spite* is its betrayal. So we may take enchantment to betray itself in spite of itself, and ask ourselves how it is possible for a thing, a thought, a theory, an exposition to betray itself in spite of itself. In proliferation, perhaps. And indeed, *perhaps. As if, perhaps. As if ~~not~~ beyond itself. ~~As if not beyond itself~~ in spite. Obliquely. Who knows? Perhaps in unforgetting...*

The unforgotten is the betrayal of enchantment...

Here in conclusion is a reenchanted science as if without betrayal, perhaps:

> In summary: the transition from the modern to a postmodern paradigm will not only resolve the theoretical mind-body problem. It will also allow the evidence of psychosomatic interaction to be taken seriously in the science of medicine, leading to significant modifications in both research and practice. Postmodern medicine will not relinquish the precision in the search for localized causes which is the glory of modern medicine; but it will include this virtue within a larger perspective which brings personal causation back into science, a development that will encourage the full recognition of individual differences, even at the level of biochemistry. Besides being more adequate in this respect, postmodern medicine will overcome the alienating depersonalization that has been the bane of modern medicine. (Griffin, *MMPM*, 161)

It will resolve, it will allow, it will take seriously, it will produce significant modifications, it will not relinquish, it will include virtue, it will encourage. It will be more adequate. It will overcome.

It will be disenchanted.

An enchanting science resolves nothing, asks everything, tells what it can and knows that every resolution is a betrayal. And still science will resolve what it can resolve, as disenchanted. And still science is enchanting...

A disenchanted science will explore psychosomatic interactions where necessary, knowing that not to do so is unscientific. An enchanting science will not produce significant changes, but reminds us that there will always be significant modifications and changes in research and practice. That is the fruit of enchantment's betrayals.

An enchanting science cannot be more adequate, knows nothing of adequacy and inadequacy, offers less alienating depersonalization, perhaps—and more; offers other fears and dangers and violences—and less. All perhaps, and as if, in proliferation...

One cannot argue for enchantment or for reenchantment, but one can ask. One can argue disenchantedly for one disenchanted position or another, but one can tell more. One such position, one such argument may be better. Enchantment knows nothing of better and worse positions and arguments, but betrays arguments and positions and the earth in wonder and abundance and asking and telling...

Enchantment will not improve the world or human life, such improvement will always be disenchanted. It will come—if and when it comes—because the earth is enchanted. It will arrive—if and when it does—from the earth's enchantments. It will be and become and arrive and go—and never be, always becoming, never arriving—in the wonder and abundance and betrayal of enchantments...

Chapter 7

Beyond Enchanting

Meters are the cattle of the gods (Calasso, *LG*, 145)

We read this in the *Śatapatha Brāhmaṇa*. We read this in calasso reading the *Ṛgveda*. We read it, hear it in our minds enchanting. We may ask what it means to tell.

> This was *the* premise, something we find hard to understand today.
>
> To understand what meters are one must go back to the gods and beyond the gods, to the unlimited from whom the gods themselves sprung. (145)

Meters are the cattle of the gods. To me, in the west, these are wonderfully enchanting words, utterly enchanting words to say and sing. And there is more.

> could it be that rather than just leading us to the gods, the meters are the gods themselves? After that thought has occurred, we won't be surprised when we come across these words: "Now, the gods who govern life are the meters, for it is thanks to the meters that all living things here below are sustained." With respect to the thirty-three Devas, the meters play a double role, at once subordinate and sovereign: humble and useful like beasts of burden who "when yoked carry weights for men, so the meters, when yoked, carry the sacrifice to the gods." But at the same time only the meters can get close to the fire without being harmed. And above all: if the gods have achieved immortality, it is the meters they have to thank for it. Once the gods roamed the earth—yearning for the sky. They knew that it was there immortality was to be found. But they didn't know how to get there. Then Gāyatri, the female creature who is the shortest and most effective of the meters, transformed herself into a *śyena*,

> a hawk or eagle. In that form she managed to steal from the sky the substance death cannot harm: *soma*. But hers wasn't the first attempt. Two other meters had tried and failed before her: Jagatī, who lost three syllables in the process; then Triṣṭubh, who lost one. When *Gāyatri* reappeared, with the *soma* in her beak, her body was made up of her own four syllables plus those her sisters had lost. Meantime the arrow of a mysterious archer, a celestial guardian, had ruffled her plumage and torn off a leaf of the *soma* plant. Loss and wound thus lurked within the meter that must heal loss and wound. From then on Gāyatri, Triṣṭubh, and Jagatī would always follow King Soma. A king can hardly turn up unattended. So who forms his retinue? The meters. (148–9)

An incredible story—and I mean to emphasize *story* and the meters that attend it. A story can hardly turn up unattended, unornamented. In our disenchanted time we in the west have relegated the attendants of story, language, exposition to ornaments—to *parerga* (if there be such) that do not convey the essence. The vedic story, with its personifications and deifications, transforms the ornaments into gods—as if they were essence when we know they are *parerga*. What we know best is that they are enchanting. I mean that we westerners know them as enchanting. I do not know what hindus know them to be. I would ask them to tell me, to chant them for me.

To me, in the west, these are among the most enchanting words I have ever heard, regardless of the hindu gods. To me, in the west, it is because each of these words in english means something different from what it means in sanskrit. Totally different? Perhaps. Certainly, however, at two levels of exposition, levels upon levels of exposition. In the vedas these are truths of exposition, told in story of what is beyond story, chanted of gods in meters beyond gods. In the west each of these terms becomes something else, again in exposition, again as if and perhaps beyond any exposition. Exposition betraying itself.

Let us listen to the words in calasso's exposition:

> *Meters.*

> When we think of meters, we may perhaps glimpse the vague outline of a rhythm, but not much more. Yet it wasn't always thus, and certainly not for the Vedic seers. (145)

> The meters are sacred power; the skin of the black antelope is the form of sacred power; he puts on shoes of antelope skin; not to be hurt, he wraps himself in meters before approaching the

> fire. The "meters," *chandas*, are the robes that the gods "wrapped around themselves," *acchādayan*, so that they might come near to the fire without being disfigured as though by the blade of a razor. Thus the gods sought to escape death. (145–6)
>
> But why are the meters so tremendously important, so much so that even the gods needed them to protect themselves. Everything that exists is permeated by two invisible powers—"mind," *manas*, and "word," *vāc*, a twinned pair whose distinguishing characteristic is that they are at once "equal," *samāna*, and "distinct," *mānā*. (146–7)

Equal and distinct—*samāna* and *mānā—idem est* again, reminiscent of spinoza;[1] the indefinite dyad, reminiscent of plato;[2] *plus d'un*, reminiscent of derrida. Being one, being two, at once both and neither. One, two, neither one nor two, both one and two, reminiscent of nāgarjūna. Unaccountable, beyond accounting, sayable, beyond saying. Enchantment, betrayal. And more. *As if, perhaps.*

> Mind alone, word alone, are impotent—or at least not powerful enough to take an offering to the gods. The horse of the mind must submit to the harness of the word, of the meters: otherwise it would lose its way. (147)

> Meter is the yoke of the word. Just as the "mind," *manas*, is so flighty in its movements—a monkey leaping from branch to branch—that it would be quite dispersed if it did not accept a yoke (and every mental discipline, every *yoga*, is above all a "yoke"); so the "word," *vāc*, omnipresent, pervasive, which "blows like the wind, sweeping across all worlds," bows to the restrictions of meter, agrees to dress up in it as if in colorful clothes, to be wrapped up, as it were, in a preordained arrangement of syllables. Only thus can it reach the heavens, like a female creature covered in bird feathers. And only thus can it make the return journey from heaven to earth. (148)

The return journey returns us to enchantments beyond enchantment:

> Such facility, such familiarity with different worlds, inevitably makes us wonder: could it be that rather than just leading us to the gods, the meters are the gods themselves? (148)

What is enchanting here for me—I hold on to my western position even as I journey with the vedas from earth to heaven and return—is that in sanskrit the *chandas* are yokes, restrictions, boundaries, while in english meters are ornaments, *parerga*, delectations.

> But there is a danger inherent in the life of the meters. Ceremonies sap their strength. Always last in everything, by the time men found the meters they had already been used up by the gods; they were worn out: "Now the strength of the meters was exhausted by the gods, because it was through the meters that the gods reached the heavens. And the chant is rapture, *mada*: the rapture that is sap, and that sap he now injects into the meters and so restores their strength; and with their vigor now renewed the sacrifice is celebrated." If we wanted to know why inspiration is necessary, here at last is an explanation. That "rapture" which we call *inspiration* is the only resource we have for reviving the meters, worn out as they are by the rash use they were once put to, not by men but by the gods. Without that "rapture" the meters would remain inert, like plants longing to be watered, mute testimony to that exploit which, through the power of a body of syllables, made the gods immortal. (150)

Perhaps they are both yokes and ornaments. Both and neither. Perhaps this *both* returns us to the indefinite dyad and the at least one that is two and more. Always in the modalities of *as if* and *perhaps*. Meters, *chandas, parerga,* are in the modalities of *perhaps* and *as if*. Enchantments *perhaps, as if* chanting.

An enchanted greek word for parerga and chandas is mimēsis, the repetition that is never duplication—one is two is not two is not one—but proliferation. The image repeats, the image does not repeat, the image neither repeats nor does not repeat, the image both repeats and does not repeat. It proliferates in its en-chant-ments...

Meters proliferate the images of words and thoughts, words and thoughts proliferate the images of things, ingredients of the earth, proliferation is enchantment, always en-chanting...

Cattle.

Calasso does not dwell on cattle as such; at one moment he replaces them by horses. The two figures he reads into cattle are yoking together, so that they may gain in strength and help us (and the gods) on our journey.

> to operate effectively they [mind and word] must team up, yoke themselves together. Mind alone, word alone, are impotent—or at least not powerful enough to take an offering to the gods. The horse of the mind must submit to the harness of the word, of the meters: otherwise it would lose its way.
>
> But how can two such disproportionate beings be yoked together? "When one of the pair in the yoke is smaller, they give it an extra support bar to the word, and like well-paired companions yoked together these two now take the sacrifice to the

so, they appear to have fled as well, to literature. Another disenchantment, no matter how enchanting literature may be.

It is possible to believe in gods, to follow the gods, to follow many gods or one, to give one's life and soul to the gods, for the gods. None of this need be enchanted, the gods do not rule over enchantment. Many gods, many myths and stories of the gods, one or many gods, are enchanted and enchanting. Even so, in a modern, industrial world, the gods and their human followers are in the grip of disenchantment, and willingly give themselves to secular goods.

Is it possible to be disenchanted in the secular world, pursuing secular goods, including scientific knowledge, technological products, and be enchanted in church or temple? Can disenchantment and enchantment be divided into separate worlds? I do not think so. I think enchantment is inescapable in the secular world, I think disenchantment is everywhere.

Is it possible to be enchanted in the secular world, pursing secular goods, etc.? Is it possible to be enchanted in the sacred world, pursuing infinite goods, etc.? I think so. Enchantment is inescapable. Disenchantment is one of its enchantments.

Enchantment without gods—or with them. Enchanted by meters, cattle, other animals, plants, the abundance of the earth—by them or without them...

The ingredients of the earth are all enchanting, all enchanted. The ingredients of the earth are all disenchanted, all disenchanting. The gods do not make it so. Literature and the arts do not make it so. We do not make it so. We are among the ingredients of the earth that are so, enchanting and disenchanting. It is the wonder and abundance and enchantment of the earth to be so. The wonder and abundance of the earth are enchanting and disenchanting...

Perhaps the wonder and abundance of the earth are not godly, not religious, are betrayed by every name. Including enchantment. Too many fairies, too much religion. Not enough asking and telling.

Time for a disenchanted interruption in the name of religion. With a disenchanted echo.

Is christianity the special form taken in the west by something that has always existed and that similarly exists elsewhere, if not everywhere, namely, religion or the religious phenomenon?...

Is religion instead an element wholly unique to western civilization, one of its most original creations?...

Is religion the west's most characteristic concept, around which it has established and developed its identity, while at the same time de-

fining its way of conceiving humankind and the world? (Dubuisson, *WCR*, 9)...[3]

> Let us consider the banal but quite significative fact that religious phenomena seem ubiquitous in Western civilization, that they inform the majority of its constituent—even simply decorative—elements. If we listed those chief works, literary or artistic, as well as the most general moral, political, scientific, or philosophical conceptions that escape the grasp of religion or its influence (if only to distance themselves from or oppose this influence), we would probably end up with very meager results. Around this privileged notion, the Christian West, spiderlike, has continued to spin its web of concepts, to wind the successive variations of its learned discourse, to superimpose its palimpsests of speculations, in brief, to affirm its own identity. Its reflections on the organization of the world, on the nature of reality, its conceptions of humanity, of life, its political theories, its most admirable or most derisory artistic triumphs, its loftiest spiritual accomplishments, as well as its most sordid crimes—all have been conceived or committed one way or another with reference to this dominant concern. From the domain of the most luminous rationality to the most constraining of superstitions, from insignificant detail to the most grandiose monuments, from the most extreme individual interiority to the vastest collective movements, no register of human experience, no order of things has ever escaped its diffuse, constant influence. (11–2)

Christianity has spun its enchanted web of disenchanted concepts, its learned discourse, superimposed its palimpsests of speculations, enchanted its virtual expositions, affirmed its own identity in the most disenchanted and—those "simply decorative elements"—in the most enchanting ways. Among these ways is the concept of religion—always christianity's religion, yet reaching out to include what is not christian, not even religious in a christian way, gathered under the umbrella of christianity, judeo-christianity, greek-judeo-christianity perhaps, as religion. Including philosophy and secularity. Betraying the other, without a name. Creating something wonderful and abundant in giving the others that name, in the midst of violence.

If only we could speak all the languages of the earth. Would that avoid eurochristianity's betrayals? I do not think so...

Dubuisson's thesis is enchanting in its disenchantments.

> every human group, in order to exist and to perpetuate itself as such, is obliged to develop and preserve a set of ideas, opinions,

> and diverse theses, themselves passed on and deepened by images, symbols, and myths concerning humankind, the world, and society. And this complex set, formed of a tangled multitude, is so indispensable, so intrinsically tied to the existence of the group itself that it finally appears (even if it is, from a metaphysical point of view, perfectly contingent) as its exclusive reference.
>
> Our word "religion" (independently of its most specifically Christian characteristics) to some degree signifies all this at one and the same time. On these grounds, it would be more judicious to include it in the vaster, more intelligible category of "cosmographic formations." This term, freed of all religious concern and all Western prejudice, has the advantage of calling attention to the fact that the formations in question possess a global coherence and are at the same time positioned with respect both to representation, that is, weltanschauung, and existence, individual or collective, in which the corresponding ideas are incarnated in the form of practices, institutions, ways of being, observances, rules for life, and corporeal expressions.[4] (69)

Freed from all religious concern and western prejudice—how could an anthropologist believe such a thing?—and thereby all enchantment—if that were possible.

Why does dubuisson, whose sophistication is unmatched about the sweep of christianity and its construction of religion, not insist that the discourse of academic neutrality, including his own, is christian, thereby entangled in religion? The disenchantment of cosmographic formations is both their enchantment and their christianization, under the heading of secularization.

> An anthropological study that began with an anthropology of the fantastic would scarcely be exaggerating, for all the rest (social, cultural, or religious anthropology) often represents only the secularized and rationalized version of it that has been gained as the result of analytical work that consists, in essence, of putting the fantastic in parentheses. As if reality, true reality, serious reality, the reality science likes to speculate about, could issue from a simple subtraction: global reality minus fantastic reality equals objective reality (the reality of laws, causal relationships, rational explanations). Contrary to the ideas that unreflective opinion frequently exhibits, fantastic shapes are not something that humanity would, after the fact, have the real world assume in order to make it less hostile or less frightening. Fantastic shapes are rather constituent of the relationship that this same humanity entertains with the world. (20)

Fantastic here merges with enchantment, still under the heading of disenchantment. Cosmographic formations are disenchanted names for what surpasses both disenchantment and enchantment—fantastically and enchantingly. Cosmographic formations are a category of what exceeds every category.

> The all-encompassing category of cosmographic formations to my mind seems the only category today that allows us to overcome the sterile old antagonisms that culminate in the idea of religion and to relativize the importance of all the debates that are defined only with reference to its intrinsic criteria—precisely because this category is capable of subsuming the totality of the global, comprehensive conceptions of the world, whatever their philosophical orientation (atheist, theist, materialist, fatalist, cynical, indifferent, or agnostic), the diversity of the elements whose existence they recognize (supernatural beings, cosmic, natural and historical laws, universal principles, vital forces or energies, transcendental concepts, ethical or political ideals, etc.), and the nature of the practices, the rules for living, and prescriptions that they imply. (17)

Subsuming the totality of the global—if there be such—is a double figure of disenchantment—or do I mean quadruple?—cosmographic, formation, totality, globality.

> Every culture is as tangible, as real as it is arbitrary, whether through its visible manifestations (institutions, practices, technical creations, etc.) or by the objectivity of the different structural relations that govern the cooperation among its diverse elements. Each culture is actually a contingent creation, which might not have existed or might have been different, even though it never appears as such to the individuals who comprise it, since, for them, it represents Reality, the reality to which their existence is attached by thousands of different threads, narrow or wide, commonplace or exceptional, prosaic or ceremonious.
>
> Each of these cultures is the result of an incalculable number of choices, accidents, conditions, and successive adaptations, just as much as it is made up of distinct human acts of volition. If we consider their individual cultural physiognomy, that is, their status at any given moment, it is obvious that none of them ought to lay claim to having derived from some kind of absolute, preexistent necessity—whether we call it destiny, providence, history or, even worse, essence—that is exterior to the changing world in which each culture finds itself entirely immersed. (18)

Each culture, with its disenchantments, is a contingent creation. Enchantment is the necessity of this contingency, a reality that exceeds any reality and any name, a reality that endlessly asks and tells of its own reality.

We are entangled again in the name. *Religion* is a name of betrayal, as are the *gods*, not to mention *philosophy* and *anthropology* and *secularity*. Even worse—if there be such a measure—it is not as if we might select a compromised name and compromise with it, affirming its betrayals.[5] Let's talk of religion sometimes, otherwise philosophy, anthropology is fine, each in its sphere. Or if not that, then rotating from one to the other as if the work of each might be done as well by the others.

All this is disenchanted, and as disenchanting as any of these names may be, they are enchanting: uncontrollable, beyond calculation, informing, controlling, diverting, producing. Their enchantments are that we can only partly know, if at all, what they are and what they do, no matter how carefully we bring them into our web of disenchantment. No matter how much we ask of them they exceed any telling.

So it is, perhaps, as if christianity's production of religion was an academic achievement, under whose disenchanted heading all sorts of wisdom has been gathered. And it is as if, at the same time, perhaps, that the production of religion was an act of imperialism, colonialism, despotism, compelling all the world's cultures to conform to an image of Christianity under the heading of their divergences. As if. Both. Perhaps.

The cultures of the world are religious, are something other than religious, are neither religious nor nonreligious, are both religious and something else...

Is that enchantment?...

The cultures of the world create cosmographic formations, create something beyond cosmographic formations, neither create cosmographic formations nor something beyond them, both create and do not create cosmographic formations...

Cosmographic formations exceed every category...

As is true for literature.

Literature.

> The gods are fugitive guests of literature. They cross it with the trail of their names and are soon gone. Every time the writer sets down a word, he must fight to win them back. The mercurial quality that heralds their appearance is token also of their evanescence. It wasn't always thus. At least not so long as we had a liturgy. That weave of word and gesture, that aura of controlled destruction, that use of certain materials rather than

> others: this gratified the gods, so long as men chose to turn to them. After which, like windblown scraps in an abandoned encampment, all that was left were the stories that every ritual gesture implied. Uprooted from their soil and exposed, in the vibration of the word, to the harsh light of day, they frequently seemed idle and impudent. Everything ends up as history of literature. (Calasso, *LG*, 3)

Literature and the gods. Not the same as *enchantment* and *disenchantment.* Not religion and religiosity. Not even cosmographic formations. Even so, calasso is speaking of enchantment.

> The world—the time has come to say it, though the news will not be welcome to everyone—has no intention of abandoning enchantment altogether, if only because, even if it could, it would get bored. In the meantime, parody has become a subtle film that has wrapped itself round everything. What in Baudelaire and Heine was just a poisoned splinter of Offenbach has now become the characterizing feature of our age. Today, everything, in whatever form it comes, appears first and foremost as parody. Nature itself is parody. Only afterwards, with great effort and subtlety, it may be that something manages to go beyond parody. But it will always be necessary to measure it against its original parodic appearance. And finally: absolute literature. What, as Baudelaire's Grand Inquisitor saw it, was still only the menace in the wings, a serpentine threat, a possible degeneration, has turned out after all to be literature itself. Or at least, the only kind of literature that I have come here to talk to you about. (23–4)

I am reminded of another understanding of literature on the scene of exposition, not to mention the scene of parody.

> In the modern age, literature is that which compensates for (and not that which confirms) the signifying function of language. Through literature, the being of language shines once more on the frontiers of Western culture—and at its centre—for it is what has been most foreign to that culture since the sixteenth century; but it has also, since this same century, been at the very centre of what Western culture has overlain.
>
> But from the nineteenth century, literature began to bring language back to light once more in its own being: though not as it had still appeared at the end of the Renaissance. For now we no longer have that primary, that absolutely initial, word upon which the infinite movement of discourse was founded and by which it was limited; henceforth, language was to grow with no point of departure, no end, and no promise. It is the traversal

> of this futile yet fundamental space that the text of literature traces from day to day. (Foucault, *OT*, 44)

> The historical sense gives rise to three uses that oppose and correspond to the three Platonic modalities of history. The first is parodic, directed against reality, and opposes the theme of history as reminiscence or recognition; the second is dissociative, directed against identity, and opposes history as knowledge. They imply a use of history that severs its connection to memory, its metaphysical and anthropological model, and constructs a counter-memory—a transformation of history into a totally different form of time. (*NGH*, 160)

And another:

> I will call the unconditional university or the university without condition: the principal right to say everything, whether it be under the heading of a fiction and the experiment of knowledge, and the right to say it publicly, to publish it. The reference to public space will remain the link that affiliates the new Humanities to the Age of Enlightenment. It distinguishes the university institution from other institutions founded on the right or the duty to say everything, for example religious confession and even psychoanalytic 'free association.' But it is also what fundamentally links the university, and above all the Humanities, to what is called literature, in the European and modern sense of the term, as the right to say everything publicly, or to keep it secret, if only in the form of fiction. (Derrida, *FPUC*, 16–7)

What about the name *literature* that—only in the secular west?—answers to and undoes the restrictions and codes of public reason? Why then, again, *literature* and not *language, exposition, being, the image, whatever*...you name it? Why literature and not art? Following calasso, the words we cannot avoid are *fugitive* and *parodic,* here words that diminish the force of the enchantments he would name. The gods are fugitive—transient, passing, ephemeral; perhaps repetitive; but also minor, elusive, inconsequent—guests of literature, not even its dwellers, its inhabitants.

Unless it is the enchantment of godliness to be elusive and inconsequent. Unless it is the enchantment of literature to be inconsequent and elusive. Unless it is enchanting to betray...

Following calasso, everything comes as parody, nature itself is parody, not to mention enchantment, the gods, and literature. And after all is that so bad, is that so unenchanting? Could it be that parody is one of the forms that enchantment takes in betrayal? That is what I imagine foucault to suggest.

In our time, history gives rise to three modalities of resistance to disenchantment. One is parodic, the second dissociative, the third counter-memory—another memory, unforgetting. Another time, enchanting.

Here, literature is the name—a disenchanted name—for the excesses and mobilities of language—enchanting exposition, the proliferation of the image. Literature compensates for the refusal of enchantment in representational language. Through literature, the enchantment of language shines on the frontiers of western culture, where it has been what western culture has most disenchanted under the names of discourse and representation.

Parody, then, is a modality of reenchantment, a resistance to disenchantment. It is not, perhaps, enchantment—though it is sometimes enchanting. It behaves as if it were enchanting. Parody is one of the gestures by which disenchanted images of nature reenchant themselves, and in doing so reveal their enchantments.

Literature, then, with *writing*, is not as such enchanting. It is a poor name for the betrayal of enchantment, a double figure of betrayal, first as *myth*, second as *communication* (even worse, *communism*), poor names themselves. Another name, *interruption*, emerges to mark betrayal. I prefer the names *asking* and *telling*.

The problem with myth—its disenchantment—is that it founds community—if community can be founded, can be found, can possess or be given or have a foundation; if myth can found anything. All disenchanting. Instead of giving and dispossessing the very limits of its togetherness—I mean enchantment. In nancy's words,[6] returning us to the name of *literature* (and *writing*) from the name of *myth*: myth interrupted, myth enchanted.

> Myth is of and from the origin, it relates back to a mythic foundation, and through this relation it founds itself (a consciousness, a people, a narrative). (Nancy, *MI*, 45)
>
> Interruption occurs at the edge, or rather it constitutes the edge where beings touch each other, expose themselves to each other and separate from one another, thus communicating and propagating their community. On this edge, destined to this edge and called forth by it, born of interruption, there is a passion. This is, if you will, what remains of myth, or rather, it is *itself the interruption* of myth. (61)
>
> A name has been given to this voice of interruption: literature (or writing, if we accept the understanding of this word that coincides with literature). This name is no doubt unsuitable. But no name is suitable here. The place or the moment of

> interruption is without suitability. What is unsuitable about literature is that it is not suited to the myth of community, nor to the community of myth. It is suited neither to communion nor to communication. (63)

> literature's revelation, unlike myth's, does not reveal a completed reality, nor the reality of a completion. It does not reveal, in a general way, *some thing*—it reveals rather the unrevealable: namely, that it is itself, as work that reveals and gives access to a vision and to the communion of a vision, essentially interrupted. (63)

Against the founding of community—against the possibility of both founding and commonality; interrupting and resisting communion and communication—literature marks sharing, another being-in-common, another universality without a name.

> the being-in-common of which I am speaking—and that many of us are trying to speak about, that is to say, to write—has nothing to do with the myth of communion through literature, nor with the myth of literary creation by the community. It designates that singular ontological quality that *gives* being *in* common. that does not hold it in reserve, before or after community, as an essence of man, of God, or of the State but that makes for a being that is only when shared *in common*, or rather whose quality of being, whose nature and structure are shared (or exposed). (64)

> we would not write if our being were not shared. And consequent this truth also: if we write (which might also be a way of speaking), we share being-in-common, or else we are shared, and exposed, by it. (69)

We would not write—or sing or dance or paint or think or chant or be—if our being were not enchanted, if being—nature itself—were not enchanting. We write—literature, or anything else, we write to be read; we dance—together, apart, on stage, in solitude, we dance to be enchanting in our bodies, to expose our bodies' enchantments; we live—in ourselves, with others, enchantingly. It is necessary, it is inescapable, it is glorious, it is disenchanting. It is necessary that enchantments be disenchanting.

Enchantment is nothing in common but being uncommon, uncommonality, excess, interruption, more and less than any identity, any name...

This is the parody of literature—to be more and less than literature, always, to be disenchanting and enchanting as literature, always. This is the parody of nature—to be more and less, to be in wonder and abundance, to be given form—to be disenchanted form, and thereby enchanting, abundant, wonderful beyond enchantment. To betray.

A nature parodic of itself—of its ingredients and forms—is enchanting, betrays every form...

Disenchantment exceeds itself in enchantments beyond enchantment, enchantments that could not be, could not be enchanting, could not enchant without disenchantment, could not enchant without betrayal...

> This new creature that appeared we don't know quite when and that still lives among us may be defined as "absolute literature." "Literature" because it is a knowledge that claims to be accessible only and exclusively by way of literary composition; "absolute" because it is a knowledge that one assimilates while in search of an absolute, and that thus draws in no less than everything; and at the same time it is something *absolutum*, unbound, freed from any duty or common, cause, from any social utility. Sometimes proclaimed with arrogance, elsewhere practiced in secret and with subtle cunning, this knowledge first becomes perceptible in literature, as presence or premonition, in the early days of German Romanticism, and seems destined never to leave it. Like a sort of irreversible mutation, you can celebrate it, you can loathe it, but either way it now belongs to the very physiology of writing. (Calasso, *LG*, 170–1)

Why absolute? Why literature? Calasso's answers are not answers, neither to these two questions nor to some others. Why german? Why romantic? Why european?

The answer to all of these, most of all perhaps to the last, is enchantment. These are local, disenchanting names of enchantment.

> I am European, I am no doubt a European intellectual, and I like to recall this, I like to recall this to myself, and why would I deny it? In the name of what? But I am not, nor do I feel, European in every part, that is, European through and through. By which I mean, by which I wish to say, or must say: I do not want to be and must not be European through and through, European in every part. Being a part, belonging as "fully a part," should be incompatible with belonging "in every part." My cultural identity, that in the name of which I speak, is not only European, it is not identical to itself, and I am not "cultural" through and through, "cultural" in every part.
>
> If, to conclude, I declared that I feel European among other things, would this be, in this very declaration, to be more or less European? Both, no doubt. Let the consequences be drawn

> from this. It is up to the others, in any case, and up to me among them, to decide. (Derrida, *OH*, 82–3)

Derrida is european—a european intellectual. No doubt. If these words mean anything at all. Who would deny it? I am american—an american intellectual. If there be such. Yet what is it to be european, not to mention intellectual? Who is to say? Who is to decide? And in what part, how many parts, more than one, altogether? Derrida is not wholly european because *european* is not identical to itself, not to mention *intellectual* and *cultural* and *identity*—not to mention *derrida* and *derrida's identity*—not identical in every part, identical in no particular way. Each identity betrays the others, betrays itself. Each part betrays itself, betrays the others. To be european, to be american, to be any adjective, to think in the adjectival, is to think disenchantedly of what—the whole, the part, the adjective, the identity, the name—exceeds and betrays any identity, adjective, part, whole, or name. Enchantedly.

Enchantment exceeds and betrays any identity. Identity betrays and exceeds itself, exceeds and betrays its disenchantments. As enchantment. And for that matter, betrays and exceeds enchantment as disenchanted identity. Betrayal betrays the boundaries of every name, every identity, every disenchantment. As enchantment...

Absolute literature betrays and exceeds every absolute—as literature; exceeds and betrays every literature—as absolute, and as other absolute and nonabsolute literatures. Not to mention other arts, other images, sciences, philosophies, and histories.

Every identity is disenchanted under a name. Every name is disenchanted as a name. Every disenchanted name is enchanted as a name, a word, an identity. Given boundaries it is impossible to gather under that or any name.

Every identity is enchanted, is disenchanted, is neither enchanted nor disenchanted, is both enchanted and disenchanted. As identity. As a name. As itself...

Relation. Finally, then, let us gather these names together—meters, cattle, the gods, literature, absolute—under a heading that might express their enchantments. *Relation, relationality*. To be is never only to be *that*. To be requires—it is necessary—being *that* and *more than that*, embodied, enformed, relational. Meters, cattle, the gods, literature, the absolute are names of forms beyond form, forms that engender other forms—enchanted forms—forms that can can be enchanted only in relation, emerging from disenchanted form; forms that can be told only in asking.

Let us attend to the names. Names are always disenchanted, yoked to truth. Names are always enchanted, freed in exposition. Calasso speaks of enchantments in the names of forms, in the words of names, that must be disenchanted in order to speak of enchantments.

These are not the only such names. We have seen others. And still others:

air, earth, fire, water;

love, life, death, desire;

betrayal—treachery, revolt, interruption, revelation, heresy; enchantment—magic, witchcraft, bewitchment, incantation, sorcery, wizardry, delight, ecstasy, bliss, joy, nirvana, paradise, rhapsody, rapture, charisma, charm, allure, attraction, aura, beguilement, fascination, enticement;

irreverence—desecration, blasphemy, heresy, parody, impiety, violation, sacrilege;

asking—telling beyond telling;

telling—beyond asking;

all as if, perhaps, might be, contingency; proliferation, multiplication, simulation, abundance, extravagance, generosity;

all in the modality of the subjunctive.

Let us imagine the following:

Enchantment can be spoken of under its name, enchantment has no name, enchantment can either be spoken of under its name or has no name, enchantment can both be spoken of under its name and cannot be spoken of under any name.

Disenchantment. Ditto.

Ditto for any name. Ditto for calasso's names.

Literature, writing, myth, language, the image: all these names express enchantment, all these words are enchanting, all exceed any accounting, all are disenchanted, create boundaries, claim to be accountable.

Enchantment betrays the boundaries of disenchanting names...

> The continuous is entrusted to a breath that may run out at any moment and to a flame that an unknown hand must constantly tend. But that is precisely what the rites are for: to weave continuity. Otherwise life would fall apart in broken stumps. Above all this is what the meters are for: to give continuous measure to our breathing.
>
> Passing the baton like relay runners, the meters act first and foremost upon time; *they make sure that it isn't interrupted*. What

> emerges quite dramatically here is the fear that time will be broken, that the day's progress will suddenly be interrupted, that the whole world may be left in a state of irretrievable dispersion. This fear is far more radical than the fear of death. A sense of precariousness so extreme, intense, and lacerating as to make the continuity of time appear as an improbable gift forever on the point of being withdrawn. (Calasso, *LG*, 159–60)

We may be reminded of descartes's fear at the discontinuity of the world, the interruption of time. We may recall that only a god can guarantee continuity. Perhaps that is the fear that guarantees the gods. Enchantment has no guarantees to offer. And indeed, the continuity of time may guarantee nothing, not even disenchantment. Nothing but interruption . . .

The fear is radical. The fear is great. The fear is extreme, intense, and lacerating. Yet in the interruptions and betrayals is time itself, enchantingly enchanted...

I fear the continuity.

In the name of absolute literature perhaps something else...

Reading the "Monologue" of Novalis:

> The true conversation is a pure play of words. What's amazing, in fact, is that people should make such a ridiculous mistake as to imagine they are speaking of things. Precisely what is most characteristic of language—that it attends only to itself—everybody ignores. As a result it is a wondrous and fruitful mystery—to the point that, if one speaks purely for the sake of speaking, one expresses the most splendid, the most original truths. But if a person wishes to speak of some particular thing, that capricious creature language has him say the most ridiculous and muddle-headed of stuff. Which explains the hatred some serious people have for language. They see its mischievousness, but they don't see that contemptible chatter is the infinitely serious side of language. If only one could have people understand that what applies to mathematical formulas applies to language too. They form a world apart, they play with each other, expressing only their own prodigious nature, which is precisely why they are so expressive—precisely why the strange play of relationships between things finds its reflection in them. Only by means of their freedom are they members of nature, and only in their free movements does the spirit of the world manifest itself and make itself the delicate measure and pattern of things. The same is true of language.[7] (Quoted in Calasso, *LG*. 178–9)

> Heidegger was right not to trust that page of Novalis. It announced a knowledge that refused to be subject to any other, and at the same time would seep into the cracks of all others.

> Literature grows like the grass between the heavy gray paving stones of thought. Despite Heidegger's grandiose determination to demonstrate the contrary in two volumes and a thousand pages, Nietzsche was the first attempt to escape from a cage of categories whose origin we find in Plato and Aristotle. What may or may not lie beyond that cage has not yet been established. But many travelers have reported that literature is the passport most readily accepted in that terra incognita where—so one hears tell—all the mythologies now pass a largely indolent life in a no-man's-land haunted by gods and vagrant simulacra, by ghosts and Gypsy caravans in constant movement. (183–4)

Under the name of literature—what might be another name?—one can travel to enchantment, with ghosts, gypsies, fairies, gods. I persist in thinking that the name *literature* is also *the image* and its proliferations. Not to mention the names *science* and *art, asking* and *telling.* All names, all exposition, all enchantments. Every word is a betrayal, betrays itself, betrays the others, and in that betrayal exposes itself, the others, and still others. Betrayal is what is enchanting in enchantment, betraying every name.

As soon as the enchantment of being is conveyed before us it is betrayed in the said that dominates the saying that states it. The otherwise than being is stated in a saying that must also be unsaid in order to extract the otherwise than being from it, a being otherwise...[8]

> *everything can be said in literature...*
> *literature betrays everything...*
> *everything is being, nature, reality...*
> *science tells us the truth of being, nature, reality...*
> *science betrays the truth of reality, nature, being...*
> *everything is language...*
> *language betrays everything...*
> *everything is parody...*
> *parody betrays enchantment...*
> *everything is exposition, expression...*
> *everything is enchanted...*
> *everything is enchanting...*
> *everything enchantingly betrays enchantment...*
> *everything asks, everything is asking, asking is everything...*
> *and telling...*

Here is another story.

I am not a really good academic. I am not a really good person. If there be such. For me, intellectual work is related to what I call "aestheticism," to transforming myself. I am not interested in the status of what I am doing because my problem is my own transformation. This transformation of one's self by one's own knowledge is, I think, something rather close to the aesthetic experience. Why should artists work if they are not transformed by their own art?...[9]

Why live and work except as if we are transfigured by enchantments?...

Perhaps...

I would hazard that this is an enchanted transformation. I would hazard that it offers a place where enchantment meets disenchantment, where religion meets secularity: the point of self transformation in the opening of the world, of every thing.

Intellectual work perhaps all work perhaps life itself finally or otherwise are related to what I call enchantment meaning transforming oneself, being transformed, beyond knowledge and calculation. Knowledge understanding expression exposition asking telling as if perhaps transformation. As if perhaps self transformation, as if perhaps transforming an excessive exalted enchanted self. An enchantment that helps to imagine an excess of "I," an "I" exalted (Wittig, *MG*, 87)...

Here in conclusion is an enchantment in proliferation under the name of science. Haunted by ghosts and ciphers. Haunted by the betrayals of enchantment under any name.

I have suggested—perhaps too seriously—that an aesthetic or dionysian or enchanted science; or academic discipline or philosophy or art or theory—the plethora of names is endless—would be one whose questions could not be brought to rest, whose askings took place in régimes of power and knowledge but which as science etc., as enchanted etc., as asking and telling etc., could not accept any régime except contingently. Such a science—I mean, of course, every form of asking—you name it, enchanted, disenchanted, etc. etc.—no matter what images it forms of itself, whatever its names—takes place under the authority of an image, a mask, that endlessly proliferates into other images. One might call this disenchantment, whose proliferation is enchanting. One might call it citation. The images that mark the truth that proliferates from the régime—a truth that moves and wanders and succeeds itself—are the enchantments and betrayals of the mask. This is the enchantment of the image, the betrayals of the image—at which we must learn to laugh. The mask—in this case the truth, the image of enchanting truth—gives rise through imitation to endless other images that mark, establish, repeat, reiterate, cite, and mask that truth to mark it as true. To expose it and betray it. To mask it, and mask masking, thereby betraying asking and telling. To disenchant it, enchantingly...

All these marks, names, images, citations, askings, tellings are aesthetic, appear in the proliferation of images. The relation of the images that proliferate by imitation, the aesthetic in the phenomenon, is the relation of as if, make believe, of exposition and enchantment. They repeat the image as if they were the image again. They present the image again through the endless proliferation of masks as if they were the image, the life and multiplication and proliferation of the image. All enchanting...

Is this science? There can be no science without this. The call and obligation and responsibility, the ethics at the heart of a science that would be truthful and honest, lies in the endless proliferation of askings and tellings—the images that proliferate and mask, the enchantments that disenchant...

Here in conclusion I am asking a different question: what kind of truth—enchanted of course—can such an aesthetic or dionysian or enchanted science provide if it is engaged in the endless proliferation of images of that truth? One image of the image is make believe: does enchanted science give make believe truth? Another image is the mask: masked truth? Here is a serious example: in the textbooks that proliferate in the pedagogical wards of science are images of scientific truths: stories of scientific experiments, stories of scientific lives, narratives, images of science at work. These are images of scientific truth. Not in the sense that they are false—though a plausible case can be made for their falsity, at least in certain respects. But if so, it is a falsity that in no way undermines their truth. It is a textbook truth, a bit misleading, a bit naive, a bit pedagogical, a bit disenchanted. The proliferation of these make believe procedures, descriptions, principles, masks expresses their truth. If the education of children were not so serious a matter, we might laugh—as some have—at the incongruities of the images that clutter up the textbooks and disenchant their truths.

An established truth would be true without citations, without masks, without questions. That is what some would say. Yet in scientific practice, truths presented before their time fall by the wayside. Later we remember that someone suggested them long ago but the world was not ready for them—they could not be established as true. I would suggest the following: there is no scientific truth, no knowledge, that can be said to belong to science that does not require being established by certain procedures—confirmed, verified, validated—and these procedures collectively are a proliferation of the images, masks, askings, citations, practices that establish truth. I would add that once this proliferation begins it never comes to rest. It enchants enchantingly. It asks and tells surprisingly. In this sense the proliferation is the truth, the knowledge; in this sense each image taken by itself is the make believe and masking of the image, makes believe it is the image itself, makes us believe in the image and its truth, makes us believe in disenchantment. The truthfulness lies in the making and the believing and disenchanting. These give us plenty to laugh at—sometimes to weep at—no matter how committed we are to truth...

It follows that we are not to imagine enchantment as if anything goes, as if everything were as acceptable as anything else, but as if anything and everything might follow, proliferate, multiply, mask—that is, as if anything and everything were a reality in the mode of as if, wearing masks, enchanting and betraying. The "might" is not a possibility or a potentiality but a reality, that of asking, telling, proliferating, multiplying, simulating, of abundance, wonder, extravagance, and generosity. The image, the truth, proliferates as if the images that follow might be the image again. And of course they are the image again, but for the gaps, caesuras, that open up in the proliferation. But for the betrayals that are for givings. And the perhaps. But for the palimpsests of masks...

If you want the truth you must be prepared to ask it, give it, proliferate it, tell it, expose it, cast it upon the waters, enchant it, not so that it will be returned intact but so that it may live. Anything (the image) might be itself as if by way of enchantment. We live as if, as it were, perhaps, in the modality of the subjunctive, even by way of the force of history. Science functions for us as if it might give us the possibility of a truth to hold onto. Our responsibility is to hold onto that possibility by way of proliferation, thereby by not holding...

Enchantment shatters every idea, ruptures every form, masks every mask, proliferates every truth as if it were countless truths. This is perhaps why the world as image of aesthetics is not metaphysical—though metaphysics and science are among the proliferating images. It is not-metaphysical as an image, another image of enchanted truth, in the sense that the metaphysical is always moving away from itself, asking of itself, proliferating as if it were otherwise. It is disenchanted as an image, another image of enchanted truth, always betraying itself, proliferating as if it were otherwise. This is true in the affirmative mode—the image is (as if it were) this image and (as if it were) the endless images that proliferate. And it is true in the negative mode—the image is (as if it were) this (disenchanted) and not that (enchanted), not masked, where the not proliferates into endless other images of what is (and is not) disenchanted and what is (and is not) enchanting and enchanted... (Ross, *WAP*, 181–4)

Notes

Preface

1 Quotations are repunctuated throughout, especially in the italicized sections, with omissions and additions, all directed toward enchantment, in abundance and wonder.

2 See pp. 5–10, especially nn. 13 and 14.

3 I include the *posts* of our time, however silently: postmodernity, poststructuralism, postcoloniality, postmarxism, postsecularism, postchristianity, postenlightenment, postrationality, etc. They do not speak of disenchantment or of reenchantment, yet I take them to be speaking of nothing more.

4 Many tongues... many tellings...

> The language we speak today, the idiom of Renaissance and Enlightenment humanism, veils the processes of nature with its own cultural obsessions. It is as if we had compressed the entire buzzing, howling, gurgling biosphere into the narrow vocabulary of epistemology, to the point that someone like Georg Lukács could say, "nature is a societal category"—and actually be understood.
>
> In contrast, for animistic cultures, those that see the natural world as inspirited, not just people, but also animals, plants, and even "inert" entities such as stones and rivers are perceived as being articulate and at times intelligible subjects, able to communicate and interact with humans for good or ill. In addition to human language, there is also the language of birds, the wind, earthworms, wolves, and waterfalls. (Christopher Manes, *NS*, 43)

The late John Fire Lame Deer comments that although the whites imagine earth, rocks, water, and wind to be dead, they nevertheless "are very much alive."

> "You ask stones for aid to find things which are lost or missing. Stones can give warning of an enemy, of approaching misfortune." Butterflies, coyotes, grasshoppers, eagles, owls, deer, especially elk and bear all talk and possess and convey power. "You have to listen to all these creatures, listen with your mind. They have secrets to tell." (J. Baird Callicott, *TAIWEA*, 200)

Perhaps without interruption.

> *Nature is a societal category...*
> *Gurgling buzzing howling...*
> *Inspirited expressive expository...*
> *Listen listen listen to what they tell tell tell...*
> *Ask ask ask...*

5 The term *ingredient* replaces, enriches, supplements, and interrupts such terms as *subject, object, thing,* and *substance,* in part to avoid the historical and conceptual weight these carry, but also to evoke enchantment. The ingredients of the earth are enchanted, proliferating in abundance. The ingredients of the earth are for asking, for giving, and for telling.

See my *RR, PE,* and *GSSEB.*

6 See here chap. 5, p. 287.

7 *Enchant = in-cant = sing (against, in, out)*

> In 1988, two researchers probing caves in the south of France made a remarkable discovery. Unlike previous visitors, Reznikoff and Dauvois focused their attention on the rather unconventional question of how they sounded. Carefully mapping the acoustical properties of different parts of the caves, they reached the significant conclusion that the very places where the paintings were located were those that demonstrated the greatest acoustical resonance. The people who made these paintings must have gathered around them for singing, chanting, or other forms of music making. And the music making was so important to them that the location of the images—some of them in places almost impossible to reach—was dictated by the need to create the loudest sounds possible.
>
> Here, at the first stirrings of music as a social enterprise, it appears already linked to the economic basis of the community. But even more striking, the "work song" of the hunter—if such we can call it—was already much more than a rhythmic accompaniment to labor. It also carried a power of enchantment, served as a spur to courage, and acted as a force of social solidarity. ("The First Stirrings of Music," Ted Gioa, pianist, composer, and one of the founders of Stanford University's jazz-studies program, in *Work Songs*, published by Duke University

Press; from *The Chronicle of Higher Education Review* (Melange) (6/30/06)

Here, the first stirring of enchantment and of music, together, reminds us, if we have forgotten it, that enchantment is song, singing, incantation. The disenchantment of the world is the quelling of its sound and music. If they can be stilled, if they can go unheard. Of course, we may become deaf, or not listen.

See here pp. 50–2.

8 What Derrida calls the *non-contemporaneity with itself of the living present*. See the introduction here, p. 122.

9 See the discussions of Morris Berman in this preface, pp. 63–73, and of Carolyn Merchant in the introduction, pp. 104–5, 120–1. See also the wonder and abundance of ecologies.

10 I envisage proper names as if enchanted, some, like *Plato* (or *plato*), publicly and visibly. The recurrent question is how to understand the historical and textual phenomenon in which the name *Plato* (or *Hegel*) is regarded as disenchanted even among those who pursue enchantment—Nietzsche, Heidegger, and Deleuze for example.

By capitalization, ellipsis, and erasure I mean to bring this question of the (im)propriety of the name—including common names—to the forefront of the stage. I mean, that is, to speak of *plato... hegel... nietzsche... heidegger... and deleuze...* among others, including *language...* and *history...*, to think beyond the name of *Plato* to the endless enchantments... of exposition...

11 See especially Roberto Calasso, *LG*, and the discussion here in chap. 7. See also the discussion of plato and platonism in chap. 1, pp. 79–102.

12 This irresistible condition is a repetition of what Deleuze and Guattari speak of as the appearance of strata betrayed in an earth enchanted by univocity and a body without organs.

> There has only ever been one ontological proposition: Being is univocal. There has only ever been one ontology, that of Duns Scotus, which gave being a single voice.... A single voice raises the clamour of being. We have no difficulty in understanding that Being, even if it is absolutely common, is nevertheless not a genus. (Gilles Deleuze, *DR*, 35)

> The essential in univocity is not that Being is said in a single and same sense, but that it is said, in a single and same sense, *of* all the individuating differences or intrinsic modalities.... Being is said in a single and same sense of everything of which it is said, but that of which it is said differs: it is said of difference itself. (p. 36)

> the Earth—the Deterritorialized, the Glacial, the giant Molecule—is a body without organs. This body without organs is permeated by unformed, unstable matters, by flows in all directions, by free intensities or nomadic singularities, by mad or transitory particles.... There simultaneously occurs upon the earth a very important, inevitable phenomenon, that is beneficial in many respects and unfortunate in many others: stratification. Strata are Layers, Belts. They consist of giving form to matters, of imprisoning intensities or locking singularities into systems of resonance and redundancy, of producing upon the body of the earth molecules large and small and organizing them into molar aggregates. (Gilles Deleuze and Félix Guattari, *TP*, 40)

13 I am speaking of language, writing, images, expression, meanings—and of course, asking and telling—when I speak of *exposition*, in their surprising, excessive, unfamiliar wonder and abundance. The world in wonder and abundance is given in exposition, in asking, calling, telling, which must always strike us as unsettling, strange. In their many expositions.

I must add the word *queer*, another figure of unsettling, doubling in its generality—the universe is queer—and its local specificity—queer as sexual, gender, intimate and personal derogation, transformed by queering into celebration—calling queerly to queer queering. See p. 50.

14 And more: as *aisthēsis, mimēsis, poiēsis, catachrēsis, technē*; as image, aesthetics, beauty, art; as unearthing, revelation, disclosure; calling as giving; interrupting in betrayal; performing as undoing.

The doubling figures of asking and telling are all betraying: revelation and violation. Queering if you will.

15 A project unfolded in questioning, in the light of giving, with Heidegger in mind. Expressed in Gilles Deleuze's words: "the Heideggerian *Not* refers not to the negative in Being but to Being as difference; it refers not to negation but to questioning" (Deleuze, *DR*, 64).

Deleuze links questioning with difference. Heidegger links it (at least in relation to art and truth) with strangeness and unfamiliarity. "A beginning always contains the undisclosed abundance of the unfamiliar and extraordinary, which means that it also contains strife with the familiar and ordinary" (Heidegger, *OWA*, 76). I associate asking with enchantment, which in its abundance is always surprising, which in its wonder is always unsettling.

I express my thanks to Michael Gelven, whose *The Asking Mystery* made it possible for me to question questioning in such a way as to ask beyond it. Even so, we differ in what we take to be the truth of asking, even as we grant its mystery. Here is an example:

> We do not ask in order to learn, but learn in order to ask. Only those made wise through reading, reflection, celebrating,

> suffering, and courage can ask in this way, and when such asking takes place there is fundamental awe; for nothing not the founding of empires nor the splitting of atoms nor the procreation of the species is as spectacular as this. To ask greatly surpasses discovering greatly. The innumerable discover; only the rare and few ask. The loftiest arts ask and do not tell, the noblest sacrifice asks and tells not, the deepest thinkers do not tell; the deepest thinkers ask. (Gelven, *AM*, 7)

I do not share the height even as I would ask us to ask. Indeed we ask, and we may ask to ask, not only to tell. Though perhaps difficult, asking is not reserved for the lofty. Of all that we should ask, height and greatness come early.

16 Here, in this moment and place, I promise my ongoing project of giving over to asking and telling. Even so, this is less a transformation than an overflowing. Giving and asking exceed every limit. Promising exceeds every expectation.

This overflowing, this beyond, promises itself in every time and place, affirming the finiteness of every limit, whose limits then are limited, finite, impossible to limit finally. In this way, finite limits betray themselves inexhaustibly.

asking beyond questions
giving beyond having
enchanting beyond disenchanting
performing beyond desiring
desiring beyond wanting
promising beyond grasping
betraying beyond telling
proliferating beyond being
expressing beyond knowing
imagining beyond framing
telling beyond saying
surprising beyond requiring
requiring beyond anticipating
calling beyond claiming
invoking beyond predicting
responding beyond expressing
saying beyond asserting
knowing beyond reasoning
coming beyond going
becoming beyond being
going beyond halting
staying beyond arriving
wandering beyond remaining
remaining beyond staying
dispossessing beyond possessing

wonder beyond possession
abundance beyond accounting
profusion beyond complexitgy
flourishing beyond experiencing
compassion beyond ethics
cherishment beyond care
sacrifice beyond suffering
plenishment beyond anything
traveling beyond borders
resisting beyond authority
mystery beyond explaining
unsettling beyond remaining
unknowing beyond knowing
conjuring beyond magic
inhuman beyond humanity
reason beyond rationality
asking beyond asking
telling beyond telling
authority beyond authority
discipline beyond disciplines
for giving beyond generosity
etc. etc.

Here the language of giving gives itself over to asking, each beyond the other. The language of the good is nothing, still beyond itself. As asking and telling. First:

The Gift of Beauty: The Good as Art
The Gift of Truth: Gathering the Good
The Gift of Touch: Embodying the Good
The Gift of Kinds: The Good in Abundance
The Gift of Property: Having the Good
The Gift of Self: Shattering, Emptiness, Betrayal

Now:

Beyond Disenchantment: Asking, Telling, Enchanting
Unsettling by Asking, Undoing in Telling
Asking, for Telling, by Doing, as if Betraying

17 On another line or trace, "*in order to be-tray* [to treat, triturate, trice, in-trigue, trace, track]"; to "be framed" (Derrida, *TP*, 151). *Framing* is a wonderful term of art, conceiving and conspiring.

18 Guattari speaks of three ecologies, but there may be as many as there are enchantments, as enchanting as anything in the earth may be.

19 This relation of disenchantment to enchantment is analogous to the relation of Power (« *le pouvoir* ») to power (*pouvoir*) and resistance

as Foucault describes them, and indeed power may be another name of enchantment and its disenchantments:

> Power is everywhere, not because it embraces everything, but because it comes from everywhere. And "Power," insofar as it is permanent, repetitious, inert, and self-reproducing, is simply the over-all effect that emerges from all these mobilities, the concatenation that rests on each of them and seeks in turn to arrest their movement....
> —Power is not something that is acquired, seized, or shared, something that one holds on to or allows to slip away; power is exercised from innumerable points, in the interplay of nonegalitarian and mobile relations.
> —Relations of power are not in a position of exteriority with respect to other types of relationships (economic processes, knowledge relationships, sexual relations), but are immanent in the latter; they are the immediate effects of the divisions, inequalities, and disequilibriums which occur in the latter, and conversely, they are the internal conditions of these differentiations;....
> —Power comes from below; that is, there is no binary and all-encompassing opposition between rulers and ruled at the root of power relations, and serving as a general matrix....
> —Power relations are both intentional and nonsubjective. If in fact they are intelligible, this is not because they are the effect of another instance that "explains" them, but rather because they are imbued, through and through, with calculation: there is no power that is exercised without a series of aims and objectives. But this does not mean that it results from the choice or decision of an individual subject;....
> —Where there is power, there is resistance, and yet, or rather consequently, this resistance is never in a position of exteriority with respect to power....These points of resistance are present everywhere in the power network. Hence there is no single locus of great Refusal, no soul of revolt, source of all rebellions, or pure law of the revolutionary. Instead there is a plurality of resistances, each of them a special case: resistances that are possible, necessary, improbable; others that are spontaneous, savage, solitary, concerted, rampant, or violent; still others that are quick to compromise, interested, or sacrificial; by definition, they can only exist in the strategic field of power relations.... (Foucault, *HS*, vol. 1, 93–6)

Where there is disenchantment it is enchanting beyond names. Among these namings beyond names are *wonder* and *abundance*; *enchantment, ecology, power,* and *aesthetics*: the exteriorities of humanity beyond any exteriority. Power interrupts itself as resistance. Disenchantment interrupts itself enchantingly.

20 Understanding its vocation as inseparable from metaphysics, logocentrism, and ethnocentrism as Derrida describes them, from:

> 1. *the concept of writing* in a world where the phoneticization of writing must dissimulate its own history as it is produced;
> 2. *the history of (the only) metaphysics,* which has, in spite of all differences,... always assigned the origin of truth in general to the logos:....
> 3. *the concept of science* or the scientificity of science—what has always been determined as *logic*—a concept that has always been a philosophical concept, even if the practice of science has constantly challenged its imperialism of the logos, by invoking, for example, from the beginning and ever increasingly, nonphonetic writing. No doubt this subversion has always been contained within a system of direct address which gave birth to the project of science and to the conventions of all nonphonetic characteristics. It could not have been otherwise. (Derrida, *G*, 3)
>
> Is not the idea of knowledge and of the theory of knowledge in itself metaphysical? (5)
>
> What can a science of writing begin to signify, if it is granted:
> 1) that the very idea of science was born in a certain epoch of writing;
> 2) that it was thought and formulated, as task, idea, project, in a language implying a certain kind of structurally and axiologically determined relationship between speech and writing;
> 3) that, to that extent, it was first related to the concept and the adventure of phonetic writing, valorized as the telos of all writing, even though what was always the exemplary model of scientificity—mathematics—constantly moved away from that goal;
> 4) that the strictest notion of a general science of writing was born, for nonfortuitous reasons, during a certain period of the world's history (beginning around the eighteenth century) and within a certain determined system of relationships between "living" speech and inscription;
> 5) that writing is not only an auxiliary means in the service of science—and possibly its object—but first, as Husserl in particular pointed out in *The Origin of Geometry,* the condition of the possibility of ideal objects and therefore of scientific objectivity. Before being its object, writing is the condition of the *epistémé.*
> 6) that historicity itself is tied to the possibility of writing; to the possibility of writing in general, beyond those particular forms of writing in the name of which we have long spoken of peoples without writing and without history. Before being the object of a history—of an historical science—writing opens the field of history—of historical becoming. (27)

Enchanting writing. said to be disenchanted...

21 Something of this view can be found in Calasso, *LG*. See here chap. 7. See also this preface, n. 11.

22 Weber says something much stronger than believing: *mastering or imploring* the spirits. Mastery is a relative of disenchantment.

23 Including those that Foucault associates with *governmentality* (Foucault, *TS*, 18–9). See here pp. 23–5.

24 Such an understanding can be found in reading Thrasymachus in Plato's *Republic* as presenting Socrates with the greatest challenge to his authority.

> You think, do you, that it was with malice aforethought and trying to get the better of you unfairly that I asked that question? I don't think it, I know it, he said, and you won't make anything by it, for you won't get the better of me by stealth and, failing stealth, you are not of the force to beat me in debate. (Plato, *Republic*, 341ab)

Thrasymachus understands Socrates' arguments as another use of force, and capitulates only when outnumbered. "Revel in your discourse, he said, without fear, for I shall not oppose you, so as not to offend your partisans here" (Plato, *Republic*, 352b). The issue of injustice remains unresolved by reason, and indeed may be a matter of force.

> Socrates, is it your desire to seem to have persuaded us or really to persuade us that it is without exception better to be just than unjust?
>
> Really, I said, if the choice rested with me.
>
> Well, then, you are not doing what you wish. (Plato, *Republic*, 357b)

See my *IR*, chap. 7.

25 See my *IR*.

26 Derrida's audience as well.

27 See Bruno Latour, *PH*, and Isabelle Stengers, *IMS* and *PI*.

28 I mean something quite different from what Derrida means, speaking of reason: "The unsurpassable, unique, and imperial grandeur of the order of reason, that which makes it not just another actual order or structure (a determined historical structure, one structure among other possible ones), is that one cannot speak out against it except by being for it, that one can protest it only from within it; and within its domain, Reason leaves us only the recourse to strategems and strategies" (Derrida, *CHM*, 36). To the contrary, I would say, it is the wonder and abundance of reason, its askings, that mark its enchantments.

29 Of scientific inspiration. See here pp. 20–1.

30 Levinas is an exception, speaking of an *anarchic reason* founded on the non-indifference of the proximity of the one and the other before indifference and agreement.

> The difference in proximity between the one and the other, between me and a neighbor, turns into non-indifference, precisely into my responsibility. Proximity thus signifies a reason before the thematization of signification by a thinking subject, before the assembling of terms in a present, a pre-original reason that does not proceed from any initiative of the subject, an anarchic reason. It is a reason before the beginning, before any present, for my responsibility for the other commands me before any decision, any deliberation. Proximity is communication, agreement, understanding, or peace. (Levinas, *OB*, 166)

Anarchic reason before reason has appeared in philosophy as skepticism.

> The periodic return of skepticism and of its refutation signify a temporality in which the instants refuse memory which recuperates and represents. Skepticism, which traverses the rationality of logic of knowledge, is a refusal to synchronize the implicit affirmation contained in saying and the negation which this affirmation states in the said. (167)

Skepticism is the irresistible return of enchantment to anarchic reason as reason itself. Skepticism betrays reason's enchantment. Including science. With *perhaps* and *as if*, skepticism is *asking*.

31 As Lyotard describes meta-narratives in *PMC*.

32 See here n. 23.

33 But perhaps not individual people governing themselves.

34 Here is another view of the caesura with a different relation to disenchantment:

> 1587: The inhabitants of the village of Saint-Julien took legal action against a colony of weevils. . . .
>
> Forty or so years earlier, in 1545, an identical trial had taken place against the same creepers (or at least their ancestors). The affair ended in victory for the insects, who, were defended by . . . the episcopal judge. The latter had refused to excommunicate them, arguing that as creatures of God the animals possessed the same rights as men to consume plant life; . . . . (Ferry, *NEO*, ix)
>
> What kind of breach must have opened within humankind for the ritual performed in all seriousness in one era to turn to high comedy in another? (p. xvi)

35 See Germain, *DOD*, for a helpful discussion in relation to Habermas of the issues of disenchantment in the critique and defense of reason and their relation to politics and technology.

36 This is Pseudo-Dionysos's vision of beauty, images of the world endlessly answering to one another and to God.

37 But not, perhaps, the western, european, greek-judaic-christian epoch of metaphysics. See here n. 20.

38 See here pp. 55–6.

39 See here n. 7.

40 See here pp. 43–4.

41 See also:

> "Zarathustra! Zarathustra! Guess my riddle! Speak, speak! Guess the riddle that I, am. Speak then: who am I?"
>
> "I recognize you well," he said in a voice of bronze; "*you are the murderer of God*! You could not bear him who saw you—who always saw you through and through, you ugliest man!"
>
> "But he *had* to die: he saw with eyes that saw everything; he saw man's depths and ultimate grounds, all his concealed disgrace and ugliness. The god who saw everything, *even man*—this god had to die! Man cannot bear it that such a witness should live." (Nietzsche, *Z*, Pt. 4, #7)

42 See chap. 7 here, pp. 354–5.

43 See also the conclusion here, pp. 350–1.

44 And to Gablik. See here chap. 4.

45 See my *WAP*.

46 See chap. 3.

47 See here pp. 40–2.

48 Maurice Blanchot speaks of the step *(pas)* not *(pas)* beyond *(au-delà)* (and not a step) *(Le pas au-delà)* (Blanchot, *SNB*). I speak of *beyond* as incessantly traversing this *not*, this impossibility: the limits of limits betrayed *as if ~~not beyond~~* themselves, enchanted. Perhaps.

49 "The perpetual penality that traverses all points and supervises every instant in the disciplinary institutions compares, differentiates, hierarchizes, homogenizes, excludes. In short, it *normalizes*" (Foucault, *DP*, 183). See here p. 23 and n. 19.

50 Communities of pagans are disenchanted.

Introduction

1 A phrase allied with Carolyn Merchant's *The Death of Nature*. I draw upon her work in the context of the earth's enchantments.

2 See the preface here, pp. 11–13, and chap. 6.

3 The one betrays the other and itself. See the preface here, p. 42.

4 See the preface here, n. 10.

5 See the preface here, pp. 7–14, 20–3.

6 See here p. 84.

7 See here p. 91.

8 See my *GKGA*, chap. 2, for a detailed reading of *Sophist*.

9 See here p. 90.

10 If *madness* is the word, if this is madness, for us today. I think of it as enchantment, interrupting sanity and madness.

11 As I have suggested repeatedly, all the *posts* of our time express enchantment beyond the grip of disenchantment.

12 See my *GBGA*, chap. 3.

13 See the preface here, p. 65, for the complete quotation.

14 In Derrida's words:

> *Before the question (which always presupposes language) there is a consent to language, which belongs to it without truly belonging to it. This Heidegger calls Zusage. Zusage is a manner of consenting, of saying "yes," to language, to the call, more originary than the questioning* (Derrida, *N*, 40)...

More originary, as if the disenchanted origin of a disenchanted world, or perhaps the wondering enchantment from which all askings emerge.

15 Derrida reads it in relation to the gift, an important and neglected reading.

> Now it seems to me that *The Origin* can also be read as an essay on the gift *[Schenkung]*, on the offering: one of the three senses, precisely in which truth is said to come to its installation, its institution, or its investiture *[Stiftung]*. One of the two other senses, the "founding" *[Gründen]*, is not without its links with the ground. On the other hand, *The Origin* also says of this truth which is, Heidegger says, "nontruth" which "comes about *[geschieht]* in Van Gogh's picture" (a statement on which

Schapiro exercises his irony), that its essence rather opens onto the "abyss." (Derrida, *R*, pp. 261–2)

16 More completely expressed as an *architectural|ethical|political|epistemological|territorial|economic project*. See my *GTGG*.

17 See the preface here, pp. 64–5.

18 "Kata to chreōn didonai gar auta dikēn kai tisin allēlois tēs adikias." The entire fragment from Simplicius is canonically translated as: "Into those things from which existing things have their coming into being, their passing away, too, takes place, according to what must be; for they make reparation to one another for their injustice according to the ordinance of time, as he puts it in somewhat poetical language" (Simplicius *Phys.*, 24, 18 [DK 12 B 1]) (Robinson, *EGP*, 34). See my *IR*.

Chapter 1

1 See the introduction here, pp. 90–1.

2 See my *WAP*, chap. 2.

3 See chap. 5, p.257, for the full quotation.

4 See the preface here, and pp. 179–80.

5 Eternal objects are *Pure Potentials or Forms of Definiteness* (Alfred North Whitehead, *PR*, 22).

6 See my *PWM*, especially chaps. 9 and 10.

7 See my *TA*.

8 For example:

> Difference is not diversity. Diversity is given, but difference is that by which the given is given as diverse. Everything which happens and everything which appears is correlated with orders of differences: differences of level, temperature, pressure, tensions, potential, *difference of intensity*. Intensity is the form of difference in so far as this is the reason of the sensible. Every intensity is differential, by itself a difference. The reason of the sensible, the condition of that which appears, is not space and time but the Unequal in itself, *disparateness* as it is determined and comprised in difference of intensity, in intensity as difference. (Gilles Deleuze, *DR*, 222–3)
>
> the Earth—the Deterritorialized, the Glacial, the giant Molecule—is a BwO. This BwO is permeated by unformed, unstable matters, by flows in all directions, by free intensities or nomadic

> singularities, by made or transitory particles. There simultaneously occurs upon the earth a very important, inevitable phenomenon, that is beneficial in many respects and unfortunate in many others: stratification. Strata are Layers, Belts. They consist of giving form to matters, of imprisoning intensities or locking singularities into systems of resonance and redundancy, of producing upon the body of the earth molecules large and small and organizing them into molar aggregates. (Gilles Deleuze and Félix Guattari, *TP*, 40)
>
> After all, is not Spinoza's *Ethics* the great book of the BwO? The attributes are types or genuses of BwO's, substances, powers, zero intensities as matrices of production. The modes are everything that come to pass: waves and vibrations, migrations, thresholds and gradients, intensities produced in a given type of substance starting from a given matrix. (153)
>
> Spinoza asks: what can a body do? We call the *latitude* of a body the affects of which it is capable at a given degree of power. *Latitude is made up of intensive parts falling under a capacity, and longitude of extensive parts falling under a relation.* (256–7)

9 I am speaking now of these works of Justus Buchler, *TGT, NJ, CM, MNC, ML*, and of my *TOM, PM, IHB, LL, LPJ*.

10 When I wrote my *TOM* and *PM* I was uncertain, and I remain uncertain, whether my reading of Buchler's categories of natural complex and ordinality and his principle of ontological parity into the enchantments of locality and inexhaustibility was felicitous for him, or whether his concern for precision and rigor would have led him to reject them, to regard enchantment as a frivolous notion. In terms of this book, enchantment is the most serious subject for us to consider at this time, at any time, under whatever name. If anything be serious as enchanted.

11 See Derrida's temptation in the introduction here, pp. 93–4.

12 See also this chapter, pp. 149–52.

Chapter 2

1 See the introduction, n. 18.

2 See here chap. 6, p. 297.

3 See the introduction here, pp. 125–6.

4 See the preface here, pp. 20–1.

5 See the introduction here, pp. 119.

6 See the introduction here, pp. 84–90, and the extended discussion of *Phaedrus* in my *IR*, chaps. 9 and 10.

7 See the preface here, pp. 31–2.

8 See also the asking of a dionysian science, in chap. 4.

9 These are guidelines to plenishment rewritten in memory of the gathering of truth, rewritten again in memory of enchantment. See my *PE*, 318–22. Plenishment is the meeting place of enchantment and disenchantment on the side of enchantments.

10 See here chap. 1, pp. 145–54.

Chapter 3

1 See the preface here, p. 70, n. 48.

2 See the introduction here, pp. 102–3.

3 See here chap. 1, p. 155.

4 See the preface here, p. 27.

5 Compare Derrida's meditation on the "syllable *gé*, with which we shall never be done, however it is transcribed (the letter *g*, the whole word 'jet,' the word fragment 'gé,' as in *génie* or *généalogie* or *générique*" (Derrida, *GGGG*, 28).

6 See my *GPHG*, especially the excursus on genitivity in the introduction, n. 1.

Chapter 4

1 The *architectural|ethical|political|epistemological|territorial|economic project* of modernity. (Ross, *GSSEB*, 195)... See the introduction here, p. 116.

2 See here chap. 3, p. 229.

3 See chap. 3 here, p. 202.

4 See the preface here, pp. 39–44.

5 For example:

> A short time ago, a "community activist" from my neighbourhood suggested that one way of practising "respect for the environment" while fostering "community responsibility" would be to form a committee or group to inspect neighbour-

> hood garbage. In a way it is refreshing to hear someone speak so openly about the surveillance, regulation and censure informing their idea of community, but it is, at the same time, chilling to have it spoken in the name of what passes for "progressive" or radical politics. (Jowett, *OOPN*, 26)
>
> I am confused about the meaning of community, having never had the experience of choosing to belong or being forced to leave one. I feel naive in these matters, thinking that community is something about which you have no choice. You are born in a certain place, amongst certain people and for better or for worse this settings and these relations are the givenness of your community. (13)
>
> Where I come from matters to me and I didn't choose it and it is not always a source of strength or pleaure and it confers unearned privilege on me and there is no way of discounting it except through acts of hypocrisy and bad faith. It is a contingent and essential "given" which is the occasion for both ethics and the refusal of ethics. My absence of choice about it is the situation in which the possibility of ethics arises. (16)

These Levinasian reflections on ethics are directly relevant to the issues of Gablik's new social paradigm and of enchantment and disenchantment. If community as Jowett describes it is not group or police surveillance, it is the givenness of relationality. As such, it is enchantment itself, capable in anyone's hands of becoming disenchanted, and historically of being imposed on anyone in the name of best practices. Including artists.

Yet also historically, but especially in the time of our toxic culture, those who have most openly resisted such authoritarian and pervasive forms of disenchantment have been artists, resisted the ways in which the most visible and invisible forms of culture pervade our lives and practices and thinking and being. Even the most toxic artists illuminate the toxicity in strange, enchanted ways. And if we discount the rich and famous, there are multitudes of other artists struggling to transform the landscape of their toxic culture, sometimes unknowingly, frequently fully aware of what they are doing.

Multitudes of artists, arts, ecologies, and ecosophies.

6 See the introduction here, p. 83.

7 See here chap. 3, pp. 211–5.

8 See also chap. 6, pp. 320–3.

9 See the preface here, p. 31.

10 See chap. 2 here, p. 161.

11 See the preface here pp. 40–2, especially n. 36.

Chapter 5

1 See here chap. 1, pp. 132–9.

2 See here chap. 1, p. 135.

3 See instead Priest, *BLT, IC*.

4 If they are strict and invariant. Perhaps they are evolutionarily adaptable. At least that is not impossible, even if it echoes the impossible. See Davies, *CJ*.

5 See my *RR*.

6 See also the preface here, p. 70.

7 See my *GTEG*, introduction and chap.7.

8 See the preface, chap. 1, and chap. 4 here, pp. 238–48. See also Levene, *DLY*.

9 See the preface here, pp. 29–31.

10 See the discussion of ordinality here in chap. 1, pp. 146–54.

11 In Artaud's enchanting language, determination (the organs of the body) is cruelty. Oh to have a body without organs!

> The pre-Columbian Indians were a strangely civilized people who knew a civilization based on the exclusive principle of cruelty.
>
> Cruelty, it's to extirpate through the blood and as far as the blood god, the bestial risk of unconscious human animality, wherever it may be encountered.
>
> Man is sick because he is badly constructed.
> We must decide to strip him in order to scratch out this animalcule which makes him itch to death,
>
> god,
> and with god
> his organs.
>
> For tie me down if you want to,
> but there is nothing more useless than an organ.
> When you have given him a body without organs,
> then you will have delivered him from all his automatisms and restored him to his true liberty. (Artaud, *THDJG*, 304–7)

And a theater of cruelty.

The organs of the body are cruel. A body without organs and a magical, dangerous theater are enchanted.

> We cannot go on prostituting the idea of the theater, whose only value lies in its excruciating, magical connection with reality and with danger.
>
> Stated in this way, the question of the theater must arouse general attention, since theater, because of its physical aspect and because it requires *expression in space* (the only real expression, in fact), allows the magical means of art and speech to be practiced organically and as a whole, like renewed exorcisms. From all this it follows that we shall not restore to the theater its specific powers of action until we have restored its language.
>
> That is to say: instead of relying on texts that are regarded as definitive and as sacred we must first of all put an end to the subjugation of the theater to the text, and rediscover the notion of a kind of unique language halfway between gesture and thought. (Artaud, *TC1*, 242–3)

12 See chap. 4 here, pp. 238, 243.

Chapter 6

1 See my *IR*.

2 See here chap. 5, n. 11.

3 I should say something of those other enchantments in which griffin takes on the betrayals of American iconic history generally known as 9/11. See Griffin, *Christian Faith and the Truth Behind 9/11: A Call to Reflection and Action [CFT911]; The 9/11 Commission Report: Omissions And Distortions [911CR]; 9/11 Contradictions: An Open Letter to Congress and the Press [900C]; The New Pearl Harbor: Disturbing Questions About the Bush Administration and 9/11 [NPH]; Debunking 9/11 Debunking: An Answer to Popular Mechanics and Other Defenders of the Official Conspiracy Theory [D911D]; The New Pearl Harbor Revisited: 9/11, the Cover-Up, and the Exposé [NPHR]*; David Ray Griffin, John B. Cobb, Richard A. Falk, and Catherine Keller, *The American Empire and the Commonwealth of God: A Political, Economic, Religious Statement [AECG].*

At the risk of offense, I suggest that conspiracy theories are enchanting. That is not, however, all that they are.

4 See here chap. 4, pp. 235–9.

5 As I have suggested in my *PWM*.

6 See here chaps. 2, 4, and 5.

7 Nor Gablik's and Berman's. It is closer to the alchemical side of berman, and the love that drives the world and ourselves in macy. All without betraying betrayal.

8 The implausibility of griffin's assumptions from the standpoint of current physics marks the latter as far more enchanted than his organicist theory. I continue to explore his anthology not to criticize but to betray.

9 See chap. 4, pp. 246–8, and this chap., pp. 319–21.

10 See here chap. 4, pp. 246–8.

11 An exception is Isobelle Stengers's view that science is most successful and authoritative where the technology enables experimental instruments to tell the truth of the world (Stengers, *IMS*).

12 See here chap. 4, pp. 245–8.

13 See the preface here, pp. 38–9.

Chapter 7

1 See here chap. 1, pp. 132–40.

2 See the introduction here. See also the preface, n. 10.

3 See the preface here, pp. 59–60.

4 For the full quotation see the preface here, p. 60.

5 This is again the choice we cannot make, the choice that is not a choice, the choice we cannot avoid. See the introduction here, pp. 93–4.

6 See here chap. 3, pp. 212–4.

7 See also:

> Matters concerning speech and writing are genuinely strange; proper conversation is a mere play of words. We can only marvel at the laughable error people make—believing that they speak about things. No one knows precisely what is peculiar to language, that it concerns itself merely with itself. For that reason, it is a wonderful and fertile mystery—that when someone speaks merely in order to speak, one precisely then expresses the most splendid and most original truths. Yet if one wishes to speak of something determinate, then temperamental language has them say the most laughable and perverse things. That is the reason too for the hatred that so many earnest people have toward language. They recognize their own willfulness, but do not observe that contemptible chatter is the infinitely earnest side of language. If only one could make people grasp that the case of language is similar to the case of mathematical formulae—they constitute a world for themselves—they play with themselves alone, express nothing other than their won-

derful nature, and precisely for that reason they are so expressive—precisely for that reason they mirror in themselves the curious play of relations in things. Only by way of freedom are they members of nature and only in their free movements does the world soul give utterance, making them a delicate standard of measure and blueprint for things. Thus it is with language too—whoever has a subtle sense of its application, its cadence, its musical spirit, whoever perceives in oneself the delicate effects of its inner nature, and moves one's tongue and hand in accordance with it will be a prophet; in contrast, whoever knows it but does not have sufficient ear and sensibility for language, writes truths such as these, will be held hostage by language itself and will be mocked by human beings, as was Cassandra among the Trojans. If I believe I have hereby declared most precisely the essence and office of poesy, I know nonetheless that no human being can understand it, and that I have said something quite foolish, for the mere reason that I wanted to say it, so that no poesy comes to be. Yet what would happen if I had to talk? and if this linguistic drive to speak were the characteristic of inspiration of language, and of the efficacy of language in me? and if my will only willed precisely everything that I had to will—then in the end this could be without my knowledge or belief poesy and could make a mystery of language comprehensible? and thus I would be a writer by vocation, inasmuch as a writer is only an enthusiast of language? (Novalis, Friedrich von Hardenberg, "Monologue." From The Philosophical and Theoretical Works, pp. 438–439. Translation by Ferit Güven. Also, *Novalis: Philosophical Writings [NPW]*. Trans. and Ed. Marjorie Mahony Stoljar. Albany, NY: State University of New York Press, 1997: 83–4).

8 See here chap. 6, p. 297.

9 See the preface here, p. 44.

Bibliography

Abbott, Sally. "The Origins of God in the Blood of the Lamb" [*OGBL*]. In Diamond and Orenstein, eds., *Reweaving the World*.

Abram, David. *The Spell of the Sensuous: Perception and Language in a More-Than-Human World* [*SS*]. New York: Pantheon, 1996.

Acker, Kathy. "Against Ordinary Language: The Language of the Body" [*AOL*]. In Kroker and Kroker, eds., *Last Sex*.

Ackerman, Robert John. *Heterogeneities: Race, Gender, Class, Nation, and State* [*H*]. Amherst: University of Massachusetts Press, 1996.

Adams, Carol J. *The Sexual Politics of Meat* [*SPM*]. New York: Continuum, 1992.

Adams, Nicholas. *Habermas and Theology* [*HT*]. Cambridge: Cambridge University Press, 2006.

Adams, Robert L. "Alain Locke Revisited: The Reconsideration of an Aesthetic" [*ALR*]. In Young, ed., *Art, Culture, and Ethnicity*.

Abram, David. *The Spell of the Sensuous: Perception and Language in a More-Than-Human World* [*SS*]. New York: Vintage, 1996.

Addelson, Kathryn Pyne. *Impure Thoughts* [*IT*]. Philadelphia: Temple University Press, 1991.

——. "The Man of Professional Wisdom" [*MPW*]. In *Impure Thoughts*.

Adorno, Theodor W. *Aesthetic Theory* [*AT*]. Trans. C. Lenhardt. New York: Routledge & Kegan Paul, 1984.

——. *Negative Dialectics* [*ND*]. Trans. E. B. Ashton. New York: Continuum, 1983.

Aeschylus. *Oresteia* [*O*]: *Agamemnon* [*A*]; *Libation Bearers* [*LB*]; *Eumenides* [*E*]. Trans. Christopher Collard. Oxford: Oxford University Press, 2002.

Agamben, Giorgio. *The Open: Man and Animal* [*O*]. Trans. Kevin Attell. Stanford, CA: Stanford University Press, 2004.

——. *Language and Death: The Place of Negativity* [*LD*]. Trans. Karen E. Pinkus with Michael Hardt.

——. *The Man without Content* [*MWC*]. Trans. Georgia Albert. Stanford, CA: Stanford University Press, 1999.

Agar, Herbert, and Allen Tate, eds. *Who Owns America? A New Declaration of Independence* [*WOA*]. Freeport, NY: Books for Libraries Press, 1970.

Allen, Douglas. "Social Constructions of Self: Some Asian, Marxist, and Feminist Critiques of Dominant Western Views of Self" [*SCS*]. In Allen, ed., *Culture and Self.*

Allen, Douglas, ed. *Culture and Self: Philosophical and Religious Perspectives, East and West* [*CS*]. Boulder, CO: Westview, 1997.

Allen, Paula Gunn. *The Sacred Hoop: Recovering the Feminine in American Indian Traditions* [*SH*]. Boston: Beacon Press, 1986.

Allen, Robert. "The Land Monopoly" [*LM*]. *Green Revolution* 9, 10 (October 1971): 7, 16.

Althusser, Louis. *Althusser: A Critical Reader* [*ACR*]. Ed. Gregory Elliott. Oxford: Oxford University Press, 1994.

———. *Essays on Ideology* [*EI*]. New York: Verso, 1984.

———. *For Marx* [*FM*]. New York: Verso, 1996.

———. *The Humanist Controversy and Other Writings* [*HC*]. New York: Verso, 2003.

———. *Writings on Psychoanalysis: Freud and Lacan* [*WP*]. New York: Columbia University Press, 1996.

Althusser, Louis, and Étienne Balibar. *Reading Capital* [*RC*]. Trans. Ben Brewster. London: NLB, 1970.

Altizer, Thomas J. J., ed. *Toward a New Christianity: Readings in the Death of God Theology* [*TWC*]. New York: Harcourt, Brace & World, 1967.

Altizer, Thomas J. J., and William Hamilton. *Radical Theology and the Death of God* [*RT*].

Alverson, Hoyt. *Mind in the Heart of Darkness: Value and Self-Identity Among the Tswana of Southern Africa* [*MH*]. New Haven, CT: Yale University Press, 1978.

Ames, Roger T. "Putting the *Te* Back into Taoism" [*PTBT*]. In Callicott and Ames, eds., *Nature in Asian Traditions of Thought.*

Ames, Roger T., ed. *Self as Person in Asian Theory and Practice* [*SPATP*]. With Wimal Dissanayake and Thomas P. Kasulis. Albany: State University of New York Press, 1994.

Ames, Roger T., with Thomas P. Kasulis and Wimal Dissanayake. *Self as Image in Asian Theory and Practice* [*SIATP*]. Albany: State University of New York Press, 1998.

———. *Self as Person in Asian Theory and Practice* [*SPATP*]. Albany: State University of New York Press, 1994.

Andersen, Margaret L., and Patricia Hill Collins, eds. *Race, Class, and Gender: An Anthology* [*RCG*]. 2nd ed., Belmont, CA: Wadsworth, 1995.

Anderson, Walt. *The Future of the Self: Inventing the Postmodern Person* [*FS*]. New York: T. P. Tarcher, 1997.

Andolsen, Barbara Hilkert, Christine E. Gudorf, and Mary D. Pellauer, eds. *Women's Consciousness, Women's Conscience* [*WCWC*]. New York: Winston, 1985.

Andreach, Robert. *Creating the Self in the Contemporary American Theatre* [*CSCAT*]. Carbondale: Southern Illinois University Press, 1998.

Andrews, Ted. Animal Wise: *The Spirit Language and Signs of Nature* [*AW*]. Jackson, TN: Dragonhawk, 1999.

——. Enchantment of the Faerie *Realm: Communicate with Nature Spirits & Elementals* [*EFR*]. Woodbury, MN: Llewellyn Publications, 1993.

Anzaldúa, Gloria. *Borderlands/La Frontera: The New Mestiza* [*B/F*]. 2nd ed., San Francisco: Aunt Lute Books, 1999.

Appelbaum, David. *Everyday Spirits* [*ES*]. Albany: State University of New York Press, 1993.

——. *The Interpenetrating Reality: Bringing the Body to Touch* [*IR*]. New York: Lang, 1988.

Appiah, Kwame Anthony. "Racisms" [*R*]. In Goldberg, ed., *Anatomy of Racism*.

Apter, Andrew: *Black Critics & Kings: The Hermeneutics of Power in Yoruba Society* [*BCK*]. Chicago: University of Chicago Press, 1992.

Aquinas, Thomas. *Basic Writings of St. Thomas Aquinas* [*BWTA*]. Ed. Anton C. Pegis. 2 vols. New York: Random House, 1945.

——. *Summa Theologica* [*ST*]. Trans. Fathers of the English Dominican Province. London: Burns, Oates & Washbourne, 1912–36.

Ardener, E. "Belief and the Problem of Women" [*BPW*]. In J. La Fontaine, ed., *The Interpretation of Ritual* [*IR*]. London: Tavistock, 1975. Reprinted in S. Ardener, *Perceiving Women*.

Ardener, S. *Defining Females: The Nature of Women in Society* [*DF*]. London: Croom, Helm, 1978.

——., ed. *Perceiving Women* [*PW*]. London: Dent, 1975.

Arendt, Hannah. *Eichmann in Jerusalem: A Report on the Banality of Evil* [*EJ*]. Rev. and enl. ed., New York: Viking, 1964.

——. *The Human Condition* [*HC*]. Chicago: University of Chicago Press, 1958.

Arens, W., and I. Karp, eds. *Creativity of Power* [*CP*]. Washington, DC and London: Smithsonian Press, 1989.

Aristotle. *The Basic Works of Aristotle* [*BWA*]. New York: Random House, 1941.

——. *The Complete Works of Aristotle* [*CWA*]. Ed. Jonathan Barnes. 2 vols. Princeton: Princeton University Press, 1984. All quotations from Aristotle are from this edition unless otherwise indicated.

——. *On Memory* [*OM*]. In *Complete Works.*

——. *Poetics* [*P*]. In *Basic Works of Aristotle.* Reprinted in part in Ross, ed., *Art and Its Significance.*

Armstrong, Isobel. *The Radical Aesthetic* [*RA*]. Oxford: Blackwell, 2001.

Artaud, Antonin. *Antonin Artaud: Selected Writings* [*SW*]. Ed. Susan Sontag. Trans. Helen Weaver. Berkeley: University of California Press, 1988.

——. *Artaud Anthology* [*AA*]. Ed. Jack Hirschman. San Francisco: City Lights Books, 1965.

——. *Heliogabalus, or, The Anarchist Crowned* [*H*]. Trans. Alexis Lykiard. London: Creation Books, 2003.

——. *The Monk* [*M*]. London: Creation, 2003.

——. *The Peyote Dance* [*PD*]. Trans. Helen Weaver. New York: Farrar, Straus and Giroux, 1976.

——. *The Theater and Its Double* [*TD*]. New York: Grove Press, 1966.

——. "The Theater of Cruelty (First Manifesto)" [*TC1*]. In *Selected Writings*.

——. "To Have Done with the Judgment of God" [*THDJG*]. In *Watchfiends & Rack Screams*.

——. *Watchfiends & Rack Screams: Works From the Final Period by Antonin Artaud* [*WRS*]. Trans. Clayton Eshleman with Bernard Bador. Boston: Exact Change, 1995.

——. *Works on Paper*. Ed. Margit Rowell. New York: Museum of Modern Art. Distributed by Abrams, 1996.

Asch, Michael. "To Negotiate into Confederation: Canadian Aboriginal Views on Their Political Rights" [*NC*]. In Wilmsen, ed., *We Are Here*.

Ash, Timothy Garton. "On the Frontier" [*OF*]. *New York Review of Books*, Vol. 49, no. 17 (November 7, 2002): 60–1.

Athanasiou, Tom. *Divided Planet: The Ecology of Rich and Poor* [*DP*]. Boston: Little, Brown & Co., 1997.

Atkinson, Adrian. *Principles of Political Ecology* [*PPE*]. London: Belhaven Press, 1991.

Augustine. *Basic Writings of Saint Augustine* [*BWA*]. Ed. and int. Whitney J. Oates. New York: Random House, 1948.

——. *The City of God* [CG]. In *Basic Writings of Saint Augustine*.

Avalos, David, with John C. Welchman. "Response to The Philosophical Brothel" [*RPB*]. In Welchman, ed., *Rethinking Borders*.

Baack, Ben. "The Development of Exclusive Property Rights to Land in England: An Exploratory Essay" [*DEPRLE*]. *Economy and History* 22, no. 1 (1979): 63–74.

Bachelard, Gaston. *The Poetics of Reverie: Childhood, Language, and the Cosmos* [*PR*]. Trans. Daniel Russell. Boston: Beacon Press, 1969.

——. *The Poetics of Space* [*PS*]. Trans. Maria Jolas. Boston: Beacon Press, 1964.

——. *The Psychoanalysis of Fire* [*PF*]. Trans. Alan C. M. Ross. Pref. Northrop Frye. Boston: Beacon Press, 1964.

——. *The Right to Dream* [*RD*]. Trans. J. A. Underwood. Dallas, TX: Pegasus Foundation; Dallas Institution Publications, 1988.

——. *Water and Dreams: An Essay on the Imagination of Matter* [*WD*]. Trans. Edith R. Farrell. Dallas, TX: Pegasus Foundation; Dallas Institution Publications, 1983.

Bacon, Francis. *Novum Organum* [*NO*]. In Burtt, ed., *English Philosophers from Bacon to Mill*.

Badiner, Allan Hunt, ed. *Dharma Gaia: A Harvest of Essays in Buddhism and Ecology* [*DG*]. Berkeley: Parallax Press, 1990.

Badiou, Alain. *Ethics: an Essay on the Understanding of Evil* [*E*]. Trans. and int. Peter Hallward. London: New York: Verso, 2001.

——. *Infinite Thought: Truth and the Return to Philosophy* [*IT*]. Trans. and ed., Oliver Feltham and Justin Clemens. New York: Continuum, 2003.

Baechler, Jean. "Liberty, Property, and Equality" [*LPE*]. In Pennock and Chapman, eds., *Nomos XXII*, 269–88.

Bailey, Lee Worth. *The Enchantments of Technology* [*ET*]. Champaign, IL: University of Illinois Press, 2005.

Bakhtin, Mikhail Mikhailovich. *Discourse in the Novel* [*DN*]. Reprinted in part in Ross, ed., *Art and Its Significance*. In *Dialogic Imagination*. Ed. Michael Holquist. Trans. Caryl Emerson and Michael Holquist. Austin: University of Texas Press, 1981.

Balibar, Etienne. *Masses, Classes, Ideas: Studies on Politics and Philosophy before and after Marx* [*MCI*]. Trans. James Swenson. New York: Routledge, 1994.

——. "Paradoxes of Universality" [*PU*]. In Goldberg, ed., *Anatomy of Racism*.

——. *Spinoza: From Individuality to Transindividuality* [*S*]. Delft: Eburon, 1997.

Balibar, Etienne, and Immanuel Wallerstein. *Race, Nation, Class: Ambiguous Identities* [*RNC*]. Trans. Chris Turner. New York: Verso, 1991.

Bar On, Bat-Ami, ed. *Modern Engendering: Critical Feminist Readings in Modern Western Philosophy* [*ME*]. Albany: State University of New York Press, 1994.

Barnard, Kathryn E., and T. Berry Brazelton, eds. *Touch: The Foundation of Experience* [*T*]. National Center for Clinical Infant Programs. Madison, CT: International Universities Press, 1990.

Barrow, John D. *The Artful Universe* [*AU*]. Oxford: Clarendon Press, 1995.

——. *Impossibility: The Limits of Science and the Science of Limits* [*I*]. Oxford: Oxford University Press, 1998.

Barthes, Roland. *Criticism and Truth* [*CT*]. Trans. and ed., Katrine Pilcher Keuneman. London: Athlone Press, 1987.

——. *Image, Music, Text* [*IMT*]. Sel. and Trans. Stephen Heath. London: Fontana, 1977.

——. *A Lover's Discourse: Fragments* [*LD*]. Trans. Richard Howard. New York: Hill and Wang, 1978.

——. *The Pleasure of the Text* [*PT*]. Trans. Richard Miller. New York: Noonday Press, Farrar, Straus and Giroux, 1975.

——. *The Rustle of Language* [*RL*]. Trans. Richard Howard. New York: Hill and Wang, 1986.

——. *Sade, Fourier, Loyola* [*SFL*]. Trans. Richard Miller. New York : Hill and Wang, 1976.

——. *S/Z*. Trans. Richard Miller. New York, Hill and Wang, 1974.

——. *Writing Degree Zero, and Elements of Semiology* [*WDZ*]. New York: Beacon Press, 1970.

Basham, A. L. *The Wonder that was India* [*WI*]. London: Sidgwick and Jackson, 1967.

Baskin, Yvonne. *The Work of Nature: How the Diversity of Life Sustains Us* [*WN*]. Washington, DC. Island Press, 1997.

Bataille, Georges. *The Accursed Share: An Essay on General Economy* [*AS*]. Trans. Richard Hurley. 2 vols. New York: Zone Books, 1988 and 1993. Translation of *La Part maudite, L'Histoire de l'érotisme,* and *La Souveraineté* (*Consumption* [1]; *The History of Eroticism* [2]; *Sovereignty* [3]). In Georges Bataille, *Oeuvres Complètes*. Paris: Gallimard, 1976.

——. *The Bataille Reader* [*BR*]. Ed. Fred Botting and Scott Wilson. Oxford: Blackwell, 1997.

——. *The Collected Poems of Georges Bataille* [*CP*]. Trans. Mark Spitzer. Chester Springs, Pa.: Dufour Editions, 1999.

——. *The Impossible* [*I*]. Trans. Robert Hurley. San Francisco: City Lights Books, 1991.

——. *Inner Experience* [*IE*]. Trans. Leslie Anne Boldt. Albany: State University of New York Press, 1988. Translation of *L'Expérience intérieure.* Paris: Gallimard, 1954.

——. *Méthode de Méditation* [*MM*]. In *L'Expérience intérieure.* Quoted in Derrida, "From Restricted to General Economy."

——. "The Notion of Expenditure" [*NE*]. In *Visions of Excess.*

——. *Oeuvres Complètes* [*OC*]. Paris: Gallimard, 1970–71.

——. *On Nietzsche* [*ON*]. Trans. Bruce Boone. New York: Paragon House, 1992.

——. *Story of the Eye by Lord Auch* [*SE*]. Trans. Joachim Neugroschel. San Francisco: City Lights books, 1967.

——. *The Tears of Eros* [*TE*]. Trans. Peter Connor. San Francisco: City Lights Books, 1989.

——. *Visions of Excess: Selected Writings, 1927–1939* [*VE*]. Trans. Allan Stoekl, with Carl R. Lovitt and Donald M. Leslie, Jr. Minneapolis: University of Minnesota Press, 1985

Batchelor, Martine. "Buddhist Economics Reconsidered" [*BER*]. In Badiner, ed., *Dharma Gaia.*

——. "Even the Stones Smile: Selections from the Scriptures" [*ESS*]. In Batchelor and Brown, eds., *Buddhism and Ecology.*

——. "The Sands of the Ganges" [*SG*]. In Batchelor and Brown, eds., *Buddhism and Ecology.*

Batchelor, Martine, and Kerry Brown, eds. *Buddhism and Ecology* [*BE*]. New York: Cassell Publishers, 1992.

Batchelor, Stephen. "Buddhist Economics Reconsidered" [*BER*]. In Badiner, ed., *Dharma Gaia.*

Battersby, Christine. *The Phenomenal Woman: Feminist Metaphysics and the Patterns of Identity* [*PW*]. New York: Routledge, 1998.

Baudrillard, Jean. *America* [*A*]. Trans. Chris Turner. New York: Verso, 1988.

——. *Cool Memories* [*CM*]. Trans. Chris Turner. New York: Verso, 1990.

——. *Forget Foucault* [*FF*]. New York: Semiotext(e), 1987.

——. *Impossible Exchange* [*IE*]. Trans. Chris Turner. New York: Verso, 2001.
——. *The Mirror of Production* [*MP*]. Trans. Mark Poster. St. Louis: Telos Press, 1975.
——. "Perfect Crime" [*PC*]. In *Selected Writings.*
——. *Selected Writings* [*SW*]. Ed. and int. Mark Poster. Trans. Jacques Mourrain and others. Stanford, CA: Stanford University Press, 2001.
——. *Simulacra and Simulations* [*SS*]. Trans. Sheila Faria Glaser. Ann Arbor: University of Michigan Press, 1994.
——. *Simulations* [*S*]. Trans. Paul Foss, Paul Patton. and Philip Beitchman. Semiotexte.
——. *The Transparency of Evil: Essays on Extreme Phenomena* [*TE*]. Trans. James Benedict. New York: Verso, 1993.
——. *The Vital Illusion* [*VI*]. Ed. Julia Witwer. New York: Columbia University Press, 2000.
Beard, Henry. *Poetry for Cats: The Definitive Anthology of Distinguished Feline Verse* [*PC*]. New York: Villard Books, 1994.
Beauvoir, Simone de. *4e cahier* [*4c*]. Holographic manuscript. Paris: Bibliothèque Nationale, 1927.
——. *All Men are Mortal* [*AMM*]. Trans. Euan Cameron based on the original translation by Leonard M. Friedman. London: Virago, 1995. Translation of *Tous les hommes sont mortels.* Paris: Gallimard, 1946.
——. *All Said and Done* [*ASD*]. Trans. Patrick O'Brian. New York: Putnam, 1974. Translation of *Tout compte fait.* Paris: Gallimard, 1972.
——. *The Coming of Age* [*CA*]. Trans. Patrick O'Brian. New York: Putnam, 1972. Translation of *La Vieillesse.* Paris: Gallimard, 1970.
——. *Djamila Boupacha: The Story of the Torture of a Young Algerian Girl Which Shocked Liberal French Opinion* [*DB*]. With Gisèle Halimi. Trans. Peter Green. London: André Deutsch, 1962. Translation of *Djamila Boupacha.* Paris: Gallimard, 1962.
——. *The Ethics of Ambiguity* [*EA*]. Trans. Bernard Frechtman. New York: Citadel Press, 1991. Translation of *Pour un moral de l'ambiguité.* Paris: Gallimard, 1947.
——. *Memoirs of a Dutiful Daughter* [*MDD*]. Trans. James Kirkup. New York, Harper & Row, 1959. Translation of *Mémoires d'une jeune fille rangée.* Paris: Gallimard, 1958.
——. "Must We Burn Sade?" [*MWBS?*]. Trans. A. Michelson. In *The Marquis de Sade.* New York: Grove Press, 1966. Collected in *Privilèges.* Paris: Gallimard, 1955: 9–29. Translation of "Faut-il brûler Sade?" *Les Temps Modernes* (December 1971), vol. 7, no. 74: 1002–33.
——. *The Second Sex* [*SS*]. Trans. and edited H. M. Parshley. New York: Vintage Books 1989, 1952. Translation of *Le Deuxième sexe.* Paris: Gallimard, 1949.
——. *She Came to Stay* [*SCS*]. Trans. Yvonne Moyse and Roger Senhouse. Cleveland: World Publishing, 1945. Translation of *L'invitée.* Paris. Gallimard, 1943.

——. *When Things of the Spirit Come First: Five Early Tales* [*WTSCF*]. Trans. Patrick O'Brian. New York: Pantheon Books, 1982. Translation of *Quand prime le spirituel*. Paris: Gallimard, 1979.

Becker, Anne E. "Nurturing and Negligence: Working on Others' Bodies in Fiji" [*NN*]. In Csordas, *Embodiment and Experience*.

Becker, Lawrence C. "The Moral Basis of Property Rights" [*MBPR*]. In Pennock and Chapman, eds., *Nomos XXII*, 187–220.

Behe, Michael J. *Darwin's Black Box* [*DBB*]. New York: Touchstone Books, 1998.

Bellany, Ian. *The Environment in World Politics: Exploring the Limits* [*EWP*]. Brookfield, VT: Edward Elgar, 1997.

Bender, Barbara: *Landscapes: Politics and Perspectives* [*L*]. New York: Berg, 1993.

Benedict, Ruth. *The Chrysanthemum and the Sword: Patterns of Japanese Culture* [*CS*]. Boston: Houghton Mifflin, 1946. In Allen, ed., *Culture and Self*.

Benjamin, Walter. *Erfahrung und Armut* [*EA*]. Passages quoted in Derrida, "Letter to Peter Eisenman."

——. *Illuminations* [*I*]. Trans. Harry Zohn. New York: Harcourt Brace & World, 1968.

——. "On Language as Such and on the Language of Man" [*LSLM*]. In *Reflections*.

——. "On the Mimetic Faculty" [*OMF*]. In *Reflections*.

——. Reflections: Essays, Aphorisms, Autobiographical Writings [*R*]. Trans. Edmund Jephcott. New York: Schocken, 1978.

——. "The Work of Art in the Age of Its Technical Reproducibility" [*WAATR*]. Reprinted in part in Ross, ed., *Art and Its Significance*. Selections from "The Work of Art in the Age of Mechanical Reproduction." In *Illuminations*.

Bennett, Jane. *The Enchantment of Modern Life: Attachments, Crossings, and Ethics* [*EML*]. Princeton, NJ: Princeton University Press, 2001.

Bennett, Lerone, Jr. *The Challenge of Blackness* [*CB*]. Chicago: Johnson Publishing Co., 1972.

Benso, Sylvia. *The Face of Things: A Different Side of Ethics* [*FT*]. Albany: State University of New York Press, 2000.

Bergson, Henri. *Laughter* [*L*]. In Sypher. *Comedy*.

——. *Matter and Memory* [*MM*]. Trans. Nancy Margaret Paul and W. Scott Palmer. London: George Allen and Unwin, 1911.

Berleant, Arnold. "Aesthetic Perception" [*EA*]. In Nasar, *Environmental Aesthetics*.

Berman, Morris. *The Reenchantment of the World* [*RW*]. Ithaca, NY: Cornell University Press, 1981.

Bermùdez, José Luis. *The Paradox of Self-Consciousness* [*PS*]. Cambridge, MA: MIT Press, 1998.

Bermùdez, José Luis, Anthony Marcel, and Naomi Eilan, eds. *The Body and the Self* [*BS*]. Cambridge, MA: MIT, 1995.

Bernal, Martin. *Black Athena: The Afroasiatic Roots of Classical Civilization, Volume 1: The Fabrication of Ancient Greece 1785–1985* [*BA*]. New Brunswick: Rutgers University Press, 1987.

Bernasconi, Robert, and David Wood, eds. *The Provocation of Levinas: Rethinking the Other* [*PL*]. New York: Routledge, 1988.

Bernstein, J. M. Adorno: *Disenchantment and Ethics* [*A*]. New York: Cambridge University Press, 2001.

Berofsky, Bernard. *Liberation from Self: A Theory of Personal Autonomy* [*LS*]. New York: Cambridge University Press, 1995.

Berry, Wendell. *Home Economics* [*HE*]. San Francisco: North Point Press, 1987.

Betelheim, Bruno. *The Uses of Enchantment: The Meaning and Importance of Fairty Tales* [*UE*]. New York: Vintage, 1989.

Bhabha, Homi K. "Interrogating Identity: The Postcolonial Prerogative" [*II*]. In Goldberg, ed., *Anatomy of Racism.*

Bhargava, Rajeev. *Secularism and its Critics* [*SC*]. New Delhi: Oxford University Press, 1998.

Binswanger, Ludwig. "Dream and Existence" [*DE*]. In Hoeller, ed., *Dream and Existence.*

Birch, Charles. "The Postmodern Challenge to Biology" [*PCB*]. In Griffin, ed., *Reenchantment of Science.*

Birch, Thomas H. "The Incarceration of Wildness: Wilderness Areas as Prisons" [*IW*]. In Oelschlaeger, ed., *Postmodern Environmental Ethics.*

Blake, William. *The Book of Urizen* [*BU*]. Ed. and comm. Kay Parkhurst Easson and Roger R. Easson. New York: Random House, 1987.

——. *The Complete Poetry of William Blake*. In *The Complete Poetry of John Donne and the Complete Poetry of William Blake* [*JDWB*]. New York: Random House, 1941.

Blanchot, Maurice. *The Book to Come* [*BC*]. Trans. Charlotte Mandell. Stanford: Stanford University Press, 2003.

——. *The Infinite Conversation* [*IC*]. Trans. Susan Hanson. Minneapolis: University of Minnesota Press, 1993.

——. *The Space of Literature* [*SL*]. Trans. Ann Smock. Lincoln, Nebraska: University of Nebraska Press, 1982. Translation of *L'espace littéraire* [*el*]. Paris: Gallimard, 1955.

——. *The Step Not Beyond* [*SNB*]. Trans. and Int. Lycette Nelson. Albany: State University of New York Press, 1992. Translation of *Le Pas Au-Delà.*

——. "Two Versions of the Imaginary" [*TVI*]. In *Space of Literature.*

——. *The Writing of the Disaster* [*WD*]. Trans. Ann Smock. Lincoln: University of Nebraska Press, 1995.

Blumer, Herbert. "Fashion: From Class Differentiation to Collective Selection" [*F*]. In Roach-Higgins, Eicher, and Johnson, eds., *Dress and Identity.*

Bockover, Mary I. "Ethics, Relativism, and the Self" [*ERS*]. In Allen, ed., *Culture and Self.*

Bohm, David. "Postmodern Science and a Postmodern World" [*PSPW*]. In Griffin, ed., *Reenchantment of Science.*

Bonhoeffer, Dietrich. *Ethics* [*E*]. Trans. REginald Fuller, Frank Clark and others; additional material by John Bowden. New York: Touchstone, 1997.

——. *Letters and Papers from Prison: Enlarged Edition* [*LPP*]. Ed. Eberhard Bethge.

——. *Meditating on the Word* [*MW*]. Trans. David McI. Gracie. Cambridge, MA: Cowley Publications, 2000.

——. *Meditations on the Cross* [*MC*]. Trans. Douglas W. Stott. London: Westminster John Knox Press, 1998.

——. *Testament to Freedom: The Essential Writings of Dietrich Bonhoeffer* [*TF*]. Ed. Geffrey B Kelly and F. Burton Nelson. San Francisco: HarperCollins, 1995.

——. *Who is Christ for Us?* [*WCU*]. Trans. Craig Nessan and Renate Wind. Minneapolis, MN: Fortress Press, 2002.

Bookchin, Murray. *The Ecology of Freedom* [*EF*]. Palo Alto, CA: Cheshire Books, 1982.

——. *Post-Scarcity Anarchism* [*PSA*]. Berkeley: Ramparts Press, 1971.

——. *Re-enchanting Humanity: A Defense of the Human Spirit Against Antihumanism, Misanthropy, Mysticism, and Primitivism* [*RH*]. New York: Cassell, 1995.

——. *Remaking Society: Pathways to a Green Future* [*RS*]. Boston: South End Press, 1990.

——. "Social Ecology versus 'Deep Ecology': A Challenge to the Ecology Movement" [*SEDE*]. In *Green Perspectives, Newsletter of the Green Program Project* 4–5.

Bordo, Susan. "The Cartesian Masculinization of Thought and the Seventeenth-Century Flight from the Feminine" [*CMT*]. In Bar On, ed., *Modern Engendering.*

——. "Hunger as Ideology" [*HI*]. In Scapp and Seitz, eds., *Eating Culture.*

——. *Unbearable Weight: Feminism, Western Culture, and the Body* [*UW*]. Berkeley: University of California Press, 2004.

Borges, Jorge Luis. "The Analytical Language of John Wilkins" [*ALJW*]. In *Other Inquisitions, 1937–1952.*

——. *Collected Fictions* [*CF*]. Trans. Andrew Hurley. New York: Penguin, 1998.

——. *Ficciones* [*F*]. Trans. Emecé Editores. New York: Grove Press, 1962.

——. *Labyrinths: Selected Stories and Other Writings* [*L*]. Trans. Emecé Editores. New York: New Directions, 1962.

——. *Other Inquisitions, 1937–1952* [*OI*]. Trans. Ruth L. C. Simms. Austin, TX: University of Texas Press, 1964.

——. "Pierre Menard, Author of *Don Quixote*" [*PM*]. In *Ficciones.*

Bormann, F. Herbert, and Stephen R. Kellert, eds. *Ecology, Economics, Ethics: The Broken Circle* [*EEE*]. New Haven: Yale University Press, 1991.

Botkin, Daniel. *Discordant Harmonies: A New Ecology for the Twenty-first Century* [*DH*]. Oxford: Oxford University Press, 1990.

Bourgeois, Verne Warren. *Persons: What Philosophers Say about You* [*P*]. Waterloo, ON: Wilfred Laurier University Press, 1995.

Bourdieu, Pierre. *The Logic of Practice* [*LP*]. Trans. Richard Nice. Cambridge: Polity Press, 1990.

Bowden, Ross. "Sorcery, Illness and Social Control in Kwoma Society" [*SISC*]. In Stephen, ed., *Sorcerer and Witch.*

Brace, C. Loring, George R. Gamble, and James T. Bond, eds. *Race and Intelligence* [*RI*]. Washington: American Anthropological Assocation, 1971.

Brague, Rémi. *The Wisdom of the World: The Human Experience of the Universe in Western Thought* [*WW*]. Chicago: University of Chicago Press, 2003.

Braidotti, Rosi. *Nomadic Subjects: Embodiment and Sexual Difference in Contemporary Feminist Theory* [*NS*]. New York: Columbia University Press, 1994.

——. *Patterns of Dissonance: A Study of Women and Contemporary Philosophy* [*PD*]. Trans. Elizabeth Guild. New York: Routledge, 1991.

Braidotti, Rosi, et al. *Women, the Environment and Sustainable Development: Towards a Theoretical Synthesis* [*WESD*]. London: Zed Books with INSTRAW, 1994.

Brennan, Andrew. *Thinking About Nature: An Investigation of Nature, Value and Ecology* [*TN*]. Athens, GA: University of Georgia Press, 1988.

Brown, Jonathon D. *The Self* [*S*]. Boston: McGraw-Hill, 1998.

Brown, Norman O. *Love's Body* [*LB*]. New York: Vintage Books, 1966.

Brueggemann, Walter. *The Land: Place as Gift, Promise, and Challenge in Biblical Faith* [*L*]. Philadelphia: Fortress Press, 1977.

Bryant, Bunyon, ed. *Environmental Justice* [*EJ*]. Washington, DC: Island Press, 1995.

Buber, Martin. *I and Thou* [*IT*]. Trans. R. G. Smith. New York: Scribner's, 1927.

Buchler, Justus. *The Concept of Method* [*CM*]. New York: Columbia University Press, 1961.

——. *The Main of Light: On the Concept of Poetry* [*ML*]. New York: Oxford University Press, 1974.

——. *Metaphysics of Natural Complexes* [*MNC*]. New York: Columbia University Press, 1966.

——. *Nature and Judgment* [*NJ*]. New York: Columbia University Press, 1955.

——. *Toward a General Theory of Human Judgment* [*TGT*]. New York: Columbia University Press, 1951.

Buckner, S. Clark, and Matthew Statler, eds. *Styles of Piety: Practicing Philosophy after the Death of God* [*SP*]. New York: Fordham University Press, 2006.

Buddhadâsa, Bhikkhu. *Me and Mine: Selected Essays of Bhikkhu Buddhadâsa* [*MM*]. Ed. Swearer, Donald K. Albany: State University of New York Press, 1989.

Bullard, Robert D. "Anatomy of Environmental Racism and the Environmental Justice Movement" [*AEREJM*]. In Bullard, ed., *Confronting Environmental Racism.*

——. "Conclusion: Environmentalism with Justice" [*EJ*]. In Bullard, ed., *Confronting Environmental Racism.*

——., ed. *Confronting Environmental Racism: Voices from the Grassroots* [*CER*]. Boston: South End Press, 1993.

Bullough, Edward. "'Psychical Distance' as a Factor in Art and as an Aesthetic Principle" [*PD*]. Reprinted in Ross, ed., *Art and Its Significance.* Originally published in *British Journal of Psychology* (1912): 87–98.

Burke, Kenneth. *A Grammar of Motives* [*GM*]. New York: Prentice-Hall, 1945.

——. *A Rhetoric of Motives* [*RM*]. New York: Prentice-Hall, 1950.

Burnett, John. *Plenty and Want: A Social History of Diet in England from 1815 to the Present Day* [*PW*]. London: Methuen, 1983.

Burtt, Edwin A., ed. *The English Philosophers from Bacon to Mill* [*EPBM*]. New York: Modern Library, 1959.

Butler, Judith. *Bodies that Matter: On the Discursive Limits of "Sex"* [*BM*]. New York: Routledge, 1993.

——. *Excitable Speech: a Politics of the Performative* [*ES*]. New York: Routledge, 1997.

——. *Gender Trouble: Feminism and the Subversion of Identity* [*GT*]. New York: Routledge, 1999.

——. *The Judith Butler Reader* [*JBR*]. Edited by Sara Salih, with Judith Butler. Oxford: Blackwell Pub., 2004.

——. *Precarious Life: The Powers of Mourning and Violence* [*PL*]. New York: Verso, 2004.

——. *The Psychic Life of Power: Theories in Subjection* [*PLP*]. Stanford, CA: Stanford University Press, 1997.

Calasso, Roberto. *Literature and the Gods* [*LG*]. New York: Vintage, 2001.

Callicott, J. Baird. *In Defense of a Land Ethic* [*DL*]. Albany: State University of New York Press, 1989.

——. "Traditional American Indian and Western European Attitudes Toward Nature: An Overview" [*TAIWEA*]. In Oelschlaeger, ed., *Postmodern Environmental Ethics.*

——., ed. *Companion to* A Sand County Almanac*: Interpretive and Critical Essays* [*CSCA*]. Madison: University of Wisconsin Press, 1987.

Callicott, J. Baird, and Roger T. Ames, eds. *Nature in Asian Traditions of Thought: Essays in Environmental Philosophy* [*NATT*]. Albany: State University of New York Press, 1989.

Calvino, Italo. *All at One Point* [*AAOP*]. In *Cosmicomics.*

——. *The Castle of Crossed Destinies* [*CCD*]. Trans. William Weaver. New York: Harcourt, Brace & Co., 1969.

——. *Cosmicomics* [C]. Trans. William Weaver. New York: Harcourt, Inc. 1965.

——. *Six Memos for the Next Millenium* [SMNM]. New York: Vintage, 1988.

Candrakîrti. *The Entry into the Middle Way* [EMW]. In Huntington, Jr., *Emptiness of Emptiness.*

Capra, Fritjof, and Charlene Spretnak. *Green Politics: The Global Promise* [GP]. New York: Dutton, 1984.

Caputo, John D. *Against Ethics: Contributions to a Poetics of Obligation with Constant Reference to Deconstruction* [AE]. Bloomington: Indiana University Press, 1993.

Card, Claudia, ed. *Feminist Ethics* [FE]. Lawrence: University Press of Kansas, 1991.

Caro, Manuel J., and John W. Murphy. *The World of Quantum Culture* [WQC]. Westport, CN: Praeger, 2002.

Carrier, David. *The Aesthetics of Comics* [AC]. University Park, PA: The Pennsylvania University Press, 2000.

Carter, Alan. *The Philosophical Foundations of Property Rights* [PFPR]. New York: Harvester Wheatsheaf, 1989.

Cassam, Quassim. *Self and World* [SW]. New York: Oxford University Press, 1997.

Cavell, Stanley. *The Claim of Reason: Wittgenstein, Skepticism, Morality and Tragedy* [CR]. New York: Oxford University Press, 1979.

——. *Philosophy the Day after Tomorrow* [PDT]. Cambridge, MA: Belknap Press of Harvard University Press, 2005.

——. *The World Viewed: Reflections on the Ontology of Film* [WW]. Enlarged Edition. Cambridge, MA: Harvard University Press, 1979.

Céline, Louis-Ferdinand. *Journey to the End of the Night* [JEN]. Trans. John H. P. Marks. Boston: Little, Brown, 1934.

Certeau, Michel de. *The Certeau Reader* [CR]. Ed. Graham Ward. Oxford: Blackwell Publishers, 2000.

——. *Culture in the Plural* [CP]. Ed. Luce Giard. Trans. Tom Conley. Minneapolis: University of Minnesota Press, 1998.

——. *Heterologies: Discourse on the Other* [H]. Trans. Brian Massumi. Minneapolis: University of Minnesota Press, 1986.

——. *The Practice of Everyday Life* [PE]. Trans. Steven F. Rendall. Berkeley: University of California Press, 1984.

——. *The Practice of Everyday Life. Volume 2, Living and Cooking* [PE2]. Ed. Luce Giard. Trans. Timothy J. Tomasik. Minneapolis: University of Minnesota Press, 1998.

——. *The Writing of History* [WH]. Trans. Tom Conley. New York: Columbia University Press, 1988.

Chapman, John W. "Justice, Freedom, and Property" [JFP]. In Pennock and Chapman, eds., *Nomos XXII*, 289–324.

Chazan, Pauline. *The Moral Self* [MS]. New York: Routledge, 1998.

Cheal, David. *The Gift Economy* [GE]. New York: Routledge, 1988.

Cheney, Jim. "Eco-feminism and Deep Ecology" [EDE]. *Environmental Ethics* 9, no. 2 (Summer 1987): 115–45.

——. "Postmodern Environmental Ethics: Ethics as Bioregional Narrative" [*PMEE*]. In Oelschlaeger, ed., *Postmodern Environmental Ethics.*

Chief Seattle. *The Eyes of Chief Seattle* [*ECS*]. Exhibition Catalogue. Seattle: The Suquamish Museum, 1985.

Christ, Carol P. "Reverence for Life: The Need for a Sense of Finitude" [*RL*]. In Cooey, Farmer, and Ross, eds., *Embodied Love.*

——. "Spiritual Quest and Women's Experience" [*SQWE*]. In Christ and Plaskow, eds., *Womanspirit Rising.*

Christ, Carol P., and Judith Plaskow, eds. *Womanspirit Rising* [*WR*]. New York: Harper & Row, 1979.

Cixous, Hélène. "Birds, Women, and Writing" [*BWW*]. In *Three Steps.*

——. *The Book of Promethea = Le Livre de Promethea* [*BM*]. Lincoln: University of Nebraska Press, 1991.

——. *Firstdays of the Year* [*FY*]. Trans. Catherine A. F. MacGillivray. Minneapolis: University of Minnesota Press, 1998.

——. *Hélène Cixous Reader* [*HCR*]. Ed. Susan Sellers. New York: Routledge, 1994.

——. "Laugh of the Medusa" [*LM*]. In Marks and Courtivron, eds., *New French Feminisms.*

——. *Stigmata: Excaping Texts* [*S*]. New York: Routledge, 1998.

——. *The Third Body* [*TB*]. Trans. Keith Cohen. Evanston, IL: Northwestern University Press, 1999.

——. *Three Steps on the Ladder of Writing* [*TS*]. Wellek Library Lectures at the University of California, Irvine. Trans. Sarah Cornell and Susan Sellers. New York: Columbia University Press, 1993.

——. *Vivre l'orange = To Live the Orange* [*LO*]. Trans. Ann Liddell and Sarah Cornell. Paris: Éditions des Femmes, 1979.

Cixous, Hélène, and Catherine Clément. *The Newly Born Woman* [*NBW*]. Trans. Betsy Wing. Int. Sandra M. Gilbert. Minneapolis: University of Minnesota Press, 1975.

Cixous, Hélène, and Jacques Derrida. *Veils* [*V*]. Trans. Geoffrey Bennington. Stanford, CA: Stanford University Press, 2001.

Clark, Cedric X. "Some Implications of Nkrumah's Consciencism for Alternative Coordinates in NonEuropean Causality" [*SINC*]. In Ruch and Anyanwu, eds., *African Philosophy.*

Clark, Lorenne M. G. "Women and John Locke; or, Who Owns the Apples in the Garden of Eden?" *Canadian Journal of Philosophy* 7, no. 4 (December 1977): 699–724.

Clément, Catherine. "The Guilty Ones" [*GO*]. In Cixous and Clément, *Newly Born Woman.*

——. *Syncope: The Philosophy of Rapture* [*S*]. Trans. Sally O'Driscoll and Deirdre M. Mahoney. Minneapolis: University of Minnesota Press, 1994.

Clifford, James. "On Collecting Art and Culture" [*CAC*]. Reprinted in Ross, ed., *Art and Its Significance.* In Russell Ferguson et al. eds. *Out There: Marginalization and Contemporary Cultures.* New York: New

Museum of Contemporary Art and Cambridge: MIT Press, 1990, 141– 46, 151–65.
Cobb, John, Jr. "Christian Existence in a World of Limits" [*CEWL*]. In Oelschlaeger, ed., *Postmodern Environmental Ethics.*
——. "Ecology, Science, and Religion: Toward a Postmodern Worldview" [*ESR*]. In Griffin, ed., *Reenchantment of Science.*
Cobham, Rhonda, and Merle Collins, eds. *Watchers and Seekers: Creative Writing by Black Women in Britain* [*WS*]. London: Women's Press, 1987.
Codiga, Doug. "Zen Practice and a Sense of Place" [*ZPSP*]. In Badiner, ed., *Dharma Gaia.*
Cohen, Tom, ed. *Jacques Derrida and the Humanities: A Critical Reader* [*JDH*]. Cambridge: Cambridge University Press, 2001.
Cohn, Jan. *Romance and the Erotics of Property: Mass-Market Fiction for Women* [*REP*]. Durham: Duke University Press, 1988.
Cole, Eve Browning, and Susan Coultrap-McQuin, eds. *Explorations in Feminist Ethics: Theory and Practice* [*EFE*]. Bloomington: Indiana University Press, 1992.
Coleridge, Samuel Taylor. *Biographia Literaria* [*BL*]. Ed. J. Shawcross. London: Oxford University Press, 1949.
Collingwood, R. G. *The Philosophy of Enchantment: Studies in Folktale, Cultural Criticism, and Anthropology* [*PE*]. Ed. David Boucher, Wendy James, and Philip Smallwood. New York: Oxford University Press, 2005. Comstock, Gary. "Pigs and Piety: A Theocentric Perspective on Food Animals" [*PP*]. *Between the Species* 8, no. 3 (Summer 1992): 121–35.
Collingwood, R. G. *The Principles of Art* [*PA*]. Oxford: Oxford University Press, 1972.
Conley, Verena Andermatt. *Ecopolitics: The Environment in Poststructuralist Thought* [*E*]. New York: Routledge, 1997.
Connolly, *William E. Pluralism* [*P*]. Durham: Duke University Press, 2005
——. *Why I Am Not a Secularist* [*WNS*]. Minneapolis: University of Minnesota Press, 1999.
Cooey, Paula M. "The Word Become Flesh: Woman's Body, Language, and Value" [*WF*]. In Cooey, Farmer, and Ross, eds., *Embodied Love.*
Cooey, Paula M., Sharon A. Farmer, and Mary Ellen Ross, eds. *Embodied Love: Sensuality and Relationship as Feminist Values* [*EL*]. San Francisco: Harper & Row, 1987.
Cook, Francis H. "The Jewel Net of Indra" [*JNI*]. In Callicott and Ames, eds., *Nature in Asian Traditions of Thought.*
Cooper, David E., and Joy A. Palmer, eds. *The Environment in Question: Ethics and Global Issues* [*EQ*]. New York: Routledge, 1992.
Cornell, Drucilla. *Beyond Accommodation: Ethical Feminism, Deconstruction, and the Law* [*BA*]. New York: Routledge, 1991.
——. *The Imaginary Domain: Abortion, Pornography and Sexual Harassment* [*ID*]. New York: Routledge, 1995.

——. *The Philosophy of the Limit* [*PL*]. New York: Routledge, 1992.

Cornell, Drucilla, Michel Rosenfeld, and David Gray Carlson, eds. *Deconstruction and the Possibility of Justice* [*DPJ*]. New York: Routledge, Chapman and Hall, 1992.

Corrington, Robert S. *Nature's Self: Our Journey from Origin to Spirit* [*NS*]. Lanham, MD: Rowman & Littlefield, 1996.

Cose, Ellis. *A Nation of Strangers* [*NS*]. New York: William Morrow and Co., 1992.

Court, Elsbeth. "The Self in African Children's Drawings of Persons" [*SACD*]. In Maw and Picton, eds., *Concepts of the Body/Self in Africa.*

Cox, Harvey. *Many Mansions: A Christian's Encounter with Other Faiths* [*MM*]. New York: Beacon Press, 1992.

——. *The Secular City: Secularization and Urbanization in Theological Perspective* [*SC*]. New York: Macmillan, 1965.

——. *The Seduction of the Spirit: The Use and Misuse of People's Religion* [*SS*]. New York: Simon & Schuster, 1973.

——. *The Feast of Fools: A Theological Essay on Festivity and Fantasy* [*FF*]. Cambridge, MA: Harvard University Press, 1969.

——. *Transformations: Recollective Imagination and Sexual Difference* [*T*]. New York: Routledge, 1993. Cranny-Francis, Anne. *The Body in the Text* [*BT*]. Melbourne: Melbourne University Press, 1995.

Crawford, M. D. C. "The Eyed Needle" [*EN*]. In Roach-Higgins, Eicher, and Johnson, eds., *Dress and Identity.*

Croll, Elisabeth. "The Exchange of Women and Property: Marriage in Post-Revolutionary China" [*EWP*]. In Hirschon, ed., *Women and Property—Women as Property.*

Crosby, John F. *The Selfhood of the Human Person* [*SHP*]. Washington, DC: Catholic University of America Press, 1996.

Csordas, Thomas J. *Embodiment and Experience: The Existential Ground of Culture and Self* [*EE*]. Cambridge: Cambridge University Press, 1994.

Curley, E. M. *Spinoza's Metaphysics: An Essay in Interpretation* [*SM*]. Cambridge, MA: Harvard University Press, 1969.

Curtin, Deane. "Toward an Ecological Ethic of Care" [*TEEC*]. In Warren, ed., *Hypatia*, 60–4.

Curtiss, Susan. *Genie: A Psycholinguistic Study of a Modern-Day "Wild Child"* [*G*] New York: Academic Press, 1977.

Dalby, Liza. "Geisha and Kimono" [*GK*]. In Roach-Higgins, Eicher, and Johnson, eds., *Dress and Identity.*

Daly, M. Catherine, Joanne B. Eicher, Tonye V. Erekosima. "Male and Female Artistry in Kalabari Dress" [*MFA*]. In Roach-Higgins, Eicher, and Johnson, eds., *Dress and Identity.*

Daly, Mary. "After the Death of God the Father: Women's Liberation and the Transformation of Christian Consciousness" [*ADGF*]. In Christ and Plaskow, eds., *Womanspirit Rising.*

——. *Gyn/Ecology: The Metaethics of Radical Feminism* [*G/E*]. Boston: Beacon Press, 1990.

Daniel, E. Valentine. "The Individual in Terror" [*IT*]. In Csordas, *Embodiment and Experience.*
Danto, Arthur. *After the End of Art: Contemporary Art and the Pale of History* [*AEA*]. Princeton: Princeton University Press, 1997.
——. "Approaching the End of Art" [*AEA*]. In *State of the Art.*
——. "The Artworld," *The Journal of Philosophy* 61 (1964): 571–84.
——. *Beyond the Brillo Box: The Visual Arts in Post-Historical Perspective* [*BBB*]. New York: Farrar, Straus, Giroux, 1992.
——. *Encounters & Reflections; Art in the Historical Present* [*ER*]. New York: Farrar Straus Giroux, 1990.
——. *The Philosophical Disenfranchisement of Art* [*PDA*]. New York: Columbia University Press, 1986.
——. *The State of the Art* [*SA*]. New York: Prentice Hall Press, 1987.
——. *The Transfiguration of the Commonplace: A Philosophy of Art* [*TC*]. Cambridge: Harvard University Press, 1981.
Darwin, Charles. *On the Origin of Species by Means of Natural Selection, or the Preservation of Favoured Races in the Struggle for Life* [*OOS*]. Cambridge, MA: Harvard University Press, 1964. Facsimile of first edition, 1859.
——. *The Descent of Man, and Selection in Relation to Sex* [*DM*]. Princeton: Princeton University Press, 1981.
Davies, Paul. *Cosmic Jackpot: Why Our Universe is Just Right for Life* [*CJ*]. Boston: Houghton Mifflin Co., 2007.
Dawkins, Richard. *The Fifth Miracle: The Search for the Origin and Meaning of Life* [*FM*]. New York: Simon and Schuster, 1999.
——. *The Mind of God: The Scientific Basis for a Rational World* [*MG*]. New York: Simon and Schuster, 1993.
——. *A Devil's Chaplain: Reflections on Hope, Lies, Science and Love* [*DC*]. Boston: Houghton, Mifflin, 2003.
——. *The Blind Watchmaker* [*BW*]. New York: W. W. Norton, 1986.
——. *The God Delusion* [*GD*]. New York: Mariner Books, 2006. Dawkins, Richard. *The Selfish Gene* [*SG*]. Oxford: Oxford University Press, 1976.
——. *The Greatest Show on Earth: The Evidence for Evolution* [*GSE*]. New York: Free Press, 2009.
——. *Unweaving the Rainbow: Science, Delusion and the Appetite for Wonder* [*KUR*]. New York: Mariner Books, 2000.
Debord, Guy. *The Society of the Spectacle* [*SS*]. New York: Zone Books, 1995.
——. *The Society of the Spectacle Revisited* [*SSR*].
de Silva, Lily. "The Hills Wherein My Soul Delights: Exploring the Stories and Teachings" [*HWSD*]. In Batchelor and Brown, eds., *Buddhism and Ecology.*
de Silva, Lynn A. *The Problem of the Self in Buddhism and Christianity* [*PSBC*]. New York: Harper & Row, 1979.
de Silva, Padmasiri. *Environmental Philsophy and Ethics in Buddhism* [*EPEB*]. New York: St. Martin's Press, 1998.

de Waal, Frans. *Good Natured: The Origins of Right and Wrong in Humans and Other Animals* [*GN*]. Cambridge: Harvard University Press, 1996.

Dean, Carolyn J. *The Self and its Pleasures: Bataille, Lacan, and the History of the Decentered Subject* [*SP*]. Ithaca, NY: Cornell University Press, 1992.

Delacampagne, Christian. "Racism and the West: From Praxis to Logos" [*RW*]. In Goldberg, ed., *Anatomy of Racism*.

Deleuze, Gilles. *Difference and Repetition* [*DR*]. Trans. Paul Patton. New York: Columbia University Press, 1994. Translation of *Différence et répétition*. Paris: P.U.F., 1968.

——. *The Logic of Sense* [*LS*]. Trans. Mark Lester with Charles Stivale. New York: Columbia University Press, 1990. Translation of *Logique du sens*. Paris: Editions de Minuit, 1969.

Deleuze, Gilles, and Félix Guattari. *Anti-Oedipus: Capitalism and Schizophrenia* [*A-O*]. Trans. Robert Hurley, Mark Seem, and Helen R. Lane. Minneapolis: University of Minnesota Press, 1983.

——. *Expressionism in Philosophy: Spinoza* [*EPS*]. Trans. Martin Joughin. New York: Zone, 1992.

——. *A Thousand Plateaus: Capitalism and Schizophrenia* [*TP*]. Trans. Brian Massumi. Minneapolis: University of Minnesota Press, 1987.

——. *What is Philosophy?* [*WP*]. Trans. Hugh Tomlinson and Graham Burchell. New York: Columbia University Press, 1994.

Deloria, Vine, Jr. *God is Red* [*GR*]. New York: Dell, 1973.

Dennett, *Daniel. Breaking the Spell: Religion as a Natural Phenomenon* [*BS*]. New York: Penguin, 2007.

——. *Darwin's Dangerous Idea* [*DDI*]. New York: Simon and Schuster, 1995.

Depillars, Murry Norman. "Multiculturalism in Visual Arts Education: Are America's Educational Institutions Ready for Multiculturalism?" [*MVAE*]. In Young, ed., *Art, Culture, and Ethnicity*.

Derrida, Jacques. *Adieu to Emmanuel Levinas* [*A*]. Trans. Pascale-Anne Brault and Michael B. Naas. Stanford, CA: Stanford University Press, 1999.

——. *Archive Fever: A Freudian Impression* [*AF*]. Trans. Eric Prenowitz. Chicago: University of Chicago Press, 1996.

——. "Cogito and the History of Madness" [*CHM*]. In *Writing and Difference*.

——. *Circumfession* [*C*]. In *Jacques Derrida*.

——. *Dissemination* [*D*]. Trans. and int. Barbara Johnson. Chicago: University of Chicago Press, 1981.

——. "'Eating Well,' or the Calculation of the Subject" [*EW*]. Trans. Peter Connor and Avital Ronell. In *Points*.

——. "Economimesis" [*E*]. *Diacritics* 11, no. 2 (June 1981): 3–25.

——. "Force of Law: The 'Mystical Foundation of Authority'" [*FL*]. In Cornell, Rosenfeld, and Carlson, eds., *Deconstruction and the Possibility of Justice*. Reprinted from *Cardozo Law Review* 11, nos. 5–6 (July/August 1991): 919–1045.

——. "Fors" [*F*]. Preface to Nicolas Abraham and Maria Torok. *The Wolf Man's Magic Word.* Trans. Barbara Johnson. Minneapolis: University of Minnesota Press, 1986.

——. "From Restricted to General Economy: A Hegelianism without Reserve" [*FRGE*]. In *Writing and Difference.*

——. "The Future of the Profession or the University Without Condition (Thanks to the 'Humanities,' What *Could Take Place* Tomorrow)" [*FPUC*]. In Cohen, ed., *Jacques Derrida and the Humanities* [*JDH*].

——. *Geneses, Genealogies, Genres, & Genius: The Secrets of the Archive* [*GGGG*]. Trans. Beverley Bie Brahic. New York: Columbia University Press, 2006.

——. "Geschlecht: Sexual Difference, Ontological Difference" [*G1*]. *Research in Phenomenology* 13 (1983): 65–83.

——. "*Geschlecht* II: Heidegger's Hand" [*G2*]. Trans. John P. Leavey, Jr. In Sallis, ed., *Deconstruction in Philosophy: The Texts of Jacques Derrida.*

——. *The Gift of Death* [*GD*]. Trans. David Wills. Chicago: University of Chicago Press, 1994.

——. *Given Time* [*GT*]. Trans. Peggy Kamuf. Chicago: University of Chicago Press, 1992.

——. "Heidegger's Ear: Philopolemology (*Geschlecht* IV)" [*G4*]. In Sallis, ed., *Reading Heidegger.* Bloomington: Indiana University Press, 1993.

——. *Jacques Derrida* [*JD*]. *Derridabase* [*D*] by Geoffrey Bennington and *Circumfession.* Trans. Geoffrey Bennington. Chicago: University of Chicago Press, 1993.

——. "Letter to Peter Eisenman" [*LPE*]. In *Assemblage* 12: 7–13.Reprinted in Ross, ed., *Art and Its Significance.*

——. *Margins of Philosophy* [*MP*]. Trans. Alan Bass. Chicago: University of Chicago Press, 1982.

——. *Negotiations: Interventions and Interviews* [*N*]. Stanford, CA: Stanford University Press, 2002.

——. *Of Grammatology* [*OG*]. Trans. Gayatri Chakravorty Spivak. Baltimore: The Johns Hopkins Press, 1974.

——. *Of Hospitality* [*H*]. Trans. Rachel Bowlby. Stanford, CA: Stanford University Press, 2000. Translation of *De l'hospitalitê: Anne Dufourmantelle invite Jacquest Derrida à réponde.* Paris: Calmann-Lévy, 1997.

——. *Of Spirit: Heidegger and the Question* [*OS*]. Trans. Geoffrey Bennington and Rachel Bowlby. Chicago: University of Chicago Press, 1989.

——. *The Other Heading: Reflections on Today's Europe* [*OH*]. Int. Michael B. Naas. Trans. Pascale-Anne Brault and Michael B. Naas. Bloomington: Indiana University Press, 1992.

——. "Parergon" [*P*]. In *Truth in Painting.* Reprinted in part in Ross, ed., *Art and Its Significance.*

——. "Passe-Partout" [*P-P*]. Intro. to *Truth in Painting.* Reprinted in Ross, ed., *Art and Its Significance.*

——. "Plato's Pharmacy" [*PP*]. In *Dissemination.*

——. *Points . . . : Interviews, 1974–94* [*P . . .*]. Trans. Peggy Kamuf and others. Stanford, CA: Stanford University Press, 1995.

——. *The Politics of Friendship* [*PF*]. Trans. George Collins. London: Verso, 1997.
——. "The Politics of Friendship" ["*PF*"]. *The Journal of Philosophy* 85 (November 1988): 632–44.
——. "Restitutions" [*R*]. In *Truth in Painting*. Reprinted in part in Ross, ed., *Art and Its Significance.*
——. *Specters of Marx: The State of the Debt, The Work of Mourning, and the New International* [*SM*]. Trans. Peggy Kamuf. Int. Bernd Magnus and Stephen Cullenberg. New York: Routledge, 1994.
——. *The Truth in Painting* [*TP*]. Trans. G. Bennington and I. McLeod. Chicago: University of Chicago Press, 1987.
——. "Tympan" [*T*]. In *Margins of Philosophy.*
——. "Violence and Metaphysics: An Essay on the Thought of Emmanuel Levinas" [*VM*]. In *Writing and Difference.*
——. "White Mythology: Metaphor in the Text of Philosophy" [*WM*]. In *Margins of Philosophy.*
——. *The Work of Mourning* [*WM*]. Trans. Pascale-Anne Brault and Michael B. Naas. Chicago: University of Chicago Press, 2001.
——. *Writing and Difference* [*WD*]. Trans. Alan Bass. Chicago: University of Chicago Press, 1978.
Descartes, René. *Description of the Human Body* [*DHB*]. In *Philosophical Writings of Descartes,* vol. 1.
——. *Discourse on the Method of Rightly Conducting the Reason and Seeking Truth in the Sciences* [*DM*]. In *Philosophical Writings of Descartes,* vol. 1.
——. *Early Writings* [*EW*]. In *Philosophical Writings of Descartes,* vol. 1.
——. *Meditations* [*M*]. In *Philosophical Writings of Descartes,* vol. 2.
——. *Objections and Replies* [*OR*]. In *Philosophical Writings of Descartes,* vol. 2.
——. *Optics* [*O*]. In *Philosophical Writings of Descartes,* vol. 1.
——. *The Passions of the Soul* [*PS*]. In *Philosophical Writings of Descartes,* vol. 1.
——. *The Philosophical Writings of Descartes* [*PWD*]. Trans. John Cottingham, Robert Stoothoff, and Dugald Murdoch. 2 vols. Cambridge: Cambridge University Press, 1985.
——. *Principles of Philosophy* [*PP*]. In *Philosophical Writings of Descartes,* vol. 1.
——. *Rules for the Direction of the Mind* [*RDM*]. In *Philosophical Writings of Descartes,* vol. 1.
——. *Treatise on Man* [*TM*]. In *Philosophical Writings of Descartes,* vol. 1.
——. *The World* [*W*]. In *Philosophical Writings of Descartes,* vol. 1.
Devall, Bill. *Simple in Means, Rich in Ends: Practicing Deep Ecology* [*SMRE*]. Salt Lake City: Peregrine Smith, 1990.
Devall, Bill, and George Sessions. *Deep Ecology: Living as if Nature Mattered* [*DE*]. Salt Lake City: Peregrene Smith, 1985.
Devi, Mahasweta, *Imaginary Maps: Three Stories* [*IM*]. Trans. Gayatri Chakravorty Spivak. New York: Routledge, 1995.
Devisch, René. "The Human Body as a Vehicle for Emotions among the Yaka of Zaire" [*HBVE*]. In Jackson and Karp, eds. *Personhood and Agency: The Experiences of Self and Other in African Cultures.*

Dewey, John. *Art and Experience* [*AE*]. New York: Putnam, 1934. Reprinted in part in Ross, ed., *Art and Its Significance*.

———. "Body and Mind" [*BM*]. In *Philosophy and Civilization*.

———. "Context and Thought" [*CT*]. In *Experience, Nature, and Freedom*.

———. *Experience and Nature* [*EN*]. 2nd ed., New York: Dover, 1958.

———. *Experience, Nature, and Freedom* [*ENF*]. Ed. and int. Richard J. Bernstein. Indianapolis: Library of Liberal Arts, 1960.

———. *Human Nature and Conduct* [*HNC*]. New York: Holt, 1922.

———. *Logic: The Theory of Inquiry* [*L*]. New York: Henry Holt & Co., 1938.

———. "Nature in Experience" [*NE*]. In *Experience, Nature, and Freedom*.

———. "The Need for a Recovery of Philosophy" [*NRP*]. In *Experience, Nature, and Freedom*.

———. *Philosophy and Civilization* [*PC*]. New York: Minton, Balch, 1931.

———. *Quest for Certainty* [*QC*]. New York: Minton, Balch, 1929.

———. *Theory of Valuation* [*TV*]. Chicago: University of Chicago Press, 1939.

Dews, Peter. *The Limits of Disenchantment: Essays on Contemporary European Philosophy* [*LD*]. New York: Verso, 1995.

Diamond, Irene. "Babies, Heroic Experts, and a Poisoned Earth" [*BHEPE*]. In Diamond and Orenstein, eds., *Reweaving the World*.

Diamond, Irene, and Gloria Feman Orenstein, eds. *Reweaving the World: The Emergence of Ecofeminism* [*RW*]. San Francisco: Sierra Club Books, 1990.

Dimen, Muriel. "Power, Sexuality, and Intimacy" [*PSI*]. In Jaggar and Bordo, eds., *Gender/Body/Knowledge*.

Dion, Mark, and Alexis Rockman, eds. *Concrete Jungle: A Pop Media Investigation of Death and Survival in Urban Ecosystems* [*CJ*]. Juno Books, 1996.

Dixon, Vernon J. "World Views and Research Methodology" [*WVRM*]. In King, Dixon, and Nobles, eds., *African Philosophy*.

Dombrowski, Daniel A. *Babies and Beasts: The Argument from Marginal Cases [BB]*. Urbana: University of Illinois Press, 1997.

———. *Hartshorne and the Metaphysics of Animal Rights* [*HMAR*]. Albany: State University of New York Press, 1988.

———. *The Philosophy of Vegetarianism* [*PV*]. Amherst: University of Massachusetts Press, 1984.

Dorter, Kenneth: *Plato's* Phaedo*: An Interpretation* [*PP*]. Toronto: University of Toronto Press, 1982.

Dostoevsky, Fyodor. *The Brothers Karamazov* [*BK*]. Trans. Constance Garnett. New York: Modern Library, 1950.

Douglas, Mary. *Purity and Danger: An Analysis of Concepts of Pollution and Taboo* [*PD*]. New York: Praeger, 1966.

Douglas, Mary, and Baron Isherwood. *The World of Goods: Toward an Anthropology of Consumption* [*WG*]. New York: W. W. Norton, 1979.

Drakulić, Slavenka. "The War on People—and on the Truth—in Croatia" [*WPC*]. *The Chronicle of Higher Education* (June 11, 2004).

Dryzek, John S. "Green Reason: Communicative Ethics for the Biosphere" [*GR*]. In Oelschlaeger, ed., *Postmodern Environmental Ethics*.

——. *Rational Ecology: Environment and Political Economy* [*RE*]. New York: Blackwell, 1987.

duBois, Page. *Sowing the Body: Psychoanalysis and Ancient Representations of Women* [*SB*]. Chicago: University of Chicago Press, 1988.

——. *Torture and Truth* [*TT*]. New York: Routledge, 1991.

Du Bois, W. E. B. *A W. E. B. Du Bois Reader* [*WEBDR*]. Ed. Andrew G. Paschal. New York: Macmillan, 1971.

——. "The Concept of Race" [*CR*]. In Hord and Lee, eds., *I Am Because We Are.*

——. "The Conservation of Races" [*CR*]. In *Du Bois Reader.*

Dubuisson, Daniel. *The Western Construction of Religion: Myths, Knowledge, and Ideology* [*WCR*]. Trans. William Sayers. Baltimore: The Johns Hopkins Press, 2003.

Duerr, Hans Peter. *Dreamtime: Concerning the Boundary Between Wilderness and Civilization* [*D*]. Trans. Felicitas Goodman. Oxford: Blackwell, 1985.

Dupré, John. *Human Nature and the Limits of Science* [*HNLS*]. Oxford: Oxford University Press, 2001.

——. *The Disorder of Things: The Metaphysical Foundations of the Disunity of Science* [*DT*]. Cambridge, MA: Harvard University Press, 1993.

Dworkin, Andrea. *Intercourse* [*I*]. New York: Free Press, 1987.

——. *Pornography: Men Possessing Women* [*P*]. New York: G. P. Putnam's Sons, 1981.

Dussel, Enrique. *Philosophy of Liberation* [*PL*]. Trans. Aquilina Martinez and Christine Morkovsky. Maryknoll, NY: Orbis Books, 1985.

——. "Principles, Mediations, and the 'Good' as Synthesis (from 'Discourse Ethics' to 'Ethics of Liberation')" [*PMG*]. Trans. Eduardo Mendieta. *Philosophy Today* (Supplement 1997): 55–66.

——. "'Sensibility' and 'Otherness' in Emmanuel Lévinas" [*SOEL*]. Trans. John Browning with Joyce Bellows. *Philosophy Today* (Summer 1999): 126–34.

Dworkin, Ronald. "Feminists and Abortion" [*FA*]. *New York Review of Books* 40, no. 11 (June 10, 1993): 27–29.

——. *Law's Empire* [*LE*]. Cambridge: Harvard University Press, 1986.

——. Review of MacKinnon, *Only Words* [*OW*]. *The New York Review of Books* 40, no. 17 (October 21, 1993): 36–42.

Eagleton, Terry. *The Ideology of the Aesthetic* [*IA*]. Malden, MA: Blackwell Publishers, 2001.

Eberhardt, Jennifer L., and Susan T. Fiske, eds. *Confronting Racism: The Problem and the Response* [*CF*]. Thousand Oaks, Calif.: Sage Publications, 1998.

Ebrey, Patricia. "Women, Marriage, and the Family in Chinese History" [*WMFCH*]. In *Heritage of China.* Ed. Paul Ropp. Berkeley: University of California Press, 1990.

Ecker, Gisela, ed. *Feminist Aesthetics* [*FA*]. Trans. Harriet Anderson. Boston: Beacon Press, 1985.

Eckersley, Robyn. *Environmentalism and Political Theory: Toward an Ecocentric Approach* [*EPT*]. Albany: State University of New York Press, 1992.

Ehman, Robert R. *The Authentic Self* [*AS*]. Buffalo, NY: Prometheus Books, 1994.

Ehrenfeld, David. *The Arrogance of Humanism* [*AH*]. New York: Oxford University Press, 1978.

——. "The Management of Diversity: A Conservation Paradox" [*MD*]. In Bormann and Kellert, eds., *Ecology, Economics, Ethics.*

Eicher, Joanne B. "Cosmopolitan and International Dress" [*CID*]. In Roach-Higgins, Eicher, and Johnson, eds., *Dress and Identity.*

Eiseley, Loren C. *Darwin's Century: Evolution and the Men Who Discovered It* [*DC*]. New York: Doubleday Anchor, 1961.

——. *The Immense Journey* [*IJ*]. New York: Time Life Books, 1981.

——. *The Unexpected Universe* [*UU*]. New York: Mariner Books, 1972.

Eliade, Mircea. *Shamanism: Archaic Techniques of Ecstacy* [*S*]. Princeton: Princeton University Press, 1972.

El Sadaawi, Nawal. *The Hidden Face of Eve: Women in the Arab World* [*HFE*]. Trans. Sherif Hetata. Boston: Beacon Press, 1980.

Engels, Friedrich. *The Origin of the Family, Private Property and the State* [*OFPPS*]. In Marx & Engels, *Selected Writings.*

Epstein, Richard. *Takings: Private Property and the Power of Eminent Domain* [*T*]. Cambridge: Harvard University Press, 1985.

Erikson, Erik H. *Identity and the Life Cycle* [*ILC*]. New York: International Universities Press, 1959 (*Psychological Issues* 1, no. 1).

——. *Insight and Responsibility* [*IR*]. New York: Norton, 1964.

——. *The Life Cycle Completed* [LCC]. Extended version. New York: Norton, 1997.

Erodes, Richard. *Lame Deer: Seeker of Visions* [*LD*]. New York: Simon & Schuster, 1976.

Euripides, *Hecuba* [*H*]. Trans. E. P. Coleridge. In Oates and O'Neill, eds., *Complete Greek Drama.*

Fanon, Frantz. *Black Skin, White Masks* [*BSWM*]. Trans. Charles Lam Markmann. New York: Grove Press, 1967.

——. *Wretched of the Earth* [*WE*]. Trans. Constance Farrington. Pref. Jean-Paul Sartre. New York: Grove Press, 1965.

Felski, Rita. *Beyond Feminist Aesthetics: Feminist Literature and Social Change* [*BFA*]. Cambridge, MA: Harvard University Press Press, 1989.

——. Felski, Rita, *Doing Time: Feminist Theory and Postmodern Culture [DT*]. New York: New York University Press, 1956.

——. Why Feminism Doesn't Need an Aesthetic (and Why it Can't Ignore Aesthetics). In *Doing Time.*

Feng, Yu-lan. *A History of Chinese Philosophy* [*HCP*]. Trans. Derk Bodde. Princeton: University of Princeton Press, 1952–53.

Fernea, Elizabeth W., and Robert A. Fernea. "Symbolizing Roles: Behind the Veil" [*SR*]. In Roach-Higgins, Eicher, and Johnson, eds., *Dress and Identity.*

Ferré, Frederick. "Religious World Modeling and Postmodern Science" [*RWMPS*]. In Griffin, ed., *Reenchantment of Science.*

Ferry, Luc. *The New Ecological Order* [*NEO*]. Trans. Carol Volk. Chicago: University of Chicago Press, 1995.

Feyerabend, Paul. *Against Method: Outline of an Anarchistic Theory of Knowledge* [*AM*]. Atlantic Highlands, NJ: Humanities Press, 1975.

Finley, Karen. *Quotes from a Hysterical Female* [*QHF*]. In *Shock Treatment.*

——. *Shock Treatment* [*ST*]. San Francisco: City Lights, 1990.

Fortes, Meyer. "Strangers" [*S*]. In Fortes and Patterson, *Studies in African Social Anthropology.*

Fortes, Meyer, and Patterson, Sheila. *Studies in African Social Anthropology* [*SASA*]. New York: Academic Press, 1975.

Foster, Patricia, ed. *Minding the Body: Women Writers on Body and Soul* [*MB*]. New York: Doubleday, 1994.

Foucault, Michel. *Archaeology of Knowledge* [*AK*]. Trans. A. M. Sheridan-Smith. New York: Pantheon, 1981.

——. *Religion and Culture* [*RC*]. Ed. Jeremy R. Carrette. New York: Routledge, 1999.

——. "The Birth of Biopolitics" [*BB*]. In *Ethics, Subjectivity, and Truth.*

——. *The Birth of the Clinic: An Archaeology of Medical Perception* (1963). Translated by A. M. Sheridan-Smith. New York: Vintage, 1975.

——. *The Care of the Self* [*CS*]. Trans. Robert Hurley. New York: Pantheon, 1986.

——. *Discipline and Punish: The Birth of the Prison* [*DP*]. Trans. Alan Sheridan. New York: Vintage, 1979.

——. "Discourse on Language" [*DL*]. In *Archaeology of Knowledge.*

——. "Dream, Imagination, and Existence" [*DIE*]. In Hoeller, ed., *Dream and Existence.*

——. *The Essential Foucault* [*EF*]. Ed. Paul Rabinow and Nikolas Rose. New York: New Press, 2003.

——. "The Ethics of the Concern of the Self as a Practice of Freedom" [*ECSPF*]. In *Ethics, Subjectivity and Truth.*

——. *Ethics, Subjectivity and Truth* [*EST*]. Ed. Paul Rabinow. Trans. Robert Hurley and others. New York: New Press, 1997.

——. *Folie et déraison: Histoire de la folie à la l'âge classique* [*FD*]. Paris: Plon, 1961.

——. "The Hermeneutic of the Subject" [*"HS"*]. In *Ethics, Subjectivity and Truth.*

——. *History of Sexuality, Vol. 1* [*HS*]. Trans. R. Hurley. New York: Vintage, 1980.

——. *Language, Counter-Memory, Practice* [*LCP*]. Trans. Donald F. Bouchard and Sherry Simon. Ed. and int. Donald F. Bouchard. Ithaca, NY: Cornell University Press, 1977.

——. *Madness and Civilization: A History of Insanity in the Age of Reason* [*MC*]. Trans. Richard Howard. New York: Random House, 1965. Translation and abridgment of *Folie et déraison.*

——. "Michel Foucault: Interview by Stephen Riggins" [*MF*]. In *Ethics, Subjectivity and Truth.*

——. "Nietzsche, Genealogy, History" [*NGH*]. In *Language, Counter-Memory, Practice.*

——. "On Popular Justice: A Discussion with Maoists" [*OPJ*]. In *Power/Knowledge.*

——. "On the Genealogy of Ethics: An Overview of Work in Progress" [*OGE*]. In *Ethics, Subjectivity and Truth.*

——. *The Order of Things: An Archaeology of the Human Sciences* [*OT*]. New York: Vintage, 1973.

——. "The Political Technology of Individuals" [*PTI*]. In *Ethics, Subjectivity and Truth.*

——. *Power/Knowledge* [*P/K*]. Ed. and trans. C. Gordon. New York: Pantheon, 1980.

——. "A Preface to Transgression" [*PT*]. In *Language, Counter-Memory, Practice.*

——. "Questions on Geography" [*QG*]. In *Power/Knowledge.*

——. *Remarks on Marx* [*RM*]. Trans. R. James Goldstein and James Cascaito. New York: Semiotext(e), 1961.

——. "Theatrum Philosophicum" [*TP*]. In *Language, Counter-Memory, Practice.*

——. *Technologies of the Self: A Seminar with Michel Foucault* [*TS*]. Ed. Luther H. Martin, Huck Gutman, Patrick H. Hutton. Amherst: University of Massachusetts Press, 1988.

——. "Technologies of the Self" [*"TS"*]. In *Ethics, Subjectivity and Truth.*

——. "Truth and Power" [*TrP*]. In *Power/Knowledge.*

——. "Two Lectures" [*2L*]. In *Power/Knowledge.*

——. *The Use of Pleasure: The History of Sexuality, Vol. 2* [*UP*]. Trans. Robert Hurley. New York: Pantheon, 1985.

——. "What is an Author?" [*WA?*]. In *Language, Counter-Memory, Practice.*

——. "What is Enlightenment?" [*WE?*]. In *Ethics, Subjectivity and Truth.*

Frederickson, Owen P. *The Psychology of Ownership* [*PO*]. Washington, DC: The Catholic University of America Press, 1954.

French, Lindsay. "The Political Economy of Injury and Compassion: Amputees on the Thai-Cambodian Border" [*PEIC*]. In Csordas, *Embodiment and Experience.*

Freud, Sigmund. *The Basic Writings of Sigmund Freud* [*BW*]. Trans. A. A. Brill. New York: Modern Library, 1995.

——. *Collected Papers* [*CP*]. New York: Basic Books, 1959.

——. *The Ego and the Id* [*EI*]. Trans. Joan Riviere. Rev. and ed., by James Strachey. New York: W. W. Norton & Co., 1960.

——. "Femininity" [*F*]. In *New Introductory Lectures on Psychoanalysis.*

——. *A General Introduction to Psychoanalysis* [*GIP*]. Trans. Joan Riviere. Garden City, New York: Doubleday, 1953.

——. *The Interpretation of Dreams* [*ID*]. In *Basic Writings.*

——. "Mourning and Melancholia" [*MM*]. In *Collected Works,* Vol. 4: 152–71.

——. "A Mythological Parallel to a Visual Obsession" [*MPVO*]. Trans. C. M. J. Hubbock. In *Creativity and the Unconscious*. First published in *Zeitschrift*, Bd. IV, 1916.

——. *On Creativity and the Unconscious: Papers on the Psychology of Art, Literature, Love, Religion* [*CU*]. Ed. Benjamin Nelson. New York: Harper & Row, 1958.

——. *The Psychopathology of Everyday Life* [*PEL*]. In *Basic Writings*.

——. "The Uncanny" [*U*]. In *Creativity and the Unconscious*.

——. "The Relation of the Poet to Day-Dreaming" [*RPD*]. Reprinted in Ross, ed., *Art and Its Significance*. In Sigmund Freud, *Collected Papers*, vol. 4. Article trans. I. F. Grant Duff. New York: Basic Books, 1959.

——. *The Standard Edition of the Complete Psychological Works of Sigmund Freud*. Ed. James Strachey, 24 vols. London: Hogarth Press, 1953–74.

——. *Totem and Taboo* [*TT*]. In *Basic Writings*.

——. *Wit and Its Relations to the Unconscious* [*WRU*]. In *Basic Writings*.

Freyfogle, Eric T. *Justice and the Earth: Images for Our Planetary Survival* [*JE*]. New York: Free Press, 1993.

Frodeman, Robert. "Radical Environmentalism and the Political Roots of Postmodernism: Differences that Make a Difference" [*REPRP*]. In Oelschlaeger, ed., *Postmodern Environmental Ethics*.

Fry, Tony, and Anne-Marie Willis. "Aboriginal Art: Symptom or Success?" [*AA*]. In *Art in America* (July 1989): 111–16, 159–61. Reprinted in part in Ross, ed., *Art and Its Significance*.

Frye, Northrop. *The Modern Century* [*MC*]. Toronto: Oxford University Press, 1967.

Fuller, Steve. *Controversial Science: From Content to Contention* [*CS*]. Albany: State University of New York Press, 1993.

——. *Philosophy of Science and Its Discontents* [*PSD*]. Boulder, CO: Westview Press, 1989.

——. *Social Epistemology* [*SE*]. Bloomington and Indianapolis: Indiana University Press, 1988.

Fuss, Diana. "A Supper Party" [*SP*]. Scapp and Seitz, eds., *Eating Culture*.

Gaard, Greta. *Ecofeminism: Women, Animals, Nature* [*E*]. Philadelphia: Temple University Press, 1993.

Gablik, Suzi. *The Reenchantment of Art* [*RA*]. New York: Thames and Hudson, 1991.

Gadamer, Hans-Georg. *Truth and Method* [*TM*]. New York: Seabury Press, 1975.

Galletti, R., K. D. S. Baldwin, & I. O. Dina. "Clothing of Nigerian Cocoa Farmers' Families" [*CNCFF*]. In Roach-Higgins, Eicher, and Johnson, eds., *Dress and Identity*.

Gallop, David. *Plato:* Phaedo [*PP*]. Oxford: Clarendon Press, 1975.

Gallop, Jane. *Anecdotal Theory* [*AT*]. Durham: Duke University Press, 2002.

——. *The Daughter's Seduction: Feminism and Psychoanalysis* [*DS*]. Ithaca, NY: Cornell University Press, 1982.

——. *Intersections, a Reading of Sade with Bataille, Blanchot, and Klossowski* [*I*]. Lincoln: University of Nebraska Press, 1981.

——. *Reading Lacan* [*RL*]. Ithaca: Cornell University Press, 1985.

——. *Thinking Through the Body* [*TTB*]. New York: Columbia University Press, 1988.

Galsworthy, John. *The Man of Property* [*MP*]. Moscow, Foreign Languages Publishing House, 1950.

Garb, Yaakov Jerome. "Perspective or Escape? Ecofeminist Musings on Contemporary Earth Imagery" [*PE*]. In Diamond and Orenstein, eds., *Reweaving the World*.

Gard, Richard A., ed. *Buddhism* [*B*]. New York: George Braziller, 1962.

Gates, Jr., Henry Louis. "Critical Remarks" [*CR*]. In Goldberg, ed., *Anatomy of Racism*.

——., ed. *"Race," Writing, and Difference* [*RWD*]. Chicago: University of Chicago Press, 1986.

Gates, Paul W. "Recent Land Policies of the Federal Government" [*RLPFG*]. Section 5 in Forest Service, Department of Agriculture and The Land Policy Section, Agricultural Adjustment Administration for the Land Planning Committee of the National Resources Board, *Certain Aspects of Land Problems and Government Land Policies: Part VII of the Report on Land Planning*. Washington, DC: 1935.

Gauchet, Marcel. *The Disenchantment of the World: A Political History of Religion* [*DW*]. Trans. Oscar Burge. Princeton, NJ: Princeton University Press, 1997.

Geis, Deborah R. "Feeding the Audience: Food, Feminism, and Performance Art" [*FA*]. In Scapp and Seitz, eds. *Eating Culture*.

Gelven, Michael. *The Asking Mystery: A Philosophical Inquiry* [*AM*]. University Park, PA: Pennsylvania University Press, 2001.

Genet, Jean. *Prisoner of Love* [*PL*]. Trans. Barbara Bray. Hanover, NH: University Press of New England, 1992.

Germain, Gilbert G. *A Discourse on Disenchantment: Reflections on Politics and Technology* [*DOD*]. Albany, NY: State University of New York Press, 1993.

Giffney, Noreen. "Queer Apocal(o)ptic/ism: The Death Drive and the Human" [*QA*]. In Giffney and Hird, eds., *Queering the Non/ Human*.

Giffney, Noreen, and Myra J. Hird, eds. *Queering the Non/Human* [*QN/H*]. Burlington, NH: Ashgate Publishing Co., 2008.

Gilbert, Bil. "Crows by Far and Wide, But There's No Place Like Home." *Smithsonian* 23, no. 5 (August 1992): 101–11.

——. *Our Nature* [*ON*]. Lincoln: University of Nebraska Press, 1986.

Gilbert, Jess, and Craig K. Harris. "Changes in Type, Tenure, and Concentration of U.S. Farmland Owners" [*CTTCFO*]. In *Focus On Agriculture*. Ed. Harry K. Schwarzweller. Greenwich, CN: Jai Press, 1984.

Gilead, Amihud. *The Platonic Odyssey: A Philosophical-Literary Inquiry into the* Phaedo [*PO*]. Amsterdam: Rodopi, 1994.

Gilligan, Carol. *In a Different Voice: Psychological Theory and Women's Development* [*IDV*]. Cambridge: Harvard University Press, 1982.

Gillis, Malcolm. "Economics, Ecology, and Ethics: Mending the Broken Circle for Tropical Forests" [*EEE*]. In Bormann and Kellert, eds., *Ecology, Economics, Ethics.*

Glass, James M. *Shattered Selves* [*SS*]. Ithaca, NY: Cornell University Press, 1993.

Glass, Newman Robert. *Working Emptiness: Toward a Third Reading of Emptiness in Buddhism and Postmodern Thought* [*WE*]. Atlanta, GA: Scholars Press, 1995.

Gluckman, Max. *Politics, Law and Ritual in Tribal Society* [*PLRTS*]. Chicago: Aldine, 1965.

Godway, Eleanor M., and Geraldine Finn, eds. *Who Is This "We"?: Absence of Community* [*WW*]. Montréal: Black Rose Books, 1994.

Goldberg, David Theo, ed. *Anatomy of Racism* [*AR*]. Minneapolis: University of Minnesota Press, 1990.

Golding, Sue. *The Eight Technologies of Otherness* [*ETO*]. London; New York: Routledge, 1997.

——. "The Excess" [*E*]. In Kroker and Kroker, eds., *Last Sex.*

Goodman, Nelson. *Languages of Art: An Approach to a Theory of Symbols* [*LA*]. 2nd ed., Indianapolis: Hackett, 1976.

——. *Ways of Worldmaking* [*WW*]. Indianapolis: Hackett, 1978.

——. "What is Art" [*WA?*]. In *Ways of Worldmaking.*

Goosens, William K. "Underlying Trait Terms" [*UTT*]. In Schwartz, ed., *Naming, Necessity, and Natural Kinds.*

Gordon, Eleanore, and Jean Nerenberg. "Everywoman's Jewelry: Early Plastics and Equality in Fashion" [*EJ*]. In Roach-Higgins, Eicher, and Johnson, eds., *Dress and Identity.*

Gordon, Mel. *Lazzi: The Comic Routines of the Commedia dell'Arte* [*L*]. New York: Performing Arts Journal Publications, 1983.

Gore, Charles. *Property: Its Duties and Rights, Historically, Philosophically and Religiously Regarded* [*P*]. New York: Macmillan, Co., 1922.

Gottlieb, Alma. "Witches, Kings, and the Sacrifice of Identity or The Power of Paradox and the Paradox of Power among the Beng of Ivory Coast" [*WKS*]. In Arens and Karp, eds., *Creativity of Power.*

Göttner-Abendroth, Heide. "Nine Principles of a Matriarchal Aesthetics" [*MA*]. Trans. Harriet Anderson. Reprinted in Ross, ed., *Art and Its Significance.* In Ecker, ed., *Feminist Aesthetics.*

Gould, Stephen Jay. "The Golden Rule" [*GR*]. *Natural History* (September 1990).

Gramsci, Antonio. *An Antonio Gramsci Reader: Selected Writings 1916–1935* [*AGR*]. New York: Schocken Books, 1988.

——. *Gramsci* [*G*]. Paris: Seghers, 1966.

——. *The Open Marxism of Antonio Gramsci* [*OM*]. Trans. Carl Marzani. New York: Cameron Associates, 1957.

Graves, Robert. *The Greek Myths* [*GM*]. Baltimore: Penguin, 1955.

Gregory, C. A. "The Emergence of Commodity Production in Papua New Guinea" [*ECPPNG*]. *Journal of Contemporary Asia* (1979): 389–409.

Grey, Thomas C. "The Disintegration of Property" [*DP*]. In Pennock and Chapman, eds., *Nomos XXII*, 69–85.

Griebel, Helen Bradley. "The African American Woman's Headwrap: Unwinding the Symbols" [*AAWH*]. In Roach-Higgins, Eicher, and Johnson, eds., *Dress and Identity*.

Griffin, David Ray. *The 9/11 Commission Report: Omissions and Distortions* [*911CR*]. Fowlerville, MI: Olive Branch Press, 2004.

——. *9/11 Contradictions: An Open Letter to Congress and the Press* [*900C*]. Northampton, MA: Interlink Publishing Group, 2008.

——. *Christian Faith and the Truth Behind 9/11: A Call to Reflection and Action* [*CFT911*]. Louisville, KT: Westminster John Knox Press, 2006.

——. *Debunking 9/11 Debunking: An Answer to Popular Mechanics and Other Defenders of the Official Conspiracy Theory* [*D911D*]. Rev. ed. Fowlerville, MI: Olive Branch Press, 2007.

——. *The New Pearl Harbor: Disturbing Questions About the Bush Administration and 9/11* [*NPH*]. Northampton, MA: Interlink Publishing Group, 2004.

——. *The New Pearl Harbor Revisited: 9/11, the Cover-Up, and the Exposé* [*NPHR*]. Fowlerville, MI: Olive Branch Press, 2008

——. "Of Minds and Molecules: Postmodern Medicine in a Psychosomatic Universe" [*MMP*]. In Griffin, ed., *Reenchantment of Science*.

——. *Reenchantment Without Supernaturalism* [*RWS*]. Ithaca, NY: Cornell University Press, 2001.

Griffin, David Ray, ed. *The Reenchantment of Science: Postmodern Proposals* [*RS*]. Albany: State University of New York Press, 1988.

Griffin, David Ray, John B. Cobb, Richard A. Falk, and Catherine Keller, *The American Empire and the Commonwealth of God: A Political, Economic, Religious Statement* [*AECG*].

Griffin, Susan. *A Chorus of Stones* [*CS*]. New York: Doubleday, 1992.

——. *Pornography and Silence* [*PS*]. New York: Harper & Row, 1981.

——. *Woman and Nature: The Roaring Inside Her* [*WN*]. New York: Harper & Row, 1978.

Griffiths, Ieuan Ll. *An Atlas of African Affairs* [*AAA*]. New York: Routledge, 1994.

Grigsby, Eugene, Jr. "Afro-American Culture and the White Ghetto" [*AAC*]. In Young, ed., *Art, Culture, and Ethnicity*.

Grodin, Debra, and Thomas R . Lindlof, eds. *Constructing the Self in a Mediated World* [*CSMW*]. London: Sage Publications, 1996.

Grosz, Elizabeth. *Jacques Lacan: a Feminist Introduction* [*JL*]. London; New York: Routledge, 1990.

——. *Sexual Subversions: Three French Feminists* [*SS*]. Winchester, MA: Unwin Hyman, 1989.

——. *Space, Time, and Perversion: Essays on the Politics of Bodies* [*STP*]. New York: Routledge, 1995.

——. *Volatile Bodies: Toward a Corporeal Feminism* [*VB*]. Bloomington: Indiana University Press, 1994.

Grosz, Elizabeth, ed. *Becomings: Explorations in Time, Memory, and Futures* [*B*]. Ithaca, NY: Cornell University Press, 1999.

——. *Sexy Bodies: The Strange Carnalities of Feminism* [*SCF*]. London; New York: Routledge, 1995.

Gruen, Lori, and Dale Jamieson, eds. *Reflecting on Nature* [*RN*]. Oxford: Oxford University Press, 1994.

Grunebaum, James O. *Private Ownership* [*PO*]. New York: Routledge & Kegan Paul, 1987.

Guattari, Félis. *Chaosmosis: an Ethico-aesthetic Paradigm* [C]. Trans. Paul Bains and Julian Pefanis. Bloomington, IN: Indiana University Press, 1995.

——. *The Three Ecologies* [*TE*]. Trans. Ian Pindar and Paul Sutton. London: The Athlone Press, 2000.

Guidieri, R. "Les sociétés primitives aujourd'hui" [*SPA*]. In *Philosopher: les interrogations contemporarines*. Ed. Ch. Delacampagne and R. Maggiori. Paris: Fayard, 1980.

Guy-Sheftall, Beverly, ed. *Words of Fire: An Anthology of African-American Feminist Thought* [*WF*]. New York: New Press, 1995.

Habermas, Jürgen. *Communication and the Evolution of Society* [*CES*]. Ed. T. McCarthy. Boston: Beacon Press, 1979.

——. *Religion and Rationality: Essays on Reason, God, and Modernity* [*RR*]. Ed. Eduardo Mendieta. Cambridge, MA: MIT Press, 2002.

——. *The Philosophical Discourse of Modernity* [*PDM*]. Trans. Frederick Lawrence. Cambridge, MA: MIT Press, 1987.

——. "Volkssouveränität als Verfahren" [*VV*]. In *Faktizität und Geltung*. Frankfurt am MainL /sygrjanom 1992.

——. *The Theory of Communicative Action, Volume One: Reason and the Rationalization of Society* [*TCA1*]. Trans. Thomas McCarthy. Boston: Beacon Press, 1983.

——. *The Theory of Communicative Action, Volume Two: Lifeworld and System: A Critique of Functionalist Reason* [*TCA2*]. Trans. Thomas McCarthy. Boston: Beacon Press, 1985.

Haila, Yrjö, and Chuck Dyke, eds. *How Nature Speaks: The Dynamics of the Human Ecological Condition* [*HNS*]. Durham, NC: Duke University Press, 2006.

Haldane, John Burdon Sanderson. *Possible Worlds and Other Essays* [*PW*]. New York: Harper & Brothers, 1928.

Hall, David L. "To Be or Not to Be: The Postmodern Self and the Wu-Forms of Taoism" [*TBNB*]. In Ames, ed., *Self as Person in Asian Theory and Practice*.

Hallen, Barry. "Phenomenology and the Exposition of African Traditional Thought" [*PEATT*]. In *Proceedings of the Seminar on African Philosophy/La Philosophie Africaine*. Ed. Claude Sumner. Addis Ababa: Chamber Printing House, 1980.

Hallen, B., and J. O. Sodipo. *Knowledge, Belief & Witchcraft: Analytic Experiments in African Philosophy* [*KBW*]. London: Ethnographica, 1986.

Hamilton, C. H. "The Idea of Compassion in Mahâyâna Buddhism" [*ICMB*]. *Journal of the American Oriental Society* 70: 145–51.
Hamilton, Cynthia. "Coping with Industrial Exploitation" [*CIE*]. In Bullard, ed., *Confronting Environmental Racism.*
Hamilton, William. "The Death of God Theologies Today" [*DGTT*]. In Altizer and Hamilton eds., *Radical Theology.*
——. *On Taking God out of the Dictionary* [*TGOD*]. New York: McGraw-Hill, 1974.
——. *A Quest for the Post-Historical Jesus* [*QPHJ*]. New York: Continuum, 1994.
Hamilton-Grierson, P. J. "Strangers" [*S*]. In *Encyclopaedia of Religion and Ethics*. Ed J. Hastings. Edinburgh: T. & T. Clark, 1921. Vol. 11: 883–896.
Hannoosh, Michele. *Baudelaire and Caricature: From the Comic to an Art of Modernity* [*BC*]. University Park, PA: The Pennsylvania State University Press, 1992.
Haraway, Donna. *Crystals, Fabrics, and Fields: Metaphors of Organicism in Twentieth-Century Developmental Biology* [*CFF*]. New Haven, CT: Yale University Press, 1976.
——. *The Haraway Reader* [*HR*]. New York: Routledge, 2004.
——. *How Like a Leaf: an Interview with Thyrza Nichols Goodeve* [*HLL*]. New York: Routledge, 2000.
——. *ModestWitness@SecondMillennium.FemaleManMeetsOncoMouse: Feminism and Technoscience* [*MW*]. New York: Routledge, 1997.
——. *Primate Visions: Gender, Race, and Nature in the World of Modern Science* [*PV*]. New York: Routledge, 1989.
——. *Simians, Cyborgs, and Women: The Reinvention of Nature* [*SCW*]. New York: Routledge, 1991.
Hardin, Garrett. "The Tragedy of the Commons" [*TC*]. *Science* 162 (December 13, 1968): 1245–48.
Harding, Sandra. "The Curious Coincidence of Feminine and African Moralities: Challenges for Feminist Theory" [*CCFAM*]. In Kittay and Meyers, eds., *Women and Moral Theory.*
——. "The Instability of the Analytical Categories of Feminist Theory" [*IACFT*]. *Signs* 11, no. 4 (Summer 1986): 645–64.
——. *The Science Question in Feminism* [*SQF*]. Ithaca, NY: Cornell University Press, 1986.
——. *Whose Science? Whose Knowledge?: Thinking from Women's Lives* [*WSWK*]. Ithaca, NY: Cornell University Press, 1991.
Hargrove, Eugene C. *Foundations of Environmental Ethics* [*FEE*]. Englewood Cliffs, NJ: Prentice Hall, 1989.
——., ed. *Religion and Environmental Crisis* [*REC*]. Athens, GA: University of Georgia Press, 1986.
Harman, Lesley D. *The Modern Stranger* [*MS*]. Amsterdam: Mouton de Gruyter, 1988.
Harman, Willis W. "The Postmodern Heresy: Consciouosness as Causal" [*PH*]. In Griffin, ed., *Reenchantment of Science.*

Harper, Clifford. *Anarchy: A Graphic Guide* [*A*]. London: Camden Press, 1987.

Harris, Cheryl I. "Whiteness as Property" [*WP*]. *Harvard Law Review* 106, 8 (June 1993): 1707–91.

Harris, Daniel. *Cute, Quaint, Hungry and Romantic: The Aesthetics of Consumerism* [*CQHR*]. New York: Basic Books, 2000.

Harris, Leonard. "Postmodernism and Utopia, an Unholy Alliance" [*PU*]. In Hord and Lee, eds., *I Am Because We Are.*

Harrison, Beverly Wildung. "Our Right to Choose" [*RC*]. In Andolsen, Gudorf, and Pellauer, eds., *Women's Consciousness, Women's Conscience.*

Hatcher, Evelyn Payne. *Art as Culture: An Introduction to the Anthropology of Art* [*AC*]. 2nd ed., Westport, CT: Bergin & Garvey, 1999.

Haug, Wolfgang Fritz. *Critique of Commodity Aesthetics: Appearance, Sexuality and Advertising in Capitalist Society* [*CCA*]. Trans. Robert Bock. Minneapolis: University of Minnesota Press, 1986.

Hegel, G. W. F. *Aesthetics: Lectures on Fine Art* [*A*]. Trans. T. M. Knox. London: Oxford University Press, 1975. Introduction reprinted in part in Ross, ed., *Art and Its Significance* as "Philosophy of Fine Art" [*PFA*].

——. *Hegel's Science of Logic* [*L*]. Trans. A. V. Miller. New York: Humanities Press, 1969.

——. *Jenenser Realphilosophie I, Die Vorlesungen von 1803–1804* [*JR1*]. Ed. J. Hoffmeister. Leibzig: 1932. Quoted and translated in Agamben, *Language and Death.*

——. *Jenenser Realphilosophie II, Die Vorlesungen von 1803–1804* [*JR2*]. Ed. J. Hoffmeister. Leipzig: 1932. Quoted and translated in Agamben, *Language and Death.*

——. *The Logic of Hegel, translated from the Encyclopaedia of the Philosophical Sciences* [*EL*]. Trans. William Wallace. Oxford: Oxford University Press, 1892.

——. *The Phenomenology of Mind* [*PM*]. Trans. and int. James Baillie. London: George Allen & Unwin, 1910.

——. *The Phenomenology of Spirit* [*PS*]. Trans. A. V. Miller. Oxford: Oxford University Press, 1977.

——. *The Philosophy of Right* [*PR*]. Trans. T. M. Knox. Oxford: Oxford University Press, 1934, 1967.

Heidegger, Martin. "The Age of the World Picture" [*AWP*]. In *Question Concerning Technology and Other Essays.*

——. "The Anaximander Fragment" [*AF*]. In *Early Greek Thinking.*

——. *Basic Writings* [*BW*]. Ed. David Farrell Krell. New York: Harper & Row, 1977.

——. *Being and Time: A Translation of* Sein und Zeit [*BT*]. Trans. John Macquarrie and Edward Robinson. New York: Harper & Row, 1962. Translation of *Sein und Zeit* [*SZ*].

——. *Being and Time: A Translation of* Sein und Zeit [*BT(S)*]. Trans. Joan Stambaugh. Albany: State University of New York Press, 1996. Translation of *Sein und Zeit* [*SZ*].

——. *Discourse on Thinking: A Translation of* Gelassenheit [*DT*]. Trans. John M. Anderson and E. Hans Freund. New York: Harper & Row, 1966.
——. *Early Greek Thinking* [*EGT*]. Trans. D. F. Krell and F. A. Capuzzi. New York: Harper & Row, 1984.
——. *Identity and Difference* [*ID*]. Trans. and int. Joan Stambaugh. New York: Harper & Row, 1969.
——. *Introduction to Metaphysics* [*IM*]. Trans. Ralph Manheim. Garden City, NY: Doubleday, 1961.
——. "Language" [*L*]. In *Poetry, Language, Thought.*
——. "Language in the Poem" [*LP*]. In *On the Way to Language.*
——. "Letter on Humanism" [*LH*]. In *Basic Writings.*
——. "Martin Heidegger interrogé par *Der Spiegel.* Réponses et questions sur l'histoire et la politique." (Martin Heidegger interviewed by *Der Spiegel*: Responses and Questions on History and Politics.) Trans. William J. Richardson S. J. as "'Only a God Can Save Us': The *Spiegel* Interview." In Sheehan, ed., *Heidegger, the Man and the Thinker.*
——. "The Nature of Language" [*NL*]. In *On the Way to Language.*
——. "On the Being and Conception of *Physis* in Aristotle's *Physics* B. 1" [*OBCP*]. Trans. T. J. Sheehan. *Man and World* 9, no. 3 (August 1976): 219–70.
——. "On the Essence of Truth" [*OET*]. In *Basic Writings.*
——. *On the Way to Language* [*OWL*]. Trans. Peter D. Hertz. New York: Harper & Row, 1971.
——. *On Time and Being* [*OTB*]. Trans. Joan Stambaugh. New York: Harper & Row, 1972.
——. "The Onto-theo-logical Constitution of Metaphysics" [*OTLCM*]. In *Identity and Difference.*
——. "The Origin of the Work of Art" [*OWA*]. Reprinted in part in Ross, ed., *Art and Its Significance.* In *Poetry, Language, Thought.*
——. *Poetry, Language, Thought* [*PLT*]. Trans. Albert Hofstadter. New York: Harper & Row, 1971.
——. "The Question Concerning Technology" [*QT*]. In *Basic Writings.*
——. *The Question Concerning Technology and Other Essays* [*QTOE*]. Trans. William Lovitt. New York: Harper & Row, 1977.
——. "Time and Being" [*TB*]. In *On Time and Being.*
——. *Was ist das—die Philosophie* [*WP*], 1955. Quoted in Derrida, "Heidegger's Ear."
——. "The Way to Language" [*WL*]. In *On the Way to Language.*
——. "What Calls for Thinking?" [*WCT*]. In *Basic Writings.*
Hein, Hilda. "Refining Feminist Theory: Lessons from Aesthetics" [*RFT*]. In Hein and Korsmeyer, eds. *Aesthetics in Feminist Perspective.*
Hein, Hilda, and Carolyn Korsmeyer, eds. *Aesthetics in Feminist Perspective* [*AFP*]. Bloomington: Indiana University Press, 1993.
Heller, Morton A., and William Schiff, eds. *The Psychology of Touch* [*PT*]. Hillsdale, NJ: Lawrence Erlbaum Associates, 1991.
Hendrix, Harville. *Getting the Love You Want: A Guide for Couples* [*GLW*]. New York: Pocket Books, 2001.

——. *Keeping the Love You Find: A Personal Guide* [*KLF*]. New York: Pocket Books, 1992.

Herdt, G. *Guardians of the Flutes: Idioms of Masculinity* [*GF*]. Stanford: Stanford University Press, 1980.

Hermann, Anne. "*'Passing' Women, Performing Men*" [*PWPM*]. In Roach-Higgins, Eicher, and Johnson, eds., *Dress and Identity.*

Hester, Jr., Randolph T. "Sacred Structures and Everyday Life: A Return to Manteo, North Carolina" [*SSEL*]. In Seamon, ed., *Dwelling, Seeing, and Designing.* (271–98).

Hirschon, Renée. "Introduction: Property, Power and Gender Relations" [*PPGR*]. In *Women and Property—Women as Property.*

——., ed. *Women and Property—Women as Property* [*WPWP*]. New York: St. Martin's Press, 1984.

Hisamatsu, Hoseki Shin'ichi. *Die Fülle des Nichts* [*FN*]. Trans. Takashi Hirata and Johanna Fisher. Pfullingen: Neske Verlag, 1984.

——. *Zen and the Fine Arts* [*ZFA*]. New York: Kodansha International, 1974.

Hix, H. L. *Spirits Hovering Over the Ashes: Legacies of Postmodern Theory* [*SHOA*]. Albany: State University of New York Press, 1995.

Hoagland, Sarah Lucia. "Lesbian Ethics and Female Agency" [*LEFA*]. In Cole and Coultrap-McQuin, eds., *Explorations in Feminist Ethics.*

——. "Some Thoughts about 'Caring'" [*STC*]. In Card, ed., *Feminist Ethics.*

Hoard, Adreinne Walker. "The Black Aesthetic: An Empirical Feeling" [*BA*]. In Young, ed., *Art, Culture, and Ethnicity.*

Hobbes, Thomas. *Complete Works* [*CW*]. Ed. William Molesworth. English Works, 11 vols., 1839. Latin Works, 5 vols., 1845.

——. *De Cive* [*DCV*]. In *Complete Works.*

——. *Elements of Philosophy* [*EOP*]. In *Complete Works,* vol. 4.

——. *Leviathan* [*L*]. In *Complete Works,* vol. 1.

Hoeller, Keith, ed., *Dream and Existence. Review of Existential Psychology and Psychiatry* [*DE*]. Trans. Forrest Williams and Jacob Needleman. Vol. XIX, no. 1 (1984–5).

Hölderlin, Friedrich. *Friedrich Hölderlin Poems and Fragments* [*FHPF*]. Trans. Michael Hamburger. Ann Arbor: University of Michigan Press, 1966.

——. "Patmos" [*P*]. In *Friedrich Hölderlin Poems and Fragments.*

Homann, Margaret. *Bearing the Word: Language and Female Experience in Nineteenth-Century Women's Writing* [*BW*]. Chicago: University of Chicago Press, 1986.

Hoppe, Hans-Hermann. *The Economics and Ethisc of Private Property* [*EEPP*]. Boston: Kluwer Academic Publishers, 1993.

Hord, Fred Lee (Mzee Lasana Okpara), and Jonathan Scott Lee, eds. *I Am Because We Are: Readings in Black Philosophy* [*IABWA*]. Amherst: University of Massachusetts, 1995.

Horkheimer, Max. *Critique of Reason* [*CR*]. Trans. Matthew J. O'Connell et al. New York: Continuum, 1974.

——. *Eclipse of Reason* [*ER*]. Trans. Alfred Schmidt. New York: Oxford University Press, 1947.

Horkheimer, Max, and Theodor W. Adorno. *Dialectic of Enlightenment* [*DE*]. Trans. John Cumming. New York: Continuum, 1972.

Horovitz, Irving Louis, ed. *The Anarchists* [*A*]. New York: Dell, 1964.

Hoseki Shin'ichi Hisamatsu, *Die Fülle des Nichts* [*FN*]. Trans. Takashi Hirata and Johanna Fisher. Pfullingen: Neske Verlag, 1984.

Hubbard, Jamie, and Paul L. Swanson, eds. *Pruning the Bodhi Tree: The Storm Over Critical Buddhism* [*PBT*]. Honolulu: University of Hawaii Press, 1997.

Hume, David. *An Enquiry Concerning Human Understanding* [*EHU*]. New York: Prometheus, 1988.

——. "Of the Standard of Taste" [*OST*]. Reprinted in Ross, ed., *Art and Its Significance.*

——. "On National Characters" [*ONC*]. In T. H. Green and T. H. Grose, eds., *Philosophical Works* [*PW*]. vol. 3. Aalen: Scientia Verlag, 1964.

——. *A Treatise of Human Nature* [*T*]. London: Oxford University Press, 1888.

Huntington, Jr., C. W. *The Emptiness of Emptiness* [*EE*]. With Geshé Namgyal Wangchen. Honolulu: University of Hawaii Press, 1989.

Husserl, Edmund. *Ideas: General Introduction to Pure Phenomenology* [*I*]. Trans. W. R. Boyce Gibson. New York: Collier Books, 1962.

Hyde, Lewis. *The Gift: Imagination and the Erotic Life of Property* [G]. New York: Random House, 1979.

Illich, Ivan. *Gender* [G]. New York: Pantheon, 1982.

——. "Toward a History of Gender" [*THG*]. *Feminist Issues* 3, no. 1 (Spring 1983). Includes symposium on his work.

Inada, Kenneth K. "Environmental Problematics" [*EP*]. In Callicott and Ames, eds., *Nature in Asian Traditions of Thought.*

Irigaray, Luce. "Any Theory of the 'Subject' Has Always Been Appropriated by the 'Masculine'" [*ATS*]. In *Speculum of the Other Woman.*

——. *Between East and West* [*BEW*]. Trans. Stephen Pluhàček. New York: Columbia University Press, 2002.

——. "The Culture of Difference" [*CD*]. In *Je, tu, nous.*

——. *Elemental Passions* [*EP*]. Trans. Joanne Collins and Judith Still. New York: Routledge, 1992.

——. *An Ethics of Sexual Difference* [*ESD*]. Trans. Carolyn Burke and Gillian C. Gill. Ithaca, NY: Cornell University Press, 1993. Translation of *Éthique de la Différence sexuelle* [*ÉDS*]. Paris: Minuit, 1984.

——. "The Fecundity of the Caress: A Reading of Levinas, *Totality and Infinity,* 'Phenomenology of Eros'" [*FC*]. In *Ethics of Sexual Difference.*

——. "He Risks Who Risks Life Itself" [*HR*]. In *Irigaray Reader.*

——. *I Love to You: Sketch of a Possible Felicity in History* [*ILTY*]. Trans. Alison Martin. New York: Routledge, 1996.

——. "The Invisible of the Flesh: A Reading of Merleau-Ponty, *The Visible and the Invisible,* 'The Intertwining—The Chiasm'" [*IF*]. In *Ethics of Sexual Difference.*

——. *The Irigaray Reader* [*IR*]. Ed. and int. Margaret Whitford. Oxford: Blackwell, 1991.

——. "Je-Luce Irigaray" [*J*]. Ed. and trans. Elizabeth Hirsh and Gaëton Brechotte. Interview in *Hypatia* 10, no. 2 (Spring 1995): 93–114.

——. *Je, tu, nous: Toward a Culture of Difference* [*JTN*]. Trans. Alison Martin. New York: Routledge, 1993.

——. *Marine Lover of Friedrich Nietzsche* [*ML*]. Trans. Gillian C. Gill. New York: Columbia University Press, 1991.

——. "The 'Mechanics' of Fluids" [*MF*]. In *This Sex Which Is Not One.*

——. "*La Mystérique*" [*M*]. In *Speculum of the Other Woman.*

——. "The Necessity for Sexuate Rights" [*NSR*]. In *Irigaray Reader.*

——. *L'oubli de l'air: Chez Martin Heidegger* [*OA*]. Paris: Minuit, 1983.

——. "The Power of Discourse and the Subordination of the Feminine" [*PDSF*]. In *This Sex Which Is Not One.*

——. "Questions" [*Q*]. In *Irigaray Reader.*

——. "Questions to Emmanuel Levinas" [*QEL*]. In *Irigaray Reader.*

——. "Sexual Difference" [*SD*]. In *Irigaray Reader.*

——. *Sharing the World* [*SW*]. Trans.? New York: Continuum, 2008.

——. *Speculum of the Other Woman* [*SOW*]. Trans. Gillian C. Gill. Ithaca, NY: Cornell University Press, 1985. Translation of *Speculum de l'autre femme.* Paris: Minuit, 1974.

——. *This Sex Which Is Not One* [*SWNO*]. Trans. Catherine Porter. Ithaca, NY: Cornell University Press, 1985.

——. "This Sex Which Is Not One" [*TSWNO*]. In *This Sex Which Is Not One.*

——. "The Three *Genres*" [*TG*]. In *Irigaray Reader.*

——. "Volume-Fluidity" [*VF*]. Translation of "L'incontourable volume" *(Volume without Contour).* In *Speculum of the Other Woman.*

——. "When Our Lips Speak Together" [*WOLST*]. In *This Sex Which Is Not One.*

——. "Why Define Sexed Rights?" [*WDSR*]. In *Je, tu, nous.*

——. "Women on the Market" [*WM*]. In *This Sex Which Is Not One.*

——. "Wonder: A Reading of Descartes, *The Passions of the Soul*" [*W*]. In *Ethics of Sexual Difference.*

Isasi-Diaz, Ada Maria. "Toward an Understanding of *Feminismo Hispano* in the U.S.A." [*FH*]. In Andolsen, Gudorf, and Pellauer, eds., *Women's Consciousness, Women's Conscience.*

Jablonka, Eva, and Jarion J. Lamb. *Evolution in Four Dimensions: Genetic, Epigenetic, Behavioral, and Symbolic Variation in the History of Life* [*EFD*]. Cambridge, MA: MIT Press, 2006.

Jackson, Jean. "Chronic Pain and the Tension between the Body as Subject and Object" [*CP*]. In Csordas, *Embodiment and Experience.*

Jackson, Michael. "The Man Who Could Turn into an Elephant: Shapeshifting Among the Kuranko of Sierra Leone" [*ME*]. In Jackson and Karp, eds. *Personhood and Agency.*

Jackson, Michael, and Ivan Karp, eds. *Personhood and Agency: The Experiences of Self and Other in African Cultures* [*PA*]. Washington, DC: Smithsonian Institution Press, 1990.

Jackson, Wes, et al., eds. *Meeting the Expectations of the Land* [*MEL*]. San Francisco: North Point Press, 1984.

Jacobs, Jane. *Systems of Survival: A Dialogue on the Moral Foundations of Commerce and Politics* [*SS*]. New York: Random House, 1993.

Jacobs, Janet Liebman. *Divine Disenchantment: Deconverting from New Religions* [*DD*]. Bloomington, IN: Indiana University Press, 1989.

Jacobson-Widding, Anita. "The Shadow as an Expression of Individuality in Congolese Conceptions of Personhood" [*SEI*]. In Jackson and Karp, eds. *Personhood and Agency.*

Jacoby, Karl. "Slaves by Nature? Domestic Animals and Human Slaves" [*SN*]. *Slavery & Abolition: A Journal of Slave and Post-Slave Studies* (April 1994): 89–97.

Jaggar, Alison M., and Susan R. Bordo, eds. *Gender/Body/Knowledge: Feminist Reconstructions of Being and Knowing* [*GBK*]. New Brunswick: Rutgers University Press, 1989.

James, William. *Essays in Radical Empiricism* [*ERE*]; *A Pluralistic Universe* [*PU*]. New York: Longman's Green, 1912.

——. *Pragmatism, and Four Essays from* The Meaning of Truth [*P*]. New York: Meridian Books, 1955.

——. *The Will to Believe* [*WB*], *and Other Essays in Popular Philosophy; and Human Immortality* [*HI*]. New York: Dover, 1956.

——. *Varieties of Religious Experience* [*VRE*]. New York: Modern Library, 1994. Jameson, Frederic. "Postmodernism, or The Cultural Logic of Late Capitalism" [*P*]. *New Left Review* 146, no. 4 (July–August, 1984): 53–93.

Johnson, Mark. *The Body in the Mind: The Bodily Basis of Meaning, Imagination, and Reason* [*BM*]. Chicago: University of Chicago Press, 1987.

Jonas, Hans. "De la Gnose au Principe Responsabilité: Entretien avec Hans Jonas" [*GPR*]. *Esprit* 171 (May 1991): 5–21.

——. *The Imperative of Responsibility: In Search of an Ethics for the Technological Age* [*IR*]. Chicago: University of Chicago Press, 1984.

Jowett, Donna. "Origins, Occupations, and the Proximity of the Neighbour" [*OOPN*]. In Godway and Finn, eds., *Who Is This "We"?*

Judson, Olivia. *The Wild Side* [*WS*]. *New York Times Blog.*

——. "Optimism in Evolution" [*OE*]. *The Wild Side* (August 12, 2008).

——. "Pineapple Dreams" [*PD*]. *The Wild Side* (March 18, 2008).

Jung, Carl Gustav. *Modern Man in Search of a Soul* [*MMSS*]. Trans. W. S. Dell and Cary F. Baynes. New York: Harcourt Brace Jovanovich, 1955.

——. "Psychology and Literature" [*PL*]. Reprinted in Ross, ed., *Art and Its Significance.* In *Modern Man in Search of a Soul.*

Jussawalla, Adil. *Missing Person* [*MP*]. Bombay: Clearing House, 1976.

Kafka, Franz. *The Complete Stories* [CS]. Ed. Nahum N. Glatzer. New York: Schocken, 1971.
——. "In the Penal Colony" [*IPC*]. In Kafka, *Complete Stories.*
Kant, Immanuel. *The Conflict of the Faculties, Der Streit der Fakultäten* [*CF*]. Trans. Mary J. Gregor. New York: Abaris, 1979.
——. *Critique of Judgment* [*CJ*]. Trans. J. H. Bernard. New York: Hafner, 1951. Translation of *Kritik der Urteilskraft.* In *Kritik der Urteilskraft und Schriften zur Naturphilosophie.* Wiesbaden: Insel-Verlag Zweigstelle, 1957.
——. *Critique of Practical Reason* [*CPrR*]. In *Kant's Critique of Practical Reason and Other Works on the Theory of Ethics.* Trans. T. K. Abbott. London: Longman's Green, 1954.
——. *Critique of Pure Reason* [*CPR*]. Trans. J. M. D. Meiklejohn. Buffalo: Prometheus, 1990. Trans. Norman Kemp Smith [*CPR (NKS)*]. New York: St. Martin's, 1956. Translation of *Kritik der reinen Vernunft* [*KRV*]. 2 Band. Berlin: Deutsche Bibliothek, 1936.
——. *Fundamental Principles of the Metaphysics of Morals* [*FPMM*]. In *Kant's Critique of Practical Reason and Other Works on the Theory of Ethics.*
——. *Lectures on Ethics* [*LE*]. Trans. L. Infield. New York: Harper & Row, 1963.
——. *The Metaphysical Principles of Virtue* [*MPV*]. Indianapolis: Bobbs-Merrill, 1968.
——. *The Metaphysics of Morals* [*MM*]. Trans. Mary Gregor. Cambridge: Cambridge University Press, 1991.
——. *Observations on the Beautiful and the Sublime* [*OBS*]. Trans. John T. Goldthwait. Berkeley: University of California Press, 1960.
——. "An Answer to the Question, What is Enlightenment?" [*WE?*]. *Konigsberg in Prussia,* September 30, 1784. Http://eserver.org/philosophy/kant/what-is-enlightenment.txt (2004). Also available in a different translation at *Internet Modern History Sourcebook,* http://www.fordham.edu/halsall/mod/kant-whatis.html.
Kasulis, T. P. "Researching the Strata of the Japanese Self" [*RSJS*]. In Ames, ed. *Self as Person in Asian Theory and Practice.*
——. *Zen Action, Zen Person* [*ZAZP*]. Honolulu: University of Hawaii Press, 1981.
Katz, David. *The World of Touch* [*WT*]. Trans. Lester E. Krueger. Hillsdale, NJ: Lawrence Erlbaum Associates, 1989.
Katz, Eric. "The Call of the Wild: The Struggle against Domination and the Technological Fix of Nature" [*CW*]. In Oelschlaeger, ed., *Postmodern Environmental Ethics.*
——. *Nature as Subject: Human Obligation and Natural Community* [*NS*]. Lanham: Rowman & Littlefield, 1997.
Keightley, Thomas. *The World Guide to Gnomes, Fairies, Elves and Other Little People* [*WGGFE*]. New York: Avenel, 1978.
Keller, Mara Lynn. "The Eleusinian Mysteries: Ancient Nature Religion of Demeter and Persephone" [*EM*]. In Diamond and Orenstein, eds., *Reweaving the World.*

Kheel, Marti. "Ecofeminism and Deep Ecology: Reflections on Identity and Difference" [*EDE*]. In Diamond and Orenstein, eds., *Reweaving the World*.

——. "The Liberation of Nature: A Circular Affair" [*LN*]. *Environmental Ethics* 7, no. 2 (Summer 1985): 135–50.

Kierkegaard, Søren. *Either/Or* [*E/O*]. Trans. David F. Swenson and Lillian Marvin Swenson. Rev. Howard A. Johnson. 2 vols. Garden City, NY: Doubleday, 1959.

——. *Fear and Trembling/The Sickness Unto Death* [*FT*]. Trans. W. Lowrie. Garden City, NY: Doubleday, 1954.

——. *The Self in Society* [*SS*]. New York: St. Martin's Press, 1998.

Kigunga, Raphael. *The Anthropology of Self—Person and Myth in Africa: A Philosophyical Reflection on Man in South-East Africa* [*AS*]. New York: Peter Lang, 1996.

Kim, Hee-Jin. *Flowers of Emptiness* [*FE*]. Lewiston, NY: The Edwin Mellen Press, 1985.

King, Deborah K. "Multiple Jeopardy, Multiple Consciousness: The Context of a Black Feminist Ideology" [*MJMC*]. In Guy-Sheftall, ed., *Words of Fire*.

King, Lewis M. "On the Nature of a Creative World" [*ONCW*]. In Ruch and Anyanwu, eds., *African Philosophy*.

King, Lewis M., Vernon J. Dixon, and Wade W. Nobles, eds. *African Philosophy: Assumptions & Paradigms for Research on Black Persons* [*AP*]. Los Angeles: Charles R. Drew Postgraduate Medical School, 1976. Fanon Research and Development Center Publication, Area 8, no. 2.

King, Roger J. H. "Caring about Nature: Feminist Ethics and the Environment" [*CN*]. In Warren, ed., *Hypatia*, 75–89.

King, Sallie B. *Buddha Nature* [*BN*]. Albany: State University of New York Press, 1991.

King, Ynestra. "The Ecology of Feminism and the Feminism of Ecology" [*EFFE*]. In Plant, ed., *Healing the Wounds*.

——. "Healing the Wounds: Feminism, Ecology, and the Nature/Culture Dualism" [*HW*]. In Diamond and Orenstein, eds., *Reweaving the World*.

Kirkham, Richard L. *Theories of Truth: A Critical Introduction* [*TT*]. Cambridge, MA: MIT Press, 1992.

Kittay, Eva Feder, and Diana T. Meyers, eds. *Women and Moral Theory* [*WMT*]. Totowa, NJ: Rowman & Littlefield, 1987.

Klemm, David E. and Günter Zöller, eds. *Figuring the Self: Subject, Absolute, and Others in Classical German Philosophy* [*FS*]. Albany: State University of New York Press, 1998.

Kline, Linus W. and C. J. France. "The Psychology of Ownership" [*PO*]. *The Pedagogical Seminary* 6, 3 (September 1899): 421–70.

Klossowki, Pierre. *Nietzsche and the Vicious Circle* [*NVC*]. Trans. Daniel W. Smith. Chicago: University of Chicago Press, 1997.

——. *Roberte Ce Soir and the Revocation of the Edict of Nantes* [*RCS*]. Trans. Austryn Wainhouse. Normal, IL: Dalkey Archive Press, 2002.

——. *Sade my Neighbor* [*SMN*]. Trans. Alphonso Lingis. Chicago: Northwestern University Press, 1991.

Klossowki, Pierre, and Maurice Blanchot. *The Decadence of the Nude* [*DN*]. London: Black Dog Publishing, 2001.

Kokole, Omari H. "The Political Economy of the African Environment" [*PEAE*]. In Westra and Wenz, eds., *Faces of Environmental Racism: Confronting Issues of Global Justice.*

Kondo, Dorinne. "The Aesthetics and Politics of Japanese Identity in the Fashion Industry" [*APJI*]. In Roach-Higgins, Eicher, and Johnson, eds., *Dress and Identity.*

Krell, David Farrell. *Daimon Life: Heidegger and Life-Philosophy* [*DL*]. Bloomington: Indiana University Press, 1992.

——. "Eating Out" [*EO*]. In Scapp and Seitz, eds., *Eating Culture.*

——. *Intimations of Mortality* [*IM*]. University Park: Pennsylvania State University Press, 1986.

Krippner, Stanley. "Parapsychology and Postmodern Science" [*PPS*]. In Griffin, ed., *Reenchantment of Science.*

Kristeva, Julia. *About Chinese Women* [*ACW*]. Trans. Anita Barrows. London: M. Boyars, 1977. Translation of *Des Chinoises.* Éditions de Femmes, 1974.

——. *Black Sun: Depression and Melancholia* [*BS*]. Translation of *Soleil noir: dépression et mélancolie.* Paris: Gallimard, 1987.

——. *Desire in Language: A Semiotic Approach to Literature and Art* [*DL*]. Trans. Leon S. Roudiez. New York: Columbia University Press, 1980.

——. *In the Beginning was Love: Psychoanalysis and Faith* [*IBL*]. Trans. Arthur Goldhammer. New York: Columbia University Press, 1987. Translation of *Au commencement était l'amour: psychoanalyse et foi*. Paris: Hachette, 1985.

——. *The Kristeva Reader* [*KR*]. Ed. Toril Moi. Trans. Alice Jardine and Harry Blake. New York: Columbia University Press, 1986.

——. *Powers of Horror: An Essay on Abjection* [*PH*]. Trans. Leon S. Roudiez. New York: Columbia University Press, 1982. Translation of *Pouvoirs de l'horreur.* Paris: Éditions de Seuil, 1980.

——. *Revolution in Poetic Language* [*RPL*]. Trans. Margaret Waller. New York: Columbia University Press, 1984.

——. "Stabat Mater" [*SM*]. In *Tales of Love*, 234–63.

——. *Strangers to Ourselves* [*SO*]. Trans. Leon S. Roudiez. New York: Columbia University Press, 1991. Translation of *Étrangers à nous-mêmes.* Paris: Fayard, 1988.

——. *Tales of Love* [*TL*]. Trans. Leon S. Roudiez. New York: Columbia University Press, 1987. Translation of *Histoire d'amour.* Paris: Denouël, 1983.

——. "Women's Time" [*WT*]. In *Kristeva Reader*, 187–213. Published as "Le temps des femmes." *Cahiers de recherche de sciences des textes et documents* 5 (Winter 1979).

Kroker, Arthur and Marilouise Kroker, eds. *The Last Sex: Feminism and Outlaw Bodies* [*LS*]. New York: St. Martin's, 1993.

Lacan, Jacques. *Écrits: a Selection* [*É*]. Trans. Alan Sheridan. New York: W. W. Norton & Co., 1977.

——. *Feminine Sexuality* [*FS*]. Ed. Juliet Mitchell and Jacqueline Rose. Trans. Jacqueline Rose. New York: Norton, 1985.

——. "God and the *Jouissance* of ~~The~~ Woman" [*GJW*]. In *Feminine Sexuality*.

——. "A Love Letter" [*LL*]. In *Feminine Sexuality*.

——. "Seminar on *The Purloined Letter* [*SPL*]." Trans. Jeffrey Mehlmann. *Yale French Studies*, no. 48 (1972).

LaChapelle, Dolores. *Earth Wisdom* [*EW*]. San Diego: Guild of Tudors, 1978.

Lacoue-Labarthe, Philippe. *The Subject of Philosophy* [*SP*]. Trans. Thomas Trezise, Hugh J. Silverman, Gary M. Cole, Timothy D. Bent, Karen McPherson, and Claudette Sartiliot. Ed. Thomas Trezise. Minneapolis: University of Minnesota Press, 1993. Translation of *Le Sujet de la philosophie* [*Sp*]. Paris: Aubier-Flammarion, 1979.

Lacoue-Labarthe, Philippe, and Jean-Luc Nancy. *Retreating the Political* [*RP*]. Ed. Simon Sparks. New York: Routledge, 1997.

Lafferty, William M., and James Meadowcroft, eds. *Democracy and the Environment: Problems and Prospects* [*DE*]. Cheltenham: Edward Elgar, 1996.

LaFleur, William. "Sattva: Enlightenment for Plants & Trees" [*S*]. In Badiner, ed., *Dharma Gaia*.

Lahar, Stephanie. "Ecofeminist Theory and Grassroots Politics" [*ETGP*]. In Warren, ed., *Hypatia*, 28–45.

Laing, R. D. *The Divided Self: An Existential Study in Sanity and Madness* [*DS*]. New York: Penguin Books, 1969.

Langer, Susanne Katherina Knauth. *Feeling and Form: A Theory of Art Developed from Philosophy in a New Key* [*FF*]. New York: Scribner's, 1953.

——. *Philosophy in a New Key: A Study in the Symbolism of Reason, Rite, and Art* [*PNK*]. Cambridge, MA: Harvard University Press, 1957.

——. *Problems of Art; Ten Philosophical Lectures* [*PA*]. New York: Scribner, 1957.

Largey, Gale Peter, and David Rogney Watson. "The Sociology of Odors" [*SO*]. In Roach-Higgins, Eicher, and Johnson, eds., *Dress and Identity*.

Latour, Bruno. *Pandora's Hope: Essays on the Reality of Science Studies* [*PH*]. Cambridge, MA: Harvard University Press, 1999.

——. *Politics of Nature: How to Bring the Sciences into Democarcy* [*PN*]. Trans. Catherine Porter. Cambridge, MA: Harvard University Press, 2004.

——. *Science in Action: How to Follow Scientists and Engineers Through Society* [*SA*]. Cambridge, MA: Harvard University Press, 1987.

——. *We Have Never Been Modern* [*WNM*]. Trans. Catherine Porter. Cambridge, MA: Harvard University Press, 1993.

Laughlin, Robert B. "Reinventing Physics: The Search for the Real Frontier" [*RP*]. *Chronicle of Higher Education* (February 11, 2005): B6–8;

adapted from *A Different Universe: Reinventing Physics From the Bottom Down* (New York: Basic Books), 2005.

Lebra, Takie Sugiyama. "*Migawari*: The Cultural Idiom of Self-Other Exchange in Japan" [*M*]. In Ames, ed., *Self as Person in Asian Theory and Practice.*

Lefkovitz, Lori Hope, ed., *Textual Bodies: Changing Boundaries of Literary Representation* [*TB*]. Albany: State University of New York Press, 1993.

Leibniz, G. W. F. "The Exigency to Exist in Essences: Principle of Plenitude" [*EEE*]. In *Leibniz Selections.*

——. *Leibniz Selections* [*LS*]. Ed. P. Wiener. New York: Scribner's, 1951. All references to Leibniz are from this edition.

——. "The Monadology" [*M*]. In *Leibniz Selections.*

Leiss, William. *The Limits to Satisfaction: An Essay on the Problem of Needs and Commodities* [*LS*]. Montreal: McGill-Queen's University Press, 1988.

Leopold, Aldo. *Game Management* [*GM*]. Madison: University of Wisconsin Press, 1986.

——. "The Land Ethic" [*LE*]. In *Sand County Almanac.*

——. *A Sand County Almanac* [*SCA*]. New York: Ballantine Books, 1970.

——. "Thinking Like a Mountain" [*TLM*]. In *Sand County Almanac.*

——. "Wilderness" [*W*]. In *Sand County Almanac.*

Levinas, Emmanuel. *Alterity and Transcendence* [*AT*]. Trans. Michael B. Smith. New York: Columbia University Press, 1999. Translation of *Altérité et transcendence.* Paris: Éditions Fata Morgana, 1995.

——. *Basic Philosophical Writings* [*BPW*]. Ed. Adriaan T. Peperzak, Simon Critchley, Robert Bernasconi. Bloomington: Indiana University Press, 1996.

——. *Collected Philosophical Papers* [*CPP*]. Trans. Alphonso Lingis. Pittsburgh: Duquesne University Press, 1998.

——. *Difficult Freedom: Essays on Judaism* [*DF*]. Trans. Seán Hand. Baltimore: Johns Hopkins Press, 1990.

——. "Diachrony and Representation" [*DR*]. In *Time and the Other.*

——. *Ethics and Infinity: Conversations with Philippe Nemo* [*EF*]. Trans. Richard A. Cohen. Pittsburgh: Duquesne University Press, 1985. Translation of *Ethique et infini.* Paris: Fayard, 1982.

——. "Ethics as First Philosophy" [*EFP*]. In *Levinas Reader.*

——. *Existence and Existents* [*EE*]. Trans. Alphonso Lingis. The Hague: Martinus Nijhoff, 1978.

——. *God, Death, and Time* [*GDT*]. Trans. Bettina Bergo. Stanford: Stanford University Press, 2000.

——. *Humanism of the Other* [*HO*]. Trans. Nidra Poller. Urbana, IL: University of Illinois, 2003. Translation of *Humanisme de'autre homme.* Paris: Éditions Fata Morgana, 1972.

——. *The Levinas Reader* [*LR*]. Ed. Seán Hand. Oxford: Blackwell, 1989.

——. "Martin Buber and the Theory of Knowledge" [*MBTK*]. In *Levinas Reader.*

——. "The Old and the New" [*ON*]. In *Time and the Other.*

——. *Of God Who Comes to Mind* [*OGWCM*]. Trans. Bettina Bergo. Stanford: Stanford University Press, 1996.

——. *On Escape* [*OE*]. Trans. Bettina Bergo. Stanford: Stanford University Press, 2003.

——. *Otherwise than Being or Beyond Essence* [*OB*]. Trans. Alphonso Lingis. The Hague: Martinus Nijhoff, 1978. Translation of *Autrement qu'être ou au-delà de l'essence* [*AÊ*]. The Hague: Martinus Nijhoff, 1974.

——. *Outside the Subject* [*OS*]. Trans. Michael B. Smith. Stanford, CA: Stanford University Press, 1994. Translation of *Hors sujet*. Saint Clement: Éditions Fata Morgana, 1987.

——. "The Paradox of Morality: an Interview with Emmanuel Levinas" [*PM*]. With Tamra Wright, Peter Hughes, Alison Ainley. Trans. Andrew Benjamin and Tamra Wright. In Bernasconi and Wood, ed., *Provocation of Levinas.*

——. *Proper Names* [*PN*]. Trans. Michael B. Smith. Stanford: Stanford University Press, 1996.

——. "Reality and Its Shadow" [*RS*]. Trans. Alphonso Lingis. In *Levinas Reader.*

——. "Reality and Its Shadow" [*RS2*]. In *Unforeseen History.*

——. "Substitution" [*S*]. In *Levinas Reader.*

——. *Time and the Other (and additional essays)* [*TO*]. Trans. Richard A. Cohen. Pittsburgh: Duquesne University Press, 1987.

——. *Totality and Infinity* [*TI*]. Trans. Alphonso Lingis. Pittsburgh: Duquesne University Press, 1969.

——. "The Transcendence of Words" [*TW*]. Trans. Seán Hand. In *Levinas Reader.*

——. *Unforeseen History* [*UH*]. Trans. Nidra Poller. Chicago: University of Illinois Press, 2004. Levine, David P. *Subjectivity in Political Economy: Essays on Wanting and Choosing* [*SPE*]. New York: Routledge, 1998.

Levine, Donald N. "Simmel at a Distance: On the History and Systematics of the Sociology of the Stranger" [*SD*]. In Shack & Skinner, eds., *Strangers in African Societies.*

Levine, George. *Darwin Loves You: Natural Selection and the Re-Enchantment of the World* [*DLY*]. Princeton: Princeton University Press, 2006.

Lévi-Strauss, Claude. *The Elementary Structure of Kinship* [*ESK*]. Trans. James Harle Bell, John Richard von Sturmer, and Rodney Needham. Boston: Beacon Press, 1969.

Lewontin, Richard. *Biology as Ideology: The Doctrine of DNA* [*BI*]. New York: Harper, 1993.

——. *It Ain't Necessarily So: The Dream of the Human Genome and Other Illusions* [*IANS*]. New York: New York Review of Books, 2000: 52.

——. *The Triple Helix* [*TH*]. Cambridge, MA: Harvard University Press, 2002.

Lewontin, Richard, Steven Rose, and Leon J. Kamin. Not in Our Genes [NOG], New York: Pantheon, 1984.

Lewis, James A. *Landownership in the United States, 1978* [*LUS*]. Washington, DC: Natural Resource Economics Division; Economics, Statistics, and Cooperative Services, U.S. Department of Agriculture, Agricultural Information Bulletin 435, April, 1980.

Liddell, Henry George, and Robert Scott. *An Intermediate Greek-English Lexicon, Founded Upon The Seventh Edition of Liddell and Scott's Greek-English Lexicon* [*IGEL*]. Oxford: Oxford University Press, 1991.

Lingis, Alphonso. "Appetite" [*A*]. In Scapp, ed., *Eating Culture*.

——. *Foreign Bodies* [*FB*]. New York: Routledge, 1994.

Linsky, Leonard, ed. *Semantics and the Philosophy of Language* [*SPL*]. Urbana: University of Illinois Press. 1952.

Lipietz, Alan. *Green Hopes: The Future of Political Ecology* [*GH*]. Cambridge, MA: Polity Press, 1995.

Lipka, Richard P., and Thomas M. Brinthaupt. *Self-Perspectives Across the Life Span* [*SPALS*]. Albany: State University of New York Press, 1992.

Lispector, Clarice. *The Passion According to G. H.* [*PGH*]. Trans. Ronald W. Sousa. Minneapolis: University of Minnesota Press, 1988.

——. *O Lustro* [*OL*]. Rio de Janeiro: Editora Nova Fronteira, 1982.

Locke, Alain. *Negro Art: Past and Present* [*NAPP*]. Washington, DC: Associates in Negro Folk Education, 1936.

——. *The Negro in Art: A Pictorial Record of the Negro Theme in Art* [*NA*]. Washington, DC: Associates in Negro Folk Education, 1940.

Locke, John. *An Essay Concerning Human Understanding* [*E*]. Ed. Alexander Campbell Fraser. New York: Dover, 1959.

——. *Two Treatises of Government* [*TT*]. Student ed., Ed. Peter Laslett. Oxford: Cambridge University Press, 1988.

Loewental, Kate. "Property." *European Journal of Social Psychology* 6, no. 3 (May–June 1976): 343–51.

Lorde, Audre. "Age, Race, Class, and Sex: Women Redefining Difference" [*ARCS*]. In Andersen and Collins, eds., *Race, Class, and Gender*.

Lovelock, James. *Gaia: A New Look at Life on Earth* [*G*]. Oxford: Oxford University Press, 1979.

Lowrie, Robert H. *Primitive Religion* [*PR*]. New York: Boni and Liveright, 1924.

Lozano, Luis-Martin. *The Magic of Remedios Varo*. Trans. Elizabeth Goldson and Liliana Valenzuela. Washington, DC: National Museum of Women in the Arts, 2000.

Lubar, Steven, and W. David Kingery, eds. *History from Things: Essays on Material Culture* [*HS*]. Washington, DC: Smithsonian Institution Press, 1993.

Ludwig, Arnold N. *How Do We Know Who We Are?: A Biography of the Self* [*HDWKWWA?*]. Oxford: Oxford University Press, 1997.

Lugones, Marìa C. "On the Logic of Pluralist Feminism" [*OLPF*]. In Card, ed., *Feminist Ethics*.

——. "Playfulness, 'World'-Travelling, and Loving Perception" [*PWTLP*]. *Hypatia* 2, no. 2 (Summer 1987): 3–20.

Lukács, György. *The Destruction of Reason* [*DR*]. Trans. Peter Palmer. London: Merlin Press, 1980.

——. *The Ontology of Social Being* [*OSB*]. Trans. David Fernbach. London: Merlin Press, 1980.

Lury, Celia. *Prosthetic Culture: Photography, Memory and Identity* [*PC*]. London: Routledge, 1998.

Lyon, M. L., and J. M. Barbalet. "Society's Body: Emotion and the 'Somatization' of Social Theory" [*SB*]. In Csordas, *Embodiment and Experience.*

Lyotard, Jean-François. *Le Différend* [*D*]. Paris: Minuit, 1983.

——. *The Differend: Phrases in Dispute* [*DPD*]. Trans. Georges Van Den Abbeele. Minneapolis: University of Minnesota Press, 1988.

——. "Europe, the Jew, and the Book" [*EJB*]. In *Political Writings.*

——. "German Guilt" [*GG*]. In *Political Writings.*

——. "The Grip *(Mainmise)*" [*G*]. In *Political Writings.*

——. *Heidegger and "the jews"* [*HJ*]. Trans. A. Michel and M. Roberts. Minneapolis: University of Minnesota Press, 1990.

——. "Heidegger and 'the jews': A Conference in Vienna and Freiburg" [*"HJ"*]. In *Political Writings.*

——. *The Inhuman: Reflections on Time* [*I*]. Trans. Geoffrey Bennington and Rachel Bowlby. Stanford: Stanford University Press, 1991.

——. *Lessons on the Analytic of the Sublime* [*LAS*]. Trans. Elizabeth Rottenberg. Stanford, CA: Stanford University Press, 1994.

——. *Libidinal Economy* [*LE*]. Trans. Iain Hamilton Grant. Bloomington: Indiana University Press, 1993.

——. *The Lyotard Reader* [*LR*]. Ed. Andrew Benjamin. Oxford: Blackwell, 1989.

——. *"Oikos"* [*O*]. In *Political Writings.*

——. *Peregrinations* [*P*]. New York: Columbia University Press, 1988.

——. *Phenomenology* [*Ph*]. Trans. Brian Beakley. Albany: State University of New York Press, 1991.

——. *Political Writings* [*PW*]. Trans. Bill Readings and Kevin Paul Geiman. Minneapolis: University of Minnesota Press, 1993.

——. *The Postmodern Condition: A Report on Knowledge* [*PMC*]. Trans. Geoff Bennington and Brian Massumi. Minneapolis: University of Minnesota Press, 1984.

——. "The Sign of History" [*SH*]. In *Lyotard Reader.*

——. "What Is Postmodernism?" [*WP?*]. Reprinted in part in Ross, ed., *Art and Its Significance.* In *Postmodern Condition.*

Lyotard, Jean-François, and Jean-Loup Thébaud. *Just Gaming* [*JG*]. Trans. Wlad Godzich. Minneapolis: University of Minnesota Press, 1985.

MacDonald, Anne-Marie. *Belle Moral: A Natural History* [*BM*]. Toronto: Playwrights Canada Press, 2006.

Mack, Carol K., and Dinah Mack. *A Field Guide to Demons, Fairies, Fallen Angels, and Other Subversive Spirits* [*FGD*]. New York: Henry Holt & Co. 1998.

MacKinnon, Catharine A. "Feminism, Marxism, Method, and the State: An Agenda for Theory" [*FMMS1*]. *Signs* 7, no. 3 (Spring 1982): 515–44.

——. "Feminism, Marxism, Method, and the State: Toward Feminist Jurisprudence" [*FMMS2*]. *Signs* 8, no. 4 (Summer 1982): 635–58.

——. *Feminism Unmodified: Discourses on Life and Law* [*FU*]. Cambridge: Harvard University Press, 1987.

——. *Only Words* [*OW*]. Cambridge: Harvard University Press, 1993.

——. "Sexuality" [*S*]. Chapter 7 in *Toward a Feminist Theory of the State.*

——. *Toward a Feminist Theory of the State* [*TFTS*]. Cambridge: Harvard University Press, 1989.

——. "Toward Feminist Jurisprudence" [*TFJ*]. Chapter 13 in *Toward a Feminist Theory of the State.*

Macpherson, C. B. "The Meaning of Property" [*MP*]. In Macpherson, ed., *Property: Mainstream and Critical Positions* [*P*].

——. *The Political Theory of Possessive Individualism: Hobbes to Locke* [*PTPI*]. Oxford: Oxford University Press, 1962.

——., ed. *Property: Mainstream and Critical Positions* [*P*]. Toronto: University of Toronto Press, 1983.

Macy, Joanna. *World as Lover, World as Self* [*WLWS*]. Berkeley, CA: Parallax Press, 1991.

Maddock, Kenneth. "Involved Anthropologists" [*IA*]. In Wilmsen, ed., *We Are Here.*

Malhotra, Ashok K. "Sartre and Samkhya-Yoga on Self" [*SSYS*]. In Allen, ed., *Culture and Self.*

Manderson, Desmond. *Songs Without Music: Aesthetic Dimensions of Law and Justice* [*SWM*]. Berkeley: University of California Press, 2000.

Manes, Christopher. *Green Rage: Radical Environmentalism and the Unmaking of Civilization* [*GRF*]. Boston: Little, Brown and Co., 1990.

——. "Nature and Silence" [*NS*]. In Oelschlaeger, ed., *Postmodern Environmental Ethics.*

Marcel, Gabriel. *Ghostly Mysteries* [*GM*]. Trans. Katharine Rose Hanley. Milwaukee: Marquette University Press, 2004.

Margalit, Avishai. *The Ethics of Memory* [*EM*]. Cambridge, MA: Harvard University Press, 2002.

Margolis, Diane Rothbard. *The Fabric of Self: A Theory of Ethics and Emotions* [*FS*]. New Haven, CT: Yale University Press, 1998.

Margolis, Joseph. *Art and Philosophy* [*AP*]. Atlantic Highlands, NJ: Humanities Press; Hassocks: Harvester Press, 1980.

——. *Culture and Cultural Entities* [*CCE*]. Dordrecht: D. Reidel, 1984.

——. *Interpretation Radical But Not Unruly: The New Puzzle of the Arts and History* [*IRNU*]. Berkeley: University of California Press, 1995.

——. *The Language of Art and Art Criticism: Analytic Questions in Aesthetics* [*LAAC*]. Detroit: Wayne State University Press, 1965.

——. *Pragmatism without Foundations: Reconciling Relativism and Realism* [*PWF*]. Oxford: Basil Blackwell, 1986.

——. *Reinventing Pragmatism: American Philosophy at the End of the Twentieth Century* [*RP*]. Ithaca, NY: Cornell University Press, 2002.

——. *Texts without Referents: Reconciling Science and Narrative* [*TWR*]. Oxford: Basil Blackwell, 1989.

——. *What, After All, Is a Work of Art?* [*WWA?*]. Lectures in the Philosophy of Art. University Park: Pennsylvania State University Press, 1999.

Marion, Jean-Luc. *Being Given: Toward a Phenomenology of Givenness* [*BG*]. Trans. Jeffrey L. Kosky. Stanford, CA: Stanford University Press, 2002.

——. *Étant Donné: Essai de la phénoménologie de donation* [*ÉD*]. Paris: Presses universitaires de France, 1997.

——. *Reduction and Givenness: Investigations of Husserl, Heidegger, and Phenomenology* [*RG*]. Trans. Thomas A. Carlson. Chicago: Northwestern University Press, 1998.

——. *Réduction et donation: recherches sur Husserl, Heidegger et la phénoménologie* [*Rd*]. Paris: Presses universitaires de France, 1989.

Marks, Elaine, and Isabelle Courtivron, eds. *New French Feminisms: An Anthology* [*NFF*]. New York: Schocken, 1981.

Martin, James J. *Men Against the State: The Expositors of Individualist Anarchism in America, 1827–1908* [*MAS*]. DeKalb, IL: Adrian Allen Associates, 1953.

Marx, Karl. *Capital: A Critique of Political Economy* [*C*]. 4th ed., 3 vols. Ed. Friedrich Engels. Trans. Ben Fowkes. London: Penguin Books in association with New Left Review, 1976.

——. *Capital: A Critique of Political Economy* [*C3*]. 3rd ed., 3 vols. Ed. Friedrich Engels. Trans. Samuel Moore and Edward Aveling. New York: International Publishers, 1967.

——. *The German Ideology* [*GI*]. In Karl Marx and Friedrich Engels, *Collected Works*, vol. 5. New York: International Publishers, 1976.

——. "Marx to Schweitzer" [*MS*]. In *Poverty of Philosophy*.

——. *The Poverty of Philosophy* [*PP*]. New York: International Publishers, 1963.

——. *A World Without Jews* [*WWJ*]. 4th ed., Ed. and int. Dagobert D Runes. New York: Philosophical Library, 1960.

Marx, Karl, and Friedrich Engels. *Selected Works* [*SW*]. 2 vols. Marx-Engels-Lenin Institute. Moscow: Foreign Languages Publish House, 1953. London: Lawrence and Wishart, 1953.

Massumi, Brian. "The Bleed" [*B*]. In Welchman, ed., *Rethinking Borders*.

Matilal, Bimal Krishna. "The Perception of Self in Indian Tradition" [*PSIT*]. In Ames, ed., *Self as Person in Asian Theory and Practice*.

Mathews, Freya. *The Ecological Self* [*ES*]. Savage, Md.: Barnes & Noble Books, 1991.

Mauss, Marcel. *The Gift: Forms and Functions of Exchange in Archaic Societies* [*G*]. Trans. Ian Cunnison. Glenco: Free Press, 1954. Also *The Gift: The Form and Reason for Exchange in Archaic Societies*. Trans. W. D. Halls. London: Routledge, 1990.

Maw, Joan, and John Picton, eds. *Concepts of the Body/Self in Africa* [*CBS*]. Vienna: Afro-Pub, 1992.

May, Todd. *The Political Philosophy of Poststructuralist Anarchism* [*PPPA*]. University Park, PA: The Pennsylvania State University Press, 1994.

Mbiti, John S. *African Religions and Philosophy* [*ARP*]. London: Heinemann Educational Books, 1969.

McConnell, Theodore A. *The Shattered Self: The Psychological and Religious Search for Selfhood* [*SS*]. Philadelphia: Pilgrim Press, 1971.

McCoy, Edain. *A Witch's Guide to Faery Folk* [*WGFF*]. St. Paul, MN: Llewellyn Publications, 1994.

McGrath, Alister. *The Reenchantment of Nature: The Denial of Religion and the Ecological Crisis* [*RN*]. New York: Galilee, 2003.

McIntosh, Peggy. "White Privilege and Male Privilege: A Personal Account of Coming to See Correspondences through Work in Women's Studies" [*WPMP*]. In Andersen and Collins, eds., *Race, Class, and Gender.*

McLaughlin, Andrew. *Regarding Nature: Industrialism and Deep Ecology* [*RN*]. Albany: State University of New York Press, 1993.

Meiling, Jin. "Strangers on a Hostile Landscape" [*SHL*]. In Cobham and Collins, eds., *Watchers and Seekers.*

Merchant, Carolyn. *The Death of Nature: Women, Ecology, and the Scientific Revolution* [*DN*]. New York: Harper & Row, 1980.

———. *Radical Ecology: The Search for a Livable World* [*RE*]. New York: Routledge, 1992.

Meredith, George. *An Essay on Comedy* [*EC*]. In Sypher, *Comedy.*

Merleau-Ponty, Maurice. *Eye and Mind* [*EM*]. Trans. Carleton Dallery. Reprinted in part in Ross, ed., *Art and Its Significance.* In *Primacy of Perception*, 282–98.

———. *Phenomenology of Perception* [*PhP*]. Trans. Colin Smith. London: Routledge & Kegan Paul, 1962.

———. *The Primacy of Perception* [*PrP*]. Ed. James M. Edie. Evanston: Northwestern University Press, 1964.

———. *The Visible and the Invisible* [*VI*]. Ed. Claude Lefort. Trans. Alphonso Lingis. Evanston: Northwestern University Press, 1968.

Merriam-Webster Dictionary of English Usage [*MWDEU*]. Springfield, MA: Merriam-Webster, 1989.

Meyer, Christine, and Faith Moosang, eds. *Living with the Land: Communities Restoring the Earth* [*LL*]. Gabriola Island, BC: New Society Publishers, 1992.

Mignolo, Walter D. *Local Histories/Global Designs: Coloniality, Subaltern Knowledges, and Border Thinking* [*LH*]. Princeton: Princeton University Press, 2000

Mill, John Stuart. *On Liberty; with The Subjection of Women and Chapters on Socialism* [*L*]. New York: Cambridge University Press, 1989.

———. *Utilitarianism and Other Essays* [*U*]. New York: Penguin, 1987.

Miller, Mara. "Views of Japanese Selfhood: Japanese and Western Perspectives" [*VJS*]. In Allen, ed., *Culture and Self.*

Milton, Katharine. "Real Men Don't Eat Deer" [*RMDED*]. *Discover* 18, no. 6 (June 1997): 46–53.

Minogue, Kenneth. "The Concept of Property and Its Contemporary Significance" [*CPCS*]. In Pennock and Chapman, eds., *Nomos XXII*, 3–27.

Moore, Thomas. *The Re Enchantment of Everyday Life* [*REL*]. New York: Harper, 1997.

Morgan, Lewis. *Ancient Slavery, or Researches in the Lines of Human Progress from Savagery through Barbarism to Civilization* [*AS*]. London: MacMillan, 1877.

Morgan, Robin, ed. *Sisterhood Is Powerful: An Anthology of Writings from the Women's Liberation Movement* [*SP*]. New York: Random House, 1970.

Morris, Brian. *Anthropology of the Self: The Individual in Cultural Perspective* [*AS*]. London: Pluto Press, 1994.

Morton, A. I., ed. *Freedom in Arms: A Selection of Leveller Writings* [*FA*]. New York: International Publishers, 1974.

Mote, Frederick W. *Intellectual Foundations of China* [*IFC*]. New York: Alfred A. Knopf, 1971.

Mouffe, Chantal. *The Return of the Political* [*RP*]. New York: Verso, 1993.

———., ed. *Deconstruction and Pragmatism* [*DP*]. New York: Routledge, 1996.

———., ed. *Dimensions of Radical Democracy: Pluralism, Citizenship, Community* [*DRD*]. New York: Verso, 1992.

Mudimbe, V. Y. *The Invention of Africa* [*IA*]. In *Invention of Africa: Gnosis, Philosophy, and the Order of Knowledge*. Bloomington: Indiana University Press, 1988.Reprinted in part in Ross, ed., *Art and Its Significance*.

Munzer, Stephen R. *A Theory of Property* [*P*]. Cambridge: Cambridge University Press, 1990.

Murti, T. R. V. *The Central Philosophy of Buddhism: A Study of the Mâdhyamika System* [*CPB*]. 2nd ed., London: George Allen and Unwin, 1960.

Myers, Fred. "Burning the Truck and Holding the Country: Pintupi Forms of Property and Identity" [*BTHC*]. In Wilmsen, ed., *We Are Here*.

Nadotti, Maria. "Karen Finley's Poisoned Meatloaf" [*KFPM*]. *Artforum* 27 (March 1989).

Naess, Arne. *Ecology, Community and Lifestyle: Outline of an Ecosophy* [*ECL*]. Trans. David Rothenberg. Cambridge: Cambridge University Press, 1989.

———. "The Shallow and the Deep: Long Range Ecology Movement" [*SD*]. *Inquiry* 16 (1973): 95–100.

Nagakawa, Keiichirō, and Henry Rosovsky. "The Case of the Dying Kimono: The Influence of Changing Fashions on the Development of the Japanese Woolen Industry" [*CDK*]. In Roach-Higgins, Eicher, and Johnson, eds., *Dress and Identity*.

Nāgārjuna, *Elegant Sayings* [*ES*]. Ed. Sakya Pandit. Emeryville: Dharma Publishing, 1977.

———. *The Philosophy of the Middle Way* [*PMW*]. Trans. int., and commentary David J. Kalupahana. Albany: State University of New York Press, 1986.

Nagel, Thomas. *Moral Questions* [*MQ*]. Cambridge: Cambridge University Press, 1979.

Nancy, Jean-Luc. *The Birth to Presence* [*BP*]. Trans. Brian Holmes and Others. Stanford: Stanford University Press, 1993.

——. *The Experience of Freedom* [*EF*]. Trans. Bridget McDonald. Fwd. Peter Fenves. Stanford: Stanford University Press, 1993.

——. *The Inoperative Community* [*IC*]. Trans. P. Connor, L. Garbus, M. Holland, and S. Sawhney. Minneapolis: University of Minnesota Press, 1991.

——. *Literary Communism* [*LC*]. In *Inoperative Community.*

——. *The Muses* [*M*]. Trans. Peggy Kamuf. Stanford, CA: Stanford University Press, 1996.

——. "Of Divine Places" [*DP*]. In *Inoperative Community.*

——. *The Sense of the World* [*SW*]. Trans. and fwd. Jeffrey S. Librett. Minneapolis: University of Minnesota Press, 1997.

——. "Shattered Love" [*SL*]. In *Inoperative Community.*

Nasar, Jack L., ed. *Environmental Aesthetics: Theory, Research, and Applications* [*EA*]. Cambridge: Cambridge University Press, 1988.

Nash, Roderick. *The Rights of Nature* [*RN*]. Madison: University of Wisconsin, Press, 1989.

——. *Wilderness and the American Mind* [*WAM*]. 3rd ed., New Haven: Yale University Press, 1982.

Naukkarinen, Ossi. *Aesthetics of the Unavoidable: Aesthetic Variations in Human Appearance* [*AU*]. Saarijärvi: Gummerus Kirjapaino Oy, 1998.

Negri, Antonio. *Marx Beyond Marx: Lessons on the Grundrisse* [*MBM*]. South Hadley, MA: Bergin & Garvey, 1984.

——. *Revolution Retrieved: Writings on Marx, Keynes, Capitalist Crisis and New Social Subjects* [*RR*]. London: Red Notes, 1988.

——. *The Savage Anomaly: The Power of Spinoza's Metaphysics and Politics* [*SA*]. Trans. Michael Hardt. Minneapolis: University of Minnesota Press, 1991.

Neither Nationalisation Nor Privatisation: An Anarchist Approach [*NP*]. London: Freedom Press, 1989.

Nelson, Lynn Hankinson. *Who Knows* [*WK*]. Philadelphia, Temple University Press, 1990.

Nerburn, Kent, ed. *The Wisdom of the Great Chiefs: The Classic Speeches of Chief Red Jacket, Chief Joseph, and Chief Seattle* [*WGC*]. San Rafael, CA: New World Library, 1994.

Nietzsche, Friedrich. *The Antichrist* [*A*]. In *Portable Nietzsche.*

——. "Attempt at a Self-Criticism" [*ASC*]. In *Basic Writings.* Reprinted in Ross, ed., *Art and Its Significance.*

——. *Basic Writings of Nietzsche* [*BWN*]. Trans. Walter Kaufmann. New York: Random House, Modern Library Giant, 1968.

——. *Beyond Good and Evil* [*BGE*]. In *Basic Writings.*

——. *Birth of Tragedy* [*BT*]. In *Basic Writings.* Reprinted in part in Ross, ed., *Art and Its Significance.*

——. *Ecce Homo* [*EH*]. In *Basic Writings.*

——. *The Gay Science* [*GS*]. Trans. with comm. Walter Kaufman. New York: Vintage, 1974.
——. *Genealogy of Morals* [*GM*]. In *Basic Writings.*
——. *Human, All Too Human* [*HATH*]. Trans. R. J. Hollingdale. Cambridge: Cambridge University Press, 1996.
——. *On the Advantage and Disadvantage of History for Life* [*OADHL*]. Trans. P. Preuss. Indianapolis: Hackett, 1980.
——. *The Portable Nietzsche* [*PN*]. Ed. and trans. Walter Kaufmann. New York: Viking Press, 1954.
——. *Seventy-Five Aphorisms from Five Volumes* [*75A*]. In *Basic Writings.* From *Dawn* [*D*]; *Gay Science* [*GS*]; *Human, All-Too-Human* [*H*]; *Mixed Opinions and Maxims* [*MOM*]; *The Wanderer and His Shadow* [*WS*].
——. *Thus Spake Zarathustra* [*Z*]. In *Portable Nietzsche.*
——. *Thus Spake Zarathustra* [*Z2*]. Trans. Thomas Common. Mineola, NY: Dover, 1999.
——. *Twilight of the Idols* [*TI*]. In *Portable Nietzsche.*
——. *The Will to Power* [*WP*]. Ed. Walter Kaufmann. Trans. Robert Hollingdale and Walter Kaufmann. New York: Vintage, 1968.
——. *Unfashionable Observations* [*UO*]. Trans. Richard T. Gray. Stanford, CA: Stanford University Press, 1995.
Nishida Kitarō. *A Study of Good* [*SG*]. Trans. V. H. Viglielmo. New York: Greenwood Press, 1988.
Nishitani. *Religion and Nothingness* [*RN*]. Trans. Jan. Van Bragt. Berkeley: University of California, 1982.
——. *The Self-Overcoming of Nihilism* [*SON*]. Trans. Graham Parkes with Setsuko Aihara. Albany: State University of New York Press, 1990.
Nodding, Nel. *Caring: A Feminine Approach to Ethics and Moral Education* [*C*]. Berkeley: University of California Press, 1984.
Nozick, Robert. *Anarchy, State, and Utopia* [*ASU*]. New York: Basic Books, 1968.
Nussbaum, Martha. *The Fragility of Goodness* [*FG*]. Cambridge: Cambridge University Press, 1986.
——. *Love's Knowledge: Essays on Philosophy and Literature* [*LK*]. New York: Oxford University Press, 1990.
——. *Poetic Justice: The Literary Imagination and Public Life* [*PJ*]. Boston, MA: Beacon Press, 1995.
——. *The Therapy of Desire: Theory and Practice in Hellenistic Ethics* [*TD*]. Princeton, NJ: Princeton University Press, 1994.
——. *Women, Culture, and Development: A Study of Human Capabilities* [*WCD*]. Oxford: Clarendon Press, 1995.
Oates, W. J., and E. O'Neill, eds. *The Complete Greek Drama* [*CGD*]. New York: Random House, 1938.
Obenchain, Diane B. "Spiritual Quests of Twentieth-Century Women: A Theory of Self-Discovery and a Japanese Case Study" [*SQTW*]. In Ames, ed., *Self as Person in Asian Theory and Practice.*

O'Donovan-Anderson, Michael, ed. *The Incorporated Self: Interdisciplinary Perspectives on Embodiment* [*IS*]. Lanham, MD: Rowman & Littlefield, 1996.

Oelschlaeger, Max, ed. *The Wilderness Condition: Essays on Environment and Civilziation* [*WC*]. San Francisco: Sierra Club Books, 1992.

——. *Postmodern Environmental Ethics* [*PMEE*]. Albany: State University of New York Press, 1995.

Ogunwale, Titus A. "Traditional Hairdressing in Nigeria" [*THN*]. In Roach-Higgins, Eicher, and Johnson, eds., *Dress and Identity.*

Olalquiaga, Celeste. "Vulture Culture" [*VC*]. In Welchman, ed., *Rethinking Borders.*

Olson, Carl. *Zen and the Art of Postmodern Philosophy: Two Paths of Liberation from teh Representational Mode of Thinking* [*ZPP*]. Albany: State University of New York Press, 2000.

Omolade, Barbara. "Hearts of Darkness" [*HD*]. In Guy-Sheftall, ed., *Words of Fire.*

Ophuls, William. *Ecology and the Politics of Scarcity* [*EPS*]. San Francisco: W. H. Freeman, 1977.

Osoro, R. *The African Identity in Crisis* [*AIC*]. Hudsonville, Mich.: Bayana Publishers, 1993.

Otnes, Per. *Other-wise: Alterity, Materiality, Mediation* [*AMM*]. Oslo: Scandinavian University Press, 1997.

Oudshoorn, Nelly. "A Natural Order of Things: Reproductive Sciences and the Politics of Othering" [*NOT*]. In Robertson, Mash, Tickner, Bird, Curtis, and Putnam, eds., *Futurenatural.*

Outlaw, Lucius. *Philosophy, Ethnicity, and Race: The Alfred B. Stiernotte Lectures in Philosophy* [*PER*]. Hamden, CT: Quinnipiac College, 1989.

——. "Philosophy, Ethnicity, and Race" ["*PER*"]. In Hord and Lee, eds., *I Am Because We Are.*

——. "Toward a Critical Theory of 'Race'" [*TCTR*]. In Goldberg, ed., *Anatomy of Racism.*

Owens, Craig. "The Discourse of Others: Feminists and Postmodernism" [*DO*]. In Hal Foster, ed., *The Anti-Aesthetic: Essays on Postmodern Culture.* Port Townsend, WA: Bay Press, 1983. Reprinted in Ross, ed., *Art and Its Significance.*

Oxford English Dictionary [*OED*]. Compact Edition. Oxford. Oxford University Press, 1971.

Pagels, Elaine H. "What Became of God the Mother? Conflicting Images of God in Early Christianity" [*WBGM*]. In Christ and Plaskow, eds., *Womanspirit Rising.*

Parrinder, Geoffrey. *Witchcraft: European and African* [*WEA*]. London: Faber and Faber, 1970.

Peirce, Charles Sanders. *The Collected Papers of Charles Sanders Peirce* [*CP*]. 6 vols. Ed. Charles Hartshorne and Paul Weiss. Cambridge: Harvard University Press, 1931–35.

——. *The Essential Peirce: Selected Philosophical Writings, Volume 1 (1867–1893)* [*EP1*]. Bloomington, IN: Indiana University Press, 1992.

——. *The Essential Peirce: Selected Philosophical Writings, Volume 2 (1893–1913)* [*EP2*]. Bloomington, IN: Indiana University Press, 1998.
——. "The Fixation of Belief" [*FB*]. In *Philosophical Writings.*
——. *The Philosophical Writings of Peirce* [*PP*]. Ed. Justus Buchler. New York: Dover, 1955.
Pennock, J. Roland,and John W. Chapman, eds. *Property: Nomos XXII* [*P*]. New York: New York University, 1980.
Pepper, David. *Eco-socialism: From Deep Ecology to Social Justice* [*E*]. New York: Routledge, 1993.
Pepper, Stephen Coburn. *Aesthetic Quality; A Contextualistic Theory of Beauty* [*AQ*]. Westport, CN. Greenwood Press 1965.
——. *The Basis of Criticism in the Arts* [*BCA*]. Cambridge, MA: Harvard University Press, 1945.
——. *Principles of Art Appreciation* [*PAA*]. New York: Harcourt, Brace, 1949.
——. *The Sources of Value* [*SV*]. Berkeley, CA: University of California Press, 1958.
——. *The Work of Art* [*WA*]. Bloomington, IN: Indiana University Press, 1955.
Picton, John. "Masks and Identities in Ebira Culture" [*MIEC*]. In Maw and Picton, eds., *Concepts of the Body/Self in Africa.*
Pinker, Steven. *The Blank Slate: The Modern Denial of Human Nature* [*BS*]. New York: Viking, 2002.
——. *How the Mind Works* [*HMW*]. New York: W. W. Norton, 1997.
Plant, Christopher, and Judith Plant, eds. *Green Business: Hope or Hoax?* [*GB*]. Gabriola Island, BC: New Society Publishers, 1991.
Plant, Judith, ed. *Healing the Wounds: The Power of Ecological Feminism* [*HW*]. Philadelphia: New Society Publishers, 1989.
Plato. *The Collected Dialogues of Plato* [*CDP*]. Ed. Edith Hamilton and Huntington Cairns. Princeton: Princeton University Press, 1961. All quotations from Plato are from this edition unless otherwise indicated.
——. *The Dialogues of Plato.* Trans. Benjamin Jowett. New York: Random House, 1920.
——. *Phaedo* [*PP*]. Ed., with int., and notes by John Burnet. London: Oxford University Press, 1963.
——. *Phaedo.* Trans. Harold North Fowler. Loeb Classical Library. Cambridge: Harvard University Press, 1914. All Greek passages from *Phaedo* are from this edition.
——. *Phaedo.* Trans. Benjamin Jowett. In *The Dialogues of Plato.*
——. *Phaedrus.* Trans. Harold North Fowler. Loeb Classical Library. Cambridge: Harvard University Press, 1914. All Greek passages from *Phaedrus* are from this edition.
——. *Protagoras.* Trans. Benjamin Jowett. 3rd ed., London: Oxford University Press, 1982.
——. *Republic.* Trans. Benjamin Jowett. In *The Dialogues of Plato.*

——. *Symposium*. Trans. Benjamin Jowett. In *The Dialogues of Plato*. 3rd ed., London: Oxford University Press, 1982. All quotations in English from *Symposium* are from this edition.Reprinted in part in Ross, ed., *Art and Its Significance*.

——. *Symposium*. Trans. W. R. M. Lamb. Loeb Classical Library. Cambridge: Harvard University Press, 1925. All Greek passages from *Symposium* are from this edition.

Plotinus. *The Philosophy of Plotinus*. Ed. and sel. Joseph Katz. New York: Appleton-Century-Crofts, 1950.

Plotkin, Bill. Soulcraft: *Crossing into the Mysteries of Nature and Psyche* [*S*]. Novato, CA: New World Library, 2003.

Pollack, Robert. *The Missing Moment: How the Unconscious Shapes Modern Science* [*MM*]. Boston: Houghton Mifflin, 1999.

Ponge, Francis. *Things* [*T*]. Trans. Cid Corman. New York: Grossman Publishers, 1971.

Porteous, J. Douglas. *Environmental Aesthetics: Ideas, Politics and Planning* [*EA*]. New York: Routledge, 1996.

Poster, Mark. "Postmodern Virtualities" [*PV*]. In Robertson, Mash, Tickner, Bird, Curtis, and Putnam, eds., *Futurenatural*.

Priest, Graham. *Beyond the Limits of Thought* [*BLT*]. 2nd ed. New York: Oxford University Press, 2003.

——. *In Contradiction: A Study of the Transconsistent* [*IC*]. New York: Oxford University Press, 2006.

Priest, Graham, J. C. Beall, and Bradley Armour Garb, eds. *The Law of Non Contradiction: New Philosophical Essays* [*LNC*]. New York: Oxford University Press, 2004.

Proudhon, Pierre-Joseph. *What is Property?: An Inquiry into the Principle of Right and of Government* [*WP?*]. Ed. and trans. Donald R. Kelley and Bonnie G. Smith. Cambridge: Cambridge University Press, 1993.

Purchase, Graham. *Anarchism and Ecology* [*AE*]. Montreal: Black Rose Books, 1997.

Quigley, Peter. "Rethinking Resistance: Environmentalism, Literature, and Poststructural Theory" [*RR*]. In Oelschlaeger, ed., *Postmodern Environmental Ethics*.

Quine, Willard Van Ormine. "Natural Kinds" [*NK*]. In Schwartz, ed., *Naming, Necessity, and Natural Kinds*.

——. *Word and Object* [*WO*]. Cambridge: MIT Press, 1960.

Rachels, James. "Why Animals Have a Right to Liberty" [*WARL*]. In Regan and Singer, eds., *Animal Rights and Human Obligations*.

Radin, Margaret Jane. "Market-Inalienability" [*MI*]. *Harvard Law Review* 100 (1987): 1849–1937.

——. "Property and Personhood" [*PP*]. *Stanford Law Review* 34 (1982): 957–1015.

——. *Reinterpreting Property* [*RP*]. Chicago: University of Chicago Press, 1993.

Randall, Jr., John Herman. *Aristotle* [*A*]. New York: Columbia University Press, 1960.

——. *Plato: Dramatist of the Life of Reason* [*P*]. New York: Columbia University Press, 1970.
Random House Dictionary of the English Language [*RHD1*]. Unabridged. New York: Random House, 1966.
——. [*RHD2*]. 2nd ed., Unabridged., New York: Random House, 1987.
Ransaw, Lee A. "The Depiction of Black Imagery Among the World's Masterpieces in Art" [*DBI*]. In Young, ed., *Art, Culture, and Ethnicity.*
Rapaport, David. "A Historical Survey of Psychoanalytic Ego Psychology" [*HSPEP*]. In Erikson, *Identity and the Life Cycle.*
Rawls, John. *A Theory of Justice* [*TJ*]. Cambridge: Belknap Press of Harvard University, 1971.
Reed, A. W. *Myths and Legends of Australia* [*MLA*]. Sydney: A. H. and A. W. Reed, 1971.
Regan, Tom. *All That Dwell Therein: Animal Rights and Environmental Ethics* [*ADT*]. Berkeley: University of California Press, 1982.
——. *The Case for Animal Rights* [*CAR*]. Berkeley: University of California Press, 1983.
Regan, Tom, and Peter Singer, eds. *Animal Rights and Human Obligations* [*ARHO*]. 2nd ed., Englewood Cliffs: Prentice Hall, 1989.
Reich, Charles. "The New Property" [*NP*]. *Yale Law Journal* 73 (1964): 733–87.
Reich, Wilhelm. *Selected Writings: An Introduction to Orgonomy* [*SW*]. New York: Noonday Press, 1960.
Reiter, Rayna R., ed. *Toward an Anthropology of Women*. New York: Monthly Press, 1975.
Richard, Nelly. "The Cultural Periphery and Postmodern Decentring: Latin America's Reconversion of Borders" [*CPPD*]. In Welchman, ed., *Rethinking Borders.*
Ricoeur, Paul. *Memory, History, Forgetting* [*MHF*]. Trans. Kathleen Blamey and David Pellauer. Chicago: University of Chicago Press, 2004.
Ricoeur, Paul. *Oneself as Another* [*OA*]. Chicago: University of Chicago Press, 1992.
Rigby, Peter. *Cattle, Capitalism, and Class: Ilparakuyo Maasai Transformations* [*CCC*]. Philadelphia: Temple University Press, 1992.
Rigterink, Roger J. "Warning: The Surgeon Moralist Has Determined That Claims of Rights Can Be Detrimental to Everyone's Interests" [*W*]. In Cole and Coultrap-McQuin, eds., *Explorations in Feminist Ethics.*
Ritzer, George. *Enchanting a Disenchanted World: Revolutionizing the Means of Consumption* [*EDW*]. 2nd ed. Thousand Oaks, CA: Pine Forge Press, 2005.
Roach, Catherine. "Loving Your Mother: On the Woman-Nature Relationship" [*LM*]. In Warren, ed., *Hypatia*, 46–59.
Roach-Higgins, Mary Ellen, and Joanne B. Eicher. "Dress and Identity" [*DI*]. In Roach-Higgins, Eicher, and Johnson, eds., *Dress and Identity.*
Roach-Higgins, Mary Ellen, Joanne B. Eicher, and Kim K. P. Johnson, eds. *Dress and Identity* [*DI*]. New York: Fairchild Publications, 1995.

Robertson, George, Melinda Mash, Lisa Tickner, Jon Bird, Barry Curtis, and Tim Putnam, eds. *Futurenatural: Nature, Science, Culture* [*FN*]. New York: Routledge, 1996

Robinson, John Manley. *An Introduction to Early Greek Philosophy* [*EGP*]. Boston: Houghton Mifflin, 1968. All Greek fragments are quoted from this edition unless otherwise indicated.

Rocheleau, Dianne, Barbara Thomas-Slayter, and Esther Wangari. *Feminist Political Ecology: Global Issues and Local Experience* [*FPE*]. London: Routledge, 1996.

Rochlitz, Rainer. *The Disenchantment of Art: The Philosophy of Walter Benjamin* [*DA*]. Trans. Jane Marie Todd. New York: The Guilford Press, 1996.

Rolston, Holmes, III. *Environmental Ethics: Duties to and Values in the Natural World* [*EE*]. Philadelphia: Temple University Press, 1988.

———. "Environmental Ethics: Values in and Duties to the Natural World" [*EEVDNW*]. In Bormann and Kellert, eds., *Ecology, Economics, Ethics.*

Rorty, Richard. *Consequences of Pragmatism* [*CP*]. Minneapolis: University of Minnesota Press, 1982.

———. *Contingency, Irony, and Solidarity* [*CIS*]. Cambridge: Cambridge University Press, 1989.

———. *Essays on Heidegger and Others: Philosophical Papers II* [*EHO*]. Cambridge: Cambridge University Press, 1991.

———. *Objectivity, Relativism and Truth: Philosophical Papers I* [*ORT*]. Cambridge: Cambridge University Press, 1991.

———. *Philosophy and the Mirror of Nature* [*PMN*]. Princeton: Princeton University Press, 1979.

———. "Philosophy in America Today" [*PAT*]. In *Consequences of Pragmatism.*

Rose, Carol. "Possession as the Origin of Property" [*POP*]. *University of Chicago Law Review* 52 (1985): 73–88.

Rosemont, Henry, Jr. "Classical Confucian and Contemporary Perspectives on the Self: Some Parallels and Their Implications" [*CCCPS*]. In Allen, ed., *Culture and Self.*

Rosenberger, Nancy. *Japanese Self of Self* [*JSS*]. Cambridge: Cambridge University Press, 1992. In Allen, ed., *Culture and Self.*

Ross, Stephen David. *The Gift of Beauty: The Good as Art* [*GBGA*]. Albany: State University of New York Press, 1996.

———. *The Gift of Kinds: The Good in Abundance* [*GKGA*]. Albany: State University of New York Press, 1999.

———. *The Gift of Property: Having the Good* [*GPHG*]. Albany: State University of New York Press, forthcoming.

———. *The Gift of Self: Shattering, Emptiness, Betrayal* [*GSSEB*]. Binghamton, NY: International Studies in Philosophy Monograph Series—Interdisciplinary Studies in Philosophy, Interpretation, and Culture, 2005.

———. *The Gift of Touch: Embodying the Good* [*GTEG*]. Albany: State University of New York Press, 1998.

——. *The Gift of Truth: Gathering the Good* [*GTGG*]. Albany: State University of New York Press, 1997.
——. *Ideals and Responsibilities: Ethical Judgment and Social Identity* [*IR*]. Belmont, CA: Wadsworth, 1998.
——. *Inexhaustibility and Human Being: An Essay on Locality* [*IHB*]. New York: Fordham University Press, 1989.
——. *Injustice and Restitution: The Ordinance of Time* [*IROT*]. Albany: State University of New York Press, 1993.
——. *In Pursuit of Moral Value,* Freeman, Cooper & Co., 1974.
——. *Learning and Discovery* [*LD*]. New York: Gordon and Breach, 1981.
——. *The Limits of Language* [*LL*]. New York: Fordham University Press, 1993.
——. *Literature and Philosophy: An Analysis of the Philosophical Novel,* Appleton-Century-Crofts, 1969.
——. *Locality and Practical Judgment: Charity and Sacrifice* [*LPJ*]. New York: Fordham University Press, 1994.
——. *The Meaning of Education,* Martinus Nijhoff, 1966.
——. *Metaphysical Aporia and Philosophical Heresy* [*MAPH*]. Albany: State University of New York Press, 1989.
——. *Moral Decision,* Freeman, Cooper & Co., 1972.
——. *The Nature of Moral Responsibility,* Wayne State University Press, 1973.
——. *Perspective in Whitehead's Metaphysics* [*PWM*]. Albany: State University of New York Press, 1983.
——. *Philosophical Mysteries* [*PM*]. Albany: State University of New York Press, 1981.
——. *Plenishment in the Earth: An Ethic of Inclusion* [*PE*]. Albany: State University of New York, 1995.
——. *The Ring of Representation* [*RR*]. Albany: State University of New York Press, 1992.
——. *The Scientific Process,* Martinus Nijhoff, 1971.
——. *A Theory of Art: Inexhaustibility by Contrast* [*TA*]. Albany: State University of New York Press, 1983.
——. *Transition to an Ordinal Metaphysics* [*TOM*]. Albany: State University of New York Press, 1980.
——. "Translation as Transgression" [*TT*]. In *Translation Perspectives,* vol. 5. Ed. D. J. Schmidt. Binghamton: Binghamton University, 1990.
——. *Un-Forgetting: Re-Calling Time Lost [U].* International Studies in Philosophy Monograph Series in Interdisciplinary Studies in Philosophy, Interpretation, and Culture, 2 volumes, 2009.
——. *The World as Aesthetic Phenomenon.* International Studies in Philosophy Monograph Series in Interdisciplinary Studies in Philosophy, Interpretation, and Culture, 2 volumes, 2008.
——., ed. *Art and Its Significance: An Anthology of Aesthetic Theory* [*AIS*]. 3rd ed., Albany: State University of New York Press, 1994.
Roszak, Theodore. Introduction to Schumacher, *Small is Beautiful.*

Rousseau, Jean-Jacques. *The Basic Political Writings* [*BPW*]. Trans. Donald A. Cress. Int. Peter Gay. Indianapolis: Hackett, 1987.

——. *A Discourse on the Origin of Inequality* [*DOI*]. In *Basic Political Writings.*

——. *A Discourse on Political Economy* [*DPE*]. In *Basic Political Writings.*

——. *The Social Contract* [*SC*]. In *Basic Political Writings.*

——. *The Social Contract and Discourses* [*SCD*]. Trans. G. D. H. Cole. New York: Dutton, 1950.

Rovane, Carol A. *The Bounds of Agency: An Essay in Revisionary Metaphysics* [*BA*]. Princeton: Princeton University Press, 1998.

Rowlands, Michael. "Accounting for Personal Success in Bamenda" [*APSB*]. In Maw and Picton, eds., *Concepts of the Body/Self in Africa.*

Rubin, Arnold. *Marks of Civilization: Artistic Transformations of the Human Body* [*MC*]. University of California, Los Angeles: Museum of Cultural History, 1988

Rubin, Gayle. "The Traffic in Women: Notes on the 'Political Economy' of Sex" [*TW*]. In R. Reiter, ed., *Toward an Anthropology of Women.*

Ruch, E. A., and K. C. Anyanwu, eds. *African Philosophy: An Introduction to the Main Philosophical Trends in Contemporary Africa* [*AP*]. Rome: Catholic Book Agency, 1984.

Ruether, Rosemary. *New Woman, New Earth* [*NWNE*]. New York: Seabury Press, 1975.

Ryan, Alan. *Property and Political Theory* [*PPT*]. New York: Blackwell, 1984.

Sachs, Wolfgang. *Global Ecology: A New Arena of Political Conflict* [*GE*]. London: Zed, 1993.

Sacks, Oliver. *The Man Who Mistook His Wife for a Hat and Other Clinical Tales,* published in four volumes as *Awakenings* [*A*]; *A Leg to Stand On* [*LSO*]; *The Man Who Mistook His Wife for a Hat and Other Clinical Tales* [*MMWH*]; and *Seeing Voices* [*SV*]. New York: Quality Paperback Book Club, 1990.

Sadler, Barry, and Allen Carlson. *Environmental Aesthetics: Essays in Interpretation* [*EA*]. Western Geographical Series Vol. 20. Victoria, BC: Department of Geography, University of Victoria, 1982.

Salleh, Ariel. "Class, Race, and Gender Discourse in the Ecofeminism/Deep Ecology Debate" [*CRGD*]. In Oelschlaeger, ed., *Postmodern Environmental Ethics.*

Sallis, John, ed. *Deconstruction in Philosophy: The Texts of Jacques Derrida* [*DP*]. Chicago: University of Chicago Press, 1987.

——. *Reading Heidegger: Commemorations* [*RH*]. Bloomington: Indiana University Press, 1993.

Salomon, Charlotte. *Charlotte: Life or Theater?: An Autobiographical Play by Charlotte Salomon* [*CLT*]. Trans. Leila Vennewitz. Int. Judith Herzberg. New York: Viking Press, 1981.

——. *Leven? of Theater? Life? or Theatre?* [*L?T?*]. Int. Judith C. E. Belinfante, Christine Fisher-Defoy, and Ad Petersen. Amsterdam: Joods Historisch Museum, 1992.

Sanders, Clinton R. "Drill and Frill: Client Choice, Client Typologies, and Interactional Control in Commercial Tattooing Settings" [*DF*]. In Roach-Higgins, Eicher, and Johnson, eds., *Dress and Identity*.
Santayana, George. *The Life of Reason* [*LR*]. New York: Scribner's, 1953.
——. *Obiter Scripta*. Justus Buchler and R. Schwartz eds. New York: Scribners, 1936.
——. "Philosophical Heresy" [*PH*]. In *Obiter Scripta*.
——. *The Realm of Essence* [*RE*]. *Realms of Being 1*. New York: Scribner's, 1927.
——. *Reason in Art* [*RA*]. New York: Scribner's, 1905.
——. *The Sense of Beauty: Being the Outlines of Aesthetic Theory* [*SB*]. New York: Modern Library, 1953.
Sartre, Jean-Paul. *Anti-Semite and Jew* [*ASJ*]. Trans. George J. Becker. New York: Grove Press. 1948.
——. *Being and Nothingness: a Phenomenological Essay on Ontology* [*BN*]. Trans. Hazel E. Barnes. Humanities Press, 1956.
——. *Colonialism and Neocolonialism* [*CN*]. Trans. Steve Brewer, Azzedine Haddour, Terry McWilliams. New York: Routledge, 2001.
——. *Critique of Dialectical Reason* [*CDR*]. New York: Verso: 1991.
——. *Existential Psychoanalysis* [*EP*]. Trans. Hazel E. Barnes. Washington, DC: Regnery Pub., 1962.
——. *Existentialism and Human Emotions* [*EHE*]. New York: Carol Pub. Group, 1995, 1985.
——. *The Imaginary: a Phenomenological Psychology of the Imagination* [*I*]. Trans. Jonathan Webber. New York: Routledge, 2004.
——. *Nausea* [*N*]. Trans. Lloyd Alexander. New York: New Directions, 1964.
——. *No Exit & The Flies* [*NE,F*]. Trans. Stuart Gilbert. New York: Alfred A. Knopf, 1946.
——. *The Psychology of Imagination* [*PI*]. New York: Carol Publishing Group, 1991.
——. *Search for a Method* [*SM*]. Trans. Hazel E. Barnes. New York: Vintage Books, 1963.
——. *Transcendence of the Ego: an Existentialist Theory of Consciousness* [*TE*]. Trans. Forrest Williams and Robert Kirkpatrick. New York: Hill and Wang, 1957.
——. *The Wall (Intimacy) and Other Stories* [*W*]. Trans. Lloyd Alexander. New York: New Directions, 1948.
Scapp, Ron, and Brian Seitz, eds. *Eating Culture* [*EC*]. Albany: State University of New York Press, 1998.
Schapiro, Meyer. "The Still Life as a Personal Object" [*SLPO*]. In Marianne M. Simmel, ed., *Reach of the Mind: Essays in Memory of Kurt Goldstein*. New York: Springer, 1968. Discussed in Derrida, "Restitutions," in *Truth in Painting*.
Schelling, Friedrich Wilhelm Joseph von. *The Ages of the World* [*AW*], Fragment from the Third Version. Trans. and int. Jason M. Wirth. Albany, NY: State University of New York Press, 2000.

——. *The Ages of the World* [*AWB*], Trans. and int. Frederick deWolfe Bolman, Jr. New York: AMS Press, 1967.
——. *On the History of Modern Philosophy* [*OHMP*]. Trans. and int. Andrew Bowie. Cambridge: Cambridge University Press, 1994.
——. *Philosophical Inquiries into the Nature of Human Freedom* [*NHF*]. Trans. James Gutmann. Las Salle, IL: Open Court, 1936.
——. *Philosophy of Art* [*PA*]. Trans. and ed., Douglas W. Stott. Minneapolis: University of Minnesota Press, 1989.
——. *System of Transcendental Idealism* [*STI*]. Charlottesville, VA: University of Virginia Press, 1978.
Scheper-Hughes, Nancy. "Vernacular Sexism: An Anthropological Response to Ivan Illich" [*VS*]. In *Feminist Issues* 3, no. 1 (Spring 1983): 28–36.
Scherer, Donald, and Tom Attig, eds. *Ethics and the Environment* [*EE*]. Englewood Cliffs, NJ: Prentice Hall, 1983.
Schleuning, Neala. *To Have and To Hold: The Meaning of Ownership in the United States* [*THTH*]. Westport, CT: Praeger, 1977.
Schönborn, Christoph. "Finding Design in Nature" [*FDN*]. *New York Times* (July 7, 2005): http://www.nytimes.com/2005/07/07/opinion/07schonborn.html.
Schopenhauer, Arthur. *The World as Will and Representation*. 2 Vols. Trans. E. F. J. Payne. New York: Dover, 1968.
Schor, Naomi. "This Essentialism Which Is Not One: Coming to Grips with Irigaray" [*TEWNO*]. *Differences: A Journal of Feminist Cultural Studies* 2, no. 1 (Summer 1989): 38–58.
Schrag, Calvin O. *The Self After Postmodernity* [*SAP*]. New Haven, CT: Yale University Press, 1997.
Schultz, David A. *Property, Power, and American Democracy* [*PPAD*]. New Brunswick, NY: Transaction Publishers, 1992.
Schumacher, E. F. *A Guide for the Perplexed* [*GP*]. New York: Harper and Row, 1977.
——. *Small Is Beautiful: Economics as if People Mattered* [*SB*]. Pref. John McClaughry, Kirkpatrick Sale. Int. Theodore Roszak. New York: Harper & Row, 1989.
Schutte, Ofelia. *Cultural Identity and Social Liberation in Latin American Thought* [*CISL*]. Albany: State University of New York Press, 1993.
Schutz, Alfred. "The Homecomer" [*H*]. *American Journal of Sociology* 60, no. 5 (1945): 369–76.
——. "The Stranger: An Essay in Social Psychology" [*S*]. *American Journal of Sociology* 49, no. 6 (1944): 499–507.
Schwartz, Stephen P., ed. *Naming, Necessity, and Natural Kinds* [*NNNK*]. Ithaca, NY: Cornell University Press, 1977.
Scott, Charles E. *The* **Question** *of Ethics: Nietzsche, Foucault, Heidegger* [*QE*]. Bloomington: Indiana University Press, 1990.
Scott, G. E. *Moral Personhood: An Essay in the Philosophy of Moral Psychology* [*MP*]. Albany: State University of New York Press, 1990.
Scott, Russell. *The Body as Property* [*BP*]. New York: Viking, 1981.

Seager, Joni. *Earth Follies: Coming to Terms with the Global Environmental Crisis* [*EF*]. New York: Routledge, 1993.

Seamon, David, ed. *Dwelling, Seeing, and Designing* [*DSD*]. Albany: State University of New York Press, 1993.

Seed, John, Joanna Macy, Pat Fleming, and Arne Naess. *Thinking Like a Mountain: Toward a Council of All Beings* [*TLM*]. Philadelphia: New Society Publishers, 1988.

Selfe, Lorna. *Nadia: A Case Study of Extraordinary Drawing Ability in an Autistic Child* [*N*]. New York and London: Harcourt Brace Jovanovich, 1977.

Sen, Amartya. "More Than 100 Million Women Are Missing" [*MMWM*]. *New York Review of Books* (December 20, 1990): 61–66.

Senghor, Léopold Sédar. "Negritude: A Humanism of the Twentieth Century" [*N*]. In Hord and Lee, eds., *I Am Because We Are.*

Serequeberhan, Tsenay. *African Philosophy: The Essential Readings* [*AP*]. New York: Paragon House, 1991.

Serres, Michel. *The Natural Contract* [*NC*]. Trans. Elizabeth MacArthur and William Paulson. Ann Arbor: University of Michigan Press, 1995.

Serres, Michel, with Bruno Latour. *Conversations on Science, Culture, and Time* [*CSCT*]. Trans. Roxanne Lapidus. Ann Arbor: University of Michigan Press, 1995.

Sessions, Robert. "Deep Ecology versus Ecofeminism: Healthy Differences or Incompatible Philosophies?" [*DEE*]. In Warren, ed., *Hypatia*: 90–107.

Setton, Mark. *Chông, Yagyong: Korea's Challenge to Orthodox Neo-confucianism* [*CY*]. Albany: State University of New York Press, 1997.

Shack, William A. "Open Systems and Closed Boundaries: The Ritual Process of Stranger Relations in New African States" [*OSCB*]. In Shack and Skinner, eds., *Strangers in African Societies.*

Shack, William A., and Elliot Skinner, eds. *Strangers in African Societies* [*SAS*]. Berkeley: University of California Press, 1979.

Shantideva. *Bodhicaryavatara* [*B*] 8:114. Trans. Stephen Batchelor. In *A Guide to the Bodhisattva's Way of Life* [*GBWL*]. Dharamsala, India: Library of Tibetan Works and Archives, 1979.

Sharma, Ursula. "Dowry in North India: Its Consequences for Women" [*DNI*]. In Hirschon, ed., *Women and Property—Women as Property.*

Sharper, Stephen D. *Redeeming the Time: A Political Theology of the Environment* [*RD*]. New York: Continuum, 1997.

Shcherbatskoi [Stcherbatsky], Fedor Ippolitovich. *Buddhist Logic* [*BL*]. New York: Dover Publications, 1962.

———. *The Central Conception of Buddhism and the Meaning of the Word "Dharma"* [*CCB*]. Delhi: Motilal Banarsidass, 1970.

———. *The Conception of Buddhist Nirvânaą* [*CBN*]. New York: Gordon Press, 1971.

Sheehan, Thomas, ed. *Heidegger, the Man and the Thinker* [*HMT*]. Chicago: Precedent Publishing, 1981.

Sheldrake, Rupert. "The Laws of Nature as Habits: A Postmodern Basis for Science" [*LNH*]. In Griffin, ed., *Reenchantment of Science*.

Shepard, Paul. *Nature and Madness* [*NM*]. San Franciso: Sierra Club Books, 1982.

Shimomura Toratarō. "Nishida Kitarō and Some Aspects of His Philosophical Thought" [*NK*]. In Nishida, *Study of Good*.

Shiva, Vandana. "Development as a New Project of Western Patriarchy" [*DNPWP*]. In Diamond and Orenstein, eds., *Reweaving the World*.

———. *Staying Alive* [*SA*]. London: Zed, 1989.

Shiva, Vandana, and Ingunn Moser, eds. *Biopolitics: A Feminist and Ecological Reader on Biotechnology* [*B*]. London: Zed Books, 1995.

———. Silko, Leslie Marmon. *Ceremony* [*C*]. New York: New American Library, 1977.

Shoemaker, Sidney. *The First-Person Perspective and Other Essays* [*FPP*]. New York: Cambridge University Press, 1996.

Siebers, Tobin. *The Subject and Other Subjects: On Ethical, Aesthetic, and Political Identity* [*SOS*]. Ann Arbor: University of Michigan Press, 1998.

Sillah, Memuna M. "Bundu Trap" [*BT*]. *Natural History* (August 1996): 42–53.

Simmel, Georg. *Sociologie* [*Soc*]. Leipzig: Duncker & Humblot, 1908.

———. "The Stranger" [*S*]. In Donald N. Levine, *On Individuality and Social Forms*. Chicago: University of Chicago Press, 1971.

Simons, Margaret A. "From Murder to Morality: The Development of Beauvoir's Ethics" [*FMM*]. *International Studies in Philosophy* 31, no. 2 (1999): 1–20.

Singer, Joseph W. "The Reliance Interest in Property" [*RIP*]. *Stanford Law Review* 40 (1988): 611–51.

———. "Sovereignty and Property" [*SP*]. *Northwestern University Law Review* 86, no. 1 (1991): 1–56.

Singer, Linda. "Defusing the Canon: Feminist Rereading and Textual Politics" [*DC*]. In *Erotic Welfare: Sexual Theory and Politics in the Age of Epidemic*. Ed. and int. Judith Butler and Maureen MacGrogan. New York: Routledge, 1993.

Singer, Peter. *Animal Liberation: A New Ethics for Our Treatment of Animals* [*AL*]. New York: Avon, 1975.

Sini, Carlo. *Images of Truth: From Sign to Symbol* [*IT*]. Trans. Massimo Verdicchio. Atlantic Highlands, NJ: Humanities Press, 1993.

Slicer, Deborah. "Your Daughter or Your Dog" [*DD*]. In Warren, ed., *Hypatia*, 108–23.

Smith, Adam. *An Inquiry into the Nature and Causes of the Wealth of Nations* [*WN*]. Ed. R. H. Campbell, A. S. Skinner, and W. B. Todd. Oxford: Clarendon Press, 1976.

Smith, Bradley. "Assimilationism: Learning How to Learn the Beauty of It All" [*A*]. In Young, ed., *Art, Culture, and Ethnicity*.

Smith, Mick. "Cheney and the Myth of Postmodernism" [*CMP*]. In Oelschlaeger, ed., *Postmodern Environmental Ethics*.

Smuts, J. C. *Holism and Evolution* [*HE*]. New York: Macmillan, 1926.

Soper, Kate. "Nature/'nature'" [*NN*]. In Robertson, Mash, Tickner, Bird, Curtis, and Putnam, eds., *Futurenatural.*

Sophocles. *Oedipus the King* [*OK*], *Antigone* [*A*], *Oedipus at Colonus* [*OC*]. All trans. R. C. Jebb. In Oates and O'Neill, eds., *Complete Greek Drama.*

Sorabji, Richard. "Aristotle on Demarcating the Five Senses" [*ADFS*]. *Philosophical Review* 80 (1971): 55–79.

Soyinka, Wole. *Art, Dialogue, and Outrage: Essays on Literature and Culture* [*ADO*]. New York: Pantheon, 1994.

———. *The Burden of Memory, the Muse of Forgiveness* [*BMMF*]. New York: Oxford Oxford University Press, 1999.

Spelman, Elizabeth V. *Inessential Woman: Problems of Exclusion in Feminist Thought* [*IW*]. Boston: Beacon Press, 1988.

———. *Repair: The Impulse to Restore in a Fragile World* [*R*]. Boston: Beacon Press, 2002.

Spencer, Colin. *The Heretic's Feast: A History of Vegetarianism* [*HF*]. Hanover: University Press of New England, 1995.

Spiegel, Marjorie. *The Dreaded Comparison: Human and Animal Slavery* [*DC*]. Rev. ed., New York: Mirror Books, 1996.

Spinoza, Benedict de. *Collected Works of Spinoza* [*CWS*], vol. 1. 2nd printing with corr. Ed. and trans. Edwin Curley. Princeton: Princeton University Press, 1988.

———. *Descartes' Principles of Philosophy* [*DPP*]. In *Collected Works*, vol. I.

———. *Ethics* [*E*]. In *Collected Works*, vol. I.

———. *Ethics* [*EG*]. Trans. William Hale White. Rev. Amelia Hutchinson Stirling. Ed. and int. James Gutmann. New York: Hafner, 1949.

———. *Ethics and Selected Letters* [*ESL*]. Trans. Samuel Shirley. Ed. and Int. Seymour Feldman. Indianapolis: Hackett, 1982.

———. *A Theologico-Political Treatise* [*TPT*] *and A Political Treatise* [*PT*]. Trans. and int. R. H. M. Elwes. New York: Dover, 1951.

———. *Short Treatise on God, Man, and His Well-Being* [*STG*]. In *Collected Works.*

———. *Treatise on the Emendation of the Intellect* [*TEI*]. In *Collected Works.*

Spretnak, Charlene. *The Resurgence of the Real: Body, Nature, and Place in a Hypermodern World* [*RR*]. New York: Addison-Wesley, 1997.

———. *The Spiritual Dimension of Green Politics* [*SDGP*]. Santa Fe, NM: Bear and Co., 1986.

Stambaugh, Joan. *The Formless Self* [*FS*]. Albany: State University of New York Press, 1999.

Starhawk [Miriam Simos], "Ethics and Justice in Goddess Religion" [*EJGR*]. In Andolsen, Gudorf, and Pellauer, eds., *Women's Consciousness, Women's Conscience.*

———. "Witchcraft and Women's Culture" [*WWC*]. In Christ and Plaskow, eds., *Womanspirit Rising.*

Starr, June. "The Legal and Social Transformation of Rural Women in Aegean Turkey" [*LSF*]. In Hirschon, ed., *Women and Property—Women as Property.*

Stengers, Isabelle. *The Invention of Modern Science* [*IMS*]. Trans. Daniel W. Smith. Minneapolis: University of Minnesota Press, 2000.

——. *Power and Invention: Situating Science* [*PI*]. Trans. Paul Bains. Minneapolis: University of Minnesota Press, 1997.

——. "Turtles All the Way Down" [*TAWD*]. In *Power and Invention.*

Stephen, Michele. "Contrasting Images of Power" [*CIP*]. In Stephen ed., *Sorcerer and Witch.*

——. "Master of Souls: The Mekeo Sorcerer" [*MS*]. In Stephen ed., *Sorcerer and Witch.*

——., ed. *Sorcerer and Witch in Melanesia* [*SWM*]. New Brunswick, NJ: Rutgers University Press, 1987.

Stirner, Max. *The Ego and His Own* [*EO*]. Trans. Steven T. Byington. New York: Dover, 1973.

Stone, Christopher D. *Earth and Other Ethics* [*EOE*]. New York: Harper & Row, 1987.

——. "Moral Pluralism and the Course of Environmental Ethics" [*MPCEE*]. In Oelschlaeger, ed., *Postmodern Environmental Ethics.*

Stone, Gregory P. "Appearance and the Self" [*AS*]. In Roach-Higgins, Eicher, and Johnson, eds., *Dress and Identity.*

Strathern, Marilyn. *The Gender of the Gift: Problems with Women and Problems with Society in Melanesia* [*GG*]. Berkeley: University of California Press, 1988.

——. "Subject or Object? Women and the Circulation of Valuables in Highlands New Guinea" [*SO*]. In Hirschon, ed., *Women and Property—Women as Property.*

Strawson, Peter F. *Individuals: An Essay in Descriptive Metaphysics* [*I*]. Garden City, NY: Doubleday & Co., 1959. Strong, Marilee. *A Bright Red Scream: Self-Mutilation and the Language of Pain* [*BRS*]. New York: Viking, 1998.

Sumner, Claude. *The Source of African Philosophy: The Ethiopian Philosophy of Man* [*SAP*]. Stuttgart: Franz Steiner Verlag Wiesbaden GMBH, 1986.

Suzuki, Daisetz T. *The Essence of Buddhism* [*EB*]. Kyoto: Bunko, 1948.

——. "How to Read Nishida" [*HRN*]. In Nishida, *A Study of Good.*

——. *Zen and Japanese Culture* [*ZJC*]. Princeton, NJ: Princeton University Press, 1993.

Swift, Jonathan. *Gulliver's Travels and Other Writings* [*GT*]. Int. Louis A. Landa. Cambridge: Riverside, 1960.

Swimme, Brian. "The Cosmic Creation Story" [*CCS*]. In Griffin, ed., *Reenchantment of Science.*

Sypher, Wylie. *Comedy* [*C*]. Baltimore: Johns Hopkins University Press, 1956.

Tambiah, Stanley Jeyaraja. *Magic, Science, Religion, and the Scope of Rationality* [*MSR*]. New York: Cambridge University Press, 1990.

Tanahashi, Kazuaki, ed. *Moon in a Dewdrop* [*MD*]. San Francisco: North Point Press, 1985.

Tannen, Deborah. *You Just Don't Understand: Women and Men in Conversation* [*YJDU*]. New York: Ballantine, 1990.

Tarski, Alfred. "The Semantic Conception of Truth" [*SCT*]. *Philosophy and Phenomenological Research* 4:341–76 (1944). Reprinted in Linsky, ed., *Semantics and the Philosophy of Language*. All page references to Linsky.

Taylor, Charles. "Modes of Secularism" [*MS*]. In *Bhargava, Secularism and its Critics.*

——. *Sources of the Self: The Making of Modern Identity* [*SS*]. Cambidge, Mass.: Harvard University Press, 1989.

Taylor, Dorceta E. "Environmentalism and the Politics of Inclusion" [*EPI*]. In Bullard, ed., *Confronting Environmental Racism.*

Taylor, Mark C. *Altarity* [*I*]. Chicago: University of Chicago Press, 1987.

——. *Hiding* [*H*]. Chicago: University of Chicago Press, 1997.

——. *The Moment of Complexity: Emerging Network Culture* [*MC*]. Chicago: University of Chicago Press, 2001.

Taylor, Mark C., and Era Saarinen. *Imagologies: Media Philosophy* [*I*]. New York: Routledge, 1994.

Taylor, Paul. *Respect for Nature: A Theory of Environmental Ethics* [*RN*]. Princeton: Princeton University Press, 1986.

Tellenbach, Hubertus, and Bin Kimura. "The Japanese Concept of 'Nature'" [*JCN*]. In Callicott and Ames, eds., *Nature in Asian Traditions of Thought.*

Theroux, Paul. "Self-Propelled" [*SP*]. *The New York Times Magazine* (April 25, 1993): 22–24.

Thomas, Elizabeth Marshall. "Reflections (Lions)" [*L*]. *The New Yorker* (October 15, 1990): 78–101.

Thompson, Robert Farris. *Flash of the Spirit; African & Afro-American Art & Philosophy* [*FS*]. New York: Vintage, 1984.

Tobias, Michael. "Ecological Aesthetics" [*EA*]. In Tobias and Cowan, eds., *Soul of Nature.*

Tobias, Michael, and Georgianne Cowan, eds. *The Soul of Nature: Visions of a Living Earth* [*SN*]. New York: Continuum, 1994.

Tolstoy, Leo. *What Is Art?* [*WA*]. Reprinted in part in Ross, ed., *Art and Its Significance.*

——. "What is To Be Done" [*WD*]. In Horovitz, ed., *Anarchists.*

Topan, Farouk M. "Body and Self in a Spirit Mediumship Cult of Mombasa" [*BS*]. In Maw and Picton, eds., *Concepts of the Body/ Self in Africa.*

Trinh, T. Minh-ha. "An Acoustic Journey" [*AJ*]. In Welchman, ed., *Rethinking Borders.*

——. "Nature's *R*: A Musical Swoon" [*NR*]. In Robertson, Mash, Tickner, Bird, Curtis, and Putnam, eds., *Futurenatural.*

——. *Woman, Native, Other: Writing Postcoloniality and Feminism* [*WNO*]. Indianapolis: Indiana University Press, 1989.

Trippi, Laura. "Untitled Artists' Projects by Janine Antoni, Ben Kinmont, Rirkrit Tiravanija" [*UAP*]. In Scapp and Seitz, eds., *Eating Culture.*

Trumbull, H. C. *The Threshold Covenant* [*TC*]. New York: Scribner's, 1896.
Tu Wei-ming. "The Continuity of Nature: Chinese Visions of Nature" [*CN*]. In Callicott and Ames, eds., *Nature in Asian Traditions of Thought.*
——. "Embodying the Universe: A Note on Confucian Self-Realization" [*EU*]. In Ames, ed., *Self as Person in Asian Theory and Practice.*
Tuan, Yi-Fu. *Passing Strange and Wonderful: Aesthetics, Nature, and Culture* [*PSW*]. New York: Kodansha America, 1995.
Tucker, Benjamin Ricketson. *Instead of a Book, By a Man Too Busy to Write One; A Fragmentary Exposition of Philosophical Anarchism* [*IB*]. 2nd ed., New York: Gordon Press, 1972.
Turner, Victor. *The Ritual Process* [*RP*]. Chicago: Aldine, 1969.
Tyler, Edward B. *Primitive Culture* [*PC*]. New York: Holt and Co., 1889.
Underkuffler, Laura S. "On Property: An Essay" [*OP*]. *Yale Law Journal* 100 (1990): 127–48.
Valiente, Doreen. *Witchcraft for Tomorrow* [*WT*]. Custer, WA: Phoenix, 1987.
Vattimo, Gianni. *The End of Modernity* [*EM*]. Trans. J. R. Snyder. Cambridge: Polity Press, 1988.
Vale, V. and, Andrea Juno. *Modern Primitives* [*MP*]. San Francisco: Re/Search Publications, 1989.
Van Sertima, Ivan. *The African Presence in Ancient America: They Came Before Columbus* [*APAA*]. New York: Random H ouse, 1976.
Vaughan, Genevieve. *For-Giving: A Feminist Criticism of Exchange* [*F-G*]. Austin, TX: Plain View Press, 1997.
Veblen, Thorstein. "The Beginnings of Ownership" [*BO*]. *The American Journal of Sociology* 4 (November 1989): 352–65.
——. *The Portable Veblen* [*PV*]. Ed. Max Lerner. New York: Viking, 1972.
——. *The Theory of the Leisure Class* [*TLC*]. New York: Modern Library, 1934.
Victoria, Brian (Daizen) A. *Zen at War* [*ZW*]. New York: Weatherhill, 1997.
Waldron, Jeremy. *The Right to Private Property* [*RPP*]. Oxford: Clarendon Press, 1988.
Warren, Karen J. "Feminism and Ecology: Making Connections" [*FEMC*]. *Environmental Ethics* 9, no. 1 (Spring 1987): 3–20.
——. "The Promise and Power of Ecological Feminism" [*PPEF*]. *Environmental Ethics* 12, no. 2 (Summer 1990): 125–46.
Warren, Karen J., ed. *Hypatia* 6, no. 1 (Spring 1991). Special Issue on Ecological Feminism.
Warren, Karen J., and Jim Cheney. "Ecological Feminism and Ecosystem Ecology" [*EFEE*]. In Warren, ed., *Hypatia*, 179–97.
Watkins, Susan M. "Stitchless Sewing for the Apparel of the Future" [*SSAF*]. In Roach-Higgins, Eicher, and Johnson, eds., *Dress and Identity.*
Weber, Max. "Science as a Vocation" [*SV*]. *From Max Weber: Essays in Sociology.*
——. *From Max Weber: Essays in Sociology* [*FMW*], Trans. H.H. Gerth and C. Wright Mills. New York: Oxford University Press, 1946.

Weber, Renée, "A Philosophical Perspective on Touch" [*PPT*]. In Barnard and Brazelton, eds., *Touch*.

Weiss, Paul. *Creative Ventures* [*CV*]. Carbondale, IL: Southern Illinois University Press, 1992.

——. *Nine Basic Arts* [*NBA*]. Carbondale, IL: Southern Illinois University Press, 1961.

——. *The World of Art* [*WA*]. Carbondale, IL: Southern Illinois University Press, 1961.

Welchman, John C. "The Philosophical Brothel" [*PB*]. In Welchman, ed., *Rethinking Borders*.

——. *Rethinking Borders* [*RB*]. Minneapolis: University of Minnesota Press, 1996.

Welwood, John, and Ken Wilber. "On Ego Strength and Egolessness" [*ESE*]. In John Welwood, ed., *The Meeting of the Ways: Explorations in East/West Psychology* [*MW*]. New York: Schocken Books, 1979.

Wenders, William. *Wings of Desire* [*WD*]. Screenplay by Wenders and Peter Handke. 1988.

Wenz, Peter S. "Just Garbage" [*JG*]. In Westra and Wenz, eds., *Faces of Environmental Racism: Confronting Issues of Global Justice*.

West, Cornel. *Keeping Faith: Philosophy and Race in America* [*KP*]. New York: Routledge, 1993.

——. "Race Matters" [*RM*]. In Andersen and Collins, eds., *Race, Class, and Gender*.

Weston, Anthony. "Before Environmental Ethics" [*BEE*]. In Oelschlaeger, ed., *Postmodern Environmental Ethics*.

Westra, Laura, and Peter S. Wenz, eds. *Faces of Environmental Racism: Confronting Issues of Global Justice* [*FER*]. Lanham, MD: Rowman & Littlefield, 1995.

Westwood, Sallie. "'Fear Woman': Property and Modes of Production in Urban Ghana" [*FW*]. In Hirschon, ed., *Women and Property—Women as Property*.

White, Daniel R. *Labyrinths of the Mind: The Self in the Postmodern Age* [*LM*]. Albany: State University of New York Press, 1998.

White, Stephen L. *The Unity of the Self* [*US*]. Cambridge, MA: MIT Press, 1991.

Whitehead, Alfred North. *Adventures of Ideas* [*AI*]. New York: Macmillan, 1933.

——. *Modes of Thought* [*MT*]. New York: Capricorn, 1938.

——. *Process and Reality* [*PR*]. Corrected edition. Ed. D. R. Griffin and D. W. Sherburne. New York: Free Press, 1978.

——. *Science in the Modern World* [*SMW*]. New York: Macmillan, 1925.

Whitehead, Ann. "Women and Men; Kinship and Property: Some General Issues" [*WMKP*]. In Hirschon, ed., *Women and Property—Women as Property*.

Whitman, Walt. *Song of Myself* [*SM*]. In *Works*.

——. *Works* [*W*]. New York: Viking Press, 1982.

Wikse, John R. *About Possession: The Self as Private Property* [*AP*]. University Park, PA: The Pennsylvania State University Press, 1977.

Wilcox, Finn, and Jeremiah Gorsline, eds. *Working the Woods, Working the Sea* [*WW*]. Port Townsend, Wash.: Empty Bowl, 1986.

Willis, Janice. *On Knowing Reality: The* Tattvārtha *Chapter of Asaṅga's* Bodhisattvabhûmi [*OKR*]. New York: Columbia University Press, 1979.

Wilmsen, Edwin H., ed. *We Are Here: Politics of Aboriginal Land Tenure* [*WAH*]. Berkeley: University of California Press, 1989.

Wilson, David Sloan. *Darwin's Cathedral* [*DC*]. Chicago: University of Chicago Press, 2002.

——. *Evolution for Everyone: How Darwin's Theory Can Change the Way We Think About Our Lives* [*EE*]. New York: Delta, 2008.

Wilson, Edward O. *The Diversity of Life* [*DL*]. Cambridge: Harvard University Press, 1992.

——. *Consilience: The Unity of Knowledge* [*C*]. New York: Knopf, 1998.

——. *Sociobiology* [*S*]. Cambridge, MA: Harvard University Press, 1980.

Wilson, Peter J. *The Domestication of the Human Species* [*DHS*]. New Haven: Yale University Press, 1988.

Winkler, Cathy (with Kate Wininger). "Rape Trauma: Contexts of Meaning" [*RT*]. In Csordas, *Embodiment and Experience.*

Wittgenstein, Ludwig. *The Blue and Brown Books* [*BB*]. New York: Harper & Row, 1958.

——. *Philosophical Investigations* [*PI*]. Trans. G. E. M. Anscombe. Oxford: Blackwell, 1963.

——. *Tractatus Logico-Philosophicus* [*TLP*]. Trans. D. F. Pears and B. F. McGuinness. London: Routledge & Kegan Paul, 1961.

Wittig, Monique. "The Category of Sex" [*CS*]. In *Straight Mind.*

——. "Homo Sum" [*HS*]. In *Straight Mind*, 46–58.

——. *The Lesbian Body* [*LB*]. Trans. David Le Vay. Boston: Beacon Press, 1975. Translation of *Le Corps Lesbien* [*CL*]. Paris: Minuit, 1973.

——. "The Mark of Gender" [*MG*]. In *Straight Mind*

——. "One Is Not Born a Woman" [*OBW*]. In *Straight Mind.*

——. "The Straight Mind" [*SM*]. In *Straight Mind.*

——. *The Straight Mind and Other Essays* [*SME*]. Boston: Beacon Press, 1992.

Wollheim, Richard. *Art and its Objects : with Six Supplementary Essays* [*AO*]. New York: Cambridge University Press, 1980.

——. *On Art and the Mind* [*OAM*]. Cambridge, MA: Harvard University Press, 1974.

——. *Painting as an Art* [*PA*]. Princeton, NJ: Princeton University Press, 1987.

——. *The Sheep and the Ceremony* [*SC*]. Cambridge: Cambridge University Press, 1979.

Worster, Donald. *Rivers of Empire* [*RE*]. New York: Pantheon, 1985.

Young, Bernard, ed. *Art, Culture, and Ethnicity* [*ACE*]. Reston, VA: National Art Education Association, 1990.

Young-Bruehl, Elizabeth, and Faith Bethelard. *Cherishment: A Psychology of the Heart* [C]. New York: Free Press, 2000.

Zack, Naomi. *Bachelors of Science: Seventeenth-Century Identity, Then and Now* [*BS*]. Philadelphia: Temple University Press, 1996.

Zimmerman, Michael E. *Contesting Earth's Future: Radical Ecology and Postmodernity* [*CEF*]. Berkeley: University of California Press, 1994.

——. "Quantum Theory, Intrinsic Value, and Panentheism" [*QTIVP*]. In Oelschlaeger, ed., *Postmodern Environmental Ethics.*

Žižek, Slavoj. "Eastern Europe's Republics of Gilead" [*EERG*]. In Mouffe, ed., *Dimensions of Radical Democracy.*

INDEX